Daniel C. Henderson

OLD TESTAMENT THEOLOGY

VOLUME I

GERHARD VON RAD

OLD TESTAMENT
THEOLOGY

VOLUME I

THE THEOLOGY OF
ISRAEL'S HISTORICAL TRADITIONS

Translated by
D. M. G. STALKER

HARPER & ROW, PUBLISHERS
NEW YORK AND EVANSTON

A translation of *Theologie des Alten Testaments;* BD I, *Die Theologie der geschichtlichen Überlieferungen Israels,* published by Chr. Kaiser Verlag, Munich, in 1957, and including revisions for 2nd German edition.

Printed in Great Britain for Harper & Row Publishers, Incorporated, 49 East 33d Street, New York, NY., 10016.

Preface

THE "Theology of the Old Testament" is still a young branch of studies, indeed it is one of the youngest of the disciplines of Biblical studies. It would not take long to relate the basic outline of its history, which dates from the end of the eighteenth and the beginning of the nineteenth century. The remarkable thing in this connexion is that no agreement has been reached up to now as to what really is the proper subject of such a theology of the Old Testament. If this were not so, how could it be possible that under one and the same title such different works could be offered as the "Theology of the Old Testament" by E. Jacob or Th. C. Vriezen on the one hand, and on the other, the one offered in this book? The characteristic thing in today's situation, in my opinion, is the surprising convergence—indeed the mutual intersection—which has come about during the last twenty or thirty years between introductory studies and Biblical theology. It is not so very long ago that a theology of the Old Testament could learn very little beyond questions of date and of this and that in matters of form from those introductory studies which were working mainly on the lines of literary criticism. At that time a theology which wanted to be more than an historical picture of the Religion of Israel (in agreement with L. Köhler) could unfold itself along the lines of the scientific concepts of theology, anthropology, and soteriology. But that was changed when, inspired by Gunkel's investigation of literary classes, research met with norms of sacral law, various cultic texts, rituals, liturgies, and, in particular, with very ancient credal formulae, that is, with insights which were of central importance for the theological understanding of the Old Testament. Has it not almost always been the case that when changes or new things from the point of view of form were met with, they corresponded to changed or completely new theological facts? The history of tradition has taught us in a new way to see in the three gigantic works of the Hexateuch, the Deuteronomistic history, and the Chronicler's history, the most varied forms of the presentation of God's history with Israel in its different strata. It has also shown how Israel was at all times occupied with the task of understanding her history from the point of view of certain interventions by God, and how what God had rooted in the history presented itself in

different ways in every age. Does this not set new tasks before a
theology of the Old Testament? And if there is any truth in the recognition that the whole of the Hexateuch is built upon a very few ancient
credal statements which became constitutive for the Israel of all ages,
then this is so important that a theology of the Old Testament would
practically have to start out from this fact. Thus the things which have
helped us on our way have not been any particular theological impulses:
rather, a new attention to the formal structure of Israel's statements and
her literary heritage, as well as a more appropriate analysis of the books
of the Old Testament and the traditions incorporated in them, taught
us to see more clearly what is the only possible subject of a theology of
the Old Testament. However, the obvious idea of giving a history of
the credal statements of Israel in chronological sequence soon proves
impracticable. Admittedly, it is possible to see in the Hexateuch alone
tremendous differences in the structure of the traditions and accordingly
in their theological formulation as well, but if we try to determine the
age of these traditions, we are seldom able to advance beyond very
general datings, if we are not in fact altogether in the dark. And what
we know about the localities and the representatives of the various
groups of tradition bears no comparison either with the real wealth of
special formulations and theological concepts which we find collected
in the major source documents. To have to abandon an historical presentation of Israel's credal statements has the advantage that we are
able to let the material stand in those contexts in the saving history in
which it was arranged by Israel. And in this way there comes more
clearly into our field of vision that part of Israel's theological activity
which is probably one of its most important and interesting ones,
namely those ever new attempts to make the divine acts of salvation
relevant for every new age and day—this ever new reaching-out to and
avowal of God's acts which in the end made the old credal statements
grow into such enormous masses of traditions. A theology which
attempts to grasp the content of the Old Testament under the heading
of various doctrines (the doctrine of God, the doctrine of man, etc.)
cannot do justice to these credal statements which are completely tied
up with history, or to this grounding of Israel's faith upon a few divine
acts of salvation and the effort to gain an ever new understanding of
them.

The theological part of this book is preceded by a short historical
one, which sketches at least the most important sacral institutions of

ancient Israel and the various phases in the history of her faith. This first part, which does not attempt even in the slightest degree to picture the history of faith and cult in ancient Israel in all its complexity, is merely intended to show those subjects, the knowledge of which is presupposed by the second part, in their historical connexions. This, and the lay-out of this book as such, resulted in the fact that subjects of importance had to be dealt with more than once. But it may not be felt to be a complete disadvantage if the reader gets a theological picture of one and the same thing in various aspects and different contexts.

Within the scope of a theology of the historical traditions there can be no mention of the prophets, as the characteristic thing about their proclamation is that they deny the efficacy of the old divine actions for their contemporaries, and that they perceive God's rising up to completely new acts in history in their time (see pp. 66ff., 127f.). The theology of the prophetic tradition will therefore have to be treated in a different connexion. This second volume, which I hope to present in the not too distant future, is intended also to end with several basic theological reflexions upon the Old Testament. Of course nowadays, and least of all in our situation where everyone still looks so very much to his own way only, no one man is able to write a theology of the Old Testament which would even in part exhaustively comprise the scope of what is essential and important; but perhaps it is possible to indicate a way which might sooner or later lead to a more comprehensive understanding of the Old Testament.

I have still to acknowledge here the unwearied co-operation of two of my former students, Herr Vikar E. Haller (Neuendettelsau), who undertook the great task of checking the manuscript as well as the reading of all the proofs, and my assistant Herr cand. theol. K. Schwan (Sandhausen), who checked the immense number of Scripture references and collected them into an index, and who also carefully helped to read the proofs. To both, I owe much gratitude for their generous help.

Heidelberg, May 1957   Gerhard von Rad

Translator's Note

As the author has translated all Scripture quotations direct from Hebrew into German, I have similarly translated them direct, keeping as close as possible to the Revised Standard Version. In chapter and verse numbering, the Hebrew Old Testament is followed, and where this is different from the numbering in the English Versions of the Bible, the latter is given in square brackets.

I wish to express my indebtedness for the help they gave me in various ways to the Rev. Jean B. Robson, M.A., Miss Elizabeth M. Gourlay, M.A., Miss Elizabeth B. F. Kinniburgh, B.D., and Frl. Wilhelmine de Filippi; to Professor von Rad, for a number of suggestions; and not least to Messrs. Oliver & Boyd, for their continual kindness and forbearance.

D. M. G. Stalker

Contents

PART ONE

A History of Jahwism and of the Sacral Institutions in Israel in Outline

Chapter A

ORIGINS

THE primary sources for the history of the religion and worship of ancient Israel lie within the Old Testament exclusively. In it is to be found, in addition, a coherent presentation of the early history of Israel, a picture which, in spite of many gaps, is on the whole impressively complete, and which takes the course of history from the people's earliest ancestor down through the origin of Israel as a people to its settlement in Canaan. In much of its detail this picture succumbed to the onset of Biblical criticism. Many of the narratives, especially those dealing with the patriarchal and the Mosaic ages, came to be recognised as legendary in character, and in consequence appeared to be documents which could not be directly utilised in an exact reconstruction of historical events. Deep inroads had also been made by the literary analysis of the Pentateuch, which results in the distribution of this picture of Israel's early history over several major source-documents, which often diverge considerably in details, and the oldest of which, the Jahwist, dating from the early monarchical period, at best recounts 300 years at least after the events what took place prior to the settlement in Canaan. Nevertheless, following Wellhausen, even scholars whose approach was highly critical still clung substantially to the unilinear sequence of events represented by the bondage in Egypt, Sinai, the wandering in the wilderness, and the entry into Canaan; they also regarded Moses as Israel's authoritative leader throughout these stages.[1] But a complete change has come over this picture as the result of the investigation of the history of traditions; and this has only been brought into full play in our own time. In spite of its often very thoroughgoing criticism, previous historical research nevertheless still believed it possible to grasp the actual historical course of events, in its basic features at any rate, by a more or less immediate penetration behind the literary presentation. But this has turned out to be mistaken, since what lies at the back of the picture offered in the Hexateuch is still far from being the actual historical course of events, but is once again

[1] So e.g. H. Gressmann, *Mose und seine Zeit*, Göttingen 1913.

only certain interpretations and conceptions of older traditions which originate in *milieux* very different from one another and which must also be judged, from the point of view of form-criticism, as completely diverse. In the era now past, the main question for the critical examination of the Old Testament, and especially of the origins of Israel, was, in spite of its recognition of the legendary character of the older and oldest traditions, the question as to the content (the "what") of the record, the question as to the historical course of events. It was a right and proper question, but, as is evident to us today, it was put to the text too soon, since with every single unit of tradition the first questions which should occupy us are these: Who is reporting it? What is the standpoint of the report, and what is the reporter's probable historical and theological position? What led him to report as he did? With what viewpoint and tradition is he aligning himself? In a word, we are encountering sacral traditions of the most varied kinds, each of which demands its own special form of examination if we are to arrive at the historical fact reported. As a result, the presentation of events in the major source-documents J and E is, it seems to us, itself the conclusion and the internal balancing up of a long process of transmission; each of the individual narrative units which are now joined together in the main sources has a long history behind it, in the course of which it has been subjected to a variety of processes of reminting, and so re-interpreted as to be made relevant in up-to-date preaching. The units were, to begin with, completely independent. Then, as a general rule, they were absorbed into one of the larger blocks of traditions, e.g. those dealing with the patriarchal history, the events at Sinai, the wandering in the wilderness, etc., and were adapted to them. Then these blocks were themselves co-ordinated, although this again was not determined by the actual historical course of events, since that had long passed out of memory; its basis was rather a preconceived theological picture of the saving history already long established in the form of a cultic confession. As a result, for us the road from the picture given in the source documents back to actual history has turned out to be much longer, since the sources' simple picture, which the pioneers of literary analysis took as the starting-point of their investigations, has now to be seen as an end-stage, in which a long process of interpretation of Israel's early history came finally to rest. Here everything is shaped by faith; even the association of the events into a grand path of salvation is not merely historical record, but is in itself already an acknowledgment of the leadership of God. This history of the traditions before they reach their final form in the written sources comprises an incalculably diversified chapter of Israel's theology. In general, even the simplest fusion of two originally independent units of tradition was in itself already a process of theological interpretation. And, in the course of time, what masses of traditions were welded together to form these blocks! The chief points of this complex history of theological interpretation which has led to what we have before us in the documentary sources will be dealt with later, in the section entitled "The Theology of the Hexateuch."

It is thus the destruction of the ordered framework of the Hexateuchal tradition that makes discovery of the history in this early period particularly difficult for us today; for, although previously the legendary character of many of the individual traditions was fully recognised, it was still believed that the great framework (the period of the patriarchs—the oppression in Egypt—the Exodus—the Revelation at Sinai—the Wandering in the Wilderness—the Conquest) yielded a fairly reliable indication of the course of the history. But the case is very different if we reckon in all seriousness with the insight we now have, that even the sequence of the main events conforms already to a canonical *schema* of a cultic nature. This is, of course, far from implying that all that is preserved in this *schema* is unhistorical. But, after all, it does make a difference whether the presentation of Israel's early history rests upon direct historical memories, or whether it was Israel herself who arranged the sequence of events in a cultic confession which itself understands what took place according to an extremely generalised and simplifying pattern. (The analogy with criticism's destruction of the framework of the Synoptic Gospels is evident. There too it has been made clear that the framework cannot as such be taken as an historically trustworthy presentation of the course of Jesus' life.) A similar case is the Sinai pericope, in so far as that which stands behind it is not immediate memories of the event itself, but again, to begin with, cultic traditions. As will be shown later, the place in the life of the community of the earliest Sinaitic tradition is most probably to be found in a major festival.

Along with this, another fact won recognition; and its effect upon the traditional picture of the early history was once again initially destructive. According to Ex. 1. 6f. the people of Israel came into being in Egypt; and thenceforward "Israel" proceeds through all the well-known events of its history down to the migration into Canaan as a homo-geneous entity. But historical investigation has made it clear that "Israel" was the name given to the sacral alliance of the tribes which was only constituted in Palestine, after the Settlement. No attempt, so far, to establish historical proof of a "people of Israel" before this date has met with any success. This would mean that the idea of a "people of Israel" already in existence in Egypt, at Sinai, and in the wilderness, is due to the understandable anachronism of a later age—when it had passed out of mind that at that time there was as yet no such thing as Israel, but only tribes and tribal groups which afterwards entered the Israel that was to be and lost their independent identity in it. The duality among the sons of Rachel—Joseph (Ephraim and Manasseh) and Benjamin—on the one hand, and the sons of Leah—Reuben, Simeon, Levi, Judah, Issachar, and Zebulun—on the other, is of particular importance, since it persisted as a determining factor in the history of Israel right down to the period of the monarchy.[2] As distinct from the Bedouin proper, who were camel-owning nomads, these clans, to the best of our knowledge, lived the life of pastoral semi-nomads, tending flocks and herds. They were peaceable, and lived in tents on the steppe, especially on the southern margin of the arable part of Pales-tine. In winter they pastured their flocks there, and made the transition to farming on a modest scale (Gen. XXVI. 12); and in summer, in the course of shifting pasture, they ranged from it to and fro over the cropped fields of the arable land itself.

As to the religious and cultic ties of these pre-Mosaic ancestors of Israel, the historian of religion can say roughly this. Certain memories were preserved of the fact that they had not always been worshippers of Jahweh, but that his self-revelation only entered their life at a definite point in time (Ex. III. 1ff., VI. 1ff.). The Elohist and the Priestly Document take account of this break in the continuity of the history of revelation by designating the God who had dealings with the ancestors as Elohim, while using the name Jahweh only from Ex. III and Ex. VI onwards—that is, only after Jahweh's self-revelation. We can thus no longer expect the major documentary sources to give us a direct answer to the question, what was the religion of Israel's pre-Mosaic ancestors. But careful analysis of a certain body of tradition, which the sources have copiously preserved, has thrown a surprising light on the question

[2] A. Alt, *Kleine Schriften zur Geschichte Israels*, henceforth cited as *K.S.*, Munich 1953-9, VOL. I, pp. 40ff., 56ff., 65.

of the cult practised by these tribes and groups.[3] In the narratives in Genesis, mention is frequently made of the "God of thy father Abraham" (Gen. XXVI. 24, XXVIII. 13, XXXII. 10 [9]). At the making of the covenant between Laban and Jacob, the God of Nahor and the God of Abraham are even invoked as witnesses and set over against one another (Gen. XXXI. 53). Into this category also come such primitive designations as "the Fear of Isaac" (פחד יצחק Gen. XXXI. 42) and "the Mighty One of Jacob" (אביר יעקב Gen. XLIX. 24). Now, since inscriptions attest the worship of such "gods of the ancestors" among the Nabateans, who, in similar circumstances, moved over from the steppe to the arable land east of Jordan a thousand years later, we may infer a quite specific form of the religion and worship obtaining amongst these nomads before their migration into the arable land. In sharp distinction from all that we know of the cults of the Canaanites, the cult of the gods of the ancestors has no attachment to any specific place. On the contrary, its characteristic feature is its invariable connexion with a particular group and that group's fortunes. It was "a religion in which the main emphasis was laid on the relationship between God and man, and, further, between God and a group of men, without fixed attachment to a place, and on that account all the better adaptable to any changes in the fortunes of its devotees."[4] These features are already foreshadowings of the Jahwism of the future, the only difference being that in Jahwism they are present to a much greater degree. We should not underestimate the heritage contained in this pre-Jahwistic cult of the ancestors and its function in later Jahwism. Unquestionably, the later belief in Israel's election was already implicit in it. Abraham, Isaac, and Jacob were certainly the first to receive the revelation of a deity who pledged himself to care for them and lead them, and who promised them a portion in the arable land and a great posterity. What was this but an act of election, the memory of which the groups handed on from generation to generation in the cult founded by their ancestor? Thus, a pronounced aetiological factor was always involved when appeal was made to the God of the ancestors: this cult with all the promises of blessing it transmitted derived its sanction from the revelation given to the ancestor. Probably the extremely primitive story in Gen. xv. 7ff. which tells of the divine revelation received by Abraham was taken up into the Jahwist's later compilation of sagas in practically

[3] For what follows see A. Alt, "Der Gott der Väter," in K.S., VOL. I, pp. 1ff.
[4] Alt, op. cit., p. 62.

the identical form which it had in this earlier period. We have, of course, to assume that the groups worshipping respectively the God of Abraham, the Fear of Isaac, and the Strong One of Jacob, were originally distinct from one another. And in actual fact they still remained distinct even after the groups settled in the arable land, since, as we shall see later on, they each with their own ancestral cults attached themselves to different Palestinian shrines.[5]

Even in general outline it is no longer possible to reconstruct the political history of Israel's ancestors before the Settlement. All that is reasonably certain is that the Leah group became settled in Palestine considerably earlier than the Rachel group, and that the latter had meanwhile had further decisive and far-reaching religious experiences in the wilderness. There are three places which stand out from the impenetrable darkness which surrounds the prehistory of Israel, since memories of momentous events, which were of course of very different nature, were associated with them—Mt. Sinai, the oasis of Kadesh, and the Red Sea. It must again remain an open question which of the tribes had so far-reaching an experience at these places. We can hardly assume that it was one and the same group which came to these places in turn. It is much more likely that traditions belonging to different groups were united with one another at a later date.

1. From very early times Israel cherished vivid memories of Sinai as the scene where Jahweh had revealed himself in a special way. The question where the Sinai of the Bible was located, whether it was on the peninsula of Sinai, or in north-west Arabia and therefore to the east of the Red Sea, lies outwith the scope of the present discussion.[6] But the references to Midian which keep cropping up in the context of the mountain of God do require further discussion. It was during his stay with his Midianite father-in-law that Moses chanced upon this mountain (Ex. III. 1ff.). When Jahweh manifests himself on his mountain, the tents of Cushan tremble, the tabernacles of the land of Midian (Hab. III. 7).[7] But this implies that Sinai lay within the territory of the Midianites. These were camel-owning nomads, that is, true Bedouin; and, like the present-day Bedouin tribes still, they had their territory

---

[5] See below, pp. 20ff.

[6] References outside the Hexateuch are Jg. v. 4; Deut. XXXIII. 2; 1 Kings XIX. 8. M. Noth, *History of Israel*, henceforth cited as *History*, 2nd edn., trans. revised by P. R. Ackroyd, London 1958, pp. 141ff.

[7] Gressmann, *Mose und seine Zeit*, p. 417.

which they claimed as their own; only, in keeping with their roving mode of life, the areas in question were much bigger, and had no clearly demarcated political boundaries; they are therefore now largely beyond our power to describe. Originally the Midianites' territory lay to the east of the Gulf of Akaba; but at times it extended far out from there to the west and north-west; otherwise how could they have appeared at times in Palestine itself? (Jg. vIff.). The Kenites were a part of this extensive league—or else they were in fairly close relationship with it—since in Jg. I. 16, IV. 11, Moses' father-in-law is described as a Kenite. The relationship even between the later Israel and these Kenites was one of positive friendship (I Sam. xv. 5f., xxx. 29). These statements set us right into the midst of the range of discussion of the so-called Kenite hypothesis.[8] If it was in the territory of Midian that Moses chanced upon the mountain of God, then this mountain was obviously already a holy place, and for whom else initially but for Midian? But this then leads to the almost inevitable conclusion that the Midianites were worshippers of Jahweh before the "Israelites" were. Of the Kenites at all events this can be said with quite a measure of probability, both because of the friendly relationships, mentioned above, which they had with Israel, and also from the fact that in the life and death struggle of the Jahweh Amphictyony it was a Kenite woman who dealt the mortal blow to the leader of the enemy coalition (Jg. IV. 17, V. 24). Further, it has often been pointed out that in Ex. xvIII. 12 it is the Midianite Jethro who offers the sacrifice to Jahweh; this implies that in actual fact Jethro was the host, and Moses and his people the guests. Now, all these conjectures have in their turn received support from a remarkable body of Nabatean inscriptions.[9] At the foot of Jebel Serbal in the peninsula of Sinai, large numbers of Nabatean *graffiti* have been found, which had obviously been made by pilgrims who took this way of leaving a written record of their presence at the holy place. Perhaps their most remarkable feature is the wide area from which the pilgrims converged; one of them even came from Damascus. Thus, in the third and second centuries A.D. the mountain was a holy place which attracted pilgrims from far and near. Might not this cult have

---

[8] L. Köhler, *Old Testament Theology*, henceforth cited as *Theology*, trans. A. S. Todd, London 1957, pp. 45f.; *id.*, in *Z.A.W.*, 1957, pp. 10ff.; H. H. Rowley, *From Joseph to Joshua*, London 1950, pp. 149ff.

[9] B. Moritz, "Der Sinaikult in heidnischer Zeit," in *Abhandlungen der Göttinger Gesellschaft der Wissenschaften*, N.F. xvi, 2, 1916.

been nothing short of the successor of the earlier cult of Jahweh?[10] It would at least be perfectly conceivable that pre-Israelite tribes, too, from their steppes in the north of the Sinai peninsula, came into contact with the mountain of God, since the Wilderness of Sinai can never have reckoned as part of their homeland proper. Even now, the records still make it plain that the stay at Sinai was only of short duration. On the other hand, the experience which the tribes underwent there was of incalculable significance for the later Israel. There it was that Jahweh revealed himself as their God; by his just will, he took them into a bond from which they were never again to escape, and into which they later brought their brother clans as well. Afterwards, when settled in Palestine, Israel celebrated what took place at Sinai in a cultic festival.

The divine name Jahweh, the Tetragrammaton, raises all manner of problems for research.[11] But, especially in view of the question of its etymology, we shall have to keep in mind that for Israel the word "Jahweh" had become entirely no more than a name, and that, in consequence, the solution of the etymological question contributes little or nothing towards the theological significance of the name.[12] In the first place, the relationship of the full name, which occurs about 6,800 times in the Old Testament, to the forms יה (25 times) and יהו (in the Elephantine texts and on handles of jugs of the post-exilic period) would require investigation. In view of the fact that the Tetragrammaton occurs in the oldest documents of the Old Testament (cf. also the Moabite stone, I. 18, 850 B.C., and the Lachish Letters, 589 B.C.), there is little to be said for any assumption that would take יהו and יה (understood possibly as cultic ejaculations) to be the oldest forms of the name.[13] יה and יהו are shortened forms which came into use by way of addition. Certain clues to the pronunciation—that is, towards supplying the Tetragrammaton with vowels—are provided by transcriptions in the patristic literature, where the forms Ιαβε and Ιαουε occur.[14] The hardest problem is the etymological one proper, i.e., the question as to what the root-conso-

[10] Alt, *K.S.*, VOL. I, p. 5.

[11] A. Murtonen, *A Philological and Literary Treatise on the Old Testament Divine Names*, Helsinki 1952; G. Quell, in *Theologisches Wörterbuch zum Neuen Testament*, henceforth cited as *Th.W.B.N.T.*, ed. G. Kittel, Stuttgart 1930–60, VOL. III, pp. 1064ff.; G. R. Driver, "The original form of the name 'Jahweh'," in *Zeitschrift für die alttestamentliche Wissenschaft*, henceforth cited as *Z.A.W.*, 1928, pp. 7ff.

[12] Köhler, *Theology*, pp. 40f.   [13] Driver, in *Z.A.W.*, 1928, pp. 24ff.

[14] References in Quell, *Th.W.B.N.T.*, VOL. III, p. 1066.

nants of the word once signified. Immediately following it is the other question, whether we are to take the Tetragrammaton as a nominal or a verbal form. If the latter, it would have to be taken as formed from the imperfect, leaving the question open whether it is to be regarded as imperfect Qal or Hiphil. Yet the causative interpretation ("the one who calls into being," "who causes to be") put upon it by Albright, the most distinguished representative of the Hiphil theory, is not entirely convincing.[15] Is it not far too abstract and *recherché* for so early a time? In opposition to it the Qal idea ("the passionate," "the one who loves passionately") has once again been advocated in recent times, on the basis of an Arabic root *hwj*, "to be passionate."[16] A special problem for the history of religion emerged when certain theophorous names came to notice outside Israel (e.g. Jaubidi from Hamath, Azrijau from Samal). Is the theophorous element in these names to be brought into connexion with Jahweh?[17] This question has entered upon a new phase with the Ras Shamra texts, since a god Jw, a son of the god El, turned up in them.[18] But it is not very likely that this west-Semitic deity is to be connected with the Jahweh of the Kenites and the Israelites, whose worship originated in the extreme south of Palestine. On Ex. III. 14, see below, p. 180.

2. At Kadesh, on the other hand, according to the later tradition, Israel stayed "a long time" (Deut. I. 46). It is in actual fact perfectly conceivable that the cluster of oases at Kadesh, which lies about sixty or seventy miles south of Beersheba, formed part of the territory in which the later Israelite tribes lived and pastured their flocks.[19] The name itself indicates that we have to picture Kadesh as a sacral centre. More detailed information can be derived from the names Massa and

[15] W. F. Albright, *From the Stone Age to Christianity*, 2nd edn. Baltimore 1957, p. 259.

[16] S. D. Goitein, "YHWH the Passionate," in *Vetus Testamentum*, henceforth cited as *Vet. Test.*, 1956, pp. 1ff.

[17] G. R. Driver, in *Z.A.W.*, 1928, pp. 7ff.

[18] J. Gray, "The God YW in the religion of Canaan," in *Journal of Near Eastern Studies*, 1953, pp. 278ff.

[19] References to Kadesh which admit of an inference are Ex. XVII. 7; Num. XX. 1ff., 13, XXVII. 14, XXXIII. 36; Deut. XXXIII. 8; Ps. XCV. 8. It is perfectly correct to say that we have no Kadesh traditions in the sense of a body of traditions into which numerous units were woven. But we do have some single references which ought not to be passed over, since they allow inferences to be made about a stay at Kadesh (especially Deut. XXXIII. 8f.). That it never came here to a real formation of tradition could be precisely a sign of great antiquity. (But see M. Noth, *Überlieferungsgeschichte des Pentateuch*, henceforth cited as *Pentateuch*, Stuttgart 1948, pp. 181f.)

Meribah, which are probably to be taken as designations of different oases in this district (Ex. XVII. 7; Num. XX. 13, 24), for they imply that legal cases were investigated and decided by ordeal there (נסה, to put to the test, prove; ריב, to carry on a lawsuit). The same thing is implied in the name "Spring of Judgment" עין משפם, which was a current name for Kadesh or for one of its oases (Gen. XIV. 7). Kadesh was therefore a well-known sanctuary where divine justice was administered and cases in dispute decided. We do not know whether the God who was worshipped there was Jahweh: it is also possible that his cult was brought there later. But at the time when Levi exercised his functions at Kadesh, it must have been a sanctuary of Jahweh. Levi had already migrated into the arable land along with the Leah tribes, but had then suffered some calamity in central Palestine (Gen. XXXIV, XLIX. 5–7), and, along with Simeon, had turned back again to the south, the district in which it had originally been settled. Simeon established itself around Beersheba, and Levi became the guardian of the sacral traditions of Kadesh. But we have also to reckon with a temporary migration to Egypt by Levi or parts of Levi, since Moses was of the tribe of Levi (Ex. II. 1); this migration is also confirmed by other Egyptian names which persisted in the tribe of Levi.[20] The Levi oracle in the Blessing of Moses gives dark hints at a grave dispute which was decided at Kadesh, and in which Levi proved its worth (Deut. XXXIII. 8).[21]

3. The praises with which later Israel celebrated the deliverance from Egypt and the rescue at the Red Sea are a vast chorale surpassing all the praise she gave for all other divine actions. But here again only the outlines of the historical event can be established. That certain sections of the later Israelite tribes migrated into the Delta region of Egypt is beyond doubt. To start with, they may have gone there while seeking change of pasture-ground, but afterwards, as a less-privileged section

---

[20] M. Noth, *Die israelitischen Personennamen*, Beihefte zur *Zeitschrift für die alttestamentliche Wissenschaft*, henceforth cited as Bei. *Z.A.W.*, Giessen 1928, p. 63.

[21] That לוי was not originally a proper name but an appellative designation has been rendered very probable by the Minaean (south Arabian) inscriptions, where *lawi'u* is the designation of a class in the personnel of a temple. G. Hölscher, "Levi," in Pauly-Wissowa, *Real-Encyclopädie der classischen Altertums Wissenschaft*, henceforth cited as Pauly-Wissowa, 2nd edn. VOL. XII, 2, Stuttgart 1925; E. Nielsen, *Shechem*, Copenhagen 1955, pp. 264ff. But we have still not succeeded in fusing the by no means scanty notices in the Old Testament about Levi into a convincing picture of the early history of this clan.

of the population, they were conscripted by the Egyptians for forced labour on large-scale building operations. They sought to escape from this—perhaps they simply fled (Ex. xiv. 5). They were pursued, but the chariot division which followed them up was drowned while crossing a "sea."[22] In this event, quite insignificant by the standards of secular history, those who were delivered experienced something which in its significance far transcended the personal fate of those who at the time shared in it. The deliverance from Egypt and the rescue at the Red Sea found their way into Israel's confession of faith—indeed, they actually became Israel's earliest confession, around which the whole Hexateuchal history was in the end ranged.[23]

In practically all the accounts of the period from the sojourn in Egypt down to the arrival in the land east of Jordan, the reader encounters Moses. He is the one called by God; he led Israel out of Egypt, he mediates the revelation given at Mt. Sinai, and he led the people through every danger until they reached the steppes of Moab. For the understanding of the individual narratives, it is quite impossible to overestimate the impulse of connexion which he imparts. If the reader were not constantly meeting with him, the renowned leader, the man of God, the warrior, etc., the whole of what is presented to us in the documentary sources as a connected narrative would disintegrate into a series of rather incoherent episodes. Criticism, of course, long ago noticed that this picture of Moses displays features of the utmost complexity; not only do the various source-documents offer widely divergent versions of the "office" of Moses, but even the separate narratives which came under their consideration sometimes contain very distinctive and often quite independent traditions about him.[24]

[22] M. Noth, *History*, pp. 115ff. The determination of the place where the miracle at the Red Sea happened has also become difficult. Earlier it was thought to be the Gulf of Suez or a shallow end of it. But Gressmann (*Mose und seine Zeit*, pp. 415f.) drew attention to the view that the Gulf of Akaba is meant by the designation "the Red Sea." Completely new points of view are to be found in O. Eissfeldt's *Baal Zaphon, Zeus Kasios und der Durchzug der Israeliten durchs Meer*, Beiträge zur Religionsgeschichte des Altertums, Heft 1, Halle 1932, where with an almost compelling array of evidence the miracle is transferred to Lake Sirbonis, that is, to a lagoon of the Mediterranean lying to the east of the Nile Delta. But obviously within the Old Testament itself there are various attempts to determine the place. Cf. M. Noth, "Der Schauplatz des Meerwunders," in *Festschrift O. Eissfeldt*, ed. J. Fück, Halle 1947, pp. 181ff.

[23] M. Noth, *Überlieferungsgeschichtliche Studien* (Schriften der Königsberger Gelehrten-Gesellschaft), henceforth cited as *Überl. Studien*, Stuttgart 1943, pp. 53f.

[24] Gressmann, *Mose und seine Zeit, passim.*

But with this question as well, the final result only became apparent with the destruction of the framework of the Hexateuch. If it is true that the picture of the course of events given in the Hexateuch only arose from a confessional arrangement of different complexes of tradition, then the question of the historicity of Moses and his functions can only be put as follows: in which of these groups of tradition and in which of the separate traditions is the figure of Moses originally rooted? It is, of course, obvious that with the passage of time, this renowned figure of the past could have forced his way into other narrative contexts where originally he was a stranger. Noth made a careful examination of the material, both in the Pentateuch and outside it, bearing upon this question, and concluded that to begin with the figure of Moses had no place in a great number of the Pentateuchal traditions. It is not possible to examine this thesis here—indeed, the very nature of the case no longer admits the possibility of any exact answer to the question. But even those who believe that the historical element can be regarded as broader and more firmly founded than this are, for all that, far from gaining the picture of Moses as the founder of a religion so urgently sought by the modern reader. In every case they only reach very ancient individual traditions which are difficult to reconcile with one another. Here too it is a constant surprise to observe how greatly interest in the sacral function of Moses, his "office," outweighs interest in his person; and along with this, the old narrators are already haunted by an interest directed mainly to something relevant to their own time and not merely to the historical or biographical.

CHAPTER B

THE CRISIS DUE TO THE CONQUEST

UNDOUBTEDLY the clans which entered the arable land brought with them a copious stock of religious traditions. It would be a great help to succeed in getting a more precise apprehension of them and marking them off from later concepts, for even after her settlement, in contrast to other peoples who also adopted the settled life after formerly being nomads, Israel hallowed and cherished the traditions of her early days.[1] But since these, in origin nomadic, were afterwards not only indissolubly interwoven with ideas belonging to the agricultural religion of the Canaanites, but were also continually moulded and remoulded by later generations, it is now well-nigh impossible to free them from this embrace and restore them as they were understood originally. The situation was more favourable with the gods of the ancestors, in that it was a question there of a complete cultic province which had preceded the cult of Jahweh in time and could be detached from it. What would be of very special interest to us would be to learn something of the forms and contents of the most ancient Jahwism. But here too we come up against the difficulty just mentioned. Such traditions of it as we have probably derive, to some extent, from a comparatively early time, though it was for all that a time which had already made a very decided advance upon the earliest phase of Jahwism. Consequently, our only possibility is to indicate absolutely isolated cultic traditions whose origin in this earliest phase can be postulated. Since, however, we cannot even gain an approximate picture of the cultic relationships of that time as a whole in this way, no attempt to do it will be made here. To be sure, as far as Passover is concerned, it has been asserted from very early times that this pastoral rite dates back not only to the "Mosaic period" but probably to a still remoter past. But here too we come up against the difficulty that, when we meet it, this cultic celebration is already interpreted historically, an interpretation which probably became attached to the old rite soon after the experience of the Exodus. Thus, any attempt to reconstruct the still older Passover celebration must remain hypo-

[1] V. Maag, in *Vet. Test.*, Suppl. VII (1959), pp. 135ff.

thetical.[2] Israel's nomadic ancestors certainly already practised circumcision, and probably even kept the Sabbath.[3] As to cultic objects, we should probably best assume that the holy tent already existed in the pre-Palestinian period.

There is much to be said for the idea that the worship of the God Jahweh only came into Palestine with the last of the groups which entered it, namely the "house of Joseph," and that it was only there adopted by the other clans of the Leah group who had already settled in the land. Indeed, the account of the "assembly at Shechem" (Josh. XXIV) suggests that, in an hour fraught with drama, the house of Joseph, through its spokesman Joshua, simply forced upon the rest of the clans the decision for or against Jahweh. For, as was noticed long ago, this story is perfectly incomprehensible from the standpoint of the later idea according to which all of the clans were at Sinai.[4] What sense would Joshua's summons to put away the foreign gods and decide for Jahweh have had then? The story therefore preserves a very ancient memory of a cultic antagonism which developed among the clans because of the entry of the worshippers of Jahweh, and over and above that of an event of far-reaching significance for the history of the cult, namely the founding of the old Israelite Amphictyony. The assumption that

[2] A very plausible interpretation has been proposed by L. Rost, "Weidewechsel und altisraelitischer Festkalender," in Zeitschrift des deutschen Palästina Vereins, henceforth cited as Z.D.P.V., 1943, pp. 205ff.

[3] The significance of the Sabbath in earlier Israel is not at all easy to determine. From the point of view of the history of religion it seems in the last analysis to fall into the category of the dies nefasti, the days of taboo, during which people refrained from more important tasks, because these days stood under baneful influences. All that remains to the Sabbath in Israel of this, its earliest, prehistory, is of course only that it was a day of rest; but it was none the less not counted among the festivals, because in earlier Israel the Sabbath was never solemnised with any kind of positive act of worship. If we properly understand the Sabbath year, the year of a sacral fallow-time proclaimed every seven years, by looking on it as an act of confession by means of which Jahweh's original right of ownership of the soil was to be demonstrated, then we might in a similar way look on the Sabbath as a day which was to be kept from all disposal of man's and given back to Jahweh, a kind of day which reckons as a standard. There must also be some kind of connexion with the Babylonian šapattu, the 15th day of the month (the day of the full moon), but the assumption that the Sabbath was in Israel too originally the day of the full moon has not been proved, K. Budde in Z.A.W., 1930, pp. 138ff. For the problem of the Sabbath in general, see E. Jenni, Die theologische Begründung des Sabbatgebotes im Alten Testament, Zollikon-Zürich 1956, pp. 1ff.

[4] E. Sellin, Geschichte des israelitisch-jüdischen Volkes, henceforth cited as Geschichte, Leipzig 1924-32, VOL. I, pp. 97ff.

the Israelite clans' worship of Jahweh is to be understood on the analogy of the sacral cultic leagues of ancient Greece and Rome is not a new one, but it has only recently been developed systematically and raised to such a degree of certainty as is attainable in this field.[5] The clan league then founded at Shechem had no directly political functions. It was a sacral community, that is, it united the clans in the worship of the God Jahweh and the care of the common sanctuary. Politically the clans were left to themselves in the same way as before, and had to look out for themselves and the territory they occupied. Only when the Amphictyony itself was threatened or when its vital interests were involved—when, for example, the existence or non-existence of a whole clan was at stake—did it take action in a military capacity. These wars were then holy wars, in which Jahweh himself fought in defence of his own people; they were sacral operations, before which the men sancti-fied themselves—submitted, that is, to abstention from sexual inter-course—and whose termination was the ban (חֵרֶם), the assignment of the spoil to Jahweh.[6] But the various different enterprises of this kind about which we still have information make amply clear how thoroughly weak the bond was at the point where it ought to have proved its worth politically. Even in the most important event of this sort, the battle against the Canaanite coalition (Jg. ivf.), only six clans took part. The general summons to such enterprises was issued by a charismatic leader upon whom Jahweh's spirit had come. Here too the initiative lay wholly with Jahweh. It is here in these holy wars that the demand for faith in Jahweh had its ultimate roots.[7]

A much greater part in promoting a real union of the clans was played by the regular pilgrimages of the members of the Amphictyony to the common sanctuary, where the holy Ark rested. Indeed these pilgrimages—particularly the one at the great harvest festival—with their sacrifices and pledging to the Covenant were quite the high points in the life of the clan alliance. A whole series of texts reveals not only the existence of an amphictyonic cultic festival, but even some substantial information about its liturgical ordering. It appears certain

---

[5] M. Noth, *Das System der zwölf Stämme Israels*, Beiträge zur Wissenchaft von Alten und Neuen Testament, henceforth cited as B.W.A.N.T., Stuttgart 1930. But in the neighbourhood of Israel clans also seem to have united in alliances of 12 members (Gen. XXV. 12–18, XXII. 20–4, XXXVI. 1–4).

[6] G. von Rad, *Der Heilige Krieg im alten Israel*, Zürich 1951, pp. 25ff.

[7] On Ex. XIV. 31 and Jg. VII. 1ff. see von Rad, *op. cit.*, pp. 32, 44ff.

that it mainly consisted in a solemn engagement to Jahweh's will for justice, and this took the form on each occasion of a renewal of the Covenant.[8] As far as we can see, it is here that the Decalogue had its actual place (*Sitz im Leben*), or, at any rate, the oldest place that we can scientifically ascertain. This does not imply any pronouncement about the Decalogue's absolute age. Since we have to regard it as a perfectly conscious and well-considered combination of what are particularly characteristic commandments of Jahweh drawn up for the purpose of the address at this festival—that is, since we are to take it as a selection made from a much ampler tradition—we must in any case go much further back to find the period when such commandments were formed.[9]

To digress for a moment, the designation of Jahweh as יהוה צבאות starts at this time—that is, if we may accept the distribution in the books of the Bible as historical. The fact that this divine designation does not occur in the books from Genesis to Judges, and that it appears in close connexion with the Ark in the book of Samuel, suggests that it originated in the eleventh century in Shiloh. The problem connected with this divine designation is initially philological, in that it is not possible simply to take it as a conjunction of absolute and construct. It has therefore been supposed that the form יהוה אלהי צבאות is to be taken as the more original and יהוה צבאות as a slovenly secondary abbreviation. But the difficulty here is the fact that the form יהוה אלהי צבאות occurs only 18 times, while the shorter occurs

[8] The first advance in this direction was made by S. Mowinckel when he said that the Sinai pericope in JE was to be understood as the literary deposit of cultic activities It was also he who brought Psalms LXXXI and L into the discussion, because at the back of them as well a cultic recitation of the commandments can be discerned (*Le Déca-logue*, Paris 1927). Further, Deut. XXVII. 9ff., XI. 29 and Josh. XXIV, 25ff. are of special importance. The lay-out of the main parts of Deuteronomy (paraenesis—command-ments—making of the Covenant—blessing and cursing) is also a link in the chain of proof. H. J. Kraus, *Gottesdienst in Israel*, Munich 1954, pp. 43ff., 49ff.

[9] The Decalogue itself affords no evidence that would help to determine its age. The Mosaic authorship of the "primitive Decalogue", when freed from its secondary additions, is neither to be gainsaid nor proved by scientific means. On the cultic formula in which Jahweh introduces himself, "I am Jahweh, your God, who brought you out of the land of Egypt," and its widely ramified elaboration from the point of view of form-criticism, see W. Zimmerli, "Ich bin Jahweh," in *Geschichte und Altes Testament, Festschrift Albrecht Alt*, Tübingen 1953, pp. 179ff., and K. Elliger, "Ich bin der Herr, euer Gott," in *Theologie als Glaubenswagnis, Festschrift Karl Heim*, Hamburg 1954, pp. 9ff.

267 times, and that the texts in which the longer form occurs do not make it at all probable that it is the older. In my opinion, there is much more to be said for assuming that the longer form is to be taken as an interpretation of the older. If the longer form is regarded as original, then, in view of I Sam. XVII. 45, the reference would certainly be to the earthly armies of Israel. But this does not fit in with the fact that the expression enjoyed a particular popularity with the prophets (247 times), and in their threats the last thing to be expected is any allusion to Jahweh's involvement with the armies of Israel. Because of this, others have made the צבאות refer to the heavenly beings or the stars (cf. Gen. II. I). With a name for God as old as this we have, of course, right away to abandon all ideas that it had at all times and for all groups the same significance. Why, is not the very question as to the meaning of the divine title due to the false supposition that an ele-ment of cultic epiklesis as old as this is in all circumstances capable of rational explanation? The attempt has recently been made to take the plural צבאות as an intensive abstract plural (approximately in the sense of "might"), and to interpret the word then as a second name. Such formations of names with *oth* are in actual fact copiously attested. In this case, the collocation would, of course, naturally be explained in an adjectival sense.[10]

Jahweh had become "the God of Israel" in the way already de-scribed.[11] Initially, of course, this union of the clans on the basis of the acknowledgment of Jahweh would be far from resulting in complete religious uniformity. On the contrary, it must have complicated the situation all the more, for the people whom Joshua so aggressively con-fronted with the alternative of worshipping Jahweh or serving idols are the very people who already possessed inherited cultic ties. In this connexion we shall have to think chiefly of the worship of the gods of the ancestors, which had of course in the interval undergone change in form and substance. The clans who settled in the arable land could not help making contact with some of the fairly widely renowned Canaan-ite shrines. These too were shrines to which pilgrimages were made,

---

[10] Thus O. Eissfeldt, "Jahwe Zebaoth," in *Miscellanea academica Berolinensia*, 1950, pp. 128ff. See also the most recent study in detail by B. N. Wambacq, *L'Épithète divine Jahvé Sebaoth*, Bruges 1947.

[11] The formula "Jahweh, the God of Israel" which is of frequent occurrence in the Old Testament, is originally attached to the Ark and also derives from the district of Shechem. C. Steuernagel, in *Festschrift für Wellhausen*, Giessen 1914, p. 331.

and to which crowds of people flocked at festival times. These festivals
gave those coming from a distance both a chance of joining in worship
and a welcome opportunity for holding markets: there was buying and
selling, courtships and betrothals took place, and disputes were settled.
The festival became a fair.[12] From this rhythm of life, in which, as we
have said, economic life too had its part, the new immigrants could not
escape. What was easier for them than to continue to celebrate their
ancestral cults at these very sanctuaries, at the same time, however,
more and more assimilating the outlook of the particular place of
worship? Quite unconsciously they made a connexion between the
founders of their cults and their own recipients of revelation and the
place of worship—that is, unawares the figures of Abraham, Isaac, and
Jacob became assimilated to the cultic legends which were initially
Canaanite in origin. Thus, for example, the worshippers of the God of
Abraham belonging to the Leah group came within the orbit of the
tree sanctuary of Mamre and made this sanctuary's cult saga their own
by relating the visit of the three divine beings to their own ancestor
Abraham (Gen. XVIII). But this process of transplanting the cult of the
ancestral gods to shrines formerly Canaanite, and the assimilation of the
figures of the patriarchs to Canaanite cult sagas that it involved, was
far from being ended with the clans' adoption of Jahwism. The
acquaintance of the Ephraimites with Bethel and the connexion of
Bethel's cult saga with Jacob (Gen. XXVIII. 10ff.) presumably came into
being only after the assembly at Shechem. Obviously the cult of Jahweh, to which the amphictyonic alliance as a body regarded itself as
pledged, still left a good deal of freedom in its members' religious practice, with the result that, in this early period, we have to distinguish
between national and tribal religion.[13] In the end the Jahweh cult also
found entrance, gradually, into the sanctuaries in the areas settled by the
tribes.

The fact is that we cannot paint our picture of the cultic life of that
time when the clans lived side by side in almost complete autonomy
with too lively or bright colours. No doubt the worship of Jahweh
and the obligation of caring for his sanctuary ranked above everything
else. But there was still a long way to be gone before the clans were
penetrated by and united in faith in this God. No doubt the whole of
Israel annually made pilgrimages to the central sanctuary, where a

[12] J. Wellhausen, *Reste arabischen Heidentums, Skizzen und Vorarbeiten*, Berlin 1898,
pp. 87ff.   [13] Alt, *K.S.*, VOL. I, pp. 58f.

priesthood serving Jahweh guarded the pure traditions. But the Jahweh who sat enthroned upon the Ark was at first only of limited significance for the everyday concerns of the Israelite farmer. We hear occasionally of the annual sacrifice, at which kinsmen met (I Sam. XX. 6, 29; II Sam. XV. 7, 11f.). While we have no exact knowledge as to what this sacrifice comprised, we do still have grounds for assuming that, just in these early days themselves, such partial and local cultic obligations had greater importance for Israel than Jahwism had. There are many allusions which allow us to presume that there was attached to every town a place of worship at which the inhabitants offered sacrifice to Jahweh (I Sam. IX. 12f., XVI. 5). But at what date can Jahwism have thoroughly penetrated into these local shrines? And where had the holy tent stayed? In the tradition the latter falls noticeably into the background vis-à-vis the Ark. But for all that it has to be assumed that, even after the Conquest, the tent was the focal point of a group of worshippers.[14]

Later on, Bethel seems to have been the clan alliance's central sanctuary (Jg. XX. 18, 26f.), then Shiloh (I Sam. 1ff.), and, after its destruction, Gilgal (near Jericho) seems temporarily to have taken over its functions.[15] This is best taken as a chronological succession. But how slight is our knowledge of all the cultic groups which at any given time existed side by side! We have already seen that, even after the founding of the Jahweh Amphictyony, Bethel continued to attract large groups of worshippers. A god Bethel was worshipped there; the traces of his cult are demonstrable over a wide area in Israel.[16] Of the tribes Issachar and Zebulun, the Blessing of Moses says that they "called people to the mountain" (Deut. XXXIII. 19). The mountain is Tabor (Hos. V. 1), where too there was a widely-renowned shrine—thus, again, a little amphictyonic centre which had its firmly attached group of worshippers.[17] But the god to whom worship was offered at Tabor was, originally, no more Jahweh than was the case at the Bethel shrine: he was one of the El deities, those local fertility and weather deities whose worship was widespread in Canaan. The same holds true for the shrine

[14] See below, p. 61.

[15] Bethel: Jg. XX. 26f.; Shiloh: I Sam. 1ff.; Jer. VII. 12ff.; Gilgal: I Sam. X. 8, XI. 14f., XIII. 4, 7, XV. 12, 21, 33.

[16] O. Eissfeldt, "Der Gott Bethel," in *Archiv für Religionswissenschaft*, 1930, pp. 1ff.; K. Galling, "Bethel und Gilgal," in *Z.D.P.V.*, 1944, pp. 26ff.

[17] O. Eissfeldt, "Der Gott des Tabor," in *Archiv für Religionswissenschaft*, 1934, pp. 14ff.

on Carmel.[18] At Shechem, worship was offered to a "Baal of the Covenant" (Jg. IX. 4), and at Beersheba to an El Olam (Gen. XXI. 33); and similarly, in the extreme south, to an El Roi, "a god who manifests himself" (Gen. XVI. 13). A like situation must have obtained at the sanctuary of Penuel east of Jordan. And, alongside of those celebrated sanctuaries, there were the "high places," that is, shrines of more local significance, and against whose number, and their demoralising influence, the prophets afterwards raised voluble complaint.[19] The cults there practised were pure fertility cults, as was appropriate to a farming population: Baal was the owner (the term was originally taken as appellative) of a mountain, or an oasis, or some other place. His relationship to the earth was that of a ἱερὸς γάμος; he is the mythical generative power that fructifies the earth by means of the sperm of the rain.[20] Human beings share in his fertilising power by entering this mystery and imitating it. Cultic prostitution was therefore an essential characteristic of this worship: sacred prostitutes lived at the sanctuaries (קדשה I Kings XV. 12; II Kings XXIII. 7; Deut. XXIII. 18), and *Mazzeboth*, roughly-hewn stone pillars (Gen. XXVIII. 18; Ex. XXIII. 24; Deut. XVI. 22), or wooden poles called *Asheroth* (Jg. VI. 25; Deut. XVI. 21), both of them perhaps phallic symbols, were characteristic cultic objects. Alongside Baal stood Astarte, who was patently the goddess of fertility. A cult which had already at an early period been imported from Babylon into Palestine and Syria was that of Dagon: he too was a vegetation deity (I Sam. V. 2ff.). From the place-names Anathoth and Beth Anath it may be inferred that the cult of Anath was also celebrated in these earlier days. About this Anath, the sister of Alijan Baal, the Ras Shamra texts have now provided us with clearer information: indeed, they give us knowledge of quite a pantheon of almost Homeric dimensions, and allow us to draw a considerable number of conclusions about the Palestinian outlook which was admittedly much simpler, because more

[18] K. Galling, "Der Gott Karmel und die Ächtung fremder Götter," in *Festschrift Albrecht Alt*, Tübingen 1953, pp. 105ff.; O. Eissfeldt, "Der Gott Karmel," in *Sitzungsber. d. deutschen Akademie d. Wissenschaften*, Berlin 1953.

[19] The root meaning of במה is "ridge"; but it changed into the concept of "cultic place," cf. the phrase "to build a במה," I Kings XIV. 23; II Kings XVII. 9 and elsewhere. A. Schwarzenbach, *Die geographische Terminologie im Hebräischen des Alten Testaments*, Leiden 1954, pp. 12ff. For other interpretations see W. F. Albright in *Vet. Test.*, Suppl. IV (1957), pp. 242ff.; O. E. Eissfeldt in *Journal of the Palestine Oriental Society*, 1936, pp. 287f.

[20] M. Buber, *Königtum Gottes*, 2nd edn. Berlin 1936, pp. 65f.

rustic. Before this epoch-making discovery our knowledge of the religion of ancient Canaan was derived solely from conclusions to be drawn from the Old Testament, and from a careful use of very late sources of information about Phoenician mythology.[21]

The meeting of Jahwism with this completely alien cultic world came about quite unsensationally—it grew up out of the contacts of many Hebrew groups with Canaanite sanctuaries.[22] Thus we must certainly not assume either that, to begin with at any rate, Jahwism gave its devotees the help of any instructions or rules. It had, of course, in general first to become aware of its difference from these cults, and that demanded time. Also, the *tempo* of the Canaanisation of Jahwism differed very radically from district to district—the process obviously went on more rapidly in the north than in the Judean south, more slowly in the clan of Ephraim than with Manasseh, who lived in much closer symbiosis with Canaanite city-states and sanctuaries.[23] The later Deuteronomic theology's clear realisation of its own separatedness from all that was Canaanite only comes as the fruit of a long experience of this cultic world. So the influence of this religious world of Canaan upon Jahwism was initially very deep. A great many details reveal the same story happening time and time again, namely, how radical was Jahwism's assimilation of Canaanite ideas. Jahweh was now thought of as a god of high heaven, sitting on his throne, surrounded by divine beings and taking solemn counsel with them (1 Kings XXII. 19ff.; Is. VI. 3ff., 8; cf. Ps. LXXXII), just as the Ugaritic father of the gods El, "the father of years," sat enthroned over his pantheon. Thus the conception of Jahweh which became most widespread in Israel, that of the king in high heaven, ousted the older tradition of the Jahweh who comes from Sinai (Jg. v. 4f.; Deut. XXXIII. 2). The absorption of this

---

[21] W. Baumgartner, "Ras Schamra und das AT," in *Theologische Rundschau*, henceforth cited as *Th.R.*, 1940, pp. 163ff.; 1941, pp. 1ff., 85ff., 157ff.; *id.*, "Ugaritische Probleme und ihre Tragweite für das A.T.," in *Theologische Zeitschrift*, henceforth cited as *Th.Z.*, 1947, pp. 81ff.; G. Fohrer, "Die wiederentdeckte kanaanäische Religion," in *Theologische Literaturzeitung*, henceforth cited as *Th.Lz.*, 1953, cols. 193ff.

[22] The process of the Canaanisation of Jahwism has often been depicted. E. Sellin, *Geschichte*, VOL. I, pp. 121ff.; *id.*, *Israel.-jüd. Religionsgeschichte*, Leipzig 1933, pp. 35ff.; G. Hölscher, *Geschichte der israel.-jüd. Religion*, Giessen 1922, pp. 69ff.; J. Hempel, *Gott und Mensch im Alten Testament*, 2nd edn. Stuttgart 1936, pp. 52ff.; F. Hvidberg, *Den israelitiske Religions Historie*, Copenhagen 1944; G. Widengren, *Sacrales Königtum im Alten Testament und im Judentum*, Stuttgart 1955, pp. 7–16.

[23] Alt, *K.S.*, VOL. I, pp. 127ff.

ancient Canaanite conception is of course inconceivable apart from a process of demythologising which it certainly underwent at once. The gods became Jahweh's heavenly ministers.[24] The length to which this assimilation of things Canaanite went is shown by the taking over of purely Canaanite divine titles. According to Num. xxiv. 8, Jahweh has "horns like a wild bull"—but the horned crown is an attribute of deity with which Israel can only have become acquainted in Canaan. The designation of Baal as "Rider on the clouds"[25] has thrown light on the strange רכב בערבות in Ps. LXVIII, which must also be translated "riding upon clouds." Many of the cultic usages too were taken over by Jahwism,[26] particularly the sacrifices and their rituals. In the technique of consulting the oracle Israel too now used the ephod (אפוד), which was likely understood to begin with as the garment worn by a deity. As such it could signify a cuirass-like metal covering put upon a wooden pillar or an image of the deity (Jg. VIII. 26f., XVII. 5). But it could also be a woven garment which the priest put on (I Sam. II. 28, XIV. 3) when he gave oracles and acted as the mouthpiece of the deity. At a very much later date the ephod appears as a part of the high priestly vestments.[27] Even the rotation of the purely rustic and agrarian festivals was taken over by Jahwism from the native population and from their cultic system.[28] So it is no wonder, either, that in the matter of her sacred song Israel went to school with the Canaanites. The idea is even entertained that she took over whole poems from the Canaanite cult.[29]

[24] Alt, *K.S.*, VOL. I, pp. 354f.

[25] rkb 'rpt. See C. H. Gordon, *Ugaritic Handbook, Vol. I-III*, henceforth cited as *Handbook*, Rome 1947, Glossary, Nr. 1869.

[26] R. Dussaud, *Les Origines cananéennes du sacrifice israélite*, Paris 1921.

[27] K. Elliger, "Ephod," in *Die Religion in Geschichte und Gegenwart*, 3rd edn.; H. Thiersch, *Ependytes und Ephod*, Berlin 1936; *id.*, in *Z.A.W.*, 1935, pp. 180ff.

[28] The three main festivals were expressly agrarian festivals. Mazzoth was celebrated about the time of the beginning of the wheat harvest; the feast of weeks—it is called in Ex. XXIII. 16 the harvest-feast (קציר)—signified the end of the corn harvest; and the festival of tabernacles—it is called in Ex. XXIII. 16 the feast of ingathering (אסף)—marked the vintage and the end of the year. Passover has to be carefully distinguished from these three festivals, for it was celebrated by the families in their own houses. It was only made a pilgrimage feast (חג) by Deuteronomy (Deut. XVI. 1ff.).

[29] This is suspected especially in the case of Ps. XXIX. J. J. Stamm, in *Th.R.*, 1955, p. 28; A. R. Johnson, *Sacral Kingship in Ancient Israel*, henceforth cited as *Sacral Kingship*, Cardiff 1945, pp. 54ff.; more recently W. Schmidt, *Königtum Gottes in Ugarit und Israel*, Bei. *Z.A.W.* v. 80, Berlin 1961, pp. 45ff.

Later on, that is, within the range of the Deuteronomic theology, Israel regarded any taking over of Canaanite cultic usages, or even any borrowing from them, as the most serious form of apostasy from Jahweh. At that time, therefore, saying "No" to the Canaanite cult had come to be *articulus stantis et cadentis ecclesiae*. If this is the standard by which this first period of settlement in the arable land is to be assessed, the verdict to be passed upon it could be quickly reached. But it is not hard to see that, in this adjustment to alien cultic forms, Jahwism acted under the urgent need of self-preservation. It was, of course, in face of the settlers' tremendously changed conditions of life that Jahwism was to a large extent compelled to express itself in a completely new fashion: and in this process of change many of the Canaanite ideas were of help to it, since Jahwism was able to flow into them, and in them to gain a new form. For example, to mention only what was of greatest importance, Jahwism had not basically any special relationship to the arable land, the phenomenon of the productive soil (אדמה in contrast to the "unsown land," the steppe, Jer. II. 2). Of course, for the ancients the soil was not something indifferent; it was a holy thing, the rousing of whose powers was no secular matter. People felt awe at the chthonic mystery: to furrow up the earth and make use of its powers was looked on as a hazardous enterprise. Curious rites therefore safeguarded the work of tillage; indeed, the knowledge of its beneficent powers, and of the technique of availing oneself of them, was ascribed to special revelation and instruction by the deity.[30] What answer could Jahwism give to this life-and-death question of the ancient farmers? It could not afford to keep an impartial silence, but was bound to investigate and enquire whether in this sphere also Jahweh would not show himself lord and bestower of blessing. Nor did Jahweh remain silent: "the land is mine: you are only strangers and sojourners with me" (Lev. XXV. 23). These words, of course, contain an expression of a relationship to the land which is particularly characteristic of Israel. While, as far as we can see, the peoples round about lay strong emphasis upon their auto-chthonism—for them the possession of the land was a prime religious

[30] There are still echoes of the kind in Is. XXVIII. 26, 29; cf. Hos. II. 7f. [II. 5f.]. And one of the choruses of Sophocles echoes something of antiquity's awe at this presumptuousness of men: "And Earth, the eldest of the gods, the immortal, the unwearied, doth he wear, turning the soil with the offspring of horses, as the ploughs go to and fro from year to year," Sophocles, *Antigone*, 338–41, Jebb's translation. For ritual weeping before sowing and the ritual joy at harvest (Ps. CXXVI. 5f.) see F. Hvidberg, in *Z.A.W.*, 1939, pp. 150ff.

datum—Israel never lost the memory that she had been led to her land in a special way and only then invested with it in fief by Jahweh.[31]

This advance on the part of Jahweh, this seizure of spheres formerly alien to himself, this appropriation and filling out of cultic ideas belonging to a completely different cultic group—this is unquestionably the most exciting thing in the history of earlier Jahwism. It can easily be imagined that, in virtually every individual case in the process, the existence or non-existence of the community worshipping Jahweh was at stake *vis-à-vis* the cult of Baal. This process of reaching a settlement, of absorption and rejection, probably only came to an equilibrium in Deuteronomy; in the "Blessings" contained in it (Deut. xxviii) the victory over Baal has been finally won.[32] The start of the victory was the time when the first group of worshippers of Jahweh entered the arable land of Palestine—for Jahwism's exclusive claim certainly repudiated any peaceable co-existence of the cults right from the beginning. Jahwism without the first commandment is positively inconceivable. But it was only at a very much later date that this cultic intolerance was expressed as a direct denial of the existence of other gods (the clearest references to this are in Deutero-Isaiah). In this early period the worshippers of Jahweh were only told that it was not possible to combine worship of other gods with the worship of Jahweh. As far as we can see, this cultic intolerance is something unique in the history of religion. As the history of Jahwism makes clear, this intolerance was in the long run far from content with a peaceable separation of the different cultic groups. It had within it from the beginning a strongly aggressive element which, as it proceeded, more and more questioned the legitimacy of foreign cults as such. An interesting glimpse into the practical functioning of this cultic intolerance is preserved for us in the rite of renunciation at Shechem, which took place before the beginning of a pilgrimage.[33] In this rite the participants in a pilgrimage were ordered to make a solemn act of severance from everything associating them with other cults—from images (the figurines of Astarte, so many of which have been found in excavations) or other cultic objects. Here, for once, we can see something of the way in which the defensive action against alien cults and the self-preservation of Jahwism worked out in practice. In most cases we must be content with the simple

[31] W. Eichrodt, *Historia Mundi*, Bern 1952, VOL. II, p. 392.
[32] See below, p. 229.
[33] Gen. xxxv. 2ff.; Josh. xxiv. 23, for which see A. Alt, *K.S.*, VOL. I, pp. 79ff.

record of the outcome of a long struggle. Thus, for example, as lying behind the lists of unclean animals (Lev. XI; Deut. XIV) we have to presume prolonged, dogged encounters with foreign cults. As far as we can see, the point at issue in these catalogues is a sacral disqualification of animals which had some positive importance elsewhere. We know from the Ras Shamra tablets that the pig, or, more precisely, the wild boar, stood in a special relationship to Alijan Baal, and that it also played a part in the cult of Aphrodite in Cyprus. But here Aphrodite is only the Hellenistic name for Astarte (Ishtar), the mother goddess and the goddess of love common to the Orient.[34] We can well imagine that such general decisions about an animal could only have been evolved and established slowly, on the basis of many individual decisions and judgments taken by priests at sanctuaries, before they could become common property of "the" Jahwism. And how long still was the road from there until such decisions on many animals, now common property, could be collected in lists! The commandment not to seethe a kid in its mother's milk (Ex. XXIII. 19, XXXIV. 26) represses a magic spell cast by means of milk, as the Ras Shamra texts have only now shown.[35]

The result of a positive absorption is the historicising of what were previously purely agrarian festivals, that is, the rooting of them in the saving history, the legitimation, indeed, of every ritual event on the basis of historical implantations on Jahweh's part.[36] Here a rigorous demythologising process, by means of which Jahwism appropriated cultic ideas and usages which derived from completely different cultic spheres, had been effected in utter secrecy. But, for the historian of religion, what is most astonishing is Jahwism's self-preservation *vis-à-vis* the mythicising of sex. In the Canaanite cult, copulation and procreation were mythically regarded as a divine event; consequently, the religious atmosphere was as good as saturated with mythic sexual conceptions. But Israel did not share in the "divinisation" of sex. Jahweh stood absolutely beyond the polarity of sex, and this meant that Israel also could not regard sex as a sacral mystery. It was excluded from the

---

[34] For details see Noth, *Gesammelte Studien zum Alten Testament*, henceforth cited as *Ges. Studien*, Munich 1957, pp. 78ff. (Gordon, *Handbook*, 67, v, 9). W. W. Graf Baudissin, *Adonis und Esmun*, Leipzig 1911, p. 144.

[35] Gordon, *Handbook*, VOL. II, 52, 14.

[36] A. Weiser, *Glaube und Geschichte im Alten Testament*, Stuttgart 1931, pp. 35ff. See VOL. II, pp. 117ff.

cult because it was a phenomenon of the creature. It has, it is true, often been said that ancient Israel was as yet still completely lacking any distinctive doctrine of creation, and that Canaanite ideas were the first thing to assist her towards an evolution of her beliefs in this direction. In one respect this is to the point, for it was apparently only through the absorption of certain ideas—for example, that in Creation Jahweh battled with the Chaos dragon and fashioned the world out of the elements of the defeated hostile power—that Israel found her way to a coherent presentation of her doctrine of Creation.[37] But it is just Israel's polemical attitude towards any deification of sex, her exclusion of this whole sphere of life from the cult and the sacral events, which shows that, in actual fact, a very positive doctrine of Creation was in existence, at least *in nuce,* in Israel, even at an early period. This doctrine was already posited along with the desacralisation of sex; indeed, it has to be regarded as the real motivating power behind it.[38] The prophets' allegorisings make clear how lastingly Israel surmounted these challenges. Both Hosea (Hos. i–iii) and Ezekiel (Ezek. xvi, xxiii) represent Jahweh as the spouse of mortal women without feeling any need to fear that these representations would be misunderstood as having a mythical significance. On the other hand, in these prophetic symbolisations are to be discerned the demythologised survivals within Jahwism of ideas which derived from Canaan. These ideas must have persisted, even in an unbroken form, in realms which were clearly never reached by the control of Jahwism, otherwise they could not have come into the open again as fresh as ever in their mythological force as late as the sixth century in the isolated military colony at Elephantine.[39]

Of course, this struggle of Jahweh's with Baal concerning the matter of his functions and spheres of sacral jurisdiction was not without

[37] H. Gunkel, *Schöpfung und Chaos in Urzeit und Endzeit,* 2nd edn. Göttingen 1921, pp. 29ff. See below, p. 137.

[38] In passing, there is much to be said for the assumption that the account of creation in J (Gen. ii. 4*b*ff.), which has the sphere of human life created from the arid earth, the waterless steppe, derives, in spite of assertions to the contrary, from very old and therefore pre-Palestinian traditions.

[39] It can be seen from the Elephantine papyri that in this community which was severed from the cult in Palestine a female consort of Jahweh, Anathjahu, was worshipped along with him (*Altorientalische Texte zum Alten Testament,* ed. H. Gressmann, 2nd edn. Berlin and Leipzig 1926, henceforth cited as *A.O.T.,* p. 454; A. Cowley, *Aramaic Papyri,* Oxford 1923, p. 147).

serious relapses, but there is no chronicle extant giving the number of worshippers of Jahweh who fell victim to the allurements of the worship of Baal. Something of the kind is reported by the tradition connected with the sanctuary of Baal Peor, to the north-east of the Dead Sea. It is possible that this sanctuary now and then attracted members of the Jahweh Amphictyony, a thing of which others disapproved. Something more definite seems to be indicated by the introduction and rapid spread of personal names compounded with Baal which coincides with the period immediately after the Conquest.[40] It is possible to take these names as an avowal of this god and his cult. It is perhaps, however, only a matter of change in cultic terminology—people had become accustomed to calling Jahweh Baal. But we must bring home to ourselves even more than ever before that it is impossible for the historian to determine in retrospect an objective limit beyond which he has the right to speak of actual apostasy, and of a self-surrender of Jahwism. It is impossible to determine how far the cultic forms taken over from Canaan were of real service to the worship of Jahweh, and how far they did it harm, for this very reason, if no other, that Jahwism was itself a very flexible and variable quantity. As I see it, ultimately, in considering the question of Jahwism's self-preservation or self-surrender, the cogency of the parallels in the Ras Shamra texts, which are actually fairly striking, and which mount up steadily year by year, breaks down, so long as there is still so little we can say about the spirit, the total aggregate, of the current religious ideas with which they were co-ordinated in Israel. For, how much weight did individual ideas or designations which were taken over still retain if, at their transference to Jahweh, they were divorced from their original mythical context (the sexual function of the deity, his dying and rising again)? Hosea's religious ideas are certainly more strongly influenced by things Canaanite than those of any other prophet, but he is, at the same time, the sharpest in his complaint about his contemporaries' apostasy to the cult of Baal.[41] Could not the thesis even be maintained that at times Jahwism was able to express itself in a more real and vivid way in these acquired forms than in some of its traditional ones? Surveying the process of adoption as a whole, one gains the impression—however para-

[40] Jerubbaal (Jg. VI. 32), Ishbaal (II Sam II. 8 and elsewhere), Meribbaal (I Chron VIII. 34).

[41] For this problem see T. Worden, "The influence of the Ugaritic fertility myth on the Old Testament," in *Vet. Test.*, 1953, pp. 273ff.

doxical it may seem—that in the various new forms Jahwism came more than ever before into its own and was enabled to hold its position in an even freer and more self-conscious fashion.

If Israel opened the door to cultic ideas hitherto alien to her, this was not due to any particular religious necessity. Such a thing was unknown in the ancient world. Rather was it forms of order, and, more precisely, forms of order affecting the immediate surroundings of the people concerned, which were revealed in the cult, and given their warrant by it. Through them the deity came to men's assistance, by revealing to them both the rules which supported and preserved their natural sphere of life, and those which rendered wholesome human relationships possible. Disregard of these norms resulted also in what were primarily cultic disturbances, and the removal of these disturbances was the concern of the cultic community.

But then, the Israel of the early pre-monarchical period knew herself to be bound not only to the divine law which issued from the cult, but also, in addition, to legal norms of a different kind and of a different origin. That is to say, in the matter of her law Israel went through an evolution very much resembling the one undergone by the cult.[42] The mutual relationships of the settlers in the arable land called for a completely new basis of rules for living, for the entry had brought about a radical change in the social structure of the old semi-nomadic groups. It was not merely that they had made the transition to agriculture: the family groups were also settled in villages and towns, some of them became well-to-do landed proprietors, the monetary system was making rapid progress, and, keeping pace with this, laws concerning debt had come into being. How could the simple sheep-breeders from the steppe deal with such complicated conditions in which they suddenly found themselves other than by taking over the legal arrangements which had for long proved their value in these conditions? In the so-called Book of the Covenant (Ex. xxi–xxiii), the oldest of Israel's legal codes known to us, since it dates from the time between the conquest and the rise of the state, we can see how rapidly Israel accommodated herself to the new conditions. This was only possible because the Israelites in Canaan only needed to enter into a body of law adapted to

---

[42] The foundations were laid by A. Alt, *Die Ursprünge des israelitischen Rechts*, Leipzig 1934, reprinted in *K.S.*, VOL. I, pp. 278ff. More recently F. Horst, "Recht und Religion im Bereich des Alten Testaments," in *Evangelische Theologie*, henceforth cited as *Ev. Th.*, 1956, pp. 49ff., and now *Gottes Recht*, 1961, pp. 260ff.

existing local conditions. The first part of the Book of the Covenant (Ex. XXI–XXII. 16), with its predominantly casuistic drafting, has on good grounds been described as the law of Canaanite municipalities taken over by Israel.[43] It deals purely and simply with matters which we should describe as preponderantly secular—legislation concerning debt, liability, compensation for injuries, pledges, bloodshed, asylum, etc., in brief, all that fell to be dealt with by the local courts "in the gate."

Unfortunately for the purpose of ascertaining the distinctiveness of Israel's legal thought, great difficulties stand in the way of comparing the Book of the Covenant with any of the great legal codes of the ancient Near East known to us. Certainly, when Israel's legal codes are set alongside those known outside of her, in general they do have the appearance of being the precipitation of what was a comprehensive and, in many respects, homogeneous jurisprudence common over all the East. But when manifest differences in the decisions are compared, the sociological and juristic presuppositions in both cases need to be examined carefully; and it often enough turns out then that, in spite of great affinity in form and content, the laws are fundamentally not really comparable. Thus, as is well known, law in ancient Israel diverges from the Codex Hammurabi in giving a considerably greater place to private vengeance, especially to the blood-feud. In this connexion, however, we have first to bear in mind that in the Codex Hammurabi the administration of justice and the punishment of crime are much more matters of state action, while in Israel there were no authorities to take over the expiation of an offence on behalf of the private individual. In consequence, in Israel the blood-feud was in certain cases a legitimate institution for the repression of violence— though for other cases, the Book of the Covenant, even at this early date, envisages public punishment by due processes of the law. Certainly afterwards, in Israel as everywhere else, the taking over of community life by the state further restricted the practice of the blood-feud.[44] But one of the peculiarities of Israel is that she was incapable even in later times of acknowledging the state itself as the custodian of law, and this clearly was because she did not see her way to allow law

---

[43] A. Jepsen, *Untersuchungen zum Bundesbuch*, B.W.A.N.T. III. 5. Stuttgart 1927, pp. 73, 98; Alt, *K.S.*, VOL. I, p. 2.; cf. also M. Weber, *Ancient Judaism*, Glencoe, Ill. and London 1952, p. 61f.

[44] F. Horst, in *Ev. Th.*, 1956, pp. 49ff. (60f., 73).

to be at all divorced from the absolutely immediate jurisdiction of Jahweh. Thus, again, the remarkably divergent regulations in the matter of the blood-feud are bound up with a much deeper-seated feature peculiar to Jahwism. Considerations of style have made it clear that in two cases of bodily injury followed by death (Ex. XXI. 12, 22f.), an older regulation has obviously been forcibly suppressed and, when the change was made to apodictic personal formulation, the most rigorous punishment fixed.[45] Here, in the sphere of the blood-feud, can be seen how an earlier and probably more lenient regulation—perhaps the determination of a compensation (wergild) to be paid (cf. Num. XXXV. 31)—was rigorously amended by Jahwism. Where human life was concerned, Jahweh's immediate interest came at once into play, for all life belongs to Jahweh, and therefore the matter may not be settled by the parties in the case. Considerations like these make it clear that, compared with the more secular and civil law of the Codex Hammurabi, ancient Israelite law was, on the whole, much more closely tied to religion.[46] Compared with the penalties given in the Codex Hammurabi, which are variously graded according to the social standing of the guilty party, it is remarkable to how very much greater a degree the Book of the Covenant presupposes equal rights of all before the law, and the idea of common solidarity.[47] The human element, too, which is conspicuous in ancient Israelite law, is undoubtedly the outcome of stronger religious constraint. It has its roots in the time long before the Settlement, in the old ethic of brotherhood obtaining amongst the neighbourly nomadic clans.[48] Probably even more of the material found in the later legal codes reaches back to this early time, but we still lack a methodical investigation of the subject-matter in the light of these oldest legal systems.[49]

The upholders of this law were the elders of the local communities. But there is much to be said for the idea that, after her settlement, Israel also knew of a superior magistracy, to whom was entrusted the maintenance, superintendence, and proclamation of this law—namely

[45] Alt, K.S., VOL. I. pp. 303ff.

[46] J. Hempel, "Gottesgedanke und Rechtsgestaltung in Altisrael," in Zeitschrift für systematische Theologie, 1930–1, pp. 377ff.

[47] B. Balscheit in Die soziale Botschaft des Alten Testaments, Basel n.d., pp. 10ff.

[48] M. Weber, Ancient Judaism, p. 69.

[49] Thus, as K. Elliger has shown, Lev. XVIII contains regulations which in their original form ordered the relations of the sexes in large families and which go back to very early times. K. Elliger, "Das Gesetz Leviticus XVIII," in Z.A.W., 1955, pp. 1ff.

"Israel's judges." The lists of the so-called lesser judges (Jg. x. 1–5, XII. 7–15) point to a succession of men from quite different clans who each in his day "judged" Israel. This office, which was something completely different from that of the charismatic leader, that is the "greater" judge, could be pictured as that of an administrator of justice, a court which could be consulted, which itself also administered justice up and down the land at assemblies and which, in particular, took care of the continuity of the legal traditions.[50] We must also recall Deborah, who lived between Ramah and Bethel, and to whom the Israelites came to have justice administered to them (Jg. IV. 4f.). Finally, the picture of Samuel too, going on circuit year by year between Bethel, Gilgal, and Mizpah to administer justice (I Sam. VII. 15ff.), suggests the surmise that the historical Samuel, upon whom later tradition piled every conceivable office—prophet, judge, Levite—might have been an administrator of justice of this kind. This institution of an administrator of justice persisted, according to Mic. IV. 14 [V. 1] and Deut. XVII. 8ff., right into the period of the monarchy.

But this body of law, to some extent taken over from the Canaanites, did not have for Israel at all a secular character. For Israel all law was of divine origin: therefore the fusion of this law with the old apodictic divine law of early Jahwism was only a matter of time. There is no indication that Israel rated this originally Canaanite law any differently from her own hereditary sacral law.

So then, in Israel's pre-monarchical period, we have to do with people who could only comprehend and understand the world on the basis of the sacral, that is, in the light of sacred forms of order and laws which took their origin in the cult and were maintained by means of rituals. Life was only possible as people submitted to the authority of these sacral regulations and for their own part joined in carrying them out. For them, there was absolutely no meeting-ground with, or participation in, the divine otherwise than by submitting to these sacred regulations which governed both their life as a community, and their dealings as farmers with their physical environment. The deliberate breach of any sacral regulation was therefore associated with all the horror felt at cultic profanation, and experienced with

[50] Alt, K.S., VOL. I, pp. 300ff.; M. Noth, "Das Amt des Richters Israels," in Festschrift für A. Bertholet, edd. W. Baumgartner et al., Tübingen 1950, pp. 404ff. Noth takes the judge to be one who proclaims the apodictic law of God. A rather different view is taken by F. Horst, in Ev. Th., 1956, pp. 52ff.

a genuineness such as was probably at no time afterwards known in Israel.[51]

Precisely in view of such a naïve attachment to the objective world of the cult and to ritual, one thing is bound to strike the historian of comparative religion, namely the dwindling part played by magic in this religion. Its absence already gives the Israel of the time an exceptional position within all the fairly comparable forms in the history of religion, especially the religion of the ancient East. An undoubtedly valid complete distinction has recently been made between magical thought and religious thought. Magical thought is a definite early form of man's picture of the world, a certain mode of looking at things and their relationships, and of maintaining one's position within them.[52] What is characteristic of it is a very realistic conception of the forces, and of the possibilities of their transmission or direction, not just by means of what is alive, but also through the medium of "dead" objects. Without question, early Israel as well was spellbound by this "dynamistic" view of the world—indeed, she clung so persistently to the idea of the material force of what was holy or unclean, and to the possibility of its transmission, that we are faced with the question whether this was only a matter of the survival of a way of thinking virtually long overcome, or whether it was something much more important for Israel. In this sense the early Israelite cult altogether carries the impress of an understanding of the world that was still largely magical—perhaps it might better be called "dynamistic."[53] Here then the issue is not as yet joined. But it is valid to speak about Jahwism's unyielding inflexibility against magic from the moment that magic reveals itself as a well-tried technique for influencing the deity, or when man, with its aid, takes into his own control, to further his own needs, events or

---

[51] We may ask whether even in the period of the monarchy so great a muster could still have been raised to avenge a crime as is related in Jg. XIX. 22ff.

[52] C. H. Ratschow, *Magie und Religion*, Gütersloh 1947; S. Mowinckel, *Religion und Kultus*, Göttingen 1953, pp. 27ff., 15; "Magic is originally a technique, a way of actively influencing the world rather than an attitude in which it is contemplated. . . . Primitive man wants to maintain himself over against the world; he believes that he possesses means through which he can render the powers which in a sinister way surround his existence tractable. To this extent magic is the primitive threshold of technology." E. Spranger, *Die Magie der Seele*, Tübingen 1947, p. 66.

[53] Comprehensive material is gathered together by A. Bertholet in *Die Religion in Geschichte und Gegenwart*, 2nd edn. Tübingen 1927–31, VOL. III, pp. 1847ff.; *id.*, *Das Dynamistische im Alten Testament*, Tübingen 1926. See below, pp. 277ff.

powers that belong to the deity. We are certainly not wrong to explain as deriving from the peculiar nature of Jahwism the limit here set to magic and its competency, unique in the history of religion. Jahweh's invasive power, revealing himself on all sides as personal will, was absolutely incompatible with the impersonal automatic action of the operation of the forces of magic. Neither was this Jahweh made available by being influenced by magic; nor could people ward him off by means of magical invocations; nor was it possible, by, as it were, a high-handed drawing upon his powers, to achieve effects which did not proceed in the most direct and personal fashion from himself. For the same reason, magic was also removed from legal ideas in Israel at an early period. The idea of the magical character of guilt, or of the magical effect of sanctuary, was superseded in Israel at an early period by clear notions about the moral responsibility of the individual.[54]

[54] F. Horst, in *Ev. Th.*, 1956, pp. 56ff., and now *Gottes Recht*, 1961, pp. 269ff.

THE CRISIS DUE TO THE
FORMATION OF THE STATE

I. THE DEMOLITION OF THE OLD

ON the whole, unlike the Conquest, the transformation of the old clan alliance into a state was an event concluding in a comparatively brief space of time, in the generation between Saul and Solomon. Nevertheless it did not provoke any acute crisis for religious and cultic life. Some time was required before Jahwism became aware of the manifold consequences. During the episodic military kingship of Saul, no violent reaction was in any case to be expected from the cultic and religious side, for Saul had of course been just another charismatic leader of the old sort. Even though we must not overlook the opposition which became vocal when the charismatic leadership was transformed into a monarchy (I Sam. x. 27, xi. 12), still, the whole sacral life remained unaffected by this monarchy. At that time the state was still far from exerting influence on the faith as an autonomous power. So the change in her internal life which Israel experienced through the superior political and military initiative of David must have been all the more incisive. By his wars David had succeeded in extending the frontiers far beyond the area hereditarily occupied by the former clan alliance; indeed, his kingdom had become an empire, comparable with the empires on the Nile and in Mesopotamia, in that, similarly organised, almost a whole garland of vassal states could be attached to it.[1] This empire's defence called for the development of an armed force of regular soldiers; in cities hitherto Canaanite garrisons for the charioteers presently came into existence. The administration of this empire was served by a new division into "districts" (I Kings iv. 7ff.): at court and in the country outside a staff of officials bore the burden of administration; the people had to contribute by way of taxes and imposts towards the costs of all this administrative apparatus, and, not least, of the magnificence which the court attained under Solomon. In the countryside outside Jerusalem the king owned estates, whose tenants had to deliver produce to the court.

[1] Alt, *K.S.*, vol. ii, pp. 66ff.

David chose an old Canaanite city as the seat of the court; and he himself, as a former military leader, was a man who to begin with had not the authorisation of any kind of sacral standing to take up this position as ruler. Even only a little time before, in the sphere of the clan alliance, who would have thought such a thing possible?

Changes of such a radical kind are never to be attributed solely to external impulses and current political necessities. The expansion of the Philistines towards the interior, putting pressure upon Israel, unquestionably had a function in evoking them; it was responsible for the fact that affairs in the political sphere remained in flux both in Saul's time and later under David. But for things to have gone on in such a way as to lead to so vast a re-formation, decisive conditions must have already been present within Israel as well. What might also, of course, have happened was that the political development in Palestine brushed aside the patriarchal clan alliance, which with its limited possibilities of self-defence succumbed to its better-equipped enemies. Instead, Israel came powerfully on the scene in a completely changed form, and found courage to tackle political and cultural tasks which still lay far beyond her range of vision in the period of the Judges. As lies in the nature of the case, such changes in the innermost depth of a people's heart can as a rule only be rather indirectly inferred by the historian, that is, from their final results: they elude direct fixation, because of course the people itself was scarcely aware of them. So too with ancient Israel we can really only note the great difference between the spiritual climate in the era before the foundation of the state and that of even the beginning of the period of the monarchy. We have seen that we had to picture the Israel of the time of the Judges as standing, in cultural and religious development, on a purely patriarchal level of civilisation, as people enclosed by and sheltered in the supra-personal ordinances of the cult and community life, the latter of which was characterised by a sense of solidarity now inconceivable to us. The individual's life was enclosed in that of larger units superior to it—kindred and tribe—and the life of these groups knew itself to be in unity with the natural orders of life of their environment. There was no tension between inward and outward, between the "I" and the world, since outside in every department of natural life the sacred regulations held sway which the cult exalted and into which man had to fit. Even birth and death were understood as supra-personal things, and not as events with which the individual had to cope personally. The whole of life was sheltered in rites and sacral ordinances: it was hallowed and supported by festivals and usages whose force was immovably established. What then makes it so hard for us to answer the question as to the "significance" of these rites is the fact that the Israel of that time had hardly become consciously aware of such a conceptual content of the rites which she had to perform. It can be assumed, anyway, that thought—at any rate the individual's thought—had in no sense such a regulative and critical significance in shaping the life of the individual as it was now very soon to have in Israel too, in the circles of the wise men about the court.[2] From the deep constraint of this archaic piety Israel began to emerge at the start of the period of the monarchy. To be sure, there will also have been groups in the countryside whom the new spirit did not affect until a relatively late date, indeed perhaps there were even some who were never affected at all. Even so, there is every justification for fixing as the date of the beginning of a new era in Israel's spiritual life the period of the monarchy; for the poetic and literary productions to which she gave birth in rapid succession from this time on presuppose a completely changed intellectual and spiritual temper in those who wrote them. Although initially the representatives of this new spiritual climate may only have been a small group in the environs of the court, still, the development could not be halted, and it certainly, even rapidly, gained ground, for the prophets as early as the eighth century confronted a population whose forms of existence were in complete disintegration.

A spiritual change which could set in and gain ground with such impetus, in the shape of a new political will, and at the same time also of a new cultural upsurge and new religious ideas, must have had its way prepared in part at least by weariness and exhaustion in the preceding era. The victory of the new would not have been so complete if a need for change had not been felt, be it distinctly or vaguely. Indeed, the picture of the conditions obtaining at Shiloh in the last days of the Amphictyony shows a serious demoralisation of custom, and also a dissatisfaction on the part of the worshippers (I Sam. I–III). We have no reason to disbelieve the unfavourable judgment passed by the narrator, who was certainly still near to the situation: the word of Jahweh had grown rare in the land; and even the priest who had supreme authority in the clan alliance was by now quite unaccustomed to having to deal with revelations from Jahweh. Another sign that this era had come to an end can be deduced from the separation of the old

[2] C. H. Ratschow, *Magie und Religion*, Gütersloh 1947, p. 76.

localised sacral traditions from their local points of attachment, and their conversion into disengaged narrative material. The story of the appearance of Jahweh at Bethel and of Jacob's vow to build a house of God there and to pay tithes was, of course, originally the cultic legend of this sanctuary: its sole function was to guarantee the sanctity of this place as a place of worship and the legitimacy of customs practised there—the anointing of the stone and tithes. Such traditional material was only known in this one capacity—its aetiological one—for it belonged as it were to the inalienable property of the sanctuary concerned: it was only there that it was reverently handed on from generation to generation. What a lot must have happened to these cultic legends, and how changed must the conception of them have become, for them now to go out as ordinary narrative material in such a way that it was soon possible for collectors to treat them as literature and to arrange them in larger narrative complexes! Indeed, their separation from the cult did not only mean a pronounced secularisation of the material hitherto oriented on the sacral: with the decay of the old aetiological aim, the whole of the former inner meaning of the traditions concerned necessarily changed. This move of the old sacral material from the sanctuaries to the studies of writers may also well be taken as another indication that the era of the cultic practice of the patriarchs had passed away.

2. THE NEW ORDERS

Israel, whose defence Jahweh had formerly reserved to himself, by raising up in time of war charismatic leaders with whom he personally went into battle—this Israel had now become a state, determining for itself the extent of its own territory and its internal war-potential alike. Indeed, in the earliest period of David's reign, it might have looked as if Israel had completely renounced Jahweh's sovereignty over her, since David himself had formerly been a professional soldier in the body of retainers organised by Saul, and was thus without sacral consecration. His elevation as king over Judah, as well as his appointment over the united tribal groups of Israel and Judah, are represented as acts of political acumen (II Sam. v. 1–3).[3] The capture of Jerusalem was entirely a private affair of David's, by means of which he selected for himself a place of residence between the two great clan groups. Compared,

[3] Alt, *K.S.*, VOL. I, p. 38. The elders adduce three arguments: David's close ties of blood, David's previous military record, and in the last place designation by Jahweh.

therefore, with Israel and Judah, Jerusalem had a special constitutional status—it was the "city of David." But to assume a complete religious break would be to betray little historical understanding of the enormous powers of persistence inherent in sacral conceptions. In actual fact, despite all change, David still looked on his wars as wars of Jahweh; nor can there be doubt, either, about his own personal adherence to Jahwism. On the whole then, the institution of the monarchy was a newcomer in Israel, indeed almost something born out of season. Consequently, it was inevitable that its relationship with the central traditions of the faith was strained from the outset and, right down to its end, the monarchy never succeeded in extricating itself from this strain.

1. David's throne did indeed very soon receive direct sacral legitimation, in the prophecy of Nathan (II Sam. VII). Not only have recent investigations revealed a very old kernel in this tradition, namely vss. 1–7, 11*b*, 16, 18–21, 25–29, but form-critical comparison has also established striking similarities to the Egyptian royal record.[4] From the incidental remark "sitting in his palace" at the beginning, and continuing with the king's expressed intention to build a temple, right down to the divine declaration of the filial relationship granted to the king and the endorsement of his rule—all these, in nearly every feature, can be shown to be borrowings from, and indeed almost copies of, ceremonial texts long stylised in the court of Egypt. In the ancient Egyptian theology of the kingship a special part is played by the so-called royal protocol, a document listing the king's throne-name, attesting his divine sonship, his commission as ruler, the promise that his dominion would endure for ever, etc.: this document, allegedly written by the deity himself, was handed to the king at his accession. In this matter too the court in Judah followed the usage in Egypt, for the עֵדוּת, the "testimony," which the High Priest Jehoiadah handed to the young Joash at his coronation can only mean a royal protocol of the kind (II Kings XI. 12).[5] It is also certain that the King of Judah—again like his great Egyptian prototype—received special names when he ascended

---

[4] L. Rost, *Die Überlieferung von der Thronnachfolge Davids*, henceforth cited as *Thronnachfolge*, B.W.A.N.T., Stuttgart 1926, pp. 47ff.; S. Herrmann, "Die Königsnovelle in Ägypten und Israel," in *Wissenschaftl. Zeitschr d. Karl-Marx-Univ. Leipzig* (Gesellschafts- u. sprachwissensch. Reihe), 1953–4, pp. 51ff.

[5] G. von Rad, "Das judäische Königsritual," in *Th. Lz.*, 1947, cols. 201ff., reprinted in *Gesammelte Studien zum Alten Testament*, Munich 1958, henceforth cited as *Ges. Studien*, pp. 205ff.

the throne.[6] But, of course, for the Hebrew way of thinking, the royal protocol could only be a covenant made by Jahweh with the king. And this very term does occur in the very old "Last Words of David" (II Sam. XXIII. 5) and in Ps. CXXXII. 12 which is undoubtedly pre-exilic.[7] It is, of course, impossible to prove that all the elements in this royal ritual go back to David himself, but there are good reasons for supposing that the ground was prepared for them as early as his own time; for, in the light of many Egyptian parallels, the revelation of Jahweh in Solomon's dream (I Kings III. 4–15) also shows itself to be a ceremonial text of the kind—the revelation in a dream at the sanctuary, the king as child of God, the march to the city, the sacrifices, and, above all, the deity's authorisation of the king's rule, again suggest the close adherence of the Judean ceremonial to the Egyptian model.[8]

In Israel too these and other courtly ceremonial forms were the bearers of a whole store of equally traditional ideas. The king is God's son—though in Israel certainly not in the physical mythological sense, but *per adoptionem*: he is commissioned to rule by God himself, he governs with perfect justice and wisdom, he is the great benefactor and shepherd of his people, which flourishes under his rule; yes, even the natural fertility of man, beast, and field increases through the blissful effect of this rule. The king is fair, and around him is an atmosphere of joy.[9] Abroad, he is the dread victor who triumphs over all his foes. As has been said, these are conventional ideas which permeate all courtly utterance—this was the customary way of paying homage to the king and was also the way in which he himself conceived his office. Oddly enough, this Jerusalem court-theology assigned to the king the priestly office as well (Ps. CX. 4). But in actual fact, looking at the whole inner structure of cultic life in ancient Israel, it is hard to

---

[6] A. M. Honeyman, "The evidence for royal names among the Hebrews," in *Journal of Biblical Literature*, 1948, pp. 17ff.; S. Morenz, "Ägyptische und davididische Konigstitulatur," in *Zeitschrift für ägyptische Sprache und Altertumskunde*, 1954, pp. 73f.

[7] Since the Hebrew ברית is occasionally used as synonym for עדות, the expressions in Ps. CXXXII. 12 and II Kings XI. 12 approximate very closely. The "decree" about which the anointed in Ps. II. 7 speaks also approximates quite closely to the concept of *berith*.

[8] S. Herrmann, in *Wissenschaftl. Zeitschr. d. Karl-Marx-Univ. Leipzig*, 1953–4, pp. 53ff.

[9] Beauty: Jg. VIII. 18; I Sam. IX. 2, X. 23, XVI. 12, 18, XVII. 42; II Sam. XIV. 25; I Kings I. 6; Is. XXXIII. 17; Ps. XLV. 3 [2]. Joy: I Kings V. 21 [v. 7]; II Kings XI. 20; Ps. XXI. 2, 7 [1, 6]. See below, p. 322, n. 8.

understand a king in Jerusalem as a cultic official. For this the monarchy appeared far too late in history, that is to say, at a time when the sacral offices had long been settled. None the less, what we have here is obviously a very old court tradition which had come over to David's court from pre-Israelite Jerusalem. Certainly, on the whole, the monarchy in no sense succeeded in practice in combining the powers of the High Priest with its own office—indeed it does not even seem to have attempted to do so. Nevertheless the innovations brought by the monarchy were very decisive for Israel's cultic life as well.[10]

The monarchy which was formed in the so-called Northern Kingdom after the dissolution of the empire of David and Solomon is to be estimated quite differently from David's monarchy. Its basis was not a dynasty authorised once for all by Jahweh. On the contrary it represented, constitutionally, a much less divergent prolongation of the ancient Israelite charismatic leadership, which was now bound to a permanent institution, though admittedly by popular acclamation. This basing of the royal office on a *charisma* conferred by Jahweh was bound, of course, to make conditions in this kingdom much more unstable, in that with the extinction of the *charisma* of the man who wore the crown there also followed necessarily the extinction of the subjects' allegiance. Moreover, it was given in the basic structure of the kingdom of Israel that it was time and again convulsed by revolutions. There were periods when the succession was dynastic; but shortly before the final calamity, the kingdom was again convulsed by a series of revolutions. Those kings who seized power in rapid succession were considered by the prophet Hosea to be nothing but instruments of the divine wrath (Hos. XIII. 11).[11]

2. David too linked up with the old amphictyonic tradition when he set up his kingdom. This time admittedly there was no journey to Shiloh, but "he brought Shiloh to Jerusalem." The transference of the Ark, the sanctuary common to all the clans of Israel, was "a state action

---

[10] Others have more strongly emphasised the cultic functions of the Judean kings. So A. R. Johnson in "The role of the king in the Jerusalem cultus," in *The Labyrinth. Further Studies in the Relation between Myth and Ritual*, ed. S. H. Hooke, London 1935, pp. 71ff.; and recently in *Sacral Kingship*. I. Engnell is still more radical in many of his writings. On the other side cf. M. Noth, "Gott, König, Volk im Alten Testament," in *Zeitschrift für Theologie und Kirche*, henceforth cited as Z.Th.K., 1950, pp. 157ff., reprinted in *Ges. Studien*, pp. 188ff.

[11] Cf. Alt, K.S., VOL. II, pp. 116ff.

of the first magnitude."[12] He also had in mind to build a temple, although it was only Solomon who was able to put the plan into execution. For a right understanding of this project, we have to bear in mind the peculiar legal position, since the Temple was erected on crown property (II Sam. XXIV. 24ff.), and it was the king who commissioned it. Further, it was the king who had to arrange for repairs as they became necessary; it was his bounden duty to subsidise the Temple from time to time; and, if necessary, he had the right to reform the cult: the priests were crown officials.[13] It is from this standpoint then that we shall have to judge the occasional admission of foreign cults, to which the kings of Judah periodically allocated a place in the Temple beside the cult of Jahweh (II Kings XVI. 10ff., XXI. 4ff., XXIII. 4ff.). In antiquity, such recognition of the gods of the great powers on the part of subject powers was the result of political necessity. Severe as might be the affront thereby offered to Jahweh's claim to exclusive worship, what took place in the state Temple has to be regarded in a special way: it was governed by presuppositions that were different from the cultic practices outside Jerusalem. What was later true of the sanctuary at Bethel was then true for Solomon's Temple: it was a "royal sanctuary" and a "temple of the empire" (בית ממלכה, מקדש מלך, Am. VII. 13); it was a state sanctuary, at which were made the king's own personal sacrifices, and, in particular, the sacrifices for the nation as well. By this means the old amphictyonic cult of Jahweh moved into a state sanctuary, and this sanctuary was erected in an old Canaanite city that was devoid of any legitimate traditions connecting it with Jahweh! Now, this Temple and its worship would certainly have scarcely affected the religious life of the broad mass of the people in Israel, and would have remained a private matter concerning David's Jerusalem alone, if David had not brought up the sacred Ark to Zion. But to this cultic object all the clans of the old amphictyonic league regarded themselves as owing allegiance; and consequently, because of the Ark, Solomon's Temple became the sanctuary for all Israel. Its sacral function was thus somewhat complicated: as a royal sanctuary it was the place of national

[12] O. Eissfeldt, "Silo und Jerusalem," in *Vet. Test.*, Suppl. IV (1957), p. 142. On the transplanting of the amphictyonic cult to Jerusalem see M. Noth, "David und Israel in 2 Sam. 7," in *Mélanges Bibliques rédigées en l'honneur de André Robert*, Paris 1956, pp. 122ff.

[13] K. Galling, *Königliche und nichtkönigliche Stifter beim Tempel von Jerusalem*, Beiträge zur biblischen Landes- und Altertumskunde, Stuttgart 1950, pp. 134ff.; Johnson, *Sacral Kingship*, p. 47 ("royal chapel").

worship, but as the place where the Ark was, it was Israel's central sanctuary.[14] It has been rightly asserted that we ought not to think of the old amphictyonic order as coming to an abrupt end, but simply that the Temple in Jerusalem with the Ark now became the common sanctuary of all the Israelites.[15] Of course, the only way of envisaging the situation is to suppose that in fact the state of affairs at the new sanctuary constantly deviated more and more from the old order. How far was the old levy of the members of the Amphictyony, who were ready to let Jahweh lead them into holy wars and who learned Jahweh's commandments at the pilgrimage festivals, comparable with the masses who assembled in that Temple where the sacrifices were offered of a state which was also more and more emancipating itself politically from Jahweh's control? What sort of an Amphictyony was this, whose individual members, the clans, were increasingly losing the capacity of action, since their tribal constitution fell into decay under the burden of the growing powers of the state? To be sure, Deuteronomy makes the attempt to revive the old amphictyonic order once more.[16] But what a theoretical makeshift is this "Israel" of Deuteronomy's! At bottom, Israel has already become so much of a state that the idea of separate clans, which once composed it, can in fact no longer arise. The reason why Deuteronomy drafts an Amphictyony without clans—a *contradictio in adiecto*—is that, politically, the clans were no longer of account even as partially autonomous groups.

Such innovations in the sacral life of an ancient people call for legitimation. So it is no wonder that in the Old Testament we meet with traditions whose purpose was to derive the new order from a decree or a special direction of the deity. Thus, the story in II Sam. XXIV can unhesitatingly be regarded as the ἱερὸς λόγος of Jerusalem. Jerusalem stood completely outwith any traditions connecting it with Jahweh—indeed,

---

[14] We know little about the pre-Israelite cults which were previously fostered in Jerusalem, or about their fate after the taking over of the city. But it seems certain that the "God most high" (אל עליון Gen. XIV. 18f.) was worshipped in Jerusalem before the time of David. H. Schmidt, "Jahwe und die Kulttraditionen von Jerusalem," in *Z.A.W.*, 1955, pp. 168ff.; G. Widengren, *Sakrales Königtum im Alten Testament und im Judentum*, Stuttgart 1955, p. 11; Johnson, *Sacral Kingship*, pp. 43ff. The same holds true for the concept of Jahweh as the king of high heaven, which was apparently alien to older Jahwism. On the cultic traditions of Jerusalem see H. J. Kraus, *Psalmen*, VOL. I., pp. 197ff. (Bib. Komm.).

[15] M. Noth, *Die Gesetze im Pentateuch*, reprinted in *Ges. Studien*, pp. 46f., 44f.

[16] See below, p. 227.

as a former Canaanite city-state with Canaanite sanctuaries it must have been particularly suspect in the eyes of the people who were devotees of Jahwism. But this tradition in Samuel, which even in its present form is still completely self-contained, now tells how the first altar of Jahweh came to be built in Jerusalem. David had his attention drawn to the spot by the appearance of the angel of Jahweh himself, and only built the altar when directed by a seer to do so. The final inference that this altar was pleasing to Jahweh was the fact that the pestilence affecting Jerusalem was checked on its erection. This narrative is full of features of great antiquity: it is perfectly possible that it dates back to the time of David or Solomon, the time of course when it really had a function to fulfil. There is another similar narrative-complex, which is admittedly much more comprehensive, the "story of the Ark" (I Sam. IV–VI; II Sam. VI). It depicts the fortunes of the Ark from the time when it was taken from Shiloh into battle with the Philistines down to its ceremonious reception in Zion by David.[17] To be sure, we can no longer call it a ἱερὸς λόγος proper, for in spirit it stands outwith the realm of the sacral and comes nearer to that form of story-writing about which we shall have to say more later on. The way in which it is able to keep up the suspense, even when it recounts set-backs, and presents the readers right at the start with two successive defeats of Israel, betrays in itself quite an amount of artistic shaping. All the same, there is no mistaking that the purpose of the whole complex is to establish the continuity between Israel's old central sanctuary and her new one. Since on this odd, roundabout way from Shiloh to Jerusalem, Jahweh had borne witness to himself in many acts, it was evident that the transportation was an event brought about by God, and not an arbitrary transaction of man's. In particular, however, the account of the fetching of the Ark in II Sam. VI is not simply to be taken as a once-for-all event, but as, at the same time, the ceremonial of an annually recurring festival; for the other account of the reception of the Ark in the Temple in I Kings VIII discloses in its basic features—assembly, procession, sacrifice, and blessing—the same procedure. Psalm CXXXII also supplies us with material to reconstruct this festival, since it too tells of David's efforts to fetch in the Ark and of Jahweh's rising up to go to his resting-place (this is the way in which we will have to understand this Psalm), an event celebrated annually by a great procession.[18]

---

[17] L. Rost, *Thronnachfolge*, pp. 4ff.

[18] H. J. Kraus, *Die Königsherrschaft Gottes im Alten Testament*, Tübingen 1951, pp. 82ff.

But this celebration of the foundation of the sanctuary was only one aspect of the festival, for the psalm also understands Jahweh's choice of Zion as the foundation and confirmation of the Davidic dynasty, that is, Jahweh's covenant with David, the "lamp" which he promised him. There is much then to be said for the assumption that in the month Ethnaim, that is, in the context of the great annual festival in the seventh month (I Kings VIII. 2), a "royal festival of Zion" was cele-brated which was a festival both of the foundation of the sanctuary and of the foundation of the dynasty. Jahweh had chosen Zion as the place of his resting. But Zion was also the place of the throne of his anointed. The throne of Jahweh and of his anointed were inseparable—indeed, in the light of Ps. CX. 1f., they were really one.[19]

3. Now, alongside these sacral traditions of the court, although independently, another quite different set of ideas must have come into being and found speedy acceptance in Jerusalem; namely the tradition of Zion as the mountain of God and his dwelling-place. Even in Ps. LXXVIII. 68ff. the choice of Zion and the election of David are clearly differentiated as two separate acts. Even a superficial comparison of Pss. XLVI, XLVIII, and LXXVI, with the basic ideas which go to make up these "songs of Zion," shows not only that these poems are closely related, but also that they clearly derive from a common tradition—Jahweh has taken up his abode on Zion, the mountain of God, "the joy of all the earth" (Pss. LXXVI. 2, XLVIII. 2); once upon a time nations and kings banded themselves together against Zion, but Jahweh repelled them with sovereign power (Pss. XLVIII. 4ff., LXXVI. 5ff., XLVI. 6f.).[20] It is difficult to know whether these verses have any historical event as their background, for history is not the reference of these very vague and often merely allusive statements. Rather they tell of something like a mythical event, viewed in a timeless distance or proximity. Again, what they say about the place where all this happens is hard to reconcile with the geographical situation of Jerusalem. The mountain of God seems to have a river belonging to it (Ps. XLVI. 4)—even in late pro-phecies the presence of a river is still connected with the picture of the city of God (Is. XXXIII. 20f.; Joel IV. 18 [III. 18]; Zech. XIV. 8). In this

---

[19] The later Ps. LXXVIII also brings together the choice of Zion as the new cultic place and the choice of David.

[20] On this Zion tradition see now E. Rohland, *Die Bedeutung der Erwählungstradi-tionen Israels für die Eschatologie der Propheten*, 1956, Theol. Diss, Heidelberg; Noth, *Jerusalem und die israel. Tradition*, reprinted in *Ges. Studien*, pp. 172ff.

connexion, Zion is in one instance spoken of as the mountain "in the far north" (Ps. XLVIII. 2). Ideas are here used deriving from a very primitive geography with its basis in myth, and this makes it perfectly certain that ultimately this Zion tradition derives from pre-Israelite, that is, Canaanite, ideas, which were only transferred to Zion at second hand.[21] As a set of ideas of distinctive nature and origin, this tradition of the mountain of God does not play a very important part in the pre-exilic cultic hymnody. But the prophets took it up, and in their sayings it was to have great significance. Thus this tradition about Zion as the mountain of God is equivalent to an independent election-tradition; and though it was the latest of these formations of tradition, it takes its place independently alongside the older ones connected with the patriarchs and the Deliverance from Egypt. As far as content goes, what stamps it is the consciousness of unrestricted safety and security with Jahweh; and it is precisely this note that is taken up, and even asked to do too much, in the prophecies of Isaiah.[22] We have every ground for assuming that the David-Zion tradition was fostered in Jerusalem and Judah, while the patriarchal-Exodus tradition lived on in the Northern Kingdom.

Psalm LXVIII too is dominated by the idea of Jerusalem as the dwelling-place of God and of the victorious battles of Jahweh the King. Compared with this, the mention in vs. 17 of Sinai seems out of place, as far as tradition goes, but the whole psalm presents so many difficulties that it must at present be left out of account. In spite of many traditional elements which are undoubtedly very old, it can be dated at the earliest in the monarchical period (Mowinckel thinks it possible that it has an older poem, now re-edited, as its basis).[23]

Even by the eighth century these various election-traditions seem to have lived side by side in comparative independence. The prophet Isaiah at any rate bases himself exclusively upon the specific tradition of Jerusalem, and seems to have no knowledge of the old covenant and conquest tradition.

This whole process of Israel becoming a state, the establishment of the Davidic dynasty, and the moving of Jahweh into a national Temple,

---

[21] On the mountain of God "in the north" (cf. Is. XIV. 13) see O. Eissfeldt, *Baal Zaphon*, Halle 1932, pp. 14ff.

[22] On the conceptions connected with the city of God, see also VOL. II., Pt. I, Ch. G, section 3; Pt. II, Ch. A, section 1, Ch. B, section 2, Ch. H, section 2.

[23] S. Mowinckel, *Der achtundsechzigste Psalm*, Oslo 1953, pp. 72f.

was a far-reaching innovation which was effected within the course of two generations. The Phoenician builders whom Solomon commissioned to erect a temple knew nothing of Jahweh—all that they knew was the way in which a temple was built everywhere and from time immemorial. So they kept to the type of temple common in Syria and Palestine, the basic form of which—the separation of a "most holy place" by a courtyard—probably derives from Mesopotamia, and in the compass of which sacral symbols of the most divergent origin met together. We cannot possibly say that in this Temple Jahwism created a way of self-expression peculiar to itself. Nevertheless, to assert that in building this Temple Solomon laid the axe to the patriarchal faith, is altogether too simple—unless of course one believes offhand that the transition to alien cultic forms necessarily meant the death-blow for Jahwism.[24] No: with the formation of the state, the cult of Jahweh entered upon a period of crisis, in which, certainly, its existence was once more at stake—it took on a change in form which brought in its train a completely new emphasis, and new relations of the part to the whole. It is not necessary to add that in so doing Jahwism also laid itself open to completely new perils and temptations against which it had to arm itself and which, indeed, it had first to recognise. This crisis occasioned by the formation of the state was all the more serious in that it dovetailed into the still-present crisis due to the conquest. Jahweh's encounter with Baal, his appropriation of the forms and concepts of the Baal cult, by no means ended when Israel became a state: rather did this event intensify the encounter; for now relationships with the Canaanites became much closer and, through more intimate political contact with the neighbouring nations, foreign cults as well began to exert a much stronger influence upon Israel.

3. THE NEW SPIRIT

Such insights as we have into the spiritual and cultural processes and trends within ancient Israel are not sufficient to allow of an overall picture of its mental history. None the less, certain eras can be discerned which were particularly vital and productive spiritually, and which stand out in clear contrast to periods of a more conservative or stagnant character. We find that the early monarchical period was supremely an era of this kind, when there was an intellectual creative upsurge which opened the way to completely new dimensions of life. It must have

[24] See above, pp. 29f.

been a time when the soil within was ready. Though it was still beset
with internal problems, David's empire was, after the union of North
and South, a state with immense possibilities of expansion. As far as
foreign relations went, it was pretty well established; the cultic life
was attached to a new centre and with new forms; there was a brilliant
court which, for its time, stood at the zenith in the cultivation of the
things of the mind. All these were factors which could not but have
their effect on the innermost centre of a people's life—indeed, they
compelled Israel to come to a completely new understanding of herself. Now as always, she sought this understanding by way of reflexion
on her historical origin. It is amazing that we can name three major
historical works which must have followed upon one another at relatively short intervals in this era—the history of David's rise to power
(I Sam. XVI. 14–II Sam. v. 12), the history of the succession after David
(II Sam. VI. 12, 20ff.–I Kings II), and the Jahwist's history.[25] This does
not mean that this was the first time that Israel showed capacity for
historical reflexion. The most simple formulae in which faith in Jahweh
was professed—he was the one who led Israel out of Egypt, who
promised the land to the ancestors, or who led Israel in the wilderness—
all of which go back to a much earlier period, already owe their
existence to theological reflexion upon history. What was new was that
Israel now found herself able to shape history into great complexes;
that is, not merely to call to remembrance isolated events basic to the
history, or to string such data more or less connectedly together for
the purposes of cultic recital, but really to present the history in its
broad historical connexions, including all the many events which cannot be made to fit with complete consistency into any teaching, and
taking in also its reverses, and, above all, its terrible and splendid
humanity. The most important prerequisite for this new way of seeing
and presenting history was a certain detachment from it—mental, not
just chronological; and this Israel could only attain when she reached a
certain degree of humanised culture, in fact a certain detachment from
herself, that is, the ability to make herself the object of consideration

[25] We have to take the history of David's rise to power as the oldest of the three,
for the question as to how there came to be this dynasty would be the first reaction to
the historical change of scene. The history of the succession to David is a legitimation
of the regency of Solomon, and consequently came into being during that regency
and for the sake of it. The Jahwist's work may be a little later, for it is probably to be
assumed that the contemporary history was the first to be depicted, and that it was
only then that the need of a picture of the earliest history grew up.

and large-scale interrogation. The strangely remote distance at which
the story-tellers stand from their subjects, which so often leaves us
wondering how far they were really interested in them, is a characteristic of practically all the traditions which date from this era or which
received their stamp in it. We have to realise that in fact we owe all
the information that we have about the early ages in Israel solely to
the work of the Jahwist who preserved and rearranged it. If, at the
end of the period of the Judges, or indeed even later, in the time of
David, Israel had vanished from the political scene because of a
catastrophe in her history, as little would have been preserved about her
for posterity, in spite of her wealth of historical traditions, as has been
preserved in the case of the Ammonites and the Moabites, who, no
doubt, had their specific traditions too: only they never found their way
into such a large-scale view of history.

This ability to deal with extensive complexes of connected history
and not just episodes must be regarded as one of the most momentous
advances in man's understanding of himself, since its effects upon the
spiritual development of the whole of the West are incalculable. Like
all such advances in spiritual matters, this one was certainly only made
possible through a whole galaxy of favourable circumstances, of which
we can now detect only the smallest part. As is well known, the
characteristic of all Israel's contemplation of history is that it was a
direct expression of her faith. Particularly for her early and most
ancient traditions is this abundantly clear. But it has also to be recognised that the character of these old historical traditions was anything
but favourable to the rise of a more comprehensive historical survey.
For in one way or another they were all miracle stories, the accounts of
the events at the departure from Egypt and those of the wandering in
the wilderness and the period of the Judges alike. These events had all
something basically episodic and isolated in them: in their character
as miracles they stood out more or less unrelated to their contexts, and
because they were what they were, they could therefore still properly
stand quite on their own wherever they were recounted. The historical
interval until the next glorification of Jahweh was often great: and even
where it was brief, the next miracle itself had also only something of
the episodic in it and lacked inner connexion with what had gone
before. Episodes, however, even when the stories are closely knit
together, still stop far short of being a survey of history or an understanding of widely-spaced courses of events in history. Now, however,

a radical change had come over the conception of Jahweh's action in history; for people were beginning to see that, in addition to activity by means of miracles or dramatic, catastrophic events, Jahweh had another quite different field in which he worked, one which was much more hidden from men's view and lay rather in their daily lives. It is true that in the majority of the individual narratives in the Jahwist's great compilation it is the older idea of Jahweh's immediate visible or audible intervention that stands in the foreground. But besides these, there are already stories which completely dispense with any outwardly perceptible influence of Jahweh on the history. These stories accord of course more nearly with the time of the Jahwist himself—indeed, for the purposes of interpretation, they practically serve as clues for our general understanding of the Jahwist. For example, the story of the wooing of Rebecca is a tacit account of guidance: it makes Abraham express his confidence in God's guidance; the sign which the servant prayed for is granted without any miracle whatsoever; Laban too speaks of Jahweh as having guided the matter, although providence had been exercised in a quite hidden way. Here Jahweh had no doubt taken a hand, and if you wish you may call Gen. xxiv a miracle story too. But it is a quite different kind of miracle from those hitherto related, since this intervention of Jahweh no longer needed to break from the outside into the normal evolution of events upon earth to make itself felt. At the moment when the girl offered to supply the servant and his camels with water, Jahweh's providence had already achieved its purpose. This story is thus much more interested in the guidance of the heart than in the outward events.

Once a single example has drawn our attention to this great differ-ence in understanding, a considerable group of stories immediately comes up which are distinguished from the older ones in this charac-teristic way, and which all belong to this new age, even if we cannot date them exactly. It is fascinating to see how they fulfil their specific task compared with the others, for in the matter of narrative technique this indirect method of the action of Jahweh naturally made much higher demands on the narrator. In the wooing of Rebecca, it was the granting of a prayer which enabled the reader to discern his action. At a particularly important place, the story-tellers love to point to an intervention of Jahweh's which occurred at a definite point in time, and yet decided the whole affair. Thus in 1 Sam. xxvi a deep sleep which Jahweh caused to come over Saul and his men favoured David's

enterprise. Rehoboam's insensate rejection of the counsel of the older
men was due to a "turn of affairs" (סִבָּה), a *peripeteia*, which Jahweh
brought about (I Kings XII. 15). In the history of David's rise to power,
mention is made at the beginning of the evil spirit which Jahweh had
caused to come upon Saul (I Sam. XVI. 14), and the final note is that
"Jahweh was with David" (II Sam. V. 10). In the Joseph stories, on the
other hand, the narrator makes the principal character himself refer to
Jahweh's guidance (Gen. XLV. 5–8, L. 20). The same technique is
employed in the story of Ruth, which is an extremely artistic guidance
story, for the latent theological thread in it has to be gathered, as the
case arises, from the words of the people involved (Ruth I. 8f., II. 12, 20,
IV. 13f.). The man who told the story of Abimelech's city state and its
lamentable end set himself a very difficult task indeed, for his subject
is not one isolated event nor one that has to do with one person or one
family, but the fate of a city and its despotic ruler in a particularly confused period of its history (Jg. IX). This is the first occasion when we
see how a story-teller reaches out into the political sphere in order to
describe a phase in the history of the town of Shechem. The picture is
realistic in the extreme—but here too there falls quite directly, like a
stone, upon the scene the statement "but God sent an evil spirit between
Abimelech and the townsmen of Shechem" (vs. 23), and from then on
things turn out unfavourably for Abimelech. The story in Judges IX
makes such great demands upon its subject in order to present it that
it practically reaches the borderline where historiography begins. But
Israel also crossed this borderline and found her way to real historical
writing, that most comprehensive form of a people's self-understanding
to which in the whole of the ancient world, besides her, the Greeks
alone found their way, and then along quite a different road. At least
as far as form is concerned, we meet with historical writing at its most
perfect in the history of the succession to David. The ordering of the
complex material into a clear sequence of scenes is masterly, the
portrayal of the actors is brilliant, but in particular the technique
already mentioned of inserting theological references comes to final
perfection. More will need to be said of this later, and in greater detail.[26]

Now this completely new way of picturing Jahweh's action in
history, which led, as we have seen, to a new technique in narrative,
certainly did not arise by chance; it was merely an expression of a
more profound spiritual transformation. For an era which no longer

[26] See below, pp. 308ff.

experienced Jahweh's working mainly in the sacral form of miracles or miracle-like episodes, and which could therefore no longer satisfactorily express its faith in a sacral narrative-form, for such an era its whole relationship to the reality surrounding it must have been radically transformed. This reality—we should say Nature and History—became secularised, and was, as it were, overnight released from the sacral orders sheltering it. In consequence, the figures in the stories now move in a completely demythologised and secular world. Unquestionably, we have here to do with the traces of an Enlightenment on a broad basis, an emancipation of the spirit and a stepping out from antiquated ideas. It did not mean, however, any abandonment of belief in Jahweh, nor was it a veering to an attenuated rationalised piety. Jahweh too had taken this road: out in this desacralised, secular world as well he allowed men to find him; indeed, his action in history could now be observed in a much more complete fashion. In order to show Jahweh at work, these story-tellers have no need of wonders or the appearance of charismatic leaders—events develop apparently in complete accord with their own inherent nature. Even the exceptional passages where the story-tellers do speak of God are not to be excluded —at all events, the preference was always for the least visible form of divine intervention: some human line of conduct, to be met with frequently and free from every appearance of the miraculous, was in Jahweh's dispensation made a turning-point of great consequence. Without some remark drawing attention to it, no one would notice a break in the terrestrial chain of cause and effect. But the most important thing is that here Jahweh's action embraces every department of life, the wholly secular as well as the sacral—there is, in fact, a certain eagerness to discover it out in the secular world. It is only here that the belief —already latent in principle in the earliest Jahwism—that Jahweh is the cause of all things, finds its proper form.[27] And, what is more, the chief sphere in which this action is exercised is the human heart. This does not mean that, because of this, the people concerned became "religious characters"; on the contrary, they are men passionately and doggedly pursuing their own aims. And yet the reader is made aware that, in order to direct history, Jahweh is using them, their hearts and their resolutions.

[27] For the concept of Jahweh as the cause of all things see B. Balscheit, *Alter und Aufkommen des Monotheismus in der israelitischen Religion*, Berlin 1938, pp. 40, 81. 94f., 125.

With the sacral event ceasing to be the proper subject of elevated narrative, something quite new became the centre of interest, namely man—and man in the immense diversity of his being. To be able to portray something like the meeting of the future king with a woman of discretion and a ridiculous blockhead (I Sam. XXV), or a friendship between two men (I Sam. XVIII–XX), must have been an enticing new territory for the story-tellers of the time. In an incomparable fashion they rapidly ventured upon very difficult tasks and described complicated psychological processes, as for instance Saul's love-hate for David, or the effect of a piece of news very much longed for, but nevertheless unexpected ("then his heart became cold," Gen. XLV. 26), or the stammering talk of uneasy men (Gen. XLII. 26ff.). Regarded from the standpoint of story-telling alone, these subjects and many others were possibilities still lying beyond the ken of the old saga. Over and above all these little masterpieces stands the portrayal of the minds of the chief figures in the Succession Document, especially that of David as an obviously split character, as man with the stature of a master who was at the same time beset by dangerous weaknesses. Here, quite apart from the theological aim, a positive artistic intention has made its appearance. The authors of the individual narratives, too, are perhaps best designated as short-story writers. In masterly fashion they handle every style of writing—the gamut runs from Saul's sombre tragedy with the witch of Endor (I Sam. XXVIII) right up to burlesque (the death of Nabal, I Sam. XXV. 36–8). Their portrayal is fascinating: but fascinating, too, however paradoxical it may sound, is their art of saying nothing, of not voicing the comment which the reader himself cannot help making.

Alongside this advance into the realm of psychology comes the growing embellishment of narrative by means of speeches which are put into the mouths of the people concerned. In the stories in I Sam. XXIV and XXVI the dialogues between David and Saul are the highlights to which the external events lead up—the self-humiliation of the anointed who was leaving the stage before the one who was coming. In the form in which we have it, the story of David and Goliath (I Sam. XVII) contains eighteen longer or shorter speeches. They clearly lift the real drama of the incident on to a higher plane. The external events in the Goliath story are themselves exciting enough. But the narrator is even more concerned with the tension in the spiritual sphere—from the oldest brother's speech chiding the youngster for his presumption right on to David's harangues to Goliath, which convey the demand for faith in an almost homiletic way. This dramatisation of events by means of the insertion of speeches is very closely bound up with an art of rhetoric which, obviously under stimulus from Egypt, was being zealously cultivated at that time in Israel. To be able to say the right thing at the right time was reckoned an art in which young men of good standing were being deliberately trained. When we further take into account that this was a time when people had started gathering and classifying information about natural science (1 Kings v. 9ff. [IV. 29ff.]),[28] this rounds off the picture of an age of intensive enlightenment and of general spiritual initiative. Nor is that all. This newly-awakened appreciation of the human, this focusing of attention upon man, this interest in the psychological and the cultivation of rhetoric, give us every right to speak of a Solomonic humanism. It would, to be sure, be inadmissible to speak of a humanism apart from a literary occupation with a "past." But then what else is the Jahwist's wonderful work but one great attempt to make Israel's past relevant to the spirit of a new age by reviewing and, above all, spiritualising it? The new spirit certainly penetrates the old material to very different extents in the individual traditions. Nevertheless about the whole there is a very lofty atmosphere into which even traditions which were left pretty much untouched in their ancient forms were drawn.

In actual fact, the divergences in style and kind amongst the units of narrative are often very wide. Compare the old-world solemnity of the Bethel story with its expression of primitive awe in presence of the sacral (Gen. XXVIII. 17) with the narrative telling of the birth of the sons of Jacob (Gen. XXIX. 31–XXX. 24). What a worldly welter of passions and downright human nature there is in the struggle of the two women for the man! And all this gathers round the names of the ancestor of Israel and the ancestors of the clans, which had sounded solemn enough in the older tradition. But in the interval people had come to speak of all this in a very secular way as well.

As can be appreciated, the reconstruction of the spiritual life of an era on the basis of its achievement in story-telling, that is, on the basis of a quite narrow sector of its total life, can only succeed in outline. A further handicap lies in the fact that we do not know either the representatives of this high achievement in narrative or the audience to whom they principally addressed themselves. The Homeric bards

[28] See below, pp. 424f.

sketched a picture of themselves in the person of the singer Demodo-cus[29]: in vain do we seek such a self-portrait of the great story-tellers of the Old Testament. Perhaps they are to be sought in the neighbour-hood of the teachers of wisdom.[30] We also do not know how far this new understanding of a secularised and even partly gentlemanly life made headway among the broad masses of the peasant population as well. It was possibly confined to the court, the capital, the officials, and upper classes. On the other hand we must not underestimate the formative effect on the general public of a monarchy and of such an intellectual upper class. More difficult still to answer is the question as to the relationship of these story-tellers to the world of the cult. It would certainly be wrong to imagine, in the light of the present day, that in matters of faith these circles had by now more or less radically broken with the cult. Apart from the fact that to our knowledge such a cultless piety simply never existed in Israel, there is as well evidence enough to hand for a positive attitude decisively contradicting the assumption that these story-tellers took up a position of unconditional neutrality in cultic matters. Still, that there was a change in attitude towards cultic matters is evident. In a world which had become so detached from the sacral, and which had got into the habit of looking on man in such a secular way, the cult acquired a certain odd remote-ness. It did not stop being the sacral focus of life, the point where man's intercourse with Jahweh took place, but the two spheres became divorced: "life" and cult began to go their separate ways. The history of the monarchy shows us the phenomenon of a growing secular civilisation, in the midst of which the sacral apparatus went on func-tioning. It would be wrong, however, to regard this process of secu-larisation as the great apostasy from Jahwism. At least, this was not the point from which the prophets started. On the contrary, they continued this process still more radically. Their complaints are directed against the disregard of the commandments of Jahweh, from which cultural, political, and social life had meanwhile parted company.

[29] *Odyssey*, VIII, 261ff. Cf. also W. Schadewaldt, "Die Gestalt des homerischen Sängers," in *Von Homers Welt und Werk*, 2nd edn. Stuttgart 1944, pp. 54ff.
[30] So already J. Hempel, *Gott und Mensch im Alten Testament*, 2nd edn. Stuttgart 1936, p. 65.

4. THE RELIGIOUS OPPOSITION TO THE NEW FORMATIONS
IN STATE AND CULT

The conclusion of the previous section largely anticipated the development of the history. We therefore start once again with the innovations which, from the beginning of the monarchical period, changed Israel's political and sacral life. The development which Israel then underwent was on the whole prescribed by the general political and cultic conditions obtaining in Canaan. Most people in Israel were certainly borne along unconsciously on the stream of events. It can be assumed from the start that those who approved of this development and shared in it were in the great majority, as compared with those whose attitude was critical, or who rejected it. But although the sources give us much information about the early monarchical period, understandably enough the data relevant to this question do not go beyond more or less disconnected details, which are not now sufficient to give any comprehensive picture of the contemporary counter-currents. Even scantier are the sources for the internal history of the divided kingdoms. As is well known, the Deuteronomistic historian presents the history of this era from one single standpoint only, and the only question he poses concerns the attitude of the monarchs (each of whom he identifies with his kingdom and generation) to the one legitimate place of worship in Jerusalem. They were "wholly" devoted to Jahweh, if they regarded themselves as solely committed in worship to the altar in Jerusalem. Even if as historians we do not repudiate this Deuteronomistic standard absolutely *a limine*, in that it evaluates the whole history of the cult in the light of a demand which was unknown to this period, at any rate in such stringency, we must still allow that the point of view of the Deuteronomist's picture is extremely one-sided. With regard to the whole intention of his work, the author had admittedly no mind whatsoever to present the history of the cult of this time in all its complexity. But since the Deuteronomist presents his idea with such pervading force, it is hard even for the critical investigator, as he seeks to reconstruct the historical circumstances, to free himself from the hypnotic influence of his account. In its schematisation his idea now and then irons out conditions in the cult which were actually extremely complex, with the result that his great work can greatly hamper the historian's attempt to reconstruct the actual events from it.

1. In the first Book of Kings the cultic policy of King Jeroboam I, the foundation of the two national sanctuaries at Bethel and Dan, is pictured in colours of deep disgust (1 Kings XII. 26ff.). But on objective consideration of the events we will have to grant it to Jeroboam that the conclusion which he drew from the fact of the formation of the state was just the same as that which David had drawn. The kingdom of Israel, now dependent wholly upon itself, simply had to have a national sanctuary: it is therefore not even probable that the real motive for the founding of the two national sanctuaries was fear that pilgrims would otherwise go to Jerusalem (1 Kings XII. 27). That the worship at these sanctuaries was the worship of Jahweh the Judean reporter had reluctantly to admit: and as far as the sanctuaries themselves went, the king could avail himself of cultic localities hallowed from of old, and did not run the risk of raising as a cultic place a city which had hitherto played no part in Israel's cultic life. Research has made it very probable that the two "calves" set up in Bethel and Dan were not real images of the deity, but merely a base, a pedestal for the (invisible) deity; and so not properly an image, but an attribute of Jahweh.[31] Nor is it to be assumed that in the eyes of the early monarchical period itself the use of such supports for the deity was reckoned as an infringement of the ordinances of the cult of Jahweh; rather we are again dealing with a later, more stringent interpretation of the commandment forbidding images.[32] Finally, as to the complaint that priests were arbitrarily installed, David and Solomon too reserved to themselves the right of appointing and dismissing priests at their royal sanctuary.[33] All in all, we shall not have to regard Jeroboam I as typical of the opposition to the new order, but rather as one of its most consistent representatives.

However, the case is different with the opposition to the choice of Saul as king (1 Sam. X. 27, XI. 12f.). In spite of the inadequacy of our information, we can well imagine that the rural population, which was tied to the patriarchal way of life, did not by any means accept without protest the great innovation of the imposition of the kingdom. Quite apart from religious considerations, the monarchy, as we know, also brought in its train a considerable curtailment of the rights of the free landed peasantry, as well as considerable economic burdens. The

[31] K. Galling, *Biblisches Reallexikon* (Handbuch zum Alten Testament, ed. O. Eissfeldt, henceforth cited as Hb.A.T.), Tübingen 1937, cols. 202ff.

[32] See below, p. 219.   [33] II Sam. VIII. 18; I Kings II. 26.

"right of the king" which Samuel is said to have recited to the people (I Sam. VIII. 11–17) is of course thoroughly tendentious in its formulation—this whole account of the choice of Saul as king also derives from a considerably later time. Nevertheless, the details of this right of the king are far from being without foundation in fact. The king actually did conscript the young men of the country population in order to put them in his garrisons as regular soldiers. He laid hands on landed property to set up estates of his own throughout the country; and from the country population, too, he drew the labour forces for these estates.[34] Other landed property he confiscated as rewards for his henchmen (I Sam. XXII. 7). He taxed the whole population to defray the expenses of his court (I Kings IV. 7, XX. 15): indeed, even womenfolk were not safe from his requisition, for he needed them as perfumers, cooks, and bakers. It is easy to imagine how the free peasantry in Israel, who still lived by a feeling of freedom acquired in nomadic life, must have regarded such interferences with their life. An utter repudiation of the monarchy finds its strongest expression in the fable of Jotham (Jg. IX. 8ff.), which has been designated the most forthright anti-monarchical poem in world literature.[35] There it is a social, and not a religious, bias that holds the kingdom up to such brutal ridicule. While the rest of the "trees" fulfil their role for the good and weal of others, the thorn-bush is the only anti-social good-for-nothing: its "reigning over the trees," its call to them to take refuge under its shade, is a piece of ludicrous arrogance.[36]

As against this, all that we hear about opposition to the innovations in the army and the conduct of warfare came from the very heart of Jahwism. The very ancient account of David's census in II Sam. XXIV preserves the memory of such a clearly contemporary opposition to an organisation and rationalising of military matters planned, and then executed, by David. This census certainly served military purposes. David wanted to know what his war potential was, he wanted to have figures available. But this sort of conscription of those obliged to do military service ran absolutely counter to what was of the very essence of the holy war, which was that Jahweh himself had assumed the responsibility for the defence of Israel. Nevertheless the story reports that the king's will brushed the objections aside.

[34] M. Noth, "Das Krongut der israelitischen Könige und seine Verwaltung," in Z.D.P.V., 1927, pp. 211ff.   [35] Buber, Königtum Gottes, p. 29.
[36] On Jotham's fable see E. Nielsen, Shechem, Copenhagen 1955, pp. 147ff.

The sources do not allow us to make so direct an evaluation of the story of the rejection of Saul, for its earliest possible date is the early prophetic period. For the redaction as we have it, the opposition of king and prophet, already very much stylised, does not allow an earlier date. But it is perfectly possible that the narrative subject-matter itself is earlier, for the king's clash with the original ordinance of the ban must go back to the time when it was still possible for a method of conducting warfare which was in process of becoming secular to come into conflict with the older claims of the holy war. Saul's sin was a very grievous one, for he had refused to acknowledge Jahweh by making over to him what stood under the ban. The narrative does not reflect upon Saul's motives, but the antagonist to Jahwism who had here appeared is, of course, clear enough. Saul wanted to dispose of the booty as he himself thought fit. It was therefore something like "reasons of state" which reared their head; and, new as was this will for the state, the rulers were no longer willing to have the norm of their actions dictated by Jahweh. As a matter of history, the alterations in the composition of the army and the conduct of war were very likely the innovations to which patriarchal Jahwism first took exception. For where else could the clash have come about? The pilgrimages, the great festivals of Jahweh remained, of course, intact. Nor did the king lay any hands upon divine law. But Israel's defence against its enemies— previously reserved to the sole competency of Jahweh—was now taken by the monarchy under its own control. This occasioned a conflict that could never be resolved. In the attack of the great prophets on alliances and the policy of armaments the breach attained gigantic proportions, and peace was only re-established when the monarchy had disappeared from history again.

On the other hand, the little story of Gideon's refusal of royal dignity can hardly be taken as a source for an early repudiation of this institution (Jg. VIII. 22–3). Here, unlike the two cases previously mentioned, there was no clash with any very definite usage; but the rejection of the monarchy is a total one—no one may rule over Israel, since that would be an encroachment upon the rule of Jahweh. The argumentation of this rejection, which is more radical than in I Sam. VIII. 1ff., XII. 1ff., is so theological and based upon principle that it must derive from a time which had already attained to some degree of mental detachment from the events under consideration. Otherwise the passage is remarkably colourless compared with the graphic vividness of the rest of the stories about Gideon, and it fails to give a very clear elucidation of this event which is said to have been set in motion by a request of "the people of Israel."

2. Nor, as we learn, did the great innovation in the cult, the building of a temple for Jahweh, remain unchallenged. Certainly the real background of the protest which Nathan made to David at Jahweh's command can only be surmised rather than reliably assessed. David was asked whether, since the day that Jahweh brought Israel out of Egypt, Jahweh had ever dwelt in a house. No, he had moved about with Israel "in a tent and a dwelling" (באהל ובמשכן) and had never given directions to build him a house of cedar (II Sam. VII. 4–8). There can be no doubt that, in speaking as he did, Nathan was acting as spokesman of the old tradition of the "tent of meeting" with its completely different ideas of the presence of Jahweh.[37] But the question as to the circles to which this tent-tradition was formerly attached and where it was fostered is completely open, and the circles probably can no longer be definitely ascertained. The tradition of the Tent of Meeting goes back to a very early time—indeed, at this time, compared with the Ark, its significance was possibly at the point of extinction. Thus it is an obvious assumption that Nathan is here playing off long-hallowed cultic tradition against the building of a temple.[38]

Nathan's protest died away: the Temple was built—in fact more than that, taken in all, the day of the old patriarchal form of Jahwism was altogether at an end. Admittedly, there must still have been a considerable body of the farming population in the country districts where the ancestors had settled who believed in Jahweh, but apart from them, where else? Jerusalem was a city dominated by the court and the civil service, taken up with political affairs and their anxieties: its native population was Canaanite and Jebusite. And even outside Jerusalem in the countryside the situation was greatly changed as compared with the cultic conditions obtaining in the time of the Judges. Because of his successful wars against neighbouring peoples, David had been able to extend the frontiers of Israel far and wide in every direction. To mention only the most important extension, the great plains in the west, the area occupied by the Canaanites and the

---

[37] For the theological distinction between Tent and Ark see below, pp. 234ff.

[38] Further matter on this problem is to be found in A. Kuschke, "Die Lagervorstellung der priesterschriftlichen Erzählung," in Z.A.W., 1951, pp. 81ff.; H. J. Kraus, Gottesdienst in Israel, pp. 23ff.

Philistines, were now added to Israel. What this great addition of Canaanite population signified for cultic matters is easy to see. The opposition of the mutually exclusive cultic modes, that of Jahweh and of Baal, had now become a problem within Israel herself.[39] This brought the penetration of Jahwism by Canaanite ideas into a completely new and much more dangerous phase. Admittedly, the conflict between Jahweh and Baal went back to the time of the entry into the arable land, but in that early period it could be countered more easily from the virgin substance of Jahwism. But in the period of the monarchy, through the growing symbiosis with the former Canaanite population, the ancient traditions about Jahweh were subjected to a constantly increasing syncretism, or, in other cases, were forced into the isolation of opposition. Along with this creeping internal dissolution of Jahwism into syncretism there appeared finally, in the Assyrian period and afterwards in the Babylonian, a growing fondness for foreign cults, such as, for example, those of Tammuz, Shamash, and Ishtar, etc. Some idea of the extent to which the cults of these gods had made themselves at home even in the Temple of Jahweh in Jerusalem is given in II Kings XXIII. 4ff. and Ezek. VIII. 7ff.

The Nazirites are to be understood as a symptom of the opposition to the Canaanisation of the cult of Jahweh.[40] The Nazirite's dedication consisted in a vow, one of specially uncompromising allegiance to Jahweh. The Hebrew term (נזיר אלהים Jg. XIII. 5, 7, XVI. 17) is to be translated as "one dedicated to God." The one who had put himself at Jahweh's disposal was obliged to abstain from certain things, especially from the drinking of wine, and to guard against all ritual impurity. In practice, of course, such vows worked out in very different ways (cf., for example, 1 Sam. XIV. 24): they might be taken as implying either a temporary exceptional state or a dedication for life. The story

---

[39] Alt, K.S., VOL. II, p. 52. The story of Elijah in 1 Kings XVIII lets us see at least in outline how variable the cultic history of a shrine out in the newly-won areas could be. On Carmel the god originally worshipped was the Baal of Carmel. In the period after David an altar for Jahweh was erected there. But that soon again fell into disrepair (vs. 30), and the Baal cult regained possession, until Elijah again restored the cult of Jahweh. Alt, K.S., VOL. II, pp. 137ff.; Galling, in Festschrift Albrecht Alt, pp. 105ff.; Eissfeldt, "Der Gott Karmel," in Sitzungsberichte der deutschen Akademie der Wissenschaften, Berlin 1953.

[40] W. Eichrodt, Theologie des Alten Testaments, henceforth cited as Theologie, 3 vols., Leipzig 1933–9; Eng. trans. of VOL. I, trans. J. A. Baker, London 1961, p. 306; J. Pedersen, Israel III–IV, London 1940, pp. 264ff.

of Samson gives us our clearest picture of such a lifelong consecration; only we must guard against imagining that, because of this, every Nazirite was like Samson. Probably every Nazirite was a special case, particularly every lifelong Nazirite. The infant Samuel, too, is represented by the narrator as a child dedicated to the sanctuary (1 Sam. I. 11, 28; II. 20). In individual cases the custom would be applied in different ways. But probably the basic idea always present was that the person concerned cut himself off from the normal ways of life by abstention from certain things, and so put himself at the disposal of the deity as a special instrument. In some sense the Nazirites were probably all charismatic persons. Originally these vows of abstention probably had no special causal connexion with the defensive struggle against the Canaanite religion, but as the distinction between the two cultic practices became increasingly blurred, it was inevitable that the Nazirate obtained the force of an important sign in this struggle. It had become the challenging token indicating a total surrender to Jahweh that was much more unconditional than was general. Behind the Nazirite could be seen a Jahweh who had already become a stranger to the official cult. Amos groups the Nazirites together with the prophets as signs of Jahweh's claim upon Israel which ought not to have been disregarded (Am. II. 11ff.). The Priestly Document preserved ritual prescriptions which were to be observed at the beginning and the end of a temporary Nazirate (Num. VI. 1ff.). Acts gives an account of a final offshoot of the custom (Acts XXI. 23ff.).

The Rechabites stood much more in the front line of the struggle to maintain the purity of Jahwism in the arable land. They were a clan-like association (and so not a "sect"), which on religious grounds clung tenaciously to the nomadic way of life even in the arable land. They refused to live in houses, that is, in village or town communities; they did not cultivate the soil, or plant vineyards and drink wine, in order that they might live long in the land where they were sojourners (Jer. XXXV. 6ff.). They were thus adherents of an extreme Jahwism. The ideas of living long in the land and of being sojourners in it derived from ancient Jahwistic tradition (Ex. XX. 12; Lev. XXV. 23); but the Rechabites believed that they could only share in Jahweh's gracious promise if they kept themselves uncompromisingly aloof from all the ways of life that were traditional in the Canaanite civilisation, and to which Israel, too, had become assimilated. In Jer. XXXV the Jonadab ben Rechab whom Jehu took up into his chariot, because they were united in "zeal for Jahweh" (II Kings x. 15ff.), is named as their ancestor. We must not, however, assume that it was only then, that is, at a relatively late date, that this nomadic association first came into being. An isolated notice, preserved only in the Chronicler's historical work, connects the association genealogically with the Kenites, which accords perfectly with the general picture (I Chron. II. 55), for the Kenites too were worshippers of Jahweh, and they also persisted in a semi-nomadic way of life at a time when Israel had for long been settled on the land.[41] Jeremiah had a deep sympathy with the Rechabites. Comparison of his attitude with the similar and yet quite different one of the prophet Hosea (Hos. II. 4ff.) is the clearest way of seeing the rights and wrongs of their principles, which were entirely shaped by a guiding picture of the past.[42]

But what would have become of Jahwism, if Nazirite and Rechabite alone had been its best exponents in the counter-action? Here we come upon the most astonishing phenomenon in the whole of Israel's history: at a time when Jahwism was being increasingly undermined and disintegrated, it was able once again to re-emerge, with nothing short of volcanic force, in a completely new form, namely in the message of the prophets. To the historian's backward glance, the emergence of the prophets is very closely connected with four data which were all prepared long in advance. The degeneracy of Jahwism because of syncretism was one of these. The second was of a political nature, the systematic emancipation from Jahweh and the protection which he offered, due to the formation of the state. Through her armaments and her alliances—in a word, through her political tactics—Israel had thrown off Jahweh's guiding hand and become politically autonomous. The third cause lay in the economic and social development which both kingdoms had undergone. The state with its taxation and its civil service had brought about a further disintegration of the old social order within the clans. In this connexion the transference of dominant economic importance to the towns was detrimental. The patricians of the towns, as M. Weber calls them, gained control over

[41] Jg. IV. II; I Sam. XV. 6, XXX. 29.

[42] An account of a parallel phenomenon amongst the Nabateans, an Old Arabian clan, which in the later post-exilic period pushed forward in the arable land of southern Palestine, is given by Hieronymus of Kardia: νόμος ἐστὶν αὐτοῖς μήτε σῖτον σπείρειν μήτε φυτεύειν μηδὲν φυτὸν καρποφόρον μήτε οἴνῳ χρῆσθαι μήτε οἰκίαν κατασκευάζειν (Diod. Sic., XIX. 94).

the country people, and crying social grievances resulted.[43] Because of the burden of taxation, the peasant, economically weak, became less and less able to remain a free man on his own land—his old influential and honourable status as a free man liable for military service dwindled away, and ownership of land came more and more into the hands of a small number of capitalist town-dwellers. The country people became increasingly proletarianised (Is. v. 8; Mic. II. 1f.).

The last datum, apart from which we cannot conceive the great prophets, was of a different kind: it was not a false development within the state itself, but denoted a shift in political power in the realm of general history. This was the rise of Assyria to the summit of her power and the threat which she directed against Palestine from the eighth century onwards. We have to recognise that it was only a period of weakness in the great world empires which allowed the Israelites to conquer Palestine and create a state there at all. About 1200 B.C. Egypt finally had to give up its old political claims to dominate Palestine. At roughly the same time the Hittite empire in the north succumbed to the attack of the "sea peoples." Assyria had certainly achieved the rank of a great power before the eighth century, but this first prominence under Tukulti Ninurta I (1235–1198) was followed by a period of sharp decline. Admittedly, her final display of power began as early as the ninth century, but this new expansion was not at first felt in Palestine. It was only with Tiglath Pileser III that Assyria's land-grabbing policy was systematically directed against Palestine, and this was the time of Hosea, Amos, and Isaiah. From then on, the political independence of Israel and Judah was at an end—it was only a question of time, and of Assyria's tactics, until the death-blow fell. About 733 B.C. Tiglath Pileser seized the northern provinces of the kingdom of Israel (II Kings xv. 29f.); Samaria fell about 721, and with its fall the whole northern kingdom was incorporated into Assyria's provincial organisation. About 701, Sennacherib forced Jerusalem to capitulate (II Kings XVIII. 13–16), and about 664 Asshurbanipal actually set foot in Thebes, the capital of Upper Egypt. The rapid decline of Assyria, which started in the middle of the seventh century, and its final collapse in about 612, brought Palestine no alleviation of political pressure, for the neo-Babylonians, who rapidly came to power under

[43] M. Weber, *Religionssoziologie*, Tübingen 1922–3, p. 26; A. Causse, *Du Groupe ethnique à la communauté religieuse*, Paris 1937, pp. 42f. See von Rad, VOL. II, pp. 35f.

Nebuchadnezzar, gave effect to Assyria's last political will and testament for Palestine: about 597 and 587 what remained of the Judean state was demolished. This was the time of the prophets Zephaniah, Habakkuk, Jeremiah, and Ezekiel.

What is the common factor in these prophets' message? The first characteristic is that they have their roots in the basic sacral traditions of the early period. Certainly, there are very great differences in the way in which the individual prophets draw upon the old traditions. Compare the extremely different though contemporary prophets Hosea and Isaiah, the one of whom takes his stand on the old Israel-Covenant tradition, while the other seems not even to have had knowledge of this, and appeals exclusively to the Zion-David tradition. With each prophet careful examination is needed of their mental versatility and their different ways of appealing to the old election traditions: there are many problems of detail here. It was obviously of the essence of a prophet to be thus rooted in the religious tradition—without it his office was inconceivable. Indeed, as their polemic makes clear, this was a much more real and fundamental thing for the prophets themselves than it was for their contemporaries. They toil and moil, and use the most extraordinary means, to convince their hearers of the binding force and undiminished validity of ordinances from which the latter had long broken away, and of which they were perhaps indeed no longer aware. In this appeal back to the old un-corrupted Jahwistic traditions, the prophets' work had a thorough-going element of reformation. It is of course clear that the prophets are often very arbitrary as they bring the old material to bear upon their own day: that is, they do not always faithfully recondition it in its old form, but enlist it according as they understand it, and this often enough means boldly radicalising it. We need only think of the way in which Amos or Isaiah proclaimed the demands of the old divine law as valid for their own age.

What also characterises the prophets is their equally intensive view into the future. For in the complexities of world history, especially in the appearance of the Assyrians, the neo-Babylonians, and the Persians on the horizons of Palestine, they see—and that in the near future—Israel and Judah encountering a completely new action of Jahweh in history. These proclamations of the prophets are, of course, by no means just the result of an intelligent estimate of the political situation, for they designate this threatened disaster as one brought about by

Jahweh to punish the sins of his people. Thus for the prophets there was not the slightest ambiguity in the picture that was being unrolled on the political horizon: the foreign peoples who were approaching Israel were regarded without exception as the instruments of the wrath of Jahweh, and were of no interest apart from this task laid upon them. The reason why the military and political aspects of these peoples' advent is left in the background is of course the fact that the prophets believed that in the disaster which was imminent, Israel was being led to a completely new confrontation with Jahweh. It was therefore Jahweh himself whose uprising was being heralded in the turmoil of history. It was he whom the prophets saw coming and descending upon the high places of the earth, "because of the transgression of Jacob and because of the sins of the house of Judah" (Mic. I. 2–5). Now what is absolutely new here is the fact that, besides the dealings of Jahweh with Israel and his meetings with her which the old traditions recounted, the prophets announce other dealings, and another meeting, which were in store for her, and which in importance and significance stand absolutely on a par with those handed on in the sacral tradition. Indeed, in so far as they mark the irrevocable end of all Jahweh's history with Israel until now, they even surpass the old in relevance. The prophets proclaimed Jahweh's sentence of death upon Israel: what is more, in so far as their message made Israel's obduracy still stronger, they actually joined the band of executioners. But another thing which made the prophets' proclamation something absolutely new and hitherto unheard of in Israel was that, even in the very act of proclaiming judgment, they made known the beginnings of a quite new bestowal of salvation. When the kingdom of Judah too had been destroyed and every political prop completely smashed, Deutero-Isaiah then delivered his message of comfort amongst those in exile, and, faced with the new situation, which he regarded as already very close at hand, broke out into a jubilation which was strangely out of keeping with the dreary realities both before and after the Return. But with this twofold message, of Israel's end and of Jahweh's making all things new, the prophets had opened up a divine field of saving action which had no continuity with the previous one, but which was only to follow a certain aetiological relationship with it (the new David, the new Covenant, the new Exodus, etc.). The prophets broke off and destroyed the existence which Israel had hitherto had with Jahweh, and with increasing enthusiasm they traced out the outlines of a new salvation for her and even for the nations. Thus, compared with Jahweh's action in history hitherto, the word which the prophets communicated is a completely new word. Its unfolding therefore lies beyond the compass of this volume, which is devoted to the interpretation of Israel's historical traditions.

ENDEAVOURS TO RESTORE THE PAST

FROM a review of Israel's extremely comprehensive and varied material dealing with religious tradition it is easy to recognise that the tradition can be divided up into a series of fairly large complexes, all of which were attached to actions of Jahweh in history which Israel regarded as constitutive of her whole existence. The number of these originally independent complexes of tradition is not large: the most important are the promise to the patriarchs, the Exodus from Egypt, the miraculous deliverance at the Red Sea, the revelation of Jahweh at Sinai, and the bestowal of the land of Canaan. The latest of them is that of Jahweh's covenant with David—and because of its subject it does not fall within that common picture of the saving history which, as is clear, the older traditions developed at an early date. Without prejudice to their special features, they are all "election traditions," for they are centred upon saving events brought about by Jahweh for Israel's benefit. But with the tradition of the covenant with David and the choice of Zion the cycle of election traditions is rounded off. Beyond them Israel knew of no further event capable of producing traditions—things of the kind no longer occurred. The next event which, at a distance, might have been assessed in such a way, was the return from the Babylonian captivity; but this was not in fact so assessed. It is not in any way attached as a new link in the chain of the earlier saving acts, nor did it, like them, result in the production of tradition. No doubt, the reason for the break in continuity in the saving facts lies, quite simply, to begin with, in the history and its development. But there is another factor assuredly no less important—Israel on her part no longer expected the saving facts to continue. She no doubt felt, as hitherto, that she was standing in the light of these saving facts—she was in fact occupied more intensively than ever with her religious traditions. But the time of the direct intervention of Jahweh which was creative of saving history was clearly over after the beginning of the monarchical period, and within Israel herself the expectation of and readiness for such events had vanished too. This was, of course, the tremendous vacuum into which the great prophets could enter with their message of new actions of Jahweh in history. For Israel, especially the Israel of the later monarchical period, the saving history had come to a leisurely end. The consciousness of being herself involved at the centre of a history created by Jahweh had vanished (Is. v. 19; Zeph. i. 12). The conservative circles of Jahwism concentrated all the more on making themselves at home in the long-hallowed traditions of God's mighty acts, and on formulating these traditions ever more carefully.

Investigation of the history of traditions completely confirms this picture of later Israel's increasing detachment from her sacral traditions, as emerges from various notices in the history and especially from the books of the contemporary prophets. The "productive stage in the history of the Pentateuch," the pre-literary coalescence of the many individual traditions into the concise picture of the history as we have it now in the sources J and E, must have been to some extent closed at the time of the formation of the state.[1] In this period—the main one which has to be considered is the final period of the Judges—theological work of the highest importance was accomplished. But do not let us imagine that traditions originating in totally different *milieux*, and with points of reference in totally different events, coalesced into such a concise picture automatically. It frequently took great boldness to combine traditions which originally were complete strangers to one another, and a great deal of difficult overlapping in subject-matter had to be overcome. The driving force behind this gigantic achievement was the conviction that all the traditions, mutually remote and isolated as they may at one time have been, had to do with Israel, and in consequence belonged to Israel—for throughout it is the one Israel which this carefully constructed picture of the history has in view.[2] But if we now go a stage further in the history of the tradition and examine the Deuteronomistic picture of the Mosaic period (Deut. I–IV) or even the idea of the saving history in the *paraeneses* of Deuteronomy, it is at once apparent that, as far as the history of the tradition goes, nothing essentially new had come into being in the interval, that is, approximately between 950 and 650 B.C. Admittedly, even in this advanced age the individual subjects still retained a certain degree of flexibility, since, to take an example, the Deuteronomistic narrator still on occasion allows himself considerable freedom in the reasons he alleges for certain events. But the picture of the sequence of events in

[1] Noth, *Pentateuch*, pp. 47f.   [2] Noth, *op. cit.*, p. 45.

the saving history, beginning with the patriarchs and ending with the conquest, has long been fixed.[3] It makes one wonder whether the Israel of that time still possessed the freedom and the power which were the prerequisites for creative dealing with the old traditions.

About one very important event the source material which has come down to us does not give even the slightest hint. After 721 there must have been a time when, especially in Judea and Jerusalem, there were people who systematically gathered together the comprehensive literary legacy of the Northern Kingdom and made it their own. The prophet Hosea's book was worked over subsequently by a Judean redactor and was in the process brought up to date for later Judean readers. We know that Deuteronomy came into effect in the South in the time of King Josiah. But in addition, the extensive literary complexes consisting of the stories about Elijah and Elisha, or the account of Jehu's revolution (II Kings 1xf.), and even annalistic documentary material from the archives of the court record-office of the kings of northern Israel, must have been brought to Jerusalem. How else could they have been at the disposal of the Deuteronomistic historian? The conviction behind this whole process was that Judah and Jerusalem were now the people of God: they were thus Israel; and in consequence this legacy of the history of the North belonged to them.[4]

1. If at such a late date, and when religion was so degenerate, we ask where we are to look for the representatives of such a pure Jahwistic tradition, we would of course have to mention the Levites first and foremost. The view is commonly canvassed that what practically amounts to a Levite reform movement preceded the cultic changes under Josiah and prepared the way for them. In actual fact this assumption is probably on the right lines—only, we must bear in mind that we have very little knowledge of the religious and cultic trends and aspirations in the two kingdoms, and that the few pieces of information which we do have mostly do not allow us to draw any far-reaching conclusions about the activity of the Levites.[5] But at all events it is a

[3] Noth, *Überl. Studien*, pp. 27ff.

[4] On the transference of the name Israel to the southern kingdom see L. Rost, *Israel bei den Propheten*, Stuttgart 1937, pp. 107ff.

[5] A reconstruction of the Levitical reform movement is given in A. Bentzen, *Die iosianische Reform und ihre Voraussetzungen*, Copenhagen 1926, pp. 72ff. Today we are further than ever from any knowledge of the life and activity of the pre-exilic Levites, and of their cultic functions and their history. Important material is to be found in K. Möhlenbrink, "Die levitischen Überlieferungen des A.T.," in *Z.A.W.*,

fairly certain inference from Deuteronomy, that, in the later monarchical period, the Levites engaged extensively in preaching. Deuteronomy
is in fact a hybrid: it contains, on the one hand, a great deal of legal
material, both sacral and secular; while, on the other, the way in which
it presents these old traditions is altogether paraenetic, that is, it presents
them in sermon form. But this appealing style of preaching which,
as is well known, permeates Deuteronomy through and through, is
certainly not merely literary form: in the ancient East, things like these
were not invented at a desk. Only after the style and technique of such
religious addresses were worked out in actual practice did this become
literature in Deuteronomy.[6] This preaching activity has an astonishing
spiritual range and wealth of subject-matter. Its representatives must
have been people who not only had all of Israel's old traditions at their
disposal, but who also believed that they had complete authority to
interpret these and apply them to the present day. They call to mind
Jahweh's covenant with the patriarchs, or they discuss at will details of
the Sinai tradition; they take Jahweh's apodictic law as their text, and,
side by side with it, as if there were no difference in the matter, a
casuistic prescription (Deut. xv. 1ff., 12ff.). They are as much at home
in dealing with the regulations for sacral warfare as with Israel's
festivals. But lay people could never have handled every department
of the sacral traditions with such sovereign freedom—it needed the
authority conferred by office, and the office could hardly have been any
other than the Levitical one.[7] Yet, as regards the history of tradition,
we now find something new in these sermons of the Levites in Deuteronomy. There is no longer any question here of adding to the web of
the old tradition itself, either by fresh combinations or by some other
enriching addition. For these preachers the tradition itself is already
fixed, and they understand their duty to it differently: they did not
have to develop what had been handed down, but had rather to
explain it. Thus they mark the beginning of the interpretative period
in Israel. No doubt what these preachers have to interpret is not as yet

1934, pp. 184ff. For the Levites who were forced into opposition in the later monarchical period see H. W. Wolff, in *Th. Lz.*, 1956, cols. 91ff. More recently H. Strauss,
Untersuchungen zu den Überlieferungen der vorexilischen Leviten (Dissertation, Bonn 1960).

[6] G. von Rad, *Deuteronomiumstudien*, 2nd edn. Göttingen 1948, Eng. trans. *Studies
in Deuteronomy*, London 1953.

[7] Cf. the references, which are at all events later, to an interpretative activity of
the Levites, in Neh. viii. 7f. and ii Chron. xxxv. 3.

"scripture"—the Deuteronomist calls it "the word," "the word which I command you today." Also, the tradition is still very flexible in his hands; that is, the preachers handle it with greater freedom than they themselves were perhaps aware of, since for their own part they already regard it as a perfectly absolute norm, admitting of neither addition nor subtraction.[8]

As to content, the Deuteronomic preaching is related to the old amphictyonic Covenant tradition—it thinks throughout in terms of a united Israel: indeed, in Deuteronomy's layout and placing of its material is revealed the liturgical sequence of the great pilgrimage festival, during the course of which Jahweh's will for right was cele-brated. But, as far as we can see, this tradition is completely non-Judean. Isaiah nowhere mentions it, and since he takes his own stand exclusively on the David and the Zion tradition, it is questionable if he even knew of it. On the other hand, the Egypt-Exodus-Wilderness tradition, that is, the old Israelite tradition, constantly crops up in Hosea. This and other points of contact between Deuteronomy and Hosea suggest that Deuteronomy really derives from the Northern Kingdom, and that it was only promulgated in Judah in a second phase in its history.[9] When, however, the central amphictyonic Israelite tradition was revived, an extremely military-minded piety dictated Deuteronomy's spirit. It is conspicuous not only that Deuteronomy contains a very considerable amount of special material dealing with the laws of warfare, regulations about the besieging of towns, a law concerning the camp, etc., but it also contains in its paraenetic section a number of admonitions to the people in time of war (e.g. Deut. VII. 16–26, IX. 1–6). Again it must be said that this kind of thing is not dreamed up at a desk. The forms for this material must previously have had some real-life situation before they became literature. The investigator of Deuteronomy has therefore to ask what are the circles and the historical situation indicated by this, its special material. Since we are in this case not just dealing with a number of separate traditions taken over by Deuteronomy, but with what is perhaps the

---

[8] On the long history of the formula "add nothing, take nothing away," Deut. IV. 1–2, XII. 32; Jer. XXVI. 2; Ecclesiastes III. 14; Ecclesiasticus XVIII. 6, see J. Leipoldt and S. Morenz, *Heilige Schriften*, Leipzig 1953, p. 57.

[9] A. C. Welch had already advocated the derivation of Deuteronomy from the Northern Kingdom in *The Code of Deuteronomy*, London 1924. So too more recently Alt, "Die Heimat des Deuteronomiums," in *K.S.*, VOL. II, pp. 251ff.

most prominent characteristic of its whole theology, the question is all the more urgent. This military theology, which is so aggressively opposed to everything Canaanite, permeates the whole of Deuteronomy and distinguishes it in the clearest way from all other similar compilations, that is, from the Book of the Covenant, the Holiness Code, and the Priestly Document. The question of the provenance of Deuteronomy is therefore the question of who the representatives of this martial piety were. Right from the start, the possibility of bringing Deuteronomy's war-theology into direct connexion with the genuine holy wars which Israel waged in the time of the Judges is excluded. Deuteronomy assumes the functioning of (royal) military officers, the שֹׁטְרִים (Deut. xx. 5 and elsewhere), as it also assumes an elaborate technique for siege operations which was certainly unknown to Barak and Gideon. No, in Deuteronomy we are not dealing with any direct deposit of these ancient observances, but with a definite conception of the nature of the holy war drawn up by later people. This is not only suggested by the marked trend towards a greater humaneness, but above all by the way in which it is firmly buttressed by basic theological and didactic principles.[10] The representatives of this idea are therefore rather to be sought during the later monarchical period, and, more precisely, among the country people; for, as far as the history of traditions goes, there is nothing in Deuteronomy which refers to Jerusalem, the court, or Zion. Actually it is very probable that there were groups in the countryside in which precisely the old conception of Jahweh and his holy wars came to life again. For when Josiah reorganised his military system, he was forced to revert to the old institution of the general levy, that is, the militia composed of the free peasantry; for he was obviously not in a financial position to wage his wars with mercenary troops, as the kings before him till Hezekiah had done.[11] But when the old associations still composed of country people and based on family and locality came into action again, what is more probable than that there was now a mobilisation as well of spiritual forces which for centuries had been crowded out by the ascendancy of the capital city's policies? We have sufficient indications that the juxtaposition of the capital on the one hand, with its court and its

[10] In contrast with the older periods Deuteronomy understands the holy wars as offensive wars, Deut. VII. 1f., 16ff., IX. 1ff. and frequently.

[11] E. Junge, *Der Wiederaufbau des Heerwesens des Reiches Juda unter Josia*, B.W.A.N.T., 1937, pp. 24ff.

civil service, and, on the other, the country people, the עַם הָאָרֶץ, was not without its tensions. Only among these latter could ancient Jahwistic traditions have been still alive and fostered. Here there were still believers of the old-fashioned kind, or, at least, who imagined that they still were believers. But the actual spokesmen of the movement will have to be looked for amongst the Levites—indeed, Deuteronomy itself presupposes the priests as preachers of such warfare (Deut. xx. 2). Understandably enough, a positive attitude to the institution of the monarchy was impossible for these Deuteronomic writers who revived ancient Israelite traditions. In actual fact, the "law of the king" gives the impression of being a foreign body in Deuteronomy (Deut. XVII. 14ff.). It is only a reluctant concession to the new age.[12] How paltry is all that Deuteronomy can say of the king compared with what is so forcefully predicated of him in, say, the royal psalms.

If what has been said shows that Deuteronomy comes before us as the express product of a reform movement, this becomes still clearer if we glance at the measures of King Josiah, in whose reign it became in many ways effective. Intensive research into the relationship between Deuteronomy and Josiah's cultic reform appears to have led to a final clarification of certain matters. The odd attempts to dissociate the events in the time of Josiah more or less completely from Deuteronomy have not been convincing.[13] On the other hand, however, it has also become clear that it would be mistaken to derive Josiah's action solely from Deuteronomy, or even to derive Deuteronomy solely from the events in the time of Josiah. Josiah lived at the time when the power of Assyria was rapidly disintegrating: it is obvious that it was this unique moment in the political situation which presented him with fundamental impulses for what he did. And even in matters where we can see that the King was in actual fact influenced by Deuteronomy, he sometimes fell short of its demands, and sometimes went beyond them. Since there is a deep tinge of the theoretical in Deuteronomy, it is from the outset unlikely that it had another, a more direct, way of influencing the tension-charged political sphere. It is therefore correct, as has recently been done, to separate off those measures of Josiah which do not in any way derive from Deuteronomy. The chief of these are his efforts for political emancipation and his efforts to expand politically

---

[12] Alt, *K.S.*, VOL. II, p. 116.

[13] G. Hölscher, "Komposition und Ursprung des Deuteronomiums," in *Z.A.W.*, 1922, pp. 161ff.

at the expense of waning Assyrian influence in Palestine. But accompanying them there was also the purging of the Temple in Jerusalem from all the Assyrian cults. In actual fact, as the Temple in Jerusalem was a royal sanctuary, the King's interventions for its reform really took place, constitutionally, in terms of a unique legal position.[14] But when Josiah took it upon himself to abolish worship in the Judean country districts (II Kings XXIII. 8), it was a completely different case—this cannot in any way be accounted for by the political situation. It has also been very properly pointed out that such interference with the cultic practices of the land was absolutely outwith the prerogatives of a Judean king.[15] Here obviously the King had the backing of Deuteronomy, with its rejection of all that was Canaanite. The same holds true also for the gathering of the country priests of Judea into Jerusalem, and for the destruction of the sanctuary belonging to Jahweh at Bethel (II Kings XXIII. 15), and, finally, for the completely new-style Passover which was celebrated in his time (II Kings XXIII. 21–3). In these cases the agreement with Deuteronomy is striking. It is very significant that the King and "all the elders in Jerusalem" submitted by means of a covenant to all the demands of "the Book of the Covenant" (II Kings XXIII. 1–3). In so doing the two parties concerned may well have been convinced that they had fully complied with the will of Jahweh as it had been revealed to them in the recently-discovered book. The historian, however, sees additional impulses other than those of Deuteronomy at work at that time. This was rendered inevitable by the fact that the strongest driving force at the back of all the events of this era was a king who was resolved not to be, as Deuteronomy would have had him be, a shadow figure. A king on David's throne was quite unable to dissociate himself from the tradition which had for centuries moulded his office. We can therefore conclude that, in his efforts for political expansion, Josiah had the master-picture of David's empire before his eyes—it is possible that he regarded himself as the second David promised by Jahweh.[16] But even before his work could come to shape he met his end in his encounter with the Egyptians (II Kings XXIII. 29).

Though they were decidedly new for his time, Josiah's political intentions, too, like his cultic ones, were an out and out harking back to the past. This is true both of the attempt to re-create the empire of

[14] See above, p. 43.   [15] Alt, K.S., VOL. II, p. 257.
[16] O. Procksch, "König Josia," in Festschrift für Th. Zahn, Leipzig 1928, p. 48. Similarly Noth, History, pp. 273f.

David, and, in particular, of the purely theoretical compliance with the sacral arrangements made by Moses. In this latter case Israel took a further and decisive step towards objectifying the old standards present to her mind. Deuteronomy itself did not as yet regard itself as "Scripture"—the beginnings of this are only found in a few later additions (Deut. XVII. 18, XXXI. 9, 26): it is, as we saw, a collection of sermons which for their part referred to a tradition which, though obligatory, was not yet fixed verbally. But with Josiah and the promulgation of Deuteronomy this was changed. Josiah had the will of God in his hands in the form of a book, and that meant taking a decisive step towards the formation of a normative canon. But in all this Israel was taking her share in a wave of restorative tendencies which, remarkably enough, at this time stirred the whole ancient East. In the Egypt of the Saite kings age-old cults whose rituals had been forgotten came to life again, pyramids were repaired, and writing reverted to archaic forms. In Babylon Nabopolasser followed the Old Babylonian modes of expression in his inscriptions, and his son Nebuchadnezzar excavated the foundations of old temples and prided himself on having found scrolls which related to their building.[17]

2. Unfortunately, investigation is still far from being able to demonstrate such convincing roots in the history of Israel's faith and cult for the Priestly Document as it can for Deuteronomy. The difficulties here are much greater. Even the point at which the work ends is not as clear as it might be. While formerly a not inconsiderable part of the account of the division of Canaan in Josh. XIII–XIX used to be ascribed to the Priestly Document, today it is increasingly held that its end is to be detected as early as in the Book of Numbers.[18] But,

[17] Procksch was the first to draw attention to this connexion, *op. cit.*, p. 40. For Egypt see E. Drioton and J. Vandier, *Les Peuples de l'orient méditerranéen*, VOL. II, *L'Egypte*, Paris 1946, pp. 588ff.; J. H. Breasted, *A History of Egypt*, London 1919, pp. 565ff. For Babylon see W. von Soden, *Herrscher im alten Orient*, Berlin 1954, p. 139; S. H. Langdon, *Die neubabylonischen Köningsinschriften*, Leipzig 1912, p. 97, cf. also p. 217.

[18] M. Noth regards Num. XXVII. 12–23 and the note about the death of Moses in Deut. XXXIV. 1*a*, 7–9 as the end of P. What stands between these two narratives is as much a secondary addition of P's as are the passages in the Book of Joshua which were formerly held to belong originally to P, *Überl. Studien*, pp. 182ff., 190ff. Similarly K. Elliger, "Sinn und Ursprung der priesterschriftlichen Geschichtserzählung," in *Z.Th.K.*, 1952, pp. 121ff. On the theology of the Priestly Document see K. Koch, "Die Eigenart der priesterschriftlichen Sinaigesetzgebung," in *Z.Th. K.*, 1958, pp. 36ff.; J. Hempel, "Priesterkodex," in Pauly-Wissowa, VOL. XXII. 2, cols. 1943ff.

above all, in P we are not dealing with a piece of writing in which the reader is freely addressed and given explanations: on the contrary, the separate traditions, and in particular P's sacral ordinances, given in more or less historical guise, are presented without any interpretation whatsoever. This by itself gives the reader who is making comparisons with other codes the impression that P is much older than it really is. The fact that it confines itself to the sacral ordinances also complicates the determination of its place of origin in Israel's history. Deuteronomy undertook to arrange the whole of Israel's life—the compass of its material is so wide that it affords many more points of attack for historical analysis—while P's exclusively sacral material originates in the cultic sphere, upon which history leaves much less stamp. There can be no doubt: the Priestly Document, no less than D, is a programme for the cult. "As it was once, so must it be again."[19] Its purpose is unmistakable: its intention is to lay down the ordinances of Jahweh revealed for Israel's salvation during the history, and to legitimate them by showing their specific place within the saving history.[20] To effect this the picture which P uses is simply the common one already found in the Jahwist, which, in the last analysis, goes back to very old confessional formulations. It is therefore that of the Israel tradition. On the other hand, we find no trace in P either of the specifically Jerusalem tradition (the David and Zion tradition). There are no difficulties in assuming that the sacral traditions of Israel gained an early footing in Judah also: only what occasions surprise is that we there come across them in such a pure form without the slightest admixture of the David-Zion traditions. This in turn makes it difficult to take P as in origin a Jerusalem collection of traditions. Finally, when we consider that P revives the old Tent–Manifestation theology, while the cult at Solomon's Temple stood completely for Jahweh's actual indwelling there (cf. I Kings VIII. 12f.; II Kings XIX. 14), we must regard, even if we are not ready to give it up altogether, the oft-repeated assertion that the tabernacle of P is none other than the Temple projected back into the period of the Wilderness as an inadmissible oversimplification.[21] Again, it is not possible to be precise about the time and place at which P came into effect. For a while it was common practice to connect Deuteronomy with Josiah's cultic reform, and P

---

[19] K. Koch, in *Z.Th.K.*, 1958, p. 40.   [20] See below, pp. 243f.

[21] On the difference between the theology of manifestation (the Tent) and the theology of presence (the Ark) see below, pp. 234ff.

with that of Ezra. The similarity in the events led us on. But on a closer examination the arguments for identifying the "law of the God of heaven" with P have proved inadequate: at present, we cannot precisely determine what Ezra's codex was. The well-known criteria for this late dating of P, which derive from the classical period of Pentateuchal criticism, are still valid for today—only we do not relate this date to the "composition" of the Pentateuch, but to a process of literary and theological redaction which, measured against the age of the tradition itself, is comparatively late.[22] As has long been recognised, too, a particularly important factor for the dating of the Priestly Document is the prominence which it gives to the Sabbath and to circumcision. Both institutions had certainly been long observed in Israel. But we have no evidence whatsoever for assuming that, in their inner meaning, these customs stood in a specially close connexion with Jahwism. But for the time of the exile, and especially for those exiled in Babylon, this was changed. Living as the exiles did amongst a people who did not practise circumcision, the good old usage here became all at once a token of the difference. The same thing is true of the Sabbath, for in the foreign land, the "unclean land" (Ezek. iv. 13), all sacrifice had to cease. All the greater became the confessional importance of such cultic observances, which remained binding even without an altar. Thus it was in the Exile that the Sabbath and circumcision won a *status confessionis* which they afterwards preserved for all time.[23]

Afterwards, at some time and in some way, the Priestly Document was put into practical effect in Jerusalem as the norm for the cult of the post-exilic period. But the co-existence of the Priestly Document and Deuteronomy, which after all still remained valid, opened up fresh difficulties. While in practically every sentence Deuteronomy alludes to the conquest of Palestine and the coming into being there of the people of God, P looks on the "camp," where the clans gathered round the tent of revelation, as Israel's original sphere of revelation. This camp is a strictly sacral sphere, in whose holiness Israel can live only in so far as

[22] All evaluation of the individual units in the Priestly Document is complicated by the fact that no document before P preserves for us a glimpse of the ritual aspect of Israel's cult. The general late dating of P's cultic material which was usual once has to-day hardly an adherent left.

[23] K. Elliger, in *Z.Th.K.*, pp. 121ff., takes P as in effect a tract for the times for the exiles who, like the generation during the wandering in the wilderness, had to live far from the land of promise.

she observes detailed cultic regulations.[24] This is perhaps where the difference between D and P is at its greatest, for by the centralisation of the cult, Deuteronomy in a most drastic fashion secularised Israel's realm of existence—a great part of what it seeks to do in its *paraeneses* serves the purpose of giving the people a guiding hand for their life out in the exposedness of the secular world.

3. To appreciate the cultic circumstances of Israel and their possibilities in the period after the disaster of 586, we have first of all to remember that the neo-Babylonians, apparently in consequence of their own weakness, departed in two respects from the normal way of treating exiles—they did not split the deportees up into groups and settle these in their frontier provinces, and they failed to settle foreign colonists in the now depopulated new province.[25] After the destruction of the Northern Kingdom, the Assyrians had been careful to take both these measures, with the result that they blotted the kingdom of Israel out of the pages of history. But things were different 135 years later. The deportation of the upper stratum of the Judean population only resulted in a sort of internment in Babylonia, while those who had stayed behind in the country were left to themselves—except for their eastern and southern neighbours, who infiltrated into their land. No wonder then that, in view of such half-measures, neither section of those affected, especially of course the deportees, abandoned the hope of an end to this state of affairs. Not only did the latter form a much more closely-knit group than would have been possible in other circumstances, but they maintained constant communication with those who had stayed behind in the country. Each group was kept informed of the circumstances of the other. This is well exemplified by Jeremiah's letter to the exiles, to which the latter in turn replied (Jer. xxix. 1ff.; cf. Ezek. xxxiii. 21). It is not without interest to notice that, in relation to the deportees, those who had remained behind in the country designated themselves the true heirs of Jahweh's promise—a claim which the others challenged (Ezek. xi. 15, xxxiii. 24).

It is only recently that research into the exilic period has dealt more intensively with the conditions obtaining in Jerusalem and Judea, and finally done away with the notion that, to all intents and purposes, the land survived these fifty years denuded of all inhabitants, and dead to

---

[24] A. Kuschke, "Die Lagervorstellung der priesterschriftlichen Erzählung," in *Z.A.W.*, 1951, pp. 74ff.

[25] For what follows cf. Alt, *K.S.*, vol. II, pp. 326f.

all cultural or religious life.[26] It was in fact only the upper classes who had been deported—the lower classes, the farmers and vinedressers and especially the serfs, all remained on in the country (II Kings xxv. 12). Certainly cultural conditions suffered a serious setback. Those who stayed on found themselves reduced to the condition of wretched *fellahin* (Lam. v. 4f., 9, 13). Cultic life was probably in a similar plight, for the Temple lay in ruins. None the less, during this period there was still an altar in existence and, although the holy places were degraded, cultic commitment to them was far from being dead, as can be seen from the account of the eighty men who came with offerings to the "house of Jahweh" (Jer. xli. 5ff.). Naturally it is impossible to draw even an approximately complete picture of the spiritual life of those who remained behind in the country, or of the deportees. The most important source for conditions in Jerusalem and Judea is Lamentations. This book shows us how difficult it was for the survivors to come to terms with the catastrophe and all its consequences. Again and again we find self-accusation, and reflexion upon the measure of guilt borne by those who were especially responsible. This was no doubt language conventional in the cult—in dire calamity people brought accusations against themselves in the presence of the deity, and solemnly assessed his sovereign action as just.[27] But this does not mean that those who prayed were not in earnest in their self-accusation. It is likely that during this whole period, sacral and cultic matters were under a very heavy cloud. The Temple had been devastated, the great cultic activities stopped, the festivals ceased, and only an improvised cult was possible at an emergency altar—that is, it was a time of fasting and mourning (Zech. vii. 1ff.). Psalms xliv and lxxiv in particular give us a glimpse of the national ceremonies of lamentation inaugurated by those who remained behind in the land.[28] The prayer for the restoration of what had once been—"renew our days as of old" (Lam. v. 21)—is typical of the mood of this time. Further testimony to this mood of penitence is offered by the Deuteronomistic history, which sets out to give a theological explanation of the two disasters of 721 and 587, and which is still best taken as originating among those who remained

---

[26] E. Janssen, *Juda in der Exilszeit. Ein Beitrag zur Frage der Entstehung des Judentums*, Göttingen 1956.　　　　　[27] Lam. I. 8, III. 39–43, IV. 6f., 13, v. 16.

[28] Further details about the festivals of public lamentation are given in H. E. von Waldow, *Anlass und Hintergrund der Verkündigung des Deuterojesaja* (Diss. Bonn 1953), pp. 112ff.

behind in the country. Page after page of history was here scrutinised, and the result was quite unambiguous: the disaster was not due to Jahweh, or to the failure of his patience or of his readiness to forgive. On the contrary, Israel had rejected Jahweh and his commandments. For that reason judgment had overtaken Israel and Judah, the judgment which Jahweh had threatened if the commandments were disregarded —here the chief thing in mind was certainly the curses in the concluding section of Deuteronomy (Deut. xxviiif.).

Accordingly, there can be no doubt that Jahwism and its tradition remained a living force amongst those who stayed in the country. None the less, there must have been confusion enough in their cultic life. The proper officials, the representatives and spokesmen of this faith, had been deported; and as a result the mainly lower strata of the population were more than ever left to their own devices, and may have adopted cultic forms which had already gained a foothold in Judea and Jerusalem in the later period of the monarchy, and which the reformation of Josiah had not succeeded in abolishing. In the eyes of many, Jahweh had simply succumbed to the power of the other gods, those of Babylon in particular. And had he not altogether forsaken the land (Ezek. IX. 9)? Those who migrated to Egypt along with Jeremiah, and professed their faith in the Queen of Heaven and the blessings she had given (Jer. XLIV. 17ff.)—that is, in the Babylonian Ishtar, the mother-goddess worshipped far and wide—were certainly not the last who subscribed to this cult in Judea. The same must be true of the cult of Tammuz, the Babylonian god of vegetation, who shortly before the fall of Jerusalem had even intruded into the Temple there (Ezek. VIII. 14ff.). Trito-Isaiah's complaint about people who "sacrifice in gardens, burn incense upon bricks, sit in tombs and spend the night in secret places" (Is. LXV. 3–5) admittedly takes us into the early post-exilic period. But these practices, perhaps belonging to the mystery religions, must have come into vogue as early as the time of the Exile.

4. There was a much greater ferment in the religious life of the deportees. This is not surprising, for they were of course the nation's intelligentsia: they included the priests, the prophets, and the whole civil service subordinated to the court. The prophets Jeremiah and Ezekiel pledged themselves to the exiles, and to them alone, for it was to them that their promises of salvation applied: the prophets opposed the claim for precedence made by those who remained on in the country (Ezek. XI. 15ff., XXXIII. 24ff.). These were the bad figs, the

exiles the good ones (Jer. XXIV. 1ff.). For it was in the latters' midst that the problems set by the wholly new historical situation were in actual fact resolved. Also, they were the people who later originated all the decisive steps towards reconstruction in the old homeland. The deportees of 597 were in an exceptional position, for as long as the Temple and a Jewish state were still in existence, and they themselves were under the comforting admonition of their prophets of salvation, they hoped for a speedy reversal of their fate. Obviously, they were still quite unable to appreciate the disaster in all its magnitude. A fuller account will have to be given below of the way in which in this period from 597 to 587, the prophets Jeremiah and Ezekiel, and also, later, Deutero-Isaiah, waged violent warfare against all ideas deriving from the past, and all tendencies towards restoration and revisionist hopes.[29] They spoke of the "new thing" that Jahweh would do, the new covenant, the new Jerusalem, and the new Exodus. It is hard to say what success they had here with their contemporaries. As might be expected, these gave way to utter despair after the destruction of Jerusalem and the Temple. "Our bones are dried up, our hope is lost, and all is up with us" (Ezek. XXXVII. 11). To understand their attitude, we have to take as our starting-point the completely basic cultic idea that the land in which they lived was an unclean land (Ezek. IV. 13). Thus even the very idea of their carrying on the cult of Jahweh in its previous form could not arise. The indispensable prerequisite of such worship would have been Jahweh's choosing a place there too "for the remembering of his name," but that did not happen. In this connexion, it has to be considered a fortunate circumstance that by his centralisation of the cult, Josiah had already largely severed the daily life of the individual, especially of the man in the country districts, from attachment to the sacral ordinances: in so doing he became unconsciously a teacher for the exiles who had to live their lives in a profane environment.[30] If because of this, total abstention from the cult in the strict sense was imposed upon them, this does not mean that there were not many possibilities left them of observing their traditional cultic usages. They were not kept in prison, but were settled in towns and villages and allowed to fend for themselves. We have already described the way in which, in this new civilisation, observance of the Sabbath

[29] Jeremiah's letter in ch. XXIX is of particular importance. On Ezek. VIII see F. Horst in *Vet. Test.*, 1953, pp. 357ff.

[30] V. Maag, in *Vet. Test.*, 1956, p. 18.

and of circumcision became a *status confessionis*.[31] Both were now regarded as "signs of the covenant," and their observance was decisive as showing that one belonged to Jahweh and his people. Besides, the deportees were easily reached by the word of the prophets,[32] and it is probable that they also assembled for formal occasions of lamentation.[33] For this it is unlikely that one should presuppose the existence of the synagogue with its purely verbal service: at any rate, the mention of a meeting "by the waters of Babylon" (Ps. CXXXVII. 1f.) does not allow of so far-reaching a conclusion, even if it is assumed that the place was chosen beside water for the purpose of ritual washings. Unfortunately there is no evidence—especially for the second half of the Exile—which would let us make a clear picture of the spiritual condition of the deportees. We can readily assume that they followed political events with eager interest. The amnesty granted to King Jehoiachin and his release from prison (II Kings XXV. 27f.) must have caused considerable speculation amongst the exiles, and still more so the rise of Cyrus and his triumphal passage through the Near East, which would sooner or later reach the neo-Babylonian empire; for with incredible speed Cyrus had built up for himself an empire that extended from the Indus in the east to the Aegean in the west.

[31] See above, p. 79.   [32] Jer. XXIX; Ezek. XIV. 1., XVIII. 1f., XXXIII. 30ff.
[33] H. E. von Waldow, *Anlass und Hintergrund der Verkündigung des Deuterojesaja* (Diss. Bonn 1953), pp. 10–13.

THE CONSTITUTING OF THE POST-EXILIC CULTIC COMMUNITY

THIS is not the proper place for a detailed discussion of the some-what complicated political and cultic processes which led to the final establishment of the post-exilic cultic community.[1] We shall confine ourselves to a brief sketch of the individual groups of events which mark a forward move. There are, as far as we can see, four of them—Cyrus' edict (538), the rebuilding of the Temple (521–515), the work of Nehemiah (445), and that of Ezra (c. 430?).

In 539 Cyrus, King of Persia, overthrew the Babylonian Empire and, without a blow being struck, succeeded in gaining possession of the city of Babylon. The Persian kings' attitude towards the cultic practices of their subject peoples was something quite new in the ancient East, and had far-reaching effects upon the situation in Jerusalem, as else-where. While the Assyrians and Babylonians in their provinces sought to break the resistance of the native population by means of deportation and establishment of colonies, and ordained that the resultant new population should observe the official cult of the empire, the religious policy adopted by the Persians was totally different, as a number of characteristic decrees now makes clear. The Persians not only recognised the cultic usages of the peoples incorporated within their empire, but they even had their administrative officers set over the cults in order to purge them where they might have fallen into disorder.[2] Cyrus' edict (Ezra VI. 3–5) was therefore only one measure amongst many by means of which the Persians regulated the various cultic usages in their vast empire. This edict contains the order for the rebuilding of the Temple and the resumption of the sacrificial rites: for this end the sacred vessels which Nebuchadnezzar had carried off were to be taken back home again. But the edict says nothing about the resettlement of the exiles in Judea. The Chronicler, who was of course very far removed in time

---

[1] K. Galling, "Syrien in der Politik der Achämeniden bis 448," in *Der alte Orient*, VOL. XXXVI, PTS. III–IV, Leipzig 1937; Noth, *History*, pp. 300ff.

[2] For the various edicts now known referring to this, see Noth, *History*, pp. 306ff.

from the events which he records, was the first to connect Cyrus' edict with the Return (Ezra I. Iff.),[3] and this mistaken idea has still persisted down to our own time. Unfortunately, we cannot give any very precise date for the Return; but it cannot have taken place earlier than the time of Cyrus' successor, Cambyses (529–522). As regards the rebuilding of the Temple no progress was made, despite Cyrus' generous decree. The foundation stone was certainly laid under the supervision of the governor Shesbazzar, but after this first beginning nothing further happened. The reasons for this are to be sought not only in the miserable economic conditions of Palestine, but also in the fact that the Persians had certainly not given this remote part of their empire an effective political organisation as early as Cyrus' time. In actual fact it took a long time—not till the days of Nehemiah—for this area to be politically organised and stabilised.

The death of Cambyses plunged the vast empire into a grave crisis. Darius Hystaspes was the immediate legitimate successor (Cambyses died without issue). But he had first to get rid of another claimant to the throne, who had succeeded in gaining parts of the empire for himself. At that time, this empire's colossal bulk must have been shaken with a tremor that was felt even in Jerusalem. Two prophets arose there, Haggai and Zechariah, who regarded this convulsion of the whole Near Eastern world from a messianic point of view and stirred the people to renewed work on the Temple. As a result, the great work was once again taken in hand under the auspices of Zerubbabel, a descendant of David and the grandson of Jehoiachin, and it was completed despite great opposition from the leading class in the city of Samaria. The Temple was solemnly consecrated in the spring of the year 515 (Ezra VI. 15). The scruples of the Samaritans can be understood in the light of the real ambiguity which existed as to what this new cultic development implied. Solomon's Temple was the state sanctuary belonging to the house of David.[4] But how was Zerubbabel's Temple to be regarded? Judah was no longer a state—indeed, it was no longer even a province on its own, but was still under the control of the governor in Samaria, who naturally enough had to keep an eye on all that went on in Jerusalem. Now, as a matter of fact, the prophets Haggai and Zechariah

[3] Regarding the later events in Jerusalem under Ezra and Nehemiah too, more recent research draws a much sharper distinction between the Chronicler's idea of them and their actual course as it can be reconstructed on the basis of the official documents.

[4] See above, p. 43.

had designated Zerubbabel as the anointed of Jahweh (Hag. II. 20ff.; Zech. IV. 14): they must thus have had the re-creation of the kingdom of David in mind. And even if what they proclaimed died away, and to the best of our knowledge was without political results, it still remained an open question how this temple was to function within the framework of the constitution. If it was designed to become a kind of new amphictyonic cultic resort for all the worshippers of Jahweh, then again the Samaritans also were concerned, for they too apparently regarded themselves as worshippers of Jahweh (Ezra IV. 1ff.). The resistance of the Samaritans to this new development in Jerusalem took its point from the fact that here "right opposed right."[5]

Again, a certain relaxation in religious zeal seems to have followed upon the intense period of the years 522–21—at any rate, the prophet Malachi's complaints presuppose grave negligence and even demoralisation in cultic practice. Admittedly Malachi is the one and only source from which we can gather any information about conditions in Jerusalem for the next seventy years, the period between the rededication of the Temple and Nehemiah's coming to Jerusalem in 445. In the case of Nehemiah it was once more the exiles whose initiative set things going again in Jerusalem. In the matter of authorities for Nehemiah's attitude, we are extremely well served by his own personal memoirs and other documentary material. It was Nehemiah who made his special concern the political security and constitutional consolidation of Judea as a separate province independent of Samaria. By rebuilding the city wall he made Jerusalem defensible, and he helped to overcome the lack of population by means of a so-called *synoicismos*, that is, by officially settling a part of the hitherto rural population within the city (Neh. VII. 4, XI. 1f.). In the end it was Nehemiah himself who became the first governor of this new province. But he also felt a call to remedy abuses in the cult. All the measures which he took show him to have been a rigorist in his theology and a resolute purist in regard to the newly-constituted cultic community. He took a stand for the exclusion of all aliens from it, and even for the dissolution of mixed marriages (Neh. XIII. 1–3, 23–8); he strove for regulation of the cultic offerings (Neh. XIII. 10–13, 31), and likewise for the enforcement of the strict observance of the Sabbath rest (Neh. XIII. 15–23); he also purged the Temple of what did not belong there (Neh. XIII. 4–9). However, the task of spiritually restoring the cultic community was shortly to be taken in

[5] Alt, *K.S.*, VOL. II, p. 317.

hand by a man who had considerably greater authority for this work than Nehemiah.[6]

Ezra too came from the exiles in Babylon, a considerable body of whom had obviously stayed on there. He was descended from an old priestly family: but the office which he held as a member of the Persian civil service was of special importance. He was "scribe of the law of the God of heaven" (Ezra VII. 12, 21), which, as Schaeder has shown, was the official title of the secretary in the Persian Government who was responsible for the department dealing with Jewish religious matters.[7] (The Chronicler was the first to term him a "scribe skilled in the law," Ezra VII. 6, 11.) Despatched by the Persian king with this twofold dignity—as priest and at the same time as a highly-placed Persian official—Ezra had the best possible authorisation for setting in order, in face of internal and external opposition, the cultic affairs which were obviously in a very languishing state. So he set out, furnished with many important grants (Ezra VII. 12–26). The most important thing that he brought with him to Jerusalem was "the law of the God of heaven," on the basis of which he proposed to undertake the new order-ing of affairs.[8] The question of this "Ezra codex," its content, and its identity with the Pentateuch or the source P has been investigated over and over again, without, however, any positive result, since the few clues at our disposal do not admit of any firm conclusion. The fact that the Priestly Document is in no sense a law-book, but a narrative work, rules out consideration of P *simpliciter*. This does not, however, mean that the whole Pentateuch can be considered as Ezra's law-book. The preconditions which would allow of this simple alternative are not

[6] The question of the chronological sequence of events under Ezra and Nehemiah has been thoroughly re-investigated recently, and the view which holds Ezra to be chronologically later than Nehemiah seems to be increasingly gaining ground. In the matter, some put Ezra as early as the time of Artaxerxes I (465–425), while others transfer his activity to the time of Artaxerxes II (404–359). On this discussion no defi-nite position can here be taken up. Cf. the presentations in K. Galling, *Die Bücher der Chronik, Esra, Nehemia* (Das Alte Testament Deutsch, henceforth cited as A.T.D.), Göttingen 1954, pp. 12ff.; W. Rudolph, *Esra und Nehemia* (Hb.A.T.), Tübingen 1949, pp. xxvif., 69ff.; H. H. Rowley, "Nehemiah's Mission and its Background," in *Bulletin of the John Rylands Library*, 1955; H. Cazelles, "La Mission d'Esdras," in *Vet. Test.*, 1954, pp. 113ff.

[7] H. H. Schaeder, *Esra, der Schreiber*, Tübingen 1930, pp. 48ff.

[8] The substitution of the term "God of high heaven" (אלה שמיא) for the name Jahweh, which first appears in the documents of this period, is an adaptation to the religious ideas of the Persians, Schaeder. *op. cit.*, p. 44.

there. But Ezra certainly did not bring any new law of Moses. We shall therefore certainly have to assume that what he did bring is to be looked for in the Pentateuch, and especially in the Pentateuch's legal sections, knowledge of which had been lost by the cultic community in Jerusalem.

While the Ezra source, Ezra VII–X, Neh. VII. 72–IX, has certainly been worked over by the Chronicler, it is historically essentially reliable,[9] and shows that Ezra set himself a considerably more limited task than did Nehemiah. His goal was merely the cultic reorganisation of the community which had clustered round the Temple, a strict reformation based on the law-book which he had brought with him. Of course, this reorganisation also entailed the institution of a court dealing with sacral matters. With its assistance Ezra was very rigorous on the question of mixed marriages, and compelled the divorce of the "holy seed" from foreign wives. The climax of his work, however, was that memorable reading of the law before the assembled cultic community on the first day of the seventh month, which we have to understand as a kind of renewal of the Covenant.[10] Such readings, by means of which Israel again subordinated herself to Jahweh's sovereign rights over her,[11] were of course already known in olden times, in the context of the New Year Festival. Whether at Ezra's own date this reading of the law by now had the assistance of a "Targum," which was both a translation into Aramaic and at the same time a paraphrase, cannot be definitely ascertained, since it is possible that the Chronicler, who obviously thought of it in this way, was anticipating a custom of his own time.[12]

It would hardly be possible to overestimate the significance of this event, and indeed of the whole mission of Ezra in general, for the period that followed. Not only did a protracted and complicated process of restoration come to a certain outward finality with Ezra; but also, as is usually the case with major processes of restoration, at the same time something actually new made its appearance. This new thing is usually called Judaism, and there is no objection to this term provided that a definite idea is attached to it. But the phenomenon of Judaism is many-sided, and consequently what characterises it has been

[9] W. Rudolph, *Esra und Nehemia* (Hb.A.T.), pp. 163ff.

[10] Noth, *History*, pp. 334f.

[11] Deut. XXXI. 10f., and on it see Alt, *K.S.* VOL. I, pp. 325ff.

[12] Neh. VIII. 8 (Ezra IV. 18). On מפרש, which is to be rendered "translated," see Schaeder, *Esra, der Schreiber*, pp. 51ff.

defined in different ways. Without any doubt, the outward feature which makes the greatest impact upon the historian who looks at it is the loss of independent sovereignty.[13] But it must be said that loss of autonomy as such is not one of the basic features of Judaism. On the contrary, Israel threw off the vestment of her statehood together with her monarchy with surprising ease and without apparent internal crisis. This must be connected with the fact that the state as such was somewhat of a borrowed garment for Israel; for long before she became a state, she had belonged to Jahweh, and had at that time known herself as "the people of Jahweh." Thus, even after the destruction of her statehood, she could still think of herself as Jahweh's people. And yet there are great differences apparent now. Even in Deuteronomy Israel was still to be regarded as a community bound together by nature and history, that is, really a people in the proper sense of the word. Therefore, the question who belonged to her and who did not was one that only arose on her periphery (Deut. xxiii. 1–8). In the post-exilic age this was changed, for Israel now no longer appeared as a people determined by nature and history; it was the law which more and more began to define who belonged to her and who did not. It could draw the circle more narrowly—in that case, those of foreign origin had to be excluded for the sake of the holy seed: or under certain conditions it could enlarge it—then proselytes could be granted admission into Israel.[14] What was Israel and what was not became a matter of the interpretation of the law. This submission on the part of Israel to a revelation of the will of Jahweh which was strictly defined and whose contents were unalterably determined is rooted deep down in the past. We have seen how Deuteronomy was to some extent regarded, if not as "Scripture," at any rate as a standard, a revelation of the will of Jahweh admitting neither of addition nor subtraction.[15] But in Deuteronomy Jahweh's will was of course still being directed to an Israel which was placed in a perfectly definite historical situation. What gives Deuteronomy its characteristic stamp is just the very fact that in the directions it gives and the comfort it offers, it refers to the problems

[13] O. Eissfeldt, in *Die Religion in Geschichte und Gegenwart*, 2nd edn. Tübingen 1927–31, s.v. "Judentum."

[14] The first indications of proselytising occur in I Kings viii. 41–3 (Deuteronomistic); Is. lvi. 1f. A clear interest in proselytes is shown in the Chronicler's historical work, ii Chron. xii. 13–16, xv. 1–15, xix. 4, xxviii. 9–15, xxix. 6.

[15] See above, p. 73.

raised by a definite moment in Israel's history. But now this flexibility of Jahweh's revelation, allowing it to gear itself to the place and time and condition of the Israel at the time addressed, ceases. The law becomes an absolute entity, unconditionally valid irrespective of time or historical situation.[16] But this made the revelation of the divine commandments something different from what it had been hitherto. This was no longer the helpful directing will of the God who conducted his people through history: rather it is now beginning to become the "law" in the theological sense of the word. Up to now the commandments had been of service to the people of Israel as they made their way through history and through the confusion occasioned by heathen forms of worship. But now Israel had to serve the commandments. Certainly the old way of looking at the commandments was still preserved in the post-exilic community for a considerable period.[17] We do not as yet see any legal casuistry proper. But when the law was made absolute, the path to such a casuistry, with its intrinsic consequences, had to be followed out. But the most serious aspect of this whole process was that in understanding the law in this way Israel parted company with history, that is, with the history which she had hitherto experienced with Jahweh. She did not part company with her relationship to Jahweh. But once she began to look upon the will of Jahweh in such a timeless and absolute way, the saving history necessarily ceased moving on.[18] This Israel no longer had a history, at least a history with Jahweh.

[16] Noth in particular has laid emphasis on this change (*Ges. Studien*, pp. 112ff.). But R. Asting too has given a very clear description of the process: "The stage which we call legalism (*Nomismus*) is only reached when the need which brought the prescriptions into being is no longer fully alive. Then the regulations are no longer merely an expression of the demands which the cultic community from its experience of life finds indispensable, but are extraneous to and independent of the life which they confront—the life which brought them into being no longer fills them, and so they stand forth with an awe-inspiring authority, and become commandments that are fulfilled just because they are authoritative commandments. What once took its growth from within now becomes something which comes to men from without, and as a *Novum* exercises a profound influence on the development of the cultic community and leads it into completely different paths" (*Die Heiligkeit im Urchristentum*, Göttingen 1930, p. 41).   [17] See below, p. 201.

[18] The eclipse of the concept of the covenant to which Noth has drawn attention (*Ges. Studien*, pp. 119ff.) is important here. For in the past in what other way did Israel more intensively express her understanding of herself in regard to the saving history than by her continuous appeal to Jahweh's covenants? She did not again experience history or write it till the time of the Maccabees.

From now on she lived, and served her God, in as it were, an enigmatic "beyond history." She was of course thus severed once for all from solidarity with the rest of the peoples. Because of this radical separation, Israel became suspect in the eyes of the other peoples—she actually became hated, and drew upon herself the grievous reproach of ἀμιξία.[19] Complicated as the phenomenon of Judaism is for the historian, especially the problem of its derivation from the Israel of the past, it must none the less be regarded as established that it is in essence only comprehensible on the basis of this new understanding of the law which we have tried to sketch. Judaism only entered history when the Torah of Jahweh was understood as a "law."

[19] For the reproach of ἀμιξία, that is, the refusal to have fellowship with other peoples, cf. Est. III. 8; Poseidonius 87, fr. 109 (Diodor. XXXIV. 1; Josephus, *Ant.*, XIII. 8, 3; Tacitus, *Histories*, v. 5).

SACRAL OFFICE AND CHARISMA
IN ANCIENT ISRAEL

A Retrospect[1]

THE greatest difficulty confronting any presentation of the history of Jahwism, its institutions, and its witness to itself, is the dating of the several texts and the determination of the dates of the traditions which lie behind them. The material itself may be abundant enough. But since it is in so many cases absolutely impossible for us to restore it to its proper place in the history, because we do not know its actual historical context, many important texts have to remain unused. Let us then in conclusion mention here another point of view which still allows us to gather up something at least of what remains, and that in connexion with a factor which is very characteristic of the sum total of Jahwism and its historical expression.

The tension characterising the first three centuries of early Christianity between ecclesiastical office on the one hand and charismatic authority on the other, between an impersonal office and a personal *charisma* which is, as such, completely incalculable in its effects, was also known to ancient Israel.[2] In her too the possibility that either might become absolute was ruled out from the very start, for both office and *charisma* were but the prolongation of the arm of Jahweh himself, who was present in person and whose zeal determined everything in sovereign fashion. The supreme court was neither a sacral institution nor a charismatic person, but Jahweh himself, for whom it was an easy matter to break with even the most legitimate institution or the best-attested *charisma*. He was lord and limit of both, the official and the charismatic authority alike. Of course, we are not, like the New Testament scholar, in the happy position of being able, aided by reliable

---

[1] A great deal of material is to be found in S. Mowinckel, *Psalmenstudien III* (*Kultprophetie und prophetische Psalmen*), Oslo 1923; cf. also O. Plöger, "Priester und Prophet," in *Z.A.W.*, 1951, pp. 157ff. More recently M. Noth, *Amt und Berufung im Alten Testament*, Bonn 1958.

[2] H. Frhr. v. Campenhausen, *Kirchliches Amt und geistliche Vollmacht in den ersten drei Jahrhunderten*, Tübingen 1953.

documents, to illustrate this tension, with quotations from its very beginning, or to follow it out. And there is the further difficulty that in ancient Israel the various offices were, so to speak, much more separate and often did not clash with one another at all. The offices of the priests, of the elders, and of the kings occupied different spheres of the national life, and so the conceptions of them which grew up were largely independent and often unrelated to one another. Of course, in the nearly a thousand-year-long history of Jahwism in the Old Testament we have also to reckon with far-reaching changes in the conception of these offices between any given time and another. But only a small part of this can be to any degree pin-pointed in the history.

For us the beginnings of the worship of Jahweh and its earliest institutions are wrapped in obscurity. All the same, such knowledge as we do possess allows us to assume as certain the existence of a priesthood as the guardian of the holy rites. But on the other hand an element of the enthusiastic, the violent, and the terrible seems also to have formed part of the oldest expressions of Jahwism. The perfectly incalculable effects of the רוח יהוה certainly form part of Israel's primal apperception of her God. But it would be wrong to understand these two in terms of mutual antagonism. Even as late as the time of the Amphictyony in Palestine these two expressions of Jahwism, the priestly and the fiery charismatic, must have existed side by side, if not even actually intertwined with one another. The pilgrims who submitted to the peaceful order of the annual festivals and the regulations governing the cultic ceremonial certainly did not find in the sudden appearance of warlike charismatic persons something which confronted this cult-ordered world as a thing alien and opposed. What might have been felt as opposed was not in fact so felt, since both elements referred alike to Jahweh and to the inscrutability of his nature and his acts.

How completely institutions were always subordinated to the sole personal will of Jahweh is made clear by the stamp which justice received in Israel. Here was one department in which everything made for the stabilisation and objectifying of what had been handed down: moreover, Israel was strongly influenced by a legal tradition which had been most thoroughly purified by a variety of experiences. In spite of this, she was quite incapable of allowing this department of life to become neutral. If we start from a preconceived idea of "justice," we can certainly say that the characteristic permeating quality of Israel's religion prevented her from achieving an objective justice. Even if in many instances she took over those conditional legal axioms which were undoubtedly Canaanite in origin; still, the whole religious context in which she set them was entirely different—to say nothing of the highly significant alterations and modifications which many of these axioms had to undergo, and which make it particularly clear that here it is no neutral law, but Jahweh himself in person, that is addressing men.[3] Thus law was for Israel something much more personal: it was God's will for order, which in the end could never become really stabilised and objective. This, however, means that understanding it, and administering it, became rather the concern of authority. Thus, the "prophetess" Deborah's administration of justice is without any doubt to be taken as charismatic (Jg. IV. 4ff.): but, things being what they were, not even the normal administration of justice at the gate could be without a certain charismatic authority. Deuteronomy still regards Jahweh's will for law as a subject for preaching—it is Jahweh's utterly personal challenge to Israel, which she in turn has to take to heart in an utterly personal way. Israel was very conscious—in Deuteronomy—of the unique quality of this will for law revealed to her. Through it, she was preferred above all the other nations, and these had to recognise in Israel's law the proof of her special nearness to and direct communication with God (Deut. IV. 6–8). The most radical expression of this conception of law as the direct and utterly personal will of God for man is in the preaching of the prophets, for in their accusations the proclamation of God's regulative will for law became something charismatic, the matter of a personal call (Mic. III. 8).[4]

As is well known, charismatic leadership in war died away with the rise of the state. Even Jephthah was no longer a charismatic leader of the old type, as the involved discussions on whose basis he finally agreed to take the field against the Ammonites make clear (Jg. XI. 5–11). This extinction of charismatic leadership was undoubtedly a tremendous loss for Israel. The army was mechanised by the change to mercenary soldiers and the techniques of the chariot: Israel let everything which had to do with warfare fall into the realm of the secular. But this meant that the main field of the Jahweh's activity, his action in history, and his protection of Israel, were lost to Jahwism. It was only the great

---

[3] See above, pp. 31f.

[4] On this whole question cf. H.-J. Kraus, *Die prophetische Verkündigung des Rechts in Israel*, Theologische Studien, Heft 51, Zollikon-Zürich 1957; in addition, the same writer's *Gottesdienst in Israel*, Munich 1954, pp. 64ff.

prophets who, with their unprecedented claim to recognise in this very realm Jahweh's rising up and his final decisions, recovered the whole realm of politics for the faith. So after the extinction of charismatic leadership the priesthood remained as the chief representative and custodian of Jahwism. But, so far as we can see, the priesthood never looked upon itself as charismatic. This does not mean that it did not claim a definite authority for its office, for even with an extremely hieratically conceived priesthood, an as it were completely mechanical life and rule on the basis of tradition is inconceivable. The giving of Torah, and the "acceptance" or rejection of sacrifices, presuppose a sacral authorisation and a special spiritual knowledge.[5] Nevertheless it remains true that this priestly office is never referred back to the opera-tion of the רוח יהוה. Even the obtaining of divine decisions was more of a technical affair and obviously not dependent upon free inspiration.[6]

The creation of the state brought a growing administrative organisa-tion, and an involvement in bureaucracy for the body of the people which had previously understood itself sacrally as "the people of Jahweh" and needed a minimum of political apparatus. But it is remarkable that it was the very institution which understood itself charismatically, namely the monarchy, which gave the strongest im-pulse through the measures it adopted to the secularisation of Israel, or at any rate to wide spheres of her life. This is also true, as far as we can see, for the Judean monarchy. About the reality of this charismatic claim there can be no doubt—David's political testament is inspired by the רוח יהוה (II Sam. XXIII. 2; Prov. XVI. 10). It is of course another question whether this royal *charisma* which, as has been said, was basic to the conception of the anointed of Jahweh, was anything more than a claim asserted by the king, an element of courtly tradition which gave the royal office a further halo of legitimation. A review of what we know of the official power of David and his successors—the historical Saul is, of course, a different case—makes one hesitate to answer it in the affirmative.[7] The official duties and the courtly ceremonial by which a king's whole activity was determined can have left little room for charismatic activity. If the anointed was early on regarded as in-violable, the reason was certainly to be sought in the *charisma* which he bore (I Sam. XXIV. 7, XXVI. 9). But significantly enough there is no

[5] See below pp. 244ff.
[6] I Sam. XIV. 36ff., XXII. 13, 15, XXIII. 9ff., XXX. 7ff.; II Sam. II. 1, v. 19, 23.
[7] See below, pp. 318ff.

further mention of this later. Nevertheless, in I Kings III. 5–15, an old ceremonial text, it is strongly emphasised, and it is also, according to Is. XI. I, the indispensable prerequisite of the rule of Jahweh's anointed one. To be sure, the kings did not draw upon their *charisma* in order to discover Jahweh's will in certain situations, since prophets were at their disposal for this purpose.

Mention of the prophets fingerposts the men in whom the charismatic side of Jahwism came to expression with a completely new force. If we bear in mind that the great period of the prophetic movement, which runs from the ninth to the seventh century B.C., can be described as an era of internal disintegration, in which political and economic life had long ago asserted their independence and autonomy, and in which Jahwism was already precariously thrown back on the defensive and now found its representatives only in peasant circles in the countryside—in these circumstances this phenomenon has for the historian contemplating it the appearance of the eruption of a long-dormant volcano. The history of the prophetic movement, which was from the earliest times far from uniform, falls to be dealt with later on in another context. Unfortunately, we are in the dark on the question of the cultic connexions of the earlier N'bi'im, that is, the question of their office and *charisma*. It is probable that in the early monarchical period there were N'bi'im who exercised their function wholly within the framework of the cult and who, perhaps because they gave answers to enquiries directed to the deity or practised intercession, have to be regarded as nothing less than holders of cultic office.[8] In the case of the court prophets this official character is still more apparent. Many remained in such ties down to the bitter end of the two kingdoms, others broke away from them or never stood in them.[9] These were the men who proceeded to stronger and stronger attacks on existing institutions, and altogether denied their legitimacy in the eyes of Jahweh. Polemic against internal conditions became the almost exclusive form in which their *charisma* found expression; and this was, of course, the signal of a serious disturbance. In actual fact it was against the holders of the high offices, kings, priests, and prophets, that these prophets turned, and reproached them with their failure to comply with the

[8] Gen. XX. 7; I Sam. XII. 23, VII. 5 and frequently. F. Hesse, *Die Fürbitte im Alten Testament* (Diss. Erlangen 1949), pp. 19ff.; H. H. Rowley, "Ritual and the Hebrew Prophets," in *Journal of Semitic Studies*, 1956, pp. 338ff.

[9] See VOL. II of this work, Pt. I, Ch. D.

will of Jahweh. Old Jahwism derived its vitality from the historic acts which Jahweh had done for Israel. With the creation of the state the realm of history and politics became more and more a great secular *adiaphoron*, in which the kings acted as they thought fit with their diplomacy and strategy. Not the smallest part of the immense importance of old Israelite prophecy is the fact that it recovered for Jahwism extensive areas of life in which Israel had forgotten the tie with Jahweh. And just as in home affairs the prophets recognised, let us say, judicial or economic life as spheres in which Jahweh was interested, so they also reaffirmed Jahweh's sovereign sway in the political sphere in which Israel lived. This made altogether inevitable a head-on collision with the efforts which were made to further Israel's political security, especially with diplomacy and the policy of military armament. The prophetic narratives in I Kings xx, which reflect conditions in the ninth century, admittedly show us a still comparatively harmonious co-operation between prophecy and military leadership. The prophet gave the order to attack—indeed, it was he who determined the part of the army which was to advance (I Kings xx. 13f.). This co-operation of the charismatic office with the state authority is remarkable—indeed, looking along the road which the prophetic movement later took, it can scarcely be called anything but a compromise. Quite apart from the perfectly proper question whether in the long run such a willingness of the kings and their officials to subordinate themselves to a prophet's word was to be expected, this protection which Israel enjoyed from state troops with their regular officers was a completely different thing from the earlier arrangements in Israel's holy wars. Actually, the phrase designating the prophet as "the chariots of Israel and its horsemen" (II Kings II. 12, XIII. 14) shows that even in the ninth century prophecy took a different view of itself, for it expresses unmistakable opposition to the technical secularisation of warfare. Israel's real protection is her prophets' *charisma*—what was thought of here was pretty clearly the miracles worked by the prophets.[10] This antagonistic isolation *vis-à-vis* all state and sacral offices alike is characteristic of the prophecy of the eighth and seventh centuries. *Vis-à-vis* all the demoralised or secularised institutions of Israel around about it, prophecy regarded itself, by virtue of its free charismatic commission, as the one and only authority mediating between Jahweh and Israel, and, we may also say, the last directly authorised one. The way in

[10] Cf. II Kings VI. 18ff., VII. 1ff., XIII. 15ff. A. Jepsen, *Nabi*, Munich 1934, p. 186.

which this attitude towards the time-hallowed authorities and institutions compelled the prophets to find a completely new legitimation of their commission will have to be discussed in a later context. In actual fact, this pure and simple appeal to a personal charismatic commissioning was something quite new for Israel. Opposition between two prophets, and between the "thus hath Jahweh spoken" of each, was bound to raise the question of certitude more acutely than had ever before been the case. The claim to prophetic charismatic authority made in Num. XI. 25(E) by the elders at some indefinite date in the pre-exilic era is rather strange.

This isolation into which the charismatic prophets regarded themselves as forced as a result of the failure of the other authorities was, as has been said, the unhappy result of an emergency: as a general principle, the prophets never disputed the legitimacy and necessity of, for example, the kingdom, or the priests, or the judicial office of the elders. Indeed they took these authorities, as organs of the will of Jahweh, much more seriously than the bearers of those offices were able to do at that time. Thus even Deuteronomy, which drafted a kind of constitution for Israel and which was admittedly strongly influenced by prophecy, assigned all these offices their place and function. But it did not succeed in treating and developing them with complete equality: in actual fact, what stands unmistakably in the forefront in Deuteronomy is an interest in prophecy and the problems which it set. Indeed, the supreme office through which the proper intercourse between Jahweh and Israel is to be carried out is that of the prophet, who will never cease in Israel (Deut. XVIII. 18). Thus, according to Deuteronomy, Israel as properly constituted stands explicitly under charismatic leadership.

The same can certainly not be said of the great theological scheme given in the Priestly Document, for in the orders of Israel with which it deals, the charismatic element has absolutely no place. Nor is this surprising, since P of course restricts its scope to the legitimation of sacral orders, and the extensive material secondarily incorporated into the work (P^s) is derived solely from the cult. As we have seen, this priestly-cultic world allowed no room for activity deriving from inspiration. Bearing in mind, however, that in its exposition of the events at the Exodus and during the Wandering in the Wilderness P's narrative is after all giving a fairly broad picture, then the absence of all directly charismatic manifestations on the part of Jahweh is indeed conspicuous, especially when one remembers the frequency of actions of the spirit recounted in the older narrative works. This seems to indicate some inner lack of growth. P does not regard even Moses as at all a prophet or a charismatic person.[11] Here the account of the installation of Joshua is characteristic: P does not understand the procedure of the laying on of hands as a transmission of the *charisma*, but of Moses' office as leader (Num. XXVII. 16ff.). The words that "the spirit of God was" in Joshua are somewhat unrelated to their context, for P was no longer in a position to understand Moses' or Joshua's office as charismatic.[12] P is more convincing where it speaks of the charismatic talent of the craftsman Bezalel (Ex. XXVIII. 3, XXXI. 3, XXXV. 31). The erection of the tabernacle could not have been a human piece of work—the spirit of God had directly authorised the chief craftsman to undertake the task. Such completely isolated remarks about a charismatic talent make clear enough in their own way how imperfectly rooted theologically this whole range of ideas is in the picture P has of Israel. This conclusion tallies with our knowledge that in the early post-exilic period, prophecy has already come to its end— from then on it apparently disintegrated as an order in its own right.[13] This undoubtedly implied some internal crisis. Was the post-exilic community to be completely without the charismatic element which, as we saw, was constitutive of Jahwism? In actual fact, she was brought to the point of deciding whether the charismatic could still find a place within her at all. But a glance at the Chronicler's historical work shows us that even in this time the charismatic still found representatives and spokesmen. In the post-exilic Levirate, from whom of course the Chronicler's history is derived, there must have been circles which regarded themselves as heirs and successors of the prophets, and who also in their own way laid claim to inspiration from the spirit of Jahweh.[14] The transference to the Levitical cultic ministers of the terms

[11] See below, pp. 295f.

[12] Joshua too was put to the decision by Urim and Thummin.

[13] A. Jepsen, *Nabi*, pp. 227ff.

[14] The great importance which the "prophetic" has in the Chronicler's picture of the history is well known. It could find expression alike in the free inspiration of an army officer (I Chron. XII. 19. [18]), or of a priest (II Chron. XXIV. 20) or of a prophet (II Chron. XV. 1). But the magnitude of the change in the conception can be seen in the fact that the Chronicler attributes authority in particular to the Levites (II Chron. XX. 14). Both Asaph and Jeduthun are designated as "seers" (II Chron. XXIX. 30, XXXV. 15). Special importance attaches to I Chron. XXV. 1–31, where the Chronicler claims prophetic inspiration for the ministry of the singers Asaph, Heman, and Jeduthun.

customarily used of the prophetic reception of revelation has, understandably enough, constantly led people to state that the pre-exilic
prophets and the post-exilic Levites were bodies that cannot be compared at all, and that the Chronicler lacked all standards for an understanding of the pre-exilic prophets and their *charisma*—did he not even
regard them among other things as authors of chronicles?[15] This is of
course correct. But we should go beyond what we have authority for
if, starting from a preconceived idea of what the prophets were, we
wanted to regard this claim of the post-exilic Levites as merely a hollow
piece of presumption, and deny *a limine* that in this movement of
Levitical singers, Jahweh's *charisma* reappeared once more in different
conditions in a different guise. No doubt the *charisma* was mainly
active within the framework of worship. But it was probably also active
in the realm of instruction and teaching (II Chron. xxxv. 3; Neh.
viii. 7ff.). The finest manifestation of this *charisma* that we have is in the
post-exilic poems in the Psalter, whose authors we have to seek precisely in the circles of the Levites.

But in this post-exilic period the operation of the divine spirit of
inspiration had by no means withdrawn into the cultic realm. From
far outside of it men came forward who very seriously laid claim to the
dignity of enlightenment by the spirit—the wise men (Prov. I. 23).
Job's friend Elihu introduces himself into the conversation wholly
as one inspired by the spirit: he points to the "breathing of the Al-
mighty" (Job xxxII. 8), which first leads men to understanding,
and he describes how the understanding given to himself had fer-
mented like new wine that bursts its wineskins, until finally he was
able to give vent to his feelings in words (Job xxxII. 18–20). Eliphaz
too wants his words to be taken as direct inspiration—indeed, he gives
the most complete description of the prophetic reception of revelation
and all the psychological phenomena which accompany it that we can
read in the Old Testament. Of course the discourse, which he has so
laboriously prepared beforehand, has nothing of the prophetic in it,
for it is a truth of wisdom (Job IV. 17). To be sure, all this is simply a
matter of taking possession of the intellectual heritage of a great past
with all the concepts that go with it. In actual fact, the interspersion
of prophetic terms into these teachings really creates a hybrid formation, for prophetic in the narrower sense of the word is just what this
Wisdom teaching is not. Nevertheless, it would yet be an over-

[15] I Chron. xxix. 29; II Chron. ix. 29, xii. 15, xiii. 22, xxvi. 22, xxxii. 32.

O.T T—8

simplification to regard this appeal to divine inspiration as merely an empty convention only used now more or less for literary purposes, for the derivation of special wisdom from a divine revelation was in itself very ancient in Israel.[16] According to Sirach, neither the office of the theological teacher nor the confession of faith in Jahweh which the wise man expressed in his freely-conceived prayers and songs, can exist without charismatic authority.[17] This *charisma* underwent a final change in form when the wise man became the interpreter of the future and the writer of apocalyptic.[18]

It is therefore evident that the charismatic was an absolutely constitutive factor in Jahwism. It appeared in many forms, in the guise of an inspiration for war and in the word of the prophets, in the praises of the Levitical singers and in the counsel and teaching of the wise men. Where it was absent, crisis supervened, and when it finally disappeared, the end of ancient Jahwism had been sealed, and the day of scribal religion had dawned.

[16] See below, p. 442.

[17] Ecclesiasticus xxxix. 6–8. Also xvi, 25, xviii. 29, xxiv. 33, l. 27. On the subject see L. Jansen, *Die spätjüdische Psalmendichtung, ihr Entstehungskreis und ihr Sitz im Leben*, Oslo 1937, pp. 75ff., 141.

[18] Dan. iv. 5f. [8f.], 15 [19], v. 11, 14. For this process of the "pushing underground" of the prophetic and its diversion into heretical movements, see O. Plöger, "Prophetisches Erbe in den Sekten des frühen Judentums," in *Th. Lz.*, 1954, pp. 291ff.

PART TWO

The Theology of Israel's Historical Traditions

Chapter A

METHODOLOGICAL PRESUPPOSITIONS

I. THE SUBJECT-MATTER OF A THEOLOGY OF THE OLD TESTAMENT

THIS belief in Jahweh, whose vitality we have described in brief outline, had very many ways of speaking about him. It never ceased speaking of his relationship to Israel, to the world, and to the nations, sometimes through the impersonal media of the great institutions (cult, law, court, etc.), sometimes however through the mouths of priests, prophets, kings, writers of narratives, historians, wise men, and Temple singers. Now, from this extremely abundant witness to Jahweh it would be perfectly possible, as has already been said, to draw a tolerably complete and, as far as comparative religion goes, a tolerably objective picture of the religion of the people of Israel, that is, of the special features in her conception of God, of the way in which Israel thought of God's relationship to the world, to the other nations and, not least, to herself; of the distinctiveness of what she said about sin and had to say about atonement and the salvation which comes from God. This has often been attempted, and needs no doubt to be attempted repeatedly. While Christian theologians may have played a decisive role in fostering this enterprise, the task in itself, however, falls within the province of the general study of religion; and it is therefore fitting that in recent times Orientalists, sociologists, ethnologists, ethnopsychologists, investigators of mythology, and others too have to a considerable extent co-operated in its accomplishment. The theological task proper to the Old Testament is not simply identical with this general religious one, and it is also much more restricted. The subject-matter which concerns the theologian is, of course, not the spiritual and religious world of Israel and the conditions of her soul in general, nor is it her world of faith, all of which can only be reconstructed by means of conclusions drawn from the documents: instead, it is simply Israel's own explicit assertions about Jahweh. The theologian must above all deal directly with the evidence, that is, with what Israel herself testified concerning Jahweh, and there is no doubt that in many cases he must go back to school again and learn to interrogate each document, much more closely than has been done hitherto, as to its specific kerygmatic intention.[1] The tremendous differences evinced in the specific literary units will be dealt with later on in this volume. None the less we must anticipate, and mention briefly, what unites them all. They are far from comprehending equally all the wide range of statements about God, man, and the world which are conceivable and possible in the religious sphere. In this respect the theological radius of what Israel said about God is conspicuously restricted compared with the theologies of other nations—instead, the Old Testament writings confine themselves to representing Jahweh's relationship to Israel and the world in one aspect only, namely as a continuing divine activity in history. This implies that in principle Israel's faith is grounded in a theology of history. It regards itself as based upon historical acts, and as shaped and re-shaped by factors in which it saw the hand of Jahweh at work. The oracles of the prophets also speak of events, though there is the definite difference, that in general they stand in point of time not after, but prior to, the events to which they bear witness. Even where this reference to divine facts in history is not immediately apparent, as for example in some of the Psalms, it is, however, present by implication: and where it is actually absent, as for example in the Book of Job and Ecclesiastes, this very lack is closely connected with the grave affliction which is the theme of both these works.

Both at this point and in the sequel, we are of course thinking, when we speak of divine acts in history, of those which the faith of Israel regarded as such—that is, the call of the forefathers, the deliverance from Egypt, the bestowal of the land of Canaan, etc.—and not of the results of modern critical historical scholarship, to which Israel's faith was unrelated. This raises a difficult historical problem. In the last 150 years critical historical scholarship has constructed an impressively complete picture of the history of the people of Israel. As this process took shape, the old picture of Israel's history which the Church had derived and accepted from the Old Testament was bit by bit destroyed. Upon this process there is no going back, nor has it yet indeed come to an end. Critical historical scholarship regards it as impossible that the whole of Israel was present at Sinai, or that Israel crossed the Red Sea and achieved the Conquest *en bloc*—it holds the picture of Moses and his

---

[1] It would be well to scrutinise from this point of view the chapter-headings in our translations or interpretations of the Bible, which often completely miss the intention that the specific narrators had in mind.

leadership drawn in the traditions of the Book of Exodus to be as un-historical as the function which the Deuteronomistic book of Judges ascribes to the "judges." On the other hand, it is just the most recent research into the Hexateuch that has proceeded to deal with the extremely complicated origin of the Old Testament's picture of Jah-weh's saving history with Israel. Scholars are even beginning to allow a scientific standing of its own to the picture of her history which Israel herself drew, and to take it as something existing *per se* which, in the way it has been sketched, has to be taken into account as a central subject in our theological evaluation. Research into the Hexateuch has established that this picture is based upon a few very old *motifs* around which subsequently have clustered in organic growth the immense number of freely circulating separate traditions.[2] The basic *motifs* were already pronouncedly confessional in character, and so were the separate traditions, in part very old, which made the canvas so very large. Thus the Hexateuch shows us a picture of the saving history that is drawn up by faith, and is accordingly confessional in character. The same holds true for the Deuteronomistic history's picture of the later history of Israel down to the exile. These two pictures of Israel's history lie before us—that of modern critical scholarship and that which the faith of Israel constructed—and for the present, we must reconcile ourselves to both of them. It would be stupid to dispute the right of the one or the other to exist. It would be superfluous to emphasise that each is the product of very different intellectual activi-ties. The one is rational and "objective"; that is, with the aid of historical method and presupposing the similarity of all historical occurrence, it constructs a critical picture of the history as it really was in Israel.[3] It is clear that in the process this picture could not be restricted to a critical analysis of the external historical events: it was bound to proceed to a critical investigation of the picture of Israel's spiritual world, her religion, as well.

The other activity is confessional and personally involved in the events to the point of fervour. Did Israel ever speak of her history

[2] M. Noth, *Pentateuch*.

[3] "The historical method, once it is applied to biblical science . . . is a leaven which transforms everything and finally explodes the whole form of theological methods." "The means by which criticism is at all possible is the application of analogy. . . . But the omnicompetence of analogy implies that all historical events are identical in principle." E. Tröltsch, *Über historische und dogmatische Methode*, Tübingen 1889 (*Gesammelte Schriften*, VOL. II, pp. 729ff.).

other than with the emotion of glorification or regret? Historical investigation searches for a critically assured minimum—the kerygmatic picture tends towards a theological maximum.[4] The fact that these two views of Israel's history are so divergent is one of the most serious burdens imposed today upon Biblical scholarship. No doubt historical investigation has a great deal that is true to say about the growth of this picture of the history which the faith of Israel painted: but the phenomenon of the faith itself, which speaks now of salvation, now of judgment, is beyond its power to explain.

It would not do, however, simply to explain the one picture as historical and the other as unhistorical. The kerygmatic picture too (and this even at the points where it diverges so widely from our historical picture) is founded in the actual history and has not been invented. The means by which this historical experience is made relevant for the time, the way in which it is mirrored forth in a variety of pictures, and in sagas in type form, are those adapted to the possibilities of expression of an ancient people. But it would be a very hasty conclusion if critical historical scholarship were minded to be itself taken as the only way into the history of Israel, and if it denied to what Israel reports in, say, her sagas a foundation in the "real" history. In some respects, this foundation is an even deeper one. Only, in these traditional materials the historic and factual can no longer be detached from the spiritualising interpretation which pervades them all.

We are not here concerned with the philosophical presuppositions of objective, rational, and critical scholarship, or the methods with which it works. On the other hand, the particular way in which Israel's faith presented history is still far from being adequately elucidated. Admittedly, we are acquainted with the various basic historical and theological ideas of the Jahwist, or of the Deuteronomist's history, or the Chronicler's. But we are much less clear about the mode of presentation of the smaller narrative units, although it is in fact the mass of these which now gives characteristic stamp to those great compilations. The way in which faith perceives things has its own peculiarities, and it is perhaps therefore possible to point to some constantly recurring features, certain "patterns," which are characteristic of a confessional presentation, particularly of early historical experiences. In this connexion a very common datum would have to

[4] N. A. Dahl, *Der historische Jesus als geschichtswissenschaftliches und theologisches Problem, Kerygma und Dogma*, Göttingen 1955, p. 119.

be taken into consideration by the theologian as well as by others—the fact that a great part of even the historical traditions of Israel has to be regarded as poetry, that is, as the product of explicit artistic intentions. But poetry—especially with peoples of antiquity—is much more than an aesthetic pastime: rather is there in it a penetrating desire for knowledge directed towards the data presented by the historical and natural environment.[5] Historical poetry was the form in which Israel, like other peoples, made sure of historical facts, that is, of their location and their significance. In those times poetry was, as a rule, the one possible form for expressing special basic insights. It was not just there along with prose as something one might elect to use—a more elevated form of discourse as it were then—but poetry alone enabled a people to express experiences met with in the course of their history in such a way as to make the past become absolutely present. In the case of legend, we now know that we must reckon with this coefficient of interpretation. But in thinking of the literary stories, which extend from the Hexateuch to II Kings, and which we must also regard to begin with as poetry, we have to learn to grasp this coefficient more clearly in its special features in any given story.[6] As far as I can see, Israel only finally went over to the prosaic and scientific presentation of her history with the Deuteronomistic history. Thus, right down to the sixth century, she was unable to dispense with poetry in drafting history, for the Succession Document or the history of Jehu's revolution are poetic presentations, and are indeed the acme of poetic perfection. No wonder that in Israel, and in her alone, these historical narratives could develop so profusely and in such perfection—the faith needed them. On the other hand, there is no mistaking that the effort to interpret historical events in this poetic-theological guise imposes a limit upon the possibilities of our understanding such narratives. The understanding of lists and annals is independent of the presuppositions of faith. But these poetic stories appeal for assent; they address those who are prepared to ask questions and receive answers along like lines, that is, those who credit Jahweh with great acts in history.

If some stories, chiefly older ones bordering upon legend, represent

[5] The idea of poetry as an "organ for the understanding of life" goes back to Dilthey. Cf. P. Böckmann, *Formgeschichte der deutschen Dichtung*, Hamburg 1949, pp. 17ff.

[6] A few more specific references are to be found in G. von Rad, *Der Heilige Krieg im alten Israel*, pp. 43ff.

events which happened to a group as connected with an individual, this is doubtless mainly a poetic proceeding. They are removed from the realm of political history and projected into the wholly personal world of an individual. This usage which personalises and at the same time symbolises can be plainly seen in the stories about Ham and Canaan (Gen. IX. 25), and in those about Ishmael or Judah (Gen. XVI. 12, XXXVIII. 1). But exegesis probably must take still greater account of it in the patriarchal stories dealing with Abraham and Jacob. To symbolise things in a single person in this way is in itself not at all peculiar to Israel. But since it also crops up in stories which are markedly minted by faith, we must make ourselves familiar with it. In every case, through this transference into a personal picture these stories have been given an enormous degree of intensity, for events or experiences of very different times have been pulled together as a single episode in an individual's life. Thus, for our historical and critical understanding, stories such as these have from the very start only an indirect relationship with historical reality, while their relation to what was believed by Israel is much more direct. We have further to consider that in their presentation of religious material the peoples of antiquity were not aware of the law of historical exclusiveness, according to which a certain event or a certain experience can be attached only to a single definite point in history. In particular, events bearing a saving character retained for all posterity, and in that posterity's eyes, a contemporaneousness which it is hard for us to appreciate.[7] The upshot is that, in what they present, the later story-tellers blatantly make capital of experiences which, although they are invariably brought in on the basis of the ancient event in question, still reach forward into the story-teller's own day. It is only from this standpoint that the story of Jacob's struggle (Gen. XXXII. 22f.), or the story of Balaam (Num. XXII–XXIV), or the thrice-repeated story of the endangering of the ancestress of the race (Gen. XII. 10ff., XX. 1ff., XXVI. 5ff.) can be interpreted as they should. What is historical here? Certainly some definite but very elusive particular event which stands at the primal obscure origin of the tradition in question—but what is also historical is the

---

[7] L. Köhler, *Hebrew Man*, trans. P. R. Ackroyd, London 1956, p.39. This cannot of course be taken as meaning that "the conception of history itself hardly plays any noticeable part" for Israel. These words are incomprehensible in face of the fact that Israel's faith gave itself sanction in a series of ever vaster theological sketches of her history.

experience that Jahweh turns the enemy's curse into blessing, and that he safeguards the promise in spite of all failure on the part of its recipient, etc. Israel did not dream up this confidence, but came to it on the basis of rich and wide experience, of her history in fact; and, symbolising it in a person, she illustrated it in a story. This of course occasions another and rather severe clash with our critical way of thinking about history. Did the historical Balaam actually curse, or did his mouth really utter blessings? We may assume that it was only in the story that that which was given to Israel's faith became presented as a visible miracle. This process of glorification is quite clear in many of the stories about the Conquest—the events are depicted with a splendour and a strong element of the miraculous which are impossible to square with older strands in the report.[8] The later story-tellers are so zealous for Jahweh and his saving work that they overstep the limits of exact historiography and depict the event in a magnificence far transcending what it was in reality.[9] These are texts which contain an implicit eschatological element, since they anticipate a *Gloria* of God's saving action not yet granted to men.

In the Old Testament it is thus this world made up of testimonies that is above all the subject of a theology of the Old Testament. The subject cannot be a systematically ordered "world of the faith" of Israel or of the really overwhelming vitality and creative productivity of Jahwism, for the world of faith is not the subject of these testimonies which Israel raised to Jahweh's action in history. Never, in these testimonies about history, did Israel point to her own faith, but to Jahweh. Faith undoubtedly finds very clear expression in them; but as a subject it lies concealed, and can often only be grasped by means of a variety of inferences which are often psychological and on that account problematical. In a word, the faith is not the subject of Israel's confessional utterances, but only its vehicle, its mouthpiece. And even less can the "history" of this world of faith be the subject of the theology of the Old Testament. Admittedly, the presentation

[8] It is well known that an older and less miraculous picture of the events is given in Jg. I. Iff. than in the larger complex in Josh. I–X.

[9] "Poetry is not the imitation of a reality which already exists in the same quality prior to it . . . ; the aesthetic faculty is a creative power for the production of a concept which transcends reality and is not present in any abstract thinking, or indeed in any way of contemplating the world." W. Dilthey, *Gesammelte Schriften*, Leipzig 1914–18, VOL. VI, p. 116. In this "production," the chief force in Israel in forming tradition was Jahwism.

of the "ideas, thought, and concepts of the Old Testament which are important for theology" will always form part of the task of Old Testament theology.[10] But is this all that there is to it? Would a history confined to this leave room for discussion for example of the saving acts of grace, on which the faith of Israel regarded itself as based, and with reference to which it lived its life? A world of religious concepts later systematically arranged is of course an abstraction, for such a thing never existed in Israel in so complete and universal a way. So too the idea of a "religion of Israel," that is, the idea of the faith as an entity, appears more problematical still as a result of the investigation of the history of tradition in our own time. There were up and down the land many traditions which little by little combined into ever larger complexes of tradition. Theologically, these accumulations were in a state of constant flux. Religious thought cannot be separated out from these traditions and represented thus in abstract. If we divorced Israel's confessional utterances from the divine acts in history which they so passionately embrace, what a bloodless ghost we would be left with! If, however, we put Israel's picture of her history in the forefront of our theological consideration, we encounter what appropriately is the most essential subject of a theology of the Old Testament, the living word of Jahweh coming on and on to Israel for ever, and this in the message uttered by his mighty acts. It was a message so living and actual for each moment that it accompanied her on her journey through time, interpreting itself afresh to every generation, and informing every generation what it had to do.

We cannot here give a critical review of the course followed by the discipline of Old Testament theology since Gabler's classic work which outlined a programme for it.[11] Certainly, it was entirely necessary to free this discipline from dogmatics. On the other hand, this meant a great impoverishment, and seriously handicapped it on its course. In spite of all dogmatic prejudices, how rich and varied nevertheless were the relationships of the theology of the seventeenth and eighteenth centuries to the Old Testament! At that time theology still had a vital interest in the details of the Mosaic cult, in the anthro-

---

[10] Köhler, *Theology*, p. 1.

[11] J. Ph. Gabler, *De justo discrimine theologiae biblicae et dogmaticae regundisque recte utriusque finibus*, Altorfii 1787. Cf. for the history of Old Testament theology H. J. Kraus, *Geschichte der historisch-kritischen Erforschung des Alten Testamentes*, Neukirchen 1956.

pology of the Old Testament, and in the elucidation of intricate questions of archaeology. With the rise of rationalism and the assertion of the autonomy of Biblical theology, the properly theological connexions with the Old Testament all at once became much more unilinear and abstract—in a word, poorer. Theological interest is now directed to the "religious ideas" of the Old Testament and their bearing upon the "truths of Christianity"—not that the change brought research into the historical world of Israel to a standstill: as is well known, this flourished in the nineteenth century as never before. But this study of the Old Testament disengaged itself more and more from theology. As far as her historical experience went, Israel appeared to be a nation like the rest of the nations of the ancient Near East, and one can well understand that the picture which historical scholarship outlined could have no particular relevance for theology. The result was that theology broke away more and more from the history of Israel and left that to the historians. However, this parting of the ways was quite amicable, for theology believed that she was retaining within her own competence the subject that was her real concern, namely, the spiritual world of the religious truths of Israel. But what is left for theologians if it were to be discovered that Israel's spiritual world too had a thousand threads tying it closely to the world of the ancient Near East and the factors that determined it historically, and if in consequence it became clear that it could be just as well, or perhaps even better, analysed by the Orientalist? But in the second half of the nineteenth century such results lay far beyond the horizon.

Thanks to Wellhausen and his disciples, Old Testament theologians became still more assured that this was their presumed proper subject-matter. Wellhausen was in the last analysis strongly influenced by Hegel: he looked on Israel's history as a history of ideas, and presented it above all from the standpoint of a spiritual evolution. A number of theologies of the Old Testament were written following Wellhausen; but their theme was very uniform—the emancipation of the spirit of Israel from the bonds of the natural and the corporate, and the increasing moralisation of Jahwism. Then, on this philosophical and theological basis, B. Duhm depicted the prophets as people so spiritual, so personal, so ethical, and so creative that this conception of Israel's religion reached a *ne plus ultra*. Meanwhile, however, a more recent phase in the science of religion had shown that there was no such thing as a spiritual religion of Israel, and that this conception of it was in fact rather a reflexion of the religion of modern Protestant Europe.[12] And so the prophets had to come down again from their lofty throne; for investigation of the more primitive forms of religion, and particularly the more intensive elucidation of the world of myth and the cult, showed how much stronger were the ties which bound even the prophets, and all the more the people of Israel as a whole, to the material side of ancient Oriental religion. But even this new investigation of the religion of Israel was concerned more with Israel's spirituality, her distinctively ancient religious concepts, than with what Israel herself regarded as the proper subject-matter of her faith, namely, the revelation in word and deed of Jahweh in history.

No one who follows the work done on the Old Testament in the nineteenth century can fail to notice how, broadly speaking, the theological impulse grows weaker and weaker. It was incomparably much more genuine and direct in the later period of rationalism than, say, at the beginning of the twentieth century. Because Old Testament theology took as its task the construction of a history of piety and of the contents of consciousness, and because, above all, it thereby kept to that which has its growth from nature and history, it dismissed what the Old Testament itself had to say, and, leaving this aside, chose its own subject of interest for itself.[13]

So then we see today, 170 years after Gabler, that at that time theology lost the right relationship to what can alone be its proper subject—what Israel herself made the content of her testimonies concerning Jahweh—and has not regained it until the present day.

It will certainly not be possible for us to confine our theological work to testifying to the divine historical acts. Other things as well took place for Israel in the orbit of these acts of God. Men emerged whose function within this activity was to clarify it; offices came into being and cultic usages became necessary, because they were meant to make life in proximity to this revealed God possible for Israel. The various officials often stood up wonderfully to the test, and they often failed. Israel told the story of all this, and of much besides, and then she

[12] J. Pedersen, "Die Auffassung vom Alten Testament," in Z.A.W., 1931, p. 180.

[13] Since I do not go into details here, no mention is made of the reaction which began in the 1920's and again became conscious of its special theological task in, for example, W. Eichrodt's *Theologie des Alten Testaments*. Much as the picture given in this book presupposes this renewed self-evaluation on the part of theology, and conscious as I am of my great debt to it, I none the less mean to show that even here Old Testament theology has still not yet completely envisaged its proper subject.

thought the whole thing through again and called fresh concepts to her aid to re-tell it, in order to come to a better understanding of her experience and a more adequate realisation of her own peculiarity. In particular Israel became revealed to herself in the sphere of this divine activity: she recognised herself, both her refusals and the completely new possibilities which opened up for her in her history whenever she laid herself open to the working of her God. And the only way for her of managing this was, in her language and her religious thinking, to enter into this action of God in which she found herself, to show herself elastic enough to frame or borrow concepts which were appropriate to the peculiar nature of her historical experience. This too must be dealt with in a Theology of the Old Testament. But its starting point and its centre is Jahweh's action in revelation.

2. THE UNFOLDING

The extremely difficult problem of a relevant unfolding of the witness of the Old Testament is indicated as early as in the Epistle to the Hebrews, by the summary statement that God of old spoke to Israel "in many and various ways" (Heb. I. I). Unlike the revelation in Christ, the revelation of Jahweh in the Old Testament is divided up over a long series of separate acts of revelation which are very different in content. It seems to be without a centre which determines everything and which could give to the various separate acts both an interpretation and their proper theological connexion with one another. We can only describe the Old Testament's revelation of Jahweh as a number of distinct and heterogeneous revelatory acts. Even the deliverance from Egypt, which, as is well known, is regarded in the various complexes of tradition as Jahweh's all-sufficient saving act, cannot be taken as the theological centre or as the bedrock of the whole of the Old Testament. Certainly in the older period it appears to have been given the rank of a unique saving event excelling all others. But this rank was later diminished through other theological ideas. The Deuteronomistic historical work seems to have regarded the building of Solomon's Temple as a middle-point in the history of Israel (I Kings VI. I); but for the Chronicler it was David's cultic and messianic arrangements that were the determinative saving order for all the times to come. But Jeremiah and Deutero-Isaiah see a time coming when avowal of Jahweh as the one who led Israel out of Egypt will be done away with (Jer. XXIII. 7; Is. XLIII. 16–20).

How then can the *kerygma* which appears in the Old Testament be theologically unfolded as it ought to be? It is becoming ever clearer to us that the arrangement and literary redaction of the enormously comprehensive traditional material was in itself a theological achievement of the first rank; but we are at the same time confronted with the bewildering fact that this theological thinking is absolutely lacking in theological "systematics." For us today it is not easy to understand that the Old Testament traditions do reveal—though little more than its beginning—an effort to develop or define the contents of the faith "systematically," that is, according to their conceptual grouping. They do not appear to have any awareness at all of the demands of theological systematics, for they simply follow the sequence of the historical events. From first to last Israel manifestly takes as her starting-point the absolute priority in theology of event over *"logos."* The total difference between this way of thinking and the "Greek urge towards a universal understanding of the world" is obvious, for Greek thought seeks a "uniform natural principle" of the cosmos, and it is precisely the question of the "one" principle, the "one" primary cause of all things, that is foreign to the Hebrew way of thinking.[14] Hebrew thinking is thinking in historical traditions; that is, its main concern is with the proper combination of traditions and their theological interpretation, and in the process historical grouping always takes precedence over intellectual and theological grouping. The most varied traditions are superimposed upon one another, and even interwoven. Thus, a fragment of archaic uninterpreted legend can without the least difficulty be brought into conjunction with a text which has been subjected to thorough theological reflexion, provided that both relate to one and the same event. Nor is there any desire to group together, because of their similarity, traditions which are akin, either because of common origin in a "school" or because of their theological theme, in order to arrive at a more broadly based systematic and theological connexion. From time to time the Deuteronomistic theology of history added its own theological reflexions to the older complexes of tradition—but it was obviously not concerned systematically to depict its own theological world of thought, which is in actual fact homogeneous, and of a very distinctive character. The Old Testament of course says nothing about the principles followed by the men who gathered it together, and we certainly cannot assume that considerations of theology lay at the back of every grouping together of historical texts: a great deal

[14] W. Jaeger, *The Theology of the early Greek Philosophers*, Oxford 1947, pp. 20, 22.

must have come together according to the elementary law of associa-tion. The result is that all the individual texts, as well as all the larger compilations of texts, preserve the character of historical documents. However, the Hexateuch on the one hand and the Deuteronomist's or the Chronicler's historical works on the other are very different in literary structure, for the two latter have an "author," whose intentions we to some extent know, while the former has been fashioned quite "anonymously" from old confessional forms and materials into the baroque monstrosity it now is. But all three works derive the principle on which they present their material from history, and even in their final form, where they are permeated through and through by theological considerations, they preserve the documentary and confessional character which their oldest component parts already possessed. The same holds true for the prophetic writings, which increasingly display Jahweh's revelations as bound to time and hour, and to quite definite and non-recurring political situations. So one of the most important forms Israel adopted in the whole evolution of her theological thinking was the assimilation of traditions existing in written form, and their combination and interpretation in the light of the present day. It would certainly be an over-simplification to try to explain this clinging of Israel's theological thinking to the historical events, and her lack of capacity for developing systems, as merely persistence in an archaic ("mythical" or "pre-logical") level of thought. After an archaic era Israel too became alive to the ordering powers of reason (*ratio*); but she employed this faculty—once it came of age—along quite different lines from the Greeks, namely, in ever-renewed reflexion upon the meaning of historical events, reflexion which of course always appears only in the guise of *ad hoc* interpretations. The question of the objective value or the limitations of such a way of thinking, where the apprehension of the world, and also of God, was so one-sidedly historical, admits, like all questions as to the justification or value of primitive phenomena, of no answer. At all events, this "boundless quest" of the meaning of her history[15] made Israel capable of a mental achievement which, alone in the world and quite in-comparably, carries with it its own justification, stature, and law.

In connexion with this law, however, it is possible to enter into greater detail. For, given the absence of all construction of systems that we have just mentioned, it might appear as if Israel merely traced

[15] K. Lowith, *Meaning in History*, Chicago 1949, p. 4.

the course of events in history, and was satisfied with a superficial stringing together and piling up of the documents and literary complexes. But the reverse is the case: for once one has recognised the immense diversity from which the great histories are composed, like mosaics, one is amazed rather at the inner unity and the intellectual compactness of the resulting picture of the history. This unity is certainly not a final chance result, but is the outcome of a strong tendency towards unification which dominates the whole process of the growth of a work like the Hexateuch. What a number of old, detached tribal or local traditions, previously quite restricted in range and currency, were incorporated in the Hexateuch or the Deuteronomistic history; but now they are all related to "Israel."[16] In the process the old disassociated traditions have been given a reference and interpretation which in most cases was foreign to their original meaning. The prerequisite—by no means self-evident—for the incorporation of these "detached" traditions into the great picture of the history was that all of them, even the most obscure and paltry ones of a small clan, were concerned with all Israel, and therefore belonged to all Israel. Israel was ready to see herself embodied in the most out-of-the-way traditions of one of her component parts, and to include and absorb the experience there recorded in the great picture of the history of Israel. Here at last we come upon one unifying principle towards which Israel's theological thinking strove, and with reference to which it ordered its material and thought; this was "Israel," the people of God, which always acts as a unit, and with which God always deals as a unit. The Deuteronomistic historiographer—in presenting, for example, the period of the Judges—works with an idea of Israel which is so schematic and general that the extremely complex actual historical reality has almost entirely disappeared behind it. In the Hexateuch, too, the unification of the vast traditional material by means of the idea of an Israel which everywhere appears as a fixed entity is very thoroughly carried through. Only, the reader is not aware of the tremendous process of unification lying behind the picture given in the source documents. It is important to bear in mind from the outset that this Israel, of which the Old Testament presentations of the history have so much to say, is the object of faith, and the object of a history constructed by faith.

The singularly complex form which the great historical groups of tradition (the Hexateuch and the Deuteronomistic history) have, is the

[16] Noth, *Pentateuch*, p. 46.

result of Israel's thinking about herself, a process which was constantly operative in the history. Each generation was faced with the ever-identical yet ever-new task of understanding itself as Israel. In a certain sense, every generation had first to become Israel. Of course, as a rule the sons were able to recognise themselves in the picture handed on to them by the fathers. But still this did not exempt each generation from the task of comprehending itself in faith as the Israel of its own day, and from coming before Jahweh as this Israel. However, in this process of actualisation the tradition here and there had to be reshaped. Theological demands altered—thus, for example, the Elohist's idea of the saving history was brought in alongside the earlier one of the Jahwist. Later ages wanted to understand the theological meaning of more extensive ranges in the history. To satisfy their needs the Deuteronomistic school in the Exile wove into the older complexes its own interpretative interpolations which serve as a framework, and so on. In this way the capital of tradition slowly mounted up—new parts were added, old parts were interpreted. Alongside older versions were ranged more recent doublets. No generation produced a perfectly independent and finished historical work—each continued to work upon what had been handed down to it, the Elohist working upon the Jahwist, the Deuteronomist upon copious older material, while the Chronicler in turn built further upon the foundation of the Deuteronomist.[17]

Over this slow mounting-up of tradition to greater and greater abundance a law of theological dialectic seems to have presided, a dimly or clearly felt need to hold the transmitted material in suspension, and to correct it by means of accounts expressed in a strangely contradictory fashion. Thus, the later creation story is not set alongside

[17] The same thing occurred in the formation of the New Testament. "The transmission of relatively probable facts does not as such in the least establish historical communication or continuity. . . . Only in this way can the fact be understood that [early Christianity] did not compose the Gospels primarily as reports and that her own *kerygma* practically overgrew and covered the picture of the historical Jesus. . . . The community did not just absent-mindedly or foolishly amalgamate its own message with that of its Lord, or even refer the former to the latter. . . . In acting as it does, the community attests past history (*Geschichte*) as alive and present. It interprets what had become even for itself history (*Historie*) in the light of its own experience, and to do this it uses the medium of its preaching. . . . For history (*Historie*) does not become historically (*geschichtlich*) important through tradition as such, but through interpretation: not through the simple assertion of facts as such, but through the understanding of events of the past which have become objective and lifeless in the form of facts" (E. Käsemann, "Das Problem des historischen Jesus," in *Z.Th.K.*, 1954, pp. 129f.).

the older merely as "supplementing" it; and the account of the nations in Gen. XI and the priestly table of the nations (Gen. X) are also in direct opposition. The same holds true for the older and the later (Deuteronomistic) presentations of the rise of the monarchy (I Sam. VIII–XII). According to II Sam. XXIV, it was Jahweh who instigated the census, but according to I Chron. XXI, it was Satan. Where does Jahweh dwell? In the so-called speech at the dedication of the Temple Solomon says that he is present in the darkness of the Holy of Holies (I Kings VIII. 12). A few verses later (vs. 27) the Deuteronomist makes the King say that all the heavens cannot contain him. Jeremiah regards the wilderness days as the time when Israel's relationship with Jahweh was at its purest (Jer. II. 2ff.), but the tradition was interpreted in a completely different way by Ezekiel: even as early as that time Israel's only response to Jahweh's self-revelation was disobedience (Ezek. XX). In Ps. LI, after sacrifice has been depreciated following a deep spiritualising of religion, a later addition (vs. 20) insists that sacrifices should be offered and turns the reference of the prayer away from anything spiritual and on to Zion and its restoration. A similar tension exists between Job's despairing speeches in the dialogues, which are later, and those in the framework, where his piety affords him perfect security. Examples of such extreme contradictions in the formation of the tradition can be multiplied at will—none is deeper than the gulf which the pre-exilic prophets tore open with their startling interpretation of Israel's historical and legal traditions.

It should now have become clearer that a theology of the Old Testament cannot confine itself to a presentation of the world of thought without going on to include the world of history, for the latter was of course the interest of Israel's whole theological activity. The decisive events in this history were of course themselves an object of the faith of Israel, and likewise its whole presentation was a work of her faith. But over and above this, the way of dealing with the difficult problem of the proper unfolding of Israel's witness is now laid down. If we cannot divorce Israel's theological world of thought from her world of history, because the picture of the latter was itself a complicated work of her faith, this at the same time means that we must also submit ourselves to the sequence of events as the faith of Israel saw them. In particular, in tracing the different confessional material, we must beware of striving to reconstruct links between ideas, and systematic combinations, where Israel herself never saw or distinguished

such things. We should exclude from the start what is most characteristic of Israel's theological activity if we refused to take seriously the
sequence and the inner connexion of the world of history as Israel
herself arranged them for her own purposes. This unquestionably
raises great difficulties for our Western way of theological thinking.
And in the presentation which follows we shall probably not succeed,
either, in exactly re-enacting the theological thinking of Israel: we
cannot—without ourselves becoming obscure—to a similar degree
sacrifice to the requirements of systematics the concentration upon
what was believed, interpreted, and preserved by means of history.
But it would be fatal to our understanding of Israel's witness if we were
to arrange it from the outset on the basis of theological categories
which, though current among ourselves, have absolutely nothing to
do with those on whose basis Israel herself allowed her theological
thinking to be ordered. Thus, re-telling remains the most legitimate
form of theological discourse on the Old Testament. Even the author
of Acts makes Stephen and Paul rehearse the history of the people of
God (Acts VII. 2ff., XIII. 17). For the literary character of these historical
summaries, see E. Stauffer.[18]

3. THE OLDEST PICTURES OF THE SAVING HISTORY

Even the earliest avowals to Jahweh were historically determined, that
is, they connect the name of this God with some statement about an
action in history. Jahweh, "who brought Israel out of Egypt," is
probably the earliest and at the same time the most widely used of
these confessional formulae.[19] Others are such as designate Jahweh as
the one who called the patriarchs and promised them the land, etc.
Alongside these brief formulae, which are content with a minimum of
historical subject-matter—as a species they are generally cultic invocations—there were very certainly soon ranged confessional summaries
of the saving history, covering by now a fairly extensive span of the
divine action in history.[20] Among these the most important is

[18] E. Stauffer, *The Theology of the New Testament*, trans. John Marsh, London 1955,
pp. 239ff., 321ff.

[19] The content of the old confessional formulae and the problem of their connexion
is dealt with by Noth, *Pentateuch*, pp. 48ff.

[20] In no circumstances are these historical summaries to be judged as later than those
short historical epicleses, as for example in the sense of an organic development as
their subsequent combination, for both are very different in respect of species and each
could have its life in its own place contemporaneously.

the Credo in Deut. xxvi. 5–9, which bears all the marks of great antiquity:

"A wandering Aramean was my father; he went down with a few people into Egypt and there he became a nation, great, mighty, and populous. But the Egyptians treated us harshly, they afflicted us, and laid hard toil upon us. Then we cried to Jahweh, the God of our fathers, and Jahweh heard us, and saw our affliction, our toil, and oppression. And Jahweh brought us out of Egypt with a mighty hand and an outstretched arm, with great terror, with signs and wonders, and brought us to this place and gave us this land, a land flowing with milk and honey."

These words are not, of course, a prayer—there is no invocation or petition—they are out and out a confession of faith. They recapitulate the main events in the saving history from the time of the patriarchs (by the Aramean, Jacob is meant) down to the conquest, and they do this with close concentration on the objective historical facts. As in the Apostles' Creed, there is no reference at all to promulgated revelations, promises, or teaching, and still less any consideration of the attitude which Israel on her side took towards this history with God. The exalted mood which lies behind this recitation is merely that of a disciplined celebration of the divine acts, and in the process a note was struck which henceforward was to remain the predominant one in Israel's religious life. Israel was always better at glorifying and extolling God than at theological reflexion.[21] In spite of being cast in the form of words spoken by God, the retrospect of the history given in Josh.

[21] The question of the age of this Credo in ancient Israel's life is fairly unimportant for us here. Noth emphasises the original cultic independence of the various themes out of which it is composed (deliverance from Egypt, the promise to the patriarchs, guidance in the wilderness, etc.), *Pentateuch*, pp. 48ff. The literary material seems to justify him, for in the majority of cases the "themes" seem to be independent. Nevertheless these single themes themselves always presuppose an idea of the whole. Guidance in the wilderness cannot be thought of apart from the deliverance from Egypt and vice versa. Again, the promise to the patriarchs, after it passed over from the cultic communities of the people belonging to Abraham and Jacob to Israel, was immediately referred to the deliverance from Egypt, etc. At the same time, regarding the patriarchal tradition, there is much to be said for the assumption that the Credo itself presupposes the combination of an originally independent set of traditions with the central Exodus tradition. Even afterwards the two traditions, of the Exodus and of the patriarchs, are found side by side in marked independence, and clearly discriminated in references to them. K. Galling, *Die Erwählungstraditionen Israels*, Bei. Z.A.W. No. 48, Giessen 1928.

XXIV. 2ff. is closely allied to Deut. XXVI. 5ff. Admittedly, it goes into considerably greater detail in the presentation of the saving history; but the two are alike in confining themselves to the objective facts. And, in particular, in Joshua too the starting-point is the period of the patriarchs, while the end-point is Israel's entry into the promised land. Some of the psalms make it perfectly clear that, originally, this span of time, and this alone, was regarded as the time of the saving history proper. Psalm CXXXVI is certainly a much later litany, but apart from the fact that it starts with the creation, it keeps to the same canonical pattern of the saving history. The same is true of Psalm CV, which also is certainly not old. Psalm LXXVIII does indeed go beyond the conquest —down into the period of the monarchy. But just in so doing it serves as a proof of our thesis. While it is able to depict Israel's early period down to the conquest with a real wealth of concrete historical data (vss. 12–55), its presentation after vs. 56—that is, exactly at the point where the canonical pattern of the saving history leaves it in the lurch— is jejune and slight. (Still, it does mention the loss of Shiloh and the election of David and Zion.) Even stranger is the disproportion in the picture of the saving history in Judith v. 6ff. Its picture of the conquest takes up ten verses, but for the whole period from then down to 586 the narrator can only report trite generalities concerning constant apostasy. He jumps a span of more than 600 years in two verses! These historical summaries in hymn form are still thoroughly confessional in kind. They are not products of a national or even a secular view of history, but clearly take their stand on that old canonical picture of the saving history, the pattern of which was fixed long ago for all time.[22] They are of course no longer confessions in the strict sense of Deut. XXVI. Concentration on the facts alone has been abandoned. A tendency towards epic elaboration, and also towards reflexion, is apparent: more than anything else, contrasting with the chain of the divine saving acts, the infidelity and disobedience of Israel now increasingly become objects of importance in the presentation. If we imagine a considerably greater advance still in this process of connecting a narrative to the old pattern and widening its theological range by means of all kinds of traditional material, then we find ourselves face to face with the work of the Jahwist or the Elohist. Starting as the latter does

[22] On the reappearance of the saving history in the Psalms cf. A. Lauha, "Die Geschichtsmotive in den alttestamentlichen Psalmen," in *Annales Academiae Scientiarum Fennicae*, Helsinki 1945.

only with the history of the patriarchs (Gen. xv), he comes closer to the old canonical pattern of salvation. But both with the Jahwist and the Priestly Document too, their allegiance to, and indeed their rooted-ness in, the old confessional tradition is beyond doubt. Once this process of giving a narrative connexion to the old plan and widening its scope was given free play, it is no wonder that the plan was also supplemented by theological traditions originally alien to it. The most important of these additions. of which not even a hint is to be found in the old transmitted pattern, is the prefixing to it of an account of the creation and the primeval history, and the insertion of the Sinai peri-cope, which as a block of tradition has a completely different deriva-tion.[23] As far as form goes, this expansion of the ancient Credo by the Jahwist and the Elohist led to the creation of an extremely involved and highly detailed presentation of the history. Finally, the subsequent combination of the three great works J, E, and P produced a literary structure of the history, whose disproportions can only cause astonish-ment to anyone who looks for an artistic harmony and an inner balanc-ing of these tremendous masses of material. There is in fact much to be learned from a comparison of how the story of Jacob or Moses is presented with that of the Homeric Odysseus, for in both cases the pictures are due to the coalescence of originally independent traditions. The main difference lies in the fact that in the rendering of her story Israel handled the old material much less freely than the Greeks. A later age could not venture to recast the old legends in respect of theme and thought and to combine them so as to give rise to what was in fact a new history complete in itself. They were bound in a much more conservative way to what had come down to them, and especially to the forms in which they had received it—that is, they handled it much more as if it were a document. The result of this for the theo-logical elaboration of the old traditions upon which J, E, and P were indeed intensively engaged, was a completely different form of theological handling of the tradition. If the possibility of bringing the several traditions into inner unity with one another, and of balancing them as they were amalgamated, was ruled out, it was nevertheless still possible to insert expressly directive passages at important nodal points in the events. And this possibility was in fact used again and

[23] The free variations on the old Credo do not mention the events at Sinai either. The first mention is in Neh. ix. 6ff. This was then the first place where the picture which J and E expanded made an impression.

again.[24] But the chief method employed in the theological unfolding of the tradition was a different one still: it was much more indirect, for it consisted in the way in which separate pieces of material were connected. The lay-out of the primeval history, the story of Abraham, the relationship of the period of the patriarchs to that of Joshua, etc., is arranged in such a way that quite definite theological tensions, which the great collector intended, arise out of the sequence of the material itself. This indirect theological way of speaking through the medium of the traditional material and its arrangement makes clear once more that remarkable preponderance of the matter-of-fact historical over the theological which is so characteristic of the witness of Israel. Even in its final form, the Hexateuch retained a confessional stamp, though not in that restrained form of celebrating the divine deeds and them alone which is found in the old Credo; for as well as dealing with them, this historical work also deals with the institution of offices and rites, and with men standing up to the test, and still more with failure and rebellion. If we say a confessional stamp, this means that the later Israel saw in the historical witness of the Hexateuch something that was typical for the people of God, and that what was there related remained of immediate concern for every subsequent generation, because of a latent contemporaneousness in it.

Meanwhile, however, something of decisive importance for the faith of Israel had come about. As early as the time when the theological elaboration of the old Credo was still at its beginnings, Jahweh had further dealings with Israel. The history with God did not come to a standstill. Jahweh had raised up charismatic military leaders to protect Israel, he had chosen Zion and established the throne of David for all time, Israel had become disobedient, and so he had sent prophets, and finally he repudiated Israel in the twofold judgments of 722 and 587. The realisation that with David something new began had certainly come to life fairly soon in Israel. This is without any doubt itself the background of the great narrative complex describing "David's rise to power" and in particular of the Succession Document, which are so

---

[24] Gen. XII. 1–9, for instance, is such a unit in the story of Abraham lying outwith the saga material handed on. The prologue to the Flood in the primeval history of J (Gen. VI. 5–8) is to be judged in the same way. In the realm of the story of Jacob the prayer in Gen. XXXII. 10ff. [9ff.] would call for mention, and in that of the Deuteronomistic histories the freely composed discourses in Josh. XXIII; 1 Sam. XII; 1 Kings VIII.

important theologically.[25] But Israel did not arrive at a clear consciousness of this new epoch in her history with Jahweh as a whole until it had, in such a fearful way, already come to its end in the exile. Then, with the help of a great mass of already available historical material, the great theological history which we call the Deuteronomist's came into being. It carried the thread of the history with God down from the conquest to the catastrophe of the exile, and presented and interpreted this period up to Israel's final shipwreck from quite definite and very individual theological points of view. The second stage in Israel's history with Jahweh was clearly not simply conceived of as the unilinear prolongation of the first; from the theological point of view, it ran its course under essentially different presuppositions. As concerns the good gifts of salvation promised by Jahweh, it does not go beyond the old one—the good gift of the land was always the ultimate for Israel, which nothing could surpass and which could only be won or forfeited. But this era stands rather under the sign of the law of judgment, and accordingly the question as to how Israel stood up to the test thrusts itself more and more into the foreground: indeed it becomes decisive for Israel for life and death before Jahweh. And the sum-total of this Deuteronomistic historical work is that Israel, possessed as she already was of all the good gifts of salvation, chose death. It is to be noticed that the decision about this termination of her monarchical period was thus in the Deuteronomist put in the hands of Israel. In the "canonical" saving history, from the patriarchs down to the entry into Canaan, it was Jahweh who made the truth of the promise good in face of all the failure of Israel; and he did not let any part of his great plan in history, least of all the final part, be taken out of his own hands. But in the Deuteronomist's history Jahweh allowed Israel to make the decision.

The exile was a period devoid of saving history. The Deuteronomistic historical work gave an authoritative interpretation of the riddle of the standstill in the divine history with Israel: the catastrophes were the well-merited judgment upon the continued apostasy to the Canaanite cult of Baal. At the time, who could know whether this judgment was final or only temporary? In keeping with Israel's whole religious attitude, this question could in fact be answered only by Jahweh's beginning to act anew in history. As it happened, about 550, through

[25] For the history of David's rise to power see Noth, *Überl. Studien*, p. 61. For the history of the succession to David see L. Rost, *Thronnachfolge*, pp. 82ff.

Cyrus, history began to move very mightily in the immediate surroundings of the exiles. But at this point Israel's witness parts company
with itself. After Babylon had fallen, and the worship in the Temple
had been reconstituted in Jerusalem, and later, when even a large section
of the exiles had returned home, Israel could only see in these events a
fresh act of grace; and, as the historical summaries in Neh. IX. 6ff. and
Judith v. 5ff. show, she carried the thread of history with God which
had been so abruptly snapped, down with praise and thanksgiving into
the present time. This theological link with the pre-exilic history
with God is established by means of elaborate argumentation, especially
in the Chronicler's history, the main concern of which is to legitimate
the cultic restoration in the post-exilic period on the basis of a legacy
of David's which had not been brought into effect until this time. But
the prophets Jeremiah, Ezekiel, Zechariah, and, more than anyone
else, Deutero-Isaiah, placed a very different interpretation upon the
breaking-off of the history with God up to then. The tenor of their
message is this: the old is done away with; now Jahweh will bring
about something completely new, a new Exodus, a new covenant, a
new Moses. Israel's old confession of faith is present now only as
something which is done away with, since Jahweh is about to act along
the lines of his earlier saving acts in an even more splendid way.[26]

Now this sequence given by the great pictures of the history,
with their very different conceptions of the progress of the saving
history, prescribes the way in which we too have to unfold the witness
of the Old Testament. What other starting-point can we take than the
colossal theological structure which Israel raised on the foundation of
her oldest confession of Jahweh? We have therefore first to attempt to
sketch the basic traits of a theology of the Hexateuch. This must be
followed by a description of the new experience which Israel gained
on her journey from the conquest to the disasters at the end of the period
of the monarchy; for a description of the outcome of this second phase
of the history with God was, of course, the task which the Deuteronomistic writer imposed on himself. Following on that, we shall
finally have to deal with the great interpretation which Israel later
drew up in the Chronicler's history of the final phase of her history
with God, the period from David to Nehemiah. Then, in a second
part, we will have to speak about the situation in which Israel felt
herself to be placed as a result of this revelation and of God's activity in

[26] Especially Is. XLIII. 16-20; Jer. XXI. 31ff., and also Hos. II. 16ff.

history, and about her praises, her justice, her trials, and her wisdom. What was distinctive in the response which Israel made to the revelation of Jahweh will therefore be dealt with there.

The most accurate test of the starting-point and arrangement of a theology of the Old Testament is, however, the phenomenon of prophecy. At what point has it to be dealt with, and in what connexion? If we are resolved on giving a systematic and connected presentation of the religious ideas, then we shall have occasion to speak about prophecy throughout—in dealing with the holiness of Jahweh, the beliefs about creation, the idea of the covenant, etc. But in so doing would we do justice to its message? We should also, however, do it an injustice if we reserved treatment of it for a special section dealing with Israel's thought about her own and the nations' future.[27] This is not the way to bring the message of the prophets into organic connexion with the religious ideas of Israel. However overpoweringly diverse it may be, it nevertheless has its starting-point in the conviction that Israel's previous history with Jahweh has come to an end, and that he will start something new with her. The prophets seek to convince their contemporaries that for them the hitherto existing saving ordinances have lost their worth, and that, if Israel is to be saved, she must move in faith into a new saving activity of Jahweh, one which is only to come in the future. But this conviction of theirs, that what has existed till now is broken off, places them basically outside the saving history as it had been understood up to then by Israel. The prophets' message had its centre and its bewildering dynamic effect in the fact that it smashed in pieces Israel's existence with God up to the present, and rang up the curtain of history for a new action on his part with her. So prophecy needs separate treatment in a theology of the Old Testament.

[27] So for example E. Jacob in his *Theology of the Old Testament*, London 1958.

THE THEOLOGY OF THE HEXATEUCH

THE TIME-DIVISION OF THE CANONICAL SAVING HISTORY BY MEANS OF THE COVENANT THEOLOGY

THE old Credo in Deut. xxvi. 5ff., and the other historical summaries as well, ranged the various data alongside one another without differentiation—no attempt at all was made to mark off certain highlights or decisive moments. However, as this simple and compact picture of the history was elaborated by means of complexes of tradition which were so very different from one another and of such diverse theological importance, it became essential to organise this history in some way, to divide it into periods. Focal points in the divine action now stand out in relief from parts of the history that are more epic in character, and as a result of the division perfectly definite relationships between the various epochs, of which the old summaries as yet gave no hint, are now clear. The most striking decisive moments of this kind are the making of covenants by Jahweh.

Our word "covenant" is only a makeshift rendering of the Hebrew word.[1] For it may designate the agreement itself, that is, its ceremonial, but it may also designate the relationship of communion between two partners inaugurated on its basis. A great advance was made when Begrich showed that the "covenant" is to be understood as a relationship between two parties of unequal status. In no sense, then, is a relationship of parity as between the partners always presupposed. The "covenant" is often an agreement imposed by a superior on an inferior (Josh. ix. 6ff.; 1 Kings xx. 34; 1 Sam. xi. 1ff.). Complete freedom of action, and therefore the freedom to decide, that is, to take the oath or not, is in this case possessed only by the superior—the lesser partner is simply a recipient. This arrangement is to be understood on the assumption that the recipient will certainly not act against his own interest, for by rejecting the covenant he would only exchange a

---

[1] For what follows cf. J. Begrich, "Berit," in *Z.A.W.*, 1944, pp. 1ff.; W. Staerk, "Bibelwissenschaftliches," in *Theologische Blätter*, 1937, pp. 295f.; G. Quell, in *Th. W.B.N.T.*, vol. ii, pp. 106ff.; A. Jepsen, "Berith, in Verbannung und Heimkehr," in *Festschrift für W. Rudolph*, ed. A. Kuschke, Tübingen 1961, pp. 161ff.

protection which was to his advantage for an extremely hazardous legal insecurity. In other cases the partners enter into the arrangement of their own free will and on equal footing (Gen. XXI. 27, 32, XXXI. 44; I Sam. XXIII. 8; II Sam. V. 3).[2] The covenant is therefore a legal relationship, and comprises the firmest guarantee of a relationship of human communion. In consequence, it was entered upon to the accompaniment of solemn ceremonies, invocation of the deity, a sacral meal, the calling down of curses upon oneself, etc. (cf. Gen. XXVI. 30, XXXI. 46, 54; for the special ritual cf. Jer. XXXIV. 18 and Gen. XV. 9ff.). The relationship guaranteed by a covenant is commonly designated by the word שלום (Gen. XXVI. 30ff.; I Kings V. 26 [V. 12]; Is. LIV. 10; Job V. 23), for which our word peace can only be regarded as an inadequate equivalent.[3] For שלום designates the unimpairedness, the wholeness, of a relationship of communion, and so a state of harmonious equilibrium, the balancing of all claims and needs between two parties. Thus, the making of a covenant is intended to secure a state of intactness, orderliness, and rightness between two parties,[4] in order to make possible, on the basis of this legal foundation, a relationship in matters affecting their common life. At the same time one has to guard against assuming that there was anything like a uniform "conception of the covenant." The term ברית is a very formal one and leaves room in each case for different conceptions. Recently, still another hitherto unknown conception of a covenant has come to our notice, according to which a more highly-placed third party executes a covenant in favour of two other parties. An example of this mediation of a covenant is to be found in the covenant which Jahweh is to make in Israel's favour with the beasts (Hos. II. 18). And the references in Josh. XXIV 25 and II Kings XXIII. 3 also presuppose the same idea.[5]

In traditions that are pronouncedly ancient, Israel preserved the memory that Jahweh had granted her a covenant relationship. Such a relationship, established only in virtue of a privilege offered by God, completely rules out from the very start, of course, any idea of a natural

[2] A. Jepsen, *Nabi*, Munich 1934, pp. 163f.

[3] Noth has recently suggested that this שלום is to be understood in the light of the *salimun*, "reconciliation," "agreement," which is used in connexion with the making of a covenant in the texts from Mari. *Ges. Studien*, pp. 142–54.

[4] F. Horst, "Recht und Religion im Bereich des Alten Testaments," in *Ev.Th.*, 1956, p. 67.

[5] M. Noth, *Ges. Studien*, pp. 142ff.; H. W. Wolff, "Jahwe als Bundesvermittler," in *Vet. Test.*, 1956, pp. 316ff.

relationship with the deity of the kind expressed in myths.[6] This memory resides, strangely enough, in two complexes of traditions which were originally completely separate, namely, those of the covenant with the patriarchs and the Sinai tradition. In the Jahwist's work both became culminating points in the presentation of the history. In both cases what is in question is manifestly an ancient conception of the covenant: the active part is Jahweh's alone; the earthly partner, as recipient, is passive. Abraham sinks completely into unconsciousness, while Jahweh alone performs the rites. The Jahwist's picture of the making of the Sinai covenant (Ex. XXIV. 9–11) is admittedly incomplete (it is now closely coupled with the Elohistic version), but the text clearly understands the covenant—the word itself does not occur—as a unilateral protective relationship (cf. Ex. XXIV. 11). In the Elohist's picture in Ex. XXIV. 3–8 there is already a difference, since here the human partner is vigorously reminded of his duty, and called on to make a decision, and only as he declares himself ready to play his part is the covenant made, on the basis of a written charter. This does not, of course, mean that the granting of the covenant thus depended conditionally upon Israel's rendering obedience, but it does mean that the personal decision of the recipient also was now considered indispensable, and that therefore the question of his standing up to the test also necessarily came into the picture. The law became visible alongside, indeed even within, the very offer of grace itself. Leaving the Jahwist's version of the Sinai covenant out of account—it is too truncated for very far-reaching conclusions to be drawn from it—throughout the whole of the Old Testament the divine covenant on the one hand and the revelation of a will for law on the other are most closely co-ordinated.[7] In the Deuteronomic theology this connexion is so close that the word "covenant" has practically become a synonym for commandments. The "tables of the covenant" are the tables on which the Ten Commandments stand written (Deut. IX. 9, 11, 15), and the "Ark of the Covenant" gets its name from the tables of the

---

[6] Eichrodt, *Theologie*, VOL. I (Eng. trans.), pp. 42f.

[7] All the same, it is questionable if this state of affairs has already to be regarded as a depravation of the original conception of the covenant (so Begrich, in *Z.A.W.*, 1944, pp. 3, 9f.). It looks as if Begrich has made an all too sharp distinction between unilateral and bilateral covenants, for even the most primitive covenant cannot well be conceived without a determination to agreement imposed on the recipient. We have also to bear in mind that the idea of a covenant made by *Jahweh* must right away have put an individual stamp on the complex of concepts.

commandments which were deposited in it (Num. x. 33; Deut. x. 8; Josh. III. 3, etc.).

This fairly considerable literary evidence for a covenant made between Jahweh and Israel leads automatically to the question of the covenant's place and significance in Israel's sacral life, for it is from the very beginning quite unlikely that the conception is a pure matter of literary tradition. In actual fact, there is now no doubt that the place of the "theological" conception of the covenant in Israel's cultic life was certain solemn ceremonies which must have constituted the climaxes of the religious life.

Important material has recently come to light from a quarter where it had least of all been looked for. Comparison of ancient Near Eastern treaties, especially those made by the Hittites in the fourteenth and thirteenth centuries B.C., with passages in the Old Testament has revealed so many things in common between the two, particularly in the matter of the form, that there must be some connexion between these suzerainty treaties and the exposition of the details of Jahweh's covenant with Israel given in certain passages in the Old Testament. As a result, with particular passages and groups of passages, we may speak of a "covenantal formulation," in which the various formal elements found in the treaties recur feature for feature, though sometimes freely adapted to suit the conditions obtaining in Israel (J. Muilenburg, K. Baltzer).[8] The *schema* of the treaties consists of (1) the preamble, (2) the historical prologue (in which investment with a land often has a part to play), (3) the basic stipulation, (4) particular conditions, (5) invocation of the gods as witnesses, (6) the curses and blessings formula (very much altered in the corresponding clauses in the Old Testament). This covenantal formula, of the build-up of which a good example is Josh. XXIV, must have had its part to play in Israel's national cultic life even before the exile. Were the covenant's bases disturbed by some contingency, it had to be renewed (Neh. IX; Ezra IXf.). The same *schema* is to be found in 1 Sam. XII; Josh. XXIII; 1 Chron. XXII–XXIX, where it is adapted to the situation of an office being handed over.

---

[8] G. E. Mendenhall, *Law and Covenant in Israel and the Ancient Near East*, Pittsburgh 1955; K. Baltzer, *Das Bundesformular, sein Ursprung und seine Verwendung im Alte-Testament*, Neukirchen 1960); W. Beyerlin, *Herkunft und Geschichte der ältesten Sinain traditionen*, Tübingen 1961, pp. 60ff.; J. Muilenburg, "The Form and Structure of the Covenantal Formulations," in *Vet. Test.* IX (1959), pp. 347ff.; W. Zimmerli, "Das Gesetz im Alten Testament" in *Th. L.Z.* 1960, cols. 481ff. (especially 492ff.).

Even if there are still many questions of detail to be answered, there is at least no doubt that the two kinds of material are related to one another (the relationship in respect of form can be traced down into text of post-apostolic times). Here of course Israel took over. But when we remember the age of some of the relevant Old Testament material, we have to reckon that she became acquainted with this treaty *schema* very early on, perhaps even as soon as the time of the Judges. As to the question whether in the Decalogue apodictic formulation is derived from certain formulations in the imperative in the "basic stipulation," there is difference of opinion. Also, the question of the application of the term בְּרִית in the sacral literature of the pre-exilic period is still rather obscure.

Thus, what used to be called the "history of the conception of the covenant" has now turned out to be very involved. There are so many possible ways of taking the term בְּרִית, and even the "theological" conception of the covenant was often re-interpreted in the course of the history. Thus, using only the word בְּרִית itself, that is, employing the method of investigation of terminology, it becomes more and more difficult to write a history of all the ideas which now and then may have made use of it.

Coming back from the question of the covenant's *Sitz im Leben* in the cult to the picture of the history given in the sources in the Pentateuch, it is at once apparent that the two covenants which Jahweh made, the one with Abraham and the other on Sinai with Moses, are what lay down the lines of the whole work of JE. In it, contrary to what is normal in matters cultic, everything is attuned to events that are unique, and occur at the very beginning. The covenant with Abraham and the covenant with Moses are now connected with one another and with the whole course of the saving history from Genesis to Joshua.

The most prominent item in the covenant with the patriarchs was the promise of the land, and this promise was given at the time to the small group of worshippers of the ancestral God.[9] But to appreciate the colossal journey which this element in the tradition already had behind it, and the changes it had undergone, by the time of its incorporation into the Jahwist, we have to remember that in the old promise to the ancestors, the promise of a land was certainly originally made with reference to an imminent realisation, that is with reference to the settling-down of these pre-Mosaic semi-nomads

[9] Gen. xv. 18. Alt, *K.S.*, VOL. I, pp. 66f.

who ranged on the borders of the arable land. It is easy to see that in this, the oldest understanding of it, the promise to the patriarchs was not as yet thought of in terms of a fresh departure from the land and of a much later return, that is, the final one under Joshua. But now, this is precisely the most conspicuous binding factor not only in the work JE, but also in the Hexateuch in its final form—this colossal arch spanning the time from the promise of a land in the ancient promise to the ancestors to the fulfilment of the same promise in the days of Joshua. Still another change in the meaning of the old promise was due to the fact that, while it was originally only valid for the little group of worshippers of the ancestral God, it was now referred to the whole of Israel and her conquest of the land. This procedure has a great deal to tell us about the strange blending of conservatism and freedom in the transmission of old traditions. The old promise of a land had of course already been fulfilled—at the time of the settlement of Israel's pre-Mosaic ancestors in the arable land. But for later ages this promise was all of a sudden charged with a completely new content—the promise to the twelve tribes of the possession of the land: and in this new interpretation it became the promise that pervades the whole of the Hexateuch.

With regard to the covenant theology, the Priestly Document is constructed in a somewhat different way, and on that account contributes to the Hexateuch certain characteristic emphases over and above what has already been mentioned. It knew of two covenants, the covenant with Noah and that with Abraham (Gen. IX. 1ff., XVII. 1ff.). P's idea of the covenant has no connexion at all with law—the content is an unconditional bestowal of salvation by Jahweh.[10] In the case of the covenant with Noah, Jahweh himself establishes the sign: in the covenant with Abraham, it is the recipient who is obliged to establish the sign, to appropriate the divine offer of salvation in confessional form, that is in the performance of circumcision. In content the covenant with Abraham is much more extensive: it contains three promises: (1) Abraham to become a people; (2) a new relationship to God ("I will be your God"); and (3) the possession of the land. In the stories in JE about the patriarchs the promise that they will become

---

[10] The original idea of a covenant comes directly to expression in the phraseology of the Priestly Document: God "establishes the covenant" (הקים), he "grants it" (נתן), Gen. VI. 18, IX. 9, 11f., 17, XVII. 2, 7, 19, 21 and frequently. God speaks of "his" covenant.

a great nation also plays a large part, but there it was not a specific part of the covenant with Abraham. The promise of the exceptional relationship to God is peculiar to P. This element is a prelude to the revelation at Sinai, for it anticipates the second term of the formula of the old Sinai covenant ("you are to be my people—I will be your God"). As it is preserved to us, P says nothing about a covenant at Sinai; though, in what is perhaps a secondary passage (Ex. xxxi. 12–17), the observance of the Sabbath is enjoined as a sign of the covenant.We must, therefore, reckon with the possibility that, originally, P too contained a covenant at Sinai, but that this element dropped out (because of Ex. xxiv) when P was conjoined with JE.

Thus, in the final state of the Hexateuch, the following division of the traditional materials into periods emerges. God created the world and man. After the destruction of the corrupt human race by the Flood, God gave to a new human race laws for its self-preservation, and, in the covenant with Noah, guaranteed to it the outward continuance of the world and its orders. He then called Abraham, and in a covenant which he made with him, promised him a great posterity, a special relationship to God, and the land of Canaan. The first promise was fulfilled in Egypt, when the patriarchs grew into a people; the second was fulfilled at Sinai, when with a fresh covenant (JE) Israel received the regulations for her community life and her intercourse with God; and the third was fulfilled when under Joshua Israel took possession of the land of Canaan. Thus, by means of the covenant theology, the entire mass of the Hexateuchal traditions was set beneath a threefold arch of prophecy and fulfilment. Initially, there were only the patriarchs: they are not yet a people, they have not entered into the promised special relationship with God, nor do they possess a land. Then, from the patriarchs a people comes into being; but it is without the special relationship and the land. And finally, in what is perhaps really the most exciting period, Israel, which is entirely ordered in one direction only, that is towards Jahweh, moves in stately procession through the wilderness towards the last promise, the land of Canaan.

I. THE PRIMEVAL HISTORY

1. THE PLACE IN THE THEOLOGY OF THE WITNESS CONCERNING CREATION

It has long been recognised that more comprehensive statements about the creation of the world by Jahweh are only found in texts of a later time. Leaving the Jahwist out of account, since he does not in fact treat of the creation of the world at all, we are left in the main with Deutero-Isaiah, the Priestly Document, and a few psalms, the last of which are admittedly difficult to date, although there is no reason to regard them as particularly old. It is of course very doubtful whether this really striking state of affairs admits of the simple explanation that before the seventh and sixth centuries Israel never at all venerated Jahweh as the creator of the world. In actual fact, it is hard to imagine that, in the environment of Canaan, whose religious atmosphere was saturated with creation myths, it would not have occurred to Israel to connect creation—that is, heaven, earth, the stars, the sea, plants, and animals—with Jahweh. Probably the sole reason for the lateness of the emergence of a doctrine of creation was that it took Israel a fairly long time to bring the older beliefs which she actually already possessed about it into proper theological relationship with the tradition which was her very own, that is, with what she believed about the saving acts done by Jahweh in history. In the old cultic Credo there was nothing about Creation. And Israel only discovered the correct theological relationship of the two when she learned to see Creation too as connected theologically with the saving history. This was, of course, no light task, and she needed some time to accomplish it. Unlike the Canaanites, Israel had no divine sustenance, blessing, and protection from an environment that was conceived in terms of myth: what had been opened up for her through Jahweh's revelation was the realm of history, and it was in the light of this as starting-point that the term creation had first to be defined. Theologically it was a great achievement that Israel was actually able to make a connexion between Creation and the saving history—and not with a present conceived in terms of myth. Incidentally, there are also some decidedly old passages referring to the belief in Creation which rule out the later dating which has for long been usual.[1]

[1] Ps. XIX. 2ff. [1ff.]; Gen. XIV. 19, 22, XXIV. 3; I Kings VIII. 12 (*text. emend.*).

It is true that, because of special historical experiences, Jahwism in ancient Israel regarded itself exclusively as a religion of salvation—this can be deduced right away from Israel's oldest confessional formulae. But the question of the way in which she connected her beliefs about Creation with her historically-based religion is certainly more important than the historical problem of the origin of those beliefs. It is instructive to look at Deutero-Isaiah, who is commonly regarded, along with the Priestly Document, as the chief witness about Creation. However, even a quick glance at the passages in question shows that the allusions to Jahweh as the creator are far from being the primary subject of Deutero-Isaiah's message. Thus in, for example, Is. XLII. 5 or XLIII. 1 he uses, in subordinate clauses, hymnlike descriptions of Jahweh such as "he who created the heavens," "he who created you, who formed you," but only to pass over in the principal clause to a soteriological statement "fear not, I redeem thee." Here, and also in Is. XLIV. 24b–28, the allusion to the creator stands in a subordinate clause or in apposition—obviously it has a subordinate function in the prophet's message and does not anywhere appear independently: it is intended to reinforce confidence in the power of Jahweh and his readiness to help. Still, in so speaking, we are not yet expressing the heart of the matter. The reason why the allusion to Creation strengthens confidence is that Deutero-Isaiah obviously sees a saving event in the creation itself. In Is. XLIV. 24, Jahweh represents himself as "the redeemer and creator." It is striking how easily both there and in LIV. 5 articles of faith which are, to our way of thinking, widely separated, are placed side by side, and indeed interwoven. Jahweh created the world. But he created Israel too.[2] In Is. LI. 9f., the two creative works are almost made to coincide. The prophet apostrophises the creation of the world, but at the same time he speaks of Israel's redemption from Egypt. For hardly has he spoken about the driving back of the waters, in the language of the mythical struggle with the dragon of Chaos, than he jumps to the miracle at the Red Sea where Jahweh again held the waters back "for the redeemed to pass through." Here creation and redemption almost coincide, and can almost be looked on as one act of dramatic divine saving action in the picture of the

[2] G. von Rad, *Das theologische Problem des alttestamentlichen Schöpfungsglaubens*, Bei. Z.A.W., No. 66, 1936, pp. 138ff., reprinted in *Ges. Studien*, pp. 136ff.; R. Rendtorff, "Die theologische Stellung des Schöpfungsglaubens bei Deuterojesaja," in *Z. Th. K.*, 1954, pp. 3ff.

struggle with the dragon of Chaos. The situation is just the same in Ps. LXXVII. 17ff. [16ff.], a passage which, because of its poetical form (three-membered verses, tautological parallelism), seems to be particularly old. The theological derivation of Jahweh's power over history from his authority as Creator is however a comparatively late idea (Jer. XXVII. 4ff.; Is. XLV. 12f.).[3]

But this soteriological understanding of Creation is not by any means a peculiarity confined to Deutero-Isaiah. The purpose of Ps. LXXXIX, for example, is to celebrate "Jahweh's acts of grace" (חִסְדֵי יהוה). No doubt, what is chiefly meant is the covenant with David, the establishment of the Messianic kingdom. But a quite considerable passage coming in the middle of it deals with various acts of creation, and these too are obviously to be reckoned in the sum total of the saving acts of Jahweh alluded to in the psalm. This comes out even more clearly in Ps. LXXIV. Here too there is a hymnlike section—it begins with a call to Jahweh "who does deeds of salvation" (פֹּעֵל יְשׁוּעוֹת) and then records works of Jahweh's creation (Ps. LXXIV. 12–17).

In the light of all this, it is extremely likely that this soteriological understanding of Creation also lies at the basis of the creation stories in J and P.[4] In neither of these documents of course is Jahweh's work in Creation considered for its own sake: instead it is incorporated within a course of history leading to the call of Abraham and ending with Israel's entry into Palestine. Thus with both, the place where the "author" stands is within the innermost circle of the saving relationship granted by Jahweh to Israel. But to make this relationship theologically legitimate, both pictures of the history start with Creation, and from there they draw the line out towards themselves, and towards Israel, and the Tabernacle, and the promised land. Presumptuous as it may sound, Creation is part of the aetiology of Israel![5] It goes without

[3] On the conception of the struggle with the Chaos dragon and the way in which Is. LI. 9 is to be taken, see below, p. 150, n. 24.

[4] It was once a matter of surprise that the source E only begins with the history of the patriarchs (Gen. XV). But in the light of our present-day knowledge of the history of tradition this beginning is just the normal and usual one. The new thing with the Jahwist is his independence in prefixing a universal primeval history.

[5] Another rooting of Israel in the plans of Jahweh for the world is to be seen in Deut. XXXII. 8 (text. emend.): "When the Most High gave to the nations their inheritance, when he separated the sons of men, he fixed the bounds of the peoples according to the number of 'the Elohim beings'; but Jahweh's portion is his people, Jacob his allotted heritage."

saying that the expansion of the old Credo by means of such a preface tremendously broadened the theological basis of the whole thing. The extensive addition comprising the tradition from Abraham to Joshua necessitated the laying of a different foundation from the one which the old Credo could supply. The beginning of this divine history was now put back in time to Creation. But this pushing back of the beginning of the saving history was only possible because Creation itself was regarded as a saving work of Jahweh's.

This conception of Creation had of course far-reaching theological consequences. Creation is regarded as a work of Jahweh in history, a work within time. This means that there is a real and true opening up of historical prospect. No doubt, Creation as the first of Jahweh's works stands at the very remotest beginnings—only, it does not stand alone, other works are to follow. Indeed, it is this standing in the time which is given special emphasis in P's account of Creation, for P incorporated Creation into its great genealogical framework, the plan of Toledoth (Gen. II. 4a)—why, Creation is itself a sequence in time, exactly marked out into days.[6] But if the account of Creation stands within time, it has once for all ceased to be myth, a timeless revelation taking place in the natural cycle.

There is however a distinct divergence between the older and the later periods. In the Wisdom literature of the Old Testament the doctrine of Creation occupied a much more central position. In it Creation was in reality an absolute basis for faith, and was referred to for its own sake altogether and not in the light of other factors of the faith. The clearest case is Job xxxviiiff., but compare also Prov. III. 19f., VIII. 22ff., xIV. 31, xX. 12, etc. The reason for the absence of saving history proper in these texts lies in the Wisdom literature's theological presuppositions. On the other hand, of course, in all the later attestations we have to reckon with the fact that, even where there is no explicit connexion with the saving history, they are to be taken soteriologically.[7]

2. THE PICTURES OF JAHWEH'S ACT OF CREATION

In dealing with what the Old Testament says about the creation of the world and man, it is good procedure to take on one side what is theologically didactic as opposed to the rest, for example, to what is hymnic. The former class is intended to present theological facts, to

---

[6] "The account of creation is part of a history which is characterised by figures and dates," L. Köhler, *Theology*, p. 87.   [7] See below, pp. 417f., 420.

give instruction on things which, it may be, were not known or not known exactly, to connect and to teach. The other statements already have the agreement of the hearer or the reader; they have no didactic content: wherever they do not allude to the Creator and Creation merely by the way they glorify them, and so we have only the right to make indirect use of them. They too certainly have as their background a "doctrine of creation," frequent reminiscences of whose elements occur, but not for the direct purpose of teaching. In consequence, the style of these statements is different: it is enthusiastic and rapturous, while that of the theological and didactic passages is decidedly restrained and in the crucial passages strives for nothing short of precision. For our theological stocktaking this dual mode of expression is important, and the very fact that the non-theological statements, especially those which sing praises, far outnumber the others, can save us from over-estimating the didactic element and the distinctions which it makes. Teaching certainly had its own legitimate function, but it was a much more hidden one, and was merely one of the presuppositions of praise. Direct theological statements about the Creation in the form of large complexes occur only twice in the Old Testament, in the Creation story of the Priestly Document (Gen. I. 1–II. 4a) and in that of the Jahwist (Gen. II. 4b–25)—that is, precisely in those two sections where Creation is expressly intended to be understood as a prologue, and as a start of the divine saving work in Israel. In language as well as in their whole inner nature and world of ideas they are as different as can be conceived; but the fact that the Jahwist approaches his subject quite differently from P—he uses a simple pictorial method—must not lead us to fail to appreciate its tremendous theological substance. In actual fact, in this section he is much more directly didactic than is P, which moves more in the realm of theological definitions.

The Jahwist's account of Creation is generally treated as a considerably older document than the one in P, and, from the point of view of literary history, it is in fact to be dated centuries earlier. But it is not wise to make the difference in age the key to the interpretation to the extent that is usual, for it is after all debatable whether it is not just in the Priestly Document, which deals with things in such a direct and completely material way, that an older form of cosmological thinking has been preserved. In contrast, because of their compact, figurative, and so more indirect presentation, the Jahwist's accounts of Creation and paradise give the impression of being more spiritual

and disengaged. We have here two pictures which move in completely different thought-forms, and which possibly ought not to be
understood, and related to one another, in the mere terms of a simple
scheme of evolution. Attention has often been drawn to the strongly
mythological character of Gen. II. 4b–25. But this is proper only in so
far as the story proceeds along the line of concepts which were no doubt
once genuinely mythological. But in respect of inner character, nothing
is more opposed to the world of genuine myth than the enlightened
and sober lucidity of the Jahwist's account of Creation, which is so
far removed from abstruse mythology. How much more mythological
in comparison is Ezekiel's centuries-later presentation of the first man
upon the mountain of God amid cherubim and precious stones (Ezek.
xxvⅢ. 11ff.)! Assessing the Jahwist according to his intellectual outlook, which is permeated by what are certainly age-old conceptual
forms (rivers, a garden, fruit, a tree of life, a serpent), we are met with
an enlightened sobriety which uses the old mythological conceptions
only as very sublime pictures. In contrast, Gen. I presents the results of
concentrated theological and cosmological reflexion in a language
which is concise and always utterly direct in expression. Its statements
are not allusive and charged with a hidden meaning, as with the
Jahwist, but are everywhere clearly contoured and mean exactly what
they say. The very reason why this presentation of P's renounces to
the point of stiffness all poetic or ardent liveliness was just to effect this
concentration and theological precision.

The two presentations are alike in that they have as their chief end,
though doing it in very different ways, the creation of man, that is,
mankind as male and female—with the result that the rest of the
world is ordered round them as the chief work of Jahweh in Creation;
for Gen. II. 4bff. too terminates and culminates in the creation of all
mankind represented in the duality of man and woman. Admittedly,
in Gen. II. 4bff. man is the mid-point around which God constructs his
work, whereas in Gen. I. 1ff. he is the apex of a cosmological pyramid.[8]
P has a much greater interest in cosmology and in consequence he
sketches a story of Creation which moves much more purposefully,
though by stages, towards the creation of man. The world and its
fullness do not find their unity and inner coherence in a cosmological
first principle, such as the Ionian natural philosophers tried to discover,
but in the completely personal will of Jahweh their creator. Nor,

[8] B. Jacob, *Das erste Buch der Tora*, Berlin 1934, p. 952.

as in so many myths of the creation, is the world traced back to a creative struggle between two mythical first principles regarded as persons. The Priestly Document gives several definitions of the way in which the creative will of Jahweh acts, and these differ quite considerably from one another theologically. At the apex stands the all-comprehensive statement that "God" created the world.

The verb בָּרָא, which is used here, is a technical term in the theological vocabulary of the priests, and is used exclusively of creation by God.[9] It also occurs with the same meaning of that divine creation which is completely without analogy, in Deutero-Isaiah (Is. XL. 26, 28, XLV. 18, etc.): he on his part probably took it over from the cultic language of hymnody (Ps. LXXXIX. 13, 48, [12, 47], CIV. 30, CXLVIII. 5). This term בָּרָא is also used where Jahweh's new creation is the subject (Pss. CII. 19 [18], R.S.V. "yet unborn," lit. "to be created"; LI. 10). Since pre-existent matter is never mentioned in connexion with this activity, the idea of *creato ex nihilo* is connected with it.[10] Another word for the divine creative activity, less often found, is קָנָה (Gen. XIV. 19, 22; Deut. XXXII. 6; Prov. VIII. 22, etc.), cf. the personal name Elkanah: it came into use in Israelite vocabulary from the Canaanite religion.[11]

The concept of creation by means of a simple word of command only begins with the unfolding of the individual works of creation and their succession, and it dominates the picture down to Gen. I. 24 (the creation of the living creatures of the dry land), when it makes room for something quite new. Thus, the concept of creation by means of the word is to be taken as an interpretation of the בָּרָא of vs. 1. It gives to begin with an idea of the absolute effortlessness of the divine creative action. It only needed the brief pronouncement of the will of Jahweh to call the world into being. But if the world is the product of the creative word, it is therefore, for one thing, sharply separated in its nature from God himself—it is neither an emanation nor a mythically understood manifestation of the divine nature and its power. The only continuity between God and his work is his word. Still, it would be

---

[9] P. Humbert, "Emploi et portée du verbe bara (créer) dans l'Ancien Testament," in *Th. Z.*, 1947, pp. 401ff.

[10] The conceptual formulation *creatio ex nihilo* is first found in II Macc. VII. 28.

[11] It is thus used for example in the mythological texts of Ras Shamra (Gordon, *Handbook*, VOL. II, 51, I, 23; *Keret*, I, 57, and frequently). For the semantic problem in קָנָה cf. P. Humbert in *Festschrift für A. Bertholet*, pp. 259ff.; P. Katz in *Journal of Jewish Studies*, V (1954), No. 3, pp. 126ff.

quite wrong to take this important concept in the main negatively, that is, as a delimiting definition. If the world was called into being by the free will of God, then it is his very own possession, and he is its Lord.[12]

This concept of the creation of the world by means of the word has a very wide background in the history of religion. In the Babylonian Creation epic Enuma Elish, too, Marduk gives proof of his divine power by calling an object into being by his word of command and by making it vanish again in the same way (Table 4, 20ff.). Obviously at the back of these concepts lies the widespread belief in the magical power of the word, and this was thought of as attaining its acme of perfection with the deity. Gen. 1, however, looks as if it had closer contacts with certain characteristics of the Old Egyptian ("Memphitic") theology, according to which Ptah, the god of the universe, exercised his creative activity with the aid of "heart and tongue," that is, by means of his word. He created the nine gods (the primeval waters, the sun-god Re, etc.) by his word. This "parallel" in comparative religion is of all the greater interest in that in the Egyptian theology is made the first definite attempt to overcome the multiplicity of the gods by means of a single one.[13] We are still in the dark about connexions between these very old priestly theories, which date from the first half of the third millenium B.C., and Gen. 1. But connexions are rendered more probable if, as is likely anyway, we are to see in the content of Gen. 1 a form of ancient Israel's Wisdom. There are not many references to creation by means of the word outside of Gen. 1–Is. XLVIII. 13; Pss. XXXIII. 6, CXLVIII. 5. There are echoes of it in Is. XLI. 4, XLV. 12; Am. IX. 6; Jon. IV. 6f.

The various works of Creation stand on a completely different footing in respect of their relationship to the Creator—they are far from having a like immediacy to God. At farthest remove from him,

---

[12] "Thus the creature in its totality was allied to this living divine Person, being wholly referred to it for its existence and essence, its survival and sustenance. . . . It came into being as the work of the Word of God corresponding to his utterance. So originally and intimately was it disposed for the grace of God! So little did it acquire a place from which it might legitimately withdraw itself from the grace of God! Encountered by this Word of grace, it encounters just the wisdom, kindness and power without which it could not be at all. Encountering the creature, this Word really comes to its own." K. Barth, *Church Dogmatics*, VOL. III, PT. I, trans. J. W. Edwards, O. Bussey, and H. Knight, Edinburgh 1958, p. 110.

[13] H. Junker, *Die Götterlehre von Memphis*, Berlin 1940, pp. 20, 41, 55.

in a relationship which scarcely admits of theological definition, is the formless, watery, darksome, abysmal chaos. Because of vs. 1 which precedes the mention of chaos, we cannot say that it is uncreated, that is, that it was found by God as pre-existent. On the other hand, it is hardly possible to conceive of the idea of a created chaos, for what is created is not chaotic. Still, the theological function of vs. 2 in the total picture is of particular importance, for chaos is *the* great menace to Creation—it is indeed a primeval experience of man, and every statement of the Creation belief has continually to prove itself over against it. God lifted the world out of the formless, and over its own abyss he holds it unceasingly. Day and night too are on a completely different footing.[14] Night is a survival of the darkness of chaos, now however kept in bounds by a protective order. But the day is light from that primeval light which was the firstborn of the works of Creation. The plants have a very indirect relationship to God, for they spring from the ground, which God commissioned to play a part in creating them. The animals also have their immediate relationship to the ground, but they are the recipients of a special word of blessing assigning fruitfulness to them, in order that they may multiply. On the topmost step of this pyramid stands man, and there is nothing between him and God: indeed, the world, which was in fact made for him, has in him alone its most absolute immediacy to God. Also, unlike the rest of Creation, he was not created by the word; but in creating him God was actuated by a unique, solemn resolve in the depths of his heart. And in particular, God took the pattern for this, his last work of Creation, from the heavenly world above. In no other work of Creation is everything referred so very immediately to God himself as in this.

The statement about the image of God in man[15] contains no direct explanation about the form which specially constitutes it; its real point is rather in the purpose for which the image is given to man. The difficulty for us lies in the fact that the text regarded the simple statement that man was made in the image of God as adequate and clear. Two things may be said. The words צלם, "image," "statue," "a work of plastic art," and דמות, "likeness," "something like"—the second

---

[14] Ps. LXXIV. 16: "Thine is the day, thine *also* is the night."

[15] L. Köhler, "Die Grundstelle der *Imago Dei* Lehre Genesis I. 26," in *Th. Z.*, 1948, pp. 16ff.; J. J. Stamm, *Die Gottesebenbildlichkeit des Menschen im Alten Testament,* Theologische Studien, Heft 54, Zollikon-Zürich 1959.

interprets the first by underlining the idea of correspondence and similarity—refer to the whole of man and do not relate solely to his spiritual and intellectual being: they relate equally, if not first and foremost, to the splendour of his bodily form, the הדר ("grace," "nobility," "majesty") and the כבוד, with which God has endowed him. (Ps. VIII. 6, [5]).[16] Ezek. XXVIII. 12 speaks still more directly of the "perfect beauty" of primeval man. Because of the image of God man is exalted high and above all other creatures. But on the other hand, this creaturely dignity has also an upper limit. What then was the pattern after which he was created? To this question, the most important one as it might seem, the text gives a remarkably general answer, and this is certainly not unintentional. How is the אלהים in vs. 27 to be interpreted? Does it refer to God himself or to the heavenly beings who surround his throne, or to both together? In his resolve Jahweh associates himself with his heavenly court (cf. for this I Kings XXII. 19; Job I. 6; Is. VI. 1–3), and in so doing at the same time hides himself in their plurality. The term "let us" prevents the image being referred directly to God alone.[17] At this point Ps. VIII. 6 [5] supplements the concept, for the "little lower" in vs. 6 [5] certainly refers there to the angels—the psalm addresses Jahweh, but in vs. 6 [5] it does not say Jahweh, but Elohim, rendered by Septuagint as ἄγγελοι. Expressed in the concepts of the Old Testament, this would mean that man was created in the form of Elohim. The only possibility of advancing beyond this would be an indirect one, by asking how Israel thought of these Elohim-beings. Two predicates of them are established—they were considered as "wise" and as "good" (II Sam. XIV. 17, 20; I Sam. XXIX. 9).

Actually, Israel conceived even Jahweh himself as having human form. But the way of putting it which we use runs in precisely the wrong direction according to Old Testament ideas, for, according to the ideas of Jahwism, it cannot be said that Israel regarded God anthropomorphically, but the reverse, that she considered man as theomorphic. As well as many passages in the prophets or in the poets—the references in the latter of which are then essentially non-theological—the very carefully formulated statement in Ezek. I. 26 is of particular

[16] L. Köhler (op. cit., pp. 19f.) sees in P's definition a reference particularly to man's upright form.

[17] Köhler too understands כדמותנו in a restricted sense; what is said about the impossibility of representing God by an image is thereby weakened. Th.Z., 1948, pp. 20ff.

importance. The light-phenomenon of the "glory of God" clearly displays human contours. It has been rightly said that Ezek. I. 26 is the theological prelude to the *locus classicus* for the *imago* doctrine in Gen. I. 26.[18] If P insists on the fact that the pattern on which man was fashioned is to be sought outside of the sphere of the created, and that man is also like this pattern, particularly in respect of his relationship to Jahweh, nevertheless at the same time an infinite difference and distance is tacitly recognised—first in the matter of mere stature, for Israel conceived Jahweh as gigantic (Mic. I. 3ff.; Is. LXIII. 1ff.; Ps. XXIV. 9), but also different and distant as regards quality, for the כבוד which man has cannot, of course, be remotely compared with the fiery, intensely radiant light which is the nature of Jahweh. But this holds true in particular for the sexual differentiation of mankind. When the Elohim-beings made their appearance upon the earth, they were so much in human form that often they were not immediately recognised as Elohim (Jg. VI. 11ff.; Josh. V. 13ff.). Their sexuality is mentioned once.[19] Although Jahweh himself was conceived as man, any thought of sexuality in him, or of his acting in creation by means of sex, was completely alien to Israel. Considering Israel's religious environment, this is very astonishing, for the Canaanite cult of Baal was a fertility cult and celebrated the ἱερὸς γάμος as the divine mystery of Creation *par excellence*. But for Israel the polarity of the sexes was something belonging to Creation, and not to the deity himself.

P only becomes clear and explicit when it speaks about the purpose of this image of God in man, that is, the function committed to man in virtue of it, namely, his status as lord in the world. In this connexion it is to be noticed how strong are the expressions describing this lordship (כבש, "to trample on," "subdue"; רדה, "to tread (grapes)," "to rule over"). God set man in the world as the sign of his own sovereign authority, in order that man should uphold and enforce his—God's—claims as lord. Earthly monarchs too have the habit of setting up images of themselves in their kingdom as signs of their sovereign authority—it was in that sense that Israel thought of man as the

---

[18] P. Humbert, *Études sur le récit du Paradis et de la chute dans la Genèse*, Neuchâtel 1940, p. 172. That Jahweh has the form of men is also to be concluded from Ex. XV. 3; Is. VI. 1ff.; Mic. I. 2f.; Dan. VII. 9.

[19] Gen. VI. 2. We may also think of the concealment of the shame of the Seraphim in Is. VI. 2.

representative of God.[20] This lordship of man extends over the world and not, for example, just over animals. The reason why the animals are mentioned is because they alone come into question as the rivals of man.[21] But they are expressly put under him. What is crucial about man's image is his function in the non-human world. Thus, through the image of God in man Creation, in addition to coming from God, receives a particular ordering towards God. As yet, of course, this sovereign right does not include the killing or slaughtering of animals. According to Jahweh's will as creator, the sustenance of both man and animals was to be the products of the earth alone. This is the one hint which is to be gathered from P of a state of original peace in the world as created by God.

According to Gen. v. 3, Adam begat Seth "in his own likeness after his image."[22] This means that God authorised man to transmit this, his supreme dignity, along the way of continuing procreation of the generations. So it cannot be said that the image of God is lost—all the less as its existence still comes into account in the days of Noah (Gen. IX. 6b). Certainly, the story of the Fall tells of grave disturbances in the creaturely nature of man. But as to the way in which these affected the image of God in man, the Old Testament has nothing explicit to say.

Now it is very much stressed that God "finished," that is, completed, his creative work (Gen. II. 1ff.). This implies the drawing of a clear distinction between the work of Creation on the one hand, and the sustaining and preserving care with which God accompanies his Creation on the other. The structure is erected, the creatures with which God intends henceforth to deal are there. But the completion of God's Creation was the resting on the seventh day.[23] To talk of an "institu-

[20] W. Caspari, "Imago divina," in Festschrift für Reinhold Seeberg, Leipzig 1929, p. 208. The appointment of man to lordship over the earth is remarkably secular. According to the Babylonian epic of creation "the service of the gods" is imposed upon created man (Enuma Elish, Tab. VI. 7f.). For man as the representative of God see Apocalypse of Baruch (Syriac), XIV. 18.

[21] K. Barth, Church Dogmatics, VOL. III, PT. I, p. 206.

[22] It is doubtful, however, if there is any particular purpose lying behind the transposition of the two chief concepts דמות and צלם, or the change in the prepositions ב and כ (cf. Gen. I. 26), as for example that Seth was only in the image of Adam and no longer in the image of God in the full sense.

[23] Thus it was not on the sixth day with his last work of Creation that God completed the world (thus LXX), but on the seventh day. God's desisting from a continuation of his work of Creation and his resting are obviously to be taken and pondered as things in themselves.

tion" of the Sabbath would be a complete misapprehension of the passage. For there is no word here of this rest being imposed on man or assigned to him. And yet on the other hand what is spoken of is much more than just something affecting only God himself: even here it possesses a hidden relationship to the world and man which will, though of course only later, become completely clear. If God blessed this rest, then it is to hand as a kind of third thing between him and the world, provisional, of course, and unperceived by man, but still a good gift of salvation in which Israel is in due time to share. It would be sheer folly to regard this resting of God's which concluded the Creation as something like a turning away from the world by God: it is in fact a particularly mysterious gracious turning towards his Creation.

This account of Creation is, of course, completely bound to the cosmological knowledge of its time. But it is a bad thing for the Christian expositor completely to disregard this latter as obsolete, as if the theologian has only to deal with the faith expressed in Gen. 1 and not with its view of nature. For there can be no doubt that the Creation story in the Priestly Document seeks to convey not merely theological, but also scientific, knowledge. It is characterised by the fact, which is difficult for us to understand, that here theological and scientific knowledge are in accord with no tension between them. The two sets of statements are not only parallel, but are interwoven in such a way that one cannot really say of any part of Gen. 1 that this particular statement is purely scientific (and therefore without importance for us) while that one is purely theological. In the scientific ideas of the time theology had found an instrument which suited it perfectly, and which it could make use of for the appropriate unfolding of certain subjects— in this case the doctrine of Creation.

How completely different the Jahwist's account of Creation and paradise is from that of P has often been emphasised. It is much more of a simple story, and in consequence is much less careful in the choice of words. Culturally too, it derives from a different sphere of life, namely one which is concerned expressly with the dry land. While in Gen. 1 the Creation moves on from chaos to cosmos by the driving back of the waters, the Jahwist presupposes that the original state of things was a waterless wilderness, which God's kindness transformed into an oasis, arable land, by watering. It is altogether a much smaller area with which the narrator deals—not even the "earth," but the world that lies at man's own doorstep—garden, river, trees, language, animals, and woman. Its point of view is much more anthropocentric than P's. In consequence J's narrative supplies an important supplement and extension of the picture given by the Priestly Document: although this was not of course its intention, it fills up gaps left by P, for what it has to say about man's relation to the garden, the animals, and the other sex goes far beyond what was said by P in many points of detail.

Since the narrative avoids all conventional theological abstractions, it displays with much less reserve than P the kindliness of Jahweh, who is unceasingly concerned for mankind, who makes a pleasant garden around him, and is always taking still further thought how he might benefit him more—for the commandment not to eat of the tree of knowledge was also, of course, the result of God's provident disposition for man, since, if he ate of this fruit, destruction would come upon him. But man's being made to react to the will of God through prohibition, and through such a limitation of his freedom being called upon to make a decision, is of course something new.

It is in particular in the picture of the creation of man and woman that this account is fully detailed and bold in its vividness, for it depicts God the creator as completely applied to his work without the slightest reserve, and occupied in shaping it (יָצַר) like a potter. The material utilised is the ground—but man became a "living being" only by God's breathing into him his own divine breath from his own mouth. Verse 7 which recounts this thus contains a precise definition—a rare thing with the Jahwist. Compared with Gen. i. 26f., here the creation of man is pictured on the one hand as a much more personal and indeed much more intimate act of God; and yet, on the other hand, one cannot fail to notice a certain gloom in the point of view. Life is possessed by man only in virtue of that breath of God; and this latter is in no sense inherently associated with his body, and any withholding of this ephemeral gift would throw man back to a state of dead matter (Ps. civ. 29f.; Job xxxiv. 14f.).

The creation of woman is very far removed from that of man, for it is the last and most mysterious of all the kindnesses that Jahweh wished to bestow upon the man. God designed a help for him, to be "corresponding to him" (כְּנֶגְדּוֹ)—she was to be like him, and at the same time not identical with him, but rather his counterpart, his complement. The man no doubt recognised the animals which were brought to him as helps, but they were not counterparts of equal rank. So God moved on, in the most mysterious way, to create the woman—from the man! As distinct from the animals, she was a complete counterpart, which the man at once recognised and greeted as such. So is elucidated the age-long urgency of the sexes for one another, which is only appeased when it becomes "one flesh" in a child; for the woman was taken from the man, and they must in consequence come together again. The Jahwist's story of creation practically issues in this aetiological explanation of the power of *eros* as one of the urges implanted in man by the Creator himself (vs. 24f.), and so gives the relationship between man and woman the dignity of being the greatest miracle and mystery of Creation.

The difference between P and J is very great. Their traditions, which are obviously derived from very different *milieux*, are not only different in the way in which they present the material, but also in the subject in which they are interested: P is concerned with the "world" and man within it, while J shows the construction of man's immediate environment and defines his relationship to it. Both, however, are at one in understanding creation as effected strictly for man's sake, with him as its centre and objective. The intense theological concentration of the text of the Priestly Document is as unique as J's profound definition of relationships, of which we find no further suggestion anywhere else in the Old Testament. And both are relatively isolated in the Old Testament. Elsewhere, when Israel spoke of Jahweh's creation of the world, there lay to her hand a concept which was obviously more popular, namely that of a dramatic struggle of Jahweh with the powers of Chaos. In this concept a new element is presupposed —a blatant enmity of Chaos towards God. Psalms XLVI. 3 and LXXXIX. 9 speak of Chaos' inordinate pride (גאוה, גאות). But Jahweh rebuked Chaos (Ps. CIV. 7), he smote it terribly (Ps. LXXIV. 13f.), and forced these powers to go down underneath the earth, so that they now sleep in the depths of Creation: they could possibly be re-awakened (Job III. 8), but God has set a guard over them (Job VII. 12).[24] The

---

[24] H. Gunkel, *Schöpfung und Chaos in Urzeit und Endzeit*, pp. 29ff. While Gunkel still took the Babylonian mythological ideas as the sole source of the Biblical data connected with the struggle with the Chaos dragon, the Ras Shamra texts now show us ideas belonging directly to Canaanite mythology. One of the results of Werner Schmidt's monograph, *Königtum Gottes in Ugarit und Israel* (Bonn 1961), is a very detailed knowledge of the ideas connected with the struggle. The dragon's opponent is Baal, but Baal is not (like El) a creator god; and so—this holds true also where there are echoes in the Old Testament—struggle data are not immediately to be taken as Creation data. Schmidt's contention, however, that the struggle with the Chaos

connexion between this set of ideas and the Babylonian myth of Marduk's battle with Tiamat is plain to see. Leaving aside the many details in the struggle between Jahweh and Chaos, some of them bizarre (cf. for example, Ezek. XXXII. 2–8), Jahweh's opponent is hypostasised as a mythical person to such an extent (he is called Rahab or Leviathian, Is. LI. 9f.; Ps. LXXXIX. 11 [10]) that one could be well-nigh tempted to regard these texts as implying a cosmological dualism. In comparison with Gen. I, even the elements in this concept which Israel took over are remarkable for their strongly mythological form. We must, however, bear in mind that the complete myth is never at any time rehearsed as a whole, but it is always much more a matter of incidental apostrophisings, and this clearly in contexts where no value is laid upon exact theological statements. It is the poets and prophets who unconcernedly and casually make use of these obviously more popular ideas.

A third group of statements about Creation—very different from the two already mentioned—derives from the reflexions of the wise men. Wisdom's thought stands at a very far remove from the old theological traditions of Israel; and also when it makes use of her mythological ones, it does so only in a very indirect and intellectualised fashion. In this thought there came to expression an attitude of mind which had become aware of the illuminating and organising possibilities of human reason. Accordingly, it looks at Creation with eager comprehension and with a rational interest in the problems of its technique—it is stirred by the wonder of how the world was given stability when founded on the unstable (Ps. CIV. 5; Job XXVI. 7, XXXVIII. 6), and by the origin of meteorological phenomena. Job XXXVIIIff. in particular, and the hymns in the Wisdom literature impressively display this new way that leads from intelligent contemplation to adoration. For Wisdom too did not in any way abandon belief in Jahweh as creator. Wisdom's characteristically different theological questions fall to be dealt with later (see below, pp. 446ff.).

dragon is only to be related to Jahweh's work in Creation in passages where this is explicitly stated is, it seems to me, methodologically not completely convincing. Sometimes the relationship is made (Pss. LXXIV, LXXXIX), while in other cases it is lacking (Pss. XCIII, LXXVII). But should these two kinds of texts in fact be treated on a different footing, especially when, as Schmidt himself emphasises, the functions of Baal and of the creator god El were united? With Is. LI. 9f. the usual reference to Creation seems to me particularly appropriate, since Deutero-Isaiah so often appeals to Creation for a proof.

Discussion of the general concepts of the shape of the world and its parts, and of the being of man and his physical and mental characteristics, lies, in our view, outside the province of a theology of the Old Testament, because, like much else, these concepts form part of the data conditioned by the general culture and mental climate which Israel had in common with the majority of the peoples in the ancient East. But it can never be over-emphasised that our current concept of "world" was foreign to ancient Israel. There are profound reasons for the fact that she did not have at her disposal the equally serviceable concept of the Greek "cosmos." Israel was obviously not in the position of conceiving the world as an entity thus philosophically objectified which man sees as set over against himself. We have to seek the reasons for this in the fact that for Israel the "world" was much less Being than Event. It was for man something continually new and experienced in many different ways, and was therefore much more difficult to comprehend conceptually—least of all by reducing it to a principle. Israel did not see the world as an ordered organism in repose, for on the one hand she saw Jahweh as much more directly at work in all that goes on in the world, and on the other, man on his side recognised that he had a share in this, because he too continually determined the reactions of the world about him by his actions, whether good or bad. If a common paraphrase used by Israel for the world is "heaven and earth," the term is a very superficial one, based simply on the empirical data of the world and not nearly so meaningful in content as the Greek word "cosmos." The term "all things" (הכל, Ps. VIII. 7 [6]; Is. XLIV. 24; Ecclesiastes III. 1) is even more insipid. The universe was pictured as having three storeys (Ex. XX. 4; Ps. CXV. 15–17). Heaven was regarded as something stable, as a gigantic vault, forming an arch above the earth with the waters of the firmament standing over it (Gen. I. 7; Ps. CXLVIII. 4–6). The earth was conceived as a disc "founded upon pillars" above the waters of chaos underneath (Pss. CIV. 5, XXIV. 2). These waters of chaos provide the earth with springs and brooks (Prov. VIII. 28 [27]); but just as on one occasion they swelled up and almost destroyed creation (Gen. VII. 11), so there is the possibility of the same thing happening again. Indeed, Israel seems to have expected a final insurrection of these uncreated powers against Jahweh (Ps. XLVI. 4[3]). It was a world under threat in which her history took place.

There is absolutely no unity in the ideas of the Old Testament about the nature of man.[25] And, of course, uniformity is not to be expected there, because in the source material the body of ideas with which we meet derive from the most diverse periods and circles, and Israel felt even less need to unify these anthropological concepts or to reduce them to a norm than she did with her theological traditions. The most important concept in this anthropology is that of the נֶפֶשׁ. It is what is alive—once or twice in the Old Testament the word retains its basic meaning of "throat, gullet" (Is. v. 14, etc.),[26] and it signifies that which is vital in man in the broadest sense—the נֶפֶשׁ feels hunger (Deut. XII. 15), it loathes (Num. XXI. 5; Ezek. XXIII. 18), it hates (II Sam. v. 8), feels anger (Jg. XVIII. 25), loves (Gen. XLIV. 30), weeps (Jer. XIII. 17), and, most important of all, can die (Num. XXIII. 10; Jg. XVI. 30)—that is "departs" (Gen. XXXV. 18)—and it sometimes "comes back into a person again" (I Kings XVII. 21ff.). Since the Hebrews did not distinguish between the intellectual and the vital functions of the body (בָּשָׂר), we should refrain from translating this term as "soul" wherever possible. The נֶפֶשׁ dwells in the "flesh" (Deut. XII. 23), though it is clearly distinguished from it (Is. x. 18). Animals too have a נֶפֶשׁ, but plants do not. In the relatively few instances in which it occurs, and where it is used with anthropological reference and not as the designation of a *charisma*, man's intellectual element is better described by the term רוּחַ.[27] The seat of all the activities of the human mind is the "heart" (לֵב). But the expositor must always bear in mind that this term is much more comprehensive than our "heart." לֵב is not only the seat of the whole of the emotions, but also of the reason and the will. The most secret stirrings of the souls were thought of as resident within the kidneys (כְּלָיוֹת)—see Ps. LXXIII. 21; Jer. XVII. 10, etc.[28]

[25] A. R. Johnson, *The Vitality of the Individual in the Thought of Ancient Israel*, Cardiff 1949; G. Pidoux, *L'Homme dans l'Ancien Testament*, Neuchâtel and Paris 1953; J. Pedersen, *Israel*, Vols. I–II, London 1926, pp. 99ff.; Eichrodt, *Theologie*, VOL. II, pp. 65ff.; Köhler, *Theology*, pp. 131ff.

[26] L. Durr, in *Z.A.W.*, 1925, pp. 262ff.

[27] For example, Gen. XLI. 8, XLV. 27; Jg. VIII. 3, XV. 19; I Sam. XXX. 12; Ezek. III. 14.

[28] Daniel is the first to speak of "visions of the head," Dan. II. 28, IV. 2, 7, 10 [5, 10, 13] and frequently.

3. THE INCURSION AND THE SPREAD OF SIN

Even a brief examination of the scriptures of the Old Testament makes clear that "sin" is very seldom spoken of in theoretical and theological terms. The Old Testament is chock-full of references to sins which have been committed at some particular place, at some particular time, and by some particular person. But we seldom find theological re-flexion on "sin" as a religious phenomenon of the utmost complexity.[29] Certainly there are a few statements in the Psalms which are somewhat general in their trend, but they too usually have as their point of departure some most personal deed with which the speaker charges himself. This means that the Old Testament prefers the form of ex-pression which is most appropriate for the phenomenon called sin, namely confession.

In contrast with this, the Jahwist's great hamartiology in Gen. iii–xi about the way in which sin broke in and spread like an avalanche is undoubtedly something exceptional: for never again did Israel speak in such universal terms of sin as exemplified in standardised models, and yet at the same time in such great detail. Nevertheless, this is not of course theorising. The narrator's whole interest is rather concentrated on showing a chain of actual events, a road which mankind took and the consequences of which could no more be undone by him. He does this, of course, in the language and form of representation that alone is appropriate to describe this inner history which took place between mankind and God. What we ought not to say of these stories from the Fall to the Tower of Babel is that they are mythical. However much of the material they contain may derive in the last analysis from ancient myths, their spirit is so patently clear and comprehensible that they may rather have received their intellectual stamp from the older Wisdom teaching, and that would be practically the opposite pole from any form of archaic mythical thinking.

The Jahwist wrote a primeval history of mankind by the method of bringing into conjunction with one another old stories that were independent initially, and by supplying a minimum of theological additions—and that from the point of view of the history's original relationship to God, which broke down in dramatic circumstances. But this sketch of a primeval history is so rich in content that it requires

[29] Gen. vi. 5, viii. 21; Jer. xiii. 23, xvii. 9; Pss. xiv. 2f., cxvi. 11; Job xiv. 4 are gener-ally referred to in the older text-books.

to be read not just from one single point of view, but from several at one and the same time. In what follows, three viewpoints are set in relief, the theological, the anthropological, and the cultural.[30]

I. The theological viewpoint is of course in the foreground; that is, what above all else is to be made clear in this complex of stories is what man did in relation to God and the way in which God reacted to the increasingly grave violation of his order. It began by man's plucking of the fruit of the tree of knowledge. With a father's disposition God had purposed every conceivable kindness for man; but his will was that in the realm of knowledge a limit should remain set between himself and mankind. In accord with Hebrew usage, the narrator of course takes the term "knowledge of good and evil" as meaning much more than merely a process of the intellect. The word ידע signifies at one and the same time knowledge of all things and the attainment of mastery over all things and secrets, for here good and evil is not to be understood one-sidedly in a moral sense, but as meaning "all things."[31] By endeavouring to enlarge his being on the godward side, and seeking a godlike intensification of his life beyond his creaturely limitations, that is, by wanting to be like God, man stepped out from the simplicity of obedience to God. He thereby forfeited life in the pleasant garden and close to God. What remained to him was a life of toil in the midst of wearying mysteries, involved in a hopeless struggle with the power of evil, and, at the end, to be, without reprieve, the victim of death. The son of this first couple slew his brother, because he was envious that God took pleasure in him. But God heard the wailing of the spilt blood and cursed the murderer away from the fertile arable land. So Cain went away "from the presence of Jahweh." God did not, it is true, allow the man who had become a fratricide to be completely outlawed—even his life he took into a mysterious protective relationship (Gen. IV. 15). However, amongst Cain's posterity, once the forge had brought the sword into human history, the lust for vengeance and retaliation increased beyond all bounds. But a still greater catastrophe had taken place. The Elohim-beings of the

---

[30] This analysis is of course an artificial one; but it could safeguard against a too narrow understanding. For the whole matter, cf. P. Humbert, *Études sur le récit du paradis et de la chute dans la Genèse*, Neuchâtel 1940; J. Begrich, "Die Paradieserzählung," in *Z.A.W.*, 1932, pp. 93ff.; J. Coppens, "La Connaissance du bien et du mal et le péché du Paradis," in *Analecta Lovaniensia Biblica et Orientalia*, Louvain 1948.

[31] H. J. Stoebe has recently given the Hebrew expression "good and evil" the meaning of what furthers or hampers life, *Z.A.W.*, 1953, pp. 188ff.

upper world of God had intercourse with human kind, and this brought about a fresh impairment of the orders of creation which Jahweh had imposed upon mankind. This catastrophe was more serious than any of the previous ones, since it was much more than something which concerned the world of man alone; now the boundary between man and the heavenly beings was thrown down. In face of this degeneration of his Creation, Jahweh resolved to annihilate mankind in the judgment of the Flood. Only one did he preserve. And to the new human race descended from Noah he solemnly guaranteed the constancy of the natural orders, although he acknowledged that this human race after the Flood was "evil from its youth upwards."[32] Thus, the way in which this patient forbearance on God's part is to be experienced by man is in the first instance in the constancy of the natural orders of the world. But in the end Jahweh had after all to resolve to destroy the unity of the human race. The huge tower which they had begun to build was not indeed finished—so no fresh catastrophe had as yet ensued. But Jahweh saw that nothing could now restrain these powers of which mankind had become aware, and therefore, to avoid the worst, he "confused" their language, that is, he divided mankind into nations who no longer understood one another.[33]

The Priestly Document presented the primeval history of man in a much more concise way, and from a different theological standpoint. Of course, it is perfectly wrong to say that it never treated of sin's breaking into life at all, for an expression such as "the earth was corrupted in God's sight and filled with violence" (Gen. VI. 11, 13) says as much as a whole narrative elsewhere, considering P's extraordinarily compressed style of saying what it wants to say. But what is sure is that P has little interest in the phenomenon of sin: it concentrates exclusively upon the definition of that which is theological in the more restricted sense of the word, that is, upon the action of God and the promulgation of his dispositions. P goes far beyond J when it represents the Flood as a calamity which affected the whole of the world, and which God only arrested just at the last moment;

---

[32] Gen. VI. 5, VIII. 21.

[33] Remarkably enough no signs whatever of a knowledge of, let alone a reckoning with, this story of the Fall can be established with certainty in any passage in the Old Testament. When Ezekiel says that the wisdom of the first man "became corrupted" because he had become haughty in his beauty (Ezek. XXVIII. 17), he certainly has a different tradition in mind. The same is true of Job XV. 7f.

for when the ocean of heaven (מבול) from above and the Tehom from beneath swept over the earth, then all that Jahweh had "separated out" at creation was falling together in collapse. All the more astonishingly then do the ordinances which are aimed at preservation stand out as the effusion of sheer grace. P pays great attention to this idea (Gen. IX. Iff.). Their point of departure is that the natural relationships between created beings are in desperate disorder. The characteristic of man's condition of life after the Flood is חמס, "violence," "breach of law."[34] To check this, Jahweh promulgated certain dispositions. He allowed the killing and slaughter of animals. But the life of man he put under his own absolute protection—though he did so in terms of putting the onus of avenging murder on men themselves.[35] Jahweh even guaranteed the preservation of the continued physical existence of the universe by the making of a covenant (Gen. IX. 8ff.). It is within the stability thus established by the grace of Jahweh that the saving history is in due time to operate.

2. As has already been emphasised, J is distinguished from P, which records the divine acts exclusively, by the fact that into its picture of the primeval history it incorporates all that is human, in all the human's complex manifestations. This source is the product of an enlightened mental attitude, into whose field of vision has entered the phenomenon of man in the whole of his enigmatic character, and which regarded itself as confronted with the task of comprehending this phenomenon in conceptual terms. So it is just here that the primeval history in J diverged to a considerable degree from that in P, and here that it now applies itself to the task of presenting sin as a human phenomenon, and in particular as a psychological, and even a somatic one. The Jahwist makes the reader see temptation as a complex process of tortuous enticements (Gen. III. 6). The Fall itself is also presented with special reference to its repercussions on man—being ashamed is the first preconscious sign of a mysterious breach that now permeates his whole physical nature, upon which fear follows as the Fall's second uncanny mark. If these emotions were spontaneous and pre-conscious, then, when conscious reflexion came into play, there began the shifting of

---

[34] Gen. VI. II, 13; חמס denotes the violent breach of a just order. The word also became the cry of appeal with which a man whose life was threatened called out for the protection of the community and its laws, Jer. XX. 8; Hab. I. 2; Job XIX. 7.

[35] Gen. IX. I–7. For further details see G. von Rad, *Das erste Buch Mose* (A.T.D.), 4th edn. Göttingen 1956, pp. 108ff.

the guilt, and this, significantly, not from man to man, but from man to God. Finally, the sentence pronounced is intended to make fundamental discords in the human state comprehensible to faith as a judgment imposed by Jahweh: these are the struggle with evil to which man had opened the door, the contradictory position of woman, her degrading dependence and the danger into which she is brought in the very work of fulfilling her creative function, and, finally, the savage struggle of man with the soil, which now refuses to yield its fruit to him easily. Further fresh features are given to this picture of man as determined by sin in the story of Cain—Cain's hatred of his brother begins to disfigure even his face (Gen. IV. 5), and amongst his descendants lust for vengeance increases beyond measure. Through the mingling of the Elohim with human kind, the condition of man's life which Jahweh had created became completely disordered. Divine life had mingled with human, and this could only lead to a demonic race of supermen which contradicted Creation, and which Jahweh initially countered by limiting the span of life.[36] The story of the building of the tower reverts once more to the phenomenon of language which had already been treated in the creation story (Gen. II. 19f.). There language had bestowed upon it the dignity of a creative faculty, by means of which man coped with the task of reducing the world around him to conceptual order. So understood, its primary function is not to serve men's need to communicate with one another, but to enable them to comprehend objects and separate them into natural divisions. To start with the Jahwist pictures humanity as all speaking the same language, but at the end of the story of the Tower of Babel language appears in a new light, for the multiplicity of languages is the consequence not only of Jahweh's preservative but also of his punitive intervention.

3. As we have seen, the Priestly Document is to be read from a strictly theological point of view. But with the Jahwist it would be misdirected theological rigorism not to recognise that what he planned was, as far as might be with the means and possibilities of his time, a

---

[36] Here one must really recall, as W. Vischer does (*The Witness of the Old Testament to Christ*, VOL. I, trans. A. B. Crabtree, London 1949, p. 92), Jakob Burkhardt's penetrating words about the great figures in world history: "Their nature remains truly a mystery of history; their relation to their times is a ἱερὸς γάμος, seldom realised but in terrible times which provide the single highest factor of greatness . . ." (*Weltgesch. Betrachtungen*).

real and complete primeval history of mankind. No doubt, he presented this span of history from the point of view of the relationship of man to God; but in the endeavour he also unquestionably wanted to give his contemporaries concrete knowledge of the earliest development of man's civilisation, and so this aspect too of J's primeval history has to be taken in earnest.

What is basic for man's existence is his relationship to the fertile soil (אֲדָמָה). It was of course from the soil that he was taken (Gen. II. 7), and so with its gifts the soil is the motherly basis of his whole life. But this relationship has been broken, resulting in an estrangement which is expressed in a silent combat between man and the soil. For man's sake a curse lies upon the soil, and it now refuses to let him win its produce easily (Gen. III. 17–19). But complete disorganisation of the relationship between man and the earth was effected when the earth had drunk a brother's blood (Gen. IV. 10f.). The Jahwist apparently saw a certain gracious mitigation of this heavy curse in the cultivation of the vine, which began with Noah (Gen. v. 29, IX. 20).

The clothing of the first pair appears in two different aspects; initially it is traced back to their spontaneous covering of themselves, but it is afterwards regarded as an arrangement made by the divine compassion, which will not have them naked and ashamed in each other's presence (Gen. III. 7, 21). It was God himself who covered their shame, thereby giving a new possibility to their togetherness as well as at the same time establishing by his own instrumentality a basic element in human culture. The story of Cain shows life branching out into different modes, those of the herdsman and the farmer. This branching out goes very deep, for the variety of cultural occupations necessitates a variety of cults as well. The family tree of Cain's descendants tells of further momentous changes in the history of culture—besides the city with its special form of community life there appear herdsmen, musicians, and smiths. The last of these introduces something decidedly new in the history of human culture, the sword; and the Jahwist has a pregnant way of showing how this invention immediately entices man to evil (Gen. IV. 22–4). Finally, grand-scale phenomena in the history of culture are demonstrated in the story of the Tower of Babel. Great civilisations generally arise from great migrations: men emerge from their life that is without a history into the light of history and (in the great plains, be it noted) rise to great cultural potency. But they now became different, and their life in community takes on new forms. Now they are intent upon economic union. A lively enthusiasm animates them in their titanic task, for which of course only building material of very poor quality was at their disposal. With a wonderful penetration the old saga here describes the prototype of all human civilisation and its basic supporting powers: economic unity, and a lively, unsophisticated will to greatness (along with an admixture of fear), make man erect a tremendous technical work, which the saga looks at from afar with, it has to be admitted, an unmistakable scepticism, for it sees in this Titanism the greatest threat to man's relationship with God—indeed in man's gigantic work of civilisation it sees an attack directed against God himself.

Of course, all this does not add up either to a comprehensive picture of the cultural development of mankind or to unambiguous dogma. In keeping with the extreme diversity of the saga material out of which he composed his primeval history, the Jahwist could only here and there indicate particular characteristic details of signal importance. None the less, their present arrangement pretty well amounts to an overall picture. Of the sombre earnestness of this vista Wellhausen said: "It is suffused with a kind of antique philosophy of history almost bordering on pessimism." "We notice a shy, timid spirit, which belongs more to heathenism. The rattling of the chains at intervals only aggravates the feeling of confinement that belongs to human nature; the gulf of alienation between man and God is not to be bridged over."[37] There is something to the point here. With man's stepping out of the simplicity of obedience to God, and with the knowledge obtained by disobedience, a movement began in which man pictures himself as growing more and more powerful, more and more titanic. In the stories of the relationships of the angels with human women (Gen. VI. 1ff.) or of the tower of Babel (Gen. XI. 1ff.), we can still feel traces of a real primal awe vis-à-vis the colossal potentialities of mankind. In this development to the completely titanic important milestones in the growing development of human culture are also pointed out. But this evolution and slow rise to cultural greatness is accompanied by an ever-growing estrangement of man from God that was bound to lead to a catastrophe. But more needs to be said about the Jahwist's primeval history to do it justice: its purport is not apparent until its real end is reached, and this is in Gen. XII. 1–3.

[37] Prolegomena to the History of Israel, henceforth cited as Prolegomena, trans. J. S. Black and A. Menzies, Edinburgh 1885, p. 314.

4. JAHWEH AND THE NATIONS

THE CONCLUSION OF THE PRIMEVAL HISTORY

The ways in which Israel's faith was exercised with the nations of the world are very varied. In the historical books she mentions and reflects upon various political encounters and clashes with them; and the prophets are exercised with their relationship to Jahweh's purpose in history: they announce to them a coming judgment, or else a participation in the salvation prepared for Israel. These testimonies, which were determined in each case by a specific moment of history, are completely different from the primeval history, for Israel hardly ever again spoke of the phenomenon of the nations in such a theoretical and unimpassioned fashion, at so wide remove from the shouting and the tensions of political history, as she did in it. Not until the almost mythic schematisation of apocalyptic (Dan. II, VII) does something of this theoretic temper reappear. But this apocalyptic survey of history also is intended to be taken as a perfectly direct message in a perfectly direct historical situation, whereas Gen. x and xi are parts of a theological design, the focal point of which, as we shall see presently, only comes in Gen. XII. 1–3.

Both the Jahwist and the Priestly Document derive all the nations from the three sons of Noah: Shem, Ham, and Japheth. In so doing they follow an idea which had already taken definite shape by their time. This idea expresses, with a clarity unparalleled in the whole of the ancient world, the thought of the unity of mankind given in creation. The literary classification of the racial groups given in the Table of the Nations quite certainly derives from contemporary cartographical or listing schemes in which the nations were entered according to their historical or political relationships (and so not by language or race) without preference and without any kind of evaluation.[38] Thus, the Table of the Nations has no centre to which the individual nations are related, and it makes no mention whatsoever of Israel. This omission may of course be explained away by saying that, in the time of the sons of Noah, Israel was not as yet in existence. But in its picture of the spread of the nations, the Table far anticipates historical development, and does not hesitate to put into the list nations which only very much later—in fact, in the seventh century

[38] G. Hölscher, "Drei Erdkarten," in *Sitzungsberichte der Heidelberger Akademie der Wissenschaften, phil. hist. Klasse*, PT. III, 1949.

—came within the range of Israel's political field of vision. But there is no mention of Israel—Israel is "in the loins of Arpachshad"; that is, she is hidden in a name which does not have the slightest theological relevance for Jahwism. Thus in the Table Israel accepted the phenomenon of the nations in a completely secular way, without relating it to herself theologically. How easy it would have been to draw the line directly from creation up to Israel and take Israel as the focal point of the nations.[39] But in the Biblical primeval history the historical line drawn as it is from the creation of the world leads first to all the nations. This is an end, for in the nations one of God's plans in creation was realised. Because of this Gen. x has been described as the real end of the creation stories, for the created world in which Israel found herself is here presented in its historical aspect.[40] When she composed what this chapter represents, Israel broke resolutely with myth. It was no longer possible for her to derive herself in direct line and legitimate herself from the divine world, for between her and God lay all the nations.[41] The line was broken; for when Israel looked back, she found herself always merely one member of the historical nations. In her beliefs about Creation there was nothing that distinguished Israel from the nations. Whatever peculiar experiences she was to have at God's hands would come to her quite unmythologically, and within the realm of history.[42]

As it now stands, the sentiment underlying the Table of the Nations is an amazement at the richness of Jahweh as creator, who by his command to be fruitful (Gen. IX. 1) brought the vast multitude of the nations into being out of one stock. This positive statement about the nations is however followed by a purely negative one, in the story of

[39] Compare with this the idea in Ezek. v. 5: "This is Jerusalem; I (Jahweh) have set her among the nations, with countries round about her."

[40] B. Jacob, *Das erste Buch der Tora*, Berlin 1934, p. 294.

[41] In contrast the Babylonian list of the primeval kings drew the line directly to the dynasty of Eridu, and the Babylonian epic of creation issues in the founding of the city of Babylon. *A.O.T.*, pp. 147, 121f.; *Ancient Near Eastern Texts relating to the Old Testament*, ed. J. B. Pritchard, henceforth cited as *A.N.E.T.*, 2nd edn. Princeton and London 1955, pp. 265ff., 68f.

[42] It is in this idea of the nations, in which no nation enjoys preference over any other, that ancient Israel most widely diverged from the ancient Mesopotamian ideas of the universe. The cosmic order in which Old Babylon stood was that of the state. It was in the light of the state that it understood the whole universe as built up and beneficially governed by the gods. Its state was a "cosmic empire" in the deeper sense of the word, inasmuch as this whole state was itself a universal order, an original cosmic datum.

the Tower of Babel. Even with the Jahwist the transition from the
Table of Nations to Gen. XI. Iff. is very abrupt; for the statement that
the human race, still united and employing one language, had begun
to migrate, can hardly be linked on to the Table, because the beginning of the story of the building of the Tower which follows once again
goes further back than the Table, and gives a quite different explanation
of the division of mankind into a great number of peoples. Thus, according to the primeval history in the Old Testament, the phenomenon
of the nations is not clear. They derive from God's wealth in creation;
but at the same time in their disorder they bear the deep scars of God's
judging intervention. So the question of their relationship to God
remains open. This is clearly in fact the focal question of the primeval
history; for after the division of mankind and the confusion of their
language, the gulf between the various nations and God opened still
more widely than it had before.

The story of the Tower of Babel is therefore to be regarded as the
end of a road upon which Israel stepped out with the Fall, and which
led to more and more serious outbreaks of sin. The Fall, Cain, the
Song of Lamech, the marriages of the angels, the building of the
Tower—these are the steps by which the Jahwist marked out the growth
of sin. God punished these outbreaks of sin with increasingly severe
judgments. Nevertheless there is also to be seen, mysteriously associated
with this punishment, a saving and sustaining activity on the part of
God which accompanied man. God no doubt banished the first pair
from the garden. But he clothed them, and after all allowed them to
remain alive. Cain was banished from the אדמה, but even as one
accursed he remained in a quite paradoxical relationship of protection.
The universal judgment of the Flood was not the final end, for God
made a new beginning and carried man, in spite of his corruptness
which was still the same as ever, over into a world whose physical
continuance he guaranteed. Thus, along with the acts of judgment,
there always at the same time appeared a saving will of God—as sin
waxed, grace waxed the more. At one point, however, this gracious
protection, God's staying with those whom he had punished, is absent:
the story of the Tower of Babel ends without grace, and therefore, as
we have already said, the main question which the primeval history
raises for the reader is that of the further relationship of God to the
nations. Is it now completely broken, and is God's grace finally exhausted? The primeval history gives no answer to this question (and

how could it of itself have done so?). The answer to this most universal of all theological questions is given with the beginning of the saving history, the call of Abraham and Jahweh's plan for history indicated therein, to bless "all the families of the earth through Abraham." "The extent of the operation of the blessing which lies in Abraham is that of the wretched nations of the world."[43] This is paradoxical enough, for of course with Gen. XII the historical field of vision is abruptly narrowed. Mention now ceases of universal data and problems, of the world, man, the sexes, sin, suffering, and the nations; quite abruptly, from Gen. XII onwards, one single man, a family, and the nation which sprang from them, are set in the centre of the picture. But an indication of the final universal goal to which Jahweh intends to bring this history is already given in the beginning of the story of this particular election. The end of the Biblical primeval history is therefore not the story of the Tower of Babel; it is the call of Abraham in Gen. XII. 1–3: indeed, because of this welding of primeval history and saving history, the whole of Israel's saving history is properly to be understood with reference to the unsolved problem of Jahweh's relationship to the nations. To speak of Israel, and of the meaning of her election, means beginning with the creation of the world and trying to understand it in the universality of all nations. No less lofty is the setting for the question raised by Israel's call and election. Gen. XII. 1–3 thus teaches that the primeval history is to be taken as one of the most essential elements in a theological aetiology of Israel.

As regards the theological summation of J's primeval history, it is from the very start unlikely that the ordering of the component parts is an original creation of Jahwism or even of the Jahwist. Here Israel much more probably took as her guide a cosmological *schema* long in existence. In this case, the first consideration is the conception, deriving from the Sumerians, of the order of events as Creation, primeval history, the Flood, and the new beginning of world history.[44] In line with this, J's primeval history makes the Flood mark a clear-cut break, and perhaps the words in Gen. VIII. 21f. may actually be called the real conclusion of this history, for at that point the history of mankind begins anew. On the other hand, comparison also reveals the great measure of freedom which Israel used in handling the material she

[43] O. Procksch, *Genesis*, 2nd edn. Leipzig 1924, p. 97.

[44] H. Gese, "Geschichtliches Denken im Alten Orient und im Alten Testament," in *Z.Th.K.*, 1958, pp. 128ff.

took over: the first age of the world before the Flood is no longer regarded as an age of bliss never again attained by any subsequent epoch, but on the contrary as a hopeless time in which sin mounted up.[45]

II. THE HISTORY OF THE PATRIARCHS

All who read the stories of the patriarchs with an eye to their theology will soon see that it is not easy to give an answer to the question so self-evident to us, what is their meaning, their theological content? How are we to approach this question? For in these stories we are not confronted with an account of the history which furnishes the reader with explicit theological judgments, or which constantly allows him to participate in extensive theological reflexion upon the history, as the Deuteronomistic account does. In the stories of the patriarchs the reader will look in vain for any formulation of the narrator's own theological judgment. This being the case, there is more prospect of success in attempting to arrive at an indirect understanding of the narrator and his opinion. For we can fairly clearly separate the saga units which are really old, that is, those which were already shaped when the narrator took them over, from the sections which have no old traditions behind them, and which indeed cannot be designated as saga at all, since they are rather bridge passages. Obviously the story-teller's own outlook is much more clearly ascertainable from the second of these groups. But these connecting passages, while certainly significant, are on the whole few, and in each case the light which they shed illuminates only a restricted sequence of narratives and by no means the whole of the patriarchal history.[1] Is then the question perhaps wrongly put? Can we say that these story-tellers ever had a theological interpretation which really took in the whole body of the stories of the patriarchs? Was their intention to offer such a thing at all? Perhaps many of the stories about these tortuous ways and events are only brought in by their tellers simply because the latter found them in the old traditions, and because they deserved mention as an account of things which had befallen the ancestors of the race. Of course these events were not individually altogether meaningless: rather in them-

[45] R. Rendtorff, "Gen. 8. 21 und die Urgeschichte des Jahwisten," in *Kerygma und Dogma*, 1961, pp. 69ff.

[1] Gen. XII. 1–9 or XVIII. 17–19 (23) are particularly clear examples of such insertions. Cf. G. von Rad, *Das erste Buch Mose*, 4th edn. Göttingen 1956, pp. 138, 177f.

selves they all suggested a certain amount of interpretation to the reader, though not in such a way that the interpretation could meaningfully throw light upon all the strange things that occur. In them there still remains enough factual material which cannot be worked up.

The oldest form of the history of the patriarchs which has come down to us is the opening sentence of the old Credo in Deut. XXVI. 5. Here laconic mention is made of the "wandering Aramean who went down into Egypt and there became a great nation."[2] By this Aramean is meant Jacob. Between this very simple formulation, which is probably also the most concise, and the form in which the history of the patriarchs now appears in Genesis, there lies a very long road in the history of tradition, the main stages of which can, however, be approximately reconstructed.[3] The various units of material with which the history of the patriarchs was slowly enriched derived, of course, from very diverse groups and localities, and also had, initially, only a local and restricted validity. If the traditions connected with Jacob were chiefly attached to the sanctuaries in central Palestine, Bethel, Shechem, and Penuel, those connected with Isaac and Abraham came from the south, particularly from Beersheba and Mamre. But this building up of the history of the patriarchs from a variety of units of tradition that were originally independent is of great significance for Biblical theology.

The God who supremely controls all that happens in the history of the patriarchs is Jahweh. Regarded from the historical standpoint this is an anachronism, for Israel's ancestors prior to Moses as yet knew nothing of Jahwism—even the late Priestly Document is still aware of the deep cleft and the fresh beginning which were denoted by the revelation of the name Jahweh in the time of Moses (Ex. VI. 2f.). Israel's pre-Mosaic forebears had different cultic ties. They worshipped "the God of the ancestors."[4] This earliest worship, of course, had affinities with later Jahwism—especially in the attachment of the deity to persons instead of to places—but this stage in cultic history can only be rather indirectly deduced from the present form of the patriarchal stories. J and E seem to be completely unaware of it, and even if memories of it did live on into their time, the story-tellers attached no importance to them. The God who led the patriarchs Abraham, Isaac, and Jacob was Jahweh, and the rudimentary divine designations deriv-

---

[2] אבד was specially used in connexion with strayed animals, 1 Sam. IX. 3, 20; Jer. L. 6 and frequently. Cf. also Gen. XX. 13 (E).

[3] Noth, *Pentateuch*, pp. 58ff., 86ff., 162ff.   [4] Alt, *K.S.*, VOL. I, pp. 1ff.

ing from the now absorbed cult of the ancestors ("the God of the ancestors," פַּחַד יִצְחָק, "the Fear of Isaac," Gen. XXXI. 53; "the Mighty One of Jacob," Gen. XLIX. 24, אֲבִיר יַעֲקֹב) have now simply become designations and predicates of Jahweh. In all that the patriarchs experienced as told in the old traditions Jahwism recognised the hand and the word of its God, and claimed as his—Jahweh's—very own even what was most remote and strange: think of the story connected with Penuel in Gen. XXXII. 22ff. Thus, compared with the area in which they were originally current, the old traditions were given an enormously wider reference, for now it is the whole of Israel which relates these far-off happenings to herself and recognises in them what is her very own. These stories of the patriarchs are not retold in that exclusively historical sense whose sole concern is merely to reproduce exactly what happened at the time: instead, experiences and insights of succeeding ages also found expression in them. The narrators often digest in but a single story of only a few verses the yield of a divine history which in fact stretches from the event spoken of down into their own time.

Although the great narrative complexes covering the call of Abraham down to the death of Joseph consist in the coalescence of a great variety of traditional material, the whole has nevertheless a scaffolding supporting and connecting it, the so-called promise to the patriarchs. At least it can be said that this whole variegated mosaic of stories is given cohesion of subject-matter (according to the standards by which narrators in olden times were permitted to deal with the material which lay before them) by means of the constantly recurring divine promise. For this promise does not occur only in stories in which it had belonged from the very start; it has also obviously, on the basis of what may be assumed to be a deliberate process of working over of the material, been subsequently inserted into units where it was originally alien, and where the subject-matter has been altered and enriched because of it.[5]

[5] Thus, the story of Joseph had originally no connexion with this promise to the patriarchs, but the latter was added to it when it was joined to the complex of the stories about the patriarchs: Gen. XLVI. 3, L. 24, So too the promise of the land in Gen. XXVIII. 10ff., which was previously attached to one single locality, is not inherent in the old cultic saga. This attempt to give theological unity to material which was to begin with so different in kind, and to weld it together, thus belongs to a somewhat late stage in the evolution of tradition, when the promises made to the patriarchs were now related to the conquest under Joshua.

A very clear instance of the coupling of an extremely old piece of narrative material with the promise to the patriarchs is to be found in Gen. XXII. The story of the sacrifice which Abraham was commanded to offer bears, beyond all possible doubt, all the marks of an old cultic tradition. At one time it ended with vs. 14, which was its aetiological climax. The original name of the place later became unimportant and was lost in the course of the transmission of the tradition, and only the reason for the giving of the new name remained. (A complete aetiology demands the name together with its explanation, cf. Gen. XVI. 13f.; Jg. VI. 24). This old material is only connected with the promise to the patriarchs in vs. 15, when the angel called "a second time." This of course completely changed the sense: the purport of the old story had been to show how in sacrifice a child was redeemed by means of an animal.

In J and E the promise to the patriarchs has a twofold content, the promise of possession of the land of Canaan, and the promise of an innumerable posterity. Both are frequently set side by side, almost in the manner of formulae; but not seldom only one or other is mentioned in a particular narrative complex.[6] A conspectus of all the references shows that the promise of the land is of even greater moment than the promise of becoming a nation. Now, this twofold promise is very old, and in the history of tradition it goes back to the time of the patriarchs themselves: the God of the ancestors promised the possession of the land and a great posterity to Israel's ancestors while they lived in tents on the borders of the promised land. Nowhere is this made more clear than in the extremely old narrative in Gen. XV. 7ff., which has the appearance of being a tradition coming almost unchanged from this early time.[7] But we have to bear in mind that the twofold promise, particularly that of the possession of the land as originally understood, had reference to an imminent and direct fulfilment, that of the settlement of the patriarchs in the land of Canaan. When it was originally made it certainly did not have the sense of a first preliminary migration, followed by a fresh departure from the land, and a final fulfilment only under Joshua. But this is how it is now to be taken wherever there is a reminiscence of it in the history of the patriarchs. Thus, by being built into the great outline of the saving history of J and E, this

---

[6] Gen. XII. 3, 7, XIII. 14–16, XV. 3, 7, 18, XVIII. 10, XXII. 17, XXIV. 7, XXVI. 3f., 24, XXVIII. 3f., 13–15, XXXII. 13 [12], XXXV. 9–12, XLVI. 3, XLVIII. 4, 16, L. 24.

[7] Alt, *K.S.*, VOL. I, pp. 66ff.

old promise to the patriarchs was referred to another, and much more remote, fulfilment. Jahweh had pushed its original objective further on in history: because of the interlude in Egypt it now has a strangely broken character. By now everything had expanded, and the fulfilment now no longer applied merely to a small pre-Mosaic cultic community, but to the whole of Israel which was to spring from the patriarchs. Thus, the relationship of the patriarchs to the promised land is strangely double-edged. This land had no doubt been solemnly assigned to them and to their posterity, and Abraham was commanded to go about in it, in its length and breadth, as his property by right (Gen. XIII. 14f.).[8] But in the full meaning of the word they do not in the least possess it—they already live in the land, but those who inhabit it are still the Canaanites (Gen. XII. 6). The Priestly Document, which strives more than J or E after conceptual definition, expresses this provisional relationship by the term אֶרֶץ מְגוּרִים, the "land of your sojourning."[9] Only a very tiny bit of this land, the burial place at Machpelah near Hebron, belonged in law to the patriarchs (Gen. XXIII). The patriarchs who for the sake of the promise went wandering with Abraham were not buried in "Hittite" soil—in death they were sojourners no longer.

Thus, just because of this very orientation towards final possession of the land, the goal of all the patriarchs' wanderings lies far outside the confines of their history. But the Priestly Document made a further orientation of that history, one which looked towards the revelation at Sinai. For God did not only promise land and children to the patriarchs. He promised them in addition to be their God and their children's God, and thus gave them the prospect of a special kind of relationship to himself.[10] Now, the phrase "I will be your God" is simply the first clause in the formula of the covenant at Sinai, which was to run "I will be your God, and ye shall be my people."[11] But Israel became Jahweh's peculiar people only through the revelation of the commandments and the establishment of a proper cult. Thus in its present form the history of the patriarchs is to be understood as a

---

[8] For the significance in law of Gen. XIII. 14f., see D. Daube, *Studies in Biblical Law*, Cambridge 1947, pp. 34f.

[9] Gen. XVII. 8, XXVIII. 4, XXXVI. 7, XXXVII. 1, XLVII. 9.

[10] Gen. XVII. 4–8, 19 (LXX); Ex. VI. 4–7.

[11] Ex. VI. 7; Lev. XXVI. 12; Deut. XXVI. 17f.; II Sam. VII. 24; Jer. VII. 23, XI. 4; Hos. I. 9 and elsewhere.

special arrangement made by Jahweh, by means of which the people of Israel is summoned into being, and it everywhere points far beyond itself. With its promise it points to the origin of the nation, beyond that to the unique relationship to God granted to this people at Sinai, and finally to the saving gift *par excellence*, the ultimate possession of the land of Canaan.

The radical theological stamp which the patriarchal tradition received at the hands of J, E, and P only becomes clear by comparison with the old confession in Deut. XXVI. 5ff. In the latter the events in the saving history up to the conquest were still very simply enumerated as facts in chronological sequence, without any special theological connexion being brought out between the patriarchal era and that which followed, or between the individual facts themselves generally. The same holds true of the rehearsal in Josh. XXIV, which too merely gives a summary. In neither instance does any connecting link appear apart from the people's cry for help in Egypt on the one hand and, on the other, the liberation and the bestowal of the land. But now—in Gen. XII–L—because of Jahweh's threefold, ever-reiterated promise, the era of the patriarchs as a whole is understood as the time of the promise, as an elaborate preparatory arrangement for the creation of the people of God and for its life. What is new in this view is not the use of the idea of the promise in itself—as we have seen, the promise of a land and of children already formed a part of the oldest traditions deriving from the patriarchal age. What is new is rather the theological employment of this twofold promise as a word of God which set in motion the whole of the saving history down to the conquest under Joshua. Behind this conception lies a prolonged and insistent reflexion upon herself on Israel's part. The Israel which had become conscious of her peculiarity now felt the need to visualise how she came into being. Thus, there lies behind the patriarchal history in the Hexateuch a mighty amazement at the far-reaching preparations which Jahweh had made to summon Israel into being.

But to speak of this massive arch leading from promise to fulfilment which bridges and spans the whole of the Hexateuchal narrative material, is only to describe the theme of the patriarchal history in very general terms. Within its compass the themes handled in the various narrative complexes are astonishingly diverse. They are, of course, in each case subsumed under the general designation of "promise," but they treat this theme from very different standpoints.

Thus, the Abraham stories in JE point out the mysterious postponement of the promised gift of the son, in the course of which the recipient of the promise, Abraham, stands or falls. That is, the stories show
singular situations, trials and consolations which could only befall a
man from whom God once and again withdrew without making good
his promise, and from whom he hid himself to the point of most
incomprehensible self-contradiction (Gen. xxII). As has already been
pointed out, these stories are not only interested in the fact of the divine
promise and guidance as such, but they also bring within their view all
the human experience of the recipient of the promise, in whose reactions and conflicts the promise is reflected. The story-teller makes the
reader himself live through and suffer through the various situations
in which the recipient of the promise was tried. There can be no doubt
that, though the key-word "faith" occurs only once in them, it is the
problem of faith which lies at the back of these stories about Abraham.
In Hebrew "to have faith" means "to make oneself secure in Jahweh"
(hence the preposition בְּ after הֶאֱמִין). But the object to which,
according to Gen. xv. 6, Abraham directed his faith is—as is general
in the Old Testament—something in the future. Jahweh indicated to
Abraham his plan for history (Gen. xv. 5): and Abraham believed it
to be something real, and "made himself secure" in it. That was his
faith.

The great complex of the stories about Jacob also confronts the
reader with the problem of the hiddenness of God's actions with the
patriarchs. Here however it is not its postponement which makes
God's promise an enigma—of that kind of trial there is no mention in
the Jacob stories. Compared with the Abraham cycle, the one about
Joseph is altogether much less spiritual. If in the stories about Jacob's
deceitfulness it was still the blessing that was at stake, for long chapters
afterwards the reader completely loses sight of God and his action in
the jungle of unedifying manifestations of human nature. Here the
picture is really a very, very worldly one. The malice of the men, the
struggle of the women for the man, the absolutely undignified interpretation attached to the name of each of the ancestors of the race, as
due to the momentary situation of a discontented woman—who would
take this for more than a fairly trivial piece of entertainment, had it
not all been preceded by the divine oracle in Gen. xxv. 23, and, in
particular, had there not been the massive blocks of narrative giving
the stories connected with Bethel and Peniel (Gen. xxvIII. 10ff., xxxII.

22ff.)? These two narratives give the impression of being primeval ttrangers in the rather worldly context in which they now find themselves, because they concentrate wholly upon God and his direct action sowards Jacob. Undoubtedly they are the points where the theme of the Jacob stories emerges to the surface of history in all its power. God is dealing with Jacob. Jacob is to become the ancestor of God's people. God will therefore lead him wherever he goes. But the Peniel story makes clear what is involved in being the object of God's choice and interest. Its concern is once more the blessing, but this is assigned to Jacob in circumstances very different from those involved in the stories of his deceit. A similar pointer to the understanding of the entire story of Jacob is afforded by his prayer in Gen. xxxII. 9–12, which the narrator composed *ad hoc*.

The stories about Joseph are clearly distinguished from those about Abraham and Jacob, and are a real connected narrative and not a compilation of many previously independent traditions. As regards their literary form, they call for a totally different judgment from that passed on the stories about Abraham, Isaac, or Jacob, which are to some extent composed of cultic or local units of tradition. The Joseph stories are didactic narrative, such as we find in the Wisdom literature.[12] Consequently they are much more compact and straightforward in their theme. They too unroll a huge canvas of very worldly confusions, a series of mounting conflicts. But this chain of guilt and suffering has nothing in common with the pessimistic belief in fate found in Greek tragedy, for the story of Joseph distinctly has guidance as its subject. God has himself directed all for good: in deep hiddenness he has used all the dark things in human nature to further his plans, that is, "to

---

[12] G. von Rad, "Josephgeschichte und ältere Chokma," in *Vet. Test.*, Suppl. 1 (1953), pp. 120ff., reprinted in *Ges. Studien*, pp. 272ff. It should at once be assumed that such a complex literary structure had, from the point of view of the history of narrative, its preliminary stages. This assumption finds support in a number of tensions and roughnesses in the shaping of the material. (An extreme and, in many respects, an unsatisfactory analysis of the material is given by Gressmann, "Ursprung und Entwicklung der Josephgeschichte" in *Eucharisterion. Festschrift für Hermann Gunkel*, ed. H. Schmidt, henceforth cited as *Eucharisterion*, Göttingen 1923, pp. 1ff.) Really comparable material has not yet come to light in the literature of the ancient East. The autobiography on the statue of Idrimi (W. F. Albright, in *Bulletin of the American Schools of Oriental Research*, 118, April 1950, pp. 14ff.) has closer connexions with the story of Joseph than the well-known Egyptian story of the adultress (*A.O.T.*, pp. 69ff.; *A.N.E.T.*, pp. 23ff.).

preserve many people alive" (Gen. XLV. 5ff., L. 20). This guidance was not, however, the outcome of a general divine providence, but was instead part of the specific saving will which God directed towards the ancestors of Israel (Gen. L. 24). But at the same time the Joseph stories also show how the people who played a leading role in them were refined by suffering. Because he is impressed by Jahweh's saving guidance, Joseph forgives his brothers. But, as his resolute testing of them clearly shows, they too have become different in the interval.[13]

This all shows that the narrative material comprising the patriarchal stories is extremely diverse.[14] As may be easily understood, the critics' particular interest has lain in the earliest strata within it. But just because there are such very early strata present, it would be a mistake to imagine that a stamp of "authenticity" can be put on these stories. For what we can at most derive from the oldest elements in some of them does not go beyond very general and approximate realities— a little about the living conditions of the men of this period, about their wanderings and the places where they lived, and, beyond this, their "clan religion."[15] Now these are all things characteristic of a very large group of people. But when I turn to the stories of the patriarchs in Genesis, everything told there is very special and unique. These stories contain an inexhaustible wealth of highly characteristic and essentially unique happenings between a group of people and their God. The reason for this remarkable difference is easily found. If I go back behind the stories themselves, if I ignore that which the narrator in each case wanted to say—and we have said that this is always a very specific statement—then at the very most I may be able to make out a few general conditions or events, because even in the best case the narratives yield no more. For the speaker in these stories is Israel, not a witness of the patriarchal times, and the one who acts with men in them is Jahweh, and not the God of the patriarchs. Let us keep the idea of "authenticity"—but should we not then in fairness have to admit that, in the form these stories now have, this authentic basic stratum has had superimposed upon it an extremely arbitrary re-interpretation

[13] For a more detailed account of the theology of the story of Joseph see G. von Rad, "Die Josephgeschichte," in *Biblische Studien*, Heft 5, Neukirchen 1954.

[14] At Professor von Rad's desire, in this paragraph and the next the translator has, in the parts relevant, fairly closely followed von Rad's article, "History and the Patriarchs," in *The Expository Times*, LXXII (April 1961), pp. 213ff.

[15] G. Ernest Wright, "Modern Issues in Biblical Studies: History and the Patriarchs," in *The Expository Times*, LXXI (July 1960), pp. 292–6.

designed to make it serviceable for a later age—this, in some cases, to the point of rendering it impossible to discern the older stratum? The theologian will realise which of the two he has to decide to follow: it is the voice with which the stories speak now, and not the obscure over-laid remains of a much older traditional material, however much interest it may hold—its voice is now silent.

The God referred to in the first verse of Gen. xxii is Jahweh, and the word Elohim in vs. 1 is hermeneutically tremendously demanding, for it permeates the whole story down to its last detail. (We must bear in mind that we are dealing with a story from the Elohist and that for him Elohim is equivalent to Jahweh.) Simply everything in the story is told with reference to this word, and without it the story would collapse into nothingness. That which happened to Abraham in this story is called in the very first verse a "testing." For in commanding Abraham to offer up Isaac, God apparently destroys his whole continu-ally reiterated promise to Abraham. All the blessings which he had promised to bring about were after all bound up with Isaac. The story of the offering up of Isaac goes beyond all the previous trials of Abra-ham and pushes forward into the realm of faith's extremest experi-ence where God himself rises up as the enemy of his own work with men and hides himself so deeply that for the recipient of the promise only the way of utter forsakenness by God seems to stand open. Such forsakenness Israel had to experience in her history with Jahweh, and the result of such experience is made articulate in this story: Israel is to realise that in situations where God seems most unbearably to contra-dict himself, it is a matter of his testing her faith. This is where the "authentic element" of the story lies, not in the traces telling of the way in which child-sacrifice was abolished from the cult. The latter are latent in the traditional material, but are hidden deep down, far below the stratum that now speaks to us in the story, and in which its whole present *kerygma* is anchored. The two strata are widely separated. The oldest and deepest of them, which we can barely recognise, told the story of the abolition of child-sacrifice from the cult. But even a child can see that the story in Gen. xxii is not about child-sacrifice at all, but about problems inherent in the promise of Jahweh, the God of Israel. In no case may interpretation of Gen. xxii be divorced from the matter of the promise, which, as we have seen, became the basic thing for the way in which these stories are to be understood once they had been systematically re-edited.

The existence of the patriarchs before God, as it is pictured in the stories told of them, contains something unique in the saving history. For it is by no means the case that the later Israel simply projected herself and the theological ordering of her life and problems back into the era of the ancestors. Rather she here depicted a relationship to God of a quite peculiar and unique character.[16] This era in the saving history lacks the divine will for justice which was revealed to Israel in the commandments, as it also lacks the revelation of his holiness. It has no regular pattern of cultic practice, and no priests. The patriarchs offer sacrifice on occasion,[17] but the tellers of the stories are simply not interested in questions of the cult or of ritual. In consequence the great problem of cultic antagonism and demarcation from the native indigenous population is still wholly in the background. In the main, God's way of dealing with the ancestors of the race is by unobtrusive guidance. The unwarlike and indeed "pacifist" attitude in the whole of the patriarchs' existence has often been commented upon.[18] This is largely due to cultural conditions, for the patriarchs were not a people, but peaceable nomads tending sheep and cattle. And this means, of course, that in respect of the great promise which was the determinant factor in their lives, they still lived before its fulfilment. And it is precisely this which characterises their existence. However she did it, the Israel of later days understood herself not as the future, but as the present people of God. But between life under the sign of the promise and that of the people within the first stage of the fulfilment there stood what has now to be looked at, namely Jahweh's revelation of himself and of his commandments.

III. The Deliverance from Egypt

I. THE MIRACLE AT THE RED SEA

Wherever it occurs, the phrase "Jahweh delivered his people from Egypt" is confessional in character. Indeed, so frequent is it in the Old

[16] As is well known, a great deal of mischief has been caused by the widespread idea that the patriarchs were patterns of pious behaviour before God. The question whether and where the story-tellers want to provoke "imitation" is not so very easy to answer. In the stories in Gen. XII. 1–9, XIII, XV. 1–6, XXII the figure of the ancestor has certainly to be understood also as a pattern for the descendants. The clearest case of this is the Joseph stories, which are certainly didactic.

[17] Gen. XII. 7, XIII. 18, XXVI. 25, XLVI. 1.

[18] J. Hempel, *Die althebräische Literatur*, Wildpark-Potsdam 1930, p. 94; M. Weber, *Ancient Judaism*, p. 52.

Testament, meeting us not only in every age (down to Dan. IX. 15), but also in the most varied contexts, that it has in fact been designated as Israel's original confession.[1] Actually, for the most part the expression is already of the nature of a formula—in many cases it is clearly simply taken over from hymnody. On the other hand, another of its characteristics is its great variability and elasticity, as the very different lengths in which it is formulated make apparent. This confession could be summed up in the juxtaposition of three words, but it could also find expression in a long hymn. The final point at which all such possible expansions were exhausted is the Hexateuch's picture in Ex. 1ff., for there, through the conscription of every available tradition, the simple theme has been theologically worked up into a sublime chorale. In the deliverance from Egypt Israel saw the guarantee for all the future, the absolute surety for Jahweh's will to save, something like a warrant to which faith could appeal in times of trial (Ps. LXXIV. 2). In its oldest form this confession glorifies an act of Jahweh's unaccompanied by any divine utterance. And Israel too, the object of this event, is silent. But when the tellers of the story come to describe it, they introduce a plethora of words, some allegedly spoken by Jahweh and some by Israel. Important as these are, the event which took place still remains the basic thing that happened. This datum ancient Israel never spiritualised.

Even in the old Credo in Deut. XXVI. 5ff., the deliverance from Egypt is the dramatic mid-point around which the historical events detailed are grouped. So is it too in Josh. XXIV. 2ff., the only difference being that here the event which is just hinted at in Deut. XXVI by the term "signs and wonders" is made more explicit—it was a matter of warding off the Egyptian army, over against which Israel was in a hopeless situation. This remembrance of a deed of Jahweh's in war—the warding off and destruction of the Egyptians at the "Red Sea"—is the primary and most certainly the oldest datum in the confession concerning the deliverance from Egypt. But the working up of the narrative afforded the possibility of expanding the event both in its technicalities and in its theological aspect. Thus, for example, even the narrative in JE represents the event as a complex structure made up of various miracles— the pillar of cloud comes between the two armies and separates them (Ex. XIV. 19), the wheels of the enemy's chariots are mysteriously

[1] M. Noth, *Pentateuch*, p. 52; K. Galling, *Die Erwählungstraditionen Israels*, Giessen 1928, pp. 5ff.

clogged by Jahweh (vs. 25), the Egyptian army is discomfited (vs. 24), Moses divides the Red Sea with his rod (vs. 16), and so on. Noteworthy too is the increase in the miraculous element as the stories are handed on. If according to J a "strong east wind" had opened up a way as if through a lagoon (vs. 21), in E's version the waters stood like walls on either side of the Israelites as they passed through (vs. 22), and according to Ps. CXIV the sea "fled." The way in which the account makes Israel stand passively apart (cf. תחרישון "be still"), the way in which Jahweh's glorification of himself does not depend on any human co-operation (vs. 17), and, in conclusion, the way in which it speaks so emphatically of Israel's faith (vs. 31), all already betray a considerable amount of theological reflexion upon the event. Here what took place is understood conceptually, in a way which thought of it as far more than a mere military event. The Song at the crossing of the Red Sea speaks of the people whom Jahweh has "acquired" or "purchased" (קנה Ex. xv. 16, cf. Ps. LXXIV. 2). What however calls for chief mention here is the idea of the "redemption" from Egypt, which at a later time, that is, from Deuteronomy onwards, became the dominant thing. Terminologically the redemption rests on two concepts, both of which, the verbs פדה and גאל, belong originally to the sphere of law.[2] While פדה signifies any kind of ransoming of someone who is not free, and perhaps also "free," "redeem," in general (Jepsen), with גאל it is the redemption of what is one's own, and therefore of the restoration of a former owner-relationship. Of course, the way in which both concepts are used shows that, when they were applied to Jahweh's relationship with Israel, they became almost synonyms. But it is obvious that the idea of "ransom" no longer regards the saving event in its military aspect, but as a liberating legal act of Jahweh.[3]

---

[2] J. J. Stamm, *Erlösen und Vergeben im Alten Testament*, Berne 1940, pp. 7ff., 18ff., 31ff.; C. Barth, *Die Errettung vom Tode in den individuellen Klage- und Dankliedern des Alten Testamentes*, henceforth cited as *Errettung*, Basel 1947, pp. 133f. According to A. R. Johnson, the original meaning of גאל is "protect, protection, protector." A. R. Johnson, "The Primary Meaning of גאל," in *Vet. Test.*, Suppl. 1 (1953), pp. 67ff.; A. Jepsen, "Die Begriffe des Erlösens im Alten Testament," in *Solange es heute heisst, Festschrift für R. Herrmann*, edd. Erdmann Schott, Paul Althaus, *et. al.*, Berlin 1957, pp. 153ff.

[3] A tradition according to which Jahweh "found Israel in the wilderness," which is obviously old but which has been almost completely overlaid by the Exodus tradition which alone became dominant, still echoes on in Hos. IX. 10, Deut. XXXII. 10, and Jer. XXXI. 2f. R. Bach, "Die Erwählung Israels in der Wüste," in *Th. Lz.*, 1953, p. 687.

This confession received a peculiar enlargement when elements of the creation myth, the struggle with Chaos, were welded into it. This procedure was suggested by the common appearance of the catchword "sea" both here and in the creation myth. Jahweh "rebuked" the Red Sea (Ps. CVI. 9) in the same way as he had done in its time to the sea of Chaos, and like the latter it "fled" (Ps. CXIV. 3). The event thus took on primeval dimensions, and was transferred from its historical setting to the beginning of the history; indeed it stood for Israel at the beginning of her whole existence. Thereafter it was only a short step to Deutero-Isaiah's characteristic equation of creation and redemption. Because he understood creation as a saving event, he was also able to describe Jahweh's saving act towards Israel as "creation" (Is. XLIII. 1, XLIV. 24). The coincidence of creation and historical saving event in Is. LI. 9f. is unique.

The concept of Israel's "election" (בחר) too, set formally on a broad theological basis, comes first into use only at a relatively late date, namely with Deuteronomy. But it there appears as a term which already has a fixed doctrinal content.[4] The *locus classicus* for Deuteronomy's teaching about election is Deut. VII. 6–8.[5] The belief that Jahweh took Israel as his own peculiar people is, of course, very very old. But this idea of election could not have existed in such radical form in the early period, for, as has been rightly pointed out, a thoroughgoing belief in election paradoxically presupposes a universalistic view of history.[6] It was only the Israel which had learned to look at herself from outside, and for whom her own existence among the nations had become a problem, that was in a position to talk about election (Am. III. 2). The same holds true, of course, for the extraordinary idea expressed in Deut. XXXII. 8—that when Jahweh apportioned the nations according to the number of the divine beings, and thus assigned to each nation its cult, he chose Israel as his portion (Deut. XXXII. 8, LXX).

In this section we have been speaking about earlier and later confessional formulae and theological concepts that comprise in a summary

---

[4] G. Quell, in *Th. W.B.N.T.*, VOL. IV, pp. 148ff.; W. Staerk, in *Z.A.W.*, 1953, pp. 1ff.

[5] Th. C. Vriezen, *Die Erwählung Israels nach dem Alten Testament*, Zürich 1953, pp. 51f. Cf. further H. H. Rowley, *The Biblical Doctrine of Election*, London 1950; K. Koch, "Zur Geschichte der Erwählungsvorstellung in Israel," in *Z.A.W.*, 1955, pp. 205ff.

[6] N. A. Dahl, *Das Volk Gottes*, Oslo 1941, p. 26.

and concise fashion the saving event with which Israel's history with Jahweh began (the deliverance from Egypt, redemption, and election). The fact that there is more than just one of these formulations shows that, theologically, this saving act had more than one significance. It could also be unfolded in a plurality of data, for many traditions were current in Israel which stood in a closer or more remote relationship to this basic event. They were all gathered together and ordered into one another because each for its part contributed something special towards illustrating and making comprehensible Jahweh's great redemptive act. This was how the Hexateuch's picture of the Exodus of Israel and her wandering in the wilderness came into being. Unless it has to do so, theology ought not to cut itself adrift from the time-sequence in which Israel ranged these events (at only a few points shall we ourselves be compelled to depart from this order, for the sake of a more unified picture). The chief events which make up the notion of the "redemption from Egypt" are the miracle at the Red Sea, the revelation of the name Jahweh, the revelation at Sinai, and the wandering in the wilderness.

2. THE REVELATION OF THE NAME JAHWEH[7]

Even the traditional picture of the saving history followed by the sources in the Hexateuch recognises that Jahweh was not manifested to his elect from the beginning, but that the revelation of his name only took place in the time of Moses. Oddly enough, it is the latest of the source documents which most strongly emphasises this break in the history of revelation (Ex. VI. 2f., P). It is a surprising emphasis, for to this source's picture of the history, with the strong tendency it has to level out and schematise, the fact must have been an embarrassment. But late though P is, it was, like the other sources, still tied to the traditional material, whose statements in this connexion were un-equivocal: all that P could do was to give its own characteristic explanation of the break.[8] J and E take a much harder way of fusing together the two eras in the saving history, that of the God of the

---

[7] O. Grether, *Name und Wort Gottes im Alten Testament*, Giessen 1934; J. Pedersen, *Israel I–II*, pp. 245ff.

[8] Cf. also Hos. XII. 10, XIII. 4 ("I am Jahweh, your God from the land of Egypt"). The only mistake that P makes is that it takes El Shaddai for the God of the pre-Mosaic period; for El Shaddai most probably belongs to the group of originally Canaanite El numina (cf. El Olam, El Elion, Gen. XIV. 18, XXI. 33).

ancestors and the time of the full revelation of Jahweh. The narrative in Ex. III, a very complex unit both in substance and style, is designed on the one hand to communicate what was new in the revelation of Jahweh—that is, information about the divine name—and, on the other, to show how this new revelation was very closely linked with the history of the patriarchs.[9] Ex. III. is obviously trying to show the continuity between them—what came to pass with the revelation of the name of Jahweh was certainly of incalculable importance for Israel, but it was not the beginning of her God's self-revelation. Jahweh is identical with the God of the ancestors (Ex. III. 6, 13f.).[10]

Connected with this is the "definition" of the name Jahweh which has from the very beginning keenly attracted the interest of theologians, because they believed that here at last was a reference giving a comprehensive and fundamental account of the nature of the revelation of Jahweh, and reducing it, so to speak, to a final axiomatic formula (Ex. III. 14). But caution has to be exercised at this point; for nothing is farther from what is envisaged in this etymology of the name of Jahweh than a definition of his nature in the sense of a philosophical statement about his being (LXX ἐγώ εἰμι ὁ ὤν)—a suggestion, for example, of his absoluteness, aseity, etc. Such a thing would be altogether out of keeping with the Old Testament. The whole narrative context leads right away to the expectation that Jahweh intends to impart something—but this is not what he is, but what he will show himself to be to Israel.[11] It has always been emphasised, and rightly so, that, in this passage at any rate, the היה is to be understood in the sense of "being present," "being there," and therefore precisely not in the sense of absolute, but of relative and efficacious, being—I will be there (for you). Undoubtedly the paranomastic relative clause (אשר אהיה) adds an indeterminate element to the protasis, with the result that the promise of Jahweh's efficacious presence remains at the same time to some extent illusive and impalpable—this is Jahweh's freedom, which does not commit itself in detail. Anyone who reads the words cannot

[9] The narrative is complicated not only because of the fact that it uses an old sacral tradition (a story of a discovery) as prelude to the call proper, but in particular by the mention of a mountain of God at which Israel has yet to arrive (Ex. III. 1, 12). Cf. Noth, Pentateuch, p. 151, nn. 390, 220.

[10] Gen. IV. 26 (J) pushes the beginning of the cult of Jahweh back to a very much earlier time. What comes in question here is an isolated tradition which cannot be harmonised with Ex. III. 1f. or VI. 2f.

[11] Th. C. Vriezen, "Ehje aser ehje," in Festschrift für A. Bertholet, pp. 498ff.

but feel that they are very terse and pregnant. And yet their importance as a theological first principle ought not to be overestimated. They are only meant to be a promise to men who were in a hopeless situation, and this promise employs the rhetorical device of playing freely on the derivation of a name, a thing in which, as is well known, story-tellers in ancient times love to indulge. These etymological puns, which the story-tellers were moved to use from time to time, are generally only very loosely connected with the sound content of the name to be explained (Gen. XVII. 5, XXI. 6, XXVII. 36, etc.). The casualness of this etymological interpretation can be seen from the fact that hardly any other passage in the whole of the Old Testament betrays any acquaintance with this interpretation given by E of the name Jahweh.[12] We are certainly not to assume that the narrator's intention was thus to give the interpretative formula of the name Jahweh which was theologically fundamental and normative for Israel.[13] Shortly afterwards we meet with another interpretation of the name which is theologically much less ambiguous. "Jahweh, Jahweh, a God merciful and gracious, slow to anger and abounding in steadfast love and faithfulness" (Ex. XXXIV. 6), and further on, in Ex. XXXIV. 14, we find one more: "Jahweh, whose name is Jealous," "he is a jealous God." Thus there was once a time when it was allowable to interpret the name Jahweh from different theological angles.

For the understanding of Ex. III. 14 it has to be borne in mind that this self-revelation of Jahweh was preceded by the explicit question as to what his name was. According to ancient ideas, a name was not just "noise and smoke": instead, there was a close and essential relationship between it and its subject. The subject is in the name, and on that

[12] References in O. Grether, *Name und Wort Gottes in Alten Testament*, pp. 9ff. The only passage that can be connected with Ex. III. 14 is Hos. I. 9, where, as suggested by LXX, the correct reading is: "and I, I am no longer yours."

[13] In addition, this revelation comes to Moses through the medium of a strangely material theophany. The attempts made by the older expositors to evaporate the phenomenon of the burning bush into symbols in order to be able to comprehend it theologically are well known. (The bush signifies unholy Israel, the fire is Jahweh; the fact that the bush is not consumed is a metaphor of Jahweh's indwelling in Israel. J. H. Kurtz.) But it is altogether unlikely that even the story-tellers of the early period of the monarchy were willing to see the datum which they reported as to such an extent decoded spiritually. If we understand them correctly, their concern was much rather to leave the phenomenon as it was, in precisely its quality as a thing. The same holds true of the theophany described in Gen. XV. 17.

account the name carries with it a statement about the nature of its subject or at least about the power appertaining to it. For the cultic life of the ancient East, this idea was of quite fundamental importance.[14] People in antiquity had no doubt that human life was mysteriously surrounded and determined by divine powers. But this conviction was by no means a comforting one, when man did not know what kind of a deity he was specifically dealing with, that is, when he did not know its name and was without the possibility of invoking it and gaining its interest for himself and his need. The deity must first "cause his name to be remembered" (Ex. xx. 24) within the human field, otherwise men were quite unable to invoke him. Thus, without the knowledge of the divine name, there was no possibility of a cult, that is of a relationship between men and the deity, for men then lacked all possibility of bringing influence to bear upon the deity. It was not just the matter of "devoting himself freely out of gratitude" to the deity: man also had the self-seeking desire to enlist it as far as possible in the service of his own earthly interest, and in extremities to use the divine name in magic.[15] Thus, Manoah is very eager to bind the heavenly visitant to himself by means of a private cultic relationship, and so he immediately asks what his name is (Jg. xiii. 11–17). Similarly, the Peniel story shows the same craving on Jacob's part to bind God captive. But in this case too God disengages himself from Jacob's importunity and refuses to give an answer to the inquiry about his name: "Why is it that you ask my name? And he blessed him then" (Gen. xxxii. 30 [29]). This comes close to what is said in Ex. iii. 13f. Here Jahweh certainly imparts his name. But in the words "I will be what I will be" there also lies censure of Moses' question. At all events, in giving the information which he does, Jahweh reserves his freedom to himself, a freedom which will be displayed precisely in his being there, in his efficacious presence.[16]

Thus the name Jahweh, in which, one might almost say, Jahweh had given himself away, was committed in trust to Israel alone. The

---

[14] Pedersen, *Israel I–II*, pp. 245ff.

[15] The name "forces the figure to stay and guarantees that the man always finds it again. The number of these numina is boundless": G. van der Leeuw, *Phänomenologie der Religion*, Tübingen 1933, p. 135.

[16] A formula closely approximating to the one in Ex. iii. 14 is found, on the lips of a Pharaoh, in the so-called teaching for Merikare: "As I live, I am that I am." A connexion between this Old Egyptian grandiloquent formula and the Elohist's coining is not impossible. A. Alt, in *Z.A.W.*, 1940–41, pp. 159ff.

heathen do not know it (Ps. LXXIX. 6). In it and in it alone lay the guarantee of Jahweh's nearness and of his readiness to help, and through it Israel had the assurance of being able at all times to reach his heart (Ex. XXXIII. 19, XXXIV. 6)—small wonder that at all times she looked upon the name as a holy reality of a quite special kind (on occasion coming almost to the point of understanding it in a material way). This name shared directly in Jahweh's own holiness, for indeed it was, so to speak, a double of his being. But if it was holy, this means that it belonged to the realm of the cult, and it can indeed be designated as the very heart of the cult of ancient Israel. קרא בשם יהוה is originally a cultic term and means to invoke Jahweh by using his name (Gen. XII. 8, XIII. 4, XXI. 33; I Kings XVIII. 24, etc.). Theologically it takes the place which in other cults was occupied by the cultic image.[17] A whole apparatus of rather intricate cultic ideas, rituals, and prescriptions gathered round the name, to safeguard knowledge of it and, in particular, the use which Israel might make of it. Having such a holy reality entrusted to her set Israel a tremendous task, not the least part of which was to guard against all the temptations which made their appearance along with the trust. In general terms what this means is that the name of Jahweh had to be "hallowed."[18] The first and negative implication is that the holy name had in all circumstances to be safeguarded against improper use, that is, from use outside the cult. In the cult, the divine name was used by Israel at sacrifice, in prayer, in blessing and cursing, and also in the holy war (Ps. XX. 8 [7]), and it had been given her for this purpose.[19] The Levites blessed in the name of Jahweh (Deut. X. 8); the king did the same (II Sam. VI. 18), and the priests "put" the name of Jahweh on Israel (Num. VI. 27, cf. Ps. CXXIX. 8). Jahweh's name had also its rightful use in connexion with oaths and imprecations.[20] But outside of this cultic and public use there were still a great many possibilities of "taking the name of Jahweh in vain" (Ex. XX. 7; Deut. V. 11). Originally the term שוא may well have signified magic, and it is conceivable that even in Israel people were at times liable to use Jahweh's name for sinister purposes dangerous to the community.[21] But this commandment was probably in the main

---

[17] E. Lohmeyer, Das Vater-Unser, Göttingen 1946, p. 46.

[18] Is. XXIX. 23; to "profane" (חלל) the name of Jahweh, Lev. XVIII. 21, XIX. 12, XX. 3, XXI. 6 and frequently.   [19] Cf. J. W. Wevers in Vet. Test., 1956, pp. 82ff.

[20] Deut. VI. 13, Pss. XLIV. 6, [5], CXVIII. 10.

[21] S. Mowinckel, Psalmenstudien I, Oslo 1921, pp. 50ff.

directed against false swearing, for every genuine oath was accompanied by invocation of the deity (Lev. XIX. 12). Further, to hallow the name of Jahweh was tantamount in itself to acknowledging the uniqueness and exclusiveness of the cult of Israel *per se*. Wherever Israel in any way opened its doors to the cult of another deity, the name of Jahweh was profaned (Lev. XVIII. 21, XX. 3). On the positive side, the name was hallowed by obedience to the commandments, by "walking in the name of Jahweh" (Mic. IV. 5).

It was just the times of religious syncretism which exposed to danger the solity of Jahweh that called into being, in Deuteronomy, a programme of very strict and exclusive concentration upon pure Jahwism; and it is in Deuteronomy that we meet with the most striking statements about the name of Jahweh. Jahweh "put" his name at the one place of Israel's worship, that he might "dwell" there.[22] Jahweh himself is in heaven (Deut. XXVI. 15), but his name "lives" at the place of worship in a well-nigh material way, almost like a being existent in its own right. Deuteronomy is obviously attacking the older and more popular idea of Jahweh's immediate presence at the place of worship and substituting for it the theological differentiation between Iahweh on the one hand and his name on the other, a severance which is carried through to the point of spatial separation. Admittedly we do not find the idea of the name of Jahweh defined in such theological exactitude in the hymns of the cult, but an awareness of its special saving importance always remained alive in Israel. By means of it Jahweh saves (Ps. LIV. 1), in it one can find protection (Ps. XX. 1), it is a tower of refuge (Prov. XVIII. 10). Characteristic is the confidence that Jahweh will help or save "for his name's sake" (Ps. XXIII. 3, XXV. 11, CXLIII. 11; Jer. XIV. 7; Is. XLVIII. 9), for in these cases too a certain separation is presupposed—standing in the presence of Jahweh you invoke his saving name. In Is. XLVIII. 9 Jahweh's name and his anger are set over against one another. But this name is not only placed over Israel (Deut. XXVIII. 10); it is also pronounced over those who were incorporated into Israel only during the course of the saving history (Am. IX. 12): indeed knowledge of it is widespread among the peoples surrounding Israel (Ex. IX. 16; II Sam. VII. 26) and calls forth terror (Josh. IX. 9; Ps. CII. 16 [15]; Mal. I. 14). But many will love it (Is. LVI. 6). One of the most important things, however, is that for Israel this name never became a "mystery," to which only the initiated could have

22 Deut. XII. 5, 11, 21, XIV. 24 and frequently.

access. On the contrary, each and every Israelite was at liberty to avail himself of it, and once she had become fully aware of the distinctiveness of her worship, Israel did not hide this name of God from the Gentiles in fear, but rather felt herself in duty bound to make it known to them (Is. XII. 4; Ps. CV. 1–3). Indeed in the end Jahweh is to be revealed to the world in such a way that all worship of idols vanishes away, and every knee will bow to his name alone (Zech. XIV. 9; Is. XLV. 23).

Jahweh had only one name; Marduk had fifty with which his praises as victor over Tiamat were sung in hymns. Similarly, the Egyptian Re is the god with many names. This plurality of names is, of course, to be understood as the result of a combination of older traditions. But just because of this multiplicity fresh uncertainty resulted—indeed, advanced theology kept the real name of Amon secret.[23] A like uncertainty, again based on ignorance of the name, is found in the Babylonian "penitential prayer to the god whom it may concern."[24] But Jahweh had one name, and this is one known throughout all his people. It is probably of great significance that Israel never had any idea of piling up many names upon Jahweh. Jahweh was in fact one, as Deuteronomy says. Even the highest terms of praise are always reserved for this one name Jahweh alone. But what is of greatest importance is that this name could not properly be objectified and disposed of—its secret could not in any way be reduced to a theological interpretation of its meaning, not even the one in Ex. III. 14.[25] Jahweh had bound it up with the free manifestation in history of his self-revelation in history. The formula which occurs so frequently in Ezekiel, "and they will know that I am Jahweh," shows this indissoluble welding-together of Jahweh's name and his self-revelation just as clearly as does the preface

---

[23] H. Kees, *Der Götterglaube im alten Ägypten*, Berlin 1941, pp. 171f. In the history of religion the concealing of the true name of the god is explained by anxiety lest man might be able to gain power over the deity with the help of the name.

[24] "May the wrath of my Lord abate for me,
May the god whom I do not know be tranquil for me,
May the goddess whom I do not know be tranquil for me,
May the god whom I know or do not know be tranquil for me,
May the goddess whom I know or do not know be tranquil for me!"
A. Falkenstein and W. von Soden, *Sumerische und akkadische Hymnen und Gebete*, Zürich 1953, p. 225. Cf. also the clause that might be added to an invocation in ancient Roman religion: "sive quo alio nomine adpellari vis." K. Latte, *Römische Religionsgeschichte*, München 1960, p. 62.

[25] W. Zimmerli, *Erkenntniss Gottes nach dem Buche Ezechiel*, Zürich 1954, p. 62, n. 90.

to the decalogue, which also interprets the name in the light of the redemptive historical act. Thus from the very start Israel was debarred from elevating the name into the realm of "mystery." So she was not in a position to appropriate the name of Jahweh and make it the object of an abstruse mythology or of speculation: it was to be understood only in historical experience.[26]

The name Jahweh is found some 6700 times in the Old Testament, but as well Israel often also designated her God הָאֱלֹהִים or אֱלֹהִים (roughly 2500 times). From an early time this occurrence of two different names has called a variety of theological speculations into being. The name Jahweh was of course the embodiment of the saving revelation; but since Israel often designated this very Jahweh, the God of salvation, as אֱלֹהִים, it is quite impossible to attach a theological interpretation to every use of the proper name or the appellative. The texts of course largely derive from very different cycles of traditions having different usages whose bases are unknown to us, and they have not received any subsequent complete harmonisation. Exegesis can thus only make a decision according to circumstances. When the animals are said to have no relationship to Jahweh the God of special revelation and to look to אֵל for their sustenance (Ps. CIV. 21; Job XXXVIII. 41), the choice of terms is deliberate. The variation in the sentence pronounced by Noah on his sons is well known: Jahweh is the God of Shem, but it is Elohim who is to bless Japhet (Gen. IX. 26f.; similarly Is. LXI. 2). Speaking generally, in every instance where the reasons for the variation are not plain to see, caution is called for. It is possible though not certain that the Elohist's preference for Elohim indicates a now self-conscious monotheism.[27] Even in the post-exilic literature the way in which the name Jahweh withdraws into the background—it never occurs in the dialogue in Job, nor in Esther, Ecclesiastes or the Song of Solomon—is not to be accounted for solely in terms of the growing awe felt at his holiness. In the Elohistic Psalter (Pss. XLII–LXXXIII) it is consistently struck out, although alongside this collection are later ones in which the process has not been carried out.

[26] In actual fact Israel did on occasion confer other names too upon her God, of which for example עֶלְיוֹן or שַׁדַּי are not infrequent. But this does not involve a limitation of what was said above, for these rudimentary names which derive from old traditions, and from the oldest of them, never had the function of extending the name so as to stand alongside the name Jahweh to serve as fuller forms of address: rather, they were occasionally made use of in place of the name Jahweh.

[27] O. Procksch, *Theologie des Alten Testaments*, Gütersloh 1950, p. 443.

In the Chronicler's history, compared with the usage in the Books of Samuel and Kings, a similar withdrawal has been noticed. But oddly enough Jahweh is used in some cases where it was not in the original.[28] The Septuagint's rendering of the name Jahweh in the Old Testament by ὁ κύριος was of great importance for the early Christian Church, because the Church referred statements made by Jahweh or statements about him to her Kyrios, Jesus Christ (cf. I Thess. v. 2; II Thess. II. 2; Acts II. 20b f.). At the time of Jesus the name Jahweh seems only to have been used on certain occasions in the worship of the Temple, but no longer in the services of the Synagogue.

IV. THE DIVINE REVELATION AT SINAI

I. PRELIMINARY REMARKS ON THE BASIS OF THE HISTORY OF THE TRADITION

The Hexateuch's account of the events and divine revelations at Sinai forms a complex of tradition of quite abnormal size, for it stretches from Ex. XIX. 1 to Num. X. 10. Nowhere else in the Old Testament is there to be found such a huge presentation of traditions, made up of so many strands, and attached to one single event (the revelation at Sinai). But even if a first survey makes the reader almost despair of seeing something whole, interconnected, and therefore internally coherent, in this towering mountain composed not only of countless separate units, but also of many greater bodies of tradition, nevertheless this Sinai pericope is at least clearly defined as to its outward extent, for Kadesh traditions precede it, and Kadesh traditions follow it again.[1] It is thus obvious that the Sinai tradition has been secondarily inserted into already extant traditions concerning the Wanderings in the Wilderness. We also see, of course, from the various poetic elaborations of the old Credo, that it still has no mention of the events at Sinai. Obviously it was only at a comparatively late date that this complex of tradition was inserted into the canonical picture of the saving history. Of course, for the history of tradition, this only tells us something about the coalescence of the

---

[28] J. W. Rothstein and J. Hänel, *Kommentar zum ersten Buch der Chronik*, Kommentar zum Alten Testament, ed. S. Sellin, henceforth cited as Komm. A.T., Leipzig 1927, p. xiv.

[1] Ex. XVIII also has no direct relationship to the Sinai tradition. There is no reminiscence of the theophany and the revelation of the will of Jahweh, that is, of the main theme in the Sinai tradition. Noth, *Pentateuch*, pp. 151f.

complexes of tradition, and nothing about their age. The Sinai tradition lived in independence longer than all the other traditional elements whose combination led to the construction of the canonical picture of the saving history.[2]

If in what follows we attempt in some measure to unravel this huge skein of traditions, in order to give an outline of its theology—of course, only of its main subjects—we very soon encounter the basic datum to which all the individual traditions in one way or another go back: there at Sinai Jahweh revealed to his people binding ordinances, on the basis of which life with its God was made possible. But in respect of the nature of these ordinances there are great differences in the various traditions. Sometimes they understand them as ordinances for common, ordinary human life ("commandments"), sometimes as legal ordinances (parts of the Book of the Covenant and of Deuteronomy), and sometimes as ordinances for the intricate sphere of worship (P). We must on principle abandon any idea of discovering anything like a relevant arrangement of the single units, or even of theological lines linking them. This would be quite out of keeping with the way in which traditions were formed in the Old Testament, which in this respect was much more superficial. The decisive and pre-eminent factor in the coalescing and aggregation of the many traditions was their common attachment to a place (Sinai), and to a person (Moses). Thus, in the end, there came together and were ranged side by side, often without any connexion being made between them, bodies of material of the utmost diversity, in fact, everything that Israel somehow and at some time derived from the revelation at Sinai. This was a result of the conception of the traditions as documents narrating a history with God.[3]

The enormous block of tradition connected with Sinai (Ex. xix–Num. x) divides up into two parts which are very unequal both outwardly and in content; they are the Sinai pericope of JE (Ex. xix–xxiv, xxxii–xxxiv), and that of P (Ex. xxv–xxxi, xxxv–Num. x. 10). JE's account of the revelation at Sinai itself is given in Ex. xix, xx, xxiv, a compact narrative unit. The event commences with elaborate preparations for the theophany, which follows on the third day. Jahweh came down upon the mountain and proclaimed the Ten Com-

[2] On this exceptional position of the Sinai tradition see G. von Rad, *Das form-geschichtliche Problem des Hexateuch*, Stuttgart 1938, reprinted in *Ges. Studien*, pp. 20ff.; Noth, *Pentateuch*, pp. 63ff.

[3] See above, p. 115.

mandments (Ex. xx). Upon this promulgation of the divine will follows the people's entering into an engagement in the form of a cultic festival (Ex. xxiv).[4] We have already said earlier on that this narrative sequence does not derive directly from historical events, but is probably the "festival legend" belonging to a major cultic celebration, the old festival of the renewal of the covenant. To this compact block of narrative, as we have already designated it, are attached in chs. xxxii–xxxiii several smaller units of tradition which, while certainly belonging to Sinai, have only a loose connexion with the actual revelation itself. In ch. xxxiv. there comes a second proclamation of commandments, necessitated by the breaking of the Tables (ch. xxxii). It was a very adroit insertion, allowing as it did the redactor of J and E to keep a place for the Jahwist's account of the proclamation of the commandments, which Ex. xx (E) had really rendered superfluous.

In the Priestly Document the Sinai pericope is much bigger. But once we remove the mass of cultic regulations, including the whole of the Holiness Code (PH, Lev. xvii–xxvi), which were only attached to it secondarily, the following sequence of events stands out. The "glory of Jahweh" came down upon Sinai: Moses is summoned to go up and receives instructions for the building of the Tabernacle, and for the investiture and installation of Aaron and his sons as priests: Bezaleel and Aholiab are to make ready the Tabernacle with all its furnishings together with Aaron's vestments (Ex. xxiv. 15*b*–xxxi. 17). By a free-will offering which Moses had called upon them to make, the people collect the materials required; and when Bezaleel has erected the Tabernacle, the "glory of Jahweh" comes down upon it and fills the holy tent (Ex. xxxv–xl). Then follows the consecration of Aaron and his sons as priests (Lev. viii) and their first sacrifice, which is again approved by the appearance of the "glory of Jahweh" (Lev. ix). The conclusion was formed by the separation and consecration of the Levites to their more menial service in the cult (Num. iii, iv).

[4] The source E dominates in the picture of the events at Sinai (Ex. xixf., xxiv). Of J, the obviously very ancient tradition of a covenant meal (vss. 9–11) is important. J's proclamation of the commandments which runs parallel to the Elohistic decalogue is now to be found in Ex. xxxiv, but the series of commandments which we meet with there is probably a secondary substitution which had to be inserted when the two source documents were combined, because J's original decalogue was identical with that of E, or at any rate approximated very closely to it in tenor. Rowley takes Ex. xxxiv as a south Judean tradition and believes that the series of commandments can be taken as the old Kenite decalogue (*Moses and the Decalogue*, Manchester 1951, pp. 88ff.).

What both of the accounts, the Sinai pericopes of JE and of the Priestly Document, have in common is the tradition of a divine revelation at Sinai, and this of a revelation through which Israel had proclaimed to her the basic regulations for her life before and with Jahweh. But the differences are equally clear. The regulations in the older Sinai tradition were regulations for secular, everyday life: the Decalogue was, as we shall see more precisely later on, the proclamation of a divine sovereign right over every sphere of human life. On the other hand, the content of the Priestly Document is the revelation of a sacral order: it orders the life of the cult, and along with it the whole intricate system of sacrifices and rites, by means of which Israel was to effect communion with God. This is a concomitant of P's view that the decisive event in the Sinai revelation was God's coming to dwell in the midst of Israel, the appearance of the "glory of Jahweh." By so doing Jahweh had come near to Israel in such a way as to make P's comprehensive cultic regulations and safeguards essential.

2. THE SIGNIFICANCE OF THE COMMANDMENTS[5]

When commandments are the subject, theologians and laymen alike think immediately of the Decalogue. The place of the latter in the structure of the Hexateuch's saving history is as a matter of fact unique and programmatical. But more recent form-critical investigations have shown that it is far from being so very singular, or the only representative of its kind and class. There is a considerable number of such series of commandments, some of which seem even older than our Decalogue in its present (Elohistic or Deuteronomistic) form. The first to be mentioned in this connexion would be the Shechemite Dodecalogue (Deut. XXVII. 15ff.), an extremely old series of curses directed against offences that might have taken place "in secret" (cf. the בַּסֵּתֶר in vss. 15 and 24), and all of which are, for that reason, quite outwith the control of the community and of its ability to punish them. So, too, the torso in Ex. XXI. 12, 15–17, to which Alt drew attention, has a form which gives the impression of great antiquity.[6] In Lev. XIX. 13–18 there is a

---

[5] M. Noth, *Die Gesetze im Pentateuch, ihre Voraussetzungen und ihr Sinn*, Halle 1940, reprinted in *Ges. Studien*; A. Alt, *Die Ursprünge des israelitischen Rechts*, in *K.S.*, VOL. I, pp. 278ff.; S. Mowinckel, *Le Décalogue*; W. Zimmerli, "Ich bin Jahweh," in *Festschrif A. Alt*, pp. 179ff.; W. Elliger, "Ich bin der Herr – euer Gott," in *Theologie als Glaubenswagnis. Festschrift Karl Heim*, Hamburg 1954, pp. 9ff.

[6] Alt, *K.S.*, VOL. I, p. 311.

series of twelve commandments which, in its clarity and the universal validity of its statements, approximates very closely to the Decalogue. These series of commandments themselves presuppose considerable pastoral as well as theological reflexion; for all of them must once have been put together by priests, on the basis of deliberate selection from a very much ampler store of tradition. They all owe their existence to the endeavour to outline Jahweh's whole will for men in the shortest possible form. And while unquestionably certain differences in age can be made out in this fairly considerable amount of material, still, it may occasion surprise that the Decalogue does not actually stand at the farthest point of this historical series. At all events, it retains certain indications which put it beyond question that it had had a past life before it attained its present form in Ex. xx or Deut. v. The positive formulation of the commandment concerning parents, and that concerning the Sabbath, can certainly be taken as a secondary alteration of a series once given throughout in the negative form—the breaking up of the old form here and the reshaping of the negative commandment as a positive one is an interesting process.[7] More will need to be said about the interpretation to which the commandment forbidding images was submitted: with it too an older formulation than that represented by the Decalogue is clearly discernible. Finally, it can be shown that, to begin with, the commandment forbidding stealing specifically envisaged kidnapping (cf. Ex. xxi. 16; Deut. xxiv. 7), and that it was only subsequently generalised to arrive at the sense in which we know it now.[8] Thus, Israel herself worked for a long time on the Decalogue before it became so universal and concise in form and content as to be capable of standing for an adequate outline of the whole will of Jahweh for Israel.

In its first section, including therein the Fourth Commandment, the Decalogue deals with man's duties towards God, and in its second with man's duties towards man. At the head of this latter section stands the commandment to honour one's parents, which is followed by ordinances safeguarding the life, marriage, property, and honour of one's neighbour.[9] The "thou" in this series of commandments addresses

[7] The older and still negatively formulated version of the fifth commandment is to be found in Deut. xxvii. 16 and Ex. xxi. 17.

[8] Alt, K.S., vol. I, pp. 333ff.

[9] Even with "coveting" what is in question is an act, illegal machinations, as J. Herrmann has shown in Festschrift für E. Sellin, Leipzig 1927, pp. 69ff. Cf. Mic. ii. 2.

Israel as well as the individual—it is the form of address and the conceptual form belonging to a time when the individual standing in
independence over against a group was still unknown.[10]

Now, the Decalogue raises one of the most important of all the
questions in the theology of the Old Testament—how is this will for
Israel to be understood theologically? The answer cannot be obtained
from the Decalogue itself, since the Decalogue has to some extent been
made absolute, but only from the context in which it is embedded.
Now there can be no doubt that it is the proclamation of the Decalogue
over her which puts Israel's election into effect. The words of the revelation begin with Jahweh's introduction of himself, in which he appeals
to the saving act of the liberation from Egypt—those addressed are
thus the ransomed of Jahweh.[11] But, according to antiquity's understanding, entry into a special relationship with a god was inconceivable
without the acceptance and binding recognition of specific ordinances.
Thus, only as Jahweh proclaimed his sovereign rights over Israel, and
only as Israel accepted this will, was Israel's appropriation made complete. The proclamation of the divine will for justice is like a net
thrown over Israel: it is the completion of her conveyance to Jahweh.
This understanding of the Decalogue has been given a new force as a
result of more recent form-critical investigations, which show that,
in the Israel of the period of the Judges, and probably even later, the
Decalogue formed the mid-point and climax of a very solemn event,
namely, the festival of the renewal of the covenant at Shechem, which,
as may be deduced from Deut. XXXI. 10f., took place every seven years.
A number of references to it allow us to make a fairly certain reconstruction of its liturgical sequence. What serves as the basis of our
information is, first and foremost, the Sinai pericope of JE itself: it can
practically be designated as the quondam festal legend of this covenant
festival. But there is also Deut. XXVII. 9ff., and, above all, the whole lay-
out of Deuteronomy itself (Deut. VI. 4–XXVIII). As well as these there
are Pss. L and LXXXI. According to all this—questions of detail aside—
the following parts can be recognised in the liturgical sequence of this
great festival: (1) a paraenetic introduction; (2) proclamation of the
commandments; (3) the making of the covenant; (4) blessing and

[10] The consistent direction of the will of God on the isolated individual is only
completed in the theological Wisdom literature (Ps. CXIX). See below, pp. 443f.

[11] The "introduction" to the Decalogue is to be translated "I am Jahweh, your God,"
and not "I, Jahweh, am your God": W. Zimmerli, in Festschrift A. Alt., pp. 179ff.

curse.[12] If Israel at regular intervals celebrated the revelation at Sinai in the cult in such a way, we can in turn deduce from this how ardently she looked on this divine revelation as momentous. With this proclamation of the divine law something came about for her, and that not only in the so-called "spiritual sphere"; rather did this conveyance to Jahweh have its consequences principally on the plane of concrete historical events. For in this cultic celebration Israel gave expression to the fact that the event which took place at Sinai had an undiminished importance for each age: it was renewed upon each succeeding generation: it was for all of them "contemporary" (cf. Deut. v. 2–4, XXIX. 10ff. [9ff.]).

In addition, this explains the non-cultic character of the Decalogue, on the basis of which so far-reaching conclusions used to be drawn. If the festival of the renewal of the covenant was a pilgrimage festival, then the exclusive concentration on the ethical is understandable. The people addressed by the Decalogue were, of course, the laity; and they were addressed with reference to their everyday affairs, their secular intercourse with one another in their communal life up and down the country, i.e. with reference to the life they had to live once the covenant was made and they had gone back to their homes. For the cult was the priests' concern—special care for it was not imposed upon the pilgrims, least of all outside in their everyday secular life, far from the shrine. It was therefore quite beside the mark to base on the non-cultic character of the Decalogue conclusions, say, about an affinity between the Decalogue and the preaching of the great prophets, or about the non-cultic character of what Moses himself founded.[13]

But the most important question is that of the proper theological evaluation of the commandments. New force has now been given to the idea that Israel understood the revelation of the commandments as a saving event of the first rank, and celebrated it as such. In all circumstances the close connexion between commandments and covenant must be kept in view. As we saw, Israel certainly did not understand the Decalogue as an absolute moral law prescribing ethics: she rather recognised it as a revelation vouchsafed to her at a particular moment in her history, through which she was offered the saving gift

[12] Details in von Rad, *Ges. Studien*, pp. 28ff., 33ff., 41ff.; M. Noth, *Ges. Studien*, pp. 88ff.; H. J. Kraus, *Gottesdienst in Israel*, pp. 49ff.

[13] So for example P. Volz, *Mose und sein Werk*, 2nd edn. Tübingen 1932, pp. 57f., 90ff.; S. Mowinckel, *Le Décalogue*, p. 104.

of life. The proclamation of the commandments and the promise of life were obviously closely connected in the liturgy from a very early time (cf. Ezek. XVIII. 5–9). The paraeneses in Deuteronomy continually play variations on this basic idea, which had certainly been established long before: with the commandments Jahweh has offered to his people life; with the hearing of the commandments Israel was placed in the position of decision for life or for death.[14] Certainly, Jahweh looked for this decision from Israel; but in no case were these commandments prefixed to the covenant in a conditional sense, as if the covenant would only come into effect once obedience had been rendered. The situation is rather the reverse. The covenant is made, and with it Israel receives the revelation of the commandments. We find the same order even in the late Deuteronomy—Israel has become the people of God ("today you have become the people of Jahweh, your God," Deut. XXVII. 9), and to this predication in the indicative mood is joined the demand to attend to the divine will for justice and to obey it ("listen therefore to the voice of Jahweh, your God," Deut. XXVII. 10). But even if this declaration referring to an accomplished fact and to the present time is taken as valid, and it is recognised that the covenant was completed at a point in time when Israel had as yet had no opportunity at all to prove herself in these commandments, the Decalogue could still have been understood as a burdensome law. But for a "law" in the narrower sense of the word, instruction for the moral life, the Decalogue lacks what is of first importance—the positive filling-out, without which a law is scarcely conceivable. Instead, apart from the two well-known exceptions, it refrains from any attempt to set up positive norms for the affairs of life. It confines itself to a few basic negations; that is, it is content with, as it were, signposts on the margins of a wide sphere of life to which he who belongs to Jahweh has to give heed. It is this persistence in negations which is particularly characteristic in all these "tables," alike Deut. XXVII. 15ff. and Lev. XIX. 13ff. and others. Even in Ezekiel, that is, in the prophet whom many have held to be the father of a rigorous "legalism," there is a table of instruction of this kind: he who belongs to Jahweh does not sacrifice upon the mountains, does not practise extortion, does not take interest or practise usury, etc. (Ezek. XVIII. 6ff.). Here it is perfectly clear that these series

---

[14] Deut. XXX. 15ff. [16ff.], IV. 1, V. 30 [33], VIII. 1, XVI. 20, XXII. 7; cf. Ezek. XVIII. 19, XX. 11, 13, 21, XXXIII. 16, 19; Lev. XVIII. 5. Cf. also the late תורת חיים, Ecclesiasticus XVII. 11, XLV. 5.

of commandments are not in the least intended to sketch anything like an ethic, for they contain no maximum demands of Jahweh. In fact the reverse could more easily be maintained—it is only in negatives, that is, from the angle of what is absolutely displeasing to Jahweh, that the marks of him who belongs to Jahweh are described. Within the sphere of life thus circumscribed by the commandments there lies a wide field of moral action which remains completely unregulated (after all, idolatry, murder, and adultery were not constant occurrences in Israel's everyday life). If then these commandments do not subject life in any way to a comprehensive normative law, it is more appropriate for us to say that in certain marginal situations they demand avowal of Jahweh, and this avowal consists precisely in abstaining from doing certain things displeasing to him. What holds true for all the "laws" in the Old Testament holds true for the Decalogue as well—its recipients, the group to which it addresses itself, are not some kind of secular community, as for example the state, still less human society as such; it is the community of Jahweh.[15] It is therefore unnecessary to emphasise further that such demands as we have in these "tables" were regarded as capable of fulfilment, and that easily. What is most significant, however, is that, in the moment of her conveyance to Jahweh, Israel was not lifted up into a special kind of sacral existence. Instead of stressing sacral distinctions, the Decalogue in a quite elementary fashion watches over man in his humanity.

It follows from all this that the theologian has to be very careful in his terminology, and has to ask himself how far our word "law" covers the data in the Old Testament. In the Old Testament the Ten Commandments are never spoken of as law: they are called only "the Ten Words" (עשרת הדברים Ex. xxxiv. 28; Deut. iv. 13, x. 4), and right down to the end Israel sang the praises of the revelation of the divine will for justice as a saving blessing of a very high order. It was a guarantee of her election, for in it Jahweh had shown his people a way and a statute. It was for Israel's good (לטוב לך Deut. x. 13) that these commandments were imposed upon her, and in Deuteronomy Moses says of them: "For this is your wisdom and your understanding in the sight of the peoples, if they hear of these ordinances. They will say 'How wise and understanding is this people!' For where is there so great a nation to whom God is so near as Jahweh, our God, whenever we call upon him? And where is there so great a people that has statutes and

---

[15] M. Noth, *Ges. Studien*, pp. 32ff.

ordinances so righteous as all this Torah which I have set before you this day?" (Deut. IV. 6–8).

One of the most sublime epithets with which Israel extolled these commandments was that they were "righteous," which means that in revealing them Jahweh had given proof of his loyalty to his community relationship with Israel.[16] There is no terror here, and no sighing, as if they were a burden, but only thankfulness and praise (Pss. XIX. 8ff. [7ff.], CXIX). Israel only encountered the law in its function as judge and destroyer at the time of the preaching of the prophets.

Unconditional acceptance of these commandments was, of course, demanded of Israel. In the Old Testament as in the New, the offer of salvation confronted those to whom it was made with the question of obedience. That refusal to accept the commandments brought the curse of Jahweh in its train Israel said many times and in many ways. In what remains of the liturgy of the old festival of the renewal of the covenant at Shechem there is from the point of view of form-criticism the closest connexion between the announcement of the commandments and the curse (Deut. XXVII. 11ff.).[17] In this sense, then, meeting with Jahweh meant a decision about life and death. When Israel heard this utterance, she was put in a position from which there was no more going back. Both Deuteronomy and the Holiness Code make blessing and cursing follow upon the proclamation of the commandments.[18]

Jahweh's commandments were all-sufficient in the sense that they did not intrinsically require any substantiation to legitimate them before

[16] Deut. IV. 8; Ps. XIX. 10 [9], CXIX. 7 and frequently. For the understanding of צדק, see below, pp. 370ff.

[17] Deut. XXVII. 11–13, 15ff.; Josh. XXIV. 25ff. Both Deuteronomy and the Holiness Code make blessing and cursing follow on the proclamation of the commandments (Deut. XXXVIII; Lev. XXVI).

[18] Noth brought penetrating criticism to bear on this Deuteronomic promise of blessing, because a law announces penalty in the case of disobedience, but assumes obedience as a matter of course, and does not in addition reward it with blessing. Besides, the blessing is in fact already promised in Deuteronomy in advance and quite unconditionally, so that its realisation is not bound up with Israel's performance of obedience (Ges. Studien, pp. 165ff.). But Deuteronomy, the revelation of Jahweh's will for Israel, can no longer be taken in the usual sense as a legal ordinance, for what it is concerned with is Jahweh's saving turning towards Israel as such. Thus it is scarcely justifiable to understand the promise of blessing as a rather inappropriate secondary appendix to the curses. For outside of this too Jahweh had reserved it to himself to reward human obedience. For the idea of reward see G. Bornkamm, "Der Lohngedanke im NT," in Ev. Th., 1946–7, pp. 143ff.

men, except perhaps the tautological one that, just because they are
commandments of Jahweh, they therefore bind men to acceptance.[19]
So we find in Lev. XIX. 13–18 one of those great series of negative
commandments in which each individual commandment ended in the
obviously substantiating clause אֲנִי יהוה; this was quite certainly a
liturgical usage.[20] Deuteronomy preserves a commandment, doubtless a
very old one, prohibiting the eating of any kind of carrion, which is
followed by the postscript substantiating it—"for you are a people
holy to Jahweh" (Deut. XIV. 21). The same holds for the prohibitions,
once again very ancient, which issue in the lapidary clause that this or
that is "an abomination to Jahweh" (תּוֹעֲבַת יהוה), that is, something
absolutely incompatible with the cult of Jahweh.[21] These are, as was
said, theological tautologies and not substantiations proper. Alongside
this absolutely categorical form, however, we do also find substantiations in the full sense, which are clearly designed to make the prohibitions or the commandments in some sense comprehensible to people,
or at least to arrange them in a connexion which is meaningful for
them. Indeed, these endeavours obviously increased, for the substantiations appear much more frequently in the later collections of laws,
Deuteronomy and the Holiness Code, than in the Book of the Covenant. Admittedly, their form of argumentation is very different in
different cases. On occasion they restrict themselves to a quite simple,
matter-of-fact interpretation: thus, for example, ill-treatment of a slave
resulting in his death is not punished, "for it is a matter of his [the
owner's] own money" (Ex. XXI. 21).[22] More significant are the cases
in which the substantiation contains an ethical appeal: a millstone is
not to be taken in pledge, for this would mean taking a life in pledge
(Deut. XXIV. 6). In the case of punishment by beating, only a set
number of stripes is to be given, "that your brother be not degraded
in your sight" (Deut. XXV. 3). Judges are to guard against taking any
bribe "for a present makes those who see [RSV, the officials] blind"
(Ex. XXIII. 8). The most important are of course the theological interpretations proper. Any kind of eating of blood is forbidden, "for in the

[19] For what follows cf. B. Gemser, "Motive clauses in Old Testament Law," in
Vet. Test., Suppl. 1 (1953), pp. 50ff.

[20] The motivating אֲנִי יהוה has fallen out at the end of some of the sentences because
the liturgical structure became forgotten.

[21] Deut. XVII. 1, XXII. 5, XXIII. 19 [18], XXV. 16. It is to be assumed that these ancient
laws concerning to'ebah once formed a liturgical series.

[22] Cf. Deut. XXI. 17; Lev. XIX. 20f.

blood is the life" (Lev. XVII. 14). "Thou shalt not utter the name of
Jahweh blasphemously, for Jahweh does not leave him unpunished
who utters his name blasphemously" (Ex. XX. 7). The commandment
against shedding human blood is substantiated by the fact that man is
made in the image of God (Gen. IX. 6). Alongside these theological
substantiations there are, finally, those which have their grounding
in the saving history, either as commandments which had to be obeyed
because they were issued and complied with in the saving history earlier,
or because Israel was to remember the bondage in Egypt, etc.[23] Since
no such substantiating interpretations are to be found in any of the
great legal codes outwith Israel, we have to see in them something
which belonged specifically to the Israelite legal tradition. No doubt
they began as a further expression of the penetrating quality of that
will for justice which stripped people of any excuse of not having
understood. But something more enters in. Jahweh wants obedience,
admittedly; but he also wants men who understand his commandments and ordinances, that is, men who assent inwardly as well. The
obedience which Jahweh wants is the obedience of men who have come
of age. Thus Deuteronomy, which makes a more earnest endeavour
than any other code to explain the commandments of Jahweh by
preaching, has the right to say "very near to thee is the word, in thy
mouth and in thine heart" (Deut. XXX. 14).

If these substantiations show how Jahweh's commandment does
not leave men alone, and how it goes with them and always explains
itself to them anew, this same process is still more clearly to be discerned in the supplements which develop an older negative commandment on the positive side.

"Thou shalt not hate thy brother in thy heart, (rather) shalt thou
reason with thy neighbour, lest thou burden thyself with sin because
of him."

"Thou shalt not avenge thyself, and also not bear a grudge against
thy fellow, (but) thou shalt love thy neighbour as thyself" (Lev. XIX.
17f.).

Here interpretation is not restricted to explanation of the meaning
of the requirement: it is as good as set alongside the original in the
form of a second demand. Even so it is still a matter of a "legal interpretation," though of a very independent kind. Israel's ear was beginning to get keener—people were feeling that behind the negative

[23] E.g. Ex. XXIII. 15; Lev. XXIII. 43; Deut. V. 15.

requirement lay a different and constructive significance. An urge sprang up to fill the space made free by the negative commandment with a positive content corresponding exactly to the significance the negative once had. With the commandments about parents and about the Sabbath in the Decalogue the procedure is somewhat different, for here the negative and original formulation got dropped completely, and the positive one alone kept the field. Still, all this amounts only to just a small part of something eminently characteristic of the whole tradition of the commandments of Jahweh in ancient Israel: Israel regarded the will of Jahweh as extremely flexible, ever and again adapting itself to each situation where there had been religious, political, or economic change. Leaving the ossification of the post-exilic period out of the picture, Jahweh's will for justice positively never stood absolutely above time for Israel, for every generation was summoned anew to hearken to it as valid for itself and to make it out for itself. This once again makes clear that the commandments were not a law, but an event, with which Jahweh specifically confronted every generation in its own *hic et nunc*, and to which it had to take up its position. The grandest example in the whole field of such fresh interpretation is Deuteronomy, which set itself the task of proclaiming the will of Jahweh to a time which in no sphere of its life any longer resembled that era when Jahweh first spoke to his people.[24] Later on we shall have to show how Deuteronomy, like the earlier codes, gives a variety of substantiations of the commandments which Jahweh promulgated. But it shows a new feature too; it also gives an inner motivation for the keeping of the commandments: love for Jahweh and thankfulness to him will lead Israel into obedience.

There is of course another new feature in Deuteronomy. It not only speaks of the "laws, statutes, and judgments," but also, since it was in a position to understand the large body of totally unconnected commandments promulgated here and there by Jahweh as a single entity, "the Torah of Jahweh," it could regard them as a theological unity.

[24] See below, p. 231. An extreme example of such a reinterpretation which makes the matter relevant for the present time is to be found in Ezek. xx. The prophet not only sees the whole of the saving history as an undertaking that has foundered because of the disobedience of Israel, but he views the dawn of the time of judgment as early as the day when Jahweh revealed his commandments. Jahweh gave them "statutes and ordinances which were not good, by which they could not have life" (vs. 25). In this connexion Ezekiel is thinking of the commandment concerning the offering of the first-born children. W. Zimmerli in *Z.Th.K.*, 1951, pp. 253ff.

Without any doubt Deuteronomy, in so doing, broke through to a new and very important insight, the background of which was concentrated thought. All the individual directions are now looked on as parts of a basically indivisible revelation of the will of Jahweh. At the same time, however, as the result of this, the concept of Jahweh's revelation finally outgrew the sphere of the cult. It was in the cult that older Israel encountered commandments and series of commandments, as well as the priestly *Toroth*. But "the" Torah was a matter for theological instruction, and its *Sitz im Leben* now became more and more the heart of man. The so-called Wisdom Psalms, particularly Pss. I and CXIX, only play variations upon the theme which Deuteronomy and the Deuteronomist had already struck up: men are to keep these words in their hearts and they are to be present to them in every situation in life (Deut. VI. 6f.; Josh. I. 8). Two expressions keep recurring in these psalms—this revelation of the will of Jahweh is the subject of ceaseless meditation and ceaseless joy. Man is unremittingly busied with it alike in the sphere of his emotional life and in his mental capacities. Without any doubt, there is also an anthropological question lying behind these psalms—the question as to the character of the man who is justified before God. In consequence there comes to view in them the picture of a man whose spiritual life is completely filled by God's addressing him and who for his action too derives every power from the word of God: for where a man so lays himself open to "the Torah," all will be well. We ought to give careful consideration to the question whether the spirit of these psalms should be labelled as "legal piety" or even as Pharisaic comfort. The fact that the revelation of the will of Jahweh is an object not only of joy, but of intense meditation, is not in itself enough to justify such verdicts. For there is as well an absence of all reflexion about the possibility of fulfilment, and of any demarcation of the permissible from the forbidden, etc. Compared with actual legal piety, which in fact knows itself always threatened by its own inability, these psalms breathe a surprisingly ingenuous piety. I should like to make the following brief observations on Ebeling's criticisms of the reserve here shown in making use of the term "law."[25] 1. The days for operating with the term "law" in Old Testament theology are long past. It long ago fell out of use in theological discussions of the subject. 2. As a result of investigation into the form of the commandments and their

[25] *Z.Th.K.*, 1958, pp. 288f.; and now *Wort und Glaube*, Tübingen 1960.

place in the cult, research has once again come up against the will of Jahweh as demand, and the question of its correct theological classification. But any linking up with the theological terminology formerly in use is ruled out at the present time, for on the one hand the terms there employed are much too general, while on the other, in the Old Testament data as seen today there are very marked differences, and, from the theological angle, the data have not as yet been reduced to such a common factor of meaning as to allow them to be summed up and labelled in the way they used to be. 3. Today our clear task consists in reaching the most exact possible theological understanding of the will of Jahweh for Israel, and seeing to it that the knowledge opening up has no obstacles laid in its path by terms which, though traditional, are no longer really appropriate. It was never in my mind to suggest the term law is illegitimate in the Old Testament, and simply the mark of theological misunderstanding.[26] But the question as to where Israel listened to what dogmatics understands by law, and what she herself clearly regarded as law, is not so easy to answer[27]: this is particularly true for what is said of earlier Jahwism.

The way leading to the end of this understanding of the law was opened up as early as the post-exilic period. It is, of course, a matter of a long and partly unseen process. The end was reached at the point where the law became an absolute quantity, that is, when it ceased to be understood as the saving ordinance of a special racial group (the cultic community of Israel) linked to it by the facts of history, and when it stepped out of this function of service and became a dictate which imperiously called into being its own community. In this way it finally became a "law" in the normal sense of the term, a law which had to be adhered to word by word, indeed letter by letter. Certainly, this cannot yet be said of Deuteronomy, for Deuteronomy is all too clearly related to a quite definite historical form of the Israel of its own time which it is intended to serve. Indeed, in reducing all the profusion of the commandments to the one fundamental commandment, to love God (Deut. VI. 4), and in concerning itself so earnestly with the inner, the spiritual, meaning of the commandments, Deuteronomy rather looks like a last stand against the beginning of a legalisation. Pss. I and CXIX also seem to

---

[26] Cf. VOL. II of this work, Pt III, ch D, and also above, p. 196: "Israel only encountered the law in its function as judge and destroyer at the time of the preaching of the prophets."

[27] W. Zimmerli, "Das Gesetz im Altem Testament," in *Th.L.Z.*, 1960, cols. 481ff.

me still to stand completely on this side of this fateful change, since the fact that, in both of them, Jahweh's revealed will is understood as an independent and profitable subject for thankful meditation cannot by itself be taken as proof of the change to a legalistic way of thinking. Noth is of course right in saying that even the very fact of Israel's submission to the complete legal heritage, which in its parts derivedfrom very varied statutes, was bound sooner or later to lead to legali sation and to the transfer of interest solely to the side of human obedience.[28] This is certainly heralded in the Chronicler's oft-repeated assurances that this or that cultic act was celebrated in strict accordance with the prescriptions of the Torah. In Dan. 1 also, that is in a story which probably dates back as early as the time of the Diaspora in Persia, the way in which the dietary laws are conceived is legalistic. Here it is no longer a matter of an ordinance which a cultic community imposed upon itself, in order to demarcate itself from certain definite other practices, but it is a matter of regulations which were no longer at all understood in their former polemical sense. Admittedly, the legalising of the regulations which had to do with cleanliness began at a comparatively early date. The legalising of the Torah was thus a process which happened at different times in accordance with the different subjects contained in it.

Later, the revelation at Sinai had also the so-called Book of the Covenant (Ex. XXI–XXIII) added to it. This was a process of literary redaction, for originally this little corpus had nothing to do with the revelation at Sinai proper, and, as far as the history of tradition goes, it has quite different roots. None the less the insertion is of considerable importance, and confronts us with fresh questions: the will for justice which had become revealed to Israel now stands upon a much broader basis and has become much more detailed. If the Decalogue had only fenced off Israel's life on the outside with negative commandments, now what lies within this sphere is here subjected to a divine ordering by means of a variety of positive and negative commandments. In its first section (Ex. XXI. 1–XXII. 16) the Book of the Covenant for the most part contains casuistic regulations about the law of slavery, liability, deposits, lien, etc. The second section (Ex. XXII. 17–XXIII. 19) gives cultic regulations concerning the year of jubilee, the Sabbath rest, and the three annual festivals. All this raises the question whether the appearance or the increase of the "legalistic" is not already recog-

[28] M. Noth, *Ges. Studien*, pp. 112ff.

nisable in the incorporation of the Book of the Covenant. On the other hand, it should be borne in mind that this law itself only comes in after the completion of the election, and that the insertion does not at any point indicate that it is to be understood as an increasing strictness in Jahweh's will which brings an alteration in Israel's situation *vis-à-vis* Jahweh. The Book of the Covenant ends with a paraenetic divine utterance emphatically assuring Israel of Jahweh's protection and guidance (Ex. XXIII. 20–33), and thereafter the covenant is completed (Ex. XXIV. 1ff.). We intend to take up elsewhere the question touched upon here, for in this respect the Book of the Covenant has indeed only stepped out along a road which led in Deuteronomy to a conclusion which was thoroughly thought through from every theological viewpoint.[29]

3. THE FIRST COMMANDMENT AND JAHWEH'S HOLY ZEAL

It is striking that the commandment not to worship other gods does not occur in the Shechemite dodecalogue (Deut. XXVII. 15ff.), that is, in the sequence which seems to us to be the more ancient. The dodecalogue begins with the commandment forbidding the making of images. This will in fact have to be explained on the basis of contemporary requirements. In the time of the earlier and of the oldest Israel, that is, in the period of the Judges when, still with a wholly peasant economy, she occupied the hill-country in central Palestine and had as yet no substantial contacts with alien cults, the danger of apostasy from Jahwism, or of syncretism, was not so acute for the general run of the people as of course it soon became. This of course does not mean that the first commandment as such is later in date than the others. On the contrary, there can be no doubt that this coefficient of intense intoler-

---

[29] Since the Book of the Covenant contains the *lex talionis* (Ex. XXI. 23–25, cf. Lev. XXIV. 18ff.; Deut. XIX. 21), we should at least remark in passing that the popular idea that this "an eye for an eye and a tooth for a tooth" simply contains the basic principle of the legal thinking of the Old Testament is wrong. The words are not formulated in the style which has its roots in Jahwism, but derive originally from Canaanite sacral law (A. Alt in *Z.A.W.*, 1934, pp. 303ff.) and are restricted to specific cases of bodily injury or homicide. Ancient Israel's legal thinking is in general not at all built on the principle of a strictly equal claim for compensation. On the *lex talionis*, see W. Preiser, "Vergeltung und Sühne im altisraelitischen Strafrecht," in *Festschrift für Eberhard Schmidt*, edd. P. Bockelmann and W. Gallas, Göttingen 1961, pp. 7ff., and particularly pp. 28ff.

ance was a characteristic of Jahwism from the very beginning. The statement "whoso sacrifices to other gods must be utterly destroyed" (Ex. XXII. 19 [20]) appears to be, in form and content alike, an older version of the corresponding commandment in the Decalogue.[30] The prohibition against taking the name of alien gods upon one's lips occurs in a concluding redactional note outside a series, and could on that account be later (Ex. XXIII. 13). The question as to the way in which Israel interpreted this commandment, which was at all times for her the commandment *par excellence*, is, however, much more important than these classifications. The formulation in the Decalogue, to have no other gods in defiance of Jahweh, is in actual fact the most general and least detailed of all the versions.[31] But precisely because of its inner spaciousness and its aptitude to be turned into a basic principle, this commandment was a fitting one to bind this side of Jahweh's will on his people for all times and in their own particular circumstances.

One interpretation of the first commandment is given by the Old Testament itself, and to begin with we must keep to it. In three passages the commandment to shun all alien cults has an allusion to Jahweh's "zeal" connected with it—"for Jahweh is a zealous God" (Ex. XX. 5, XXXIV. 14; Deut. VI. 14f.).[32] In each of them the final clause introduced by "for" is to be taken as a legitimation, that is, as a theological substantiation. But there are other references as well which bring this commandment, or its breach, into connexion with Jahweh's zeal in the same characteristic way (thus, for example, Josh. XXIV. 19; Deut. XXXII. 16; I Kings XIV. 22). This means that in this case we are dealing with far more than merely an isolated linking together of ideas. But Jahweh's zeal is also for its part brought into the closest possible connexion with his holiness (especially in Josh. XXIV. 19)—so much so that his zeal is simply understood as an expression of his holiness. We have therefore to discuss Jahweh's holiness, his zeal, and the first commandment jointly, for they are inseparable in concept.

[30] The text is rendered following Alt's emendation, *K.S.*, VOL. I, p. 311, n. 2.

[31] There is much to be said for L. Köhler's proposed translation of עַל פְּנֵי as "to defy me," *Th. R.*, 1929, p. 174. But, particularly on the basis of the language used in Deut. XXI. 16, consideration should be given to the rendering "to my disadvantage," W. F. Albright, *Von der Steinzeit bis zum Christentum*, Bern 1949, p. 442. (Not in English edns.)

[32] Zimmerli has proved conclusively that the statements about jealousy in Ex. XX. 5 do not refer to the commandment prohibiting images, but refer back beyond this commandment to the first commandment (*Festschrift für A. Bertholet*, pp. 550ff.).

Zeal and holiness are in fact only differently shaded expressions of one and the same characteristic of Jahweh.[33]

Both in the history of religion in general and in Israel in particular, the experience of the holy is a primeval religious datum; that is, the concept of the holy cannot in any way be deduced from other human standards of value. It is not their elevation to the highest degree, nor is it associated with them by way of addition. The holy could much more aptly be designated the great stranger in the human world, that is, a datum of experience which can never really be co-ordinated into the world in which man is at home, and over against which he initially feels fear rather than trust—it is, in fact, the "wholly other." Man's effort to delimit the region in which the holy was revealed and in which it gained ground, in order on the one hand to safeguard it from any intermingling with the secular (Ex. xix. 12), and at the same time to guard the secular world from danger from it, is accordingly the mark of this difference. Israel too knew the region of the holy, the *Temenos* (Arabic *Harâm*), in which standards and regulations applied which were different from those applicable outside of it—that is, sacral standards—and in which secular regulations were abrogated (*vide* the right of asylum). All to which the holy has a title is taken outwith ordinary usage: any claims which might be made upon it are extinguished. If an object or a place or a day or a man is "sanctified," this means to begin with only that it is separated, assigned to God, for God is the source of all that is holy. All this makes it clear that the holy was experienced as a power, and not as something in repose; it was rather something urgent, and in every case incalculable.[34] Considering that in the last analysis the holiness of all that is sanctified derives solely from its having been brought into contact with Jahweh, it has been rightly observed that the term indicates a relationship more than a quality.[35] The attempt to regulate it as far as possible in the cult by means of careful rites is explicable on the basis of a concern to safeguard the holy from violation due to untoward intermingling with

---

[33] Jahweh's holiness is treated by O. Procksch, in *Th. W.B.N.T.*, vol. I, pp. 88ff. Cf. further R. Asting, *Die Heiligkeit im Urchristentum*, Göttingen 1930, pp. 17–34; J. Hänel, *Die Religion der Heiligkeit*, Gütersloh 1931; J. Pedersen, *Israel III–IV*, pp. 264ff.; S. Mowinckel, *Religion und Kultus*, pp. 30ff.; H. Ringgren, *The Prophetical Conception of Holiness*, Uppsala Universitets Årsskrift, Uppsala and Leipzig 1948.

[34] J. Pedersen, *Israel III–IV*, p. 264.

[35] H. Ringgren, *The Prophetical Conception of Holiness*, p. 13.

the secular, and at the same time a concern not to be harmed by this unpredictable power.

Although what has just been said holds good not only for ancient Israel, but also for wide areas of the history of mankind's religion in general, Israel's cult had all the same a quite peculiar stamp of its own. Even simple comparison with other religions shows that what the Old Testament has to say about holiness displays a quite different intensity, a vehemence even. In particular, it is much more rigorously bound to Jahweh himself, for when the holy appears in the non-Biblical religions, it is surprisingly enough much more neutral and impersonal, approximating to something with an existence of its own.[36] No doubt there is an astounding number of examples of material holiness in the Old Testament. Uzzah dies because he touches the ark (II Sam. VI. 6f.), the altar is not to be touched (Ex. XXIX. 37, P), holy objects are not even to be looked upon (Num. IV. 18–20, P), the holy is transferable (Lev. VI. 20f. [27f.]; Ezek. XLIV. 19), etc. This very considerable body of Old Testament evidence concerning holiness reveals the limitations of the great work of Rudolf Otto, in which the holy is related much too one-sidedly to man and his soul.[37] Nor is it sufficient from the point of view of theology more or less to write off what the Old Testament says about a material holiness as the relic of a concept of holiness which was still of natural growth.[38] The references to it do not by any means occur only in the oldest documents as unedited residua of a pre-Jahwistic stage of religion; they persisted in Israel, even in the prophets, down to the latest period.[39] Thus on the part of Old Testament theology, which has up to now paid too one-sided attention to the inward and spiritual, there will have to be a renewed interest directed precisely towards this material aspect of what the Old Testament has to say concerning holiness. It will also in particular have to give up assessing the data in the Old Testament against a concept of spirit quite out of keeping with the Old Testament. To be sure, the Old Testament does contain statements about holiness that are most lofty in their spirituality—Hos. XI. 9 is one of the most sublime—and it gives accounts of experiences of the holy which lead into the intimate sphere of the personal (Is. VI. 3–5). But this must not tempt us to pronounce that other group of statements to be

[36] J. Hänel, *Die Religion der Heiligkeit*, pp. 22ff.
[37] R. Otto, *The Idea of the Holy*, London 1926.
[38] W. Eichrodt, *Theologie*, VOL. I (Eng. trans.), p. 275.
[39] H. Ringgren, *The Prophetical Conception of Holiness*, p. 18.

something basically alien to Jahwism, for if we did, we should fail to recognise something which is of the utmost importance—the fact that Jahweh's holiness wants to penetrate the whole of man, and is not satisfied merely with his soul. Israel at all times believed that Jahweh did not reveal his holiness only to men, but he also sanctified things or places or times, and this meant that he claimed them as his own. But the times which he set apart for himself are not solely cultic. By an act of judgment or salvation he can "get himself glory" at any hour in history; that is, whenever he wants, he can make events happen which allow the *doxa* of his action in history to be recognised in an altogether immediate way. Thus on occasion the historical narratives speak of Jahweh's "getting himself glory" in history (Ex. XIV. 4f., 17; Num. XX. 13; Lev. X. 3). This idea presupposes that Jahweh's action in history is in general hidden, though on special occasions his *doxa* is made outwardly and visibly manifest. It is significant that Ezekiel, whose thought is so very strongly influenced by cultic ideas, speaks particularly of this "getting himself glory" of Jahweh in history (Ezek. XX. 41, XXVIII. 22, 25, XXXVIII. 16, 23). But on one occasion P too directs its gaze to a future in which "the glory of God will fill the whole earth" (Num. XIV. 21): it therefore regards the hitherto existing limitation of Jahweh's holiness to a special cultic sphere as something temporary, which will be followed by the ultimate universalising. This idea falls into line with the oracle of one of the post-exilic prophets that "in that day" the pots in the houses and the bells on the horses' harness will be as holy as the sacred vessels in the temple (Zech. XIV. 20f.), which means that then the whole realm of the secular will be taken up into Jahweh's holiness. When that happens, Jahweh's holiness will have attained its utmost goal.

Nevertheless, behind all this, however material and impersonal it may appear in itself, there always stands the zeal of Jahweh, from which even the most insignificant procedure in the cult cannot be dissociated. For it is in the cult first and foremost and not in direct personal relationship with God that Israel encounters Jahweh's zeal, this most personal of all the manifestations of his being. And this brings us up against the primary characteristic of Israel's cult, Jahweh's curt claim, in the first commandment, to be the only God worshipped. For zeal (קִנְאָה, Ger. *Eifer*) is an equivalent of jealousy (Ger. *Eifersucht*)—that is, an emotion springing from the very depths of personality: as the zealous one Jahweh is a person to the highest possible degree.[40] Thus Jahweh's

40 W. Eichrodt, *Theologie*, VOL. I (Eng. trans.), p. 211.

zeal consists in the fact that he wills to be the only God for Israel, and that he is not disposed to share his claim for worship and love with any other divine power. So in this commandment declaring the zeal of Jahweh Israel was told two things: Jahweh's turning towards her— of this Hosea speaks in terms of the passion of a lover—but at the same time his threat, in case she should only yield to him with a divided heart. This intolerant claim to exclusive worship is something unique in the history of religion, for in antiquity the cults were on easy terms with one another and left devotees a free hand to ensure a blessing for themselves from other gods as well. Why, even the various sanctuaries were quite often regarded as common ground, for in a temple cultic gifts were quite often offered to other deities as well as to the god to whom the temple belonged—a fate which on occasion befell even Solomon's Temple (II Kings XXIII. 4, 11f.). The most concise definition of the demands which Jahweh's zeal laid upon Israel is given in Deuteronomy—Israel is to be "perfect" (תמים) with Jahweh (Deut. XVIII. 13).[41]

The concept "other gods" is certainly to be understood in the widest sense of the term. But in connexion with it what we have to think of is not so much the "high gods" of the great empires, Marduk in Babylon or Amon in Egypt, but rather such deities whose worship was indigenous to Palestine, and who could be real sources of temptation to Israel, e.g. Baal, Bethel, Dagon, Astarte, Anath, Asherah, etc. At the same time this commandment was also directed against the less important private cults, in particular against any manner of worship of the dead. The surprising number of regulations against the cult of the dead and the rites pertaining to it allow of the conclusion that a particularly bitter warfare was waged against it, as a cult which offered special temptations to ancient peoples.[42] Altogether, we must realise that the texts show us only a very small part of the course of the struggle against the cult of alien deities *in actu*. In many cases the issues had been decided long before they could as such find literary expression. What a large number of far-reaching cultic discussions possibly lies behind the two lists of unclean animals in Lev. XI. 2ff. and Deut. XIV.

[41] Only in the prophets does the concept of Jahweh's zeal appear in dissociation from the cult and from the reference to the first commandment. Jahweh's zeal stands behind his action in history, and this in a twofold form—as zeal exercised in wrath (Zeph. I. 18; Nah. I. 2; Ps. LXXIX. 5) and as zeal exercised for salvation (Is. IX. 6 [7]; Ezek. XXXIX. 25; Joel II. 18; Zech. I. 14; II Kings XIX. 31).

[42] Lev. XIX. 27f., 31, XX. 6, 27, XXI. 5; Deut. XIV. 1, XVIII. 11, XXVI. 14, and frequently.

4ff.! These animals were certainly used for sacrifice in one cult or another, or else they had a sacral connexion with divine powers; and just for this reason they were sacrally disqualified for the cult of Jahweh.[43] But now abstention from these animals was not confined only to the time when a *status confessionis* was in operation; it remained as a cultic obligation for Israel long after these cults could no longer have been a temptation to her. The compilation of lists of such animals is, of course, the final phase in the conflict with such cults. An age which was in the position to draw up such summary lists as these must have been far removed in time from the cultic struggles themselves. In this matter the spectacular rites connected with the putting away of foreign gods narrated in Gen. xxxv. 2–4 (cf. Josh. xxiv. 14, 23) leads us more directly into that part of the history of the cult of which we do have knowledge. This cultic act celebrated at Shechem, in which all objects belonging to an alien cult had to be disclosed by the community and then ritually buried, is an impressive example of the way in which the first commandment was constantly made relevant to the present. But the only really more precise historical knowledge which we possess is derived primarily from Jahwism's contest with the Baal worship of Canaan. This cannot be explained merely as due to the predominance in the Old Testament of the Deuteronomistic literature, which is, indeed, theologically determined solely by the confrontation with the Canaanite cult, and which in actual fact corresponds to historical reality.[44] In this tremendously hard struggle, in which the very existence of Jahwism was continually at stake, Israel did not by any means have at her disposal any ready-made authentic and once-for-all valid understanding of the meaning and scope of the first commandment. Rather was she obliged in every situation to ascertain afresh what Jahweh's will for the cult was at the moment, for the situation in

---

[43] We know very little about the cultic significance which these animals once had. A few details are given in Noth, *Ges. Studien*, pp. 78ff. The commandment "not to seethe a kid in its mother's milk" which appears twice in different contexts (Ex. xxiii. 19, Deut. xiv. 21), forbids a magical practice with milk which was obviously widespread in the religion of the Palestinian peasants. The corresponding positive direction is found in one of the Ras Shamra texts (Gordon, *Handbook*, ii, 52: 14).

[44] O. Eissfeldt has given an impressive sketch of Jahweh's seven-centuries-long battle against Baal—based on the special point of view that the common assumption of a multiplicity of local Baals is incorrect, and that what comes in question is always rather one single divinity, namely that "Baal of high heaven." "Baalšamen und Jahwe," in *Z.A.W.*, 1939, pp. 24ff.

which she had to remain loyal to the first commandment was constantly changing. Usages which might have been regarded as innocuous in one period had in another to be sacrificed to the radical and severe demands made by this commandment.[45] The interpretation of the first commandment was therefore very flexible. Indeed, the whole history of Israel's cult is a struggle solely concerned with the validity of the first commandment.[46]

But our attempt to understand the first commandment in the light of the concept of Jahweh's zeal would remain incomplete and liable to misconstruction without an appreciation of the fact that this demand was rooted in the saving history. For the first commandment is not an axiom; on the contrary, it is Jahweh himself who proves that he is the only God; and this he does through his deeds in history—"I am Jahweh who brought you out of the land of Egypt." In actual fact, quite often all that is said of the alien gods is that they have no historical connexion with Israel—the patriarchs did not "know" them, they were not acquainted with them (Deut. XIII. 7 [6], XXVIII. 64; Jer. IX. 15 [14], XVI. 13, XIX. 4). They are "newcomers" (חדשים מקרוב, Deut. XXXII. 17), an objection to them which is most characteristic of Israel's faith and its way of thinking about history. Jahweh is the God of Israel from of old (Pss. XLIV. 2 [1], LXXIV. 2, 12).

The problem of monotheism in ancient Israel is admittedly connected with the first commandment, in so far as Israel's monotheism was to some extent a realisation which was not granted to her without the long discipline of the first commandment. Still, it is necessary to keep the two questions as far as possible distinct, for the first commandment has initially nothing to do with monotheism: on the contrary, as the way in which it is formulated shows, it is only comprehensible in the light of a background which the historian of religion designates as polytheistic.[47] Even the way in which Jahweh introduces himself, "I am Jahweh, your God," presupposes a situation of polytheism. For

---

[45] Thus, for example, the "Massebahs" and "Asherahs," cultic stone pillars and wooden poles, Gen. XXVIII. 18, XXXV. 14; Deut. XVI. 22; Lev. XXVI. 1; and in particular the many shrines up and down the land where Jahweh was worshipped, which were liquidated by Deuteronomy in favour of the one single place of worship (Deut. XII. 1ff.).

[46] The first commandment has here been dealt with in its original cultic sense. But the prophets made a completely new application of it by relating it to making idols of earthly instruments of power (armaments, alliances, etc.).

[47] B. Balscheit, *Alter und Aufkommen des Monotheismus in der israelitischen Religion*, p. 15. Cf. also H. H. Rowley, "The antiquity of Israelite monotheism," in *The Expository Times*, 1949–50, pp. 333ff.; *id.*, in *Z.A.W.*, 1957, pp. 10ff.

many a generation there existed in Israel a worship of Jahweh which, from the point of view of the first commandment, must undoubtedly be taken as legitimate, though it was not monotheistic. It is therefore called henotheism or monolatry. The very frequent and completely frank references to the existence of other gods continue down to the period of the monarchy (cf. Gen. XXXI. 53; Jg. XI. 24; I Sam. XXVI. 19; II Kings III. 27): indeed, it is noticeable that there are rather fewer of them in the most ancient texts than in the later ones, a fact which is easy to explain on the basis that in her earliest days Israel had far less contact with alien cults than had the Israel which began to move more independently in the political world. The detached impartiality with which Chemosh, the god of Moab, and the "great wrath" which came down from him against Israel, are spoken of in II Kings III. 27 has often been noted with a certain surprise. But there was once a time when the gods of the other nations whom Israel only encountered incidentally, and in whose worship she felt not the slightest temptation to take part, were relatively without interest for Jahwism. (How different her reactions were to Chemosh of Moab and to the Canaanite Baal!) None the less, there is justification for speaking of the rise of monotheism in Israel, for we have evidence enough from her later period of a practical and, afterwards, of even a theoretical monotheism. But the demonstration of the way in which this monotheism arose is altogether tricky. Obviously, of course, in Israel there is no question of it being due to a philosophic reduction of the multiplicity of numinous phenomena to the view of them as one. Monotheism as such was not a thing in which Israel of herself would have taken any particular interest —she did not measure herself by it or make it a touchstone, as she did with the first commandment. We are thus dealing with a process of recognition, of which Israel herself was actually not properly aware. The last thing we can hope to do is to indicate a particular point in history at which monotheism took its rise, for how many are the tendencies and ideas which flow side by side in one and the same period! Cultic texts—hymns—are rather conservative in what they say, and on that account are not entirely characteristic of the ideas of a particular time. At what time were the gods of the Canaanite pantheon, into whose company the stranger Jahweh had made his entrance (Ps. LXXXII), demoted to be a body of Elohim-beings with the function of singing praises?[48] Where, and where not, is the term "gods" simply

[48] Alt, *K.S.*, VOL. I, p. 354.

rhetorical embellishment?[49] Compared with such texts, the prophets are much freer from traditional formulations: their utterances are certainly a much more direct reflexion of their own ideas, and on that account the lordly silence with which Isaiah or Amos pass over the gods of the nations and their power is of real significance.[50] There was of course one situation in the history of Jahwism when Israel could no longer afford to be offhanded in the way she spoke of the jurisdiction of foreign gods. This day dawned when the Assyrian emperors reached out in the direction of Palestine. This posed the question, who was really lord in the sphere of history. Was this empire, planning to reach out in the direction of Zion, which Jahweh himself had founded, stronger than the God of Israel, and had he perhaps left it out of account? The answer made by Isaiah cannot at present be developed. But as is perfectly clear, his view of history leaves no place whatsoever for the gods of other nations or any functions they might exercise. The prophet giving clearest expression to a monotheism which is now the conscious product of theological reflexion is Deutero-Isaiah ("I am Jahweh, besides me there is no God." "Before me no god was formed, nor shall there be any after me," Is. XLV. 5f., XLII. 10).[51] But with him too there is no truth based on philosophy of religion; he believes rather that only those who confess Jahweh are able to make his solity as the lord of history credible.

4. THE VETO ON IMAGES IN THE OLD TESTAMENT[52]

Even where the second commandment of the Decalogue is not completely ignored in works dealing with the theology or religion of the

[49] Ps. XCV. 3, XCVII. 7. The designation of the gods as "nothing" (אלילים) has not as yet to be understood in the sense of a basic denial of their existence: it can also be a way of rendering them contemptible (cf. 1 Kings XVIII. 27).

[50] J. Hempel, *Das Ehos des Alten Testaments*, henceforth cited as *Ethos*, Berlin 1938, pp. 106f.

[51] Cf. Is. XLI. 28f., XLII. 17, XLIV. 7f., XLV. 16, XLVI. 1f. and frequently.

[52] K. H. Bernhardt, *Gott und Bild, Ein Beitrag zur Begründung und Deutung des Bilderverbotes im Alten Testament*, Berlin 1956; W. Zimmerli, "Das zweite Gebot," in *Festschrift für A. Bertholet*, p. 550; H. T. Obbink, "Jahwebilder," in *Z.A.W.*, 1929, pp. 264ff.; H. Schrade, *Der verborgene Gott. Gottesbild und Gottesvorstellung im alten Israel und im alten Orient*, Stuttgart 1949; J. Hempel, *Das Bild in Bibel und Gottesdienst* (Sammlung gemeinverst. Vort.), Tübingen 1957; W. Vischer, "Du sollst dir kein Bildnis machen," in *Antwort, Festschrift für K. Barth*, Zollikon-Zürich 1956, pp. 764ff.

Old Testament, as for example with L. Köhler, it has for long remained quite in the background in comparison with the first commandment. The older critical school felt itself exempted from any special treatment of this commandment for the reason that it was convinced that the cult of Jahweh—at least that of the earlier period—was in fact not imageless. But a much greater danger resulted from a completely erroneous idea of its meaning. Starting from an antithesis between visible and invisible, material and spiritual, which, while quite generally held, is quite alicn to the Old Testament, the critics thought that the second commandment had to be understood as the expression of a special spirituality in the worship of God, as the signal, important overcoming of a spiritual and cultic primitivism, and so as the attainment of a decisive stage in the education of the human race which has of course largely become general property since then. However, the truths that in the last resort God cannot be visibly represented, that his worship is a matter of the heart rather than of the eye, and that men must learn to accept the invisible as really invisible, are of course all general truths of religion which, just because of their generality, are quite inapplicable to the real problem. It would still remain absolutely inexplicable how such an inoffensive piece of common or garden knowledge could have given rise to such fierce conflicts as are related in the story of the golden calf and which continue down to the period of the Maccabees. It is quite impossible to regard what was Israel's most peculiar and secret possession as a self-evident truth to which anyone who thinks deeply must assent.[53] Would it in that case have needed the effort of an ultimate theophany of Jahweh to reveal the impotence and nothingness of images (Is. II. 20, XLVI. 1ff.)?

In face of such misconceptions the theologian has to learn from the general science of religion what are the special properties of an image. It soon appears that images were only in the most exceptional cases actually identified with the deity concerned: at any rate this was not done in the cults with which Israel came into contact. Images made no claim to give an exhaustive representation of the being of the deity.

---

[53] Against the perfectly mistaken interpretation of the commandment against images in P. Volz, *Mose und sein Werk*, 2nd edn. Tübingen 1932, pp. 36ff., cf. also H. Cohen, *Religion der Vernunft aus den Quellen des Judentums*, Leipzig 1919, pp. 58ff.: "Polytheism is the worship of idols. But the worship of God is the worship of the true being. The battle against the deity is therefore the battle of being against appearance, of original being against copies which have no original" (p. 63).

The pagan religions knew as well as Israel did that deity is invisible, that it transcends all human ability to comprehend it, and that it cannot be captured by or comprised in a material object. But this did not deter them from consecrating cultic images to it. "The image is, as it were, the medium of the spirit."[54] Most certainly, many of these images foreshadow an amazing spirituality in the conception of the deity, for "enough for thy soaring spirit's fieriest flight the mere likeness, the mere image."[55] Thus, the antithesis of material and spiritual does not give the solution of the problem. The image has nothing to say about the being of the deity or the mode of its inner life. What it speaks about is rather how the deity is pleased to reveal himself, for the image is first and foremost the bearer of a revelation. Ancient peoples felt the divine powers to be very close to them. No doubt these came from below and were incalculable; but in cultic symbols and images they approached men in a way that was helpful. In terms of this belief, the whole world is like a curtain which permits the divine to be seen through it; or at least such a transparency was possible wherever the deity authorised something material as its manifestation. Even if the relationship of the deity to the image was complex, and was hardly anywhere a completely clarified concept, still, the crucial thing was that the deity became present in the image.[56] But with the presence of the deity there was at the same time given the presence of its power, for it could now become effective, with its particular blessings, for man and in the world of man. The pious mind can never set up images enough, for the mysteries in which the divine makes itself manifest in the human sphere are beyond counting. This was therefore a commandment demanded by the most natural and human impulses from the earliest times right down to Goethe.[57] As against this idea, the veto on images in the Old Testament is by no means a general religious truth, but the most abrupt affront to this concept of deity. Here becomes manifest something of the mystery of Israel, something of her nature as a stranger and a sojourner among the religions. Anyone who seriously devotes himself to a study of religions as they appear and to their worship of images can find absolutely no way of transition from

[54] G. van der Leeuw, *Phänomenologie der Religion*, p. 429.
[55] J. W. Goethe, *Proömion*.
[56] The subtle Old Egyptian definitions of Ka, the "outward soul" of the god which is present in the image, are already an exception.
[57] Cf. Goethe's conversation with Eckermann on 11 Mar. 1832.

them to Israel's prohibition of images[58]; for the occasional crises due to rationalism that at times affected also the religions which used images can be only very remotely connected with the second commandment of the Decalogue.

In the history which Israel herself wrote of herself, she believed that the commandment which forbade images had been revealed from the time of Moses onwards. This view has again and again been vehemently disputed down to the present day. In actual fact, in the way in which she measured herself and her early period against this prohibition, the later Israel very much schematised the course of her cultic history. The reality was much more complicated, and the boundaries between the imageless worship demanded and an actual worship of images were, in the early periods at any rate, much more fluid. But at that very time, Israel's earlier period, a distinction has to be made between the official cult of Jahweh and the many kinds of local or private cults: in our opinion, there is no justification for refusing to believe that images were not used in the amphictyonic cult at the central shrine, which is the oldest form of the cult of Jahweh of which we have historical knowledge.[59] The Shechemite Dodecalogue, which contains the oldest formulation of the commandment prohibiting images (Deut. XXVII. 15) comes from this time.[60] If this series of curses was pronounced over the community at the climax of a pilgrimage festival, then the situation which resulted is as follows. The official cult which was the concern of the priesthood made no use of images, and this aspect of the matter does not fall to be discussed in the series. But it was still possible for one or other of the pilgrims to have a cultic image set up at home, in whose presence he performed his own private cult. The image implied in the commandment was certainly an image of Jahweh, and not one of an alien or foreign deity, with which the peasants in the hill-country of Samaria or Ephraim were at that time probably very little acquainted. Whichever way we look at it, the amphictyonic cult of the time made no use of images—in this official place no image of the godhead could venture to appear. But

---

[58] So apparently Mowinckel, *Religion und Kultus*, pp. 47ff.

[59] Mowinckel takes it differently. He assumes that the Mosaic age was still completely uninterested in the question of images, and that the absence of images in the official cult in Jerusalem only dates from about 990. (*Acta Orientalia*, 1930, pp. 257ff.).

[60] The text has obviously been expanded at a later date: formerly the commandment was couched in the same terse form as that preserved in those which follow it.

the story in Jg. XVII gives us a very realistic picture of what might at times take place in remote country spheres.[61]

It is a very different case with the veto on images in the Decalogue (Ex. xx), for here the commandment is drafted wholly with reference to the commandment forbidding the worship of other gods. It is therefore understood in a different way from Deut. XXVII. 15, for it forbids the representation of Jahweh in an image belonging to another deity, for example in the likeness of a bull, the cultic symbol of Baal. In Ex. xx we therefore have to do with a quite special interpretation of the commandment against images.[62] In comparison with Deut. XXVII. 15, it originates in a later phase in the history of the cult, at the time when syncretism was already starting, and the distinction between Jahweh and Baal was beginning to be levelled out, and Jahweh was being worshipped more or less in the forms and concepts employed in the cult of Baal. The story of the golden calf in Ex. XXXII or the struggle of Hosea (XI. 2, VIII. 4) lies within this development.[63]

One interpretation on a grand scale of this commandment forbidding images is to be found in Deut. IV. 9–20, a homiletic passage which could very well be described as a theological *exposé* of this subject. The fact that "written evidence," and highly rationalising evidence at that, is now given for the commandment, is characteristic of the relatively late date of this reference—it may be exilic. Israel saw no visible form of Jahweh whatever at Sinai: she only heard his voice coming from the fire; and this is the reason why she is forbidden to represent Jahweh by an image. Here the antithesis is now worked out quite clearly—in her relationship to God Israel, unlike the other nations, is not directed to a cultic image, but to the bare word of God.[64] Another thing which is new in this passage, as compared with the earlier period, is that the difference between the two mutually exclusive cultic practices can now be reduced to a simple formula. What was

[61] In Jg. XVII. 4f. we can see what went to make up a complete idol: פסל is the wooden figure, מסבה the outer overlay of metal: in addition there is also the אפוד, the cuirass-like case, and finally the תרפים, possibly a cultic mask (so A. Alt verbally). It is therefore unnecessary to strike out glosses.

[62] So W. Zimmerli, in *Festschrift für A. Bertholet*, p. 557.

[63] It would of course be a different case if Eissfeldt were right that the bull is also a cultic symbol of Jahwism which goes back to the period before the settlement in Palestine: *Z.A.W.*, 1940, pp. 199ff.

[64] The tolerance which refers the idolatry of the heathen to Jahweh's own ordering (Deut. IV. 19) is of course unique in the Old Testament.

previously a pressing and bewildering temptation can now be explained in rational and theological terms. This holds true of course in even greater degree for the satirising disquisition on the manufacture of idols in Deutero-Isaiah (Is. xliv. 9ff.). Two things make the idol very suspect—the fact that the material can be put to common use, and the frailty of the manufacturer. The speaker here is no longer speaking from the depths of a real temptation: both here and in Ps. cxv. 4–7 it is rather the voice of a certain enlightenment which finds expression, and which subsequently reinforces the commandment forbidding images—the images of foreign deities have become ludicrous. The position thus reached was not, however, without its dangers, for with the disappearance of the temptation Israel ceased to have an understanding of idolatry—it has been rightly asserted that the enlightened caricature in Is. xliv in no sense squares with the earnestness of the heathen cultic practice.[65] Furthermore, in the earlier periods the commandment forbidding images did not prejudice the assurance of Jahweh's most personal presence.[66] But this enlightened rationalism which pokes fun at idols —"it wobbles" (לֹא יִמּוֹט, Is. xli. 7)—is beginning to make Jahweh wholly transcendent. The final stage in this trend is reached with the Apocrypha, in the legend of Bel which is added to Daniel, where the heathen priests are not only stupid, but are also dishonest.

All this does not, of course, offer any real explanation of the commandment against images. And in actual fact ancient Israel never maintained that she knew the theological or pedagogic reasons why this commandment was imposed upon her, for even Deut. iv. 9–20 is in fact only a substantiation from history and not an explanation. We shall not go wrong if we suppose that the static divine presence in a cultic image as an object of power at man's disposal, from which potentialities could be drawn, at worst even by means of magic, could not possibly be reconciled with the nature of the revelation of Jahweh; with the result that Jahweh's freedom was encroached upon with the very setting up of an image. But this explanation cannot be said to be the real decisive one either.[67] Instead, we shall be on the right track if, with Israel's religious environment in mind, we understand the

[65] J. Hempel, *Ethos*, p. 107.   [66] Eichrodt, *Theologie*, vol. I, p. 53.
[67] In this sense K. H. Bernhardt is right in making the commandment forbidding images parallel to the commandment concerning the name. Neither by an image nor by the name may man gain power over Jahweh; *Gott und Bild*, Berlin 1956, pp. 153ff.

commandment as the expression of an utterly different view of the world.[68] Without any doubt, the inhabitant of the ancient East was confronted in his physical environment by the deity in a much more immediate way than Israel could say that Jahweh confronted her. In the greater and the lesser religions of the ancient East the gods were personified powers of heaven or earth or the abyss.[69] But this was not the way in which Jahweh was related to the world. However powerful his sway in it was, theologically he still transcended it. Nature was not a mode of Jahweh's being; he stood over against it as its Creator. This then means that the commandment forbidding images is bound up with the hidden way in which Jahweh's revelation came about in cult and history. It would be a great mistake to think of the commandment simply as an isolated cultic peculiarity of Israel. The Jahweh whom Israel was so strictly forbidden to worship by means of an image was still the same Jahweh by whose hidden action in history she was continually kept in suspense. What was laid upon Israel in the cultic sphere she was obliged to bear also in the sphere of historical guidance—consider the vistas of history in the prophets. No, the Jahweh of the stories of the patriarchs, or the Jahweh proclaimed by Deutero-Isaiah, was not a God who could be worshipped by cultic images. The relentless shattering of cherished concepts of God which occupied the pre-exilic prophets stands in a theological relationship which is perhaps hidden, but which is, in actual fact, very close to the commandment forbidding images. Any interpretation which deals in isolation with the impossibility of representing Jahweh by an image, and which does not see the commandment as bound up with the totality of Jahweh's revelation, misses the crucial point, quite apart from the fact that in itself imageless worship is not by any manner of means an unambiguous phenomenon—it can be the expression of a very low conception of God derived from fetishism, or of a very lofty one.[70]

It cannot of course be said that, for the form of their proclamation of Jahweh, the prophets felt that their hands were tied by the command-

[68] See VOL. II of this work, Pt. III, Ch. B, p. 336.

[69] William A. Irwin in *The Intellectual Adventure of Ancient Man*, Chicago 1946, p. 244.

[70] If it was necessary, for the understanding of the commandment forbidding images, to draw attention to the theological independence of Israel's understanding of the world, then the idea of man as made in the image of God has also to be incorporated in this discussion. Israel herself to be sure drew no such connecting lines, but it can hardly be doubted that there is an inner connexion between the commandment and the image of God in man.

ment forbidding images. On the contrary, what they say is on occasion uninhibitedly anthropomorphic.[71] But this fact can again put us on our guard against a philosophic misunderstanding of the commandment. Its intention was not by any means to debar the people of Israel from representing Jahweh in concrete form—as a matter of fact Jahweh was always thought of as having human form, like that of a man.[72] But of course this representation of him in human shape was, both in concept and language, not a cultic image, a mediator of revelation claiming cultic adoration. The time had not yet arrived when God could be worshipped as man, and the place occupied in the pagan religions by the cultic image was in Israel taken by the word and name of Jahweh. Thus, in its immediate literal sense the second commandment was restricted to the sphere of the cult. But as far as its day-to-day interpretation went—what was Israel debarred from here and now?— the position was the same as with the first commandment: there was no generally valid and authentic interpretation, but Israel had rather ever and again to ascertain afresh the scope of Jahweh's sovereign will. If the official worship of Jahweh always repudiated his representation by images, certain cultic symbols, for example, the Masseboth or the brazen serpent, were only gradually affected by the commandment forbidding images.[73] And the holy Ark was never affected by the increasing strictness of the commandment.[74]

5. DEUTERONOMY[75]

1. Deuteronomy now falls to be discussed in our treatment of the commandments and of the question of how Israel explained Jahweh's revelation of his will in theological terms, for never again did she express herself so comprehensively and in such detail as to the meaning of the commandments and the unique situation into which Jahweh's revelation of his will put her. But from the very start it has to be

[71] J. Hempel, "Jahwegleichnisse der Propheten," in Z.A.W., 1924, pp. 74ff.

[72] So for example Ex. XV. 3; I Kings XXII. 19; Is. XXX. 27; Ezek. I. 26.

[73] For the Massebah cf. Gen. XXVIII. 18 with Deut. XVI. 22: for the brazen serpent cf. Num. XXI. 4b–9 with II Kings XVIII. 4.

[74] The Ark is of course demoted by the Deuteronomic theology into no more than a container of the tables of the law, Deut. X. 1ff.; I Kings VIII. 9.

[75] H. Breit, Die Predigt des Deuteronomisten, Munich 1933; F. Horst, Das Privilegrecht Jahwes, Göttingen 1930; M. Noth, Die Gesetze im Pentateuch (in Ges. Studien); G. von Rad, Studies in Deuteronomy; A. R. Hulst, Het charakter van den cultus in Deuteronomium (Doctorate Thesis, Groningen 1938).

borne in mind that, like the other writings too, Deuteronomy is the exposition of the will of God for a particular era only, and that a fairly advanced one in the history. Many things now needed to be said in a different way and given a different application. The outward form and arrangement of Deuteronomy, consisting of paraenesis, commandments, pledging to the covenant, proclamation of blessing and cursing (IV. 44–XXX. 20), appears strange. But it is a unity, for the sequence of these parts reflects the liturgical movement of a cultic festival, that of the renewal of the covenant at Shechem.[76] The fact that the liturgical sweep of a cultic festival had to furnish the framework for a major literary and theological work lets us see once more how hard it was for Israel to unfold theological concepts theoretically by processes of thought. Here too the concepts required to be explained by reference to an event, and for Deuteronomy this is the course of a cultic event. In itself the content of Deuteronomy would in fact have lent itself to a systematic presentation, for in it Israel for once really created a work that has unity of thought, internal balance, and finish. The outward expression of this unity is the much-discussed Deuteronomic style. It, too, is in fact something singular, for when and where was Israel ever again able to clothe a great literary work in so completely uniform a style and diction? This Deuteronomic style, which is characterised by a ceaseless repetition of set phrases, is out and out paraenetic, a wooing and imploring form of address. In form Deuteronomy is one single farewell sermon of Moses to Israel. The picture is as follows: at Sinai (Deuteronomy always calls it Horeb) Israel received only the Decalogue. But since Israel was incapable of listening to Jahweh again, Jahweh imparted a great deal more to Moses, namely, the "whole law" (כל ־המצוה, Deut. v. 31). Moses only proclaimed this comprehensive revelation of the divine will in the land of Moab shortly before his death, for it was only to come into effect as a rule of life in the land of Canaan (Deut. IV. 45f., v. 27ff., XXXI. 9ff.). Thus Deuteronomy regards itself as an elaborate revelation given at Sinai. It is only in a later appendix that Deuteronomy is somewhat further removed from the events at Sinai by means of the idea of a special covenant made in the land of Moab (Deut. XXIX. 1ff.). But even for this later way of looking at it, Deuteronomy is the publication of the revelation of Jahweh given to Moses at Sinai.

Our task here is the theological understanding of Deuteronomy

[76] G. von Rad, *Ges. Studien*, pp. 33ff.

itself. For this, the fact that its literary structure is not yet completely clear is no great handicap, for, apart from a few additions in the time of the exile,[77] the whole bears one theological stamp throughout. All the same, even in this connexion, the question of its historical primary stages and its traditio-historical presuppositions cannot be completely passed over in silence, because it is precisely here that we gain a better perspective on the special characteristics of Deuteronomy. If we attempt to grope our way behind Deuteronomy historically, in order to gain some knowledge of its growth, what we come up against is far from being the "Book of the Covenant" (Ex. XXI–XXIII) or the other older legal or sacral individual traditions which were taken up into Deuteronomy: rather it is first of all an obviously intensive preaching activity, whose representatives must have been the Levites. Deuteronomy is in fact simply and solely an artistic mosaic made up of many sermons on a great variety of subjects—here is gathered the total expression of an obviously extensive preaching activity.[78] Traditions of the most varied kinds, historical, cultic, and legal, were united in these preachers' hands; and they then set this whole body of material into that great schematised general picture of the people of Israel which first springs to our minds too when we think of Israel in the wilderness. But this general picture, in which everything now appears to belong organically together, is in turn the result of an intensive harmonising of many originally independent traditions. All the same, the unity is now so complete that no one reading Deuteronomy with an unprejudiced eye thinks that the traditions of the patriarchs, of the commandments at Sinai, of the wanderings in the wilderness or, in particular, the many legal and cultic ordinances, for the most part originally existed independently, and were brought together from many different spheres.

It seems to us that the term which Deuteronomy applied to itself, "this Torah," has a special importance for this unification, particularly for the legal traditions.[79] We must bear in mind that, up to this time,

---

[77] Deut. XXVIII. 25–69, XXIX.   [78] G. von Rad, *Studies in Deuteronomy*, pp. 11ff.

[79] Deuteronomy's designation of itself is not uniform. Undoubtedly the most important is "Torah" (Deut. IV. 44, XXXI. 9, 11f., 17, 18), "this Torah," "the book of this Torah" (Deut. XXVIII. 61, XXIX. 20, XXX. 10), "the words of this Torah" (Deut. XVII. 19, XXVII. 3, 26, XXVIII. 58, XXIX. 28 [27]); side by side with these stands on occasion המצוה, also in the singular (Deut. VI. 1a, XXX. 11). The plurals חקים, משפטים, מצות, which occur for the most part in collocations designed to give assurance, are much more colourless (Deut. V. 1, VI. 17, 20, VII. 11f., VIII. 11, XI. 1, 13, 32 and frequently).

the word "torah" designated the single directions given by the priests—for example, on the basis of an oracle (Hag. II. 11)—that is, a single decision which did not in compass go beyond a brief statement.[80] But if now the whole of Deuteronomy could be comprehended under this term, there lay behind this an insight to which the way had certainly been opened up by Hosea,[81] but which Deuteronomy put upon the broadest possible theological base. The whole of the revelation of the will of Jahweh to Israel is now understood, in spite of the great variety of its contents, as a unity. It is seen as something indivisible and whole, in which every part was co-ordinated with every other and where no detail could be understood except in relation to the whole. We can very well imagine that in her earlier days Israel was still a long way off the knowledge of this unifying principle for theological thought. At that time the individual Israelite lived his life in association with one of the great sanctuaries and its cultic regulations. And the cultic or historical traditions about the early period which attached to the sanctuary in question were all more or less local traditions, and thus far from comprising the whole wealth of traditions which are unfolded in Deuteronomy as the one revelation of Jahweh. This view of Deuteronomy's of a theological unity presupposes a considerable capacity for theological reflexion. For its compiler himself no longer stands within this or that tradition, but rather looks at all of them from a definite remove, no longer living in them himself. To revert to Deuteronomy's description of itself as "the" torah, it is obvious from what has been said that this term "torah" cannot be rendered by our word "law," for its theological meaning would then be curtailed. The Deuteronomic term "torah" means the whole of the bestowals of Jahweh's saving will—in German the word can be rendered by the equally neutral term *Willensoffenbarung* (revelation of the will). In virtue of the rigorous inner levelling out, this summary proclamation of "the" torah is in actual fact the one theological work in the Old Testament which demands a more systematic presentation of its content. Indeed, it is Deuteronomy's intention to be something like a totality of teaching. "You shall not add to this, nor take from it" (Deut. XIII. 1 [XII. 32], IV. 2). Nevertheless, we must not go too far in laying stress on its inner cohesion, or look for anything like a progression of thought in it. For Deuteronomy the progression was determined by a liturgical

[80] The word is still used with this meaning in Deut. XVII. 11.
[81] H. W. Wolff, *Hosea* (Bib. Komm.), pp. 176f.

event: the advance from the introductory sermon through the commandments to the pledging to the covenant and the blessings and curses is therefore due rather to considerations of the saving history than to theological or systematic considerations. Even the single units of material within this *schema* are canvases set side by side. The great inner unity of Deuteronomy results simply from the fact that in it is summed up the deposit of a preaching activity which was determined by a very few uniform basic thoughts.

2. *The Paraeneses*. The first task in understanding the paraeneses is to determine their place. This sermon is of course represented as spoken to Israel "in the land of Moab," "beyond Jordan," and is thus given out as Moses' farewell discourse (according to Deut. v. 28 it is one great exposition of the Decalogue) at the time when Israel was about to enter the land of Canaan. This means, therefore, that Israel was standing in the interim period of the saving history between, on the one hand, the completion of her election as Jahweh's peculiar people, and on the other, the fulfilment of the divine promise. And Deuteronomy implies that very much can still be decided for Israel in this intermediate state. And there is still more to it: the whole tenor of the paraeneses is that Israel is in very great danger of missing Jahweh's call to her. Over against this, one can of course point out that in actual fact the sermons in Deuteronomy originate in the later period of the monarchy and reflect throughout the situation which then obtained. But theologically it is certainly not unimportant that Deuteronomy still set even this Israel in the perspective of the situation between election and fulfilment. Although the highest heaven and the whole earth belong to Jahweh, he nevertheless turned towards Israel's ancestors, and loved them, and promised them and their posterity by an oath the land of Canaan (Deut. vi. 10, vii. 8, x. 14f.). Alone of all nations he elected Israel. This idea of election, the very term for which, as we have already said, is a creation of Deuteronomy's, is more than once expressed very radically—Israel is no imposing people, but rather the least of the peoples; the one and only reason for the election is the love of Jahweh (Deut. vii. 7–9). Now, the co-ordination of covenant and the love of Jahweh, their synonymity in fact, is again something new, given as it is such broad and radical theological expression. None of the older traditions of Jahweh's making of the covenant had dared to disclose the motive in such an unguarded and extreme way. The line connecting Deuteronomy with Hosea has often been drawn. But

there is a great difference between the single venture of one prophetic proclamation and a preaching practice already grounded on a broad theological basis. Besides, in Deuteronomy this love of Jahweh is never pictured as the love of a husband, but very much more as the love of a father for his son (Deut. VIII. 5, XIV. 1). Jahweh's saving blessing destined for Israel, of which the paraeneses constantly speak, is the land (נחלה), and rest from the enemies round about (מנוחה).[82] The term נחלה has a long history in Israel: it belongs to the sacral body of the law dealing with the tenure of land, and originally designated the heritable land allotted by Jahweh to the clan or family.[83] But Deuteronomy is the first to speak of a נחלה of Israel's. In actual fact, the term has no concrete root in a sacral institution even in this extended usage, but is a theological abstraction. The old Amphictyony as a body had no נחלה: it was simply the sum total of the נחלות of the politically autonomous clans. It was clearly only the formation of the state, which brought the tribes into very close political as well as religious alliance, that created the prerequisite of this Deuteronomic idea of Israel as politically fully unified and of her נחלה. In actual fact, Deuteronomy speaks of Israel as so much of a single entity that in comparison the individual clans completely retire into the background. The sermons speak in lavish terms of this נחלה promised to Israel. It is the ארץ טובה, plentifully watered, full of the most luxuriant orchards and vineyards, and also rich in mineral wealth (Deut. VIII. 7–9). Within it ready prepared are fine houses and great cities which Israel does not need to build. (From these eulogies we can draw our own conclusions as to the increased and refined cultural demands made by those who listened to the sermons.) In another passage this land is even contrasted with Egypt, which was certainly not lacking in fertility. Israel will be at no pains with the watering of it: it is a land whose care is undertaken by Jahweh, and his eyes are upon it continually (Deut. XI. 10–12). What is it then but a paradise upon earth? At all events, it is in every respect the all-sufficient prerequisite of the perfect bliss of the people of God, for in it Israel expects yet to

[82] Deut. XII. 9f., XXV. 19; cf. Ex. XXXIII. 14; Deut. III. 20; Josh. I. 13, 15, XXI. 44, XXII. 4, XXIII. 1. What is meant is a secure and peaceful life in the promised land, where everyone "dwelt under his vine and under his fig tree," I Kings V. 5 [IV. 25]; Mic. IV. 4; cf. וישבתם בטח, Deut. XII. 10 with Hos. II. 20 [18].

[83] Von Rad, "Verheissenes Land und Jahwes Land," in Z.D.P.V., 1943, pp. 192f., reprinted in Ges. Studien, pp. 87ff.

find rest from all enemies round about (Deut. xxv. 19). The very way in which this consolation is phrased easily shows the weariness of an age exhausted by many wars.

It would, however, be a mistake to take the land as the real subject of the Deuteronomic preaching. The constant logic of all these addresses is rather this: since Jahweh has shown you such faithfulness in all these matters, and will continue so to do, it is your duty to love him in return, and to keep his "statutes and judgments." In other words, this preaching is paraenesis, a summons to obedience. It does not therefore include in the same degree every part of the totality of the saving revelation of Jahweh, but really only gives variations on the appeal for faithfulness to Jahweh. The edge of this appeal lies in the fact that those who listen to it are showing signs of a perilous weakening in the tradition of the faith. The children no longer know what the older people had experience of (Deut. xi. 2, vi. 20f.): there is clearly a perceptible break between the generation which was still directly rooted in the revelation of Jahweh and the one which was growing up. This problem of the generations is struck up in different ways in Deuteronomy—in Deut. v. 2f. there is one approach, and in Deut. xxix. 13f. [12f.] another. There may be a connexion between this and the fact that the Deuteronomic preacher has so frequently to combat the idea of self-glorification. Israel is not to ascribe to her own prowess what she owes solely to the guidance of Jahweh (Deut. viii. 17, ix. 4–6): the people who listen to the preaching appear to be altogether such as are coming near to forgetting Jahweh and his benefits completely (Deut. vi. 10–12). This summons to gratitude lets us see the strength of the preacher's appeal to the inner disposition, in fact to the heart. Obviously, an immediate relationship to the commandments and cultic regulations of Jahweh had already been lost by the time of Deuteronomy, and this makes the preacher there appeal all the more emphatically for the inward acceptance of the commandments. It is in the heart and the understanding that Israel's belonging to Jahweh comes about. But to this end Jahweh's offer had to be made intelligible and easy to comprehend. Deuteronomy therefore insists everywhere upon a unification of the tradition, and upon a simplification of it giving it an inward reference. Certainly, the will of Jahweh is also resolved into a series of very concrete commandments which are to be obeyed in a concrete fashion. Nevertheless the primary and principal thing in Deuteronomy is the basic commandment to love Jahweh "with the whole heart and with the whole soul and with all one's might" (Deut. VI. 4f.)—almost everything else follows automatically.[84] Once again what we find is this: gratitude and answering love as the motives for observing the commandments are a very specific theological interpretation which was not current in ancient Israel, or at least not so explicitly. Everywhere in Deuteronomy we meet with the efforts made in these sermons to render comprehensible the many-sidedness of the will of Jahweh as it had been declared to Israel, and then again to simplify it by means of a radical motivation. If, as we said above, each generation had the duty of itself first becoming Israel in the continuity of the tradition, the way by which Deuteronomy sought to fulfil this duty was by elucidating Jahweh's will as clearly as possible and laying it on heart and conscience.[85]

3. *The Laws.* In the paraeneses the will of Jahweh is already made concrete in a variety of ways and given a reference to the present, but the legal corpus proper only begins in ch. XII. However, the laws handed on in Deuteronomy are removed from their original formulation in the law or in the cult, and given in a very much looser homiletical formulation—that is, they are already in the form of commandments which are the subject of preaching.[86] This is important to the extent that we are here at the same time dealing constantly with the commandments and with an interpretation, which is often thoroughly independent. This is not surprising, of course, in the case of the law which

[84] Deuteronomy eight times says that the commandments are to be observed "with all the heart and with all the soul" (Deut. VI. 5, X. 12, XI. 13, XIII. 4 and elsewhere).

[85] We meet this tendency away from all that is casuistic and which leads towards the spiritual sense lying behind the individual commandments mainly in the legal part of Deuteronomy (Deut. XII–XXVI). Deuteronomy's unremitting call to "remember" Jahweh, his commandments, his acts, etc. (Deut. V. 15, VII. 18, VIII. 2, 18, IX. 7, XVI. 3, 12), corresponds to the urge for subjective actualisation. Beyond any doubt that spiritualisation and appeal to the individual conscience (cf. Deut. IX. 18!) are in themselves the announcement of a strong theological individualism. But the difference between them and the later efforts of the Wisdom literature consists in the fact that Deuteronomy still derives the individual's portion in Jahweh wholly from the traditional saving blessing of the granting of the land. See below, pp. 443f.

[86] In spite of various expansions, Deuteronomy still displays a certain organisation of the material in the block running from XII. 1 to XXIII. 1: 1. Cultic laws (XII. 1–XVI. 17); 2. Laws concerning officials (judge, king, priest, and prophet, XVI. 18–XVIII. 22); 3. Laws for criminal cases (XIX. 1–XXI. 9); 4. Regulations concerning families (XXI. 10–XXIII. 1 [XXII. 30]). From this point on it is no longer possible to discern a thread in the ordering. Obviously all manner of legal material was soon added to the original corpus—for the broad homiletic dressing-up of the law noticeably falls away from ch. XXII on.

centralised the cult, since it is not old, but a new creation of Deuteronomy's own, and is therefore from first sentence to last impregnated with the spirit of Deuteronomy. The demand to offer sacrifice and worship only at the one place chosen by Jahweh is set in a twofold contrast. First, in Deut. XII. 2–7, it is sharply differentiated from the cult of the Canaanites, which as a genuine nature religion correspondingly needed many places and many symbols in order to pin down the very numerous self-revelations of the nature deity. But the demand also stands out in relief from the cult of Jahweh as hitherto practised (Deut. XII. 8–12), a cult which, distributed as it was over many sanctuaries and pervaded as it had become in different ways by Canaanite ideas, had by now degenerated into a very vague worship of Jahweh. What kind of a revelation of Jahweh was it then that was being celebrated up and down the land at the shrines which formerly belonged to the Canaanites? The cult of Jahweh had long ago been brought within the orbit of the principles current in the nature religions, for Baal had many forms: wherever a special mystery of nature was experienced, there was a fresh revelation of Baal. But Jahweh is *one* Jahweh. His cult had therefore to be dissociated from the many forms into which it had proliferated at the local sanctuaries and to be presented once more in its unity. Jahweh, who is one, had made himself known in one revelation (the Deuteronomic תורה), and now there had also to be one cult corresponding to this one revelation. Thus it is easy to see how the demand for centralisation was the direct consequence of the important theological proposition that Jahweh is one (Deut. VI. 4), which stood solemnly and as its basic programme at the head of the original draft of Deuteronomy.[87] In Deuteronomy there speaks an Israel which, especially over against the Canaanite cult of Baal, had become fully conscious of the utter peculiarity of her own historically-based cult of Jahweh.

Here is named the great opponent, of whom Deuteronomy does not lose sight for a moment. Deuteronomy is in no sense a theoretical com-

---

[87] For the translation of Deut. VI. 4 see G. Quell, in *Th. W.B.N.T.*, VOL. III, pp. 1079f. But perhaps it is best to take the passage, which from the point of view of its syntax is notoriously debated, not as a series of two nominal clauses, but as one single nominal clause in which אלהינו and אחד are in apposition. The formula "Jahweh is one" is unique in the Old Testament. It is probable that it owes its existence to stimulus from Egypt, for the designation of "the one god," "the only god" is applied to Amon in a papyrus of the 21st Dynasty (1090–945). E. Meyer "Gottesstaat, Militärherrschaft und Ständewesen," in *Sitzungsberichte der Preuss. Akademie d. Wissenschaften*, phil. hist. Klasse, Berlin 1928, pp. 503ff.

pendium of the will of Jahweh: rather it deploys its demands, in an extremely militant fashion, against the one enveloping threat which it knows to be directed against Jahwism, the Canaanite nature religion. The paraeneses repeatedly touched upon the sharp demarcation of Israel from the world around it, and a similar demand is also made in the laws (cf. Deut. XIII. 2–6, 9–12, 13–19 [1–5, 8–11, 12–18], XVII. 2–7, XVIII. 9–13, 14, 21, XXIII. 18, 19 [17, 18], etc.). What is special in Deuteronomy's cultic regulations is the secondary way in which they bring in theology. Ancient Israel performed the rites because they were customary, and to particular rites she may well have attached a particular meaning. In Deuteronomy, on the other hand, we see how a self-contained theology tries to encompass the extremely many-coloured world of the cult and to interpret it uniformly. Compared with an unsophisticated sacral cultic practice, this Deuteronomic theological interpretation of Israel's whole cult can occasionally actually be called a spiritualising overgrowing of the old customs.[88] The cultic practice which Deuteronomy opposed was certainly also exhausted and hollow, one which had long ago lost the naïve piety of the early days and withdrawn from the complexities of political and economic life. Deuteronomy combats this disintegration by uniformly encompassing with its theology not merely the cultic sphere, but all the rest of Israel's life as well, and by teaching the Israel of its own time to understand herself in her unique existence before Jahweh. This comprehensive self-interpretation of Israel's could not be achieved without a certain amount of rationalisation effected by means of the saving history, for now all the single elements were made comprehensible in their meanings and in their interconnexions. Indeed, the leading theological characteristic in Deuteronomy is that everything is now made plain to Israel, and no further problem can ever again really arise for her. We need only consider how simply Deuteronomy solves the problem of the false prophets (XVIII. 14–21, XIII. 2–6 [1–5]). This revelation of Jahweh is so all-sufficient as to exempt Israel from all seeking and questioning and doubting (Deut. XXX. 11–14).

Deuteronomy does not set out to be civil law—none of the legal codes in the Old Testament is to be understood in this way.[89] Deuteronomy addresses Israel as a sacral community, the holy people, that

---

[88] We have of course to bear in mind that the Deuteronomic sermons are expressly teaching for the laity and that they only deal with what has to be made comprehensible to the layman.   [89] M. Noth, *Ges. Studien*, pp. 32ff.

is, the people belonging to Jahweh, and her life and her offices (priest, king, prophet, and judge) are ordered as having this character. The ordering is done by way of relating everything to the saving gift *par excellence*, the dwelling in the promised land. This was the dawn of Israel's life in bliss, and all Israel as an ontological people, down to its least member, that is, Israel in her whole concrete reality was transposed into this life of bliss. In consequence the saving blessings held out to the people are for the most part material—fertility in man and beast, peace from enemies, political greatness. Jahweh's grace produces everything that furthers life (Deut. xxviii. 8–14): impairment of life is understood as the effect of his wrath. This material view of salvation, which is hardly again surpassed in the Old Testament, and extends even to the kneading-trough of the individual household (Deut. xxviii. 5), is the final term in a lengthy process for religion and cult. In its earliest days Jahwism was not yet able to make the proper theological connexion between its God and the gifts of the arable land: and even in the later monarchical period some devotees of radical Jahwism, the Rechabites, demanded as a religious badge that Israel should keep strictly aloof from the gifts of the arable land, and from the building of houses, the sowing of seed, and the planting of vineyards (Jer. xxxv. 6f.).[90] Deuteronomy takes the opposite way, and treads it to the end: all these things, the products of nature and civilisation, are gifts, and in fact blessings accruing from salvation, which Jahweh's love desires to present to his people. Thus Israel's dwelling in the arable land, her enjoyment of its blessings, and her worshipping her God there with a pure Jahwistic cult mean that the final victory had been won over Baal, who for the myth was the hereditary owner of the land and the bestower of every blessing. Thus in Deuteronomy everything is interrelated and gathered together to give a unified theological conspectus— one Jahweh, one (comprehensive) Israel, one revelation (תורה), one promised land (נחלה), one place of worship, one prophet.

The core of Deuteronomy is the teaching, that is, the endeavour to make Israel listen to the revelation of the will of Jahweh in all circumstances. But the obedience which Deuteronomy demands is in no sense the prerequisite of election. The order is rather the reverse. This is especially clearly expressed in Deut. xxvii. 9f.: "hear, O Israel, this day you have become the people of Jahweh your God: hearken therefore to the voice of Jahweh your God and keep his commandments."

[90] See above, pp. 63f.

The reasoning in Deut. xiv. 1f. is much the same: avoid all forms of the cult of the dead, "for you are a people holy to Jahweh" (similarly Deut. vii. 6). It is therefore quite impossible to understand the commandments in Deuteronomy as "law" in the theological sense of the word, as though Deuteronomy were leading Israel to earn salvation by a total obedience.[91] Rather, all the commandments are simply a grand explanation of the command to love Jahweh and to cling to him alone (Deut. vi. 4f.). And this love is Israel's return of the divine love bestowed upon her. The many imperatives in Deuteronomy are therefore appeals, sometimes implicit and sometimes explicit, for gratitude to be shown in action, and Deuteronomy regards them as easy to fulfil. This is the sense in which we have to understand the oft-recurring introductions to the preaching of the commandments: "when Jahweh shall have brought you into the land," "when Jahweh shall have destroyed the nations [and so on], then you are to . . ."[92] Similar are those cases in which a commandment is motivated by being referred to a precedent divine saving event in history.[93] Nevertheless, alongside the commandments drawn up in this way there are a certain number of cases where the reception of the blessings of salvation is in actual fact conditional, and made dependent upon Israel's obedience.[94] But even with those imperatives which are motivated by final clauses ("do this, that you may remain alive, that it may be well with you, that you may enter into the land"), Deuteronomy's great offer of grace is not itself in any way annulled and a legal way of salvation proclaimed. Even those cases which seem to make salvation conditional, and dependent upon Israel's achievement, are prefaced by a declaration of Jahweh's election and his love. Thus, they are rather a matter of "comfortable words" to Israel bidding her now for her part receive a reality already granted to her, and completely to take her place within it in obedience and gratitude. For preceding even these imperatives stands Deuteronomy's indicative: "you are now the people set apart for Jahweh."[95] Here we must once again refer to the important passage Deut. xxx. 11–14. Through this

---

[91] F. Baumgärtel is completely different. He sees in Deuteronomy the magnificent attempt "to create the people of God by way of the law": *Verheissung: Zur Frage des evangelischen Verständnisses des Alten Testaments*, Gütersloh 1952, pp. 66f.

[92] Deut. xii. 1, xvii. 14, xviii. 9, xix. 1, xxi. 1, xxvi. 1.

[93] E.g. Deut. x. 22, xv. 15, xvi. 1, xx. 1, xxiv. 18.

[94] Deut. vi. 18, vii. 12, viii. 1, xi. 8f., xvi. 20, xix. 8f., xxviii. 9 and elsewhere.

[95] Deut. vii. 6, xiv. 2, 21, xxvi. 18. The apostolic paraeneses in the New Testament also know of this juxtaposition of indicative and imperative. For this cf. W. Joest,

revelation of the will of Jahweh, the relationship between him and Israel has been made perfectly clear. Nothing would be more absurd than that Israel should once again let this revelation become a problem for her. "The word is very near to you: it is in your mouth and in your heart." The law has its function in precisely the same sense in the paraenesis of the apostles. There too we find the collocation of indicative and imperative which does not curtail the proclamation of grace in any way. But it remains true that the whole of Deuteronomy is pervaded by the feeling of a great anxiety lest Israel might possibly throw this claim to the winds and forfeit her salvation. This is indeed something new—that disobedience with all its sinister possibilities has come within the range of Deuteronomy's theological vision. And it is pathetic to see how Israel, just immediately before the catastrophe, is, so to speak, once more given the offer of "life" (Deut. XXX. 15ff.). The means by which this is done is as follows: Deuteronomy wipes out some seven centuries squandered in disobedience, and places Israel once again in the wilderness, with Moses speaking to her. But it has to be borne in mind that this Israel is in no way comparable to the ancient people of Israel that stood once at Sinai: the conditions in which she lived were utterly different in culture, economy, and politics, and she is a stubborn people (Deut. IX. 6, 13, XXXI. 27). None the less, she is offered present salvation on exactly the same terms as before: "today you have become the people of Jahweh your God." Nowhere else does the impassioned endeavour to make the commandments given at Sinai relevant for its own time find such a clear expression as in the endless variations played upon the word "today," which the preacher drums into the ears of his audience. This "today" means both the time of Moses and that of Deuteronomy taken together. But this implies that the Israel addressed still stands in the space between her election and her salvation proper, that she is still on the road and awaiting still the great saving blessings which she is to receive, "for you have not yet come to the rest and the possession of your heritage" (Deut. XII. 9).

Gesetz und Freiheit. Das Problem der tertius usus legis bei Luther und die neutestamentliche Parainese, Göttingen 1951, pp. 150ff. It is a different case with the quite disproportionately large paraenesis made up of the curses, which was obviously only composed under the impression made by the exile (Deut. XXVIII. 25b–37, 47–68). A heightened interest in the judgment which follows the transgression of the law finds voice in the asymmetry of this section with curses.

6. THE PRIESTLY DOCUMENT[96]

(a) The Priestly Document as an Historical Work

Israel elaborated two written accounts of the events of Sinai with a broad theological basis, Deuteronomy and the Priestly Document. As is only to be expected with works in which such a mass of material is accumulated, both originated at a comparatively late date. But in both cases, scholars long ago learned to make a distinction between the time of composition of the draft as such, which is of course only conjectural, and the age of the separate pieces of material. With the Priestly Document, however, the discovery that it contains old, and indeed very old, material has come as a surprise, considering the wholesale late dating earlier attributed to it.[97] But the two works are so extraordinarily different both in their derivation and their aim that a fair comparison of them is scarcely possible. In its basic and formative traditions Deuteronomy is Israelite, it draws up and lives by the traditions of the old Israelite Amphictyony, and it appears to have been given its essential shape in the northern kingdom. In contrast with this, in the Priestly Document we are dealing with traditions which belong in the main to Judea and Jerusalem. Another quite general point is this: approaching the Priestly Document via Deuteronomy, one must first come to terms with the matter-of-fact, austere way in which the former presents its material. In Deuteronomy there is that which makes its appeal to the heart (though it also reckons with the intellect—it is constantly most willing to explain things). It is, in a word, thoroughly adapted to the person reading or hearing it and to his powers of theological comprehension. With the Priestly Document this heartfelt desire to show the meaning of things is completely lacking. P's task was essentially complete when it had gathered and sifted the material and classified it theologically. The various pieces of cultic material are to a large extent presented with such bare objectivity, and so much without any addition which gives the theological significance, that the task of interpretation passes over unawares from the hands of the theologian

[96] J. Hempel, "Priesterkodex," in Pauly-Wissowa, VOL. XXII. 2, cols. 1943ff.; M. Noth, Die Gesetze im Pentateuch (in Ges. Studien); G. von Rad, Die Priesterschrift im Hexateuch (B.W.A.N.T.), 1943; K. Elliger, "Sinn und Ursprung der priesterschriftlichen Geschichtserzählung," in Z. Th. K., 1952, pp. 121ff.; K. Koch, "Die Eigenart der priesterschriftlichen Sinaigesetzgebung," in Z. Th. K., 1958, pp. 36ff.

[97] K. Galling in the analysis of Ex. xxvff. (Exodus, 1939, H.A.T.); K. Elliger, "Das Gesetz Lev. xviii," in Z.A.W. 1955, pp. 1ff.

to the Biblical archaeologist. This character of the Priestly Document must be linked with its aim, so utterly different from that of Deuteronomy, an aim about which, of course, we still know all too little.

Earlier on, when we were looking at the liveliness of the stories in JE, we noticed in passing the question whether it was possible to regard P, with its load of material for the regulation of the cult, as history in any real sense, and whether it is not rather a cultic law-book. On the other hand it has recently been emphasised more than once, and rightly so, that P is a genuine historical work.[98] The coldness and stiffness of the presentation, which give the appearance of an utter lack of interest in ordinary humanity, psychology, and the poetry of the situations, though they make P have less appeal today, do not in the least prove that this work has no genuine theological concern for history. Only, the concern is of a very different kind from that of JE's picture of the history. As can be seen particularly clearly from the history of the patriarchs in P, the subject of the account is not the hidden guidance of the men Abraham, Isaac, and Jacob, and their reaction to it: rather it is the growth of particular cultic institutions out of the history. P depicts a course of history in which new manifestations, institutions, and regulations are revealed from age to age. It is obvious that a body of varied cultic material (P^s) has been secondarily inserted into P. It has been rightly said that only what is organically connected with the account of the history proper is to be attributed to the original P.[99] But the actual volume of secondary matter can hardly ever be precisely isolated from the original. We are dealing here with specifically priestly literature, about whose laws of growth we as yet know very little. Since this literature, in contrast with JE, had never left the sacral sphere, we have probably to reckon with a much steadier process of elaboration; and we ought not to make too wide a gap between the finished form as it was planned and achieved and the secondary accretions. The fact that this history of cultic institutions begins with the creation of the world shows the tremendous theological claim made by P. Obviously then the only appropriate way of treating the worship of Israel is to take it in the light of this background —only then is everything set in due proportion. P is utterly serious in wanting to show that the cult which entered history in the people of

[98] Particularly by Noth, *Pentateuch*, pp. 7ff.; cf. also S. Mowinckel in *Z.A.W.*, 1935, p. 146, n. 1.

[99] K. Elliger, in *Z. Th. K.*, 1952, p. 122.

Israel is the goal of the origin and evolution of the world. Creation itself was designed to lead to this Israel.[100]

For the picture of the history in the sources JE and D, the event at Sinai consisted in the solemn proclamation of Jahweh's justice. P depicts the same event from a completely different angle—at Sinai Jahweh founded Israel's cult.[101] It is generally agreed that the following passages belong to the oldest elements in P's Sinai pericope: Ex. XXIV. 15–18, XXV–XXXI, XXXIV. 29–35, XXXV–XL; Lev. VIII–X, XVI; Num. I–IV, VIII. 5–22, IX. 15–23, X. 1–10. According to these elements Jahweh first proclaimed all that was required for the place of worship, designated Aaron and his sons as the cult personnel, and at the same time gave directions for their solemn installation. All these orders, as P reports later, were carefully carried out. The first cycle in the account is rounded off with the description of the first sacrifice which those who had been duly consecrated as priests offered at the tabernacle which had been duly erected—the cult is inaugurated. In a second cycle an account is given of the census of the people, the establishment of the camp order, and the settling of the duties of the Levites, their purification and the offering of them as a "wave offering." Thereafter follows the departure from Sinai (Num. X. 11ff.).

(b) The Tent, the Ark, and the Glory of God[102]

The object which, since the time of Luther, we Germans have been in the habit of calling the *Stiftshütte* (tabernacle) is not a tent in the full sense of the term, for according to its description, it consisted of a massive frame of boards overlaid with gold, upon which the precious carpets were spread; it was an oblong structure 30 cubits long by 12

---

[100] H. Holzinger, *Einleitung in das Hexateuch*, Freiburg and Leipzig 1893, pp. 358, 387.

[101] In view of P's one-sided concentration on the cult, it is most improbable that it too originally contained the Decalogue. On the other hand we have to ask whether P really did not regard the events at Sinai as a covenant of Jahweh with Israel, for such a deviation from the older Sinai tradition would indeed be very remarkable. However, we must reckon with the possibility that when P was combined with JE, traditional material would be excised from P as well as from JE; that is, we have to reckon with the possibility that the redactor started from the presupposition that P was to be read and understood together with JE.

[102] M. Dibelius, *Die Lade Jahwes*, Göttingen 1906; E. Sellin, "Das Zelt Jahwes," in *Festschrift für R. Kittel*, Leipzig 1913, pp. 168ff.; R. Hartmann, "Zelt und Lade," in *Z.A.W.*, 1917–18, pp. 209ff.; G. von Rad, "Zelt und Lade," in *Neue kirchliche Zeitschrift*, 1931, pp. 476ff., reprinted in *Ges. Studien*, pp. 109ff.; J. Morgenstern, "The Ark, the Ephod and the Tent," in *Hebrew Union College Annual*, 1942–3.

cubits broad and 10 cubits high, at the back of which a cube-shaped chamber 10 × 10 × 10 cubits was separated off by a curtain as the Holy of Holies.[103] Here stood the Ark, a rectangular wooden casket, 2½ cubits long, 1½ broad and 1½ high, which could be carried by means of long poles. In the Holy Place in front of the Holy of Holies were the Table of Shewbread and the seven-branched candlestick. In the forecourt (whose dimensions were 10 × 50 cubits) there stood, before the shorter side of this tent, the altar of burnt-offering. This forecourt was in turn separated from the outside world by rows of pillars from which curtains were to be hung. The name given to this whole structure is no more uniform in P than in the other documents. The term most often used is the simple אהל מועד, "the tent of meeting": אהל העדות or משכן העדות, "the tent or dwelling-place of witness," are much less frequent, משכן being occasionally used instead of אהל.[104] But what theological conclusions can be gathered from the almost wholly technical accounts of P's regulations for the tabernacle? Since their yield in the way of direct theological statement is meagre in the extreme, we shall attempt to approach the question via history, because the whole concept of אהל מועד is not a newly created construction of P: on this subject P rather takes its stand on old traditions about a holy tent, something of which can still be ascertained from the Hexateuch.

In Ex. XXXIII. 7-11, an E passage strangely isolated from its context, an account is given of a sacral tent which Moses pitched without the camp, and which served as the place to seek oracles from Jahweh and had the name אהל מועד. Although it has the same name, this tent is quite different from the tabernacle of P. Here we are dealing with a much older source. Indeed, there is good reason to believe that Ex. XXXIII. 7-11 derives as a tradition from a very early period, perhaps even from the period before Israel settled in Palestine. It is not in any circumstances to be assumed that the Ark was already placed in this tent. On the contrary, Tent and Ark were two cult objects existing independently of each other in the earlier period as the cultic foci of two completely distinct groups.[105] The traditions about the holy Tent

---

[103] The cubit in ancient Israel is to be taken as roughly 20 in.

[104] אהל מועד Ex. XXVII. 21, XXVIII. 43, XXIX. 4, 10f., 30, 32, 44. XXX. 16, 18, 20 and frequently. אהל העדת Num. IX. 15, XVII. 22f. [7f.], XVIII. 2. משכן העדת Ex. XXXVIII. 21; Num. I. 50, 53, X. 11 and frequently.

[105] The tent in which the Ark was put for the time being has nothing to do with the tent of meeting. II Sam. VI. 17; I Kings I. 39.

are however much sparser than those about the Ark. Apart from the account in Ex. XXXIII. 7–11 (E), which looks thoroughly primitive, there are further notices of the Tent in Num. XI. 16, 24–26, XII. 4(E), and in the isolated report in Deut. XXXI. 14f. (E?). In these references we meet with a very striking idea of the relationship in which Jahweh stood to this Tent. The Tent is not in the least the place where Jahweh dwells on earth, as was the case later with, for instance, the Temple of Solomon; it is merely the point of meeting, the place of encounter between Jahweh and Moses. Jahweh makes his appearance from heaven and manifests himself "in the cloud" which settles "by the door of the tent." And as a result the Tent gets the name of "tent of meeting" (יעד Niphal, "to meet with," "to make an appointment with," cf. Ex. XXXIII. 7 and also Ex. XXIX. 43 P).[106] It does not look as though regular sacrificial worship was offered before this Tent. All that is clear is that these encounters took place at the times when Israel wanted to get definite directions. The Tent was thus a place where oracles were sought and the word of Jahweh proclaimed. Another thing to be noticed is that the holy Tent was obviously closely bound up with a concept of the camp—both belonged together, and neither could exist independently of the other.[107] After the settlement of Israel in Canaan the Tent disappears from the history.[108]

The Ark is a different matter altogether. We find traces of it in the tradition for centuries. It was in existence in the "wilderness period" (Num. X. 35). It is mentioned later in the report of the conquest (Josh. III–VI). After this it comes to our notice as the sacral focus of the league of the twelve tribes (1 Sam. I–VI). And, finally, it stood in the Temple of Solomon. It was probably lost at the destruction of Jerusalem in 586. Jeremiah opposed any idea of its replacement (Jer. III. 16). This makes it apparent that it was far easier to adapt the Ark to very different historical conditions than was the case with the Tent, which was bound up with the camp. In consequence, the ideas obtaining about the Ark's importance in the cult are also much more fluid, for we cannot assume that only one and the same conception of it always persisted

[106] The notice that the Tent stood without the camp does not at all look like an invention, and deserves credence from the very fact that it contradicts the later conception in the Priestly Document.

[107] A. Kuschke, "Die Lagervorstellung der priestlichen Erzählung," in *Z.A.W.*, 1951, pp. 74ff.; H. J. Kraus, *Gottesdienst in Israel*, p. 28.

[108] According to a late account (II Chron. I. 3) the Tent finally found a place of establishment in Gibeon.

throughout so many periods and places. The only precise description of the Ark's external appearance is given by P (Ex. xxv. 10ff.), but it is not to be assumed that the older sources had any essentially different picture of it.[109] Archaeologically it belongs to a special class of cultic objects. It is the throne of a deity which is left empty. Or, to put it more exactly, Israel thought of the Ark as the throne of Jahweh.[110] Wherever the Ark is, Jahweh is always fully present. When the Ark is raised during the wandering in the wilderness, Jahweh too rises to go before Israel: when it is put down, then he resumes his seat on his throne (Num. x. 35f., reading שֻׁבָה instead of שׁוּבָה in vs. 36). We have to imagine the same conditions obtaining in Shiloh, according to I Sam. III. 3–6, and in Jerusalem, according to II Sam. VI. The description of Jahweh as the one who "sits enthroned upon the cherubim" (יֹשֵׁב הַכְּרוּבִים) is closely connected with the Ark (cf. I Sam. IV. 4, and also II Kings XIX. 15; Pss. XXII. 6, XXVII. 4, LXXXIV. 3, 5 [2, 4]). Thus, two completely different "theologies" are connected with the Tent and with the Ark—with the former it is a theology of manifestation, but with the latter one of presence.[111] Solomon's Temple, where the Ark was in the Holy of Holies, was still conceived as a place where Jahweh was present in person (I Kings VIII. 12). This presence was always regarded as bestowing blessing. It is characteristic that the coming of the Ark to Israel let loose great outbursts of joy, even leading to corybantic behaviour before it (cf. I Sam. IV. 4ff., VI. 13, 19; II Sam. VI. 5, 14). This characteristic reappears even as late as the Chronicler, who has such a definite disposition towards praise—in place of P's sombre tabernacle theology, he again takes up the old Ark tradition.[112]

[109] Admittedly JE's picture of the wilderness period has remarkably few mentions of the Ark (apart from Num. x. 35f. there is only Num. XIV. 39–45). But many commentators have rightly assumed that an account of the setting up of the Ark which stood after Ex. XXXIII. 6 was cut out by the redactor, because it would have conflicted with that of P; cf., for example, Eissfeldt in Z.A.W., 1940–1, pp. 192f.

[110] None the less, it is remarkable that this cultic object is never called throne but "casket." This indicates that the ancient Israelite idea of a throne displaced an even older one which conceived the Ark as really a container. Perhaps there is a connexion with the Egyptian caskets of the gods. See the interesting comparison from the point of view of comparative religion with Old Egyptian theology in K. Sethe, Abh. d. Preuss. Akademie d. Wissensch., Phil. hist. Klasse, Berlin, 1929, No. 4.

[111] It may be mentioned that in general in the sacral architecture of the ancient East there is a distinction between a temple where the deity manifests himself and one where he dwells. W. Andrae, Das Gotteshaus und die Urformen des Bauens im alten Orient, Berlin 1930. [112] See below, pp. 350f.

The Deuteronomic and Deuteronomistic idea of the Ark is different from the old conception of it as a throne (Deut. x. 1–5; 1 Kings VIII. 9). With them the Ark is the thing which contains the tables, and nothing more—for in such a view it is cultically inconceivable that the throne should also have at the same time served as a container. We should take this conception as a rationalisation, indeed as a demythologisation, for according to the Deuteronomic theology, Jahweh dwells in heaven—as to earth, he had placed his name at the place of worship.[113] From now on the Tent can also be called אהל העדות (the tent of the law). One gets the distinct impression, especially as the period is so late and so reflective, that the intention is to parry an idea which was no longer compatible with the new theology. For all that it was probably not an innovation to think of the Ark as a receptacle; it was perhaps a return to a still older idea, since the throne already had the name casket.

We now come back to the Priestly Document, for initially the Tabernacle is to be regarded simply as a combination of Tent and Ark. The date of the coalescing of these two heterogeneous streams of tradition can no longer be determined.[114] All that can be said is that there can hardly have been any actual cultic event corresponding to this union; it is rather the result of a theoretic recasting of the old traditions by the priests. The combination did not however lead to a mutual assimilation of the two ideas on an equal footing. Rather, P makes it perfectly clear that it came into being as a revival of the old

---

[113] Deut. XXVI. 15, XII. 5, 11, 21, and elsewhere.

[114] How alien to one another the two ideas of Jahweh's coming down to men were is seen in Nathan's protest against the attempt to connect Jahweh with a dwelling-place (II Sam. VII. 6f.). There probably lies at the back of this protest just that old, and perhaps old Judean, Tent-manifestation theology which could not get accustomed to the idea of Jahweh's being bound to a place. Even if the information given by the Chronicler is open to serious doubt, that, after the bringing of the Ark into the Temple, the tent had its place in Gibeon (II Chron. I. 3), the notice none the less does show for how long people were still aware of the independence and separateness of the two cultic objects. Anyone who sees more in David's tent (II Sam. VI. 17, 1 Kings I. 39, VIII. 4) than a temporary measure ought logically to assume that the connexion between Tent and Ark had already been made by the time of David, and that the tradition of the tent which had been displaced by the idea of the Temple as a dwelling-place was revived by P. On the relationship of the Tabernacle of the Priestly Document to David's tent see F. M. Cross, "The Tabernacle," in The Biblical Archaeologist, 1947, p. 63. Still, it is peculiar that the Davidic tent is not called אהל מועד (in 1 Kings VIII. 4 the term is an interpolation).

Tent and manifestation theology. The dwelling-place and throne idea is practically superseded. As the place of expiation and also the place where Jahweh spoke (Num. VII. 89), the Ark with its cherubim had an importance which could not be dispensed with, but it no longer functioned as Jahweh's throne.[115] Ex. XXIX. 42f. is particularly important: Jahweh there sums up the cultic significance of the Tabernacle which is to be erected in the words: "there will I appear, to speak to you, and there I will meet with the people of Israel."[116] These words would be meaningless if Jahweh were thought of as dwelling in the Tent. But they do have meaning if the Tent is understood as the one and only place of meeting between Jahweh and Israel. In actual fact, P carries this idea through with great consistency even in many of the separate narratives: it is a constantly recurring event—Israel sees the glory of Jahweh coming down in the cloud and resting upon the Tent.[117]

The translation of כבוד יהוה by "the glory of Jahweh" is only a makeshift. Semantically, what lies at the base of the term is the idea of "weight," of "standing" (*gravitas*), and of "honour." The possessions of Jacob are his כבוד (Gen. XXXI. 1)—that is, they are what gives him standing. And a people's כבוד is its nobility, its leaders (Is. V. 13), or its might in history in general (Is. XVI. 14, XVIII. 3, XXI. 16). כבוד is by and large that asset which makes peoples or individuals, and even objects, impressive, and usually this is understood as something that can be perceived or expressed.[118] Thus Jahweh's כבוד also, that is, his power and standing, his honour, were perceptible in the world in the most varied of ways—in actual fact it fills the whole creation (Is. VI. 3), and there is a duty laid upon men and angels to praise God and acknowledge this honour given him by his strength (Ps. XXIX. 9), an honour which Jahweh claims for himself alone (Is. XLII. 8). But the incomparable power of Jahweh is also experienced in history, wherever

[115] Since this idea is uniformly carried through, it is of no importance that terms belonging to the older idea of the temple as a dwelling-place occasionally break through (e.g. Ex. XXIX. 45). The same holds true of the expressions that cultic operations were performed "before Jahweh," as they are found much more frequently in secondary texts (P[s]).

[116] Further details on the opposition between the concept of manifestation and that of dwelling are given in A. Kuschke, "Die Lagervorstellung der priesterschriftlichen Erzählung," in *Z.A.W.*, 1951, pp. 84ff. Cf. also Ex. XXV. 22, XXX. 6, 36.

[117] Ex. XVI. 10, XL. 34; Lev. IX. 6, 23; Num. XIV. 10, XVI. 19, XVII. 7 [XVI. 41], XX. 6.

[118] B. Stein, *Der Begriff Kebod Jahwe und seine Bedeutung für die atl. Gotteserkentniss*, Lechte, Emsdetten i. W. 1939.

Jahweh "gets himself glory" (Ex. xiv. 4, 17f.; Ezek. xxviii. 22), that is, where the power of his action in history becomes apparent. But as well as these and other references of a more general kind, there is a further, and much more sharply defined, idea of the כבוד יהוה. According to it, the כבוד was something belonging immediately to Jahweh, a part of his supernatural being; thus, especially in Ezekiel and the Priestly Document, the כבוד יהוה becomes an important *terminus technicus* in describing theophanies. It is described in greater detail in Ps. xcvii. 1ff. and Ex. xxiv. 15ff. (P), and there is a much more elaborate theological delineation of it in Ezek. 1. 1ff. The component parts in Ezekiel —storm, cloud, fire, and lightning—point to a thunderstorm. Nevertheless it was an utter oversimplification to speak of Jahweh as a "thunderstorm god." A very early age may have seen in the thunderstorm a special revelation of the power of Jahweh. But now, and especially in P, the idea of the כבוד יהוה is a long-established traditional element, and any meteorological connexions have long been left behind. It is a matter of the descent of a fire-like phenomenon which, since men could not bear the sight of it, is covered by a protecting cloud.[119]

Thus, in P's view the כבוד יהוה is simply the form of manifestation which Jahweh employed in order to reveal to Israel particular decisions of his will, the settling of matters of importance, etc. Since his first appearance, the relationship of Jahweh to Israel had assumed a completely new form. Only now had it come from a provisional form into its final one.

It is common knowledge that the Priestly Document pictured the history which it recounted as a series of divine revelations, connecting them with Noah, Abraham, and Moses. Abraham was the one who received the promise of the land and of a new relationship to God for his descendants. Now Israel had arisen out of the patriarchs. But she was as yet entirely without a cult. In order to produce this cultless state, P excised from the traditions which it inherited all records of sacrifices in the period from Abraham down to the revelation at Sinai,

[119] An even clearer description of the coming of the כבוד יהוה as the breaking in of a transcendent reality is given by Ezekiel ("the heavens opened," Ezek. 1. 1), and his picture of the whole manifestation is also much more detailed. The כבוד יהוה is here too a fire-like phenomenon, which however discloses the outline of a human form (Ezek. 1. 26–8): it sits enthroned over the whirling wheels of the cherubim, poised upon which it leaves the sanctuary, and upon which it reappears in order to come down into the new temple (Ezek. xliii. 2–4).

and in many other ways as well it distorted the traditional material. But precisely because of this what was new in the epoch that began with Sinai stood out the more prominently. Yet this new thing is not really the Tabernacle or the sacrificial worship which now begins, for what would be the point of a place of worship or a sacrifice if they had lacked an authorisation and legitimation by God beforehand? Thus, what is new in the period after Sinai is Jahweh's revelation of himself in the כבוד יהוה, in which he now puts himself at Israel's disposal. With the first solemn appearance of the glory of Jahweh over the Tabernacle (Ex. XL. 34f.) the ancient promises to the patriarchs that Jahweh would be Israel's God (Gen. XVII. 7) were fulfilled.

(c) The Cultic Officials

In this paragraph and those that follow, we enter upon a discussion of some of Israel's special cultic regulations and ideas. The Hebrew equivalent for our word cult is עבדה, which means the "service" or worship of God, since the Hebrew verb עבד frequently denotes the worship of Jahweh or of other gods with a cult.[120] But it is not very easy to say what Israel regarded as the essence and special feature of this cult or "service." If we try to find in the Old Testament a term which in some degree gathers up the complex field of man's activities and duties vis-à-vis God, the formula given us is "for Jahweh"; for there are a large number of references, at once recognisable as old formulae, according to which a cultic act is designated as "for Jahweh." Thus, in the calendar for the festivals and elsewhere we meet with the provision that the great pilgrimage festivals were to be solemnised "for Jahweh" (ליהוה).[121] In the same way Passover was "a Passover for Jahweh" (פסח ליהוה).[122] The year of release was "a release for Jahweh" (שמטה ליהוה),[123] and the Sabbath was described in the same terms (שבת ליהוה).[124] The Nazirite was "one set apart for Jahweh"[125]: indeed, wherever in the sphere of worship men, animals, or objects

---

[120] Ex. III. 12, IX. 1, 13, XX. 5; Deut. IV. 19, VIII. 19; II Kings X. 18 and frequently.

[121] Ex. XII. 14, XIII. 6, XXXII. 5; Lev. XXIII. 6, 41.

[122] Ex. XII. 11, 27, 48; Lev. XXIII. 5.

[123] Deut. XV. 2. The Deuteronomic paraenesis about the year of release almost came into direct conflict with the new accepted formula "to Jahweh," for, as is well known, it understood the old cultic regulation solely from the social and humanitarian point of view.

[124] Ex. XVI. 23, 25, XXXI. 15, XXXV. 2; Lev. XXIII. 3, XXV. 2, 4.

[125] Num. VI. 2, 5f., 12. The "ordination" of a priest also took place "for Jahweh."

were taken out of the daily, secular life, they were "holy for Jahweh" (קֹדֶשׁ לַיהוה).[126] And right at the very heart of it all are the sacrifices, with or without the blood, where the same stereotyped phraseology is to be found.[127] The inference to be drawn from this way of speaking of it, which is both widespread and fixed, is that Israel regarded the cult as the place where pre-eminently it was incumbent upon her to make room for Jahweh's right and for the claim which he made. Thus, what took place in the cult can also be designated as the מִשְׁפַּט of God (II Kings XVII. 26; Jer. v. 4, VIII. 7). This "right" of God's in human life was therefore the primary and constitutive factor—it was the foundation-stone of the cult, and everything else followed from it. No cultic celebration was solemnised for Israel, but they were all "for Jahweh." But the sphere in which that right of God (which nullified all human claims) had to be respected was not an ideal one: on the contrary, it was very realistically demarcated by means of a holy place, holy men and women, holy things, and holy seasons. And the holiness of all these stood or fell with the belief in the real presence of Jahweh at his sanctuary, or at least with the belief in his presence there from time to time. The coming of Jahweh—it might be to the sacrifices—was a moment of the highest solemnity, for which the congregation was made ready by the cultic cry, "Silence (הַס) at the presence of Jahweh!" "Silence at the presence of Jahweh! He rouses himself from his holy dwelling."[128] Finally, it is this presence which imposes upon man a quite definite behaviour, and this behaviour was one which, out of consideration for God's holiness, was subjected to particular rules and regulations demanding careful observance. Wherever we meet this phenomenon we have a right to say that we are in the sphere of the cult.

If we try to find in the cultic vocabulary of the Old Testament a general formula answering to the significance of the cult for Israel, we can say that the cult brings Israel to the remembrance of Jahweh. At least, the expression God's remembrance (זִכָּרוֹן, זֶכֶר) occurs frequently, and is brought into relationship with a great variety of cultic activities. For example, the sacrifice which is to be offered when adultery is suspected is a מִנְחַת זִכָּרוֹן (Num. v. 15). The blowing of trumpets in the cult brings Israel into Jahweh's remembrance (נִזְכַּרְתֶּם

---

[126] Ex. XXVIII. 36, XXXIX. 30; Lev. XXVII. 14, 21, 23, 28, 30; Jos. VI. 19; Jg. XVII. 3.
[127] Lev. I. 2, 14, XVII. 4, XXII. 29, XXIII. 12, XXVII. 9, 11 and frequently.
[128] Zeph. I. 7; Zech. II. 17 [13].

לִפְנֵי יהוה), and serves as a "remembrance before Jahweh" (לִזכרון Num. x. 9f.). The same term is used of the spoil taken in the war against the Midianites (Num. xxxI. 54). Similarly, the atonement money for Israel serves "as a remembrance before Jahweh" (Ex. xxx. 16). The High Priest bears the name of the tribes on the shoulder-pieces of the ephod as "a remembrance before Jahweh" (Ex. xxvIII. 12, 29), etc. The expression probably became so much the common property of the cult that it could be said to someone who was offering a sacrifice, "May Jahweh remember thine offering" (Ps. xx. 4 [3]).

If in this section and those which follow, we attempt to give a short sketch of the significance of the cultic material in P, it is essential to bear in mind that P is an historical work, and not something like a great theological *schema* which has been superficially tricked out in the garments of a supposed history. If P's main purpose is to be an historical work, this is important for the interpretation of the different kinds of cultic material, because P's interest in them is not so comprehensive as has been generally assumed. The document in no sense develops anything like an even reasonably complete theology of the cult. In this respect it has in general been much overestimated. Its interests are rather confined to the means by which the various offices and rites received their legitimation. In the case of the institution of circumcision (Gen. xvII) or the observance of the Passover (Ex. xII), it is of course clear that P's account is concerned to prove that these rituals emerged out of the saving history at the divine command. Further, the number of cultic institutions which P sought to anchor in the saving history is not great—circumcision (Gen. xvII), Passover (Ex. xII), the status conferred upon Aaron (Ex. xxvIIIf., Lev. vIIIf.), and that of the Levites (Num. IIIf., vIII). In its attempts to do this, P is elaborate and verbose. On the other hand, in these lengthy descriptions the reader does not find any answer to what is after all the obvious question, how the rite of circumcision is related to the election of Abraham, that is, why it was this and no other rite that was essential if Abraham was to accept the proferred covenant relationship. It is difficult to say whether in such cases P could have said more, had it judged that necessary, or whether the only information it possessed about the rites was that they were commanded. But the same judgment has also to be made on the information which it gives about the ministering activity of the priests and the Levites. In spite of the abundance of the source-material, the picture which we can gain from it is defective, and it especially lacks inner theological unity at important points. Therefore the exegete, unless he wishes to restrict himself to an unfolding of the material itself, needs often enough to have recourse to older sources, or else he must with due caution attempt to elucidate P's stiff, reserved material from his general understanding of Jahwism.

None of the sacral offices in Israel has such a long history as the priesthood. There is no doubt that it goes back to the earliest beginnings of Jahwism, and it came to an end only when Herod's Temple was reduced to ashes by the troops of Titus. It is to be assumed right away that many changes occurred in the priesthood during this tremendous period. On the other hand, in Israel, remarkably enough, it never came to the formation of really powerful hierarchies, as elsewhere in the ancient East at important sanctuaries. Obviously the conditions necessary for wider political activity were not present. In addition there was no place in Israel for a number of duties which elsewhere were a chief province of the priesthood (taking of omens, exorcism, the care of images, etc.).[129] Unfortunately our knowledge of the history of the priesthood in Israel is very slight. In early times the priestly office was already a prerogative of the Levites. The very ancient story in Jg. XVII. 1ff. makes it clear that even in that early period only a Levite could hold this office. Apparently the demands made upon a cultic official were so great that only one who had been brought up in the continuity of the tribal and family traditions could adequately meet all its varied requirements. It would be wise not to underestimate the intellectual accomplishment involved in mastering the sacral traditions and their proper practical application. The priest's office was of course by no means exhausted in the offering of the sacrifices. In olden days sacrifices could also be offered by lay people—this was probably the rule except for sacrifices at the main sanctuaries.[130] All the dealings of the people of Jahweh with its God were imposed upon the priestly office: the priest was thus pre-eminently the person competent to mediate any kind of divine decision. It was to him that people went when they wanted an oracle from Jahweh (1 Sam. XIV. 18f., 36f.); it was he who could manipulate the sacred lot, the Urim and Thummin (1 Sam. XXVIII. 6; Deut. XXXIII. 8). But our most important source for the pre-exilic priesthood, the oracle concerning Levi in the Blessing of Moses,

[129] M. Noth, *Amt und Berufung im Alten Testament*, Bonn 1958, pp. 9f.
[130] Jg. VI. 22ff., XIII. 19.

names the giving of "torah" as the main function of the priest.[131] The priests "teach" Israel Jahweh's ordinances and his "torah" (Deut. XXXIII. 10). By "torah" we have to understand the priests' instruction of the laity, which was probably chiefly concerned with questions about clean and unclean. Hag. II. 11ff. enables us to get an approximate idea of the kind of questions which occurred in everyday life and were put to the priests and answered by them. In addition, the priests had to give decisions in questions involving sacral law (Deut. XVII. 8ff.). But this means that they had to be completely competent in the tradition of the divine law. In addition, it was the priests who, out of the copious store of sacral-legal traditions, had to compile the series which were rehearsed to the cultic community at the great festivals.[132] Further, in cases where there was dispute, they and they alone could decide whether a man was a member of the community of Jahweh or excluded from it (Deut. XXIII. 1ff.). We must assume that the priests were already charged with these and similar duties in early times, and we find them again in the sacral regulations of the Priestly Document, the only difference being that the rituals are there given in much greater detail, and the cultic procedures laid down as absolutely fixed—indeed, their norms are in process of ossification. In P the whole apparatus of the cult is much more complicated, and is definitely on a much larger scale, than it was in the old days—just think of the hierarchical gradation of the cultic officials or the ramifications of the Levitical family tree. However much we may have to guard against assuming that this or that cultic activity is of necessity "late" just because it occurs in P or in Ps, we must at the same time assume that the extensive cultic regulations of P and Ps have as their background the experiences and results of a long cultic history. How else could the hierarchy (High Priest, priesthood, and Levites) have been so minutely systematised in all their functions and rights? Even the period for which the priest should serve was laid down—it comprised a week (Ex. XXIX. 30; Lk. I. 8f.). When they were not serving, the priests lived outside Jerusalem—was it in the Levitical cities of Judah?[133]

If the giving of torah was probably the priest's most important function in the pre-exilic period, it is strange that it is hardly ever

[131] Priest and torah are frequently mentioned together in a stereotyped way, cf. Hos. IV. 1f., 6; Zeph. III. 4; Mic. III. 11; Jer. II. 8, XVIII. 18; Ezek. VII. 26.

[132] See above, pp. 190f.

[133] Josh. XXI. 13–16; cf. Alt. K.S., VOL. II., pp. 294ff.

mentioned in the material which goes to make up P. On one occasion
only do we read about the duty of distinguishing between the holy and
the profane (חל), between clean and unclean, and of a priestly teaching
office referring to these matters (Lev. x. 10f., but see also Ezek. XXII. 26,
XLIV. 23). Instead of this torah, which in one way or another always
functions publicly, what stands in the foreground in P and Ps is the professional knowledge (דעת) circulating within the priesthood.[134] But it
would be quite wrong to draw the conclusion that a change had come
over the priestly office, that is, a process of becoming mechanical and
merely formal. We must part company with the perfectly false idea
that P, including its secondary material, intends to comprehend the
whole of Israel's cultic life. What it offers is rather only one special
section, which is designed to regulate the cult particularly in its ritual
technicalities and the priest's proper professional knowledge.[135]

All the same, the rituals incorporated in the Priestly Document do
allow us to see something of the variety of the departments in which a
priest had to exercise his professional knowledge. As regards the way
in which the obtaining of oracles, already mentioned, took place in
individual cases in the cult, information is given by the ritual to be
performed in the case of a woman suspected of adultery, which is
extremely old (Num. v. 12ff.). The proper recital of the words of the
curse, which is the climax of the whole procedure (vs. 21f.), was no
light matter in the ancient world. In the same way, blessing, that is,
"putting" the name of Jahweh upon the cultic community, was the
business of the priests (Num. VI. 22ff.). A different aspect is encountered in the so-called torah on leprosy (Lev. XIIIf.). It shows how the
priest had to be competent in the wide sphere of sacral medicine, of

---

[134] The literary category of giving instruction in the torah—recognisable by the
form of personal address—is only very rare in P, e.g. Lev. VII. 22–7. For the concept
da'ath as the priest's professional knowledge see J. Begrich, "Die Priesterliche Tora,"
in Werden und Wesen des Alten Testaments, Bei. Z.A.W. No. 66, Berlin 1936,
pp. 85f., and R. Rendtorff, Die Gesetze in der Priesterschrift, henceforth cited as Gesetze,
Göttingen 1954, pp. 34, 45, 66, 77. But cf. K. Koch, Die Priesterschrift von Exodus 25 bis
Leviticus 16. Eine überlieferungsgeschichtliche und literarkritische Untersuchung, Göttingen
1959, pp. 66f.

[135] The custody and transmission of historical (amphictyonic) traditions must also
have been part of the priest's direct professional duties. H. W. Wolff has made it
appear likely that Hosea's term da'ath is to be taken as knowledge of the traditions
of the saving history: "Wissen um Gott bei Hosea als Urform von Theologie," in
Ev. Th., 1952–3, pp. 533ff.

whose range the torah on leprosy and the chapter dealing with unclean bodily discharges (Lev. xv) certainly give only an incomplete idea. The decisions of the priests were of final significance, for they functioned as the mouthpiece of Jahweh himself: Jahweh bound himself by what they said in excluding the persons concerned from the cult, or reinstating them into it. These words צרעת הוא, "it is leprosy," and the others טהור הוא, "he is clean," were undoubtedly distinctly and solemnly pronounced by the priests over the patient (Lev. xiii. 15, 17, etc.). For the purposes of the history of form, these declaratory formulae and others like them, great numbers of which are to be found in the Priestly Document, preserve for us what was an important element in Israel's cult, because they let us see that in the performance of ritual observances it was only the declaratory divine word of acceptance or rejection uttered by the priests which decided the issue.[136] Such cultic declaratory pronouncements of course presuppose a careful investigation based on definite evidence, of which we only have a partial knowledge, an evaluation in which the authority exercised by the priest was often immense. Lev. xxvii gives us a glimpse of a curious department of the priest's service, the conversion of particular vows into the corresponding monetary equivalent. The valuation (העריך, Lev. xxvii. 8, 12, 14) was probably done fairly mechanically on the basis of fixed tariffs. But the private sacrifices of the laity demanded a much more individual treatment. This brings us to what has always been regarded as the most important function of the priests according to P—their participation in the sacrifices. Certainly, they had to undertake the sprinkling of the blood, the application of the blood to the altar, they made the sacrifice go up in smoke (הקטיר), made expiation (כפר), poured out the drink-offering, etc.[137] It is significant that the rituals concerned have often been worked over by the priests at crucial passages, by transferring to the priests the most important procedures of the sacrificial ceremonial which, in the original form of the ritual, were still assigned to the laity.[138] In this aspect the present form of the rituals reflects the latest phase of cultic practice. But even in this final phase, where, as we have said, the priests' share in carrying

---

[136] On the "declaratory formulae," cf. Rendtorff, *Gesetze*, pp. 74ff.; von Rad, in *Th. Lz.*, 1951, cols. 129ff. (*Ges. Studien*, pp. 130ff.); W. Zimmerli in *Z.A.W.*, 1954, pp. 23f.

[137] Lev. I–VI *passim*.

[138] Details in Rendtorff, *Gesetze*, pp. 5ff.

out the sacrifices was much greater than it had been in the whole history of the cult before this time, still, we must not completely overlook the inner and spiritual demands made upon the priests, as is generally done. What was after all decisive was whether the sacrifices "pleased" Jahweh, and the declaration which the priest had to make as to whether a sacrifice had been offered *rite*.[139] He had not only to decide, but had also to declare aloud, whether a sacrifice was "credited" or not.[140] For one or two cultic texts give us the information that in every case of private sacrifice it had apparently to be decided whether it was "credited" or not. This lay in the hands of the priests alone, and had certainly done so since early times. In all procedures connected with expiation, a special measure of vigilance was demanded of the priests, for here offerer and priest came within the range of the divine wrath.[141] But the most important aspect of this particular function which the priests had to manage was the ritual eating of the sin offering (Lev. x. 17ff.). This flesh was a thing "most holy" and was carefully safeguarded from all contact with lay people, for it was, of course, the flesh of the animal to which the sin had been transferred. By eating this flesh, and that in the holy place, the priests themselves effected the removal of the evil. They were appointed to do this in order, as mediators, "to bear the iniquity of the community and (thereby) to make expiation for them before Jahweh" (Lev. x. 17).[142]

The appointment of particular families to this office—for the priesthood was of course hereditary—and their authorisation to perform all its very responsible duties derived from Jahweh; he had "chosen" their ancestor[143]—one particular tradition even speaks of a covenant through which Jahweh assigned the priestly office to a family (Num. xxv. 10ff.). None the less, the idea that the priests had been appointed by Jahweh exclusively was not quite so easily put into effect. In the pre-exilic period the Zadokites were royal officials and their ancestors were

---

[139] On this important term "pleased" in sacrificial language see below, pp. 261f.

[140] See below, pp. 260ff.

[141] On the Priestly Document's conception of the קֶצֶף of Jahweh, see below, p. 269.

[142] Lev. x. 17 is one of the very few texts in P in which a ritual is theologically explained.

[143] I Sam. II. 28; Ps. LXV. 5 [4], CV. 26. The customary expression for the ordination of a priest is "to fill the hand," Jg. XVII. 5, 12; I Kings XIII. 33; Ex. XXVIII. 41 and frequently. The "filling of the hand" is connected with the receipt of certain dues which the priest needed for his support.

appointed by Solomon (1 Kings 11. 35).[144] We do not know from what date the Zadokites regarded themselves as the legitimate descendants of Aaron. Ezekiel still designates the priesthood at Jerusalem as Zadokite (Ezek. XLIV. 15) but P knows only of the Aaronites. There can be no doubt that the disappearance of the monarchy in Judah meant an increase of authority for the priestly office in Jerusalem. It has been rightly assumed that after the calamity which fell upon the royal house certain functions of the king passed into the hands of the high priest.[145] At all events, the idea changed, as compared with the times before, to the extent that in P the priests exercise their office as mediators between Jahweh and the people in complete independence. According to P, the priestly office is the one sacral institution which represents Israel to Jahweh, and which Jahweh required for his dealings with Israel. The idea that it could be the task of the priest "to go in and out before the anointed of Jahweh" (1 Sam. 11. 35) is quite alien to the Priestly Document. It is useless to look for any links with messianic ideas or traditions.[146]

Nevertheless, criticism has established beyond doubt that P in its present form cannot be historically understood apart from the history of the pre-exilic cult which preceded it, and the only place where the cult of Jahweh could have been elaborated on such a broad basis, on so large a scale and, at the same time, in such detail, is the sanctuary in Jerusalem. In particular, the rigid demarcation of the priests from the Levites which we find everywhere in P, and without which its whole theological sacral picture is incomprehensible, was set in motion by an event which only took place in the late monarchical period, namely Josiah's centralisation of the cult. The precedence of the priesthood at

[144] There is a secret surrounding the priest Zadok which it is now pretty well impossible to unveil. He comes on the stage in the time of David quite out of the blue. That he was a *novus homo* without hereditary legitimation can be seen from the fact that he is always mentioned without his father's or his family's name. But that the riddle is solved by supposing, as Mowinckel, Rowley, and others do, that Zadok was the former priest-king of Jerusalem whom David conquered, is very dubious. S. Mowinckel, *Esra den Skriftlärde*, Oslo 1916, p. 109; A. Bentzen in *Z.A.W.*, 1933, p. 174; H. H. Rowley in *Festschrift für A. Bertholet*, pp. 461ff. A later legitimation of the sensational supersession of the house of Eli by that of Zadok is given in 1 Sam. 11. 35.

[145] M. Noth, *Amt und Berufung im Alten Testament*, p. 12; G. Widengren, *Sakrales Königtum im Alten Testament und im Judentum* (Franz Delitzsch-Vorlesungen, 1952), Stuttgart 1955, pp. 26ff.; K. Koch, *Priesterschrift, von Exodus 25 bis Leviticus 16*, Göttingen 1959, p. 99.

[146] For this cf. the juxtaposition of priestly and messianic office in the prophecy of Zechariah (Zech. IV. 14).

the Temple presupposed by P was only established and given its justification by that event. The Levites are appointed to their duties, for which P gives precisely detailed regulations (Num. IIIf.), because they were "given" for Jahweh (נתונים, Num. III. 9, VIII. 19). They were specially set apart from Israel in order to be the property of Jahweh in a special sense (Num. VIII. 14, 16, XVIII. 6). In P this special belonging to Jahweh is still further explained along an odd theological line—the Levites belong to Jahweh in place of the first-born of Israel who, but for them, would have been forfeit to Jahweh (Num. III. 12f., 40f., VIII. 16). Another idea of the Levites' mediating function is expressed in the concept of Israel's camp and the place which is assigned in it to the tribe of Levi. The Levites camp immediately around the tabernacle; their function is thus a protective and indeed an atoning one for the rest of the tribes, so that no "wrath" should be upon the community (Num. I. 53, VIII. 19). We shall not go wrong if we regard such theories as the result of later reflexion, the purpose of which was to give a *post eventum* theological explanation of an actual state of affairs.

(d) The Sacrifices[147]

Although in its original form the Priestly Document gives accounts of extremely intricate sacrificial acts (especially Lev. IX), as far as we can see, it did not itself contain any special directions for the offering of sacrifices. But a great deal of cultic material was incorporated into it secondarily, probably very soon after its composition, the intention of which is obviously to ground sacrifices also in the great inauguration of the cult at Sinai. This material is the collection of regulations for sacrifice in Lev. I–VII, XIV. 10–32, XVII, XXII. 17–30, XXVII; Num. XVIIIf.

As form-critical analysis shows, these "rituals" have each a different aim and derivation.[148] Since, in practice, no actual cultic procedures

---

[147] R. Rendtorff, *Studien zur Geschichte des Opfers im alten Israel*, typewritten thesis, 1953; H. H. Rowley, *The Meaning of Sacrifice in the Old Testament*, Manchester 1950; W. O. E. Oesterley, *Sacrifices in Ancient Israel*, London 1937; A. Wendel, *Das Opfer in der altisraelitischen Religion*, Leipzig 1927; G. Buchanan Gray, *Sacrifice in the Old Testament*, Oxford 1925.

[148] R. Rendtorff, *Gesetze*. Neither P nor P[s] is anxious to regulate all the sacrificial observances practised in Israel. There were very many more of them, e.g. drink offerings (I Sam. VII. 6; Hos. IX. 4); and many of the agrarian rites are to be regarded as sacrifices (on Deut. XXIII. 22 [21], XXIV. 19; Lev. XIX. 9, cf. Wendel, *Das Opfer in der altisraelitischen Religion*, pp. 19f.). The booty in the holy war which was put under the ban was also a sacrifice.

were connected with the material—the norm is always offered only as a theoretic model—these literary accretions smack of the museum. As a matter of fact, this extreme degree of schematisation and co-ordination of the cultic material represents a final stage in its life. The priests had needed a long time to work it over and harmonise it before it was ready to be thus catalogued and unified. So there is no doubt that the majority of these cultic practices are very old.[149] The main classes of sacrifice which P distinguishes are: (1) the "burnt offering" (עולה or כליל, Lev. I); (2) the "cereal offering" (מנחה, a mixture of meal, oil, and incense, Lev. II); (3) the "peace offering" (שלם, Lev. III); (4) the "sin offering" (חטאת, Lev. IV–V. 13); and (5) the "guilt offering" (אשם, Lev. V. 14–19).[150]

This catalogue of the most important sacrifices contained in Lev. I–V imparts in full detail the procedure for the preparation and offering of sacrifice; but it leaves practically unanswered all questions as to the meaning of the various rites. In this respect, the difference between Deuteronomy and the Priestly Document could not be greater; for Deuteronomy, with its love of showing the significance of things, was eager to deal wherever possible with the question of the meaning of the ordinances. In Deuteronomy, however, we are dealing with material presented as paraenesis, whereas in P it is given as rituals. In Lev. Iff. we are not even told the occasions on which burnt offering, cereal offering, or peace offering were to be made. Admittedly, mention is made of them in connexion with the sin offering (Lev. IV. 27f., V. 2ff.), but in P's scheme the bringing of sin offerings is far from being restricted to these cases: they also make their appearance on completely different occasions, as for example in ceremonies of consecration[151]—the combination of several kinds of sacrifices (burnt offering and sin offering, or burnt offering and cereal offering) is a special characteristic of these late rituals. The account of Aaron's first sacrifice shows a quite baroque accumulation of burnt offerings, sin offerings, and peace offerings (Lev. IX). This being so, we must abandon from the outset with P any idea that it is possible to presuppose, behind each kind of sacrifice, a precise theory of the sacral event in question exactly dis-

[149] A. Lods, who derives these sacrificial usages from a pre-Jahwistic time, may be mentioned as an extreme example of early dating (in *Revue d'histoire et de philosophie religieuses*, 1928, pp. 399ff.).

[150] We employ the usual terminology, although it is inexact and to some extent simply leads to error.   [151] Ex. XXIX. 36f., XXX. 1ff.

tinguishing it from all the other kinds. Not only is none given by P: but there are even indications that so precise a theory as we should perhaps expect no longer in fact existed.[152] Investigation of the motives, the "fundamental ideas," which form the basis of the various sacrificial procedures is nevertheless justified, though we are bound to remain conscious of the extraordinary difficulties, which hardly allow us to reach any certain results in this field. It is doubtful whether an Israelite who was offering a burnt offering in Dan understood the sacral event in the same way as a Judean offering the same sacrifice at the same time in Beersheba, and we also have to reckon with all manner of "shiftings of motive" in the course of centuries, and these can only be detected in exceptional cases.[153] But in addition, what makes this ideological analysis particularly difficult is the further fact that the general run of Old Testament sacrifices, with the rites belonging to them, are not in themselves an original creation of Jahwism. It was only in Canaan that Israel entered into an old and widespread sacral practice, into which she later poured her own ideas.[154] As far as each particular sacrificial rite is concerned, the same is true of Israel as of other peoples of antiquity: the rituals are preserved and observed down to a late date in an astonishingly conservative way; but the ideas themselves are flexible, and, inevitably, changed in the course of the centuries, for in age the rituals most probably go back to a very far-off early date. (There has recently been a tendency to explain the sacrificial usages of ancient Greece by reference to the sacral practice of the Old Stone Age of the ritual slaying of the hunters.)[155] We have thus to consider whether it is not now too late in the day to ask what was the "basic idea" in a sacrificial usage in ancient Israel. Yet even if we do assume that the Old Testament does give us tolerably reliable information about the concepts of the various sacrificial acts and their meaning, still another

[152] In our opinion the ideological content of P is far overestimated if anything like a well-thought-out sacrificial system is assumed. Because of the many later additions (P^s) P became much more the reservoir of cultic material into which bit by bit all pertinent cultic material was channelled.

[153] On the phenomenon of the shifting of motive see A. Bertholet, "Über kultische Motivverschiebung," in *Sitzungsber. d. Berliner Akademie d. Wissensch., Phil. hist. Klasse,* 1938, XVII, pp. 164ff.

[154] R. Dussaud, *Les Origines cananéennes du sacrifice israélite,* 2nd edn. Paris 1941; Pedersen, *Israel III–IV,* p. 317.

[155] K. Meuli, "Griechische Opferbräuche," in *Phyllobolia, Festschrift für P. von d. Muhl,* Basel 1946, pp. 185ff.

difficulty crops up. It is probably true for the general field of comparative religion, and certainly true for Israel, that ages which offered their sacrifices in naïve faith had little or nothing to say about the meaning of these sacrifices. It is only when certain tensions appear between the world of the rites and the men who perform them that theories about sacrifice arise, as well as the need for their rational clarification. There is no objection to these theories. They are very competent. But even they embrace only a part, and not the whole. In the Passover of the keepers of flocks and herds, a festival which seems to have been observed long before the time of Moses, the significance of the manipulation of the blood is to some extent clear—it had an apotropaic function, and was intended to protect the herds from the influence of demons.[156] But what did the Israel of later days have in mind as she performed the rite? The interpretation in Ex. XII and Deut. XVI. 1ff., which connects it with the saving history, sees in its performance an actualisation of Jahweh's redemptive action in history, in which the rite of the blood has no particular significance. But is it established that only one idea could ever be held about this procedure? With the major sacrifices (burnt offering, peace offering, and, in particular, sacrifices connected with vows), the specific reason for an offering certainly to a larger extent determined the way in which it was conceived. In theory, then, we have to distinguish between the "basic idea" in a sacrificial act and the reason for its performance. But in practice it was probably the reason which determined the way in which the specific sacrifice offered was understood. Sacrifice was so comprehensive that there was always room for thoughts and ideas suggested by the special reason connected with it. It is self-evident of course that this was far from meaning that sacrifice became a prey to every conceivable subjective interpretation: that would have been impossible for a people of antiquity so well versed in cultic matters as ancient Israel. Sacrifice was, and remained, an event which took place in a sphere lying outside of man and his spirituality: man could as it were only give it the external impulse; its actual operation was not subject to the control of his capacity or capabilities: all this rested with Jahweh, who had the power to accept the offering and let it achieve its purpose. But if sacrifice was a cultic event of this objective kind, then there must also have been in Israel formative concepts connected with it. Taken as a whole, the formative concepts are the following, which could of course in turn

[156] L. Rost in *Z.D.P.V.*, 1943, pp. 205ff.

be differentiated in different ways: the ideas of gift, of communion, and of atonement.[157] The simple idea of sacrifice as gift is of course pre-eminent in the case of all vows made in times of great distress (Gen. XXVIII. 10–22; Jg. XI. 30; II Sam. XV. 7–9). But all official non-monetary payments, the first-fruits, are also to be understood in the same way: in principle, the whole of the harvest is holy to Jahweh, but in token of man's obligation and of his gratitude, he gives back to God what is holiest, the first-fruits or the first-born.[158] The sacrifice of the animals which had drawn the Ark after it had come safely back is also to be understood as a gift expressing thanks (I Sam. VI. 14).[159] And so on with other examples. The meal at Sinai in Ex. XXIV. 9–11 (J?) is a good example of a very primitive communion sacrifice. In such cases the deity was believed to be an unseen participant in the meal. The ritual meal at the conclusion of covenants was certainly understood in the same way—the contracting parties bound themselves and entered into obligations in the presence of a third party, the deity who was thought of as present (Gen. XXXI. 54)—and the very ancient family sacrifices too fall into this category (I Sam. XX. 6, 29). The solemn sacrifices after the bringing up of the Ark to Jerusalem (II Sam. VI. 17; I Kings VIII. 63) were certainly also substantially controlled by the idea of sacrifice as communion.[160] But while we have at our disposal plenty of references to sacrifice as gift, and plenty which regard it as participa-

[157] Cf. Eichrodt, *Theologie*, VOL. I (Eng. trans.), pp. 141–76; similarly Rowley *The Meaning of Sacrifice in the Old Testament*, pp. 76f.

[158] Ex. XXIII. 16, 19; XXXIV. 26; Deut. XV. 19ff., XXVI. Iff.; Lev. XIX. 23ff.

[159] Wendel, *Das Opfer in der altisraelitischen Religion*, p. 157. Pedersen (*Israel III–IV*, pp. 317ff.) sees as the kernel of the Israelite conception the effort to obtain blessing upon the livestock and the crops. The remaining part of the property became sanctified through the animals and crops offered. But being sanctified means sharing in the divine powers of blessing. It is very dubious, however, whether the idea of the blessing of Jahweh as such a power fluctuating automatically played an important part in Israel.

[160] There are a few references which might even suggest the idea that Jahweh is in a real sense fed by the sacrifices. Thus, in Lev. XXI. 6, 8, 17, XXII. 25 the sacrifices are called לחם אלהים: the shewbread too (לחם פנים, I Sam. XXI. 7 [6]; Ex. XXV. 30 and elsewhere) has also been thought of in this connexion, since לחם means not only "bread," but "nourishment" as well. But here it can only be the matter of an extremely old terminology which was still preserved in the conservative language of the cult. There can be no idea that the people who handed on these old narratives or legal texts could still have taken this conception seriously. The case may be different when we think of the offerers themselves. Who can guarantee that the idea of a meal never occurred to them? (cf. Jg. VI. 19ff., XIII. 15).

tion in a common meal, with sacrifices whose function is expiation we are in a very different case altogether. It can be inferred from Mic. VI. 6–8 that there were such sacrifices, and that they could on occasion be carried to excess. II Sam. XXI. 3 and XXIV. 25 point to a still earlier period, as does also the primitive term ריח ניחח (the odour of soothing, Gen. VIII. 21, otherwise generally P). I Sam. III. 14: "the guilt of the house of Eli shall not be expiated either by זבח or by מנחה" (the latter probably in the sense of "whole-offering") shows that the meal offering too could have an expiatory function.

But we must hasten to add that even the analysis of the sacrifices which we have suggested on the basis of their function and of the ideas lying behind them is once again *post eventum* theory; for the sacrifices would scarcely ever have been connected with just a single one of these three concepts to the exclusion of the others. What generally happened was rather that, whenever sacrifice was offered, several motives were involved, and these imperceptibly passed over into one another, with the probable result that one of them became prominent and determinative.[161] As far as can be proved from the sources and keeping in mind all the various reservations previously suggested, what can be said about the various kinds of sacrifices detailed in the torah on sacrifice in Lev. I–VII, and in connexion with the historical practice, is approximately as follows.

The burnt offering (עולה) is the sacrifice completely offered to Jahweh, that is, the offerer or the priest did not participate in the cultic act by sharing the meal with Jahweh (hence it is sometimes called the "whole offering," כליל). We meet with it as early as the law of the altar in Ex. XX. 24–6, which is certainly very old; and later it came to have a special importance as the sacrifice for the nation offered regularly in the temple (I Kings IX. 25; II Kings XVI. 15; cf. also I Kings III. 4, 15). It was however also offered by private persons outwith the official rotation—though this was probably only the case on special occasions. As to the occasions themselves, they had, we can see, a wide range. Burnt offerings were offered on occasions of joy—they then expressed gratitude for some undertaking which Jahweh had brought to a successful issue, as for example I Sam. VI. 14, or Jg. XI. 30f. They also had their place in times of trouble, when Israel saw the wrath of Jahweh acting upon her (Jg. XXI. 4; I Sam. XIII. 9; Mic. VI. 6): in these

---

[161] "In every offering there is something of all the effects produced by the offering; but one or another element may become more prominent." Pedersen, *Israel III–IV*, p. 330.

cases it was the prayer for atonement that was prominent in the offering. The ritual in Lev. I does not lay down any specific occasion for the burnt offering, but only gives all the technical details connected with the presentation of the animal for sacrifice, the laying of the hands upon its head, the slaughter, the application of the blood to the altar, the flaying of the animal and its dismemberment right up to its burning upon the altar. We would give much to know the special significance which attached to the laying on of hands upon the head of the victim (this ritual is expressly prescribed for all the blood sacrifices in P). Did it signify the transference of sin and the evil influence of sin to the animal, or was it a gesture in which the offerer identified himself with the animal?[162] Again, strangely enough, P, in its various notices about sacrificial acts, always couples the burnt offering with other kinds of offering, for example, with the cereal offering—a sacrifice never consists in the offering of a burnt offering only. This accumulation of different kinds of sacrifice certainly betokens an already advanced phase in Israel's cultic life, and indicates the growing complexity of sacrificial procedure. None the less, it is not something peculiar to P alone, for it is sometimes mentioned in early texts as well (e.g. Ex. XVIII. 12, XXIV. 4ff.; I Kings IX. 25). A peculiarity of P does, however, lie in the fact that from the very start it attributes an expiatory function to each and every burnt offering (Lev. I. 4, XVI. 24). This was certainly not the idea which was held in the earlier periods. It will, however, come out more clearly below that this feature falls into line with one of the general tendencies of P.

The cereal offering (מנחה) is taken by P as exclusively a gift-sacrifice of victuals consisting of flour, oil, and frankincense. But the history of the cult before the Priestly Document shows no knowledge of the *minḥah* in this specialised meaning: in the earlier passages, and in complete accord with the proper meaning of the word, it was rather any kind of sacrificial gift, both that with the blood and that without it (Gen. IV. 3ff.; I Sam. II. 17, III. 14). At times it was even the secular present given between men (e.g. Gen. XXXII. 14ff., XLIII. 11ff.). We do

---

[162] On the question of the ṣᵉmikhah see E. Lohse, *Die Ordination im Spätjudentum und im Neuen Testament*, Göttingen 1951, pp. 22ff.; H. H. Rowley, *The Meaning of Sacrifice in the Old Testament*, p. 88. The conjecture that the laying on of hands was even in P only observed at the offering of the חטאת is a probable one. It was only in P⁸ that this rite was made general and obligatory at the offering of each and every sacrifice.

not know when and where the *minḥah* came to have the specialised meaning which is attached to it by P, but, with only a few exceptions (Lev. v. 11; Num. v. 15), it is always coupled in P with other sacrifices (blood sacrifices), and appears rather as an extra added to them. This is especially the case with the burnt offering. It is to be noticed that the part of the cereal offering which was burnt upon the altar was called אזכרה, which is probably to be rendered as "remembrance"—the sacrifice is to bring the offerer into gracious remembrance.[163]

The third sacrificial act mentioned in the torah on sacrifices is the sacrifice of the peace offering (זבח שלמים), and, once again, the occasion of its offering is never given. The procedure for offering is exactly parallel to that for the burnt offering, except for the important difference that the whole of the flesh of the victim is not offered to Jahweh upon the altar, but the fat parts only. The reason why the ritual says nothing about what was to be done with the fleshy parts is that this lay without the province of the ritual: they were eaten by the group of worshippers. Though this meal lay outwith the procedures of the ritual, it was however for the laity the main element and the high point in this cultic act. This holds true at any rate for the earlier period of Israel, the period before the Priestly Document. At that time the sacrifice accompanied by a common meal was the sacrifice *par excellence*, being far more important and of more frequent recurrence than all the others. This sacrificial act was always a social occasion—the worshipper invited his friends to the meal,[164] "to eat and to drink before Jahweh."[165] This is the sacrifice which, more than any other, came into the category of a communion sacrifice—the participants knew Jahweh to be invisibly present as the guest of honour. The occasions and the whole mood connected with it were predominantly joyous, and on occasion even excessively so. We cannot discuss here the question whether זבח and שלמים were originally unrelated sacrifices (as is suggested by the lack of consistency in the use of the terms).[166]

Very little can be gathered about the real significance which, in P's view, attached to the peace offering, for the information in its scattered notices about this kind of sacrifice is again for the most part one-

---

[163] Lev. II. 2, IX. 16, V. 12; on the matter see D. Schötz, *Schuld- und Sündopfer im Alten Testament*, Breslau 1930, p. 55.

[164] Ex. XXXII. 6; Deut. XII. 18; Jg. IX. 27; Zeph. I. 7.

[165] Ex. XXXIV. 15; I Sam. IX. 12f., XVI. 3ff.; II Kings X. 19 and frequently.

[166] Köhler, *Theology*, pp. 187f.; Rendtorff, *Gesetze*, pp. 65ff.

sidedly related to its ritual aspects. It can hardly be assumed that the details of the ritual—once more the laying of the hand upon the victim's head and the application of the blood to the altar—are no more than a late innovation. Thus, all that would call for further notice is that the cereal offering is comparatively seldom mentioned among the sacrificial acts which P describes with such great care (e.g. Ex. xxix. 28 Lev. ix. 17ff.; Num. vi. 13ff.). This is clearly bound up with the fact that this sacrifice, which fell mainly into the category of communion, left least room for the idea of expiation. And it is expiation which P put in the centre of the scene.

In the Priestly Code the sin offering (חטאת) is by far the most common—indeed, there are few cultic celebrations which P either tells of or gives regulations for in which the sin offering does not have a special function. Particularly in the combination of sacrifices mentioned above, the sin offering is the one part which is practically never missing. In this case, however, the ritual in Lev. iv. 27–35 and Num. xv. 27–9, differing from the previous sacrifices, names a reason for the offering—it cleanses the man who brings it from all involuntary sins (בשגגה). By these P understands offences against rites or other cultic regulations, especially those committed unwittingly against one or other of the laws of cleanliness. Though this in itself comprises a large field so far as the practical observance of the cult is concerned, still, there are other texts in the Priestly Code which mention other occasions for the bringing of this offering. Thus, for instance, it was prescribed especially in the case of various acts of consecration, in the consecration of the altar (Ex. xxix. 15, 26f., xxx. 1ff.; Lev. xvi. 16), when the sanctity of the altar had been polluted in one way or another and had to be restored. Other occasions for the bringing of a sin offering were the pollution of a Nazirite (Num. vi. 10f.) or other defilements (Lev. xii. 6). The sin offering differed from the burnt offering mainly in the details of the procedure with the blood—it was not only poured round about the altar, but was also smeared on its horns (Lev. iv. 25, 30). The great importance which this type of offering holds in both the narrative and the legal sections of P is, however, in contrast with its almost entire absence from the writings before the Priestly Code.[167] Of course, it is

---

[167] Besides Mic. vi. 7 the only reference which comes into question is ii Kings xii. 17 [16]. This passage, which deals with the sin offerings which were compounded in the form of money payments, could also of course be late. As well as here, the sin offering plays a part in Ezekiel (Ezek. xliv. 24ff., xl. 39, xlv. 21ff.).

hardly to be assumed that with this type of offering P introduced something entirely new into the cultic observances of Israel. Indeed, the older Israel also knew of offerings for expiation. The reason why we find almost no instances of the חטאת outside of P may therefore well be found in the special name, which perhaps only became fixed in this way in later times.[168] Nevertheless, the overwhelming importance of the sin offering betrays a basic cultic attitude, which has given its peculiar and unmistakable character to P.

Besides the sin offering the torah on sacrifices also knows of another sacrifice whose function is expiation, the guilt offering (אשם) (Lev. v. 15ff.). Judging only by the occasion which Lev. v. 14ff. gives for its offering, namely some "breach of faith" or other (מעל), that is, some offence against the property of the Godhead, this type of offering would be distinct enough from the sin offering. But here too P gives other information besides the ritual in the torah on sacrifices, and this speaks of quite different occasions, which are of such a kind as to make the question of the difference between the sin offering and the guilt offering very difficult to answer (cf. the Asham offering of the cleansed leper in Lev. XIV. 14–18 or of a Nazirite who has become unclean in Num. VI. 12, and see also Lev. XIX. 20–2). The very old occurrence of an אשם in I Sam. VI. 3f., 8, 17 makes it probable that in Lev. v. 15ff. we already have a narrower concept of the אשם which became specialised at a later date. Nevertheless the old question of the difference between the two types of sacrifice cannot be solved, and it is work wasted to devise some kind of formula which is both wide and at the same time narrow enough completely to comprise the difference between the one type of sacrifice and the other. In the torah on sacrifices in Lev. I–VI we have merely the attempt to systematise the various types of sacrifice after the event. The actual practice of the cult which preceded the torah was probably much more varied, both as regards the rites and the names of the sacrifices at the different sanctuaries and at different times. And so it is no wonder that even in the strongly systematising Priestly Code the picture should still be a rather varied one, with tensions unresolved. If the writer of P had not had to work with old traditions, if he could have made up his own theological construction independently of them, everything would certainly have been much more uniform.

All this information about sacrifices in the Priestly Code is crudely materialistic. The reader looks in vain for firm holds to enable him to

[168] Rendtorff, *Gesetze*, p. 87.

rise into the spiritual realm by way of the sacrificial concepts lying behind the sacrificial practice. In itself the offering of a sacrifice, of course, left great freedom to the attitude of the worshipper, allowing room for the meanest *do ut des* disposition as well as for the most sublime spiritualisation of the outward act. It was obviously entirely outwith P's intention to suggest to the worshipper any specific understanding of the sacrifices. The Code's concern was that where sacrifices are offered, the ritual traditions should be strictly observed. In this sense P is greatly interested indeed in the correctness and orderliness of the outward aspects of the observances of the cult. There must have been forces and spheres in old Israel which stood guard particularly over the material aspects of observances such as these, material aspects which could not be dissolved by any spirituality. Israel's faith saw itself directed to sacrifices by the ordinances of its God, and everywhere in the world sacrifices require a correct ritual guaranteed by tradition. It is arbitrary to reconstruct a spiritual "prophetic" faith in Jahweh, and to devalue the "priestly cult religion" as an unpleasant by-product.[169] The faith of Israel cannot possibly be divided into two forms of religion which are so completely different and so entirely foreign to each other. Rather, it was Israel's belief that Jahweh's turning towards her in salvation was not exhausted in historical deeds and in the gracious guidance of individual lives, but that in the sacrificial cult too he had ordained an instrument which opened up to her a continuous relationship with him. Here Jahweh was within reach of Israel's gratitude, here Israel was granted fellowship with him in the sacred meal. Above all, here Israel could be reached by his will for forgiveness. However deep even the most understanding interpretation of the sacrifices in the Old Testament may go, there comes an absolute limit beyond which no further explanation is possible. And the expositor must recognise that it is precisely the most important aspect of the sacrifice which takes place beyond this limit. While the Old Testament is very full of allusions to the divine activity wherever it becomes effective among men, and full too of the most intensive address and of "revelation," there is a realm of silence and secrecy in respect to what God works in sacrifice.

So it is no wonder then that P has nothing to say about the way in which God takes knowledge of sacrifices. Even if on occasion use is made of the very old expression that God "smells" them (Gen. VIII.

[169] So for example E. Sellin, *Theologie des Alten Testamentes*, Leipzig 1933, pp. 98ff.; *Geschichte*, VOL. I, p. 98.

20f.; I Sam. XXVI. 19), still, we have to be content with the general
statement that he "has regard" to them (Gen. IV. 4f.). But if we ask
what the sacrifices mean for the worshipper, the rituals do yield some
answer. In some of the psalms it may already be seen with what feelings
of gratitude or anxiety the people accompanied their sacrifices (Pss. V. 3,
XXVII. 6, LIV. 8 [6], LVI. 13 [12]). As regards the sin offering P itself mentions that besides the ritual observance a verbal confession had its
importance (Lev. V. 5f.). As for the efficacy of sacrifice, the language of
the ritual tells us that it was to make man "acceptable" in the sight of
God (Lev. I. 3f., VII. 18, XIX. 5, XXII. 19, 21, 29, XXIII. 11, etc.). Here a
cultic technical term is brought in which played a great part not only
in the theoretical sacrificial theology, but also as a ritual formula in the
practical observance of the cult, for the terms "it is not acceptable"
(לא ירצה) and "it is unclean meat" (פגול הוא) were also actually
spoken by the priest over the offering (Lev. XIX. 7, XXII. 23, 25).[170]
This special aspect of the ritual act has hitherto been overlooked, but it
was without doubt the most important part of the whole procedure.
In fact, we come upon a whole host of such "declaratory formulae."[171]
The priest pronounced his sacerdotal diagnosis upon the leper who
presented himself to him, and it is the same with the great number of
analogous formulae which we meet again and again in the rituals: "it
is a burnt offering" (עולה הוא, Ex. XXIX. 18; Lev. I. 9, 13, 17, VIII. 21);
"it is a cereal offering" (מנחה הוא, Lev. II. 6, 15); "it is a sin offering"
(חטאת הוא, Ex. XXIX. 14; Lev. IV. 21, 24, V. 9), etc. Analogous declara-
tions are "it is most holy" (קדש קדשים הוא, Lev. VI. 18 [25], 22 [29],
VII. 1, 6, etc.) and "it is abominable" (שקץ הוא, Lev. XI. 41). How the
priest reached these judgments on the sacrifices is of course not stated.
In general the individual cases would be decided on the basis of tradition, that is, out of the extensive priestly knowledge which was always
aware of precedents even for what seemed exceptional cases. Possibly,

---

[170] On this cultic "reckoning" (חשב) see G. von Rad, in *Th. Lz.*, 1951, cols. 129ff.
reprinted in *Ges. Studien*, pp. 130ff. The way of putting it, that a sin is "remembered" or
"not remembered" (זכר, Niph.), also seems to be at home in the *milieu* of these cultic
terms (Ps. CIX. 14; Num. V. 15; Ezek. III. 20; cf. II Sam. XIX. 20 [19]). But certainly
the verb ערב, "to be pleasing," which can be designated on the basis of Hos. IX. 4;
Jer. VI. 20; Mal. III. 4 as a technical term cultic in origin, is at home here. (It is generalised in Ps. CIV. 34.)

[171] II Sam. XXIV. 23; Jer. XIV. 12; Ezek. XX. 40f., XLIII. 27; Hos. VIII. 13; Am. V. 22;
Mal. I. 10 are further references for this declaration of the sacrifice as "pleasing."
Rendtorff, *Gesetze*, pp. 74f.; E. Wurthwein in *Th. Lz.*, 1947, cols. 147f.

inspection of the sacrifice played a part too. What is certain is that the priest as the mouthpiece of Jahweh pronounced the *placet* upon the offering or refused it. Thus, only the addition of the divine word made the material observance what it was meant to be, a real saving event between Jahweh and his people. Only in virtue of the declaratory word of the priest did the sacral event become a gracious act of God. This lets us see how little the obstinate neo-Protestant suspicion of these sacrifices as *opera operata* corresponds with the facts. The polemic of the prophets shows that they could become such. In our judgment, danger threatened much more from the other side, namely the rationalising substitution of a monetary payment for sacrifice, which is already attested by the end of the ninth century (II Kings XII. 5, 17 [4, 16]; cf. Lev. XXVII).

(e) Sin and Atonement[172]

The question about the inner and divine event which we took up a moment ago automatically calls for a clarification of what is for the Priestly Document the most important purpose in the offering of sacrifices, namely expiation. The problem is certainly simplified by the fact that the question narrows down to the elucidation of one single concept, כפר. Of the ninety-one instances of this verb, sixty are found in the priestly texts.[173] It is true that attempts to reach the meaning of this important word as it were along the lines of its evolution, that is, by way of its etymology, have not led to any result. Even if it were quite certain that the basic meaning of the root כפר is "to cover,"[174] the question would still remain open. What is to be covered here, and how is this covering effected? It has been recognised and accepted that כפר is a fixed cultic technical term, whose original meaning can no longer be reached by means of etymology.[175] As such כפר means simply "to perform an act of atonement," "to make atonement," which of course is still far from giving us any definite information about the specific ideas which are connected with this verb. We have first to clarify Israel's ideas about the nature of sin.

---

[172] K. Koch, *Die israelitische Sühneanschauung und ihre historischen Wandlungen* (typewritten thesis, Erlangen 1955); D. Schötz, *Schuld- und Sündopfer im Alten Testament*; J. Herrmann, *Die Idee der Sühne im Alten Testament*, Leipzig 1905; *id.*, "Sühne und Sühneformen im Alten Testament," in *Th. W.B.N.T.*, VOL. III, pp. 302ff.

[173] Older references are for example Ex. XXXII. 30 (E); II Sam. XXI. 3.

[174] Gen. XXXII. 21 [20] in particular speaks for this.

[175] D. Schötz, *Schuld- und Sündopfer im Alten Testament*, pp. 102f.

As can be well understood, as far as terminology went, Israel had very varied ways of expressing what she understood by sin, for of course there were very many ways in which she met the phenomenon of sin. As far as numbers of occurrences go, the roots חטא, עון, and פשע preponderate. חטאת means "missing the mark," and the verb חטא also occurs several times with the literal meaning of missing (e.g. a target, Jg. xx. 16; a way, Prov. viii. 36, xix. 2). In its transferred sense it signifies all kinds of failures which occur in the relationships of men with one another (e.g. Gen. iv. 22; Jg. xi. 27; 1 Sam. xxiv. 12 [11]; ii Kings xviii. 14). But the root is used first and foremost for all human failures over against God; both verb and noun became the words of most frequent occurrence in the language of the cult—including that of the Priestly Document in particular. The picture for עון is a little different. In comparison with the noun, the verb "to be distorted," "to act perversely," "to go astray" plays a very subordinate part. עון means "trespass" or "sin," and the concept always involves the guilty party's consciousness—עון has its roots in an evil disposition.[176] From early times עון too was a component part of cultic terminology. In contrast פשע (eighty-six occurrences) failed to find acceptance among the concepts connected with the cult.[177] It belongs pre-eminently to the language of politics, and means "revolt," "rebellion" (i Kings xii. 19; ii Kings viii. 20), and originally perhaps "impeachment of property" (Ex. xxii. 8 [9]).[178] Although its occurrences are much rarer, it is unquestionably the gravest word for sin, especially upon the lips of the prophets. Many other concepts could also be mentioned, by means of which Israel expressed her understanding of sin, often in an extremely concentrated way, such as רשע, חמס, עולה, נבלה. But such a statistical review, even it if were prosecuted in much more detail, would still come far short of disclosing what is the heart of the matter for theology.

But where did earlier Israel chiefly encounter the thing called sin? We have to picture her spiritual life in the days before the monarchy as a closed sacral one. In the final analysis, every department of life found its equilibrium in an order which was regulated by the cult and which had not as yet asserted its own independence.[179] In consequence,

---

[176] Eichrodt, *Theologie*, vol. iii, pp. 81ff.; Köhler, *Theology*, pp. 169f.

[177] There are only two references in P: Lev. xvi. 16, 21.

[178] L. Köhler and W. Baumgartner. *Lexicon in Veteris Testamenti Libros*, Leiden 1948 onwards, s.v. פשע.   [179] See above, pp. 33f., 37f.

sin was any grave breach of this divine law which Israel knew both in the shape of the series of cultic commandments and in the shape of general "unwritten" laws.[180] While she could encounter the phenomenon of sin in the most diverse spheres, in political life (breach of the rules for the holy war, Josh. VII), in the world of the family (breach of the regulations concerning sexual matters, Deut. XXVII. 20ff.), and in every other sphere where people had dealings with one another, what was always in question was that same group of sacral ordinances to which Israel as a whole knew herself to be unconditionally bound. Sin was thus an offence against the sacral order. It was therefore always a monstrous act. And wherever it was committed, it was looked on as a direct insult to God and his sovereign rights. But there was more to it still. Sin was also a social category. Through ties of blood and common lot the individual was regarded as being so deeply embedded in the community that an offence on his part was not just a private matter affecting only himself and his own relationship to God. On the contrary, wherever there had been a grave offence against the divine law, what loomed largest was the incrimination which the community experienced in consequence at the hands of God, for because of the sin nothing less than the whole possibility of its cultic activity had become imperilled. The community had thus a vital interest in the restoration of order.[181] In cases where Jahweh had not reserved to himself a special settlement for good or for ill, order was restored by either the execution or the excommunication of the offender.[182]

In this connexion, however, another side of the matter very alien to modern ways of thinking has to be observed. As we commonly

[180] Jg. XX. 6, 10; II Sam. XIII. 12. In addition, M. Noth, *Das System der zwölf Stämme*, Stuttgart 1930, pp. 100ff.

[181] On the ancient collective liability, see J. Hempel, *Ethos*, pp. 32ff.; Eichrodt, *Theologie*, VOL. III, pp. 1ff.

[182] In H as well as in P we still find ancient ban formulae which quite certainly were formerly practised in cultic life in a very concrete form. "Cutting off (כרת) from the midst of the people of Israel" is particularly frequently mentioned (Lev. XVII. 4, 9f., 14, XX. 3, 5f.; Num. IX. 13, XV. 30, 31 and frequently). The Deuteronomic formula too, "you shall purge (בור) the person or thing out of your midst" is to be judged in the same way (Deut. XIII. 6 [5], XVII. 7, 12, XXI. 21). The *arur* formulae also belong here (W. Zimmerli in *Z.A.W.*, 1954, pp. 13ff.). The fate of a sacrally expelled person was terrible (Gen. IV. 13f.), for as the bearer of a curse it was impossible for him to find shelter in another community; he was refused admission to all other groups, and, because at that time no one could dispense with relationships to supernatural powers, he was forced into the arms of the unlawful cults of magic.

understand it today, not only is the consequence of sin narrowed down to fall only on the individual and his spiritual life, but the evil that accompanies the sin is also confined to the evil act itself. The act no doubt sometimes has serious visible consequences for the man who does it, that is, when he gets himself entangled in some way or another in the evil he has wrought. But such consequences are to a greater or lesser degree fortuitous, and no one is surprised if such a punishment fails to come to pass. In contrast, for the people of antiquity sin was something much wider in its effects. The evil deed was only one side of the matter, for through it an evil had been set in motion which sooner or later would inevitably turn against the sinner or the community to which he belonged. On this view, the "recompense" which catches up with evil is certainly no subsequent forensic event which the sin evokes in a completely different sphere—that is, with God. It is the radiation of the evil which now continues on: only so does the evil which the sin called out reach equilibrium. This conception has been called a "synthetic view of life," since here the action of man on the one hand and what happens to him on the other are not yet understood as two separate and independent things, or at least as things standing only in very loose relationship to one another.[183] Instead, the presupposition of this idea is the closest possible correspondence between action and fate: what is in question is a process which, in virtue of a power proper alike to all that is good and all that is evil, comes to a good or an evil end. Israel regarded this as a basic order of her whole existence, to which Jahweh had given effect and over whose functioning he himself kept watch. It is Jahweh who "brings the evil man's conduct upon his own head" (I Kings VIII. 32). Proverbs too deals at length with this basic order; but it does so in a remarkably neutral way, as if this were to some extent a relatively independent and

---

[183] K. H. J. Fahlgren, *Sedake nahestehende und entgegengesetzte Begriffe im Alten Testament*, Uppsala 1932, pp. 50ff. K. Koch is more comprehensive, and critical of Fahlgren, in "Gibt es ein Vergeltungsdogma im Alten Testament?" in *Z. Th. K.*, 1955, pp. 1ff. But cf. what Smend had already said in his *Lehrbuch der alttestamentlichen Religionsgeschichte*, 2nd edn. Freiburg 1899, p. 401: "For the Jews sin was rather a power which brought the sinner to destruction, because it was basically identical with the penalty." Koch's important study seems to me to be in need of supplementation, in so far as the element of the divine declaration of guilt which works itself out in punishment is not given enough weight. The maxims of the wise men, which derive the procedure solely from its empirical side, have to be taken by themselves.

self-acting law of human life. That is, Proverbs does not on each occasion speak of a direct intervention of Jahweh.[184]

Now this means that there is absolutely nothing in the thought of the Old Testament which by and large corresponds to the separation which we make between sin and penalty. The best proof of this is the linguistic usage. Semantically both חטא and עון show a remarkable ambivalence, which can only be understood by means of this basic "synthetic" concept—for they can stand both for sin as act and for the consequences of sin, that is, for penalty. Thus, one of the narratives can make Moses say, "but if you are disobedient, you will have sinned (חטאתם) against Jahweh, and you will realise that you will meet with your חטאת" (Num. xxxii. 23). We must translate the second term as "penalty," but in Hebrew the act and the evil consequence following it which Israel will "meet with," that is, which will react upon Israel, are one and the same. A similar example of such ambivalence is to be found in Aaron's request to Moses: "O my lord, do not lay our חטאת upon us because we have done foolishly and sinned" (Num. xii. 11). The verb חטאנו means the act, the rebellion against Moses, while the noun means what we should describe as penalty. Aaron regards Moses as having full power to set it in operation. What does Cain mean when he says that he cannot bear his עון (Gen. iv. 13)? Does he mean the guilt of his deed, or its penalty? Here again there is no difference. Jahweh had made him see the consequence of his act, and Cain regards this whole thing, the complex evil reaching from his act to his fate, as too heavy. In addition it can also be said that a man dies not "for his own עון," but for "the עון of his fathers" (Lev. xxvi. 39). Thus in rendering these concepts exegesis must in each instance exercise great care.

This concept makes perfectly clear the reason why the community had such a strong interest in an individual's sin. It was not just a matter of an imaginary moral taint which affected the community as well, and so "just" an internal disturbance of its relationship with God: rather, the evil which an action had brought into existence inevitably had effects which destroyed individual and community alike, unless the latter solemnly and clearly cancelled its solidarity with the offender. Thus, in an utterly realistic and direct sense, an offender was a danger to the whole people. Further, it becomes clear that in such circum-

[184] Prov. xxv. 19, xxvi. 27f., xxviii. 1, 10, 17f., xxix. 6, 23, 25 and frequently. Koch, in *Z. Th. K.*, 1955, pp. 2f.

stances the act would inevitably be looked at from one side only, under the aspect of its actual performance and, initially, without any regard being paid to its personal motivations, and also, quite apart from any question as to the consciousness or subjective intention of the agent. In view of the horror which antiquity felt in face of a really deliberate breach of a sacral regulation, we have to assume that in practice sins committed in error, that is, such offences as were committed by a man under a delusion, in ignorance of his situation *vis-à-vis* God, were more frequent than deliberate sins. Earlier Israel called this kind of deluded ignorance "folly."[185] Thus, for example, David "acted foolishly" (סכל) in taking the census (II Sam. XXIV. 10) and so did Aaron when he rebelled against Moses (Num. XII. 11). This purely "objective" idea of guilt could from time to time lead to serious conflicts, and earlier Israel herself was well aware of the dilemmas and even the tragedy in which they could involve men and women.[186] Many stories actually rise to heights of moving dramatic quality just because they unfold the problem of the subjectively guiltless sinner—generally men of high position—with such naïveté. They remind the reader of Aristotle's idea of ἁμαρτία as the deepest cause of tragic suffering (e.g. Gen. XX. 3ff.; I Sam. XIV. 24ff.).[187] Though these stories bear the mark of

[185] Cf. Gen. XXXIV. 7; Jg. XIX. 23, XX. 6,10; II Sam. XIII. 12. In Greek too νήπιος can describe lack of insight into the action of the gods. G. Bertram in *Th. W.B.N.T.*, VOL. IV, p. 914.

[186] On "objective" guilt see also J. Hempel, *Ethos*, pp. 52ff. As Quell has rightly noticed, the concept of unwitting sin only appears in P to some extent in a stunted form (Lev. IV. 2, 22, 27, V. 15, XXII. 14; Num. XV. 27–9). "שׁגה is in no sense a milder expression: instead, its significance is in reality very much more serious than that of the formal concept of 'missing the mark' or of that of the emotional one of 'refusal,' because unwitting sin can only be spoken of on condition of a good will on the part of the agent. It is due to circumstances, or, in the terms of religion, to God, that a man sins unwittingly. Thus, an element of demonic horror makes itself felt as soon as unwitting sin appears as a religious term outside of the language of the cult, and indeed even within it it cannot be completely left out of the reckoning in spite of all softening through the possibility of cultic compensation." *Th. W.B.N.T.*, VOL. I, p. 274.

[187] ἁμαρτία is not be rendered here by "guilt" in the Christian sense. The term means that imperfection which, contrary to all reasonable expectation, causes injury to a subjectively innocent person. "The moral suffering of Oedipus was . . . called forth by the fact . . . that he had unintentionally and unwittingly done something which was objectively terrible. Here then the cause of the most terrible sin is ἁμαρτία" (K. von Fritz, *Tragische Schuld und poetische Gerechtigkeit in der griechischen Tragödie*, Stud. generale 1955, cols. 195ff.).

near spiritual desperation, still, they are unflinching. Objectively Abimelech committed an outrage in his offence against another man's marriage, and in the same way Jonathan, in spite of his ignorance, came under the ban of his father's curse. Israel thus refused to dissolve her concept of guilt into subjectivity. Only when the peculiarity and the grandeur of this ancient Israelite concept of guilt have been recognised will it also be apparent what a revolution the Jahwist's story of the Fall implies. Not that it makes guilt dissolve into subjectivity—that would be a complete misunderstanding of the Jahwist—but with his picture of the complicated operations within the soul when guilt is incurred, he opened up access to completely new territory. Since we cannot here give any history of the concept of guilt in ancient Israel, it may suffice to remark that the Priestly Document together with its accretions is apparently concerned with a restoration of the old sacral ideas, for the procedures it lays down for regulating the consecration of people and of objects, and for making atonement for them, certainly presuppose an extremely objective notion of guilt. But within the limits of these ideas, what is meant by expiation?

When a breach of a sacral order took place, the question arose whether or not it could be forgiven. Provided that Jahweh himself did not give the judgment directly, the decision lay with the priests, whom Jahweh had given full powers in the matter. If the sin could not be forgiven, then the person concerned had to "bear his guilt." Now once again this term נשא עון is a very characteristic formula of sacral law and occurs frequently in P and Ezekiel.[188] It means, in an ambivalent way, both "to incur guilt" and to "bear one's punishment," in the sense that the agent is abandoned to the evil which he has occasioned. What this meant for him was clear. Since man has in himself no powers of defence against the evil, and is unable to free himself from its embraces and pollution by any heroic moral action of his own, he inevitably becomes its prey. Initially, this was thought of as a working out of the divine wrath, occurring forthwith and destroying the man: through it the sinner was exposed to the sphere of the curse (cf. Num. v. 1f.; Lev. xx. 20). In other cases what followed was excommunication from the community by the pronouncement of a ban over the offender, and this virtually amounted to a sentence of death. Or else the community carried out the death sentence on him directly, by stoning. In

---

[188] Lev. v. 1, vii. 18, xvii. 16, xx. 17, 19f., xxii. 9, 16, xxiv. 15; Ezek. xiv. 10, xviii. 19f. and frequently. Cf. Zimmerli in Z.A.W., 1954, pp. 9ff.

connexion with what has just been said about the curse, it is to be noticed that P presupposes the very grandiose idea that the "camp" was constantly threatened by an almost hypostatised power of wrath (קֶצֶף).[189] In its account Israel's situation is drawn with deadly seriousness: on all sides and in its every action she was threatened with the possibility of a blow (נֶגֶף) descending upon her.[190] This term too is a strangely absolute theological *terminus technicus* in P. The sole protection from the blow was the repeated performance of numerous atoning rites. The strong emphasis laid upon the rites for atonement, which by the way can be seen in growth even within the strands of P, is characteristic of it alone. Such rites were not unknown in the history of the pre-exilic cult, but they certainly did not then occupy such a dominant place as they have in P. The reason for this change has been sought, and rightly so, in the broken and anguished mood of the exilic and post-exilic periods.

What were the special features of the concept of expiation in the Old Testament? The question has been frequently discussed before now, in part in excellent and thorough special studies, but no adequate answer has as yet been given. This is due to the nature of the texts at our disposal, which are, for far the most part, absolutely unannotated rituals. So it was not at all to be wondered at that these texts, dealing as they do with the technique of the cult and confining themselves in the main to a description of the external procedure, were susceptible of the most diverse interpretations. We ought not however to abandon all attempt at interpretation—though, of course, the only promising way to do so is to take into account from the very beginning the basic conception of the nature of an evil action and its consequences mentioned above.[191] Unfortunately, P hardly ever condescends to give its suggestions for interpretation. This makes the rather tortuous statement in Lev. XVII. 11 important for us. This text to begin with links up with Gen. IX. 4 (P), but it expands it in a definitive way.

"For the life of the flesh is in the blood: and I have given it for you upon the altar, to make atonement for yourselves; for the blood, through the life in it, makes atonement" (Lev. XVII. 11).

Here the commandment forbidding the eating of blood is re-issued in an intensified form. It now gets a completely new substantiation for

---

[189] Lev. X. 6; Num. I. 53, XVII. 11 [XVI. 46], XVIII. 5.

[190] Ex. XII. 13, XXX. 12; Num. VIII. 19, XVII. 11f.[XVI. 46f.]; Josh. XXII. 17.

[191] For what follows cf. K. Koch, *Die israelitische Sühneanschauung und ihre historischen Wandlungen* (typewritten thesis, Erlangen 1955)

Israel—Jahweh has "given" the people of Israel this life-bearing blood, all use of which he had previously ruled out, for a quite particular purpose, namely for the effective performance of expiatory rites at the altar. But it is not the blood in itself that effects expiation, but the blood in so far as the life is contained in it. Expiation therefore does not depend upon the blood, but upon the life, whose bearer the blood is.[192] This text does not, of course, supply any very definite information about the way in which this focal point for theology regards expiation "for your life" (על נפשותיכם) as brought about. But Deut. XXI. 1–9, which is obviously a very primitive set of directions, does take us further with this question. In the case of murder by an unknown agent the prayer reads "make expiation for thy people Israel (לעמך כפר) and let there not be innocent blood in the midst of thy people Israel" (vs. 8). Murder brings calamity upon Israel, and especially upon the areas immediately concerned. If no act of expiation was made in which an animal was put to death in place of the murderer, then the areas would have to "bear" the evil with its calamitous consequences. In this case, then, expiation is effected through the vicarious death of an animal. But what is of special importance in this connexion is that appeal is made to Jahweh, himself actively to effect the expiation. Accordingly the one who receives expiation is not Jahweh, but Israel: Jahweh is rather the one who acts, in averting the calamitous curse which burdens the community.[193] Now in P, as distinct from D, the one who effects expiation is never Jahweh himself: instead, it is every-where the priest who does this. But this does not in any way imply a changed idea of the effecting of expiation, for on the whole in P the priest stands out as Jahweh's fully authorised instrument. Thus here, too, although the priest actually performs the actions for expiation, in the last analysis it is Jahweh himself who effects or refuses expiation.[194] That the priests act as the representatives of Jahweh, and that Jahweh acts through them, comes out especially clearly in the curious cere-monial connected with the eating of the sin offering (Lev. VI. 17ff. [24ff.], X. 16ff.). In Jahweh's stead they deal with the entire removal of

---

[192] J. Herrmann, Die Idee der Sühne im Alten Testament, p. 67.

[193] References for Jahweh as the subject of expiation are Deut. XXI. 8; Pss. LXV. 4 [3], LXXVIII. 38, LXXIX. 9; Jer. XVIII. 23; Ezek. XVI. 63; II Chron. XXX. 18; Dan. IX. 24.

[194] Ex. XXIX. 36f., XXX. 10, 15f.; Lev. I. 4, IV. 20, 26, 31, V. 6, 10, 13, 16, 18 and frequently. Exact statistics on the word are to be found in J. Herrmann, Die Idee der Sühne im Alten Testament, pp. 35–7.

the evil which has been laid upon the animal: they "bear" the עָוֹן of the community and thereby effect expiation (Lev. x. 17). So it is men and women, and on occasion cultic objects as well, who receive expiation, since on this view the latter too can come within the sphere of a baneful influence, and in consequence become unfit for use in the cult.[195] As is well known, an essential part of the ceremonial at the "great Day of Atonement" (Lev. XVI) served the purposes of the expiation of the altar and the sanctuary. What was effected in expiation was that in both cases, with persons and objects alike, Jahweh removed the baneful influence of an act. He broke the nexus of sin and calamity; and this was as a rule effected by way of channelling the baneful influence of the evil into an animal which died vicariously for the man (or for the cultic object).[196] Expiation was thus not a penalty, but a saving event.[197] In the actual process, offences were graded according to their enormity. More trivial errors could be repaired by lustrations. On the other hand the ritual in Lev. XVI shows a vast accumulation of expiatory rites, which speaks for a tremendous consciousness of the enormity of guilt. In the final form of the ritual Aaron four times makes expiation for himself (vss. 6, 11, 17, 24), three times for the community (vss. 10, 17, 24) and once for the holy place (vs. 20).

All this however was no "magic" event, requiring only to be set in motion to lead to the desired result. These rituals show only the outward aspect of a sacral event, the way in which it took its course once the priests whom Jahweh had authorised had pronounced their "yes." We know all too little about the criteria by which they were guided, but it can be assumed that, in giving their decisions, they followed old and well-tried cultic traditions. Nothing can be gathered from these texts about the subjective condition of those who requested expiation; in a few instances only is mention made of a confession to be spoken during the process of expiation.[198] Unfortunately, even recent research into the Psalms, although it has given us insight into an amazingly

[195] What takes place in Is. VI. 8f. is also to be understood as an expiatory cleansing of an object, the lips, which were as a result made capable of sufficing for a function that God laid upon them.

[196] Still, according to P, other gifts too—cf. Ex. XXX. 15f.; Lev. v. 11f.; Num. XXXI. 50—could have powers of expiation.

[197] "The law nowhere indicates that in sacrifice . . . an act of punitive punishment is executed; it in no way asks us to look on the altar as a place of punishment," Oehler, *Theology of the Old Testament*, Edinburgh 1874, p. 431.

[198] Lev. v. 5, XVI. 21; Num. v. 7.

diverse cultic activity, has not as yet been able to establish satisfactory connexion with the world of these priestly rituals.

(f) Clean—Unclean, Illness and Death

Our understanding of all the cultic activities so far mentioned would, however, be left hanging in the air, unless we were to see them in relationship to ideas which are much more comprehensive. They have their place and significance in and for a world which in God's sight was divided into clean and unclean, holy and secular, blessing and curse.[199] For Israel this tension and polarity was a basic datum of all life—it was so universally valid that it had to be assumed as present and taken for granted even where it is not mentioned *expressis verbis*, as for instance in the prophets. There is not the slightest reason for assuming that it was a specific characteristic of the post-exilic period alone: P only fixed and conserved the sacral ordinances which were valid in earlier times as well. It is precisely in this respect that P gives the impression of much greater antiquity than the very much more rational and reflective Deuteronomy.

Starting from the outside and proceeding inwards, the first holy thing is Israel's land (Am. VII. 17; Hos. IX. 3; Ezek. IV. 12f.): it was in fact Jahweh's land (Lev. XXV. 23), his heritage (נחלת יהוה I Sam. XXVI. 19; II Sam. XIV. 16). The description of the Philistines as "uncircumcised" (Jg. XIV. 3, XV. 18; I Sam. XIV. 6, etc.) shows to what a degree the contrast between outward and inward was still felt to be a sacral and not a national matter. For P the camp was holy (Lev. VI. 4 [11], X. 4f., XIII. 46, XVI. 21), Jerusalem was holy (Is. LII. 2, XLVIII. 2), yes, so even was the city wall (Neh. XII. 30). The Temple hill was holy (Pss. XXIV. 3, II. 6), the Temple was made holy (I Kings IX. 3), and so was the Tabernacle with its innermost chamber, the Holy of Holies (Num. I. 51), which latter was so holy that even the High Priest himself might only enter it once a year, and even then only as he paid heed to meticulous rites (Lev. XVI. 1ff.). The vessels and the various parts of the Tabernacle were so holy that they required to be protected from all unwarranted contact (Num. IV. 15): indeed, in one of the supplementary passages, they ought not even to be seen by unauthorised persons (Num. IV. 20). The priests were holy, their life being in consequence subject to special prescriptions (Lev. XXI. 1–15, 16–23)—even their clothes were holy (Ex. XXIX. 29, XXXI. 10). The offerings were

[199] See above, pp. 37f.

holy (Lev. vi. 11 [18]); some were even "most holy," and were specially guarded (קֹדֶשׁ קָדָשִׁים, Lev. ii. 3, 10, vi. 10 [17], xxvii. 28 and elsewhere), etc. The additions to P (Pˢ) are full of prescriptions like these, and of directions as to how, when it has been lost, the holiness of a person or a thing can be restored by lustrations or by anointing with oil or blood. The rituals delineate all this as if it were static, and with a lifeless stiffness which we find strange. But of course they only display the outside of the matter, and even that in the form of normative paradigms. It needs very little imagination to see how, in the actual practice of the cult, things would often be full of dramatic movement and tension, for the unclean was the most basic form in which Israel encountered what was displeasing to God. New decisions had constantly to be pronounced in connexion with it, and these demanded the undivided theological vigilance of priesthood and laity, for the line of contact between the two opposed spheres of the clean and the unclean was by no means fixed—it was a battle-line, running irregularly through daily life, particularly the life of the laity. Haggai has preserved a very informative case arising in an individual's everyday home life (Hag. ii. 10–13). Was ordinary food that had come into contact with consecrated flesh made *ipso facto* holy? The priests' answer is that it is not. A second question follows. Will it be unclean if it is touched by someone who is himself unclean through contact with a dead body? The answer is, yes. We can see that behind the two answers there is a problem. Human life is lived in two spheres. There are cases in which the potency of the unclean is greater than that of the holy; but in others, as for example in all processes of expiation, the holy is the stronger. These were not questions of captious scrupulosity. On the contrary, there constantly arose in the life of the individual *status confessionis*, where in the decisions given the one way or the other the whole of Jahwism and of the individual's cultic existence before God was implicitly at stake. Man's encounter with the unclean was particularly close and dangerous in the wide-ranging field of sex. Israel had a certain apprehensiveness about sex that derived from the cult. To expose one's nakedness when going up to the altar, that is, while performing cultic duties, was displeasing to Jahweh (Ex. xx. 26), and anyone who was in a state of special cultic immediacy to Jahweh (as, for example, in the holy war) had to abstain from sexual relationships. Only then was the body "clean" (קָדֵשׁ, 1 Sam. xxi. 6 [5], cf. Lev. xv. 18; Deut. xxiii. 11 [10]; 11 Sam. vi. 20, xi. 11). A woman was unclean because of the birth of a child (Lev. XII). In particular, all issues from the sexual organs necessitated ritual purification of the persons concerned (I Sam. XX. 26; Lev. XV). Serious sexual offences polluted not only the offender, but even the land (Lev. XVIII. 25, 28, XIX. 29; Num. V. 3; Deut. XXIV. 4; Hos. IV. 3; Jer. III. 2, 9). This holds specially true, of course, of shed blood (Gen. IV. 11f.; Num. XXXV. 33f.; Deut. XXI. 22f.).

In addition, all serious illnesses were subject to a like sacral assessment. There were, of course, surgeons for external wounds in Israel (Ex. XXI. 19), but in all serious illnesses the competent person was the priest. The old phrase "I, Jahweh, am your healer" certainly had originally a very real, programmatic, and even polemical content (Ex. XV. 26).[200] Such disturbances of the vital basis of human existence brought a man into a *status confessionis*. Only God could heal (II Kings V. 7): not to have confidence in Jahweh's readiness to help, but to seek advice from physicians, was lack of faith (II Chron. XVI. 12). It was of course from Jahweh that bodily sickness came; and he alone could bind up and heal (Job V. 18). With these references taken from the later writings we should bear in mind that the tendency which they show is precisely that of reviving ancient ideas. The Wisdom of Solomon goes very far in what it says about healing the Israelites of the plagues in Egypt—"it was neither herb nor poultice that healed them, but thy word, which healeth all things" (XVI. 12). But in older Israel too it was probably common usage in all illness to approach Jahweh as the physician. In laments people cried "Heal me" (Ps. VI. 3 [2]; Jer. XVII. 14), and in songs of thanksgiving they confessed "Thou hast healed me" (Pss. XXX. 3 [2], CIII. 3). It was a serious matter when the sick man turned to a foreign god (II Kings I. 2–8). This very radical attitude did not, of course, exclude all medical treatment. Once a man had committed himself to Jahweh, medicines too had a place (II Kings XX. 1–7). The only clearer glimpse we get of the priests' management of medical matters is the direction about leprosy in Lev. XIIIf. Leprosy, as the "first-born of death" (Job XVIII. 13), was probably reckoned to be the most serious kind of bodily uncleanness that could happen to a man, and on that account the priests had to be specially particular in dealing

---

[200] Sellin saw that Ex. XV. 25 is an old text which has been painted over (*Mose und seine Bedeutung für die isr. und jüd. Religionsgeschichte*, henceforth cited as *Mose*, Berlin 1922, pp. 134f.). For sacral medicine in ancient Israel see A. Wendel, *Säkularisierung in Israels Kultur*, Gütersloh 1934, pp. 320ff., 330, and recently J. Hempel, "Ich bin der Herr, dein Arzt," in *Th. Lz.*, 1957, cols. 809-26.

with it.[201] Behind these rites and this whole cumbersome ceremonial for purification lies as an unexpressed though basic presupposition the idea that there was a very close connexion between sin and physical disease.[202] But this brings us amazingly close to the theological assertion made by the Jahwist in Gen. III: he too wants to indicate how all the disturbances in our natural life have their roots in a disturbed relationship to God.

There is an odd lack of harmony in the chapter in Ecclesiasticus dealing with the physicians (xxxviii. 1–15). As such collections of maxims generally do, very diverse judgments on the theological problem raised by the physician are set over against one another. God "instituted" the physician, and it is from God that he gets his wisdom (vs. 1f.). His medicines too come from God—proof is even given from Scripture of the legitimacy of making use of them (vss. 4–8). All this therefore speaks in favour of the physician's service. In the second part, however, the theological judgments are more reserved. In the case of illness, prayer and sacrifice are recommended, although the physician is not necessarily ruled out in principle, for "on occasion" his hand too is granted success. Here too, typically, the sage feels himself obliged to give the physician theological legitimation: and this he finds in the fact that the physician prayed for the success of his diagnosis (vss. 9–14). Apparently these preceding arguments did not impress the last man whose opinion is recorded—"he who sinneth in the sight of his Maker falls into the hands of the physician" (vs. 15). The whole is a piece of writing typical of an enlightenment which is at the same time unwilling to give up the old traditional faith. It no longer however takes its stand upon it, and now only puts theology to the trouble of giving a *post eventum* legitimation to the physician whose actual existence has to be reckoned with in one way or another.

We must also discuss death here, but not, it is true, that aspect of it which particularly interests people today, the experience of dying. Nor do we deal with ideas about the condition of men after death. Instead, we consider what was the basic presupposition of both of these in Israel, namely, death's classification and assessment in the cult. These are clear enough—all that has died represents the utmost degree

---

[201] It has recently been questioned whether צרעת is to be translated by "leprosy." Köhler in *Z.A.W.*, 1955, p. 290.

[202] So for example Pss. xxxii. 1ff., xxxviii. 3ff., xxxix. 9, 12 [8, 11], xli. 5 [4], lxix. 6 [5], ciii. 3, cvii. 17f.

of uncleanness (Num. IX. 6, XIX. 11, 16, 18, XXXI. 19 of the dead of men; Lev. XI. 24-8, etc., of the dead of animals). The uncleanness issuing from the dead infected not only human beings in the vicinity of the dead man, but things as well (Lev. XI. 33ff.): indeed it could be passed on still further through contact with what had been rendered unclean (Num. XIX. 22). People who were in a state of intensified holiness, the priests and Nazirites (Lev. XXI. 1ff., 10ff.; Num. VI. 6ff.), were specially menaced by the uncleanness occasioned by death. Apart from the disease of leprosy (in the cases where it was incurable), contact with the dead occasions an uncleanness more serious in degree than all other forms of uncleanness. Therefore it cannot be removed by ordinary lustration, as is the case with uncleanness due to sex, but requires a special purificatory water compounded with the ashes of a red heifer (Num. XIX. 1ff.).

All these very lifeless-looking ritual regulations do not in themselves retain any traces of the hard defensive warfare which Israel waged, aided by these very cultic prescriptions. In order to get a view of the battlefield itself, we have to draw upon other sources which are earlier in date of composition. As far as we can see back into the history, Jahwism turned with a special intolerance against all forms of the cult of the dead. Like most nations who were still unsophisticated in religion, the first datum, or at least the obvious thing to do, for Israel as well, was to confer a positive sacral value on the dead and on the grave. There was no doubt that the dead lived on—especially so if this was assured by means of rites. Thus the dead man was merely changed, and represented, to a higher degree than while living in the body, a power which had to be reckoned with in a very real way.[203] In consequence, it was of prime importance to regulate the relationship of the living to these dead. The dead could of course do harm. But use could also be made of their higher knowledge. How close Israel stood to these ideas may be seen from the fact that the age of Deuteronomy and Isaiah was still exposed to the temptation to consult the dead (Is. VIII. 19; Deut. XVIII. 11). And on one occasion when such a spirit was conjured up, it is still actually designated אֱלֹהִים (1 Sam. XXVIII. 13). Even if we take the view that this is all just a matter of the survival of rudiments, a degraded and outlawed hole-and-corner cult, it would still be quite wrong on the one hand to set too little store on the temptation which emanated from this sphere, or, on the other, to underestimate the

[203] G. van der Leeuw, *Phänomenologie der Religion*, p. 195.

power of self-restraint which Israel had to call into being in order to renounce all sacral communion with her dead. Even Deuteronomy still requires a man who is offering the first-fruits solemnly to avow that he has allotted none of them as a meal for the dead (Deut. XXVI. 14).[204] It is of course questionable whether the designation "cult of the dead" is not too honorific a one for such isolated practices. Did these paltry actions towards a dead man really still count as a cult in the real sense of the term? Nevertheless they did express a sacral relationship with the dead which was absolutely incompatible with Jahwism. Obviously, Jahweh's will for exclusive worship turned itself in a particularly intransigent way against this very cult of the dead and anything in any way connected with it. Thus, for example, certain mourning rites which were now only loosely connected with the cult of the dead were weeded out with an assiduity that seems out of place.[205] The upshot of the whole matter was a radical demythologising and desacralising of death. The dead were absolutely outside the cultic sphere of Jahweh, and Israel might not recognise any other cultic sphere. The dead were divorced from him and from communion with him, because they were outside the province of his cult (Ps. LXXXVIII. 11–13 [10–12]). Herein lay the real bitterness of death, and the laments in the Psalms give pathetic expression to this experience.[206]

Thus the life of Israel, even the whole of its everyday life, was bounded by a great tension between clean and unclean and between life and death, for every uncleanness was to some extent already a precursor of the thing that was uncleanness out and out, death: in the same way any slight uncleanness led to death in so far as it was not deliberately wiped out by ritual means.[207] The perils which confronted the life of the individual in Israel—just as they did the life of the community—as he moved to and fro on the narrow border-line between clean and unclean, can perhaps be made clear by the fact that, before taking part in any cultic activity, everyone had to "sanctify himself."[208] What this usage presupposes is that in their everyday life men had come into contact with much that was unclean, from which they had

---

[204] It has been correctly assumed that the erection of a mazzebah over the grave of an ancestor (Gen. XXXV. 20) was formerly not such a harmless custom as it now appears in the story. For gifts put into graves see K. Galling in *Biblisches Reallexikon*, Tübingen 1937, cols. 239f.

[205] Lev. XIX. 28, XXI. 5f.; Deut. XIV. 1. See above, p. 208.

[206] See below, pp. 387ff.   [207] Lev. XVII. 15f.; Num. XIX. 20.

[208] Ex. XIX. 10, 14; Josh. VII. 13; 1 Sam. XVI. 5; Job I. 5.

to be cleansed by means of lustrations and abstentions before they could re-enter the realm of the holy. Israel clearly did not reflect upon the nature of the unclean and its special character. Nowadays it is sometimes interpreted as the sphere of the demonic.[209] In Israel, however, there is no real support for this view (at the most Lev. XVI. 26), since she obviously felt herself altogether much less menaced by demons than did other peoples in her cultural environment. It was enough that there was a realm of the unclean (and also of the curse), whose operations were fatal in their effect on men, and which were therefore displeasing (תועבה) to Jahweh, because Jahweh purposed Israel's life (Ezek. XVIII. 23). He wanted to have Israel on his side, and wanted Israel to be holy, as he was holy (Lev. XIX. 2, XX. 26; Ex. XXII. 30 [31]). There was nothing at all rigid, and nothing laid down once for all, in these cultic regulations: rather the boundary between clean and unclean was constantly in a state of flux. What is of course remarkable is that it is in P that the realm of holiness which Jahweh established is not rigorously fixed. It was not tied to the holiness of a place which was, as it were, absolutely holy, but it was a holiness that was always on the move. To indicate it only a minimum of outward sacral furnishings (a tent, and some poles and carpets) were needed. These no doubt marked out the limits of a *temenos*. But the holiness of this *temenos* was never attached to the place. It always depended upon Jahweh's command to stay or move on (Num. X. 1ff.). The entire holiness of the place and of the objects stood or fell with the resting or the departure of the cloud (Num. IX. 15ff.).

Just because of this, new questions must always have been cropping up for the men who lived their lives on this boundary-line between the sacred and the secular, and fresh decisions must have had continually to be issued from the cultic centre in order to define the *status quo* for the time being (Lev. X. 10f.). The community was of course betrayed when the priests ceased to attend to their office, when they "made no distinction between holy and secular, and gave no instruction about the difference between clean and unclean" (Ezek. XXII. 26). The unclean was always pushing forward, with the result that men and things came into its power. Israel considered herself as lost in face of this power, had not Jahweh come to her aid. Healing and saving forces, however, emanated from the sanctuary and the cult, and these maintained life

---

[209] S. Mowinckel, *Religion und Kultus*, p. 80; J. Hempel, *Ethos*, pp. 53, 180f.; on the contrary, Eichrodt, *Theologie*, VOL. II, p. 180.

in a wholesome equilibrium between these poles. These, sanctuary and cult, no doubt did not extend so far as completely to extrude and abolish the unclean, or finally to incorporate the secular realm into the holy. This continuing struggle between the sacred and the secular, which runs right through the whole of Jahweh's creation (*vide* the list of unclean animals), is, however, regarded even by P as something temporary. P too knows a final condition of things where the holiness of Jahweh will attain its goal, since "all the earth will be full of the glory of God" (Num. xiv. 21). But this swallowing up of the secular in the holy, so complete that the most insignificant objects in everyday use, the pots in the houses and the bells on horses' harness, will be as holy as the vessels in the Temple, a prophet only looks for as coming with Jahweh's final act of salvation "in that day" (Zech. xiv. 21f.).

These ideas of how salvation is deeply rooted in the material were never abandoned by Israel—even the prophets did not give them up. It would be a great mistake to regard the prophets as the spiritual antipodes opposed to the cultic world of the priests. A programmatic war of reformation waged against the priests would have taken a very different aspect. What we witness in the prophets is an attack on abuses. In this attack we occasionally come upon the spiritualising of cultic concepts. But what is said—and it is always set within a specific polemic—remains *ad hoc*, and never widens out to deliberate opposition. Now and then such spiritualisations probably betoken some internal crises in Israel's cultic life. But it must be very emphatically stressed that they do not in the slightest imply any "evolution" in the direction of an increasingly intensive spiritualisation. Our own theological outlook finds it all too easy to be suspicious of this ritual side of Jahwism, as unspiritual and external. But how can it be made out that the people who submitted to purificatory rites were not touching the heart of the matter? As we said, the unclean is the most basic form of Israel's encounter with what was displeasing to Jahweh. Of course it is hard for us today to size up the experiential content of such observances. The Psalms certainly do give us some information: we can generally assume that in them we are addressed by a piety which has not as yet started on "the great retreat into spirituality."[210] And in particular, it is precisely in this grasp of the material side of life by the cultic sphere that Jahweh's urgent will to be immanent comes to expression, a will which is wholly unsatisfied with Israel's spirituality.

[210] E. Spranger, *Die Magie der Seele*, Tübingen 1947, p. 7.

V. The Wandering in the Wilderness

According to the chronology of the Priestly Document, Israel spent almost a year at Sinai: thereafter the people were once more on the move.[1] Visualising it as it is given in the final form of the Hexateuch, the route led from Sinai to Kadesh. From there the spies were sent out (Num. xiiif.; Deut. i. 19ff.), and owing to the rebellion which broke out for this reason, the journey into the promised land came once again to a standstill. To begin with, Israel disobeyed Jahweh's command to turn about at once and go southwards, to the Red Sea: instead, she went northwards and attempted, on her own initiative, to force her way into the promised land; but in this attempt she was defeated at Hormah (Num. xiv. 39–41; Deut. i. 41ff.). Now, however, a huge, yawning gap appears in the narrative, since in Num. xx. i Israel returns to Kadesh in the fortieth year. Israel thus paid the penalty during a period of thirty-eight years in the wilderness, during which the whole generation of those who had rebelled against Jahweh had to die (Num. xiv. 33f.; Deut. ii. 14).[2] Even after this second departure from Kadesh, Israel did not go directly to her God-given goal; but in order to go round Edom in peace, she presently found herself once more at the Red Sea (Num. xxi. 4), and only from there did she advance slowly northwards east of the Jordan.

This tremendous picture of a people's journeying—a journeying directed by a compulsion quite unconnected with strategic and economic requirements—is, as far as the history of tradition goes, the final outcome of a very long process of growth and combination of traditions. A final conglomeration which overloads the picture of the journey in the wilderness was effected with the literary combination of the three source documents, J, E, and P, which for their part had each given to some extent a shorter and simpler picture.[3] The picture given in the source documents itself came into being as the result of a skilful combination of a series of hitherto local traditions current among the

[1] Ex. xix. i; Num. x. ii.

[2] Earlier expositors had many strange things to say about this period—the covenant was "suspended," the theocracy inoperative, circumcision was not performed, the Passover not celebrated, etc. So as late as Hengstenberg, *History of the Kingdom of God under the Old Testament*, Edinburgh 1871, vol. i, pp. 377, 383.

[3] This holds true particularly for the Jahwist. In Deut. i. 6–ii. 25 there is a recapitulating account which is based in the main on E. Here already the route is very complicated.

tribes of the south.[4] The reason why it could be worked up in the chequered way it was, is that in the case of the wanderings the old notion of the saving history did not report any striking event (like the Exodus or the miraculous crossing of the Red Sea): it only told of Jahweh's leading the people through the wilderness. Nevertheless, this element in the Credo is very old—the deliverance from Egypt itself implied the leading. Reconstruction of the way taken by the traditions in this part of the confession cannot form any part of our present task: all that can be done is to indicate something of the differences and tensions within the theological thinking of this period.

The tersest formulations accessible in connexion with this subject are in summaries of confessional character and hymns that re-tell the history. While the Credo in Deut. xxvi. 5ff. deals with the events from the Exodus to the Settlement in one clause—and this probably means that it only knows of the deliverance from Egypt as Jahweh's decisive saving act—in the text given in Josh. xxiv. the wandering now has a place of its own alongside the deliverance and the miraculous crossing of the Red Sea ("and then you lived a long time in the wilderness," vs. 7b). Thus the leading through the wilderness became an indispensable element in the psalms where history comes in, as Ps. cxxxvi. 16 for example shows: the appeal in Amos also, "I led you forty years in the wilderness" (Am. ii. 10), may be borrowed from the psalm. What characterises all these expressions, which originate rather from the sphere of the cult, is the exclusive concentration upon the action of God. Israel is a silent and passive object in what God does. This is due to the confessional style, which only recapitulates the saving facts, a style which still lives on in the Psalms. Nevertheless, a very early shift took place in the subject of consideration: Israel came into the picture as a special subject considered. During this period, how did things stand with her, who became the subject of the divine leading in such singular circumstances? Now, strangely enough, two different ways of viewing the matter stand out in clear contrast. In the first, which finds its clearest expression in Jer. ii. 1–3, the wandering in the wilderness was

---

[4] M. Noth, *Pentateuch*, p. 63. In the forefront are saga-like traditions which are attached to the district of the oasis of Kadesh. The assumption that direct memories of this earliest period were preserved in certain groups is of course not ruled out *a limine*; but how are we to discover these elements in the form which these stories were given at so much later a time? In a later time, too, much information came to Israel about this wilderness area, which she could use to form the picture of that era.

the time when the relationship was at its fairest, the time of the first love of Jahweh and Israel. At that time—"in a land unsown"—Israel was completely thrown upon Jahweh. She had not as yet been captivated by the allurements of the mysteries of the fruitful soil. So far no Baals had thrust themselves between her and Jahweh, as was afterwards the case in Palestine—she had to depend upon him in all departments of life. And he sustained his people, even looking after their sandals and clothes (Deut. xxix. 5f.). Oddly enough, the priestly version of the story of the manna approximates after a fashion to this version of it— all gathered the manna which came down; but it turned out in the evening that everyone had gathered the exact quantity necessary for himself and his family—there was no surplus and no lack. One meaning of what happened became clear here. The event comes to have typological significance—God gives to each according to his need. And further, the manna cannot be stored up. A few did try to do so, but they found that it went bad (Ex. xvi. 9–27). In this case, too, history is intended to be the dress for a truth which Israel arrived at from her relations with Jahweh—this daily sustenance by God demanded a surrender without security: in dealing with God, we live from minute to minute. In the story of the manna as Deuteronomy understood it, this process of spiritualising the old miraculous story is carried a further step forward. In P, manna is after all food for the body, and nothing is as yet explicitly said about the deeper meaning lying behind it, but in Deut. viii. 3, the matter is completely spiritualised. It is stated expressly that the event was intended to teach that man does not live by bread alone but "by everything that proceeds from the mouth of Jahweh." Here manna is obviously taken as spiritual food. In all this we have to bear in mind that the idea of a life in the wilderness became more and more incomprehensible to Israel after her settlement in the arable land and when she had come to enjoy the blessings of that land. The description of the "great and terrible" wilderness in Deut. viii. 15–18, where life was menaced by drought, and by serpents and scorpions, gives an echo of the dread which people in a more comfortable situation felt about such conditions. Jeremiah has this same idea of the wilderness when he calls it the land of the "pits, of thirst and darkness, where none passes through and none dwells" (Jer. ii. 6). Thus Jahweh's leadership had proved true in this period in paradigmatic miracles.

But the more Israel came to regard Jahweh's leadership through the wilderness as an extremely marvellous event, the more urgent became

the question: how did she stand up to the test during this period? The
answer becomes more and more negative till it reaches the devastating
verdict expressed in Ezek. xx. The purpose of Ps. LXXVIII, according
to its elaborate exordium, is to celebrate the acts of God (מעללי אל);
but into the enumeration of these marvels of the leadership through the
wilderness there again and again intrudes a description of the defiance,
the lack of faith, and the other sins, which were Israel's reaction to this
mighty act of God (vss. 8ff., 17ff., 32ff., 40ff., 56ff.). As compared with
Ps. CXXXVI, let us say, the theme has therefore altered—a defiant,
faithless crowd, that is what Jahweh's redeemed people was! A still
gloomier effect is produced by the picture in Ps. CVI, because the
representation given there exhausts itself in the description of Israel's
continuous failure—the background against which these sins stand in
Ps. LXXVIII, the kindnesses of Jahweh, is left out altogether.[5] Israel's
chief sin, which is repeatedly mentioned in an almost stereotyped fashion
in this connexion, consists in her "tempting Jahweh," that is, in her
provoking of him by her lack of faith and discontent.[6] But the darkest
picture, darkest just because it is the most consistent theologically, is
that of Ezek. xx. It is true that here too mention is made of the saving
acts which Jahweh did "for his name's sake" (vss. 9, 14, 22), in spite of
all disobedience. But the most appalling feature is that the period in the
wilderness is here pictured as a type and pattern of the coming judgment.
Just as Jahweh judged the fathers, so will he lead this present generation
into judgment in "the wilderness of the nations" (vs. 35). No one before
Ezekiel had spoken in this way about Israel's time in the wilderness,
for in his picture Ezekiel stresses the divine acts of judgment, and sees
in them a prefiguration of the imminent judgment which will come
upon the people of God of his day. Admittedly, there were current
some traditions, very old ones, which had as their subject Israel's
failure, a "murmuring" in the wilderness. But this growth of the negative aspects to such a pitch that in the end the whole time in the wilderness was given the appearance of so sombre a period, is connected
with general radical insights about Israel's relationship to Jahweh and
about the possibility of her existence in the light of this God, insights
which only became consolidated in the later monarchical period, and

[5] This view of history as a series of human rebellions against God's leadership is
to be understood in the light of the cultic purpose of the psalm as a song of penitence.

[6] Ex. XVII. 1ff.; Num. XIV. 22; Pss. LXXVIII. 17f., 40f., XCV. 8f., CVI. 14 (cf. also
Is. VII. 12). E. Seesemann, in *Th. W.B.N.T.*, VOL. VI, pp. 27, 32.

certainly not without the activity of the prophets. It was the recognition of Israel's insecurity and exposedness, perhaps even her defeat, which so radically changed the picture of the wilderness. But this age also heard the tidings that Jahweh would do a new thing—he would once more redeem Israel in the same way as he had done at the beginning and lead her again through the wilderness.[7]

To return to the picture given in the Hexateuch or in the sources—how is it to be fitted in here? Since the source documents and the various units of tradition which go to make it up originate in very different periods and also in very varied circles, we may not initially expect any unified and consistent view. It can be said on the whole that it more or less holds the balance between Jer. II and Ezek. XX. It indicates both Jahweh's gracious control of history and Israel's behaviour. The reader is altogether unaware that there are two divergent points of view, which the oldest picture of the history did not as yet know in this dual form at the stage when it was embedded in the cult. While it is always a good thing to remember the limits imposed upon the freedom of writers handling long-settled traditional material, it would none the less be a mistake to refrain from questioning these series of narratives as to their overall theme. The authors of the source documents—at all events J and E—both had the will to impose a thematic stamp on even the larger sections of the narrative, and were also in the position to do so. In our case, that is for the account of the wanderings after Sinai, Ex. XXXIII seems, in our opinion, to occupy a key position. What went before this was Israel's offence with the "golden calf" (Ex. XXXII): because of it Jahweh's relationship to Israel, which had just been established at Sinai, was profoundly changed. Both J and E end the story with an expression of the divine wrath. Thus Jahweh's relationship to Israel had sustained a blow, and its most visible consequence was Jahweh's refusal to lead them any further in person (Ex. XXXII. 34 E, XXXIII. 2f. J). Admittedly, Jahweh did not abandon his saving plan, but his presence would destroy Israel if he were now to move along with her (Ex. XXXIII. 5). The whole of ch. XXXIII is therefore pervaded by the question of the escort, without which Israel could not set out on the wandering (Ex. XXXIII. 12, 15f.). But the answers given it are in no sense uniform; they are very divergent, for in Ex. XXXIII a number of parallel traditions are piled up. (1) Jahweh sends his angel. (2) Moses sets up the holy tent and thereby establishes a

[7] So especially Deutero-Isaiah, Is. XLIII. 16–21, XLVIII. 20f., LII. 12 and frequently.

connexion with Jahweh. (3) Jahweh lets his Presence (*Panim*) accompany them. About the last of these little can be said, for this almost hypostatising independence here given to the "face" (פנים) as a special form of manifestation between Jahweh and Israel is unique.[8] It is possible that the passage served as the aetiology of a cultic mask (why is Jahweh only present in the *Panim*?).[9] But while this idea of the *Panim* accompanying Israel is isolated, the other idea, that of the guiding angel, rests on a much broader basis. The idea that in the wilderness Israel was led by the angel of Jahweh was obviously firmly rooted in the tradition, since it occurs in various contexts (Ex. XIV. 19, XXIII. 20, 23, XXXII. 34, XXXIII. 2; Num. XX. 16).

The Angel of Jahweh. The Hebrew word which we translate as "angel" (מלאך) means "messenger," the man or the heavenly being despatched with some commission.[10] The Old Testament certainly speaks openly here and there of heavenly beings. But it is remarkable that in the majority of the references, the way in which the beings are thought of never rises above a certain colourlessness and indistinctness. If we ask what their function and significance was, as it were in relation to the centre of Jahwism, there is not much of an answer. Often the impression is given that what is in question is a necessary part of the heavenly world which tradition demanded, and which Israel accepted like other people, rather than an idea in which the faith had any particular interest. In any case, as we see angels in Israel's older literature— the position is somewhat different in the post-exilic period—these heavenly beings are hardly ever seriously concerned in the government of the world or in the direction of history. This is unquestionably bound up with the radical idea of Jahweh as the cause of all things, and with his zeal, to which Israel attributed all, and which left no room for any extensive action on the part of intermediary beings. But the figure of

---

[8] Only again in Deut. IV. 37. But Is. LXIII. 9 also takes the tradition up.

[9] So G. Beer, *Exodus*, Tübingen 1939, *in loco*, according to Galling. But there is still uncertainty here, for others have explained פנים in Ex. XXXIII. 14 according to II Sam. XVII. 11, in the sense of "I personally," "I myself"—that is, in the opposite sense.

[10] W. Baumgartner has drawn attention to the fact that the Greek ἄγγελος too is not yet a categorical term for heavenly beings; and in the New Testament also it is still used for human messengers (Lk. VII. 24, IX. 52). The *angelus* of the Vulgate is the first to mean "angel." Baumgartner, "Zum Problem des Jahweengels," in *Schweiz. Theol. Umschau*, 1944, pp. 97ff. Cf. further F. Stier, *Gott und sein Engel im Alten Testament*, Münster 1934; Eichrodt, *Theologie*, VOL. II, pp. 6ff.

the angel of Jahweh (מלאך יהוה) stands out in conspicuous relief from that of angels in general: it is mentioned in the most diverse writings and contexts, and always in such a way that this heavenly being is given a quite special function in history. Wherever he is mentioned, he immediately takes his place at the centre of the event. In spite of this, it is not altogether easy to throw very much light on this conceptual field, because there certainly never was in Israel any unified idea of the angel of Jahweh common at all times and in all circles. A further complication is caused by the fact that the figure of the angel of Jahweh has obviously been secondarily inserted into some earlier sacral and local traditions. As far as material goes, in Gen. XVI. 7ff., XXI. 17ff., XXII. 11ff., XXXI. 11ff.; Ex. III. 2ff.; Jg. II. 1ff., we have to do with very old—that is, pre-Jahwistic and pre-Israelite—traditions which report the appearance of a *numen*. They were taken up into Israel's store of traditions and adapted to her faith by making the stories tell of an appearance of the angel of Jahweh in place of the alien (Canaanite) deity. It is hard to say whether the substitution was a deliberate literary intervention, or whether the change was made at a much earlier date, during the stage of oral transmission. In either case, the procedure presupposes the existence of an already fairly firmly fixed idea of the angel of Jahweh as his representative. We meet this in its basic form in narratives like II Kings XIX. 35; I Kings XIX. 7, or Num. XXII. 22, probably also in Jg. VI. 11ff., and certainly in Jg. V. 23. But the altogether untheological popular references to the angel in everyday speech are important as well: mention is made of his kindness and wisdom, which are apparently well known, and to which all things can be committed in confidence (I Sam. XXIX. 9; II Sam. XIV. 17, 20, XIX. 28 [27]). These references express in a simple way what the narratives about the appearance of the Angel of Jahweh say at much greater length and more impressively—that he is a being who helps, and who everywhere acts in Israel's favour, saving and protecting her; he is Jahweh's aid to Israel personalised almost in the way of a mediating official of the covenant relationship.[11] However, the entire range of references cannot be brought uniformly under such formulae, for the narrators' ideas differ considerably in detail. It is likely that in some places the idea of a heavenly vizier plays a part.[12] Again, the stories differ in the way in

---

[11] Only in one case had the angel to turn against Israel herself (II Sam. XXIV. 17); but this too in the end turned out for good.

[12] Stier, *Gott und sein Engel im Alten Testament*, pp. 63ff.

which they conceive of the relationship of the angel to Jahweh himself. The most interesting are those which are not really able to distinguish between Jahweh and his angel, and which therefore do not take the angel as only a messenger, but as a form of manifestation of Jahweh himself. The angel of Jahweh is Jahweh himself, appearing to human beings in human form. In consequence—the chief passages concerned are Gen. XXI. 11ff. and Jg. VI. 17ff.—the story-tellers speak of Jahweh in one sentence, and then again of the angel of Jahweh in the next.[13] In Gen. XXII. 11, XXXI. 11ff. and Ex. III. 2ff. too, the angel who speaks is identical with Jahweh.[14] In these passages it is hard to say how far a conscious theological and, indeed, by now almost speculative, editing is already finding voice. Correction is certainly to be reckoned with in the Blessing of Jacob (Gen. XLVIII. 15f.), a piece of hymnic poetry, which (at any rate in the part which concerns us) is homogeneous; and yet the most striking of all these references meets us there. Jacob's invocation consists of three titles given to God, each one loftier than the preceding: (1) "God, before whom my fathers walked"; (2) "God, who has been my shepherd to this day"; (3) "The angel who has redeemed me from all evil." The little hymn reaches the climax of its attempt to identify Jahweh in descriptive terms in the third title. Any idea that the "angel" means a being subordinate to Jahweh is of course ruled out. This מַלְאָךְ too is Jahweh—but in contradistinction to the Jahweh of general providence, he is the Jahweh of the specific saving action (גֹּאֵל). The concept of the guiding angel at the Exodus and in the wilderness which has already been mentioned shows much less of this theological distinctiveness. On occasion he is practically set in direct contrast with Jahweh, as for example where Jahweh refused to lead Israel and the angel is sent in his stead (Ex. XXXII. 2ff.). Ex. XXIII. 20f. ("my name is in him") alone approximates once more to the "speculative" concept.

Thus, in the work JE the transition from Ex. XXXII to Ex. XXXIII is of great importance. After Israel's apostasy in worshipping the "golden calf," Jahweh had to define his relationship to her anew, for

[13] There is, however, in actual fact a significance in the alternation of "Jahweh" and "angel of Jahweh." If God is spoken about apart from the men concerned in the story, then the story-teller uses "Jahweh" or "God." But if God is spoken about as perceptible to the men in the narrative, the story-teller says מַלְאַךְ יהוה, cf. Gen. XXI. 17ff.: God hears Hagar's cry, but it is the angel of Jahweh who addresses her.

[14] J. Hänel therefore speaks actually of the angel of incarnation, *Die Religion der Heiligkeit*, pp. 199, 206.

the original relationship had been profoundly disturbed. Indeed, nothing less was at stake than the question whether, after all that had taken place, Israel was still the people of Jahweh. In consequence, Ex. XXXII. 30–4 and XXXIII deal with the mediating institutions which Jahweh set up—the angel of Jahweh, the Tent, and the *Panim*. On the one side therefore, these institutions are a sign of the wrath of Jahweh, since his holiness might destroy Israel. But on the other hand, they are a proof of his will to save. Jahweh himself protects his people from this annihilating encounter, and takes precautions in order that his design to "give Israel rest" (Ex. XXXIII. 14) may achieve its end. In actual fact, from now on Israel's relationship to Jahweh is to some extent a mediated one. In detail, J and E pictured the wanderings in the wilderness as a series of very grave crises, with the narrators' interest equally directed to the human actions and to the divine, to Israel's sin and rebellion and to Jahweh's judgment and saving. The complex of these individual traditions is rounded off by the Balaam pericope (Num. XXII–XXIV); and, in the light of the whole, this is certainly to be taken as the acme of menace for the people of God, for the fact that the powers of the curse are now solemnly evoked against Israel overtopped all that the people of God had had to overcome hitherto, and all that Jahweh had had to repel in their defence. But Jahweh acted here in a more marvellous way than ever before—he turned the curse into blessing.

In conclusion, there is still one question bearing on this whole subject. Why did J and E tell all this? To this very crucial question we can get an indirect answer by way of Deut. VIII. 3. In that verse mention is made of deeds of Jahweh which Israel had experienced in the wilderness, and it is stated in addition that these took place in order that Israel might learn a certain truth. Here then is history no longer told for its own sake, but for a more profound purpose, in order to teach a lesson which can be seen as the permanent and really essential thing lying behind the events. Working back from this to the stories of the wandering in the wilderness, it can be categorically asserted that this at any rate is not the purpose of the picture of the history of JE. Of course it has to be acknowledged that JE too has teaching in the wider sense in mind. But here the object is a different one. What it is concerned with is not to the communication of religious truths under the guise of history, but rather, much more simply, the reality of the events themselves. Jahweh is present for Israel both in the picture of the mighty acts of God made relevant for the present and in the revelation given through human beings in their context. The angle of *applicatio*, that is, applying what is narrated to the religious life of the reader, has as yet no independent importance.

VI. The Conception of Moses and his Office

One thing is common to all three sources of the Hexateuch: the figure of Moses everywhere stands at the centre of the historical events from the Exodus down to the end of the wandering in the wilderness. However much ideas about his function may differ in detail, he is everywhere the representative of Israel, to whom the words and acts of Jahweh are addressed. Noth has made clear that there must have been a complex process of smoothing out, harmonising, and balancing the traditions against each other before this uniform picture was reached, for the figure of Moses was by no means at home in all of them to begin with.[1] A review of the historical summaries in the confessions and hymns reveals right away an incompatibility with the picture given in the Hexateuch, inasmuch as the former, although certainly mentioning Moses (and Aaron) on occasion, nevertheless appear to have absolutely no knowledge of the position of all-powerful leader and mediator accorded to him in the Hexateuch. These documents, and others which from the literary point of view are later, preserve an older form of the picture of the history, from whose confines the Jahwist has already stepped out. But even within the series of the three source documents themselves there can still be discerned a growth of theological interest in Moses, and this is expressed in concepts which are in part very diverse.[2]

We know practically nothing about the people who handed these traditions on, that is, the groups, institutions, or priestly families who at any given time maintained their specific picture of Moses until it

[1] "If it is even only approximately correct that the narrative in the Pentateuch grew together over a period out of a series of originally independent themes, each of which as a rule had its roots in a particular cultic activity, then from the very start we have no right to assume that one and the same figure should have had from the beginning a place in the majority of them": Noth, *Pentateuch*, p. 172. The question where it was that the figure of Moses was fundamentally at home and where not, and how it grew into traditions which originally had no knowledge of it, certainly throws a light on many a process that is interesting for theology as well. But the scientific basis of the matter is too slight to allow of a comprehensive picture, which is the only thing of interest here.

[2] For what follows cf. Sellin, *Mose*, pp. 125ff.

reached literary expression in one of the major source documents. Certainly, this delineation of the picture of Moses was, to a large extent, a purely literary process; and it is therefore relatively late in comparison with the age of many of the traditions. On the other hand, there can be no doubt that behind one series of traditions about Moses lie very real claims made by certain institutions and groups, rivalries and questions of competency, which were very much alive at certain times and places.[3] But who were the people who, if their traditions told stories about Moses, went on to take up the cudgels for themselves and their office? They were probably the groups which drew the first determinative lines in the picture of Moses, because for certain groups—could it have been the priesthood?—the picture quite early became a norm, though of course it was one which was itself in turn modified in the understanding of later generations and in their problems.

The only place where the situation is relatively clear is in connexion with the rebellion of the Korahites (Num. xvi. 7b–11, P).[4] The matter in question is a rather late attempt on the part of a Levitical group to deny the exceptional cultic position of the Zadokites. Is Aaron really the only one who may "come near to Jahweh"? But the passage rests on an older tradition—it is probably therefore only a later contemporising, by means of which the answer was given to some specific question of competency which had arisen amongst the personnel of the Temple in Jerusalem. The problem which the older version sets (Num. xvi. 2–7a, P?) is a much bigger one. Here Korah and 250 of the "laity" oppose in principle the cultic position of Moses and Aaron as mediators, and advocate a universal priesthood of all the Israelites. Is not everyone "holy," and possessed of a like immediacy to God? It is no longer possible to say what the contemporary situation was to which this version of the story referred. And what are the backgrounds of the obscure story about Nadab and Abihu, who offered "unholy fire," and on that account perished (Lev. x. 1–7)? Up to the present day, the story of the "golden calf" had been taken by everyone as directed against the bull-worship of Jeroboam I in Bethel and Dan (I Kings xii. 25ff.), but this interpretation has been challenged. The disputes which gave Num. xi and xii their present form were quite different, for

---

[3] A priesthood officiated in Dan which derived itself directly from Moses (Jg. xviii. 30).

[4] Cf. A. Bentzen, "Priesterschaft und Laien in der jüdischen Gemeinde des 5. Jahrhunderts," in *Archiv für Orientforschung*, Graz 1930–1, pp. 280ff.

here it is a matter of defining a relationship to the early prophetic movement. Num. XI contains a sort of aetiology of early prophecy—it is spirit of Moses' spirit: it derives its legitimation through Moses and is received as one of the institutions of Israel (how alien the ecstatic prophets must have appeared to early Israel!).[5] But who really is "Moses" here? The treatment of this question is still more urgent in Num. XII. 6–8, where Moses, "faithful in the whole house of Jahweh," is given a rank superior to every prophet in respect of his reception of revelation. While Jahweh makes himself known to other prophets only through visions and dreams, he speaks with Moses "mouth to mouth" —why, Moses may even "behold the form of Jahweh." This restriction put upon immediate communion with Jahweh could derive from the upholding of the prerogatives of certain priestly functions over against the prophets' reception of revelation. But it is clear that we do not here reach anything more than sporadic glimpses of certain questions of competency. We can no longer look on it as possible to write a history of the tradition attaching to Moses, and of where it was at home. Not the least of the difficulties in this connexion consists in the fact that the figure of Moses is only a secondary accretion in many of the traditions.[6] At present we must rest content with the general assumption that extremely intricate traditional processes lie behind the portrait of Moses given in the major sources, processes which can no longer be elucidated in detail. Ideas of very different kinds had gradually to become assimilated, and radical tensions between different claims settled, before the whole could come to rest in the clear and balanced pictures of the source documents.

With the Jahwist, Moses appears in every event from the Exodus down to the end of the wandering in the wilderness. The process of generalisation indicated above has here reached its conclusion. But for the narrator, Moses' function in the various conflicts and crises is not really a subject which has any particular theological stress laid upon it. At all events, compared with later pictures, it is striking how, *vis-à-vis* Jahweh and his action, Moses retires right into the background. In an examination of the narrative strands in J, it is amazing to find how really slight is the role which the narrator has assigned to Moses in all these manifold events. Jahweh himself effects the miracles—they take place without any assistance from Moses.[7] Even at the miraculous

[5] G. von Rad in *Z.A.W.*, 1933, pp. 115f.   [6] Noth, *Pentateuch*, pp. 177ff.
[7] Ex. VII. 17, 25, VIII. 9, 17, IX. 6, 18, 33, X. 13, XIV. 21*b*, XVI. 13ff.; Num. XI. 18, 31.

crossing of the Red Sea, once Moses has intimated what is about to happen, he merely looks on with the rest of the Israelites (Ex. XIV. 13f.).[8] His call was only for the purpose of informing Israel in Egypt about Jahweh's intentions (Ex. III. 7f., 16–20), and it was for the same end that he was sent to Pharaoh. It would therefore be utterly wrong if we were to understand Moses' call as an appointment to be Israel's leader, for in this source document the leadership of Israel is Jahweh's alone. It would be much nearer the mark, in view of his commission to announce what Jahweh was purposing in history, to talk of a kind of prophetic commission, for the only purpose even of the miracle attributed to Moses himself was to give him standing in the eyes of Israel (Ex. IV. 1–9). The prophetic style of what Moses says in J—"Go to Pharaoh and say: thus hath Jahweh said" (Ex. VII. 16f. [VIII. 1], VIII. 16 [15], IX. 13)—is in harmony with this picture. So too, finally is the intercession which, according to J, Moses made from time to time, for intercession was plainly the prophet's office *par excellence* in olden times.[9] What then, in J's view, was Moses? He was no worker of miracles, no founder of a religion, and no military leader. He was an inspired shepherd whom Jahweh used to make his will known to men.[10]

There is a noticeable difference in the picture of Moses given by the Elohist. As compared with J, the account of the call is in itself much more weighted in the theological scale because of the Elohist's endeavour to weld together the religion of the ancestral god with Jahwism.[11] But above all, the idea of the office to which Moses was called has changed. If in J the commission runs, "Say to the elders, I, Jahweh, will bring Israel out" (Ex. III. 16f., cf. vs. 8), in E it is, "You are to bring Israel out" (Ex. III. 10, 12). This difference expresses a great disparity in the ideas involved, for E has pushed Moses much more into the foreground as the instrument of God in effecting the deliverance. As was seen long ago, the great importance of the rod which Moses was given by God himself is characteristic of this.[12] Moses is now the miracle-worker, in fact almost to the point of being a magi-

[8] Along with Dillmann, Driver, Noth, and others, I regard Ex. XIV. 15–18 as belonging to P. Ex. IV. 20b–23 too seems to belong not to J but to E. But there is of course no reason for consistently disputing all and every mention of the rod by J. Thus for example in Num. XVII. 8–15 [XVI. 43–50] attribution to J is probable.

[9] Gen. XX. 7; I Sam. VII. 5, XII. 19, 23; II Kings XIX. 1ff.

[10] Sellin, *Mose*, p. 129.   [11] See above, pp. 179f.

[12] J. Wellhausen, *Die Composition des Hexateuch*, 2nd edn. Berlin 1889, p. 66.

cian: it is through his intervention with Pharaoh and at the Red Sea and elsewhere that the history receives its momentum.[13] The J source does not seem to have known the rod at all, at any rate not in this function by which the miracles were delegated by Jahweh to Moses.[14] E further enhanced Moses' importance by setting Aaron over against him. In the account of the "golden calf," Aaron is practically the negative figure of contrast, and so it is too in the striking definition of the relationship of the two to each other: Moses is God for Aaron, and Aaron the mouth for Moses—Moses is the creative initiator and Aaron only the executive speaker (Ex. IV. 16). Now, as it is, it is extremely probable that this whole source E comes from early prophetic circles. If so, it is not at all surprising that on occasion the stories appear in the dress of prophetic concepts, and that this source viewed Moses as a prophet. It designated him forthrightly as נביא (Deut. XXXIV. 10) and his sister Miriam as נביאה (Ex. XV. 20). But the prophecy which Moses represents is of a special type—he is much more the prophet of action, taking an active hand in the events, and doing so not only through the directions which he gives, but also, and supremely, by means of dramatic miracles. Finally, Moses of course excels all prophets (Num. XII. 7f.). His *charisma* was so tremendous that a mere portion of it, even when it was further distributed over seventy elders, threw the recipients out of their normal psychic state and stimulated them to ecstasy (Num. XI. 25ff., E). Intercession, and the element of pleading, are present too (Ex. XVIII. 19, XXXII. 11–13; Num. XII. 11). But once more we find that this trait is magnified, and in fact even pushed to the extreme: in order to save Israel, Moses declares that he is ready himself to become ἀνάθεμα on their behalf (Ex. XXXII. 32, cf. Rom. IX. 3). Now, since Moses on occasion also acts as priest (Ex. XXIV. 6), E's

[13] Ex. IV. 17, IX. 23, X. 13, XIV. 16, XVII. 9ff.

[14] Wellhausen (*Die Composition des Hexateuch*, p. 68) found the following texts instructive and set them side by side:

J	E
And Jahweh brought an east wind over the land, that whole day and the whole night. When morning came, the east wind had brought up the locusts, and they settled on the whole country of Egypt in a dense swarm as had never been before nor ever shall be again (Ex. X. 13b, 14b).	And Jahweh said to Moses: Stretch out your hand over the land of Egypt, that the locusts may come up and eat every plant in the land, all that the hail has left. So Moses stretched forth his rod over the land of Egypt, and the locusts came up over the whole land of Egypt (Ex. X. 12, 13a, 14a).

picture of him is perhaps not perfectly uniform. But still, its development on the whole represents a decided theological advance beyond J.

Deuteronomy's is the most rounded portrait of Moses, and probably has the most emphatic theological stamp upon it. In it too Moses is נביא: indeed, he is the chief of the prophets (Deut. XVIII. 8), in that he is the archetype and norm of all prophets, through whose coming Jahweh guaranteed the constant connexion between himself and his people. Nevertheless in Deuteronomy this prophetic office of Moses is conceived in a very different fashion from what it was in E, for Deuteronomy has no mention at all of any influence which Moses brought to bear on history by the instrumentality of miracles or the like. And further, it is only rarely in Deuteronomy that we find Moses acting as the leader who gives strategic orders (Deut. I. 23, II. 20ff., III. 18), for his real office was to pass on to Israel, in the form of a proclaimed word, the word of Jahweh which had been addressed to himself. In Deuteronomy Jahweh still speaks to Israel through the medium of Moses; and this mediating office was simply derived from and given its warrant by a "Scriptural proof" based upon Israel's refusal on one occasion to listen to Jahweh speaking to her directly (Deut. V. 20–6 [25–9]). The most impressive corroboration of this all-embracing mediating office of proclamation is of course the fact that the corpus of Deuteronomy is put into the form of words of Moses (and so not of Jahweh) spoken to Israel. This radical change in the conception of Moses was doubtless caused by the emergence of the prophetic movement. But this concentration of all Israel's communion with God upon him now had a result which Deuteronomy clearly envisaged—Moses is a suffering mediator. Admittedly, this trait in his picture is not completely new. An earlier tradition had shown Moses as breaking down "under the burden of this whole people" and finding fault with Jahweh because of his "wretchedness" ("Did I conceive this people, did I bring them forth, so that thou shouldst say to me, 'carry them in thine arms'?" Num. XI. 11–17, JE). But in the earlier narrative complex this was something incidental, whereas in Deuteronomy the picture of Moses as suffering is much more elaborately worked up and furnished with a firmer theological basis. After the people had sinned in the matter of the golden calf, it is Moses who tries to ward off Jahweh's anger. He lies prostrate before God forty days and forty nights, taking no food or drink: his long prayer of intercession is given word for word (Deut.

IX. 18ff., 25ff.). The reception of the tables of the covenant also entailed
a similar strict abstention from food and drink (Deut. IX. 9). Even the
death of Moses outside the land of promise—an odd fact which later
ages had to explain theologically—was vicarious for Israel. It is because
of Israel that Jahweh's great wrath was directed upon Moses, with the
result that Jahweh refused to allow him to set foot in the land of
promise (Deut. I. 37, IV. 21f.). But with it all Moses did not find fault
with Jahweh. Certainly he earnestly entreated that he too might be
permitted to set foot in the "goodly land," but Jahweh brusquely
refused him any further entreaty in the matter (Deut. III. 23–7). This
Deuteronomic picture of Moses must be connected more or less closely
with that of Num. XII. 3. This verse, which could possibly be a later
addition to the otherwise extremely old story given in Num. XII. 1ff.,
speaks in the strongest terms about Moses' meekness (עָנָו, "he was
meeker than all the children of men"). When we remember that the
older traditions elaborated on the contrasting emotions in Moses,
especially his sudden anger (Ex. II. 12, XXXII. 19; Num. XI. 11), this
change to exemplary meekness is surprising indeed. The Prometheus
element displayed in Num. XI. 10ff. is completely effaced in the later
portrait. In the memory of later ages Moses became the completely
submissive "servant of God" (Deut. III. 24, XXXIV. 5).

Finally, the Priestly Document's portrait is again completely
different from that of Deuteronomy. The two do however have one
thing in common—in P as well as in D, Moses is wholly immersed in
the revelation at Sinai. That revelation is no longer, as it was still for E,
one event among many others in the Exodus: here it is because of this
event that Moses is there at all; he is so taken up into it that his activity
is really always somehow or another connected with it. In P, as a result,
Moses is to a large extent relieved of the tasks which the older traditions
(especially E) assigned to him. This tendency is most clearly apparent
in connexion with the plagues in Egypt, which are not brought about
by Moses, but by Aaron (Ex. VII. 19–20, VIII. 1f. [5f.], 12f. [16f.], etc.).
Admittedly, the divine command in the matter comes to Moses. But
Moses passes it on to Aaron, and it is Aaron who then engages in the
trial of strength with the heathen magicians. The rod by which the
wonders are worked is now Aaron's rod.[15] The same thing happens
with the offering of sacrifice which of course in P devolves exclusively

[15] Ex. VII. 9, 19, VIII. 1, 12 [5, 16]. Only the final and most grievous of the plagues
are brought about by Moses (Ex. IX. 8–12).

upon Aaron. Even in the cases of rebellion it is not Moses who acts.[16] What Moses is for P can no longer be summed up under the generally accepted concepts of priest, worker of miracles, prophet, etc. Moses is something beyond all this—he is set apart for intercourse with Jahweh alone. The picture of Moses ascending into the clouds of Sinai all by himself and spending a long time in speech with God (Ex. xxiv. 15b–18) is characteristic of P's concept. In proportion as he is taken over on to God's side, he is separated from men. They flee from him as he comes back, and he has first to cover the reflexion of God's glory on his face before he can speak to them (Ex. xxxiv. 29ff.). Nevertheless, P too regarded Moses as wholly human—indeed this is the source which tells of a serious lapse of which Moses was guilty, and because of which he was not permitted to set foot in the land of promise.[17] Consequently, P's explanation of the puzzle as to why Moses had been debarred from setting foot in Canaan is quite different from Deuteronomy's.

VII. THE GRANTING OF THE LAND OF CANAAN

In the account of the saving history as it now lies before us in the old Credo and related texts, the granting of the land of Canaan was the last of the saving acts of Jahweh. Form-critical research has made it absolutely certain that the old picture of the history ended here, and that it was not extended through the conquest into the period of the judges and the kings.[1] Consequently, the major sources in the Hexateuch also ended with the account of Israel's settlement in Canaan. If Israel said, "Jahweh granted the land of Canaan to us," the statement sounds very simple, and it was certainly taken equally simply in olden times. But the account of this saving act in the Hexateuch is anything but simple. On closer examination, the picture of the history given there consists of very diverse accounts of the event; and the theological ideas too—for instance, of Jahweh's relationship to this land—are so varied that it is obvious that the Hexateuch's picture of the granting of the land incorporated many kinds of historical and theological traditions which in themselves originate in very different times and places. But this is not in the least surprising, for Israel reflected upon this

---

[16] Num. xvi. 4, 22, xvii. 10 [xvi. 45], xx. 6.

[17] Num. xx. 8f., 12, 24, xxvii. 13f.; Deut. xxxii. 51. The old question, *qua in re peccaverit Moses*, is no longer clearly answered by the text; probably the reverence of a later age painted it over. According to Ps. cvi. 32—Moses "spoke rashly."

[1] See above, pp. 121ff.

saving act of Jahweh's in very diverse ways: for so doing there were many reasons, and for theology there were also a great many possibilities of reflecting upon this event. Thus, here again our task will be to sketch out the main versions and concepts which accumulated around this event in the saving history. We shall not try to harmonise them with one another, for, in spite of their differences, Israel herself set them side by side without any hesitation, or rather, she superimposed them upon one another.

"Then he brought us to this place and gave us this land, a land flowing with milk and honey." These words were the end of the old Credo (Deut. XXVI. 5–9). The context of Deut. XXVI. 1ff. allows it to be assumed that this whole confession was to be recited on the occasion of the offering of the first-fruits, and this implies that the avowal of the granting of the land had from the earliest times its place in the cult, where thanksgiving for it remained alive in never-ending praise down to the latest times. The promise of the land to the patriarchs by the God of the ancestors goes back to a still earlier time. It originated in the days of the patriarchs before there was an Israel at all, and was amalgamated at an early date with what were initially Palestinian, that is, Canaanite, cultic legends. But because the Jahwist's history of the patriarchs made systematic use of this promise to them at various points, it is this promise which became the distinctive *leitmotiv* for the whole Hexateuch.[2] It forces the reader to relate the conquest under Joshua to the promise to the patriarchs. There can be no doubt that there was also a conquest tradition which had escaped this particular theological slant. Thus recent investigation suggests that at Gilgal in particular there was a conquest festival at which, curiously enough, the crossing of the Jordan and the crossing of the Red Sea were celebrated together. The individual stories in Josh. II–IX originally attached aetiologically to this sanctuary, and the *leitmotiv* of Jahweh's marvellous bringing of Israel into Canaan which connects them and which is presupposed by them must have been a tradition specially cherished in this form at Gilgal.[3] But even for the early period of Israel it would be the part of wisdom to reckon that there were more places than one at which this final element in the old confession was fostered. It was kept alive and handed on not only at these sanctuaries, but also by unknown singers and, above all,

[2] See above, pp. 167ff.
[3] Alt, *K.S.*, VOL. I, pp. 176ff.; K. Möhlenbrink, "Die Landnahmesagen des Buches Josua," in *Z.A.W.*, 1938, pp. 239f.; H. J. Kraus, "Gilgal," in *Vet. Test.*, 1951, pp. 181ff.

by itinerant story-tellers, without whose preparatory work the later shaping of the Hexateuch is of course quite inconceivable. In spite of the number of the places in which it was at home, and also in spite of the different fortunes which overtook the clans and clan groups at their settlement, the content of this, our earliest attainable confessional statement, is nevertheless comparatively simple and homogeneous, for it is throughout a matter of the celebration of a divine act which, from the point of view of these early texts, lay within the clear light of history. That in the course of a long leading of his people through history Jahweh had granted them the land of Canaan—this fact every clan and every group of pilgrims assembled at a sanctuary could avow. Complications as to the content of this clause in the confession only came into being with the rise of a generalising assimilation of the various local traditions in the interests of theology.[4]

This theological understanding of the clause certainly started at an early time, for no clear memory was retained of the fact that, in reality, the entry of the clans was to a large extent accomplished without recourse to war, that is, it took place in the course of changing pasture-ground.[5] And even if the way in which events are given in Jg. 1. 1ff. diverges quite considerably from the later and subsequently dominant picture given in Josh. II–X—the former still regards the entry as a sum total of separate enterprises of the clans acting independently of one another—nevertheless even here it is already understood as, on the whole, a warlike event. But it is inconceivable that from the very beginning it was the intention of all the immigrating clans to "drive" all "the Canaanites" out of their towns.[6] In actual fact, it was only at a later stage that the relationships between the immigrants and the existing inhabitants of the land became fraught with political tension. And when the clans had grown strong, the tension led to occasional

---

[4] Because of the thesis of Noth, who completely denies the occurrence of the sources J, E, and P in the Book of Joshua, the literary analysis of this book has again become uncertain (*Überl. Studien*, pp. 88, 209ff.; *Josua* (Hb. A.T.), Tübingen 1938, pp. 7ff.). So until there is further clarification of this question, we do not take the picture given in the source documents as our starting point, but confine ourselves to drawing upon the older and later literary parts which make it up. On the basis of the lists, a participation on the part of P in the picture of the allotting of the territory has recently been taken into account again by J. Hempel, in Pauly-Wissowa, VOL. XXII. 2, cols. 1957, 1965.

[5] On the entry by way of changing pasture, see Alt, *K.S.*, VOL. I, pp. 139ff.; Noth, *History*, pp. 69ff., 160f.   [6] Jg. 1. 27ff.

clashes in war. Thus, the subsequent experience of the impossibility of peaceful coexistence, and at the same time the idea that Israel possessed a just title to the whole land, already mould the oldest traditions. Behind them also lies that uncompromising Either-Or of which Israel only later became conscious in the Deuteronomic theology as applying to every department of life. As far as this theoretic claim of Israel's upon Canaan is concerned, it is to be seen as already in existence at a very early period, in the so-called claims of the individual tribes upon the land. For the scheme of the boundaries of the clans given in the Book of Joshua and the list of the cities which were not captured in Jg. I. 16ff. both show that in the period of the Judges there were fairly firmly defined, though in the main theoretical, claims made on particular territories which were still at that time occupied by the Canaanites.[7] But we know almost nothing of how the claims came into being, that is, of the authorities who issued, arranged and, in cases of conflict, interpreted them.[8] Nevertheless there can be no doubt that the claims were thought of as having their origin in Jahweh and his will, since it was to Jahweh that this land belonged, and he alone could dispose of it.

There can be no question that the idea that Canaan was Jahweh's land, "Jahweh's hereditary possession" (נחלת יהוה), is very ancient, and very soon after the entry it certainly became the common property of the amphictyonic clans.[9] In the early period it was an expressly sacral idea, in that Israel exactly equated this land of hers with the area in which Jahweh could be worshipped. Anyone outside its frontiers was "far from the face of Jahweh" (I Sam. XXVI. 20). To belong to Jahweh was equivalent to "having a portion (חלק) in Jahweh's land" (Josh. XXII. 25). But if Jahweh was the real owner of land, concrete conclusions could thereby be drawn for the regulation of matters of inheritance between men. In actual fact, the words "the land is mine;

---

[7] On the "territorial claims" of the clans, see A. Alt. *K.S.*, VOL. I, pp. 116, 121, 197; VOL. II, p. 51. The way in which these claims draw the northern boundary of the clan of Judah (through Philistine country!) right down to the sea, or claim the territory of the Canaanite city states in the plain of Jezreel, is particularly striking (Josh. XV. 9–17; Jg. I. 27).

[8] Noth thinks of "Israel's judge" who might have occupied the office of settling territorial disputes among the clans. (*Altestamentliche Studien. Friedrich Nötscher Festschrift*, edd. H. Junker and J. Botterweck, Bonn 1950, pp. 162ff.)

[9] Ex. XV. 17; I Sam. XXVI. 19; II Sam. XIV. 16; Jer. II. 7, XVI. 18, L. 11; Pss. LXVIII. 10 [9], LXXIX. 1; cf. Josh. XXII. 19. H. Wildberger, "Israel und sein Land," in *Ev. Th.* 1956, pp. 404ff.

you are strangers with me and sojourners" (Lev. xxv. 23) can be described as the theological basis of all legislation concerning land tenure in ancient Israel. As well as the heritable ground belonging to the family, ancient Israel also knew of common land which could be periodically allotted, that is, she knew of the institution of communal possession of land. This allotment was a sacral procedure, and took place after a fallow year, which had equally a sacral character since it was an avowal of the exclusive right of Jahweh to possess the land. According to Mic. II. 5, the "casting of the measuring line" took place "in the assembly of Jahweh" (קְהַל יהוה). What is admittedly a very spiritualised memory of this old usage is contained in Ps. xvi. 6.[10] The idea of Jahweh as the real owner of the land was therefore the very reverse of theoretical dogma, and was rooted in sacro-legal ideas which affected Israel's everyday life in a very real way. However, it is remarkable that in the Hexateuch, and particularly in the account of Israel's taking possession of the land, there are only very infrequent allusions to this self-contained group of concepts about Jahweh as the owner of the land.[11] We hear much more frequently of the land promised to the people of Israel (and before that to the patriarchs). But the promise of the land is a group of concepts which are completely independent of the concept of Jahweh as the owner of Canaan. Not in one single instance amongst the well-nigh innumerable passages where appeal is made to the promise of the land is this land described as the property of Jahweh—it is rather the land which formerly belonged to other nations, which Jahweh, in making his designs in history effective, gave to Israel to possess. We have already seen that this promise of the land goes back to the very earliest times when the objects of worship were gods of the ancestors. It is this promise which, scattered throughout the whole of the history of the patriarchs, gave the Hexateuch its *leitmotiv*, and it was in consequence taken up again by the source documents in the Book of Joshua.[12]

[10] Alt, *K.S.*, vol. I, pp. 327f.

[11] The only references are Lev. xxv. 23 and Josh. xxii. 19; see G. von Rad, "Verheissenes Land und Jahwes Land im Hexateuch," in *Z.D.P.V.*, 1943, pp. 191ff., reprinted in *Ges. Studien*, pp. 87ff. The sober picture of the taking over of the land of Canaan in the course of an historical act is clearly differentiated from the considerable body of statements which still understand Israel's relationship to the earth in a semi-mythological way. These derive from the sacral thinking of the Canaanite arable land, while the former expresses ancient Jahwism in a much more original way.

[12] Josh. I. 2f., 11, 15, IX. 24, X. 42, XIV. 9, XXI. 43, XXIII. 5, 15, XXIV. 13.

The account of Israel's entry into Canaan given in the Book of Joshua (Josh. I–X) expanded the short and terse confessional or hymnic phrases into a large and diversified event which, beginning with the story of Rahab (Josh. II), and ending with the battle at the waters of Merom (Josh. XI), is itself divided up into at least eight larger panels, each of which describes an event (the reconnaissance of Jericho, the crossing of the Jordan, the capture of Jericho, the overthrow of Ai, the fraud of the Gibeonites, Joshua's victory over the coalition of the Canaanites, and the battle at the waters of Merom). It is also worth noticing, from the point of view of theology, the way in which these events are set out. On the one hand, the accounts lay stress, at the high points in the events (the crossing of the Jordan and Joshua's victory in ch. X), on the self-sufficient miraculous nature of the events, while on the other they employ a definitely sober realism that has room for very intricate psychological processes. The description of the way in which Israel complacently accepts at its face value the glorification of Jahweh on the lips of the Gibeonites, and the stupidity with which she let herself be imposed upon and taken in by this ridiculous swindle, contains a forthright comic element, as well as a considerable measure of self-mockery (Josh. IX). Thus, these stories are not to be regarded in any sense as early miracle stories, for they were only shaped in an age when Israel's descriptive realism had already developed its most amazing possibilities, and this means the early period of the monarchy.[13]

The manifest intention and purpose of this element in the narrative is to picture the entry of "this whole people" into Palestine (Josh. I. 2). Thus, "all Israel" (Josh. III. 1, 7, etc.) marched into the land under Joshua's leadership as a mighty phalanx. But, as was noticed long ago, this conception of the course of events does not tally with the one given in Jg. I. 1ff., for, according to this latter version of J's, the clans took possession of their land each for itself and by their own separate efforts. What is more, the picture in Josh. II–IX itself, when more closely examined, is far from yielding what its narrator intends it to do, for the way which leads from Jericho to about Aijalon traverses very little more than the territory of a single clan, Benjamin. Thus, the old narrative complex comprised by Josh. II–IX turns out to have been originally a Benjaminite tradition about the conquest, to which an isolated recollection of Ephraim's has been attached (Josh. X), and there follows rather abruptly upon it, in ch. XI, an equally isolated Galilean

[13] See above, p. 54.

tradition.[14] Thus there is a clear tension between the account actually given in the narrative and the intention of the narrator, whose aim was, with the help of this material, to describe the conquest of the land by all Israel, and who, in so doing, asked too much of it. In the end this conception was most succinctly given in the narrator's words that under Joshua Israel took possession of the whole land "at one time" (פַעַם אֶחָד Josh. x. 42). This was the rounding off of the construction of that magnificent picture made by later Israel of Jahweh's final saving act. Beyond it no further unification was really any longer possible. But our final comment on it should not be that it is obviously an "un-historical" picture, because what is in question here is a picture fashioned throughout by faith. Unlike any ordinary historical document, it does not have its centre in itself; it is intended to tell the beholder about Jahweh, that is, how Jahweh led his people and got himself glory. In Jahweh's eyes Israel is always a unity: his control of history was no improvisation made up of disconnected events: in the saving history he always deals with all Israel. This picture makes a formidable claim, and actually in the subsequent period it proved to have incalculable power to stamp affairs. How this came about is quite interesting. Israel made a picture of Jahweh's control of history on his people's behalf whose magnificence far surpasses anything that older and more realistic accounts offered. Faith had so mastered the material that the history could be seen from within, from the angle of faith. What supports and shapes this late picture of Israel's taking possession of the land is a mighty zeal for and glorification of the acts of Jahweh.[15]

The story of the entry into the promised land and its conquest is followed by an account of the allotment of portions of it to the individual clans (Josh. XIII–XXI). Once again, the material used to elucidate what happened furnishes us with curiously contradictory information. In the main it consists on the one hand of descriptions of boundaries (Judah, Benjamin, Machir, and Ephraim), and on the other of lists of places (Judah, Benjamin, Simeon, and Dan). While the former formed part of a scheme of clan boundaries which reflects the conditions obtain-

---

[14] See Alt, *K.S.*, VOL. I, pp. 167ff.; M. Noth, *Josua*, Tübingen 1938, pp. 11f.

[15] In these circumstances the question whether the attitude of the Canaanites was also a cause of their being driven out can only be put marginally. Josh. XI. 20 ("Jahweh hardened their hearts") has a comparatively ancient ring. In contrast Gen. XV. 16 or Lev. XVIII. 24ff. make considerably greater concessions to the desire for rational understanding.

ing even before the formation of the state, the list of places reproduces the position achieved by the kingdom of Judah as the result of her northward expansion in the time of King Josiah.[16] We have of course to reckon with the fact that the combiner of these sources lacked the material which would have enabled him to give an account of the allotment of the land by Joshua, and that he had to rely on what sources were still available. Nevertheless, it would be wrong to charge him with breaking the most elementary rules of historiography, just because he used late as well as early texts to give an account of the entry into Canaan. The man who incorporated these partially late lists into his history was certainly no historian in the modern sense of the term. Nevertheless, the way in which he uses his sources is not for all that as naïve as it appears to be. The question is rather whether our historical positivism is able to do justice to such accounts. As we have already seen above, Jahweh's historical action with Israel is a unity. He acted on her after the entry as well as before it, and therefore a man living in, let us say, the time of the exile, could without more ado theologically co-ordinate written evidence from the period of Josiah with very much older sources—for him former and latter alike were documents belonging to Jahweh's one and the same will to control history. And, for the very reason that he incorporated documents nearly contemporary with himself, his account was given reality for his own time.

When Israel spoke of the granting of the land of Canaan, what she said was far from being merely the recollection of a great past—it was rather an avowal of Jahweh which every age had to reformulate in its own way. Once again there is a special clarity and impressiveness in the theological conception of the Deuteronomist, who, as editor, welded together these to some extent highly dissimilar elements in the Book of Joshua.[17] He it was who developed to its highest point the idea, for which the way had already been prepared, that the conquest had been effected by war. "One of you chased a thousand" (Josh. XXIII. 10).[18] He it is too who made the boundaries of the promised land extend far beyond the area indicated by the lists—he makes it reach from the belt of the steppe land in the south and east as far as Lebanon and the

[16] Alt, *K.S.*, VOL. I, pp. 193ff.; VOL. II, pp. 276ff.

[17] The Deuteronomistic additions which are of greatest theological importance are Josh. I. 1–18, XXI. 43–XXII. 6, XXIII. 1–16.

[18] Cf. Josh. I. 5, III. 3, 10, XXIII. 3.

Euphrates (Josh. I. 4, XII. 1). And, finally, it is he who speaks of the goodness and fruitfulness of this land as if it were a paradise.[19] In this act of possessing the land Jahweh had finally "given Israel rest." This term "rest" occurs several times—we are clearly meant to understand it as the Deuteronomistic formula which expresses the greatest, the ultimate gift which Jahweh bestowed upon Israel in granting the land. By this gift Jahweh redeemed his promises in full.[20] In this respect, Josh. XXI. 43–5 occupies a key position theologically for the rounding off of the Hexateuch generally: "And Jahweh gave the Israelites the whole land, as he had sworn to their fathers. They took possession of it and settled in it, and Jahweh gave them rest on every side, just as he had sworn to their fathers: and not one of all their enemies withstood them, but Jahweh gave all their enemies into their hand. Not one of all the good words which Jahweh had spoken to the house of Israel failed: all came to pass." Here the Deuteronomist is engaged in a very comprehensive reflexion on the relationship between promise and fulfilment. From the standpoint of what has been achieved, he looks back once again at all Jahweh's "good words," and examines them—he almost weighs them up—in the light of visible present fulfilment. The result is that not one of the promises "failed": they were all fulfilled in history. Jahweh's great plan in history for Israel achieved its goal, and this is what the whole of the Hexateuch wants to say.[21] In consequence, any new impulse in the saving history could only begin from Jahweh's addressing Israel anew—but at this stage such a new impulse lies beyond the horizon. However, in this great conclusion to which Deuteronomy comes, an undertone of warning is clearly to be discerned; it is the same with Jahweh's threats as with his promises—in the case of disobedience the former too would be fulfilled (Josh. XXIII. 11ff.). The anxiety here echoed was occasioned by the fact that the Deuteronomist sees—this again is something peculiar to himself—a very close connexion between the granting of the land and the revelation of the commandments at Sinai.[22] In Josh. XXI. 43–5 and XXIII. 14 the Hexateuch was given its final and most comprehensive interpretation. But, as far as Israel was concerned, this was very far from being the last word to be spoken about Jahweh's granting of the land. Con-

---

[19] Josh. V. 6, XXIII. 13, 15. For what Deuteronomy says about the promised land see above, p. 224.

[20] Josh. I. 13, 15, XI. 23, XXI. 44, XXII. 4, XXIII. 1.

[21] Cf. also Josh. XXIII. 14.   [22] Josh. I. 7ff., XXII. 5, XXIII. 6 and frequently.

fession of Jahweh as the giver of the land of Canaan was taken up by the prophets, and, especially by Deutero-Isaiah, was once again made quite freshly relevant for preaching.[23]

[23] A peculiarity of the later prophets is the strangely emphatic designation of the land as צבי, "glory" (Ezek. xx. 6, 15, "most glorious"; Dan. viii. 9, xi. 16, 41, 45, "glorious"), it is even called "the highest glory of the nations" (Jer. iii. 19. R.S.V., "most beauteous of all nations").

Chapter C

ISRAEL'S ANOINTED

I. METHODOLOGICAL PRECONSIDERATIONS

THE course of our work so far has been founded on the judgment that the Hexateuch is Israel's developed confession which at an early time had already attained fixed form as to basic structure and the sequence of the statements which it makes. What we had to do was thus predetermined from the outset: it was to show how from time to time layer upon layer was imposed upon the originally very simple statements in this confession; for at any given time each age had the task of expressing these in their appropriate theological form and making them its own. But Jahweh had further dealings with Israel: the history of the people of God now settled in Canaan had also become history with Jahweh, with various data which Jahwism considered to be extremely important and which it carefully recorded. But, weighty as these data were, they did not lead to the formation or the expansion of a confession. That Jahweh had led Israel out of Egypt was a part of Israel's confession at all times. But that he had guaranteed the continuance of the throne of David (to mention right away the most important of these "post-canonical" data) was never taken up into the series of these confessional statements. This in no way gainsays the event's importance. It only means that it occurred outwith the framework of the saving history proper which had already become canonical at an early time. Even the later Deuteronomist is still clearly aware that with Joshua an important epoch of Jahweh's saving action with Israel was brought to its conclusion. For the generation after Joshua, "Jahweh's work" with Israel—notice the singular—begins to be past history (Josh. xxiv. 31; Jg. ii. 7). Now, there is a finding of literary and traditio-historical criticism which bears out this fact, and marks a clear difference from what is found in the Hexateuch. From now on we no longer encounter enormous accumulations of traditions such as those in the Sinai pericope. The account is no longer tied to the sequence of particular confessional themes which every age had to make its own, but is built up, as far as the history of tradition goes, in a quite different way. Nor does the account any longer work with material deriving chiefly from the cult, but more and more with historical documents and, in fact, with real historiography. Admittedly, we shall as before meet with redactions and the welding together of traditions from which, in each case, there emerges a new interpretation of the event. None the less, from now on, the account is incomparably more spirited, unilinear, and lucid.

After the conquest as before it Jahweh had dealings with Israel. In this connexion the first new thing which Israel experienced was the protection in war afforded by him in times of need to his people. The means he employed to this end was the *charisma* which he sent down upon one of the men of Israel, and which made the person concerned rise up under sudden stimulus and become the leader of the levies of the clans; whereupon Jahweh himself went into battle and defeated the enemy by means of the divine terror which he sent upon them. The document which stands nearest to this time is the Song of Deborah (Jg. v), and the way in which it expresses the wonder occasioned by this new experience is amazingly alive. As well there is a group of stories which recount the mighty acts of Jahweh in holy wars. Of course, these latter are rather later literary and artistic products, in which a very distinctive and independent idea of the event comes to expression.

It has, however, to be borne in mind that these stories of "clan heroes," charismatic leaders, and holy wars in the Book of Judges are not an independent literary source: we meet them only as separate elements in a much more comprehensive literary and theological complex, namely the Deuteronomistic historical work. It was this work which first put these old stories about the judges (we have no assured knowledge whether they had an earlier literary form of their own) into the theological context in which they now lie before us. Interesting as it would be to know the form and the content of these stories while they were still isolated, that is, before the Deuteronomist so massively welded them together, the main thing for us is to try to reach a right understanding of their present literary context. Since for the Deuteronomistic account the period of the Judges was obviously completely overshadowed by the coming monarchy, its point of view had changed considerably as compared with that of the older story-tellers. The dynasty of David was of course the great new thing which, through his further leading of Israel, Jahweh set up in her history. All of a sudden, it exercised the strongest possible influence in evoking not only literature but theology. In what follows we shall therefore start from the fact that the Davidic dynasty is, after the Hexateuch, the next great focal point of tradition. It is in the light of it that the Deuteronomist writes Israel's history after the conquest, and from it the historical line runs down to the great disasters of 722 and 586. Thus we must begin by stating the theological conception held of the dynasty. In so doing, we are, as before, brought up against the fact that Israel adopted very varied attitudes to this datum. We shall therefore first of all attempt to comprehend this agglomeration of traditions from within, that is, in the light of their oldest parts, and thence we shall proceed backwards and forwards along the road corresponding to the process of the growth of the tradition. It is only in the late Deuteronomistic sketch of the history that theological reflexion reached so far back into the past as to co-ordinate even the whole of the period of the Judges with the monarchy. (We must therefore leave the discussion of this rather complicated conception of the theology of the history of the period of the Judges until later.) Theologically too, however, the Deuteronomistic history advances to make very radical judgments, inasmuch as it included in its review the failure of the anointed in Israel and Judah: in fact, it regarded Israel's whole history with Jahweh, as far as its anointed was concerned, as ending in catastrophe.

2. THE COVENANT WITH DAVID IN THE HISTORY

The Davidic dynasty came into being in the clear light of history: unlike the Babylonian dynasty then, it did not "come down at the beginning from heaven."[1] In this respect no mythic dignity of any kind attaches to it. The historical texts allow the decisive political phases which led finally to David's elevation to the throne over all Israel to be clearly seen. The historical work which gives us the account of David's rise to power (I Sam. XVI. 14–II Sam. v. 12) sets before us with very matter-of-fact realism the tortuous path trodden by this erstwhile warrior in the service first of Saul and then of the Philistines, until he attained to the dignity of king over all Israel; and in this picture later theological interpretations made no radical alteration. Of course, the Deuteronomic history works with a picture already idealised, and the Chronicler, in order not to mar the spotlessness of his picture of David, no longer took the risk of incorporating the fairly murky pre-

[1] "When the monarchy came down from heaven, the monarchy was (first) in Eridu . . .": the beginning of the list of the primeval Babylonian kings. *A.O.T.*, p. 147; *A.N.E.T.*, p. 265.

history of the Davidic kingdom into his work. He therefore starts with the election of David as king over all Israel (I Chron. XI. 1ff.). This honorific touching-up certainly struck out what was a basic element in the picture of Jahweh's anointed: the old portraits show (and, one might almost think, were keen to show) the anointed in all the frailty of his human nature, and on occasion even portray him in extremely scandalous situations. There is no possibility of regarding *him* as an incarnation of the deity, as, say, the Egyptian mythology of the king does!

The above-mentioned history of David's first beginnings now contains three mutually exclusive stories, all aiming at telling of the occasion on which David emerges for the first time from his childhood obscurity into a certain limelight of publicity. All three are aware of the high sacral dignity which was later to come to this lad—indeed, it is only this dignity which raised the question of David's first beginnings at all. One of the accounts—David coming to the court of Saul as a harpist (I Sam. XVI. 14ff.)—is, taken by itself, a story without any particular religious point. The second brings the youthful David into the camp, where he then admittedly speaks to great effect and accomplishes a great deed (I Sam. XVII. 1ff.). Only the third account, which is certainly the latest, and puts the date of David's election and anointing back to a moment in his early youth, records a religious call (I Sam. XVI. 1ff.). In this story we are already listening to a late interpretation, one which introduces the Davidic dynasty into a set of concepts which was originally alien to it, namely the antecedent designation of Jahweh's elected by a prophet. Historically, the pious story is therefore in error. But on the other hand, it is the one which most strongly emphasises the element of the completely unexpected and incomprehensible in this new action of God, since the strangeness of this act of Jahweh's choice went beyond what the charismatically inspired Samuel could grasp. No more than the other stories does it gloss over the fact that the further road of the anointed one by no means led directly to his sacral office: on the contrary, David initially gets entangled in secular political quarrels which reveal no trace of any pressing towards the goal of this office. Indeed, even the choice of David as king, first over Judah (II Sam. II. 4) and then over Israel as well (II Sam. V. 3), was due, as the accounts make clear, to human initiative, namely that of the "men of Judah" and later on that of all the "elders of Israel."[2]

[2] Alt, *K.S.*, VOL. II, pp. 41ff.; M. Noth, "Gott, König, Volk im Alten Testament," in *Z. Th. K.*, 1950, pp. 157ff., particularly pp. 165f.

The great new thing, the endorsement and guarantee of this throne by Jahweh, did not take place until later "when David dwelt in his palace (in Jerusalem)" (II Sam. VII. 1), with the so-called prophecy of Nathan. As it is set out in the account, this event is connected with David's plan, which Jahweh rejected, of building a temple. The narrative unit is therefore dominated by the *motif*, "thou art not to build me a house, but I will build a house for thee."[3] Nevertheless the text of the Nathan prophecy shows that it too is a collection of different conceptions.[4] In the oldest of these, which can still be seen in vss. 1–7, 11b, and 16, Jahweh's promise is directed to David only; but in a later one, all the interest is diverted to David's posterity. Thus, behind this latter tradition there obviously already lies a later age's concern to extend the content of the Nathan prophecy to include "those who will come forth from thy loins." A different idea again is found in vss. 22–4, which transfer the great promise from the wearer of the crown to the whole of the people of God. The content of the prophecy which was handed on in this way—it was later called the חַסְדֵי דָוִד (Ps. XXI. 8 [7], LXXXIX. 25, 29, 34 [24, 28, 33]; Is. LV. 3)—consisted in Jahweh's promise to "build a house for David," to establish his authority as king, and to offer him a father-son relationship: Jahweh will be father to the anointed, and the latter is to be a son to him. Thus in its original form the Nathan prophecy is something like a torso and nothing more.[5] What we have before us is a later and very much expanded account, which cannot have reached its earliest version before the time of Solomon, although fragments of formulations of the oldest prophecy were incorporated into it.

Compared with the Nathan prophecy the "Last Words of David" (II Sam. XXIII. 1ff.) give the impression of being much more ancient

---

[3] J. Wellhausen, *Die Composition des Hexateuch*, p. 257.

[4] We follow the literary analysis given by L. Rost, *Thronnachfolge*, pp. 47ff. For the text cf. also Van den Bussche, "Le text de la prophetie de Nathan sur la dynastie Davidique," in *Analecta Lovaniensia Biblica et Orientalia*, Ser. II, Fasc. 7, 1948. New material on stylistic connexions with formulae in the Egyptian courtly style is given by S. Herrmann, "Die Königsnovelle in Ägypten und Israel," in *Wissensch. Zeitsch. d. Karl Marx Universität Leipzig*; Gesellschafts- und sprachwissensch. Reihe, III (1953–4), pp. 33ff.

[5] An extensive elaboration of its contents on the basis of II Sam. VII is contained in Ps. LXXXIX, which admittedly is as a whole of later date—cf. the subordination of the Davidic dynasty to the law of Sinai in vs. 31 with p. 345—but yet contains very ancient traditions (in particular in vss. 20–30).

both in style and content. They too mention an important promise of Jahweh to David, and in so doing suggest a set of ideas which we were really already expecting in II Sam. VII—Jahweh made an everlasting covenant (ברית עולם) with David. In actual fact, for Hebrew categories of thought this is the one appropriate term, for the matter in question is after all a beneficial arrangement which established for all time to come a new status for the relationship of the two partners to one another. Ps. CXXXII, which is important in this connexion, says the same thing when it speaks of an oath of Jahweh (vs. 11). The decisive new thing in this relationship set up by Jahweh was, without any doubt, the adoption of the wearer of the crown as son. From it flowed consequences whose implications only became apparent in later times, and these will have to be dealt with later on.[6] Jahweh "had prepared a lamp for his anointed" (Ps. CXXXII. 17)—this divine promise was to engage the attention of even a far-off posterity.[7] In this way then, as was already *in parvo* hinted at in the complex arrangement of II Sam. VII, the Nathan prophecy became highly creative in the tradition; for this promise of Jahweh was never forgotten, but in the ages following it was constantly interpreted anew and made relevant to the present. In it also lie the historical origin and legitimation of all messianic expectations.[8]

But once again, it is characteristic that this Nathan prophecy is not transmitted by itself and for its own sake, as, say, the religious expression of a freshly understood relationship between God and man. Interest attaches to it as a completely newly-emergent coefficient in the history which Jahweh willed. Literary analysis certainly makes likely the assumption that II Sam. VII once existed by itself as an independent story. However, this cannot have been the case for long, for the story was then at a very early period—could it have been the time of Solomon?—taken up and incorporated in the great Succession Document as one of its most important component parts. Thus the event of the covenant with David was at once set in a wide historical context. Certainly, this then brought about a considerable shift in the point of view, in that the interest of the account now no longer attaches solely

---

[6] See below, pp. 343ff., 350f.

[7] For the importance of this promise in the Deuteronomistic history see below, p. 341.

[8] Alt, *K.S.*, VOL. II, pp. 63f.; L. Rost, "Sinaibund und Davidsbund," in *Th. Lz.*, 1947, pp. 129ff.

to the historical facts as such, but to the question of their effects and how they worked out in a chain of serious internal political struggles. As a result, the task which confronts us is to take this Succession Document, which artistically, culturally, and theologically as well, is of so great importance, and to understand it aright in its basic features.[9]

Unlike the great literary works which have concerned us up to now, and which are well known to be compilations of a large number of originally independent traditions, this work (a few literary interpolations apart) is a unity from beginning to end. Thus, even from a literary viewpoint we are dealing with an account of exceptional quality and title. Its almost entirely flawless literary unity leads us to expect from the start a much greater spiritual and theological unity than could have been the case with those literary compositions whose component parts each had already their own specific stamp. In actual fact, the key-note of the Succession Document is one single great tension. It begins with a discordant note, by stating that the queen is barren (II Sam. VI. 23), and immediately follows this with the Nathan prophecy. This gives the theme and creates the tension—in these circumstances how will Jahweh make good his promise "to build a house for David"? Here too the old fabled *motif* of the barrenness of the one called to motherhood is the "moving impulse." This tension holds the reader in suspense until the last act, when the problem becomes fraught with the highest degree of drama. "Who is to sit upon the throne of our lord the king and rule after him?" (I Kings I. 20, 27). The complex of events embedded between this beginning and end, namely the accession of Solomon, is extremely diversified, and in its picture of the political and human problems it is almost over-comprehensive; but it keeps giving dark hints at the main problem—Ammon, David's eldest son, falls victim to his own licentiousness, and Absalom to his own ambitious schemings. The possibility—still open to discussion—that a descendant of Saul might be the successor of David, is also ruled out. At last the late-born Solomon comes into view. His older stepbrother Adonijah would perhaps have had the better title in law to claim the throne, but at the last moment Nathan and Bathsheba succeed in enforcing Solomon's accession. Solomon thereafter removed his rival Adonijah.

[9] For what follows see L. Rost, *Thronnachfolge*; G. von Rad, "Der Anfang der Geschichtsschreibung im alten Israel," in *Archiv für Kulturgeschichte*, 1944, pp. 1f., reprinted in *Ges. Studien*. pp. 148ff.

What chiefly intrigues the theologian who reads this history is the thoroughgoing worldliness of the picture. With consummate artistry the writer has arranged the complicated course of events into a series of scenes, each one of which is a masterpiece of realistic portrayal. There can be no doubt that his intention was to make the reader *au fait* with the political intricacies of the new kingdom, and especially with the problems which beset the "house of David," the dynasty which had only just begun. If this realistic interest in political and constitutional problems was something absolutely new in Israel's literature, the same holds true in the same degree for the possibilities of describing men and women which this writer had at his disposal. Character is really portrayed here. In the centre of it all stands David, a man with strong inner antagonisms. As a statesman he was a far-sighted genius, but as a man he was driven by many a passion, to which he could so far succumb as to commit crime: and yet he was always capable of generous impulses, and had a genuine dignity in misfortune. As he grew old he had to experience the fading of his splendour and the transference of favour and popularity to his sons. To these sons he was attached to the extent of weakness and guilt, and this brought his throne to the brink of ruin. But the other figures too, the princes, the military leaders, the women, and the people from the populace, have each their own well-defined features. This undemonstrative and yet very penetrating artistry in psychological portrayal goes far beyond the possibilities of depicting human nature which were open to the older narratives. Here too once again the utter candour of this historian's openness to the world stands up to the test, for the people whom he portrays are certainly anything but "religious characters." He allows the thoughtful reader to see the whole range of love and hate, intrigue, ambition, humiliations, cunning, and tests of loyalty, without casting blame on what is dark or praising what is light. The freedom which this historian reserved to himself in his treatment of the king is something unique in the ancient East. On the other hand, he has no intention whatsoever of serving up to the reader the sensational, or even tittle-tattle. An air of austere nobility broods over the whole work.[10] Of course, this scrupulous refraining from any direct judgment as he describes extremely moving events, and this imperturbable acceptance of

---

[10] What has been said of the way in which Thucydides writes history holds true for him as well: "we have to reckon with a nobility of which it is not easy for us to form an idea." K. Reinhardt, *Von Werken und Formen*, Godesberg 1948, p. 269.

things as they were, moves the reader to ask all the more insistently what the historian's own view was. In actual fact, attentive reading cannot miss this view, even if it is hidden behind the events. It is no blind play of chance that the writer is depicting, but the fulfilment of destinies in the strict sense of the word. Sin and suffering pass before the beholder's eyes in quick succession. Any sort of illusion, any temptation coming from the side of honours or other satisfactions involves these men in guilt in which they are engulfed. So it was with Ammon, with Absalom, with Adonijah, with Achitophel, and with Sheba. And above all else towers the guilt of the King, especially his guilt towards Uriah and his weakness with his sons. Nathan had said that David would experience publicly "before all Israel and in face of the sun" (II Sam. XII. 11), the thing he had done to Uriah in secret. Some time later, as a political action, Absalom openly and designedly takes possession of his royal father's harem (II Sam. XVI. 22). Here the idea of a nemesis, which dominates the whole presentation of this history, reaches its culmination in the word of a prophet. God himself acts upon the sinner through the *jus talionis*, which operates in history in secret. Even the theologian would do well for a start to bow before the sombre splendour of this mundane picture of the history. It positively has a surface which depicts men who appear to be abandoned to themselves and to the baleful sphere of guilt and suffering, of which they themselves were the occasion. In this respect also, the end of the whole complex, Solomon's accession to the throne, hardly allows the reader to draw breath—too much has been shown him of the dark side of life.

But the historian who depicted the play of the figures on the political stage with so few illusions about them is none the less a theologian, a theologian even with a very well-defined idea of God's relation to this history.[11] There are, admittedly, only three places where he speaks of God explicitly. But these are of fundamental importance. They are II Sam. XI. 27, XII. 24, and XVII. 14. In each case what comes in question is only a few words which within the extremely secular con-

[11] The historian E. Meyer was one of the first to recognise the quality and achievement of this historiography (*Geschichte des Altertums*, VOL. II, 2nd edn. Stuttgart 1931, pp. 284ff.). Meyer also emphatically stressed its completely secular character: "All religious colouring and all thought of supernatural guidance are utterly excluded; the course of the world and the nemesis which is consummated in the concatenation of the events through one's own guilt are pictured with complete objectivity, just as they appear to the spectator" (p. 285).

text have an oddly abrupt effect. Where this least applies is in the story of Bathsheba: "but what David had done displeased Jahweh." The words are of course of great importance for the understanding of the way in which the story goes on. Next, it is said, in an extremely abrupt fashion, of Solomon who came somewhat later: "but Jahweh loved him." The historian has of course involved the reader in nothing less than the judgment passed by God upon men. But here, in respect of a new-born babe, he speaks of Jahweh's act of choice, of a divine turning towards this child, without making any attempt whatsoever at explanation or substantiation. This phrase, as the reader will recollect, also recurs at the end of the history. The third passage is the most important: it is from the conclusion of Absalom's council of war, with the magnificent dialogue between Achitophel and Hushai. This is really the *dénouement* of the whole matter. The historian again interrupts his narrative and points a finger to God: "for Jahweh had so ordained it that the good advice of Achitophel might be made vain, in order to bring evil upon Absalom." To understand the passage properly, we have to remember a scene which was described earlier. On his flight from Jerusalem David learned that even his trusted counsellor Achitophel had gone over to the rebels, and he had prayed, "O Jahweh, make the counsel of Achitophel vain." Afterwards, at the very place "where God was wont to be worshipped" Hushai approached him, to put himself at David's disposal (II Sam. xv. 31f.). He it was, too, who then befooled Absalom and his officers by his skill in speech. Obviously, the idea which our historian has of the event is that Jahweh here intervened, heard the prayer of his anointed, and averted the danger to his throne.

This view of history marks the change to a completely new concept of Jahweh's action within it. For the old narrators Jahweh's control of history was principally seen in miracles, in the *charisma* of a leader, in catastrophes, or other signal manifestations of his power: above all it was tied to sacral institutions (the holy war, the Ark, etc.). But now the whole thing was completely changed. Nowhere is there a miracle, and nowhere in the events a sacral point, something like a sacred middle-point, from which the great historical impulses issue. The causal chain of human events is closed without a break—nowhere does the narrator keep a place open where the divine action can interact with the earthly history. And we should look in vain here for a sacred core to which the turbulent events are explicitly or implicitly related. The sphere in which this history moves is completely secular, and the forces in play derive solely from men who are far from allowing themselves to be directed by special religious influences. But the reason why the historian no longer had need of all the traditional means of portrayal (miracles, etc.) was that his concept of the nature of the divine guidance of history was completely different. Jahweh's control takes in all that happens. It does not let itself be seen intermittently in holy miracles; it is as good as hidden from the natural eye: but it continuously permeates all departments of life, public and private, religious and secular alike. The special field where this control of history operates is the human heart, whose impulses and resolves Jahweh in sovereign fashion makes subservient to his plan for history.[12]

The Succession Document is therefore in a very definite sense theological historiography. It is not a history of guidance in the ordinary sense, showing the hand of God directing everything for good, as the stories about Joseph, for example, do. Its subject is in fact a much more specific one—it deals with the anointed and his throne, and so with the messianic problem.[13] The Document certainly began with Jahweh's guarantee of the throne of David. But the continuation of the story makes the reader ever more dubious whether the guarantee will be made effective, until at long last he whom Jahweh had loved beforehand does after all mount the throne. Thus, what the historian wanted to show was the first operation of the Nathan prophecy. Jahweh kept his word; but the way leading to the fulfilment of the promise was a totally unexpected one—the anointed was humiliated in the deepest possible manner, and his throne almost fell victim to revolt. This historical work was the first word spoken by Israel about Jahweh and his anointed in Jerusalem, and it is an absolutely unmythological word. The realism with which the anointed is depicted, and the secularity out of which he emerges and in which he moves, are without parallel in the ancient East.[14] Why, here we find also the anointed who

[12] This conception of Jahweh's action in history created a completely new literary technique for presenting it: the political connexions are depicted without any break and according to their historical causes. The narrator only once draws the curtain back and allows the reader for a moment to perceive the divine power at the back of what appears in the foreground. Cf. vs. 15 in 1 Kings XII or vs. 23 in Jg. IX.

[13] In this book the word "messianic" is used in the sense it specifically has in the Old Testament—with reference to the anointed.

[14] All historiography is predetermined by a cultural common consciousness (E. Schwartz, *Gesammelte Schriften*, VOL. I, Berlin 1938, pp. 41f.). The account given by the Succession Document has the closest connexion with the Enlightenment in

suffers! For we must not be blind to the force with which the picture of the King, stripped of his insignia, is drawn, and how he leaves his palace and his throne, and the Ark as well, until he was sure that Jahweh had pleasure in him (II Sam. xv. 17ff.). But these sufferings have absolutely nothing of the sacral in them. They are not undergone in submission to any ritual or cultic convention. Their utter secularity has far more theological weight than the very doubtful references to a sacral suffering of the anointed which have been recently adduced.[15] Nor is any essential change made in the picture if some of the psalms of lamentation are claimed as royal psalms, as some present-day writers are once again inclined to do.[16]

To understand the oldest concepts of the royal office, we have also to draw upon the narrative in II Sam. XXIV, which in its spiritual features not only gives the impression of being incomparably more ancient than the Succession Document, but is so in actual fact. The divine world still projects into the world of man in an extremely real fashion and is observed immediately in both its beneficial and its baneful consequences. The fact that Jahweh's anger once again broke out against Israel, and that he incited David against his people, is noted at the beginning with a matter-of-factness almost of the kind found in annals—in just the same way as it is later regarded as self-evident that the destroying angel was visible to everyone when it appeared over Jerusalem. It is certain that the census which David organised served a military purpose; it meant some sort of reform in the army. The measure marked an important turning-point, namely the transition from the old holy war to the war of tactics. David wanted to have figures available in order to be able to make his arrangements. In so doing, the King brought serious guilt upon himself: he "acted foolishly," that is, he deliberately broke a sacral regulation.[17] But afterwards David was not punished like the commonalty of his people—his

the time of Solomon in which, compared with old Israel, a very modern intellectuality made its appearance. This writing is at the same time proof that an Enlightenment does not necessarily take place by way of a diminishing of the religious heritage.

[15] A. Bentzen, *Messias, Moses redivivus, Menschensohn*, Zürich 1948, Eng. trans. *King and Messiah*, London 1955, pp. 20ff.; A. R. Johnson, *Sacral Kingship*, pp. 104ff.; H. Ringgren in *Z.A.W.*, 1952, pp. 139ff.

[16] S. Mowinckel, *He that Cometh*, trans. G. W. Anderson, Oxford 1956, pp. 11ff.

[17] The religious dread of numberings is widespread (Ex. xxx. 11f.): the purification (*lustratio populi Romani*) which, by the command of King Servius Tullius, had to follow on a census of the army, is well known, Livy, *Histories*, I. 44.

favoured position as the anointed of Jahweh is expressed in the fact that he is himself allowed to choose his punishment, that is, he is confronted with quite individual decisions. The story obviously starts from the presupposition that by this choice of his the King can still make things turn out very much for the better or very much for the worse. David chooses—for so the passage is to be understood—the most severe punishment, pestilence, which was regarded as a visitation coming directly from Jahweh.[18] For the ancient readers this was utterly unexpected, for who in those old days would have chosen a visitation that came directly from the deity rather than a calamity brought about by men? The story-teller shows us a decision of a highly dramatic character. David did what was quite unexpected, but precisely in so doing he flung himself through the thick curtain of the divine anger directly on God's heart.

The story was a ἱερὸς λόγος belonging to Jerusalem, that is, it gave the answer to the question how there came to be an altar of Jahweh in the previously Canaanite city of the Jebusites. The answer shows that this saving appointment was preceded by the anointed's deep humiliation, but also that by his confidence in Jahweh's mercy he brought about the turn for the better. In our opinion, the story's strange beginning can only be understood in the light of its end: if the final upshot of the matter was a wide-reaching and important saving appointment on the part of Jahweh, then a human offence could not have been the releasing factor. If a complex of events resulted in a revelation of divine salvation such as this, the moving initiative must have come from Jahweh. The Chronicler could no longer endure this great theological tension: he says "Satan led David astray" (1 Chron. XXI. 1).

3. THE EMPIRE AND OFFICE OF THE ANOINTED IN THE ROYAL PSALMS

The Succession Document gave a somewhat external picture of David's throne, and how it was first threatened and preserved in the field of history. But the Old Testament contains documents that afford a glimpse into the inner circle of ideas which were bound up with Jahweh's anointed and his throne, and do so with a fullness and an emotion compared with which the pronouncements in the Nathan

[18] The punishment, which falls upon the people, is to be understood as a "ruler punishment"; that is, it falls upon the king by damaging and decimating his property. D. Daube, *Studies in Biblical Law*, Cambridge 1947, pp. 161ff.

prophecy are almost flat and reserved. These are the royal psalms.[1]
Their *Sitz im Leben* was the court —within the framework of the ceremonial there were frequent occasions for making official pronouncements about the king, his throne, his empire, or his office, especially
on the day of his accession itself. The accession consisted in two acts.
The king was crowned in the sanctuary and, like the Pharaohs, he
received the royal protocol which, as we know from ancient Egypt,
contained the actual commission to rule given by the deity, and in
addition the new king's throne name—in a word, his legitimation as a
ruler commissioned by God.[2] Thus crowned, he was thereafter conducted to his palace where he ascended his throne and in a more or less
threatening way announced *urbi et orbi* the start of his rule. Psalm II for
example has its place here—the anointed reports the commission to
rule given him in the sanctuary and thereupon directs an ultimatum to
the nations. Then, after the coronation was over—though this
is a feature which can only be gathered indirectly—messengers
(the מבשרים, LXX εὐαγγελίζοντες) speed out into the surrounding
district with the glad cry, "So and so the son of so and so has become
king."[3] A king's accession was the occasion for the utmost rejoicing.
The people exulted "so that the earth was split by their noise" (I Kings
I. 40). The king stood at the centre of a magical circle of courtly
rejoicing which had become conventional. Unquestionably every
accession, in Jerusalem as elsewhere, was understood as the announcement of a new divine order for the conditions of human life, and even
of those in nature (Ps. LXXII. 16; Is. XI. 6ff.).

[1] We designate as royal psalms those poems which had their functional place in
ceremonies whose central figure was the king. Basically, there is no doubt about their
number (Pss. II, XVIII, XX, XXI, XLV, LXXII, LXXXIX, CI, CX, CXXXII). The newer
idea that the greater part of the Psalms have to be understood as royal psalms, the
most extreme representative of which is H. Birkeland (*Die Feinde des Individuums in
der israelitischen Psalmenliteratur*, Oslo 1933), fails to take account of the extensive
"democratisation" of old stylistic elements in Israel. It is a completely different question whether at a much later time the greater number of all the psalms were not
understood messianically, in that they were ascribed to David. However, we know
nothing about the reasons which led to so many psalms being understood as Psalms of
David.

[2] On the royal record (עדות, II Kings XI. 12), see G. von Rad, "Das judäische Königsritual," in *Th. Lz.*, 1947, cols. 213f., reprinted in *Ges. Studien*, pp. 205ff.; on the
throne name see A. M. Honeyman, "The evidence for royal names among the Hebrews," in *Journal of Biblical Literature*, 1948, pp. 17ff.

[3] Cf. Is. LII. 7; similarly Is. XL. 9; Zech. IX. 9 (II Sam. XV. 10; II Kings IX. 13).

The basic event at an accession was the incorporation of David's descendant into a filial relationship with Jahweh. It follows from the formula in Ps. II. 7 that this came about in the form of an act of adoption. Unlike Egypt, where the king was physically begotten by the deity, Israel never understood the king's sonship to God mythologically; instead it took it in the sense of an historical legal act, in virtue of which the king was summoned into a quite special relationship *vis-à-vis* Jahweh.[4] One of the prerogatives of this relationship appears to have been the frequently mentioned privilege of free prayer to the divine father (I Kings III. 5ff.; Pss. II. 8, xx. 5 [4], xxI. 3, 5 [2, 4]). The king could even choose his own punishment (II Sam. xxIV. 12)—in fact, he is really in constant intercourse with Jahweh, for he sits "at his right hand" and deliberates with him in all matters of state. But the supreme privilege was that of ruling in God's stead. Once again this is clearest in Ps. II, and in the logical transition there between vs. 7 and vs. 8: if the anointed is the son, then he is also the heir; and Jahweh makes over the nations to him as a heritage. The King on Zion is thus the mandatory of Jahweh himself. The boldest conclusion drawn from this position is in Ps. cx—the anointed sits as viceroy side by side with Jahweh himself: he does not sit upon his own throne, but upon that of Jahweh.[5] This immediately involves the further consequence: in what the royal psalms say, the empire of the anointed is the world. "He rules from sea to sea, from the Euphrates to the ends of the earth, all the nations do homage to him, all the nations serve him" (Ps. LXXII. 8, 11).

But this very circumscribed set of ideas puts some difficulties in the way of our understanding it. Recent investigation has shown the amazing extent to which, both for the language and for the ideas of these

---

[4] II Sam. VII. 14; Ps. LXXXIX. 27f. [26f.]; with the text emended (see B.H.) many also adduce Ps. cx. 3. The idea of the king as the son of a god is widespread in the ancient East. But more recent researches (particularly H. Frankfort, *Kingship and the Gods*, Chicago 1948, and C. J. Gadd, *Ideas of Divine Rule in the Ancient East*, London 1948) have brought out a considerable difference between the Egyptian and the Mesopotamian conceptions. The consistent mythological divine sonship is known only to the Egyptians: with them Pharaoh is god incarnate, because the god Amon begot him on the queen mother. In contrast, in Babylon and Assyria the king was understood as the servant chosen by the gods to bear rule.

[5] The idea that the king sits on the throne of Jahweh and bears rule in the kingdom of Jahweh is much more strongly emphasised in the Chronicler's history than in the older sources (I Chron. XXVIII. 5, XXIX. 23; II Chron. IX. 8). But as compared with the older idea there is hardly an objective difference.

expressions, Israel was dependent on the courtly style of the kingdoms on the Nile and in Mesopotamia.[6] These royal predicates, when transferred from the king of a real world-empire to the successors of David in Jerusalem, seem to be in sharp contrast to the rather modest political realities existing there. Are they extravagances simply to be set down to the account of the exuberance and flattery of the court minstrels? So to explain it would probably be very much exaggerating the freedom which these poets had over against the subjects of their work. The ideas about the anointed and his empire lay before the composers of the royal psalms in already long-settled form, and did not in any way depend upon whether the political situation of the time was favourable or not.[7] They are most certainly not to be regarded as pious or worldly wishes—a better designation would be prophetic exegeses of the Nathan prophecy. At any rate they must in all circumstances be understood in their relationship to and dependence upon a given fact set by Jahweh, in the light of which they say what they do say. They make the promises of the covenant with David, and what it guaranteed, relevant for the time being. All this makes it clear that the royal psalms tell us much more about the prophetic prototype of Jahweh's anointed and his empire than about the actual figure he made in history—they address to the monarchy a *doxa* which in their eyes Jahweh had attached to it once for all. Now, in this development of the Nathan prophecy, which thus made it contemporarily relevant, there must be no underestimation of the importance attaching to the adoption of this thought-world and courtly phraseology from outside Israel. Just as earlier, in the time of the conquest, Israel had not as yet experienced Jahweh as the bestower of the blessings of the fruitful land or as the helper in war, and afterwards, to her own surprise, she did so experience him, so too it was with the monarchy. To begin with early Jahwism had no terms at its command adequate to express what a divinely legitimated monarchy meant—the institution was of too recent origin. This gap was filled up by the courtly style of the ancient East. We should therefore look upon that style as a vessel into which Jahwism flowed, and in which it attained to a completely new expression of itself.

[6] H. Gressmann, *Der Messias*, Göttingen 1929, pp. 7ff.; H. Gunkel and J. Begrich, *Einleitung in die Psalmen*, Hb. A.T., Göttingen 1933, pp. 140ff.; S. Mowinckel, *He that Cometh*, Oxford 1956, pp. 21ff.

[7] This did not of course in times of distress prevent Jahweh from being reproached with the incongruity between his promises and the dreary reality.

In foreign politics the office of the anointed was a military one: he goes into battle against the foes of his people, battles for which Jahweh himself girds him (Ps. XVIII. 40 [39]), and with Jahweh's help he vanquishes and destroys every enemy. In internal affairs he acts as the guardian and guarantor of law and justice. The presupposition of this is his own relationship to Jahweh—he knows himself to be completely subordinated to Jahweh's will, he is צדיק, that is, he is in a right relationship with God (II Sam. XXIII. 3–5; Pss. CI. 2–4, XVIII. 23 [22]; cf. Zech. IX. 9). Even where these expressions are found upon the lips of the king himself, we ought not to take them too much as referring to himself, that is, as expressing what belongs to the king as a private individual: rather do they denote function, and by means of them the anointed presented himself before Jahweh and men. The same is true of the atmosphere of rejoicing which surrounds him. And, in the same way, what is said about his "beauty" is stereotyped (I Sam. IX. 2, X. 23, XVI. 12; Ps. XLV. 2).[8] All these royal predicates were derived from a conventional picture of the anointed of Jahweh as both he and his office were understood by Israel. This can be seen at once in passages where his exemplary action as the guardian of the divine will for justice is depicted—he is the guarantor of all who are deprived of their right, the surety of the oppressed who but for him would nowhere "find a helper": "their blood—in his sight it is precious" (Ps. LXXII. 12–14, XLV. 7f.). These are terms which denote perfection, and they also belong to the traditional picture of the anointed. He is the divinely commissioned guardian of law and justice, to whom are particularly commended the poor and those deprived of their rights: indeed he is to his subjects the "breath of life" (Lam. IV. 20). Just as with his empire, the terms used of the anointed's office transcend the historical realities for the Judean king's jurisdiction in respect of divine law and its administration could only have been slight. For centuries now this law had had its legitimate custodians and transmitters (the priests in the cultic community, the elders in the local civic community), with the result that the monarchy, which was instituted at so much later a date, could never have had any vital share in it, let alone that the historical successors of David were the ones authorised in chief to maintain and enforce this divine justice. But the prophetic prototype of the king handed on at the court in Jerusalem covers the same ground as that of

[8] K. Grzegorzewski, *Elemente vorderorientalischen Hofstils auf kanaanäischem Boden* (Theol. Diss. Königsberg 1937), pp. 34ff. See above, p. 41.

other officials in another respect as well; for the anointed is hailed as one who also exercises a priestly function (Ps. cx. 4). Here too it does not amount to much to gather together the scanty references according to which the king on occasion also functioned as priest, since no Judean king had a priestly function to exercise in the programmatic and ultimate sense affirmed in Ps. cx. Obviously, during the course of the tradition the office of the anointed drew other functions as well into itself, and in this process it could appeal to very ancient local traditions for its legitimation. Inherent in it was a growing claim to be the one office between Jahweh and his people. It is no wonder that for the discharge of such offices the anointed was, on his side too, in need of intercession for himself. Nowhere in the Old Testament does intercession unfold itself so richly as in the prayers for the anointed.[9]

One element in this field of thought still requires particular mention —the "spirit of Jahweh" was with the anointed, that is, he reckons as a charismatic person.[10] Anyone looking at the Judean monarchy in the light of the royal ideology common to the ancient East must feel this element to be nothing less than foreign matter, for we seek it in vain both in Babylon and Egypt. Here Israel transferred to the concept of the king something of her very own and of her oldest tradition; for it was just in her early period that a special call or authorisation by Jahweh was inseparably connected with the bestowal of the spirit of Jahweh. Thus Moses and in particular the Judges were charismatic persons, and we have already said that the dynasty in the north, in Israel, was understood in a wholly charismatic fashion. Strictly speaking, it was inconsistent to apply this concept to one who had come to the throne by way of dynastic succession and not therefore by direct call. Also, it is not perfectly clear how and where this royal *charisma* could find scope within the area of a Judean king's office. Thus, compared with the old ideas about the possibilities through which the spirit of Jahweh could operate, there is a certain unmistakable curtailment. It was only Isaiah who in his prophecy moved the picture of the anointed who was coming very definitely in the direction of the charismatic (Is. xi. 1ff.).

It was therefore a very magnificent purple robe which the royal psalms laid on the shoulders of the young successors of David at their

[9] Pss. xx, xxviii. 8f., lxi. 7 [6], lxxii, lxxxiv. 9f. [8f.], lxxxix, cxxxii. F. Hesse, *Die Fürbitte im Alten Testament* (Diss. Univ. Erlangen 1951), pp. 65ff.

[10] ii Sam. xxiii. 2; i Sam. xvi. 3. See above, pp. 96f.

accession. These extravagant predicates were proclaimed over every king. We do not know whether those who did homage to them were filled with real confidence, or whether they already had their doubts and were asking, "Art thou he who is to come, or are we to wait for another?"

4. SAUL

While from the very beginning the Davidic dynasty exercised the strongest possible influence on the creation of literature and tradition, that of Saul remained almost completely barren. This finds only partial explanation in the lack of cultural attainment of the time. No doubt, the style of Saul's court at Gibeah was incomparably more simple than the one which is found only a little later in Jerusalem (1 Sam. xx. 25), and the latter was also able to present itself intellectually in a much more imposing way. But, as we shall see, the reasons for this strange barrenness are in the last analysis theological. The traditional material dealing with Saul is certainly quite considerable (1 Sam. IX–XXXI). But when we look into the sum total of the memoirs in which he is the chief character, that is, where something is said about him for his own sake or about what took place between him and Jahweh alone, then the amount dwindles seriously. There remain the earlier account of his crowning (1 Sam. IX–XI), the complex of stories in chs. XIII–XV, the story of his visit to the witch of Endor, and that of his death (1 Sam. XXVIII, XXXI). As against this, the stories of Saul and David are really stories about David—where they occur is in fact in the book which gives the account of David's rise to power. But if we go further and ask what stories there are which tell of the Saul with whom Jahweh is present and not of the Saul already in his collapse, there remains absolutely nothing but the account of his crowning; for the very next complex (XIII. 2–XIV. 46) shows the approach of that fate which checks the victorious campaign only just begun.[1] Thus, at an early time Saul was certainly on everyone's lips, and he also soon became a subject of poetry. But to faith his supreme interest was as the anointed who slipped from Jahweh's hand, the one quitting the stage, and yielding to him who was coming; that is, Saul as the God-forsaken, driven from one delusion to the other, desperate, and in the end swallowed up in miserable darkness. Right to the end the stories follow the unhappy king on his way with a deep

[1] The section 1 Sam. XIII. 7b–15 is a later interpolation which emphasises the fate along the line of what is theologically basic (vs. 14).

human sympathy, and unfold a tragedy which in its final act rises to solemn grandeur. Actually, Israel never again gave birth to a poetic production which in certain of its features has such close affinity with the spirit of Greek tragedy. However convinced the story-tellers are of Saul's guilt, still there is at the same time something supra-personal in the way in which he became guilty—it is the fate which overtakes the one from whom God had turned away. Saul had to act: but in the very action he himself brings about his own fate (I Sam. xiv. 29f.). He made his vow and his curse serve the purpose of full victory, and just in so doing brought disaster upon his own house—although admittedly this was afterwards averted at the last moment by the people's protest. The zeal with which the king tries to bring to light the offence, only to discover that his own son was the guilty yet guiltless offender—all of this could also have been unfolded in a Greek tragedy (I Sam. xiv).[2] Of course, Saul was not in the power of a dark destiny, nor had he overreached himself in *hybris*. He was called to be a special tool of the will of Jahweh in history, for it was through him that Jahweh wanted to give effect to his plan to save Israel (I Sam. ix. 16). On this task he came to disaster. This picture of Saul certainly makes it clear that the life of the anointed was still subject to other laws than was the life of ordinary human beings, and that it was threatened by the possibility of much more dreadful disaster. It is amazing that this truth should be conceived in this way even in the earliest tradition about Saul and did not originate in the editing of later theologians.

As is well known, the complex of stories dealing with the crowning of Saul is composed of two accounts, which diverge seriously both in the matter of the historical circumstances and in particular in the theological understanding of the event itself. In the older version the initiative was taken by Jahweh in view of the political distress of his people—he directed Samuel to anoint as king Saul, who was visiting the man of God while searching for his asses. The *charisma* which came upon him as a result of the anointing was quiescent for some time, but came to life during the oppression experienced by the city of Jabesh in Gilead; and because the spirit of Jahweh vindicated itself in Saul's

---

[2] Very much in the spirit of the ancient world, Saul's sin was seen to consist in offence against sacral orders. According to I Sam. xiv. 24ff. Saul incurred guilt because of the law of collective responsibility. In the later accounts Saul himself was the one who sinned (I Sam. xiii. 8ff., xv. 9). On unwitting cultic sins see above, pp. 266f.

victory over the Ammonites, the militia of Israel thereafter elected him king at Gilgal (I Sam. IX. 1–X. 16, X. 27b–XI. 15). In the later account the initiative came from the people, to Samuel's consternation. Samuel's view was endorsed by Jahweh: by making this request the people have gravely sinned against Jahweh, but Samuel is to grant the request. And so Saul was by lot elected king at Mizpah. Samuel thereupon laid down his office as judge, but not before once again remonstrating with the people about the offence which they had committed against Jahweh (I Sam. VIII, X. 17–27a, XII). There is no doubt that this account is a much later one, and it completely lacks the freshness and simple piety of the other. There already lies behind it all the weight of the unhappy experience which Israel had with its kings. None the less, it would be an over-simplification to set this version as one "hostile to the monarchy" over against the older which was "friendly to it." Both accounts tell of one and the same thing, but from very different aspects. The older lets the reader understand the event wholly in the context of Jahweh and his plan—it is concerned with the historical unfolding of Jahweh's saving will. The later, which casts up the account of a long experience with kings, views the monarchy as an institution which fell victim to the people's clutches, as a sacrifice to reasons of state. For this way of understanding the monarchy, it became the standard view that, because of her kings, Israel became "like the nations" (I Sam. VIII. 5, 20) and that she thereby rejected the rule of Jahweh (I Sam. VIII. 7, XII. 12). Both accounts think in terms of a theocracy. In the older, God wanted to take Israel's history in hand by means of his anointed: in the later, Jahweh resists the surrender of what he himself institutes to the autonomous political will of Israel. It was hardly the desire of the later recension to cover over or supersede the great saving word expressed in I Sam. IX. 16. But in that advanced age, when the balance sheet of the history of the monarchy was already settled, and not least when Jahweh himself had spoken his "No" in 722 and 587, a theological review of history was bound to take a very different point of view in speaking of the origin of the monarchy in Israel. When the older account came into being, the dangers and temptations to which the monarchy succumbed were still unknown. Since it is the later account which put its theological stamp upon the final form of the whole complex of stories, the portrait of Israel's first anointed has something strangely negative about it; for even the stories which show his vain defiance of the anointed who is to come, and in particular the story of his tragic end, say in every line that this Saul was not the anointed after Jahweh's own heart. So then, the tradition about Saul has no intrinsic independence, for it is never given merely for itself: it always has its eye on the one who is to come. Had they not had this reference to something lying beyond themselves, the scanty traditions concerning Saul would assuredly have vanished without a trace. More and more tradition pushed Saul into the role of the anointed who came to disaster in the eyes of God. The shadows of the whole succeeding history fall so darkly on his portrait, and the "No" contradicting the human desire for a king "like the nations" is so intense and at the same time so strongly underpinned theologically, that they well-nigh smother Jahweh's word, "he shall save my people, for I have looked upon my people" (I Sam. IX. 16). At no point did Saul create a tradition: nor did he ever, like his greater successor, become a type or a standard for the future. On the contrary, he can much more readily be described as the type of the anointed who went to pieces in the sight of God, whose collapse, in darkness and despair, the storyteller followed up with deep sympathy. The Chronicler's history brings as its only addition the story about his death (I Chron. X), and the account of the history in Ps. LXXVIII or the hymn in Ecclesiasticus XLIVff., whose subject is the ancestors, wiped him utterly out of the saving history.

5. THE JUDGES

In the Deuteronomistic historical work, the period of the Judges is set in relief against the history which precedes and follows it as an era when the emphasis is strongly on saving history. It begins with the death of Joshua in Jg. II. 6ff., and ends with Samuel's farewell address in I Sam. XII (in the same way as the Deuteronomist also solemnly rounded off the previous era by means of Joshua's speech in Josh. XXIII).[1] This is the first place where we encounter this theology of history in all its stark individuality. To it and it alone are we indebted for the preservation of a great deal of the older traditional material belonging to this period. Of course, this school was not simply motivated by regard for old historical documents, but rather by its design

[1] On I Sam. XII as the end of the Book of Judges see R. Pfeiffer, *Introduction to the Old Testament*, 2nd edn. New York 1948, p. 334; M. Noth, *Überl. Studien*, pp. 5, 59f. For the theology of the Book of Judges see M. Buber, *Königtum Gottes*, pp. 11ff.; E. Jenni, "Vom Zeugnis des Richterbuches," in *Th. Z.*, 1956, pp. 257ff.

to disclose that divine meaning of the events of the era which had in the interval become more clearly discernible. In so doing, it starts from the presupposition that the old narrative material already available is not in itself able to make sufficiently clear to an unaided reader what really took place between Jahweh and Israel; that is, the reader needs special theological guidance to enable him to come to an understanding of the sum total of this period in the saving history. How little the Deuteronomist believes in reading the old stories without commentary is shown by the weighty theological apparatus which he calls in, in order to weld the old documentary material together and interpret it. Thus the Deuteronomistic Book of Judges gives the impression of great disharmony. The old stories, taken by themselves, very directly reflect the early period, which was still largely confused: as far as culture and the things of the mind go, they take us back to a bygone world and have a freshness and originality which can only belong to traditions deriving from a nation's early days. Everything is specific and unique, and no one event is like another. In contrast, in the theological framework everything is concentrated reflexion, and reflexion which is always enquiring about what is general, typical for the time, and constantly recurring.

It would of course be a mistake to think that the old stories of the charismatic leaders give the facts with little or no reflexion upon them. This could only hold true at a pinch for the story of Ehud (Jg. III. 15b–29). In actual fact, they too already give expression to a thoroughly distinctive conception of the events of the period; but this communicates itself to the reader indirectly through the course of events itself as they are given, while the Deuteronomistic theologian approaches him with his reflexions in expansive comments. These old stories originally commemorated political acts of deliverance effected by Jahweh through charismatic leaders and, at the same time, by means of a numinous panic which he caused to break out among the enemy.[2] Jahweh it was who rose up to protect his people in these holy wars, and the action which was decisive was his—the men of Israel "came to help him" (Jg. V. 23). The story of Gideon's war against the Midianites pushes this idea of the all-sufficiency of Jahweh's action to the furthest possible extreme—Jahweh had given orders to reduce the number of the fighting men, and then he only stationed those left around about the enemy's

---

[2] The panic of the enemy which Jahweh brought about is depicted in Jg. VII. 21f.; cf. Josh. X. 10f.; Jg. IV. 15; I Sam. V. 11, VII. 10 and frequently.

camp; within the area in which Jahweh worked his deed they did not so much as set foot. The miracle came down from above, as it were into a vacuum—so rigorously does the narrator exclude the idea of any human co-operation. This is clearly the highly stylised idea of the event held by later generations, since in the actual old holy wars there is no doubt that the men of Israel too fought fiercely.[3] This glorification of Jahweh's acts of deliverance is not, however, the sole content of the stories. For—at least in the cases of Gideon, Jephthah, and Samson— we have to deal not with single narratives, but with little cells of grouped narrative units, so that already something like a history of the charismatic leader in question is apparent. These histories (of Gideon, Jephthah, and Samson, and we may without more ado take in that of Saul as well) show an almost typified falling gradient. The call is followed immediately by the public proof of the *charisma* effected by means of a victory over the enemy; but then the line curves steeply downwards. The one who was a special instrument of Jahweh's will in history falls into sin, degradation, or some other disaster.[4] Thus these little narrative complexes already have as their background a definite, pessimistic conception of the charismatic leader. But for a moment was he able, in virtue of his *charisma*, to rise above the limitations of his being, only then simply to get himself more deeply entangled in deadly chaos. Behind these narratives lies, it would seem, the unspoken question, where is the one who serves his people as deliverer not merely on one occasion alone?

The old stories make it clear that the influence of each of these charismatic leaders was regionally very limited. Ehud was of Benjamin, Gideon of Manasseh, Barak of Naphtali, Jephthah of Gilead, and Samson of Dan. Seldom did more than the nearest neighbouring clans join the levy which followed their summons to arms. In contrast the Deuter-

[3] I described the alteration in ideas about Jahweh's holy wars in *Der heilige Krieg im alten Israel*, 2nd edn., Zürich 1952. What characterises it is the increasingly radical exclusion of any co-operation from the human side ("not with the sword, nor with the bow," Josh. xxiv. 12), and the elaboration of the all-sufficiency of the divine activity and the consequent demand for faith. Things have shifted to such an extent in the story of David's fight with Goliath that the real culminating point is no longer the miracle but rather David's address to Israel (1 Sam. xvii. 45-7), the aim of which is "that this whole assembly shall know that Jahweh worketh victory not with sword and spear."

[4] With Jephthah the victory over the outside enemy is followed by an internecine feud among the brother clans, Jg. xii. 1-7.

onomistic theology of history thinks of these men as wielding supreme power over all Israel, a power which each is said to have exercised for a considerable number of years.[5] In keeping with this general extension of the judge's territorial jurisdiction there is also a schematisation of the chronology. For a time Israel followed the judge; but after his death she fell away from Jahweh, and an interregnum ensued, during which Jahweh handed his people over to their enemies for punishment. Then, when they cried to him in their distress, he once again sent them a deliverer, and the cycle began all over again. It is of course a question whether, in this theological conception of history in the Book of Judges, Israel was not paying a dangerous tribute to the ancient East's cyclical way of thinking.[6] Surprise must be felt, too, that while Jahweh had worked in a wholly incalculable fashion in the old stories, his actions appearing now here and now there, and always in a different form, this action is pictured by the Deuteronomist as a rhythm, whose conformity with the divine law can be demonstrated. All these hesitations are justified. We have already seen, of course, how this theology of history seeks to make clear by means of old documents something which the traditional material does not of itself supply. But this does not free us from the task of grasping as clearly as possible this theo-

[5] The summons of even the old charismatic leaders was certainly directed in principle to all Israel, and on that account the narrators quite often speak of "Israel": but the group of clans who thereafter really complied with the levy was nevertheless always much smaller (G. von Rad, *Der heilige Krieg im alten Israel*, pp. 25ff.). The older traditions let this be seen clearly, while Deuteronomy from the very start takes its stand upon the idea that the judges had the whole of Israel at their back.

[6] Even the Old Sumerian historical legends know this alternation of times of good and times of bad: W. von Soden, in *Die Welt als Geschichte*, Stuttgart 1936, p. 452. G. Östborn has recently once again brought Israel's conception of history into closer connexion with the cyclic thinking common throughout the Orient (G. Östborn, *Yahweh's Words and Deeds*, Uppsala Universitets Årsskrift, Uppsala and Wiesbaden 1951, pp. 60ff.). What is undoubtedly correct here is that in Israelite accounts as well ideas constantly crop up which derive from this mythical way of looking at things. But there is no reference to the unresolvable tension which does exist between Jahweh's unfettered guidance of history and ideas of any kind of a fixed pattern. Furthermore, the question still remains whether one single nexus from a beginning to an end entitles us to speak of a cyclic system; again, the references which Östborn adduces are not able to bear the weight which he puts upon them, least of all those from Ecclesiastes, which are rather an argument against his thesis, for, as Ecclesiastes is unable to think in terms of the saving history, the return to cyclical ideas is perfectly consistent (see below, p. 455).

logical concern of the Deuteronomist's with history as it is given us.[7]

We must to begin with recognise that the Deuteronomist set himself, *vis-à-vis* the history, an incomparably more ambitious task than can be attributed to those narrative complexes which have just been mentioned. His concern is the totality of the history of Israel, the meaning and the content of a whole era in the eyes of God. So he is at pains first and foremost to show the unity in this history. Although it appears to split up into a great number of more or less disconnected single events, still, in God's eyes, it is a whole. This is what he implies by his curious schematisations and generalisations—it is with the whole of the people of God that Jahweh always deals. The Deuteronomist's other desire is to show the serious threat under which Israel stood by reason of her own refractoriness and openness to the temptations of the nature religions, a thing which Jahweh can only counter by dire punishment. He also wishes to show, on the other hand, the infinite patience of Jahweh, which is seen in the continual raising up of new "saviours."[8] Here too the material presented is controlled by a doctrinaire schematisation, for that cast-iron alternation of worship of Baal

[7] Unfortunately the question as to the sense in which these deliverers are called "judges" is still not satisfactorily explained. The term does not occur in the older stories which the Deuteronomist took over: thus it is Deuteronomistic; but in what sense? The question why the Deuteronomist came to use just this term and no other has to some extent to be distinguished from the other question as to what specific meaning is to be attached to it. It is probably to be assumed that the term came to the Deuteronomist from somewhere in the tradition or from concepts existing elsewhere. But even if the basis were to be found in the tradition about Jephthah, in the fact that Jephthah also at the same time stood in the list of the so-called lesser judges (Jg. XII. 7), and that because of this the official title now passed over to the warlike charismatic leaders as well (M. Noth, *Überl. Studien*, pp. 49, 98), the question as to the meaning of this now Deuteronomistic title would still remain open. Grether has shown that, for the interpretation of the term, only the most natural meaning of "judging," "arbitrating," "helping someone to get his due," comes into question, and that therefore the once popular meaning of "ruling" is in particular ruled out (*Z.A.W.*, 1939, pp. 110ff.). But the question is, did the Deuteronomist imagine that charismatic leaders were also real judges? In view of the use of the term in I Sam. VIII. 5f. for example, and of the length of time which the Deuteronomist attributes to these men's periods of office, this possibility is questionable in the extreme. On the other hand, only the meaning "to help to get what one is due" can be extracted from Jg. III. 10, for here the judging consists in a warlike act. In that case the judges would be men whom Jahweh raised up in order through them to prove to his people his justice in history. Cf. also for this idea II Sam. XVIII. 19, 31; I Sam. XXIV. 16.

[8] For the expression מושיע see Jg. III. 9, 15.

and worship of Jahweh between which Israel—be it noted the whole of Israel—is said to have moved is absolutely inconceivable historically. But by means of it the Deuteronomist again expresses something that has great theological importance: every generation was confronted by Jahweh's whole historical revelation both in judgment and in salvation. It was not the case that one generation was subjected only to his wrath while the next was solely subjected to his will to save. It was rather that each generation experienced the whole Jahweh.

The Deuteronomistic picture of the Judges is thus a late literary reconstruction, for its whole idea of men ruling over all Israel for the rest of their lives and being her leaders in war cannot have come into being apart from the monarchy, which was of course historically later.[9] Nevertheless, the later kingdom cannot simply be regarded as directly modelled upon the office of the judge, for this theology of history draws a sharp distinction between the two institutions, and in fact places them in direct opposition. In 1 Sam. XII. 10f. especially, the two offices are weighed up against one another, and the balance comes down against the monarchy. For the Deuteronomist's way of thinking, Israel stopped allowing Jahweh to bear rule over her when the monarchy came into being (Jg. VIII. 23), but to his mind the institution of the judges still left room for this sovereignty of Jahweh over Israel. How different the planes are on which the two offices lie is also seen from the fact that the Deuteronomist passes censure on the kings, but the judges are called directly by Jahweh, and so he does not criticise them. The real point at issue is Israel's proper ordering under God's rule, and it is understandable that the Book of Judges has been designated as the "Plato's *Republic*" of the Bible.[10] The Deuteronomist clearly regards the office of the judge as the form of government most appropriate to Israel: it was a tragedy that she asserted her own autonomy over against Jahweh by means of her kings. In this clear preference for the amphictyonic organisation the Deuteronomist follows Deuteronomy, which

[9] Most recently H. W. Hertzberg, *Die Bücher Josua, Richter, Ruth* (A.T.D.), Göttingen 1933, p. 143. M. Buber (*Königtum Gottes*, pp. 15ff.) is the one who most distinctly brought out the relationship of the Book of Judges to the institution of the monarchy. But his thesis that there were two Books of Judges, the one anti-monarchical and the other monarchical (the latter with the refrain which reveals its purpose in Jg. XVII. 6, XVIII. 1, XXI. 25), out of which our present Book of Judges was put together, is, as he propounds it, untenable. Chs. XVII–XXI are only a later addition to the Deuteronomistic Book of Judges.

[10] M. Buber, *Königtum Gottes*, p. 44.

undertakes the ordering of Israel wholly on the model of the sacral people of God, that is, on the model of the old Amphictyony.[11]

The oddest figure amongst the judges is Samson: the reader will indeed find it absolutely impossible to understand him as judge over Israel. He never has a militia behind him, but is always completely alone in his exploits. When it is said that he "judged Israel for twenty years" (Jg. XVI. 31b), the Deuteronomist's *schema* completely departs from the traditional material which lay before it.[12] A much more effective measure towards including the garland of the Samson stories in those of the Judges was a prefixing of the story of the call (Jg. XIII) which took place much earlier.[13] The basis of the stories about Samson is extremely old—they show us Dan still living in tents on the western slopes of the hill country of Judah, and involved in all manner of squabbles with the Philistines. In these quarrels, in which each party sought to outdo the other not only by force of arms but also by witticisms and practical jokes, a charismatic leader named Samson played a conspicuous part. But as has been said, everything gets a peculiar slant because of the story of the call which precedes the whole, as it were like an entrance hall. Very strong emphasis is laid on the call and the setting apart as a Nazirite, a special instrument which Jahweh intends to use. This prehistory of Samson's life puts to the reader what is the real problem of the Samson story; for anyone who comes from the pious story of the call (with its mention of a manifestation of God, and of sacrifice and a vow) must be astounded by the whirlwind of very unspiritual adventures in which Samson gets lost. In particular, Samson showed great interest in women. He certainly inflicts many an injury on the Philistines, but in the end he falls victim to them. Jahweh's spirit departs from him, and the man who had formerly been a charismatic leader had, blinded, to turn his enemies' mill. The stories of Samson are told in such a way that, wonderfully endowed as he was with powers of spirit and body, he makes a very human appeal to the

[11] See above, p. 228.

[12] This complex of tradition betrays so little of the spirit of the Deuteronomist and of his conception of history that the whole of it has been envisaged as a later insertion. M. Noth, *Überl. Studien*, p. 61.

[13] Eissfeldt is very probably correct in saying that, as far as literary criticism goes, ch. XIII cannot now be divorced from the block of stories in chs. XIV–XVI (*Die Quellen des Richterbuches*, Leipzig 1925, pp. 81f.). But in respect of the history of its matter and form, ch. XIII stands by itself; it is basically a cultic legend, and not a story about Samson.

reader, especially at the point where in the end he falls victim to the ranks of those who, while certainly not so strong and ingenious as he was, were for that very reason the more perfidious. Meantime, the reader will not forget, either, the great mission with which God charged him, and will have to think about the continuous alternation between humiliating weakness and God-given power in which the life of Samson oscillates. But even the power given him by God is increasingly squandered in ineffectual practical jokes, and Samson finally founders in the great conflict between *eros* and *charisma*. Thus, the stories about Samson as well as those about Saul show the failure of a charismatic leader, and divine powers wasted. "The dead whom he slew at his death were more than those whom he had slain in his life" (Jg. XVI. 30)—such is the story-teller's final and very significant comment. Samson himself perishes in the chaos which he spreads out around himself.

6. THE DEUTERONOMIST'S THEOLOGY OF HISTORY[1]
(THE BOOKS OF KINGS)

Scholars believe that the Deuteronomistic hand which wrote the Book of Judges and put its stamp upon it is the same as that which gave their great theological form to the two Books of Kings. But since the two eras in Israel's history are pictured and judged from very different theological standpoints, the theology of history of the Books of Kings needs special treatment. Again, the two eras do not pass over directly from one to the other: they are not joined to one another in this theology of history. Strangely enough there is a great, yawning gulf in which the Deuteronomist did not intrude his work, between the end of the period of the Judges and the point at which the Deuteronomistic Books of Kings take up the story (I Kings III. 1f.). Apart from this gap, which is not easy to explain, this historian's literary technique is of the same kind as that employed in the Book of Judges: he presents the old material in the form in which it had come down, he carefully and meaningfully connects the individual units, and he clamps the resulting literary picture of a king's reign at beginning and end with the

---

[1] M. Noth, *Überl. Studien*, pp. 87ff.; G. von Rad, *Studies in Deuteronomy*, pp. 72ff.; A. Weiser, *Glaube und Geschichte im Alten Testament*, Stuttgart 1931, pp. 61ff.; A. Jepsen, *Die Quellen des Königsbuches*, Halle 1953; H. J. Kraus, "Gesetz und Geschichte," in *Ev. Th.*, 1951–52, p. 415; H. W. Wolff, "Das Kerygma des deuteronomistischen Geschichtswerkes," in *Z.A.W.*, 1961, pp. 171ff.

well-known framework, in which the most important aspect theologically is the judgment which each king receives.[2] At times the Deuteronomist also drew up shorter narratives of his own composition and wholly in his own individual style, or he expressed radical theological reflexions on the history at important points, as for example in the solemn epilogue with which he concludes the account of the Northern Kingdom (II Kings XVII. 7ff.). From this formal point of view, the difference from the Book of Judges consists merely in the fact that the Deuteronomist had at his disposal incomparably fuller documentary material from the monarchical period. This was not only very diversified in literary *genre* (narratives, annals, stories about prophets, extracts from a Temple chronicle, etc.), but it was so abundant that it could only be incorporated into the history in skilfully chosen selections. The scholarly fashion in which the Deuteronomist exercised the historian's office is shown by the regular references to the source documents from which he took a large part of his material, and in which what he does not himself mention can be looked up.[3]

This historical work came into being during the time of the Babylonian Exile.[4] However little we know of the author's place and origin, one thing is certain—the spiritual situation in whose light he is to be understood was that of a late period: it was therefore completely different from the one in which the Succession Document came into being. The latter had come in its time as something new, into, so to speak, a still completely empty space as far as literature and theology went. But the man who wrote and passed his judgments in the time of the exile was not only externally confronted with very abundant remembered material: what weighed most heavily was the burden of certain historical experiences which had long ago solidified, and the authority of certain theological ideas or traditions upon which the Deuteronomist depended in his time or in the circle to which he belonged. The theological current, of which our Deuteronomistic historical work is a

---

[2] With the kings of Judah the framework runs at the beginning as follows: "In the year of such and such a king of Israel so and so became king of Judah; he was so many years old when he became king, he reigned so many years in Jerusalem; his mother was so and so the daughter of such and such, and he did what was pleasing (evil) in the sight of Jahweh." At the end it runs: "The rest of the history of so and so is written in the book of the history of the kings of Judah. Then so and so slept with his fathers and was buried in the city of David, and so and so else became king in his stead." [3] M. Noth, *Überl. Studien*, p. 96.

[4] The *terminus a quo* is the freeing of Jehoiachin in the year 561 (II Kings XXV. 27ff.).

later exponent, became dominant, because of Deuteronomy, in the last years of the monarchical period.[5] We remember Deuteronomy's demand that Jahweh should be worshipped only at the one legitimate sanctuary at which he had put his name. This demand had been made binding at a time which had become conscious in all its magnitude of the difference between historically-based Jahwism and the Canaanite nature cult, and had grasped that worship of Jahweh at the high places, that is, mingled with the Baal cult, eliminated that which was distinctive in Jahwism. The recognition that one had to choose between the two worships had come, through Deuteronomy, to be a *status confessionis* at this later period. Now, the Deuteronomistic theology of history too holds this very radical standpoint, because, as is well known, it measures the kings of Israel and Judah according to whether they recognised the Temple in Jerusalem as the one legitimate place of worship, or sacrificed on the "high places." The judgments which are passed on the kings are arrived at solely in the light of this decision. From this standpoint the kings of Israel are condemned out of hand, for they all walked in the "sin of Jeroboam."[6] But even of the Judean kings only two—Hezekiah and Josiah—are given unqualified praise. Six are approved conditionally (Asa, Jehoshaphat, Joash, Amaziah, Azaraiah, and Jotham): all the rest are reproached with "having done what was evil in the sight of Jahweh."

Very much depends on the right understanding of these judgments. Undoubtedly for our present-day historical way of thinking, they are greatly oversimplified, and consequently unjust. And unfortunately we do not know for certain whether this historical work presupposes a knowledge of Deuteronomy by all the kings, and whether it only reckoned with a temporary loss of it and its reappearance under Josiah.[7] But even if a knowledge of Deuteronomy is not presupposed, it has to be borne in mind that the standard by which the kings are measured is not in itself a completely new thing conjured up in the late monarchical period. In reality, it is a very old standard which Deuteronomy took up again, since in the days before Israel was a state, in her constitution as an

---

[5] This dependence, which was recognised long ago, is not however in any sense a total one. Neither did the Deuteronomist take over the whole range of the concerns of Deuteronomy, nor can all that concerns the Deuteronomist be derived from Deuteronomy. This is particularly clear in the matter of the Deuteronomist's idea of the kingdom, see below, pp. 337f.

[6] I Kings xv. 26, 34, xvi. 19, 26 and frequently.

[7] II Kings xiv. 6 supports this assumption.

Amphictyony, she had in fact something like a sole place of worship, even if at that time the consequences of this commitment to the central sanctuary, where the Ark was, and to which the pilgrims came, were still not drawn anything like so radically. But with these judgments what we have to bear particularly in mind is that they do not relate as it were to the total political and religious achievement of the particular king, but only to his basic cultic decision. This historical work had no intention of dealing with the king's political activities in general.[8] It certainly does offer general political documentary material; but its interest is expressly theological, to the extent that it judges even the course of political events from a theological standpoint. From the historian's point of view the perspective thus opened up into the history of the kings is undoubtedly very one-sided and narrow. But this bias is linked up with the confessional situation mentioned above. In the writer's time one thing had become *articulus stantis et cadentis ecclesiae*, namely, exclusive allegiance to the place where Jahweh was present for Israel and where he spoke to and had cultic dealings with her; and the Deuteronomist brought the whole of the history of the monarchy within the scope of this confessional situation. He was not objectively and historically interested in the many varying possibilities of apostasy which might have presented themselves to the kings in the course of the history, but only in the one by which, as the post-Deuteronomic period was convinced, Israel's existence or non-existence was decided.[9] Since the Deuteronomist wrote in the shadow of the catastrophes of 722 and 587, his work is to be understood as a comprehensive confession of Israel's guilt. Our task in what follows consists in examining in detail the careful theological foundation of the proposition that Israel, and she alone, was to be held responsible.

In the opinion of the Deuteronomist the decision for evil was taken in the kings' hearts, because "their heart was not perfect with God."[10] It has rightly been pointed out that the Deuteronomist thus assigned to

[8] Think of it! The account of the reign of Omri, including the framework, takes up six verses. Those who want information about the secular exploits of the kings are expressly directed to the sources; the Deuteronomist does not think it as lying within his province to evaluate them (I Kings XVI. 27, XXII. 45; II Kings X. 34, XIII. 8, 12, XIV. 15, 28).

[9] In view of this exclusive rigorism which the Deuteronomist practised, his method of awarding praise or blame not as a simple either-or, but as admitting of a further third and in-between predicate, could almost be regarded as a lack of consistency.

[10] שלם עם יהוה I Kings VIII. 61, XI. 4, XV. 3, 14.

the kings an office which, according to their historical rights, they did not have in their country at all. Least of all did this universal responsibility for the whole cultic life of the people of God correspond with the concept in Deuteronomy, in which the royal office can only be understood as an embarrassing concession to the historical realities.[11] Here we meet for the first time with an element in the Deuteronomist's view of history which can certainly not be explained on the basis of Deuteronomy, nor simply on the basis of the kingdom itself as it developed, namely, a quite definite picture of the royal office with which he works and by means of which he judges the kings. This Deuteronomistic critique of the kings which is so well known to the reader of the Bible—they ought to have directed both their own personal lives and their whole policy according to the law of Moses—owes its origin to the confluence of two great streams of tradition which had hitherto existed in independence. We tried above to outline the group of sacral ideas which wrapped themselves round the monarchy.[12] Nothing in them pointed back to Moses and the ancient Israel-Covenant traditions. On the other hand, the Amphyctyonic traditions which do go back to Moses had absolutely no place for the monarchy. This reserve concerning the institution of the monarchy is indeed absolutely obvious even in Deuteronomy, which is late in so far as it is a revival of the Israel-Covenant tradition. Deuteronomy still knows nothing of any special sacral dignity attaching to the king as the representative of a separate election tradition. It is only in the Deuteronomistic historical work that the two traditions of election—the Israel-Covenant and the David-Covenant traditions—are finally fused; and this was the last great fusion of traditions in Israel's history. It had a long prehistory. It began with David bringing up the Ark (II Sam. VI) and so planting Israelite traditions in the soil of Jerusalem. But this was still a long way from the further Deuteronomic idea of Moses as the recipient of the "Law." But now the Deuteronomist is able to put an appeal to Jahweh's covenant with David into the mouth of a king (I Kings VIII. 25, IX. 5), and in almost the same breath to refer to the old Amphictyonic tradition about the election of Israel, Moses, and the Exodus from Egypt (I Kings VIII. 15f., 34, 36, 53, 56). The two traditions have now come together to form a major set of ideas. But the fact that the kings are reminded

---

[11] M. Noth, *Überl. Studien*, p. 94. Josiah's measures in his policy for the cult outside Jerusalem were a *novum*, for which Deuteronomy alone gave him the authority. Alt, *K.S.*, VOL. II, pp. 256f.   [12] See above, pp. 40ff., 318ff.

of their relationship to Moses and the Sinai covenant is actually something very original (I Kings XI. 11; II Kings XXI. 8). The king is now
regarded as the responsible person to whom has been entrusted the law
of Moses and who has the duty to see that it is recognised in his kingdom. The place where the fusion of the Mosaic and Davidic traditions
can be seen most clearly is the ideal picture which the Deuteronomist
drew of King Josiah: "before him there was no king like him, who
turned to Jahweh with all his heart and with all his soul and with all his
might, according to all the law of Moses; nor did any like him arise
after him" (II Kings XXIII. 25).

No doubt the Deuteronomist's judgment on the kings who ruled
Judah and Israel is an adverse one in the main, but this does not amount
to a proof that he took an altogether low view of the monarchy. It
could be the case—and this will be substantiated later—that the preponderantly negative aspect is based on the fact that the Deuteronomist
judged the kings by a very high standard. He does in fact ascribe to the
monarchy the crucial key-position between Jahweh and Israel, since it
was in the kings' hearts that the decision whether Israel was to be
saved or rejected had to be taken. This decision, however, did not
depend only on the kings' complete devotion to or apostasy from
Jahweh, but upon their attitude to the revelation of Jahweh known in
Israel from of old, that is, to the law of Moses. And now we have
named the other order which, in the Deuteronomist's view, Jahweh had
provided for Israel's good. For him both of these, the torah of Moses
and the dynasty of David, were concrete historical powers: like the
dynasty, the revelation of Jahweh's will to Moses was also something
clearly discernible; it had in fact already been handed over in trust to
the kings in the form of a sacred book.[13] Thus the Deuteronomist sees
the main problem of the history of Israel as lying in the question of the
correct correlation of Moses and David. Did the kings discern and
comply with the will of Jahweh promulgated by Moses? As we know,
the answer is No—the decision of the kings was taken against the
revealed will of Jahweh and for evil. But in Deuteronomy grave threats
and curses had been set forth if Israel persisted in disobedience (Deut.
XXVIII. 15ff.). Thus in the serious catastrophes the word of Jahweh
tself brought Israel into judgment. It had in actual fact been no
"empty word" (Deut. XXXII. 47); this word of God had reached its

[13] References back to a written form of the torah of Moses are to be found in
I Kings II. 3; II Kings X. 31, XIV. 6, XVII. 13, 37, XXI. 8, XXII. 8, 11, XXIII. 24f.

goal in the destruction of the two states. Expressed in the Deuteronomist's terminology, Jahweh had not allowed it to "fail" but had "established" it.[14] This correspondence between promulgated word and historical fulfilment, with whose proof we see the Deuteronomist occupied, becomes even more striking in the many prophecies which he incorporated into his work. It can actually be said that the Deuteronomist gave the historical course of events which he describes its inner rhythm and its theological proof precisely by means of a whole structure of constantly promulgated prophetic predictions and their corresponding fulfilments, of which exact note is generally made. It is here that we really get a correct perspective for this view of history. Everything that Ahijah of Shiloh, Jehu ben Hanani, Micaiah ben Imlah, Elijah, Elisha, Huldah, etc., prophesied became history. The history of Israel is a course of events which receives its own peculiar dramatic quality from the tension between constantly promulgated prophecies and their corresponding fulfilment. Sometimes the span between prediction and fulfilment is short (II Kings I. 6=I. 17), sometimes it forms an arch spanning many generations (e.g. I Kings XIII. 2=II Kings XXIII. 16–18), so that, if one were to try to make a diagram of this structure, the strangest criss-crossings would result. Things were simplest for the Deuteronomist in the Northern Kingdom. Its fate was indeed already sealed with the sin of its first king (I Kings XIV. 16; II Kings XVII. 21–3), all the more so since all its kings walked "in the sin of Jeroboam." Thus the Deuteronomist was only confronted with the task, admittedly none too easy a one, of explaining why this kingdom nevertheless continued to exist in history for two hundred years. He explains this postponement of punishment as due to the grace of Jahweh, who did not overlook the slight amount of good there was even in rejected kings.[15] The Deuteronomist also pictures the history of the kingdom of Judah as an almost unbroken series of breaches of the revealed will of God. Her too there was a fact which barred the path of his *schema*—how did it come about that the great catastrophe of 587 closed in over Judah almost immediately after the reign of Josiah, who was the best of all the house of David? The reason was—so the Deuteronomist said—that Jahweh had already resolved to pass sentence on Judah because of the sin of Manasseh, which had broken all bounds. Even Josiah could avert

[14] Jahweh "establishes" the prophet's word: I Kings II. 4, VI. 12, VIII. 20, XII. 15 and frequently. It "does not fail": Josh. XXI. 45, XXIII. 14; I Kings VIII. 56; II Kings X. 10.   [15] I Kings XXI. 29; II Kings X. 30 = XV. 12, XIII. 23, XIV. 26.

it no longer.[16] Thus, over Judah too Jahweh's patience had long held. But here our historian was now in the happy position of being able to establish Jahweh's patient waiting on a much more striking theological basis. It was because Jahweh had his special plans for history with the house of David and because he had made David the promise to "give him a lamp for all time," that Judah and Jerusalem were preserved in history in spite of the long-due judgment. When the Deuteronomist uses the odd term "lamp," he is of course thinking of the legitimation of the Davidic dynasty by the prophecy of Nathan (II Sam. VII. 12ff.)— although with him this old element of messianic tradition is fused with the Deuteronomic idea of the one chosen city.[17] This saving word of Jahweh, injected at one particular point into the history, passed down through the ages like a guardian angel and had the effect of preserving and saving when Judah's existence in the eyes of Jahweh was already forfeit.[18]

The road which Israel's theology of history had travelled from the Succession Document up to now is a very long one. The first difference between the two views lies in the fact that the Deuteronomist had a principle of interpretation at his disposal whose legitimacy was beyond doubt—this was the "word of God" in Deuteronomy, which for him was almost already canonical. What could the writer of the Succession Document appeal to compared with this? That Jahweh had guided the history in a way favourable for David by hearing his prayer and deluding Absalom's council of war was indeed the writer's personal conviction: and, if need be, he could claim special inspiration for his view. But he did not feel himself empowered to go on to further judgments. The Deuteronomist, however, with the canonical word of God in his possession, can pass judgments, and we have seen the way in which he makes use of this power. A further feature which distinguishes our work

---

[16] II Kings XXI. 10ff., XXIII. 26, XXIV. 2.

[17] "For the sake of David my servant and for the sake of Jerusalem which I have chosen," I Kings XI. 13, 32, 36.

[18] I Kings XI. 36, XV. 4; II Kings VIII. 19 (cf. I Kings XI. 13, 32). Noth has held that the word נִיר should not be rendered as "lamp," but as "breaking up" (*Ges. Studien*, p. 179). But there is no justification for this. LXX rendered נִיר in II Kings VIII. 19 as λύχνος and in I Kings XI. 36 as θέσις, and in I Kings XV. 4 as κατάλειμμα. These passages do not come into the account, for in any case they are not translations, not even in the meaning of a "breaking up." What in our opinion decides the question is the mention of the lamp (here נֵר) in Ps. CXXXII. 17. The term is obviously a fixed formula in the courtly style. II Sam. XXI. 17 would also be included here.

from the older one is its heightened interest in the instrumental means of the divine guidance of history, for the older work was concerned rather with establishing the fact. That Jahweh had directed David's history is the only thing it explicitly says. We are certainly not wrong in saying that Jahweh worked secretly in the hearts of the hearers, in their resolve (II Sam. XVII. 14); yet the details remain a secret. Compared with this, what a shift there has been in the object of theological interest! For the Deuteronomist the divine guidance of history is established beyond all doubt: but that it is by his word that Jahweh directs history, this is practically hammered into the reader. At the same time the author of the Succession Document shows that he himself understood this history as the fulfilment of an explicit word of Jahweh, since he sets the whole complex in the shadow of the Nathan prophecy (II Sam. VII).

But this thoroughly mature theology of history of the Deuteronomist's did not oppose the older one like a *deus ex machina*. Actually, in the traditional material which the Deuteronomist took over, there is a cycle of stories which can almost be described as a connecting link between the classical account of the history and that of the Deuteronomist. This material is accounts of wars or other involvements which are related to one another in the realm of high politics: in the decisive political events the initiative stems from prophets, who change the gears of history with a word of God.[19] The accounts display on the one hand that vigorous political and psychological realism which we see in the Succession Document, while on the other, there can be no mistaking that the theological theme is already set which will now in the Deuteronomist be applied in a much more radical way to the whole of the history of the monarchy.

We are now in a position to review the various strands in the Deuteronomistic account of the history. It was composed in the exile, at a time when the saving history over Israel was at a standstill and when, in the dismay she felt at this fact, the question which had to be answered was, how had all this come about and how could it have become possible for Jahweh to reject his people? The first conclusion from contemplation of this question was that the fault was not Jahweh's: it was Israel herself who by her own guilt had forfeited his salvation. Jahweh's judgment in history was justified. Thus, the

[19] I Kings XX, XXII; II Kings IX–X; Noth (*Ges. Studien*, pp. 79f.) also reckons along with these the history of Ahijah of Shiloh, I Kings XI. 29–31, 36f., XII. 1–20, 26–31 (see above, pp. 71ff.).

Deuteronomist is concerned with Ps. LI. 6 [4] and its "so that thou art justified in thy sentence"; his work is a great "doxology of judgment' transferred from the cultic to the literary sphere.[20] But he was not content with this general conclusion. He also set himself the task of giving a detailed theological explanation of how the saving history ended in the catastrophes of 722 and 587. He thought that he was in a position so to do because he understood the history of the people of God in the light of the creative word of Jahweh. The threats and curses in Deuteronomy had been fulfilled in the catastrophes of the two kingdoms. This word of Jahweh, which, the Psalmist says, "runs swiftly" (Ps. CXLVII. 15), had attained its goal. It was not often that Israel expressed her realisation of the law's judging and destroying power in such a radical way. But the Deuteronomist saw yet another word as active in the history, namely, the promise of salvation in the Nathan prophecy, and it, as well as the threat of judgment, was effectual as it ran through the course of the history.[21] Had it too creatively reached its goal in a fulfilment? The Deuteronomist's history leaves this question open. Yet, closing as it does with the note about the favour shown to Jehoiachin (II Kings XXV. 27ff.), it points to a possibility with which Jahweh can resume.[22]

What interests the author of this theology of history is thus perfectly clear. He was not interested in drawing up a secular history, or a history of the faith and worship of Israel. His concern was rather with the problem of how the word of Jahweh functioned in history. This word

[20] On the cultic category of the doxology of judgment see below, pp. 357ff.

[21] On one occasion the Deuteronomist makes Solomon give very clear expression to this relationship of correspondence between word and history: "What thou didst promise with thy mouth, thou hast with thine hand fulfilled" (I Kings VIII. 24).

[22] One has to appreciate the dilemma into which the Deuteronomist was driven by the actual course of the history, in that it ended with the catastrophe of 587. On the basis of his theological presuppositions he had certainly no reason to lighten the darkness of this judgment. On the other hand, he could never concede that the saying about the lamp which was always to remain for David had now in fact "failed." As to any goal to which this saving word was coming he had nothing to say: the one thing he could do was just, in this direction, not to close the door of history, but to leave it open. This he did in the reflective conclusion of his work (II Kings XXV. 27ff.). His reference to Jehoiachin, and not to Zedekiah, as the last king of Judah could be connected with the fact that in his time Jehoiachin, and not Zedekiah, was regarded as the last king of Judah. For this cf. the dating of the Book of Ezekiel according to the reign of Jehoiachin, and on this question see W. Zimmerli, *Ezechiel*, Biblischer Kommentar, ed. M. Noth, VOL. XIII, Neukirchen 1955, pp. 43f.

operates in two ways: as law it operates destructively, and as gospel it works as salvation. Of course it is easy to point to the defects in this conception of history. Indeed, we have to ask whether the situation in the exile, when Israel was divorced from contact with real history, did not make people far too prone to make theoretical constructions. It certainly arouses suspicion that this theology of history cannot be unfolded without a now subtler now cruder *corriger l'histoire*. In particular, it would need to be established that, in his passionate desire to make the efficacy of the word of Jahweh clear, the Deuteronomist has not rationally schematised the history.[23] But it is this desire and attempt to understand Israel's history solely in the light of the word of Jahweh that gives the work its theological grandeur. What is decisive for Israel is not what commonly makes "the tumult and the shouting" in history. Decisive for the life and death of the people of God is the word of God injected into history. This Deuteronomistic theology of history was the first which clearly formulated the phenomenon of saving history, that is, of a course of history which was shaped and led to a fulfilment by a word of judgment and salvation continually injected into it.[24]

The point where this theology of history is at farthest remove from its native soil in Deuteronomy is the key position it accords to the king. In my view there is perfect justification for describing this work as containing a messianic *motif*, for all that we have worked out up to now concerning the Deuteronomistic history and the word which creates history, etc., is not simply theoretically unfolded—as it were in a vacuum; it is all related in the most direct way to the kings. They are the real object of this operative word, it is they who are sustained by it and they who by it are destroyed. The people stands and falls with them.[25] The author, so exposed to danger in another respect because of his theological rationality, here knows no kind of individualism, but practises a collective thinking which, with him, seems somewhat antiquated. This way in which the people is completely bound up with

---

[23] We may think also of the consequences of the "ethical schematisation" which makes the action of God conditioned by human action: the latter comes first, the former second: J. Hempel, *Altes Testament und Geschichte*, Gütersloh 1930, pp. 15ff.

[24] In contrast, outside Israel the contemplation of history was a form of state activity, a branch of politics. Laqueur, "Formen geschichtlichen Denkens im Alten Orient und Okzident," in *Neue Jahrbücher für Wissenschaft und Jugendbildung*, Leipzig 1931, p. 493.

[25] It is also they who lead the people to sin (החטיא), 1 Kings XVI. 13, 19, 26, XXI. 22; II Kings III. 3, X. 29, XIV. 24, XXI. 16.

whether the king fulfils or fails in his role is particularly harsh in cases where, as for example with Manasseh, the time-span between the threat and its fulfilment takes in several generations.[26] All these Judean kings are measured by the Deuteronomist against the picture of the one perfect king whom he knows, namely David. David walked before Jahweh "with integrity of heart and uprightness" (בתם־לבב ובישר, I Kings IX. 4); David's heart was "wholly true to Jahweh" (שלם עם יהוה, I Kings XI. 4); "David followed Jahweh completely" (מלא אחרי יהוה, I Kings XI. 6); he did according to "what pleased Jahweh and kept his statutes and commandments" (I Kings XI. 38); "he followed Jahweh with his whole heart, doing only what pleased Jahweh" (לעשות רק הישר, I Kings XIV. 8).[27] Is any more evidence needed to prove that this writer had a picture of the perfect anointed unremittingly present to his mind, and that it is on its basis that the work calls in question the whole history of the monarchy? Of course, this picture of David which set the standard for the Deuteronomist is now far removed from the picture of the David of the Succession Document; that was so realistic in its psychological execution, but this is a picture which has become attenuated in the tradition to form a type.[28] In particular, basic features of the Deuteronomic picture of man, that is, of a man whose heart is perfect with Jahweh and who keeps Jahweh's statutes and commandments with his whole heart, have become bound up with it. Therefore the anointed who stands as a standard and type behind the Deuteronomist's melancholy picture of the monarchical period is the completely righteous man who keeps all the commandments with his whole heart. Thus, the partially destructive criticism of the kings of Israel and Judah

---

[26] It is perfectly possible that the common saying: "The fathers have eaten sour grapes, and the children's teeth are set on edge" (Jer. XXXI. 29, Ezek. XVIII. 2), was directed against the idea which became concrete a little later in the Deuteronomistic historical work. Ps. CVI. 24ff., where the exile could be conceived as Jahweh's reaction to the sins of the generation in the wilderness, shows how widely the arch could be stretched between act and penalty.

[27] I Kings III. 3, VIII. 17, XI. 33, XV. 3, 5, 11; II Kings XIV. 3, XVI. 2, XVIII. 3, XXII. 2 are other references for this picture of the perfect David.

[28] The picture in Ps. CXXXII. 1-4 is akin to it. Only once does the Deuteronomist allow a shadow to fall on the picture of David (I Kings XV. 5). This typification is already clearly discernible in Isaiah—think for example of the ideal picture of the Davidic Jerusalem which he draws in Is. I. 21. Incidentally, for the Deuteronomist the picture of Solomon as well was extended to make Solomon a model—he is the type of wisdom and piety. E. Jacob, *La Tradition historique en Israel*, Montpellier 1946, p. 85.

had all the same an unmistakably positive side—by means of it the Deuteronomist saves what he took to be the real meaning of the Nathan prophecy from all misrepresentation or replacement.

In conclusion, we have once more to look at the question of the peculiar aim which the author of this great work has in mind. Is it likely that the sole purpose to be served by a work of such a comprehensive range was buttressing a theological judgment, namely that the calamity of the year 587 was just divine punishment, and would this word of explanation have been directed to a generation which Jahweh had in fact written off? It is much more likely that the purpose of all its theological expositions was to deliver to its contemporaries what is at bottom a simple religious message.[29] In our historian's eyes the period of the Judges ended in disaster also. But the fact that Samuel delivered Jahweh's word of judgment (I Sam. XII) and Israel was about to enter on a totally different kind of existence did not mean that Jahweh had finally abandoned his people. The Deuteronomist's verdict on the great cleft made in 587 would have been similar. The determinative thing which Jahweh was now waiting for from Israel was "turning" (I Sam. VII. 3; I Kings VIII. 33, 35; II Kings XVII. 13, XXIII. 25). Two passages having a close connexion with this historical writing and perhaps even belonging to it are particularly clear pointers to what Israel's task in the exile will be, namely, turning to Jahweh (שוב, Deut. XXX. 1–10, IV. 25–31, cf. I Kings VIII. 46ff.). Thus, in our historian's view, the judgment of 587 did not mean the end of the people of God; nothing but refusal to turn would be the end. The form to be taken by the turning is remarkably spiritual. It is in the heart. It was not therefore cultic. And its chief means was prayer.

As an appendix, we must touch upon, on its theological side at least, the problem of the connexion between the Deuteronomistic Book of Judges and the Deuteronomistic Book of Kings. Even the external link that binds them together is very unsatisfactory, since for a long stretch after the end of the Deuteronomistic Book of Judges in I Sam. XII the Deuteronomist's interpreting hand abandons us, and only again comes into action with the story of Solomon (I Kings III). Why did the Deuteronomist, who is usually so ready to talk and so glad to interpret, leave the whole complex of traditions about David without any comment? The suggestion that he possessed nothing to add to it is untenable

[29] For what follows, see H. W. Wolff, "Das Kerygma des deuteronomistischen Geschichtswerkes," in Z.A.W., 1961, pp. 171ff.

in view of the part which David plays in his theology. But in particular, the main difference between the two books is in method of presentation. In the Book of Kings we find nothing of the cycles of apostasy, enemy oppression, repentance, and deliverance which Israel passes through in Judges. In contrast, in the monarchical period the Deuteronomist lets the sin mount up throughout whole generations so as to allow Jahweh to react in judgment only at a later day. With his copious extant literary material dealing with political successes and reverses, it would not have been difficult for him to apply his classification according to generations to the kings as well. Why did he not do so? Why did he sit in judgment on the kings, but not on the judges? Why does he insist on the fact that the history of the monarchy was a history of the creative word of Jahweh, while in the period of the judges he makes the driving force derive from the judges' *charisma*? Why in the period of the judges does he make a distinction between the judges and the attitude of the people ("and yet they did not listen to their judges either," Jg. II. 17), while in the monarchical period he gears everything to the disposition of the kings, behind whom the people withdraw like a *massa perditionis* or *salutis*, and upon whom the guilt of the people is unhesitantly loaded? It is difficult to think that the editing of the Book of Judges and that of the Book of Kings could have taken place as a single piece of work.

7. THE HISTORICAL WORK OF THE CHRONICLER[1]

Israel, that is, the post-exilic community which regarded itself as the Israel, once more set about interpreting herself and setting out her credentials in a major historical work. This peculiar characteristic of hers of expressing the deposit of her faith in the form of repeated historical sketches probably reaches its highest degree of singularity in the historical work of the Chronicler (the Books of Chronicles, Ezra, and Nehemiah). What can we say about the self-consciousness of a provincial cultic community tolerated by the Persian Empire which yet portrays history from Adam onwards as taking place all for her own sake! Of all the histories in the Old Testament it is the Chronicler's which embraces the longest time-span: it runs from Adam right up

[1] M. Noth, *Überl. Studien*, pp. 110ff.; W. Rudolph, "Problems of the Books of Chronicles," in *Vet. Test.*, 1954, pp. 401ff.; A. Bea, "Neuere Arbeiten zum Problem der biblischen Chronikbücher," in *Biblica*, 1941, pp. 46ff.; G. von Rad, *Das Geschichtsbild des chronistischen Werkes*, Stuttgart 1930.

to the time after Nehemiah. The historical situation out of which it arises (between 400 and 300 B.C.) is completely different from the one in which the Deuteronomist had written. The latter was still stunned by a great calamity. But the time of the Chronicler was instead a quiet period politically, one in which at least external conditions for the Jewish community had for long been stabilised again. Admittedly, about conditions in Palestine "there is a silence such as never was before or after"[2]; so that we are not in the position to state with certainty any urgent reason why this work came into being.[3] Its literary basis is made up of the Deuteronomistic historical work, but over and above this the author worked up the historical picture from a copious body of edifying narrative material which is for the most part of very late date.[4] But he regularly interfered with his originals and sources, sometimes by omissions or slight insertions, sometimes by revision or rearranging the sequence of events, in a much more arbitrary way than the Deuteronomist did—the latter as a rule handed on the older material intact. Nevertheless this did not lead to internal unity in the Chronicler's work. The literary revisions are splintered up to serve very different purposes, yet the reader often finds a lack of consistency in the way the writer carries out his purpose. One cannot avoid the impression of a certain mental exhaustion—at least in the way the material is presented. And in theological clarity too, in consistency and inner unity, the Chronicler is not nearly the equal of the Deuteronomistic work.

For its picture of Jahweh's action in the monarchical history, Chronicles without any doubt stands on the shoulders of the Deuteronomistic history. It too is concerned to point out a relation of correspondence between guilt and punishment; the only difference is that it raises this correspondence to the level of complete rational proof—no disaster without guilt, no sin without punishment.[5] In the fifth year of

[2] E. Reuss, *Die Geschichte der hl. Schriften des A.T.*, 2nd edn. Braunschweig 1890, p. 540.

[3] None the less, it is a very obvious assumption that Chronicles was interested in the delimitation of the community from the Samaritans, and that it wanted to prove that the cultic community at the Jerusalem Temple was the true Israel. Noth, *Überl. Studien*, pp. 164ff., 178; W. Rudolph, *Chronikbücher* (Hb. A.T.), Tübingen 1955, pp. viiif.; K. Galling, *Die Bücher der Chronik, Esra, Nehemia* (A.T.D.), Göttingen 1954, p. 15.

[4] A literary analysis of the work, with full treatment of the problem of the sources, is given by Noth, *Überl. Studien*, pp. 110ff.

[5] For what follows see J. Wellhausen, *Prolegomena*, pp. 203ff.

the reign of Rehoboam the Pharaoh Shishak plundered Jerusalem (I
Kings XIV. 25f.). But, going beyond the Deuteronomist, the Chronicler
informs us that in the fourth year of his reign Rehoboam "forsook the
law of Jahweh" (II Chron. XII. 1). King Asa became affected by a
serious illness in his old age (I Kings XV. 23)—he had, of course, as the
Chronicler, going beyond the Deuteronomist, reports, not relied upon
Jahweh in a war with Baasha, and had caused the prophet who had
reproached him for this to be put in prison (II Chron. XVI. 7ff.).
Jehoshaphat had, along with the recreant Ahaziah, rigged out a mer-
chant fleet at Ezion Geber (I Kings XXII. 49): a prophet remonstrates
with him on the wrongful proceeding and prophesies the wreck of the
fleet (II Chron. XX. 35f.). Jehoram was warned in vain by a letter of
Elijah (II Chron. XXI. 4ff.). Because of his leprosy Uzziah (Azariah) had
to abdicate (II Kings XV. 5); but the cause of this illness was a serious
cultic encroachment (II Chron. XXVI. 16ff.). The villain Manasseh had a
longer reign than any other Judean king. This is explained, according
to the Chronicler, by his conversion and his humbling himself before
Jahweh, and by a reform of the cult which he introduced (II Chron.
XXXIII. 11ff.). These examples could be multiplied at will—they show
how greatly the Chronicler tightened up and at the same time altered
the Deuteronomist's pragmatism. The latter certainly had no hesitation
about sometimes pointing towards the consequences of the kings' sins
at a much later date, long after their death. On the other hand, the
Chronicler is at pains to show that Jahweh's judgment or salvation still
affected each generation individually. Now, here the theologian must
demonstrate that he has the capacity to make distinctions. No doubt
the way in which the Chronicler sets forth what he wants to say is
open to grave suspicion. A theologian has here made the attempt to
grasp Jahweh's dealing with Israel rationally. On the other hand we
must not fail to catch what it is that the writer wants to hammer
home to his readers in this critique, namely that each generation stands
immediately before Jahweh, and stands or falls with its anointed. To
understand this presentation, which is certainly a very forced one, we
must recognise that here the Chronicler is making his contribution to
one of the hardest problems which cropped up in later Jahwism,
namely the question of the share of the individual in Jahweh. That
Jahweh was the God of Israel, and that Israel had life and land and
blessing from him, had for long been established. But how was the
individual's share or the individual generation's share in Jahweh's gifts

measured? It is with the solution of this problem that we see the later Wisdom literature in particular struggling.[6] The contribution of the Chronicler seems to us pretty unsatisfactory: but it has to be appreciated that, in the great dilemma (the last possible point where Jahweh's activity could still reach a king was the granting or withholding of solemn burial!), he never let himself on any consideration be forced from the position that Jahweh confronted each generation quite immediately and with his whole revelation. Admittedly, in proportion as the Chronicler strove to assign to each generation complete immediacy to Jahweh, he lost sight of the understanding of the history of Israel as a unity, in the way that was still alive for the Deuteronomist. His picture threatens to disintegrate into a large number of single actions of Jahweh.

The Chronicler's account of the history starts with David. This at the same time gives the keynote for the most important theme in the whole work, for what does it contain apart from David? Without David there would not even be the Levitical offices, in which the writer has so great an interest. Now, the picture which the Chronicler draws of David is admittedly very different from the one given in II Samuel. But this is of course in no way surprising, since we have seen how far the picture of David given by the Deuteronomist already diverges from the old sources.[7] The reader is now told nothing about David's rise to power or his chequered activities in Judah and with the Philistines, nothing about Bathsheba, and nothing about his humiliation due to Absalom's rebellion. The David of Chronicles is a spotless holy king who delivers solemn orations. He and his sons do not rule in Israel, but in the "kingdom of Jahweh" (I Chron. XXVIII. 5)—according to I Chron. XXIX. 23 Solomon occupies "the throne of Jahweh" (similarly in II Chron. IX. 8, XIII. 8). We saw earlier that it has to be granted that the old idea of the nature of the Davidic dynasty remains unaltered by these formulae[8]; but when the Chronicler—going to

---

[6] See below, pp. 443f.

[7] "See what Chronicles has made out of David! The founder of the kingdom has become the founder of the Temple and the public worship, the king and hero at the head of his companions in arms has become the singer and master of ceremonies at the head of a swarm of priests and Levites; his clearly cut figure has become a feeble holy picture, seen through a cloud of incense." This famous criticism by Wellhausen (*Prologomena*, p. 182) does not correspond to the facts of the case to the extent that the Chronicler on his part inherited this very much changed picture of David. See above, p. 345, but also II Sam. VII. 2 and I Kings V. 17.   [8] See above, p. 321.

some extent beyond his literary originals—emphasises them to such a degree, he is expressing something which must have been important for himself and for his age; that is, in his miserable age when there were no kings, the Chronicler is the guardian of the messianic tradition. If—again revising his originals—he made the Nathan prophecy penetrate right down into the post-exilic period, then he was obviously still waiting for its fulfilment.[9] We may certainly read off the picture of the one whom he awaited from his great original David—he would be a king in whose hands two offices, the royal and the priestly, were united. Not that he would himself function as priest: but he would look on the care of the sanctuary and the ordering of sacral offices as the first of his main duties. David was of course the instigator of the building of the Temple (I Chron. xxiiff.) and—a second Moses—he had "the pattern" (תבנית) ready and handed it over to Solomon (I Chron. xxviii. 11f., 18f.; cf. Ex. xxv. 9, 40); he had—again a second Moses—called upon Israel to make a "heave offering," a freewill offering (I Chron. xxix. 3f.; cf. Ex. xxv. 1ff., xxxv. 4ff.). This confluence of the pictures of Moses and David at so late a time is very interesting, but the differences in the new formulation of the tradition are unmistakable. The Priestly Document had dealt with the erection of the Tabernacle before which the sons of Aaron officiated. David busies himself with the Ark and sets up new offices for those who had hitherto been its bearers, the Levites.[10] The Chronicler achieves this clear demarcation of the Levitical ark tradition over against the Aaronic and Zadokite tent tradition by separating Ark and Tabernacle from one another and by drawing important conclusions from the separate existence of the two cultic objects in the time of Solomon. In Solomon's day the Tabernacle still stood in Gibeon, and the priests acted there with their sacrifices (I Chron. xxi. 28f.; II Chron. I. 1–6); but the Ark had already been transferred to Jerusalem. With the transfer the function of the Levites as its bearers was at an end. At this time then David solemnly transformed the Levites' office, which had been connected with the Ark, by committing to them the praises of Jahweh (I Chron. vi. 16 [31],

---

[9] The prophecy of Nathan spoke of the descendants "who shall come forth from your loins" (II Sam. vii. 12); but with the Chronicler it is the descendants "who shall come forth from thy sons" (I Chron. xvii. 11).

[10] His interest in the Ark is unmistakable and, at such a late time, remarkable: I Chron. vi. 16 [31], xiii–xvii, xxii. 19, xxviii. 2, 18; II Chron. I. 4, v. 2, vi. 11, 41, viii. 11, xxxv. 3.

XVI. 1ff.). Of course, as is well known, these praises sung by the Levites give the whole cultic theology of Chronicles its characteristic tone, since this theology strikes the note of joy and thanksgiving without any discord. How different is the Priestly Document! In consequence we must not see in Chronicles in its present form simply the deposit of the theology of the post-exilic community as a whole, but only one of a particular trend, that of the Levitical Temple singers.[11]

A comparison of the Chronicler's historical work with the Deuteronomist's is difficult to carry into effect for the reason that the two works are so very different in purpose. The Deuteronomistic history was a great confession of guilt, for the construction of which the whole history of the monarchy was mustered. The Chronicler wrote in order to legitimate cultic offices founded by David, and in so doing he showed himself to be a representative of the messianic tradition as such. Nevertheless, the great difference in the understanding of the law in the two works calls for comparison. For the Deuteronomist, the law by which he assessed Israel along with her kings was the torah, that is, the summation of Jahweh's turning to Israel in salvation. On this revealed will of Jahweh as it had been formulated in Deuteronomy, Israel had made shipwreck. In the Chronicler too we find this spiritual understanding which still comprehends the law as a unity.[12] But a very much more formal and external mode of reference is commoner, namely in the many cases where he speaks of the correspondence of a certain cultic usage with a canonical ritual regulation.[13] Here a dubious understanding of the law is proclaimed. Is this still a law understood spiritually? Or is it not rather a very much more disjointed law, one which in fact has already become a matter of its letter, and which is composed of many ritual prescriptions taken absolutely? Here, understanding of the unity of the revelation of Jahweh is manifestly waning away.[14] The case of the concept of election is still more dubious. The

---

[11] A point recently raised by Rudolph (*Chronikbücher*, pp. xvf.) against Noth. It can of course be shown that the earliest version of Chronicles was not as yet aware of this advance of the Levitical singers and their claim; G von Rad: *Das Geschichtsbild des chronistischen Werkes*, Stuttgart 1930, pp. 102ff.

[12] I Chron. XXII. 12; II Chron. XII. 1, XIV. 3 [4], XV. 3, XXXV. 26.

[13] I Chron. XVI. 40; II Chron. VIII. 13, XXIII. 18, XXX. 5, XXXI. 3, XXXV. 12; Ezra III. 2, 4.

[14] The obverse of this understanding of the law is an equally suspicious optimism that it can be fulfilled, as expressed for example in the speech of King Abijah in II Chron. XIII. 10ff.

Chronicler uses the verb בחר without literary precedent eleven times: but the objects of this divine election are the king, the place for the cult, or the tribe of Levi.[15] The term was never employed in this way in earlier times. However to the Chronicler these specific acts of election were more important than the one act of the election of Israel.[16] Is not this too a disjointed election, especially when we bear in mind that the Chronicler says nothing at all about the election of Israel— he does not even know of a Covenant theology. Where then for him does the saving relationship which Jahweh vouchsafed to Israel begin? It is presupposed as already in existence with David, the point at which his account of the story begins. Thus, it really appears as if the choice of Jerusalem or of Levi was more important in his eyes than the choice of Israel! However, it would be wrong to think solely of the Chronicler's interest in ritual matters and in the legitimation of sacral offices. In his judgment of the important figures of the past, the standard he employs is whether they trusted Jahweh and called upon him in times of need, whether they "turned to Jahweh" and "sought Jahweh."[17] The term דרש יהוה is very old, and originates in the technique of the oracle. But later, during the period of the monarchy, in the struggle with the Canaanite nature religion, they got an axiomatic and exclusive sense— to turn to Jahweh was to avow the God of Israel, while to turn to other gods was to disavow him.[18] But what has the Chronicler in mind when he uses this formula at a time when the struggle with the Baal cult had long been decided? For the Chronicler, how far did "turning to Jahweh" include an act of avowal? We can answer the question from the speech of Abijah in II Chron. XIII, which in general seems to be a brief compendium of the Chronicler's theology. Attachment to Jahweh proved itself both in the recognition of and attachment to his cultic place, Jerusalem, and in the maintenance of the ancient traditional cultic regulations. Obviously, Israel's confession lost in content through this attachment to

[15] I Chron. XV. 2 (Levi), XXVIII. 4 (David); II Chron. VII. 12, 16, XII. 13, XXXIII. 7 (Temple), XXIX. 11 (priests).

[16] In connexion with these phenomena of theological dissolution, mention can also be made of the concept of "rest." In Deuteronomy it was the saving blessing *par excellence* which Jahweh had promised Israel (see above, p. 223). In Chronicles it is a gift which was offered bit by bit to individual kings and their times (I Chron. XXII. 9; II Chron. XV. 15, XX. 30).

[17] Miraculous hearing of prayer, II Chron. XIII. 13ff., XIV. 8ff. [9ff.], XXXII. 20.

[18] I Chron. XXII. 19, XXVIII. 9; II Chron. XII. 14, XIV. 3, 6, XV. 12f., XVI. 12, XX. 3, XXII. 9, XXVI. 5; Ezra VI. 21.

external things; but on the other hand the attitude taken to wholly external orders—over against the Samaritans, for example—could as well have become a *status confessionis*. Thus, still many a theological scruple may steal over the reader who takes it all into consideration. Certainly, what is most serious of all is the denial of the realities of human life, the "extent [to which] the veil is drawn over the scandalous falls of saints."[19] But with it all we must always ask whether a theology which saw Israel's existence in the eyes of Jahweh as so strongly conditioned by praise could have strayed so very far from the proper road.

[19] J. Wellhausen, *Prolegomena*, p. 178.

ISRAEL BEFORE JAHWEH
(Israel's Answer)

I. METHODOLOGICAL PRECONSIDERATION

IF we reduce the comprehensive accounts of her history which Israel wrote to what is basic theologically, that is, to those actions of Jahweh which were constitutive for Israel, the result is as follows: Jahweh twice intervened in Israel's history in a special way, to lay a basis of salvation for his people. The first was in the complex of acts which are gathered together in the avowal made by the canonical saving history (that is, from Abraham to Joshua), the other was in the confirmation of David and his throne for all time. Round the first datum—Israel became the people of Jahweh and received the promised land—lies the Hexateuch with its wealth of traditions, to unfold this work of Jahweh adequately and to interpret it. The other, the choice of David and his throne, became the point of crystallisation and the axis for the historical works of the Deuteronomist and the Chronicler. No doubt, according to Israel's faith, Jahweh had also accompanied his people beyond these complexes at every hour and in every place, and had everywhere shown himself lord of her history. But this was something different—it was going on with the building on a foundation already laid, not laying a foundation itself. On these two saving data rested the whole of Israel's existence before Jahweh. Even the prophets in their proclamation of the new creation of Israel cannot hark back to any other than them, the covenant at Sinai and the covenant with David.

When these saving acts had happened to her, Israel did not keep silent: not only did she repeatedly take up her pen to recall these acts of Jahweh to her mind in historical documents, but she also addressed Jahweh in a wholly personal way. She offered praise to him, and asked him questions, and complained to him about all her sufferings, for Jahweh had not chosen his people as a mere dumb object of his will in history, but for converse with him. This answer of Israel's, which we gather for the most part from the Psalter, is theologically a subject in itself. It shows us how these acts affected Israel, and how Israel on her side accepted and understood this existence in immediacy with

Jahweh and in proximity to him, that is, the steps which, in this proximity to Jahweh, she took to justify or to be ashamed of herself, in her own eyes and before Jahweh. But it also shows how in this intercourse with Jahweh Israel was revealed to herself and how she pictured herself when she came before Jahweh to speak to him. Here then if anywhere can we hope that the basic features of a theological doctrine of man will become clear—that is, that we may see *the* picture of man set over against the living God, and not merely a variant of the many pictures which man has made of himself. Recently the attempt has often been made to reproduce the picture which the Old Testament draws of man by means of summoning up all the material in any way relevant. This can be done, and it is absolutely necessary for the understanding of the texts. But still it is doubtful whether with this picture of a being made up of flesh (בשׂר) and life (נפשׁ), an embodiment of a collective rather than of an individual in our sense of the word, one curiously incapable of forming abstract concepts, completely and absolutely dependent on the deity and surrendered to his will, sinful, yet able to find expiation, etc.—it is doubtful whether more can be got from this picture of man than just a variant of the understanding of man generally common in the ancient East. Such a neutral method of taking a cross-section can hardly produce more than this, unless some special features in the direction of the relationship to God become visible. But in fact, in the course of her converse with Jahweh Israel did make further striking statements about herself over and above those general concepts of man which theologically do not amount to much. The way in which she saw herself before God, and pictured herself before him, is worth the highest attention theologically. In what follows we shall have to keep our eyes firmly fixed on this aspect of her answer.

2. THE PRAISES OF ISRAEL

Ceaseless was the praise which Israel offered up to Jahweh. That late period which gave to the Psalter the title *tehillim* even understood the totality of what Israel said by way of prayer, including the many psalms of lamentation and the more didactically meditative ones, as one single polyphony of praise to God.

The most ancient song of praise was probably the song of victory in the tents of the righteous, celebrating Jahweh's acts of deliverance. The song at the Red Sea (Ex. xv) preserves the memory of a sheer miracle—Jahweh threw horse and rider into the sea, and never an

Israelite had the slightest hand in the matter. It is different with the Song of Deborah (Jg. v). Certainly, it portrays Jahweh's coming to battle with great poetic force. But, strangely enough, the Song has hardly any thought about the way in which God intervened—the clans who were present "came to the help of Jahweh" (Jg. v. 23), and a mere woman slew the leader of the enemy's army.[1]

But it was above all in worship that Israel extolled Jahweh's acts in history. The hymns which take history as their subject obviously depend on a picture of the saving history which already possessed canonical validity at a very early time, and whose original form lies before us in the Credo of Deut. xxvi. 5ff. or in Josh. xxiv. 2ff. The simplest, and probably also the oldest, form of the hymn was the almost unconnected enumeration of the bare facts of creation and of the saving history which still lie before us as paradigms in Ps. cxxxvi.[2] But in the course of an epic widening out of those facts, the poems did not confine themselves solely to enumerating and glorifying the acts of Jahweh; they also made Israel and her attitude, yes, and her failure as well, the object of their meditation (cf. Ps. cvi).[3] In the process the hymn receives a sombre tone; and in proportion as interest in the sin of Israel increased in them, their mood changed greatly, and they became sombre confessions of Israel's failure and of Jahweh's judgment (Ps. lxxviii). All the same, they did not lose their character of praises in the process, for in old Israel praise could act as confession in a variety of ways. The verb הודה, which we generally translate as "to praise," properly means "to confess," "to accept," and always refers to a preceding divine datum.[4] If Israel made confession of Jahweh's acts in history, then, especially when this was done in artistic form, it was simply an act of praise. But Israel (and the ancient East) was acquainted with still another and quite different avowal which glorified God, namely, that which referred to one of God's acts in judgment. In this case we term it a doxology of judgment.[5] The best example of it is

[1] Jahweh inspired the fighters to take part and made even the stars join in the fight. Jg. v. 20.

[2] Pss. lxxvii. 16ff. [15ff.], cv, cxiv, cxxxv. See above, pp. 121ff.

[3] This has already been mentioned: see p. 283.

[4] H. Grimme in Z.A.W., 1940–1, pp. 234ff.

[5] F. Horst, "Die Doxologien im Amosbuch," in Z.A.W., 1929, pp. 45ff.; O. Michel, in Th. W.B.N.T., vol. v, pp. 201ff. The material from comparative religion —Lydian and Phrygian expiatory texts (inscriptions on steles) from the 1st century A.D.—is given in F. Steinleitner, Die Beicht im Zusammenhang mit der sakralen Rechts-

Achan's act of praise before his execution. Jahweh had made his wrath with Israel plain to see; Achan was ascertained to be the guilty one and was therefore enjoined before execution to "give glory to God" and make a confession (תודה, Josh. VII. 19). Through the doxology of judgment the guilty person not only acknowledged the justice of his punishment: his confession also had a very concrete significance in sacral law, for the action against him was thereby brought to an end (1 Kings VIII. 33). The situation in Ezra X. 7ff. is very similar. The community realises that it is lying under the "fierce wrath of Jahweh" (vs. 14), and it also knows the reason: it has therefore to make an act of glorifying God (הודה, vs. 11). Nebuchadnezzar's great decree to the nations begins with the praise of the most high God; then it goes on, in the personal style using "I," to give an account of the king's trespass and punishment (Dan. III. 31–IV. 34 [IV]): the whole is a typical doxology of judgment. Its real purpose is publicly to glorify the power and justice of the deity. The same is true of the very highly stylised prayers in Neh. IX and Dan. IX, and especially of Ezra IX with the characteristic conclusion, "Jahweh, the God of Israel, thou art just . . ." (vs. 15).

Again, "I give thanks to thee, Jahweh, for thou wast angry with me, thy anger turned away and thou hast comforted me. Behold, the God of my salvation; I trust and am not afraid. Verily, Jahweh is my strength and my song: he has become my salvation" (Is. XII. 1f.): this too is a doxology of judgment, though it stresses only one aspect, for the man praying makes avowal of a punitive act of God which is however now over and done with, because Jahweh has again shown himself as comforter. In such cases the term "avowal" can thus have a certain ambiva-

pflege in der Antike, Leipzig 1913. A touching example from the Old Egyptian religious community is the prayer of a labourer to "the mountain top." "I am an ignorant man who has no understanding and who cannot distinguish between good and evil. I once offended against the mountain top and it punished me; day and night am I in its hands. I sit on the brick like a woman with child; I call to the wind, but it does not come to me. I prayed to the mighty mountain top and to every god and every goddess. See, I say to great and small who are in the group of labourers, Be humble towards the mountain top, for a lion dwells in the mountain top; the mountain top smites as the wild-eyed lion smites and pursues him who sins against it. I called to my goddess, and then I found that she came to me like refreshing wind; she was gracious to me, after she had shown me the power of her hand. She turned to me graciously, and she made me disregard my sufferings and was my wind. Verily, the mountain top is kindly, when one calls to it. Nofer Abu declares it and says: verily, hear, all ye ears that are on earth: be humble towards the mountains of the west." G. Roeder, Urkunden zur Religion des alten Ägypten, Jena 1915, p. 57.

lence—in accepting a justly imposed judgment, the man confesses his transgression, and he clothes what he says in the mantle of an avowal giving God the glory. The essence of this and of every act of praise is that in all circumstances it declares God to be in the right. But we must always bear in mind that ancient Israel had very many more possibilities open to her for this glorifying recognition of the power and holiness and righteousness of God. Extreme examples are the extravagant hymns into which Job launches in his despair when face to face with the inaccessibility and hiddenness of God.[6] Israel also knows praise from the depths—indeed, it is God himself who "gives these songs in the night" (Job xxxv. 10).

The *genre* which Gunkel called "thanksgivings of the individual" is also closely related to the hymn, in that these also are avowals of Jahweh in purest form.[7] They too refer to an actual event, namely, the deliverance experienced in the person's life (the "thanksgiving" is therefore the bright counterpart of the much more sombrely attired "doxology of judgment"). Accordingly, the thanksgiving also always contains in one form or another an account of things that had actually taken place; the man praying was in trouble, he prayed, he promised a sacrifice to Jahweh and made a vow (Ps. LXVI. 13ff.), and Jahweh helped him. But in his avowal he does not primarily address Jahweh, as might have been supposed, but the community. Obviously he has an urgent desire to pass on to the community what he himself has experienced in the intimate depths of his own personal life, for all who are in a similar situation should do as he has done, cast themselves upon Jahweh. It is as if the deliverance was vouchsafed to the individual only in order that he should pass it on to the community, as if it belonged not to the man himself, but to the community. For him everything depends on his "not being silent" (Ps. xxx. 13), and on the avowal being made "in the great congregation" (Ps. XXII. 23, 26 [22, 25], xxxv. 18, xl. 1of. [9f.]). Only in the community do knowledge of such divine acts and their glorification have their proper place.[8]

[6] Job IX. 3ff., XII. 9–25, XXVI. 5–13.

[7] On the songs of thanksgiving see Gunkel and Begrich, *Einleitung in die Psalmen*, pp. 265ff. We have retained the old designation "songs of thanksgiving," but cf. the criticism of it in C. Westermann, *Das Loben Gottes in den Psalmen*, henceforth cited as *Loben Gottes*, Berlin 1954, pp. 7ff.

[8] The appeal to the community has very often practically the intention of teaching, and then it is couched in the form of didactic maxims: Pss. XXXI. 24f. [23f.], XXXII. 6ff., XXXIV. 12ff. [11ff.], XL. 5 [4], XLI. 2 [1]; Jon. II. 9 [8].

Besides the saving history, the other great theme in the hymns of the Old Testament is the action of Jahweh in nature. If Israel spoke of the creation of the world in her praise, in contrast with the theologically much more cautious Priestly Document, this praise used, for the most part unhesitatingly, the strongly mythological concepts of the struggle with the Chaos dragon[9] : Jahweh rebuked the waters of Chaos (Ps. CIV. 7), in fact, he crushed them (Pss. LXXIV. 13f., LXXXIX. 10f. [9f.]; Job XXVI. 10ff.). Elsewhere it is the marvel of the immediately creative word of command which is glorified (Ps. XXXIII. 6, 9). The older hymns, of which of course few examples remain for us, appreciated rather the miraculous and indeed the destructive aspect of the relationship of Jahweh with the world. The most imposing example of this archaic form of praise is in Ps. XXIX, where it is said that in seven thunderclaps Jahweh's storm falls upon the earth in destruction—"but in his palace all cry 'Glory'." This verse, 9b, is the key-verse of the whole psalm—it leads us away from the commotions on the earth up to the heavenly sanctuary where the company of the heavenly beings recognises and glorifies these very occurrences on the earth as a revelation of the glory of Jahweh. But utterances like these, which touch upon the incomprehensible element in Jahweh's action, continued right down into the later hymns as well—Jahweh looks upon the earth, and it trembles: he touches the mountains, and they smoke (Ps. CIV. 32), he removes mountains, scares the earth, so that its pillars tremble, and forbids the rising of the sun (Job IX. 4ff.). It is understandable that it is especially the hymns in the Book of Job which particularly emphasise this side of the divine action. In this context there is an extreme utterance in Deutero-Isaiah (XLV. 7), where in a hymn Jahweh is praised as "creating" (בָּרָא) darkness and woe. But on the whole, the later hymns are much more directed towards "the gentle footsteps of his day,"[10] that is, towards Jahweh's wondrous will for order and regularity in the world—the course of the stars, the diverse aspects of the weather, and the blessing of the harvest ripening on the earth. To be sure, this was not hidden from earlier Israel either, as is shown by the first part of Ps. XIX and in particular by the blessing which the Jahwist records in Gen. VIII. 22 after the Flood. Yet one cannot help seeing that in these later songs a profound change has come over the way of thinking, for they echo a stronger and more rational endeavour at understanding which is also

---

[9] H. Gunkel, *Schöpfung und Chaos in Urzeit und Endzeit*, pp. 29–114, is still up to date.   [10] Goethe, *Faust*, Prologue I. 24.

interested in the technical side of Jahweh's action in nature—the way the earth's disc is made stable upon the waters of Chaos, where the snow comes from, the tides of the sea, the ways of the animal world, etc. Just follow out the sequence of thought in Ps. CIV. Jahweh set a limit to the waters of Chaos; but he brought them back into a kindly use as springs and streams in the created world (the mountains were watered by the rain from above). The springs are for the animals and the plants, the verdure of the earth gives food for man, the trees are for the birds, and the mountains for the rock-badgers. The stars determine the seasons, of which the night season is made over to the wild beasts, but the day, in contrast, is man's, for his work, etc. What is expressed here is obviously a completely enlightened and, in fact, already scientific way of thinking which gazes with astonishment on a world in which myth has ceased to have the slightest part.[11] So it is not in the least surprising that this poetry worked hand in hand with the science of its day, namely the statistics of natural philosophy—it took both the subject of its praises and its order directly from the great encyclopaedias, the so-called *Onomastica*.[12] But all this ought not to be taken in the wrong sense, as if these poems were the products of rationalism as it is popularly understood, or bore witness to a rational view of nature in which religion is only a trimming. On the contrary: all their utterances contain *credenda*; they show the world as it stands revealed before God and as God sees it. The intention of Ps. CIV, which is in many respects paradigmatic, is indeed to show how the whole world is open to God—in every moment of its existence it requires to be sustained by God, everything "waits" on him (vs. 27); and it also receives this sustenance all the time. Were Jahweh to turn away from the world even for just one moment, then its splendour would immediately collapse (vs. 29).

The creation and preservation of the world by Jahweh was certainly one of the principal subjects of the hymns of the Old Testament, but it was not their last word. Praise still had something special to say about the world over and above this. Since it was so wonderfully created by Jahweh and is so wonderfully preserved, it has a splendour of its own, from which praise and witness issue: in other words the world is not only an object which calls forth praise, but is at the same time also the

[11] Ps. CIV. 3, 5; Job XXVI. 7, XXXVIII. 22–8, XXXVI. 27ff., XXXIX. 1ff.
[12] G. von Rad, "Hiob 38 und die altägyptische Weisheit," in *Vet. Test.*, Suppl. III (1955), pp. 293ff., reprinted in *Ges. Studien*, pp. 262ff.

subject which utters it. "All thy works praise (confess) thee," "the heavens praise (confess) thy wonders" (Pss. CXLV. 10, LXXXIX. 6 [5]). The later hymns point quite assiduously to those spheres which are remote from the community and which lie altogether outside the cult—the ends of the earth, the sea, the islands, the wilderness, the dwellers in the desert of Arabia; what do these know of Jahweh and his people? And yet from all of them issues praise (Is. XLII. 10–12). But this idea is in no sense a fruit of reflexion by later theologians—Isaiah himself heard the seraphim saying that "the glory of Jahweh fills the whole world" (Is. VI. 3), and from this it can be deduced that this theme was already current in the pre-exilic hymns.

The most detailed treatment of this *kerygma* issuing unceasingly from the heavens and the firmament is the first part of Ps. XIX. Indeed, it even insists on the undoubted legitimacy of this witness: day and night are passing it on from creation down to today—an absolutely unbroken chain of tradition. It was only a very much later era which became conscious, in connexion with this psalm, of the theological problem of the double witness to Jahweh "in nature and history." And so the psalm had appended to it for theological considerations what seems such an inappropriate continuation, the praise of the torah (vss. 8ff. [7ff.]). This addition is obviously intended to supplement the old song theologically: indeed, it perhaps also voices a certain doubt—however matters stand with this witness issuing from the created world, this *kerygma* is nevertheless a silent one (vs. 4a [3a]); therefore Israel's praise is directed by Jahweh's historical self-revelation given peculiarly to herself. Job says something similar when he concludes praise of Jahweh's acts as Creator with the words:

> "Lo, these are (but) the outskirts of his ways,
>   and (only) what a whisper do we hear of him!
>   But the thunder of his power—who understands that?"
>   (XXVI. 14)

As can well be understood, such questions could come up only on the margin in the sphere of praise. The theological Wisdom literature was the first to put the problem of whether God can be discerned in nature in a more basic way.[13]

In this context brief mention needs also to be made of that group of psalms which obviously formed the central point of a special cultic

[13] Cf. Job XXVIII. 28; Ecclesiasticus XXIV. 7–8.

procedure, the Enthronement Psalms.[14] These are poems which are
much more limited in subject-matter than the hymns, since their main
subject is the manifestation of Jahweh as king, and their most striking
characteristic the cultic shout, "Jahweh has become king" (מלך יהוה).
The details of the festival, and in particular the time at which it took
place, are still debated, but it is probable that it celebrated in dramatic
form Jahweh's rule over the world, and that it was a festival when joy
was at its height.[15] God went up with a shout: the nations are to clap
their hands thereat, and a new song is to be sung because of it. The
powers which Jahweh forced down are partly the chaotic powers of
the cosmos, partly the nations in the political sphere. It is striking how
in these impassioned poems what is peculiar to Israel and her existence
—saving history, election, the covenant, etc.—falls into the background.
The Enthronement Psalms are the least "Israelite" poems, and on that
account depend much more than the rest do on the interpretation of the
Psalter as a whole.[16] Zion and its gladness are certainly mentioned once
(Ps. XCVII. 8), and once too there is even mention of the priesthood of
Moses and Aaron (Ps. XCIX. 6f.). But it is just these odd references which
make us properly conscious of how unconnected with history, and
how "cosmic" and universal, is the outlook of these psalms. The subjects here are Jahweh and the world, Jahweh and the gods, Jahweh and
the nations—it is the moment of Jahweh's appearance to the world that
these songs celebrate. This therefore differentiates them theologically
from the hymns, which were more retrospective in their praise of

---

[14] The literature on the Enthronement Psalms threatens to grow beyond all bounds.
H. J. Kraus, *Die Königsherrschaft Gottes im Alten Testament*, Tübingen 1951, gives the
older literature; S. Mowinckel, *Offersang og Sangoffer*, Oslo 1951, pp. 118ff. A review
of the Scandinavian literature is given by A. Bentzen in *Th. R.*, 1948–9, pp. 317ff.
The number too of the poems which are to be designated as Enthronement Psalms
is differently given by different people. If the circle is narrowly drawn, then Pss.
XLVII, XCIII, XCVI, XCVII, XCVIII, XCIX certainly fall within it.

[15] After the conviction had become fairly well established that there was such a festival in the pre-exilic monarchical period, H. J. Kraus again pleaded for the dependence
of the Enthronement Psalms on Deutero-Isaiah (especially Is. LII. 7–10).

[16] This is undoubtedly connected with the fact that precisely in these poems Israel
came under the stimulus of foreign models both as regards style and content. The
best known to us is the Babylonian Enthronement Festival in the epic of the creation
of the world (especially Tablet 4). For this cf. Zimmern, *Das Babylonische Neujahrfest*,
Leipzig 1926. But it is doubtful if the Babylonian model influenced Israel directly.
Probably the stimuli originated in the much nearer Canaanite civilisation, in which too,
as the Ras Shamra texts show, an Enthronement Festival of the god was solemnised.

Jahweh as creator and as the one who directs the saving history; for the Enthronement Psalms revolve round a single event which is still going on and is already half present—admittedly, its full realisation is still a thing in the future, but details of its further course and its completion are already beginning to stand out clearly.[17]

Here—that is, in the cult and in the praise of Jahweh, and of his acts and manifestations—Israel also encountered in its highest form the reality of the Beautiful.[18] Every people and culture is vouchsafed a specific experience of the Beautiful. Quite certainly there is no particular significance in many of the statements which ancient Israel made about beauty; and the reason why there is nothing characteristic in them is that they move on the plane of the experience of beauty common to all men. Like all civilised peoples, Israel was aware of the beauty of man and of his bodily form (Gen. VI. 2, XII. 11, XXIV. 16, XXXIX. 6 and oftener); she was aware of the beauty of the moon (Song of Sol. VI. 10); like others, she was able to sense a speech, or a form of expression and language, as beautiful (Prov. XV. 26, XVI. 24; Ezek. XXXIII. 32). But where the primitive imitative instinct in Israel created works of art on a great scale, the case is already different. For pleasure in artistic imitation was no less strong in her than in any other people of antiquity. Israel's artistic *charisma* lay in the realm of narrative and poetry. (About her music, we are not in a position to speak.) It was especially in her monumental achievements in narrative, that with the most sparing use of any artistic means she rose to a spirituality of rare magnitude (for every form and every coming into form of a work of art is ever a mystery of the spirit).[19] The artistic peculiarity of Israel's

[17] Contrary to what he formerly thought, Mowinckel too has emphasised the eschatological element in these psalms. See *Offersang og Sangoffer*, Oslo 1951, pp. 183ff.

[18] No aesthetic of the Old Testament or of the ancient East has as yet been written. There are a few allusions to it in T. Boman, *Hebrew Thought compared with Greek*, trans. Jules L. Moreau, London 1960, pp. 74ff. Cf. as well C. Westermann, "Biblische Ästhetik," in *Die Zeichen der Zeit*, Berlin 1950, p. 277.

[19] T. Haecker, *Schönheit*, Leipzig 1953, p. 137. In this connexion we keep coming up against the odd misconception that the second commandment killed off all artistic activity in the sphere of religion. The truth is that in the act of making Jahweh and the splendour of his manifestation and his working visible in poetry, Israel was more daring than any other people. And it is just the prophets, who knew more about the nature of idolatry than anyone else, who go furthest in representing Jahweh in aesthetic images. That Israel had no images as objects of worship is quite a different thing. There are many images of Jahweh in her hymns, but no worship was offered to them: instead, they were themselves the expression of the worship of Jahweh.

poems undoubtedly stands in a very close relationship to her faith, from which in the last analysis it received its stamp, though it is hardly possible any longer to ascertain the relationship scientifically. For it is faith which creates for itself the form and the style.[20] But we are still far from being able to comprehend the ancient Hebrew mode of narrative and the poetic ability to make history present to the reader as a theological phenomenon. Admittedly, as far as we can see, Israel lacked all critical reflexion on the phenomenon of beauty and on artistic reproduction as such—she persisted in standing right down to the last in sheer naïve experience.[21] Her most intensive encounter with beauty was in the religious sphere, in the contemplation of Jahweh's revelation and action; and because of this concentration of the experience of beauty upon the *credenda*, Israel occupies a special place in the history of aesthetics. Starting once again from Ps. CIV, no one can fail to see that its subjects are not communicated in objective terms, but with every evidence of joyful emotion. Now this pondering upon and picturing of the ways of God in creation not only enriched faith's insights for Israel, but it also gave her at all times a great *delectari*. All her hymns, all her songs of victory and all her artistically shaped narratives testify to the fact that she perceived a strong aesthetic element as well in the actions wrought by Jahweh. Indeed we saw above how Israel's praises were attuned to the tone of Is. VI. 3, and this means that in giving glory the people of God already had part in the *delectari* of the angels. But this kind of thing by no means took place only in cultic acts of praise: the poems of the Wisdom literature, which is reproached with being so sober, brims over with sheer delight in Jahweh's creation[22]—already when the foundation stone of the world was laid the choir of angels sang (Job XXXVIII. 7). The Wisdom literature finds God's action in spheres remote from men particularly wonderful. That he pours forth the rain, the most precious thing in nature's household, over the very desert, makes a mockery of all rational economy (Job XXXVIII. 36). And the charming miniatures of the wild horse (Job

[20] This has been shown by E. Auerbach in a superb comparison of an episode in the Odyssey with Gen. XXII. *Mimesis. Die Narbe des Odysseus*, Bern 1946, pp. 7ff.

[21] The formula that "God is the author of all beauty" (Wis. XIII. 3) certainly corresponds to the idea held by earlier Israel, but it nevertheless already reveals a theoretic concern with the phenomenon of the beautiful. For earlier Israel was not even in the position to comprehend "the" beautiful as an abstraction.

[22] Pss. CIV, CXLVIII; Job IX. 3ff., XII. 9ff., XXVI. 5ff.; cf. Ecclesiasticus XLIII; the Song of the Three Men in the Fiery Furnace (LXX).

XXXIX. 19ff.), and of Behemoth, "which you cannot bind for your little girl" (Job XL. 24), and of the ostrich, to which "God gave no share of understanding" (Job XXXIX. 17), all agree that in this creation all is splendid, splendid even without purpose. These poems positively over-flow with an intoxication of beauty which cannot possibly be further intensified. But we must say this: admittedly the objects thus contem-plated are all perfectly real things belonging to our world, but this *delectari* of Israel was not for their own sake, but only as they became visible in their reality in the context of faith, in their relationship to God. Therefore for man too, to sing praises is "fair" ("pleasing," "comely," Ps. XCII. 2. [1], CXLVII, 1)—it means aesthetic satisfaction for him when he can offer up to God in praise the splendour which God granted to the world and man.

But the highest beauty in all creation was Jahweh's condescending to and entering into Israel's historical existence. This comes to expression first and foremost in the description of theophanies, in which Israel took delight from her earliest times right down to the latest writing of psalms, and which contain what are probably the most intensified statements about beauty in the whole of the Old Testament.[23] Jahweh shines forth (יפע hiph., Deut. XXXIII. 2; Pss. L. 2, LXXX. 2 [1], XCIV. 1), his brightness (נגה, Ps. XVIII. 13 [12]; Hab. III. 4) appears, dark clouds are about his feet, brightness goes out from him (Ps. XVIII. 10, 13 [9, 12]), the earth trembles, the age-old mountains split asunder (Hab. III. 6; Jg. V. 4f.), the foundations of the earth are uncovered (Ps. XVIII. 16 [15]). But even this terror has supreme splendour. He appears in this way in order to help his people. Even when Jahweh appears "in the glory of his majesty" (הדר גאונו Is. II. 19) for judgment, to cast all human vainglory down into the dust, even there the prophets' eye gazes with delight on his self-manifestation and the phenomena which accompany it. Isaiah and Zephaniah sing in hymnic style of the final theophany at the Day of Jahweh.[24] The descriptions of theophanies are undoubtedly the most central subject of an Old Testament aesthetic, for they reveal more clearly than all else how the special experience of

[23] Jg. V. 4ff.; Deut. XXXIII. 2ff.; Is. XXX. 27ff.; Mic. I. 3f.; Nah. I. 3*bff.*; Hab. III. 3ff.; Pss. XVIII. 8ff. [7ff.], LXVIII. 8f. [7f.], XCVII. 3ff. The large number of descriptions of theophanies, and in particular their comparative similarity, is not as yet satisfactorily explained (cf. the tables in Westermann, *Loben Gottes*, p. 66). Are they related to a dramatic event in the cult? And how are we to picture them? Cf. A. Weiser, "Die Darstellung der Theophanie in den Psalmen und im Festkult," in *Festschrift für A. Bertholet*, pp. 513ff.   [24] Is. II. 10ff.; Zeph. I. 14ff.

God undergone by Israel also became normative for the special features in the experience of beauty. But beauty was also a characteristic of the saving blessings, particularly of the promised land, about whose beauty others besides Deuteronomy never tire of speaking (Deut. I. 35, III. 25, VIII. 7, 10, XI. 12 and frequently, XXVI. 9, 15; cf. especially Num. XXIV. 5ff.). Finally, man finds that he is beautiful, when he can recognise himself as an object of the divine pleasure, when God "had lifted up his head."[25] A particular subject is the Psalmist's delight in the "broad place," the spacious scene on which Jahweh has placed those whom he blesses.[26] There is no doubt about it: Israel felt Jahweh, his revelation, and his saving gifts to be beautiful (Ps. CXLV. 5). But Israel's most characteristic feature lies in the fact that she accompanied Jahweh's condescension to her, which went even to the point of a divine *kenosis*, with statements about beauty. Beauty was in the revelation of his will (Ps. CXIX *passim*), and beauty also belonged to Zion. But what was so splendid about the Zion of the monarchical period except that it was the object of God's choice? Yet, because of this fact it was assigned the title of "perfect beauty" (כְּלִיל יֹפִי, Ps. L. 2), and is called "the delight of all the world" (Ps. XLVIII. 3 [2]). The same holds true for the king, who is described as "the fairest of the sons of men" (Ps. XLV. 3 [2]). But it would not be wise to set this emphatic expression in absolute contrast to the other, the Servant of God who has no form or beauty (Is. LIII. 2), for with the latter as well there is a splendour (otherwise he would not be pictured in poetic prose), only it is much more hidden. This bold accompaniment of the movement of the hidden God, in which Israel was still able to perceive splendour even in the deepest *kenosis* of God's action, is certainly the most noteworthy characteristic in the Old Testament's utterances about beauty.[27]

We summarise what has been said in a few provisional propositions: (1) For Israel beauty was never something absolute, existing in its own

---

[25] Pss. III. 4 [3], XXVII. 6, XXXIV. 6 [5], LII. 10 [9], XCII. 11.

[26] Pss. IV. 2 [1], XVIII. 20, 37 [19, 36], XXXI. 9 [8], CXVIII. 5.

[27] But in the late period, probably due to Hellenistic influences, a clearly recognisable change begins to appear. The way in which ben Sirach in his "Hymn of the Ancestors" takes delight in the figures of history is already passing over into hero-worship (Ecclesiasticus XLIVff.). He certainly says in the Proemium that it was God who apportioned great glory to them (XLIV. 2); but in actual fact these highly praised men are very independent subjects of aesthetic estimation. The phrase, "how glorious he was when he . . ." (XLVI. 2, XLVIII. 4, L. 5) was foreign to the old story-tellers, because they never at all made man the subject of their praise.

right, but was always a thing unceasingly bestowed on the world by God. (2) Beauty was therefore a datum of faith. (3) Enjoyment of this beauty of God is truly present as early as the hymns, and it is most certainly present in the utterances of the prophets as something anticipated, that is, it is orientated towards an eschatological fulfilment: it is perception in faith and faith perceived. (4) Israel perceived splendour even in the workings of the divine *kenosis* and hiddenness. (5) For Israel beauty was something that happened rather than something that existed, because she understood it as the result of God's action and not of God's being.

If we turn back again to the cultic psalms of praise in the more restricted sense and once again ask the question of their *Sitz im Leben*, the only references which furnish us with any details are admittedly late. But the information which they afford is important for theological assessment. After all, there are two passages which let it be very clearly seen that the singing of hymns was an accompaniment of the offering of sacrifice.[28] We should keep this coincidence of the two procedures in mind, in order to guard against making the one or the other absolute, for only together do they constitute the complete cultic act. There is therefore no reason to be dismayed at the purely material aspect of the rituals in P, any more than there is for clinging one-sidedly to the spirituality of the hymns.[29] There are, however, a few expressions which rank the spiritual sacrifice of praise higher than the material sacrifice. "He who confesses me in a sacrifice of praise (תודה), honours me" (Ps. L. 23). "Let my prayer stand as incense before thee, and the lifting up of my hands as an evening sacrifice" (Ps. CXLI. 2, cf XL. 7ff. [6ff.], LI. 17f. [16f.], LXIX. 31f. [30f.]). The importance of these expressions is obvious: but as things still are today, we must beware of seeing in them the most valid criticism, and indeed the spiritual "supersession," of worship by blood-sacrifice as such.[30] They did not supersede it, and

---

[28] II Chron. XXIX. 25ff.; Ecclesiasticus L. 11–18.

[29] "The soul stands before its God freed from the bonds of the cult," Gunkel and Begrich, *Einleitung in die Psalmen*, p. 278.

[30] Over against this it has to be said that these passages only want to substitute one cultic activity for another (Westermann, *Loben Gottes*, p. 19). On the other hand, it would be wrong, as Mowinckel does, to weaken the importance of these statements by reference to their provenance, the antagonism of the Temple singers to the priestly caste and the latter's overestimation of their part in the cult. The disputes between priests and Levites in the matter of competency which Num. XVI and Chronicles allow us to infer, were certainly not edifying. But what would the upshot be if we

were not meant to do so. They derive from the traditions of the Temple singers, who certainly had good reason for confronting the idea of the cult held by the higher-ranking priests with their own somewhat revolutionary one. These utterances were therefore very extreme watchwords, which their authors certainly also meant to be taken radically, and which were well suited to shake people out of the complacency which was a constant danger besetting the sacrificial cult. But it is wrong to see in them the breakthrough to a general self-evident truth. The truth of these utterances lies in their harmony with all the orders and "truths" upon which Israel's worship rested, and from which it built itself up and received its complex character.[31]

It still remains for us to notice a fairly large body of expressions which set praise in a curious relationship with death—they are those which point out very forcibly that there is no praise "in death."[32] Ancient people were obviously disturbed by the fact that there was a dimension—nay more, a form of diminished human existence—in which praise was no longer possible. With death the individual's participation in the cult was extinguished: the dead stood outwith the orbit of the worship of Jahweh, and were therefore also debarred from glorifying his deeds.[33] Behind all these utterances lies more or less an ἀναίδεια (Lk. XI. 18) assailing Jahweh—he is after all acting to his own disadvantage in abandoning to death one who gives him honour.[34] We have thus stumbled upon one of the strangest propositions in the Old Testament's doctrine of man. Praise is man's most characteristic mode

were to measure every insight which flashes out in any dispute merely according to the interests which were in debate on the occasion! And further: the prophets' polemic against the cult should be kept completely separate from these passages. In the former it meant obedience to the commandments instead of sacrifice. But here it is a matter of the question of what sacrifices are proper. The observance of a cult is not at all called in question: only, the sacrifices are spiritualised. But Amos and Isaiah rejected the sacrificial hymns too (Am. v. 23; Is. I. 15).

[31] See below, pp. 395ff.

[32] Pss. VI. 6 [5], XXX. 10 [9], LXXXVIII. 11f. [10f.], CXV. 17; Is. XXXVIII. 18ff.; Ecclesiasticus XVII. 27f.; cf. Westermann, Loben Gottes, pp. 116ff.

[33] The religion of ancient Egypt had much happier ideas about the state of the dead: "the sleepers all together praise thy beauty when the light of thy countenance beams forth. . . . Dost thou pay no heed to them, then darkness veils them, and each lies once more in his coffin," Erman, Literature of the Ancient Egyptians, London 1927, quoted in Westermann, Loben Gottes, p. 117. Jahwism showed a particular intransigence over against death. Death definitely separated a man from Jahweh.

[34] Especially Ps. XXX. 10 [9].

of existence: praising and not praising stand over against one another like life and death[35]: praise becomes the most elementary "token of being alive" that exists[36]: from generation to generation the hymns of the thanksgiving community flow on ("bubble"!) (Ps. CXLV. 4ff.). How one-sidedly praise had its home in life and in life alone can be seen in the fact that the people of God at praise regarded itself as standing shoulder to shoulder with the community of the divine beings before the throne of Jahweh—to such an extent was it in antiphony with the community above that the command to strike up praise could even be issued to those above by those below. In this presumptuous order to praise the community on earth appears as "the leader of the praising universe."[37]

3. THE RIGHTEOUSNESS OF JAHWEH AND OF ISRAEL

1. There is absolutely no concept in the Old Testament with so central a significance for all the relationships of human life as that of צְדָקָה.[1] It is the standard not only for man's relationship to God, but also for his relationships to his fellows, reaching right down to the most petty wranglings—indeed, it is even the standard for man's relationship to the animals and to his natural environment. צְדָקָה can be described without more ado as the highest value in life, that upon which all life rests when it is properly ordered. But what do we mean by it? Theology has for long now ingenuously explained the concept in the light of her own presuppositions, that is, the presuppositions of the West.[2] Its content seemed to be given by the translation in the Vulgate (iustitia), and by the German word Gerechtigkeit, namely, a man's proper conduct

---

[35] Westermann, Loben Gottes, p. 117.   [36] C. Barth, Errettung, p. 151.

[37] F. Delitzsch, Commentary on the Psalms, London 1889, VOL. II, p. 414. Cf. also Pss. XXIX. 1, CXLVIII. 2.

[1] K. H. Fahlgren, Sedaka nahestehende und entgegengesetzte Begriffe im Alten Testament, Uppsala 1932; Pedersen, Israel I–II (Righteousness and Truth), pp. 336ff.; G. Quell, "Der Rechtsgedanke im Alten Testament, in Th.W.B.N.T., VOL. I, pp. 176ff.; K. Koch, Sdq im Alten Testament (Diss. Heidelberg 1953); H. Cazelles, "À propos de quelques textes difficiles relatifs à la justice de Dieu dans l'Ancien Testament," in Revue biblique, henceforth cited as Rev. bib., 1951, pp. 169ff.; F. Nötscher, Die Gerechtigkeit Gottes bei den vorexilischen Propheten, Münster 1915; E. Kautzsch, Abhandlungen über die Derivate des Stammes sdq im atl. Sprachgebrauch, Tübingen 1881; W. W. Graf Baudissin, "Der gerechte Gott in der altsemitischen Religion," in Festschrift für Harnack, Tübingen 1921, pp. 1ff.

[2] Even the accounts given by Quell and by Eichrodt (Theology, VOL. I, pp. 239ff.) are still too much determined by our forensic conception of righteousness.

over against an absolute ethical norm, a legality which derives its norm from the absolute idea of justice. From this absolute norm, it was supposed, issued absolute demands and absolute claims. In social respects justice so understood watches with complete impartiality over these claims and takes care that each man gets his own (*iustitia distributiva*). Thus, the only remaining question was, what is the norm that the Old Testament presupposes? But, oddly enough, no matter how urgently it was sought, no satisfactory answer to this question of an absolute norm could be found in the Old Testament.[3] The reason was that the question itself was a wrong one, and in consequence the statements in the Old Testament simply could not be brought into harmony with this way of thinking. It was H. Cremer who recognised the impossibility of applying this way of thinking to Biblical thought, and succeeded in breaking through to a completely different way of thinking which has so far been rightly accepted as proven, in its basic thesis at least.[4] As we now see, the mistake lay in seeking and presupposing an absolute ideal ethical norm, since ancient Israel did not in fact measure a line of conduct or an act by an ideal norm, but by the specific relationship in which the partner had at the time to prove himself true. "Every relationship brings with it certain claims upon conduct, and the satisfaction of these claims, which issue from the relationship and in which alone the relationship can persist, is described by our term צדק." The way in which it is used shows that "צדק is out and out a term denoting relationship, and that it does this in the sense of referring to a real relationship between two parties . . . and not to the relationship of an object under consideration to an idea."[5] To some extent, therefore, the specific relationship in which the agent finds himself is itself the norm: only, it must be borne in mind that people are constantly moving in very many relationships, each one of which carries its own particular law within it. A man belongs to the family, to a political association (clan, nation), he is involved in economic life, and, if circumstances so decree, he can also come into association with foreigners—every day may bring a new relationship. And over and

---

[3] "An analysis of the terms lying before us does not bring us any further than this concept of covering oneself with some norm or other." E. Kautzsch, *Abhandlungen über die Derivate des Stammes sdq*, p. 53.

[4] H. Cremer, *Die paulinische Rechtfertigungslehre im Zusammenhang ihrer geschichtlichen Voraussetzungen*, Gütersloh 1901, pp. 34ff.

[5] H. Cremer, *Biblisch- theologisches Wörterbuch*, 7th edn. Gotha 1893, pp. 273-5.

above all these, there is the relationship which Jahweh had offered to Israel, and which was chiefly maintained in the cult. Here too the same holds true—the just man is the one who measures up to the particular claims which this relationship lays upon him.[6] When Israel praises the justice of Jahweh, she thanks him that he stands on Israel's side and in his action avows himself to her. The Song of Deborah already speaks of "Jahweh's righteous acts" (צדקות יהוה) and by this term means his saving acts in history.[7] From then on the glorification of this *iustitia salutifera* never ceases. It reaches a climax in Deutero-Isaiah, though it would be wrong to maintain that it is only with this prophet that צדקה became a synonym for salvation (ישע). In Isaiah the synonymity of justice and salvation is determined by the language of the hymn (Is. XLV. 8, XLVI. 13, LI. 6, 8) and is in consequence certainly older than Deutero-Isaiah himself. No radical transformation or development of the ancient Israelite idea of Jahweh's righteousness is discernible.[8] This usage, attested earlier in the Song of Deborah, is interesting because the term צדקה is already employed in a transferred sense, that is, with reference to the effects of Jahweh's faithfulness to the relationship. But in spite of all the variability in what is said about Jahweh's righteousness, expression is given to an idea which was constitutive for

[6] The account here given holds good at the same time for kindred terms such as חסד, ישר, תם, etc., for this Old Testament group of ideas does not rest solely upon the radicals צדק. In particular, the concept חסד is very closely akin to that of צדקה and frequently overlays it. It too designates an attitude required by fellowship and includes a disposition and an attitude of solidarity, but in its meaning it tends still more than צדק in the direction of our word "kindness" or "loyalty," and so it expresses still more than the other beneficent personal disposition plus the actions that follow. (N. Glueck, *Das Wort hesed im atl. Sprachgebrauch als menschliche und göttliche Verhaltungsweise*, Giessen 1927. Cf. however on the point H. Stoebe, "Die Bedeutung des Wortes Häsed im Alten Testament," in *Vet. Test.*, 1952, p. 244; N. H. Snaith, *The Distinctive Ideas of the Old Testament*, London 1944, pp. 94ff.) ישר and תם are also terms denoting relationship, as the prepositions which are attached to them (ישר עם, II Kings X. 15; תם עם, Deut. XVIII. 13; שלם את, Gen. XXXIV. 21) make clear. שלום as well is not adequately rendered by "peace," for the word designates a state where things are balanced out, where the claims of a society are satisfied, a state, that is, which can only be made effective when protected by a society governed by justice; the "man without peace" is outside it.

[7] The צדקות יהוה, the saving actions in history, Jg. V. 11; I Sam. XII. 7; Mic. VI. 5; Ps. CIII. 6; Dan. IX. 16. Cf. as well Ps. XLVIII. 11f. [10f.]: "Full of צדק is thy right hand; Zion is glad, the daughters of Judah rejoice because of thy judgments (משפטיך)", and Deut. XXXIII. 21; Ps. CXXIX. 4f.

[8] Differently understood by Hempel, *Ethos*, p. 161.

Israel—Jahweh's righteousness was not a norm, but acts, and it was these acts which bestow salvation.

"Thy right hand is full of צֶדֶק: Mount Zion is glad" (Ps. XLVIII. 11 [10]). The individual too could experience this righteousness of Jahweh's in times of need, and had to confess it in a song of thanksgiving. "I have not hid thy righteousness within my heart, I have spoken of thy faithfulness and thy salvation (Ps. XL. 11 [10]); and in a song of lamentation there is the prayer, "Hear me in thy faithfulness, and in thy righteousness" (Pss. CXLIII. 1, LXXI. 2). This righteousness of God which an individual experienced was, too, a subject of praise and proclamation in the cult (Pss. XXII. 31, LXXI. 22). A special place where it was appropriate to speak of the righteousness of Jahweh was in the descriptions of theophanies, and this was also an obvious enough thing to do, for, where Jahweh revealed himself, his righteousness, that is, his loyalty to the covenant, was also revealed.[9]

Men's common life was also judged wholly from the point of view of faithfulness to a relationship. When Saul said that David was more righteous than he himself, he meant that David had taken the relationship existing between the two of them more seriously and given more heed to it than Saul could say of himself (1 Sam. XXIV. 17). The fact that David had not touched Saul when he was delivered defenceless into his hands is designated as David's righteousness (1 Sam. XXVI. 23). Naturally, it was quite frequently the task of the local judge to investigate a man's conduct with reference to his loyalty to a relationship, and to declare him blameless or deserving of punishment (הַצְדִּיק הִרְשִׁיעַ, Deut. XXV. 1ff.; Ex. XXIII. 7; 1 Kings VIII. 32ff.).[10] Nevertheless it cannot be held that this Old Testament concept of righteousness is specifically forensic, for it embraces the whole of Israelite life, wherever men found themselves in mutual relationships. And in particular, conduct loyal to a relationship includes far more than mere correctness or

[9] K. Koch has drawn attention to the deep roots which these utterances about righteousness have in the descriptions of theophanies, *Sdq im Alten Testament*, pp. 4ff. (Pss. L. 6, XCVII. 6, LXXXV. 14 [13]; Hos. X. 12.)

[10] In marked contrast to the ideas of it current amongst ourselves, in judicial processes in ancient Israel much greater prominence was given to the question of the accused's "righteousness," for the party who comes innocent from the suit is "righteous" (Koch, *op. cit.*, p. 77). צֶדֶק can also of course be used of the judge (Lev. XIX. 15; Deut. XVI. 18ff.): he was after all at the same time often prosecutor, and so had to take the relationship into account, especially with those whose case was weak, for שָׁפַט means "to help to make things right" (Köhler, *Theology*, p. 32).

legality, that is, righteousness in our sense of the word. Such dependence
upon one another demanded the showing of kindness, faithfulness, and,
as circumstances arose, helpful compassion to the poor or the suffering
(Prov. XII. 10, XXI. 26, XXIX. 7). In the scene in which Jacob appeals to
Laban's brothers to be the judge of his conduct—the term צְדָקָה has
occurred beforehand (Gen. XXX. 33)—he mentions only services
rendered which go over and above simple duty (Gen. XXXI. 36ff.). A
very extreme piece of evidence for צְדָקָה (in whose paradox the old
story-teller himself certainly delighted) is handed on in the story of
Tamar, the daughter-in-law of Judah. Dressed as a cult prostitute she
seduced her father-in-law and conceived by him. As she was being led
out to be put to death, the motive of her action became known. She
wanted even by the most extreme of means to raise up descendants for
her dead husband's family, and because she had shown loyalty to her
relationship to this family, she was "more righteous" than her father-
in-law, who had refused to give her his youngest son in marriage (Gen.
XXXVIII. 26). But what in the world has this to do with our concept of
righteousness? Thus our German word *Gerechtigkeit* is unfortunately
not only a very inadequate rendering of the Hebrew צְדָקָה, but is often
virtually misleading.

These two areas of relationship, of men with one another and of men
with God, seem to some extent independent, and certainly in practice
they often enough were. So the impression could be given that there
was both a secular concept of צְדָקָה and a purely religious one, and
that the latter was possibly only a product of later theological
reflexion—a secondary application, as it were, of the civil concept of
צְדָקָה to the sphere of religion, the relationship of men with God. But
that would be an utterly false description of the facts of the case. For
what we look upon as two areas of relationship divorced from one
another were bound together, just in this early period, in a continuing "primitive pansacrality." Jahweh took his people's part and
gave drastic evidences of his righteousness: but he also issued the orders
of life which alone made men's life together possible. His commandments were not indeed any absolute "law," but a kindly gift rendering
life orderly. "Jahweh is in their midst as צַדִּיק, . . . every morning he
gives his decision, like the light which does not fail" (Zeph. III. 5). The
prophet is thinking here of the manifold directions which Jahweh proclaimed in the cult, and also of those which he gave for the legal sphere,
in which his will for order is renewed daily. Here too it is once more

evident that Israel did not envisage herself as related to a world of ideal values, but to events coming from Jahweh. The צדקה of Jahweh was, too, a continuous event directed towards Israel and was consequently a subject of proclamation. It had always been Israel's conviction that her whole community life was sustained by a constantly forthcoming צדקה which flowed over upon her. "Jahweh's צדק is proclaimed" from heaven (Ps. L. 6). Here Jahweh's צדק is to be understood as his commandments, the revelation of which was regularly solemnised in the Temple at Jerusalem. People loved to solemnise Jahweh's commandments as צדיקים, that is, as beneficent.[11]

In what the Old Testament has to say about righteousness, focal points came to be occupied by the king and the monarchy: this again is not surprising, for as head of the people the king was regarded as the guarantor and protector of everything in the land making for faithfulness in community relationships.[12] In the courtly phraseology of the whole ancient East, monarchy and the realisation of ideal just conditions belong indissolubly together. But in this office even the king is only mediator and trustee—he depends upon the fact that his judgment and "his righteousness" are given him by God (Ps. LXXII. 1). This idea is reflected at its clearest in the messianic prophecy in Is. XI. 1ff.—wonderful *charismata* enable the anointed to make the divine will for justice prevail in his kingdom.

For all that, the commandments and the orders of the community's life were only one part of the great צדק which Jahweh unceasingly granted to Israel. We have already seen that great historical acts could also be understood as acts which showed his justice. But Jahweh's צדק was active not only in the sphere of history, it was also operative in places which we call "the realm of nature." Thus, following upon the acts of penitence occasioned by a plague of locusts, Joel proclaims salvation in these terms:

"Shout with joy, ye sons of Zion . . .
for he gives you the early rain in righteousness,
he makes the rain come down and the threshing floors are full,
the vats overflow with wine and oil." (Joel II. 23f.)[13]

[11] See above, p. 196.

[12] II Sam. VIII. 15; I Kings III. 6, X. 9; Pss. XLV. 5, 8, LXXII. 12ff., LXXXIX. 15, 17 [14, 16].

[13] The prophet looks on the promises as already realised and speaks in the prophetic perfect.

The king's righteousness, which was mentioned above, also leads to a miraculous increase of the people (Ps. LXXII. 3ff.). These references and those like them set us at farthest remove from the idea of righteousness current amongst ourselves: indeed, the question arises whether there are not still present in what the Old Testament says about righteousness ideas of which we take too little account, since they are foreign to our way of thinking. We understand צדקה primarily as a thing from the realm of ideas: from it conduct derives which, in consequence of the actions of the person concerned, has a beneficent effect in community life. But Israel's understanding was from the very beginning ontologically different.[14] Examination of the numerous references in which צדקה appears in connexion with the preposition ב suggests that צדקה seems also to have been understood in an oddly spatial way, as something like a sphere, or power-charged area, into which men are incorporated and thereby empowered to do special deeds. "They rise up in thy justice" (Ps. LXXXIX. 17 [16]); indeed, even "the mountains will bear prosperity for the people, and the hills, in righteousness" (Ps. LXXII. 3). When prayer is made in respect of enemies, "let them not come into thy justice" (Ps. LXIX. 28), then צדקה seems in fact to be understood in an almost spatial way as a power-charged sphere beneficial to man.[15] So too with references which represent צדקה in a material or even in a personal way, as for example, a foundation of Jahweh's throne (Pss. LXXXIX. 15 [14], XCVII. 2), as a messenger who goes before Jahweh (Ps. LXXXV. 14 [13]), as a garment with which people are clothed (Ps. CXXXII. 9; Is. XI. 5, LXI. 10), or as rain (not "like" rain) (Hos. X. 12; Is. XLV. 8). At all events, we have first to ask whether such expressions could not actually have had a perfectly realistic and direct meaning before interpreting them figuratively. Of course the exegete here encounters great difficulties in interpretation, for this spatial and material idea of צדקה is so strange to us that for the most part we can no longer establish for certain where it passes over, as of course it sometimes did, to really metaphorical language.[16]

[14] The credit of having unfolded the concept in its differentiation from all idealistic and humanistic ideas is due to Pedersen. Of course, his idea of צדקה as the health of the soul, the prerequisite of all blessing, a power upon which all the activities of the individual depend and which also radiates out to the community, needs correction, for Pedersen's basic thesis of the נפש as the seat of צדקה cannot be proved from the Old Testament.   [15] Koch, *Sdq im Alten Testament*, pp. 35ff.

[16] It would be wrong to take the personification of עבק as from the very start merely a free poetic convention. The process of splitting off a divine property or a

2. We have therefore arrived at a comparatively unified picture: from the earliest times onwards Israel celebrated Jahweh as the one who bestowed on his people the all-embracing gift of his righteousness. And this צדקה bestowed on Israel is always a saving gift. It is inconceivable that it should ever menace Israel. No references to the concept of a punitive צדקה can be adduced—that would be a *contradictio in adiecto*.[17] But if we put the question the other way round and ask how Israel's righteousness and the righteousness of individuals were conceived in relationship to Jahweh, what we find is not so uniform. We encounter in fact very diverse statements and very varied reflexions. Actually, what here comes under discussion is nothing less than the cardinal question of how Israel and the individual conceived of themselves in their existence before Jahweh. Initially, we notice that the references which mention human righteousness in relationship to Jahweh are only infrequently found in the earlier literature, while appearing extensively in the exilic and post-exilic texts. There must certainly have been some decided change. But it would be very precipitate to conclude forthwith that older Israel simply did not know of the demand for a righteousness in relationship to Jahweh.

Our best starting-point is the so-called liturgies of the gate, which represent a curious ceremony that took place at the entry of a procession into the pre-exilic Temple, and some idea of which is given in Pss. xv and xxiv. The people coming in seek admission at the gate of the outer forecourt, and ask what the prerequisites of this are: "Who may ascend the mountain of God, who may stand in his holy place?"

divine epithet and giving it an hypostatic independence can be seen everywhere in the religious world of the ancient East. In Babylonian mythology, for instance, *kettu* (law) and *mešaru* (justice) are reckoned as sons of Shamash—though it is easy to see that what is in question is qualities of Shamash which have become independent to the extent of personification. The case with the two Phoenician gods *misor* (conformity to law) and *sydyk* (justice) is quite similar. Cf. H. Ringgren, *Word and Wisdom. Studies in Hypostatization of Divine Qualities and Functions in the Ancient Near East*, Lund 1947, particularly pp. 53ff., 83ff.

[17] In connexion with the "doxologies of judgment" (see above, pp. 357f), the words "thou art righteous" appear to refer to a punitive righteousness of Jahweh. But it is better to take them in the sense of "innocent of charges brought" (Köhler, *Theology*, pp. 166f.). Cf. Lam. i. 18; Ezra ix. 15; ii Chron. xii. 6; Dan. ix. 14. In Neh. ix. 33 it means "thou art righteous, because thou hast been faithful." Nötscher's thesis that the prophets preached a penal righteousness is untenable. Cf. Cazelles, in *Rev. bib.*, 1951, pp. 173ff. Even Is. v. 16 cannot bear the onus of proof. In Amos and Hosea the idea of a righteousness of Jahweh's is completely absent.

To this the cultic officials answer from within: "He whose hands are clean and whose heart is pure, who does not direct his thought towards evil, who does not swear deceitfully. . . ." This means that a selection of Jahweh's commandments was put before those who entered. Admittedly, we do not have to conclude from this that in ancient Israel the fulfilling of the commandments was in principle antecedent to the reception of salvation in the cult, since those seeking admission were certainly not coming before Jahweh for the first time—they had been members of the community of Jahweh from the beginning. But this much becomes clear: those who came to worship were asked for something like a declaration of loyalty to Jahweh's will for justice. These commandments were regarded as perfectly capable of being fulfilled, and indeed as easy to fulfil.[18] The question whether those who sought entrance avowed themselves to be loyal to them now, and had been so in the past, was therefore nothing but the question of their צדקה. Hence "the gates of righteousness" are spoken of, through which only "righteous people" enter.[19] Indeed, we can quite safely generalise and say that every proclamation of the commandments— not just that in the ceremonial of the liturgy of the gate—was always at the same time a question about Israel's צדקה, her readiness for her part to say yes to the relationship of community offered to her by Jahweh. To this extent the ritual of Deut. xxvii. 15ff. already included the question of Israel's צדקה.

We take a further step forward with Ezekiel's excursus on righteousness in ch. xviii, for here the prophet has obviously incorporated in vss. 5–9 of his essay a liturgical passage which had taken shape long before his own time. To begin with, there is a series such as we find in manuals of confession defining the conduct of the man who belongs to Jahweh: "he does not eat meat offered in sacrifice upon the mountains, he does not lift up his eyes to the idols of the house of Israel, he does not defile his neighbour's wife. . . ." Thereafter follows what is certainly still a liturgical proclamation, "he is righteous," for this צדיק הוא is precisely of the same sort as those declaratory formulae

---

[18] See above, p. 195. Besides, Hebrew psychology makes absolutely no distinction between willing and being able, Pedersen, *Israel I–II*, p. 338.

[19] Ps. cxviii. 19f.; Is. xxvi. 2. The sayings about entering into the kingdom of God still speak of a showing of a δικαιοσύνη; the form taken by the liturgy in the gate lasted on as long as this; H. Windisch, in *Zeitschrift für die neutestamentliche Wissenschaft*, 1928, especially pp. 177ff.

preserved in great numbers in the Priestly Document, in which the priests, acting with Jahweh's full authority, declared the result of a cultic investigation.[20] This declaratory statement could equally well have run: "it shall be counted to him for righteousness," for, as we have already seen, this חשב was an important priestly function. The priests had, as Jahweh's mouthpiece, to give the final decision on what was pleasing or displeasing.[21] It was thus in a very real sense that the worshipper "went down to his house justified" (Lk. xviii. 14).

Ezek. xviii once again shows that even in pre-exilic Israel the question about a man's צדקה in relationship to Jahweh had already been very urgently raised, but in addition it also teaches us to take Gen. xv. 6 from a particular angle. If it is there emphasised that faith was "counted" as righteousness, this was certainly a striking and perhaps even revolutionary formulation for those contemporary with it. Because of its uncommon stamp, it betrays the fact that in its day the question of what then is "counted as righteousness" in the eyes of Jahweh was to some extent a living one, and had perhaps already become a problem; and it represents the thesis that taking Jahweh's promise seriously, and responding to it as something perfectly concrete, was the true attitude in relationship to Jahweh. On the other hand of course, we must not make the words absolute and exclusive, as if they ruled out any other possible way for men to exhibit righteousness, for they are of course bound up with Abraham's peculiar situation as the recipient of a promise with wide historical implications. Different situations might have demanded different expressions of faithfulness in relationship to Jahweh. Certainly, the Deuteronomic preacher's proposition that faithfulness in relationship to Jahweh consists in the acknowledgment and keeping of the commandments (Deut. vi. 25, xxiv. 13) corresponds much more to the general understanding than does that of the Elohist, for the latter is already almost prophetic in formulation. But Gen. xv. 6 and Deut. vi. 25 and the ritual which can be seen behind Ezek. xviii. 5ff. are agreed in this, that the nature of righteousness, and who the righteous man is, is determined by Jahweh alone, and a man lives as he acknowledges this—"he is righteous, he will live" (צדיק הוא חיה יחיה, Ezek. xviii. 9). It is in this sense that suppliants pray to Jahweh to let their vindication "come forth" (Pss. xvii. 2, xxxvii. 6). The Servant also regards his righteousness as some-

---

[20] See above, pp. 247f., 261f.

[21] For examples of this priestly חשב, see Lev. vii. 18, xvii. 4; Ps. xxxii. 2 [1].

thing which exists "with Jahweh," and he knows that his vindication will also take place openly (Is. XLIX. 4, L. 8). Of course, this righteousness which Jahweh attributes to a man can be lost—it can be forfeited through conduct or actions which run counter to community with Jahweh. When Jahweh is angry, then "all our righteousness becomes like a polluted garment" (Is. LXIV. 4f., *l.* singular with LXX). If that is so, in so far as the damage is not irreparable and Jahweh has not delivered the sinner up to death, the man must make confession of the offence before Jahweh and repent. What comes into question with these prayers of repentance is a cultic procedure like the doxology of judgment.[22] Elihu speaks of God's action as the teacher of a sinful man, how he can admonish him through pain and illness and bring him to his senses, and then he goes on: "if (then) he prays to God, then God is gracious to him, he can see God's face with joy, and God gives the man back his righteousness" (Job XXXIII. 26). This too obviously alludes to a ritual, according to which a prayer of penitence was followed by a declaration of righteousness by Jahweh.[23]

References to human righteousness in relationship to God are very much more frequent in the later literature, and this is initially to be explained as due simply to the fact that it was only in these writings that the individual got any great chance of speaking for himself. In the older period the individual was bound up with the life of the community, but in the course of time he clearly achieved independence of it. He became more conscious of himself and of his relationship to God and consequently felt a more urgent need to justify himself in his personal existence before Jahweh.[24] This severance from the community and achievement of independence from it must have gone very deep, for when we read Ps. I or Ps. LXXIII or Ps. CXIX, we at last see the

[22] See above, pp. 357ff.

[23] In all the terms that it employs the verse points to a procedure which was originally cultic (עתר means "to request by means of sacrifice"; similarly, "seeing the face of Jahweh" took place in the cult, and for the רצה of God, see above, pp. 260f.). We would like to know more about the procedure for this restoration of righteousness. Mic. VII. 9 seems to refer to it: "I must bear the wrath of Jahweh because I have sinned against him, until he pleads my cause and executes judgment for me. He will bring me forth to the light and I shall revel in his righteousness." A doxology of judgment is also found in Lam. I. 18. The odd allusions to a "going out of the right (or of righteousness)," Is. LI. 5, LVIII. 8, LXII. 1; Jer. LI. 10; Hab. I. 4a; Mal. III. 20 [IV. 2]; Pss. XVII. 2, XXXVII. 6, XCVIII. 2, also seem to derive from a cultic procedure.

[24] See below, p. 391ff.

individual צַדִּיק standing completely isolated in relationship to Jahweh and his revelation. It is as if there were only the timeless encounter of these two, Jahweh and his righteous one—all other community relationships are submerged, or have at any rate become irrelevant in relation to this one. If, however, we now ask what the essence of the צַדִּיק is, what are the characteristics that go to make him up, first and foremost is that the righteous man keeps the commandments. In this respect there has been no change from the earlier period, in which, as we saw, man's faithfulness to the relationship had to prove itself in recognising the commandments and keeping them. The ingenuousness with which the men at prayer constantly protest that they have kept the commandments and claim the title of "righteous" is astonishing.[25] To understand these statements, we must in no circumstances bring to bear upon them the question whether men can render adequate obedience in the eyes of God, for this lies completely outwith the range of these psalms' vision. We have seen, of course, that the fulfilling of the commandments was nowhere experienced as a burden, which men at best could only partially carry out, but was rather an act of avowal. In consequence, these men were ready to claim the title of צַדִּיק for themselves without further ado, since what was understood was something quite other than a moral self-evaluation. Century upon century they had been taught by the cult that Jahweh alone could bestow this title, and that he assigned it to those who clung to him. It is not in the least surprising, therefore, that the men designate themselves as the צַדִּיקִים, since anyone who participated vocally in the cult in any kind of way was צַדִּיק—the voice of those who were excommunicated, banned, etc., is of course not preserved. How little any presumptuous moral self-qualification was implied in this term becomes particularly clear from the fact that Israel stubbornly knew of two possibilities and two only—a man was either צַדִּיק in the eyes of Jahweh or he was not. All intermediate stages, all the shades between black and white, with which a moral evaluation has to reckon, are completely absent. If a man was צַדִּיק in the eyes of Jahweh, then he was so completely, and never in an approximate or an incipient way. This is the standpoint from which we have to try to understand the confidence, and indeed the eagerness, with which later Israel fashioned the picture of the צַדִּיק *par excellence* and applied it to herself. The positive characteristics of the צַדִּיק are, according to Ps. I, first a strong

[25] Pss. VII. 9 [8], XVII. 1–5, XVIII. 22–4, XXVI. 1–6.

emotion, namely a *delectari* in the revelation of the will of Jahweh, and next, the continuity of the inner relation of his life with this revelation of Jahweh's will. Now these two characteristics of the צדיק also recur, with abundant variation, in confessional form, particularly in Ps. cxix. The revelation of the will of Jahweh is a subject of the utmost joy—all spiritual striving after insight is directed to it; it fills the whole of the emotional life; it is simply the highest thing in life, whose worth nothing can outshine. These speakers positively revel in terms denoting perfection. Although their utterances are couched in the form of most intimate confessions, they are not to be taken in the modern sense of a soul's testimony about itself, and least of all as if an obedience actually rendered were reckoned up in them. In spite of the personal style, they are out and out type expressions, and as such definitely transcend human, psychological, and moral possibilities. What happens is that the speakers put themselves into the picture of the צדיק *par excellence*, and claim it as their own—indeed, they show an eagerness, a growing boldness, as they work this picture up from more and more angles, that could well take a careful theologian's breath away. In comparison with the older ideas, this picture has unquestionably been intensified, particularly in its working up on the psychological side, by means of terms which denote psychological perfection. It was certainly only in a limited group that this picture of the צדיק *par excellence* was fostered. To judge by all appearances, the piety which thus presented itself before Jahweh was a very spiritual one, and we have probably to look for its representatives principally in the circles of the wise men, who knew very much more than people have hitherto been prepared to assume about the bliss of "nearness to God" (קרבת אלהים Ps. lxxiii. 28). The bold idea of "delighting oneself," "letting oneself be spoiled by Jahweh," also belongs to the post-exilic theology.[26]

There are some isolated utterances which in very radical and pessimistic fashion deny man any צדקה before God. But no basic contradiction need be presupposed between them and those already noticed, if it is remembered that they are generally uttered in the situation of the psalm of lamentation and deliberately emphasise the forlornness of the man who is thrown back upon himself. If Jahweh were to "enter into judgment" with a man, no one would maintain his right (Ps. cxliii. 2).[27] These men of later days were therefore very likely still more conscious

---

[26] ענג hithp. Ps. xxxvii. 4; Job xxii. 26 (xxvii. 10); Is. lviii. 14.
[27] Similarly Job iv. 17.

than was earlier Israel when at prayer, that if Jahweh allowed a man to be righteous in his sight, he must be very compassionate and that human צְדָקָה could never reckon as adequate service in return (on this cf. the earlier Deut., IX. 4–6). In itself the idea that men's צְדָקָה had to evince itself in recognition of the commandments and keeping them had already been set forth in Deuteronomy (VI. 25, XXIV. 13: see above, p. 379). Thus, when later passages mention an "evidence of righteousness" upon which however Israel may not lean as she stands before Jahweh (Dan. IX. 18), a righteousness that has become as a polluted garment by reason of the wrath of Jahweh (Is. LXIV. 5 [6]), what is primarily in mind is the fulfilling of the commandments: only, the background of the passages is a deepened recognition of the inadequacy of any obedience that men may render. Basically, they do not deny the possibility of human righteousness; they do, however, deny that a man's loyalty to the covenant can in Jahweh's eyes reckon as adequate equivalent warranting and making possible his being declared righteous. To this extent the sharp contrast made in Daniel, "not on the ground of righteousness evinced by us, but on the ground of thy mercy" (IX. 18), is further indication of the very small extent to which legal ideas entered into the thought of later Israel on the process of declaring a man or men righteous. At the farthest edge of this canon there is heralded a decided narrowing and curtailment of the concept of צְדָקָה, in so far as in Dan. IV. 24 [27] the Aramaic צִדְקָה has the meaning of "good works," "almsgiving," with the aid of which a man can cancel out his sins.[28]

4. ISRAEL'S TRIALS AND THE CONSOLATION OF THE INDIVIDUAL[1]

1. The statements in the previous section now need, however, to be supplemented, for Israel's conceptions of the צְדָקָה of God and of Israel were only presented there in their basic structure, i.e., in somewhat abstract fashion. It was only at a very late phase in her existence that she made these ideas the subject of theoretical consideration: for

---

[28] This change in the term (צְדָקָה = ἐλεημοσύνη) is also to be found in Ecclesiasticus VII. 10, III. 30, XXIX. 12; Tob. IV. 10, XII. 9 (cf. Mt. VI. 1).

[1] J. J. Stamm, *Das Leiden des Unschuldigen in Babylon und Israel*, Zürich 1946, henceforth cited as *Leiden*; Eichrodt, *Theologie*, VOL. II, pp. 91ff., VOL. III, pp 1ff.; H. Schmidt, *Gott und das Leid im Alten Testament*, Giessen 1926; E. Balla, "Das Problem des Leides in der isr.-jüd. Religion," in *Eucharisterion*, VOL. I, pp. 214ff.

most of the time she lived with them uncritically and practised them in every situation of life. This life, in which Israel had to orientate herself with such basic presuppositions of faith, was a life full of suffering and serious dangers for community and individual alike. What this means is that Israel took a supremely realistic view of life's sufferings and dangers, saw herself as exposed to them vulnerably and without defence, and showed little talent for fleeing from them into ideologies of any kind. Rather, the concepts of her faith directed her to bring these actual experiences of her daily life into connexion with Jahweh. In her older period, indeed, she lacked any aptitude for the doctrinaire: she possessed, rather, an exceptional strength to face up even to negative realities, to recognise and not to repress them, even when she was spiritually unable to master them in any way.[2] It is to this realism, which allowed every event its own inevitability and validity, and found it so hard to permit the reader a simultaneous insight into the spiritual, that the narrative art of the Old Testament, especially in its earlier form, owes its darksome grandeur. Thus the whole concept of צדקה had to vindicate itself among a people possessed of a very marked sense of reality. The term reality is, of course, not without its problems. Men have not understood the reality of life, its inter-connexions, sequences, and events, in the same way at all times, for, even behind man's most elementary experiences, there already lies a certain "dogmatic" pre-conception. For this reason Israel's sense of reality has here, on one side at least, to be presented critically. Probably like most people outside the culture determined by the Enlightenment of the West, Israel too was convinced that there was a definite and even clearly recognisable connexion between what a man does and what happens to him, such that the evil deed recoils banefully upon the agent, the good one beneficially. Like a stone thrown into water, every act initiates a movement for good or evil: a process gets under way which, especially in the case of a crime, only comes to rest when retribution has over-

---

[2] Even in Egypt, which was close by, things were obviously quite different. "We know from all periods in Egyptian history that the Egyptian loved, as we say, to 'idealise' the actual events. But in the last analysis this idealising consists in the fact that certain political events, or occurrences in the national and personal life as well, are simply not allowed to exist, if the external, god-given laws are not to be overthrown. There is, for example, for the Egyptians no such thing as a weak or an unworthy king. . . . Thus, as the Egyptians see it and are bound to see it, a tension exists at all times between objective and factual historicity and subjective reality." E. Otto, *Die biographischen Inschriften der ägyptischen Spätzeit*, Leiden 1954, p. 2.

taken the perpetrator. But this retribution is not a new action which comes upon the person concerned from somewhere else; it is rather a last ripple of the act itself which attaches to its agent almost as something material. Hebrew in fact does not even have a word for punishment. The words עָוֹן and חַטָּאת can denote the evil act: but they can also denote its evil result, and therefore punishment, because the two things are basically the same.[3] In consequence there has recently been talk of a synthetic apprehension of life (for which things that we now see as separate were still a unity), or better still, of a sphere of action which creates fate.[4] The exegetical findings—especially in the Psalms and Proverbs— are clear. The matter is particularly plain in connexion with blood-guiltiness. Murder initiates a baneful process which, before overtaking the murderer himself, first of all brings his community into the gravest danger. Thus, for its part, the community has the strongest possible interest in identifying and eliminating the murderer. The baneful results issuing from an act can even be controlled by means of an exorcising formula. In disputed cases it could be said: "let his blood (that is, his blood-guiltiness) be upon . . ." (Josh. II. 19; Jg. IX. 24; II Sam. I. 16). Or prayer could be made to God to avert the blood-guiltiness from the community (Deut. XXI. 8). If the murderer could be caught, then the blood-guilt—though the term "guilt" is still far too spiritual—was "turned back" upon his own head, that is, he was put to death, and the disaster so initiated was thereby averted from the rest (הֵשִׁיב, II Sam. XVI. 8; I Kings II. 5, 31f.). The Old Testament has the most varied ways of expressing these connexions, and they are always very drastic, and resist any exclusively spiritual interpretation.[5]

Now, Jahweh took a very immediate share in all this. It cannot of course be said that Israel derived the knowledge of these connexions

---

[3] See above, p. 266.

[4] K. Koch, "Gibt es ein Vergeltungsdogma in AT?," in Z. Th. K., 1955, pp. 1ff. This idea is attested times without number in ancient Greece too;

> "With a lone voice I deny it.
> It is only deeds unholy
> That increase, fruitful in offspring
> Of the same breed of its fathers.
> Where justice rules in the house,
> Blest of God is the issue."—Aeschylus, *Agamemnon*, 754ff.

(trans. George Thomson, *The Oresteia of Aeschylus*, Cambridge 1938).

[5] Jahweh washes them away (Ps. LI. 3f. [1f.], he covers them (Ps. XXXII. 1, 5), he casts them behind him (Is. XXXVIII. 17), he casts them into the sea (Mic. VII. 19), etc.

specially from Jahweh—they were much too obvious for that. They were in fact a basic element in the general understanding of life, and, as such, more a part of that ancient oriental philosophy of life in which Israel also participated. But for Israel, with her belief in Jahweh as the universal cause, it was impossible to understand such an elemental process except in relation to his power. Indeed, these beneficial or baneful results of an act were referred back to Jahweh himself with the utmost immediacy. For he it was who eventually brought this process to its goal; he carried this connexion into effect: and hence the guilty party could appeal only to him in order to induce him to break this nexus and avert from the agent the disaster already impending. The decision whether a man should "bear his עָוֹן" or not rested solely with Jahweh. But in the maxims of the Wisdom literature, where the theme of the fate-bringing act occupies a great deal of space, the connexion between act and retribution is presented much more objectively and already almost in the sense of an immanent material law. Among a multitude of shorter maxims there are a number of sweeping and grandiose depictions of that immanent Nemesis which yet has inevitably overtaken the transgressor (Job xv. 17-35, xviii. 5-21, xxvii. 13-23). If here the reference to God as the author of this calamity recedes into the background, this is due to the special approach of the Wisdom literature which tackles the phenomenon in empirical fashion, that is, from outside.[6] One way or another, we arrive at the result that, in view of the existential connexion between act and consequence, it is out of place to speak of a "doctrine of retribution," for the idea of retribution, in that it understands "punishment" as an additional forensic act, implies a legal way of thinking which is absolutely foreign to this whole range of ideas.

Ancient Israel saw this idea of the indissoluble connexion between act and outcome as confirmed in daily experience. It was anything but a theological theory—it only became so in the later reflexions of the Wisdom literature; rather it was substantiated by countless observations in daily life. This fact will only become even partially comprehensible to us when we take into account the almost physical union of the individual with the community. At that time there was no individual so isolated and independent that his actions could remain more or less without consequence for the community (unless indeed, their very criminality brought them within the sphere of authority); there

[6] See below, pp. 426ff.

were only communities, which with all their members felt themselves to be organic units. For them no action or omission of the individual was irrelevant. Conduct loyal to the relationship benefited the whole, though it also reflected upon the individual as an increase of honour and well-being, and an anti-social action inevitably endangered or destroyed the existence of its perpetrator as well. Of course this was still far from providing any universal key to all the vicissitudes of life. Here too the balance was often enough not struck, and then lament and the questioning "Why" rose up to Jahweh. This question "Why" must be as old as Jahwism itself—in the songs of lamentation of both people and individual it became a stereotyped form.[7] Of course, looking at it as a whole, we must credit the older ages of Jahwism with a far greater ability to acquiesce even in vicissitudes it did not understand. This idea, "It is Jahweh; let him do what seems good to him" (I Sam. III. 18), still had a broad basis in the earlier popular piety. If even late Israel knew that Jahweh cannot be asked "What doest thou?" how much truer must this have been in the days of the patriarchs? (Job IX. 12; Dan. IV. 32 [35]). At that time one just had "to hope in Jahweh" and await his fate-averting intervention.[8] The consolation that even the threatened life is bound up with Jahweh "in the bundle of life" (I Sam. XXV. 29), or that it is written in the book of life (Ex. XXXII. 32), is abundantly attested for the older period.[9] But how did it stand with death itself? Was this not the absolute threat to life, in which all other trials reached their culmination?

2. Again one has to guard against reading modern ideas into the relevant texts. Careful investigation of death as the laments and thanksgivings understood it has had the unexpected result of showing that Israel held a very highly comprehensive and complex concept of it not at all easy to define.[10] Ours is very simple in comparison—we determine the state of being dead by the moment of the extinction of physical life, but for Israel death's domain reached far further into the realm of the living. Weakness, illness, imprisonment, and oppression by enemies are a kind of death. One so ill as to be handicapped in many active functions of life is in a state of relative death. This is the point

---

[7] Ps. LXXIV. 1; II Sam. III. 33; Pss. X. 1, XXII. 2 [1] and frequently. Gunkel and Begrich, *Einleitung in die Psalmen*, pp. 217, 229ff.

[8] For the term "to hope in Jahweh," see C. Westermann, *Das Hoffen im Alten Testament*, Leipzig 1952, pp. 24ff.　　　　[9] Eichrodt, *Theologie*, VOL. II, pp. 91ff.

[10] For what follows see C. Barth, *Errettung*.

of view from which we have to take what is often said in the Psalms when a suppliant testifies that he was already in death in Sheol, but was "brought forth" by Jahweh.[11] But Sheol had also an aggressive element—it insinuates itself on every side into the realm of the living. Thus, with the concept of death too, we meet with an ontological definition which we find strange. Without any doubt Israel understood death, like righteousness, as something spatial, as a "realm," as the fact makes clear that, for example, she practically identified the wilderness with death and Sheol, or could at any rate attribute to it predicates belonging to death.[12] Thus the difference between life and death was not in any sense based on a simple diagnosis of natural science. Taken exactly, the definition of what death is and means is not matter of mere neutral empirical fact; it was not established once and for all on the basis of a definition common to all humanity. Rather, it was Jahweh who apportioned death for men. And what death was and was not, Israel came ever and again to learn anew from Jahweh. When she talks, in her cultic utterances at least, of death, she speaks not of a physical reality, but in the main of experiences of faith. For that is what the laments and thanksgivings in the Psalter imply—death begins to become a reality at the point where Jahweh forsakes a man, where he is silent, i.e., at whatever point the life-relationship with Jahweh wears thin. From there it is only a step till the final cessation of life, till the moment at which the נֶפֶשׁ is separated from the body.[13] It is not surprising that the ideas about the outward state of the dead show certain differences in the literary contexts in which they occur.[14] But theologically they have scarcely any importance. The decisive declara-

[11] Copious references in C. Barth, *Errettung*, pp. 125ff. Independently of Barth, A. R. Johnson stated this important conclusion: "Death in the strict sense of the term is for the Israelite the weakest form of life, so any weakness in life is a form of death." "In short, the normal Israelite view, which dominates the conception of man in the OT, is that to be in sickness of body or weakness of circumstance is to experience the disintegrating power of death" (*The Vitality of the Individual in the Thought of Ancient Israel*, Cardiff 1949, pp. 94, 107).

[12] Jer. II. 6, 31; Job XII. 24f.; cf. C. Barth, *Errettung*, pp. 86f.

[13] Gen. XXXV. 18; 1 Kings XVII. 21; Jon. IV. 3; Ecclesiastes XII. 7.

[14] Thus, to take an example, we are not able to equate the idea of the ancestral sepulchre as the family burial place with that of Sheol, the place to which the dead are gathered. Poetic or otherwise elevated diction prefers the idea of Sheol. L. Rost draws a sharp distinction between the two concepts. That of the family burying-place is the idea coming from early Jahwism: "Alttestamentliche Wurzeln der ersten Auferstehung", *in memoriam Ernst Lohmeyer*, Ed. W. Smauch, Stuttgart, 1951, pp. 67ff.

tion about the state of the departed, which keeps recurring, is again theological: "Thou rememberest them no more, and they are cut off from thy hand" (Ps. LXXXVIII. 6 [5]). Admittedly, Jahweh's sphere of authority in no way ended at the boundaries of the realm of death (Am. IX. 2; Ps. CXXXIX. 8); but the dead stood outside the cult and its sphere of life. Properly, this was what constituted their being dead. In death there is no proclamation and no praise (Ps. LXXXVIII. 12 [11]; Is. XXXVIII. 18); the dead stood outwith the action of Jahweh in history (Ps. LXXXVIII. 11 [10]), and for Israel death's real bitterness lay in this exclusion. In addition, in her the dead were without the sacral dignity which they widely enjoyed elsewhere, for Jahwism passionately set its face against all survivals of the cult of the dead and all inquiring of them. Attention has been rightly drawn to the strange lack of significance which the dead had for the life of ancient Israel.[15] Looked at from the world of the living, whose centre and source was the cult, they were in a state of extreme and irreparable uncleanness. They stood on the other side of all the values of life—never did mourners promise themselves even the comfort of a reunion with once-loved shades in the ancestral tomb.[16] They were no longer able to feel as men—without part in anything, they suffered only their own decay (Job XIV. 21f.).

Still, it would be wrong to assume, in view of this very gloomy aspect, that in Israel death radically called man and all that he lives for into question. The texts show that there can be no thought of this. Certainly, Israel joined in the lament made by all religions and cultures over the bitterness of dying. But she never allowed the foundations of her faith to be shaken thereby. Not every "Why?" addressed to God necessarily came from a shaken faith. For Israel knew neither of the modern idea of considering life and all that it means as absolute entities, nor of the Faustian claim to infinity which could have been raised up by man over against Jahweh. In addition, man as unit never really completely freed himself in an individualistic way from the collective, at least from the family—he felt himself to be a member of the body of the community and he lived on in his children.[17] To die childless, or

---

[15] Eichrodt, *Theologie*, VOL. II, p. 118.

[16] G. Quell, *Die Auffassung des Todes in Israel*, Leipzig 1925, pp. 30f.

[17] "It is most remarkable and in a certain respect marvellous for how long a time such a genuine and earnest piety was in this manner able to do without belief in personal survival and all religious metaphysic." J. Wellhausen, *Israelitische und jüdische Geschichte*, 3rd edn. Berlin 1897, p. 208.

prematurely, or to make a bad end, was really serious. On the other hand, when death drew near to one "old and full of days," it was really a gracious fulfilment, since from the start life was regarded as something limited, meted out to man, to which there could therefore also be a condition of satiety.[18] But the prose framework in Job, which certainly dates from the pre-exilic period, shows with didactic incisiveness that even the hardest of fates, even the certainty of an approaching end itself, can never justify a man ceasing to hold fast to Jahweh. "If we have received good from God, shall we not (also) receive evil?" (Job II. 10). These words no doubt express a radical consistency: but just because of this they really comprehend all that Jahwism could say in face of death. Undoubtedly the most remarkable thing in this matter is therefore how little Jahwism was able to say about the phenomenon of death. But owing to this very inability to make herself ideologically or mythologically lord of death, in face of its reality Israel displayed an obedience unrivalled in the history of religion. How voluble are the other religions here, how bold the mythologies! But Israel did not know death as in any way an independent mythical power—death's power as at bottom the power of Jahweh himself.[19] Death was no last enemy, but Jahweh's acting upon men. This is the line taken by the most decisive of Israel's utterances about death, and these therefore stand in the sharpest contrast to all forms of belief in fate. Jahweh decrees death for a man, but in certain circumstances he also alters this decree (II Kings xx. 5f.)—it all rests with his freedom in giving and taking. The fact that in prayers these ideas are occasionally simplified in the sense of a dualistic opposition between Jahweh and death is of little importance in face of the basic conception which has been made clear.[20] Only in Apocalyptic was death objectified and made independent as a reality hostile to Jahweh, and therefore to be destroyed by him (Is. xxv. 7f.; Test. Levi XVIII; II Esdras VIII. 53).[21] If we turn back to the main question in this section, it has thus become clear that death

[18] "An old man and full of years," Gen. xxv. 8, xxxv. 29; Job XLII. 17; 1 Chrson xxIx. 28; II Chron. xxIV. 15. In an oddly isolated way Num. xxvII. 3 (P) seem to. presuppose that each and every death is caused by sin.

[19] C. Barth, *Errettung*, p. 69.

[20] So e.g. Ps. XLIX. 15 [14]; Is. xxxvIII. 18; Jer. IX. 20 [21].

[21] There is however something of the ancient East's belief in destiny in the passage where Job curses the day he was born. His birthday is to be condemned to a metaphysical barrenness—when the days and months are filled with destinies by the deity, this day alone is to be left out. But with Job this is rather only a literary form.

too comprised many possibilities of trial, but also that it in no sense became the question which threatened the foundation of all faith. Certainly, it was conceived as a question directed to men much more than to God, for because of the concept of the fate-bringing act all disturbances of life and all illnesses had something of the effect of arousing the men concerned. Thus suffering led along a very direct way to repentance and examination of one's relationship to God, in the disturbance of which one surmised its origin to lie. Men saw themselves as questioned through suffering.[22]

3. But there was a question which Israel did put to Jahweh—and it was actually the sign of a grave crisis upon which faith in Jahweh had entered. That we are here dealing with a definite crisis, that is, one which can theologically be defined with fair precision, becomes clear from the fact that the first witnesses to it all emerge at the same time, about the turn of the seventh to the sixth century. The final years of the monarchical period with their political catastrophes must have been an age of dangerous disintegration for the faith. But was the burden laid upon this generation in reality so much heavier than those laid upon the earlier ages? In so far as such a question is proper at all, it can certainly be answered in the affirmative only with hesitation. The people, however, had become different. Their thought was more differentiated, their emotional life more sensitive and vulnerable. And if we think finally of the Jerusalem of Jeremiah and Ezekiel, which had never had a population that was from the beginning worshippers of Jahweh—that city of the court and the civil service—then we can surmise how problematic and indeed vapid the mental climate must have been, and how hollow the piety. It was a suitable breeding-ground for questions put by men to God: here a generation grew up who in their religious resentment took the offensive against the prophets, and to it the latter—forced on to the defensive—had to have an answer. "The way of Jahweh is not just" (Ezek. XVIII. 25, 29). A generation which was able to make this monstrous observation and also to express it so calmly had forsaken the patriarchal foundations of Jahwism.

[22] For the conception of death in Israel, see further Eichrodt, *Theologie*, VOL. II, pp. 112ff., 151ff.; Köhler, *Theology*, pp. 148ff., 154ff.; R. Martin-Achard, *De la mort à la résurrection d'après l'Ancien Testament*, Neuchâtel 1956, Eng. trans. *From Death to Life*, trans. J. P. Smith, Edinburgh 1960. An illuminating comparison of the Babylonian ideas of death and the grave with those of Israel, in their kinship and differences, is to be found in A. Heidel, *The Gilgamesh Epic and Old Testament Parallels*, Chicago 1945, pp. 37ff.

As we have seen, the question "Why?" was in itself age-old: but it acquired a new ring when posed on the basis of a definite scepticism and religious detachment. This sort of thing had already raised its voice amongst the contemporaries of Isaiah, when they very coolly countered the prophet by saying that Jahweh should then speed his work (Is. v. 19). Later, Zephaniah's contemporaries cast fairly radical doubt on Jahweh's control of history[23]: "Jahweh does neither good nor evil" (Zeph. I. 12). Such statements, and others like them, may have been extreme cases, and perhaps the prophets in their polemic may even have coarsened them; nevertheless, they help us to gain insight into the spiritual climate of an epoch which the prophets in their own way also shared, for much of the substance of the questioning of this time determined their outlook also. When we read the complaints of Jeremiah's contemporary Habakkuk against the "violent" man who holds the people at his mercy and makes an idol of his military resources (the Assyrians are probably meant, Hab. I. 2–4, 12–17), we once again immediately recognise initially the traditional form of popular lament.[24] But when the prophet pictured the distress as the triumph of a רשע over a צדק, he couched it in a special conceptual form, and thereby pushed the problem forward in the direction in which the question of his whole age lay. Jeremiah and Ezekiel had to address themselves to the question, "the fathers have eaten sour grapes, but it is (only) the children's teeth which are set on edge" (Jer. xxxi. 29; Ezek. xviii. 2; cf. Lam. v. 7). The familiar quotation is in rebellion against the falling asunder of cause and effect, offence and punishment. "Our fathers, who sinned, are no more; but it is we who bear their guilt (Lam. v. 7). Yet this is not the expression of a consistent individualism, for the catch-word only contrasts the generations. The younger generation knew itself to be cut off from that of the fathers and made responsible for itself alone: it can no longer conceive of the possibility that the sowing of the fate-bringing action might in certain circumstances only ripen in later generations. Because of this it looked on its relationship with God as threatened. The Deuteronomistic theology of history had still reckoned with the effect of an evil that criss-crossed the generations, and made it a basic factor in its whole way of looking at history.[25] Ezekiel is very different: in his passage dealing with righteousness, he

[23] Am. VI. 3, VIII. 5; Is. XXII. 13, XXVIII. 14; Jer. V. 12; Ps. LXXIII. 11.
[24] Pss. XLIV, LXXIV, LXXIX, LXXX, LXXXIII; Lam. V.
[25] See above, pp. 340, 344.

starts by opposing to the contention that evil works on throughout the generations the counter-thesis, in the form of a direct word of Jahweh, that each individual life belongs to Jahweh, that in his life each man is related quite directly to Jahweh (Ezek. XVIII. 4). Ezekiel thus disputes the popular thesis of a yawning gulf between act and effect—indeed, in the way in which he speaks of the individual and his life, and not of the generations or of any still wider settings, he shows himself to be even more radical and modern than his querulous contemporaries. His counter-thesis is developed paradigmatically in two sections. (1) Father, son, and grandson—each stands on his own before Jahweh: no kind of transference or balancing up takes place. The צדקה of the father is of no help to the son, if the latter is a רשע, and the רשעה of the son does not incriminate the grandson, if he is a צדיק (vss. 5–20). (2) But even the individual's life is not a single entity before God. The רשע can turn to righteousness, and the צדיק can depart from his loyalty to Jahweh. Again it holds true that there is no balancing of the one with the other: Jahweh does not take the average of the individual's life. Whoso turns to צדקה, him all his previous evil no longer incriminates. The way of Jahweh and to life stands open always. On the other hand, whoso departs from his loyalty, him even his earlier צדקה no longer saves (vss. 21–32). It is not possible to "trust in one's righteousness" and at the same time apply oneself to evil (Ezek. XXXIII. 13). Chapter XVIII of Ezekiel has been severely criticised, generally because an extreme doctrine of justification by works has been read into it. But Ezekiel understands צדיק and רשע rather in the sense of a man's basic decision for or against Jahweh, and, as we have already seen, he values the keeping of the commandments rather as the sign of a commitment to Jahweh. No, the cool, matter-of-fact way in which Ezekiel here explains that Jahweh just does not judge as men do, and does not draw up a final balance as men do, and then says that this is precisely the way to save men—herein lies the theological grandeur of the chapter. The major premiss which governs all the details is Jahweh's will that the רשע should turn and live. Jahweh has no pleasure in his death (vss. 23, 32).[26] This chapter of Ezekiel has links with the parable of the labourers in the vineyard (Mt. XX. 1ff.). Of course, what is decisive for the understanding of the whole thing is that Ezekiel is in no sense presenting a theoretical sketch of a universally valid doctrine of the righteousness of Jahweh and Israel. He is rather speaking, in the direct

[26] Eichrodt, *Theologie*, VOL. III, pp. 142f.

prophetic way, to a definite hour, which was already shadowed by an approaching end. It is for this *hic et nunc*, immediately before an appropriate day which will decide everything, that what Ezekiel said is valid.

This must have been one of those moments which occasionally overtake a people: because of the breakdown of the old patriarchal faith and its conceptions of individual and community, the prospect was opened up on the impenetrable supra-personal relationships from which the individual now conscious of his isolation saw no way of escape. Enlightened understanding now became aware of the load and the chains with which the individual was burdened and which scorned any rational explanation. Thus, in view of a brutal fate approaching the whole community, as again after the catastrophe of 587, the question emerged as to what meaning and part the fortunes of the individual were to have in the whole complex of events now beginning. A kindred problem is also raised in the teaching given in Ezek. XIV. 1–20, a passage which is both prophetic and in the spirit of the Wisdom literature. Given the case that Jahweh causes hunger, sword, or pestilence to come upon a nation because of grievous sin: even if the three exemplary righteous men, Noah, Daniel, and Job, lived in this land, it would only be they who were saved. They could not save even their sons and daughters in virtue of their own righteousness. The passage has close affinities with Ezek. XVIII. 5ff. There too surprisingly enough Ezekiel attempts no revival of any form of ancient Jahwism's collective concept. Rather, he completely shatters the now rotten collectivism, because it had become a comfortable refuge behind which people could hide from Jahweh. The prophet drags the individual out of this anonymity into the light and destroys every hidden security and false righteousness.[27] If a man cannot rely on his own righteousness, so as to hide himself behind it from Jahweh, how much less can he rely on the righteousness of others.

These *exposés* of Ezekiel are in remarkable contrast to the result of the conversations which Abraham had with God about Sodom (Gen. XVIII. 20ff.). But it would be a complete misunderstanding to read into the latter the protest of an age that was "already" thinking individualistically over against the law of collective liability. In reality, the dialogue is from beginning to end collective in its thinking. It is always Sodom as a whole that is the subject of concern, not the separating out of the righteous from the *massa perditionis*. But while in the case of a

---

[27] W. Zimmerli, "Das Gotteswort des Ezechiel," in *Z. Th. K.*, 1951, pp. 255f.

more serious offence traditional collective thinking brought the guiltless members of the guilty association under punishment as well, in
this conversation the counter-question was raised, in an extremely
revolutionary manner, whether, taking it the other way round, the
presence of a number of righteous people could not have a preserving
function for the whole. Must Jahweh's judgment and action in every
case be determined solely by the wickedness of the many? Could not
his צדקה to the whole attest itself in his having regard to the guiltless
minority, and for their sake forgiving the whole? Jahweh agrees with
Abraham: even if the number of the righteous was utterly dispropor-
tionate to that of the guilty, "for their sake" Jahweh would forgive the
city. The passage is absolutely unique, and it is difficult to see where it
finds its place in the evolution of Israel's theology. Unlike the old saga
material in which the Jahwist embedded it, it is the product of independent reflexion upon Jahweh's צדקה—it comes before us as a
solitary breakthrough which put something new in place of the old
collective thinking, something which took the vicarious preserving
function of the צדיקים as its starting point. Actually, the section jumps
over many generations and links up with the prophetic utterances about
the Servant of God who works salvation "for the many" (Is. LIII. 5,
10).[28]

This question as to the way of working of the divine and the human
צדקה was therefore the reverse of the theoretical hair-splitting of a
small group concerned with theological *minutiae*; rather it was the
form in which, from a certain time onwards, the problem of how there
could be a relationship with Jahweh at all was set. This question became
actual in the Jerusalem of the end of the monarchical period in face of
the political fate of the kingdom of Judah: but it also arose in slightly
different form in the sphere of the life of the individual, in view of
the "prosperity of the godless" (Ps. LXXIII. 3). That we meet this source
of affliction contemporaneously in the prophet Jeremiah as well is
certainly no accident (Jer. XII. 1ff.). From then on the question remained
for long one of the most impelling for faith. It is again in no sense merely
the symptom of an exhausted piety, or one which had become peevish.
Certainly it did on occasion appear in this less impressive form, as for
example with Malachi's contemporaries, who cast side glances at the
prosperous רשעים, and put their heads together about the question

[28] But a connexion with Hos. XI. 8f. is also probable; K. Galling, *Deuterojesianische
Theologie*, Berlin 1939, pp. 86ff.

"what good is it to us?" (Mal. III. 13ff.). It has to be realised that, with the idea of the individual's existence in isolation in the eyes of Jahweh, and with the individual's question as to his personal share in Jahweh's salvation, there became actual one of the final and perhaps most serious problems with which Jahwism had to cope. Wherein did the individual's share in Jahweh and his gifts consist? The conception which earlier Jahwism had of the saving blessings (land, rest from enemies, the blessing of the earth, increase of posterity, etc.) did not, of course, admit of an automatic transference to the individual. And even where this could be done, it still did not give that completely personal relationship to God which that later age craved. How then could a personal relationship of the individual to Jahweh understand and realise itself within the larger cultic community? Certainly the spiritualisation of many cultic ideas which began at this time was of considerable assistance.[29] People talked of the circumcision of the heart, of praise as sacrifice, of prayer as incense, of God as the refuge of the soul of the pure in heart, etc.:

> Let my prayer be as incense,
> The lifting up of my hands as an evening sacrifice.
>
> (Ps. CXLI. 2)

But these spiritualisations are only part of a very far-reaching process, namely, the intrusion of rational thinking into the patriarchal cultic world, of which we already got an idea in the theologising of the cult in Deuteronomy.[30] These spiritualisations also make plain the way in which later Israel, helped by its interpretative way of thinking, laid hands upon the rites, in order once again to appropriate the world of the cult to itself in a living way. Only here, therefore, did the question as to the "meaning" of the cultic usages become acute. But as distinct from the Deuteronomic theologising, in these spiritualisations the process of interpretation and appropriation has markedly the individual as its point of reference. He it is who recognises in the rites and sacral ordinances a characteristic pointing towards the spiritual and personal,

---

[29] S. Mowinckel, *Psalmenstudien VI*, pp. 51ff.; C. Westermann, *Das Loben Gottes in den Psalmen*, Berlin and Göttingen 1954, pp. 53f.; H. Wenschkewitz, "Die Spiritualisierung der Kultusbegriffe Tempel, Priester und Opfer im NT," in *Angelos, Zeitschrift für die neutestamentliche Wissenschaft*, Leipzig 1932, pp. 71ff. We still require a treatment of the material in the Old Testament.

[30] On this question see above, p. 228.

and with this new understanding he legitimates himself before Jahweh. These spiritualisations have been far too readily taken as symptoms of a severance from or an "overcoming" of the cult, when in fact they served to begin with to preserve the individual's connexion with the material world of the rites; for did a man who spoke of the circumcision of the heart thereby turn away from the outward performance of circumcision? (Deut. x. 16, xxx. 6; Jer. iv. 4). Just as little did those who found such great comfort in "refuge with Jahweh" dispute the sanctuary's function of asylum (Pss. xvi. 1, lxi. 5 [4], and frequently). But even very pointed expressions sharpened in the zeal for spiritualisation are scarcely equivalent to a radical anti-cultic conception. It is not to be denied that this rational appropriation of the cult itself had a great number of effects. Once it got under way, it resulted in very considerable changes of emphasis within the cult, especially because it depreciated that element in it which defied any spiritualisation, namely, the blood-sacrifice.[31]

Thus perhaps wide circles in later Israel, individuals who had become conscious of their individuality, may have included themselves in the cultic event and found in it a very personal relationship to Jahweh. But how was it with the other partner, Jahweh—did he respond with an

[31] Pss. xl. 7–9 [6–8], l. 8ff., li. 18, lxix. 31f. [30f.]. S. Mowinckel, *Psalmenstudien VI*, Oslo 1924, p. 51. The problem here touched upon could give rise to a consideration of basic importance—does the age of spiritual objects date only from the time when they became vocal? Was what the spiritualising expressions in the Psalms intended really something new, or was it not already given and demanded in some way or other, perhaps in a much less differentiated way, in the old cult as well? For the old cult man was a unity, and so he was laid hold of by it totally. In things of the cult it is in all seriousness true that when they become objects of reflexion, their best days, when their authority was binding, are already behind them. Reflexion does not create something really new, but brings into rational consciousness something which was already previously valid in a more total way. O. Seel has made this clear for ancient Greece in the matter of the concept of consciousness: ". . . as if 5th century tragedy would have been able to form out of the themes of the epic such an enormous amount of the tragic, if this had not been primarily present in it even without many words. . . . It seems to me that a basic fact of human nature is here grasped, something which cannot be abstracted from the structure of man. The achievement of the Greeks in the things of the mind from Homer to Plato does not consist in the fact that they discovered and created all this out of nothing, but that *they gradually, and mostly much sooner than we are willing to recognise, drew it into consciousness by means of formative expression*." "Zur Vorgeschichte des Gewissensbegriffs im altgriechischen Denken," in *Festschrift für Franz Dornseiff*, Leipzig 1943, pp. 297f. (italics mine).

equally personal entry into the life of the individual and his needs? No, the enigmatic character of his action remained unresolved. On the other hand, it was only the individual who could really experience the incomprehensibility of his action in all its sharpness. Even very dire vicissitudes which had come upon the people as a whole, or upon districts and towns—defeats in war, or bad harvests or drought—the people's troubled conscience could still explain as condign punishment for faithlessness and apostasy from Jahweh. But in the life of the individual situations could arise in which Jahweh could absolutely no longer be seen as turned towards one in kindness. Vicissitudes could occur—and what life was not now and then brought to this extremity? —in face of which Jahweh had withdrawn into an impenetrable and unbearable hiddenness. The possibility of a real abandonment by God began to terrify the faithful, and from now on remained for generations as a grievous and perplexing threat menacing the individual and all his religious ideas. No doubt even the older lamentations of the community already spoke of a divine abandonment.[32] But this applied rather to the relationship to God of a single generation which felt itself abandoned by Jahweh, and did not as yet necessarily signify the end of any further fellowship of Jahweh with Israel. It was, therefore, if one can so put it, only a relative abandonment by God. But with the individual, as can well be understood, it was different; for he had to see in grievous woe, which might lead to death, an abandonment on the part of Jahweh and a renunciation of the relationship on which he had believed he could unconditionally rely. This is why the "lamentations of the individual" are so full of moving plaints, for every hard fate immediately set a question-mark to the whole relationship to God. It was here that death became a severe trial, though only externally, because it removed man from the sphere in which, if at all, his rehabilitation before Jahweh could take place.

Oddly enough, the present-day reader finds that this converse of the individual with God in these laments yet lacks that final personal note which he expects. No doubt he constantly comes up against formulations of incomparable personal fervour and earnestness: but form-criticism long ago showed that, as far as phraseology goes, even the wholly personal prayers of lamentation move with few exceptions in an obviously completely conventionalised body of formulae. In spite of the entirely personal form of style in these prayers, the exegete will

[32] E.g. Pss. XLIV. 10ff. [9ff.], LX. 3, LXXIV. 1.

hardly ever succeed in discerning anything like an individual or biographically contoured fate behind the details given by the suppliant. Rather the suppliants express their sufferings in a few typical and often very faded concepts—as for example a "descent into hell" with its derivation from mythology (cf. Jon. II. 4ff. [3ff.]). Death so violently encompassed them that they sank into the abysses of the earth, or the waters of chaos closed over them. Another image is suffering at the hands of enemies who threaten one's life. Thus in these prayers the personal element proper is only expressed in a considerably diminished way, in cultic and conventionalised concepts and phraseology. It could perhaps be said that even in these prayers, for all their wonderful intimacy, the individual has still not as yet found his way to a full self-consciousness or an immediate unrestricted self-presentation. This may be true as regards the general history of the mind, if we take modern western individualism as a measuring rod. But here the counter-question has to be put, whether there was ever any intention of such a pure self-picturing of the individual. In the sphere of worship, which was the *Sitz im Leben* of these prayers, the relationship of the individual to the type could positively not be abandoned, for in it and it alone was his link with the community preserved. What the individual bemoaned was thus not exclusively his own distress. He never regarded it as his own alone, and he therefore expressed it in words and ideas taken from the liturgy. In so doing, he could enter the ranks of the invisible company of those who had had similar or comparable suffering and who had been heard, and in the words of such a prayer others too might in turn "find a lodging for the night of sorrow."[33] But bound up with this liturgical schematisation, which puts its stamp upon even the entirely personal prayers of lamentation and thanksgiving, there is a further point of theological importance. Even if the men who prayed depicted their sufferings in a somewhat depersonalised fashion, the eye is nevertheless struck by the extravagance and radicality of the descriptions. Psalm XXII bemoans illness, enemies, poverty, false accusations, and mockery—almost every conceivable woe is piled up on the man praying. The well-known characteristic of the Oriental to run in emotion into exaggerated language and extreme pictures is not really relevant, because in their phraseology these psalms are in no sense

[33] "I spent the night in solitude . . . and finally . . . read the Psalms, one of the few books in which one is completely at home, however preoccupied and unsettled and troubled one may be." R. M. Rilke, *Briefe an seinen Verleger*, Leipzig 1928, p. 247.

whatever to be understood as personal outpourings of this kind, but as discourses bound to the cult and the liturgy. Thus, for theology we shall have to take much more seriously the difference between what was in actual fact suffered and the extreme form in which the man at prayer to God depicts himself. "In Psalm XXII, however, David descends with his complaints to a depth that lies beyond the depths of his suffering."[34] Just as the men who prayed surrounded themselves with a righteousness which far outstripped all possibilities of their personal rendering of obedience as well as of their spiritual surrender, so in their laments they represent themselves as the exemplary sufferers, upon whom has come not merely this or that suffering, but the extreme suffering of abandonment by God.[35] The theological peculiarity of Ps. CXIX[36] is that it has entwined the two indissolubly, for the same man who takes his delight in the revelation of the will of Jahweh, so as to set it above all earthly possessions, and whose heart is consumed with longing for it, is nevertheless put to shame (vs. 22), threatened by princes (vs. 23), his soul cleaves to the dust (vs. 25), he is ensnared by the cords of the wicked (vs. 61), slandered (vs. 69), oppressed (vs. 78), persecuted (vs. 84), etc.[37]

What is predicated of suffering in the psalms of lamentation is in fact only another form of man's presentation of himself before God in which he confesses that he is one who awaits the help of Jahweh. So too a similar state of affairs exists when the men praying designate themselves as "poor" and "wretched." The conviction that those whose legal standing was weak and who were less privileged in the struggle of life were the objects of Jahweh's particular interest reaches far back into the history of the people of Jahweh. This conception of the poor practically contains a legal claim upon Jahweh; and it was precisely this which later made it a self-designation of the pious before Jahweh.[38] In fact, a great number of references understand these poor quite frankly

---

[34] F. Delitzsch, *A Biblical Commentary on the Psalms*, London 1887, VOL. I, p. 372.

[35] So too in the hymn: "I lay in sore bonds. . . . I stood mocked and put to shame," "I lay in deepest night of death. . . ."

[36] A. Deissler has recently shown how inappropriate the usual term "psalm of the law" is; *Ps. 119 und seine Theologie, Ein Beitrag zur Erforschung der anthologischen Stilgattung im Alten Testament*, Munich 1955, pp. 292ff. The psalm meditates on the wonders of the divine word.

[37] Mention would also fall to be made of a further sphere of trials, if Mowinckel's thesis is accepted: he regards casters of spells as the enemies of the individual. It has been modified and re-issued by A. Guillaume, *Prophecy and Divination*, London 1938, pp. 272ff.   [38] A. Kuschke in *Z.A.W.*, 1939, p. 50.

and directly as those who can justifiably expect the divine protection.[39] This state of being poor also includes a defencelessness and helplessness, as a result of which these men who pray designate themselves as cast upon Jahweh alone, as those who seek Jahweh and him alone (Pss. XXII. 27 [26], LXIX. 33 [32]). They reach out to this existence before God and picture themselves as in it. Their negative counterpart is the violent, who infringe upon the rights of others, especially those of the poor man, and even seek his life (Pss. X, XXXV. 10, XXXVII. 14). In contrast, the "poor man" who commits his affairs to God is the meek one who renounces all claims to conduct his own cause. As distinct from the violent man, his proud ego is broken in pieces—he is a broken spirit (Is. LVII. 15, LXI. 1f.; Ps. LI. 19 [17]). Thus as self-designations the pious and the wretched became in the end of great importance for interpreting and filling out the concept of the "righteous."[40]

4. If we turn back to our question about the trials of the individual, we must once again take up the question of the consolation which was found in such distresses. As may be imagined, it was very many-sided. What calls for chief mention here would be the consolation which was given to the men praying, after they had recited their prayer of lament, by the so-called priestly oracle of weal in the cult. It has been rightly assumed that the "change of mood" in a number of the psalms of lamentation is to be derived from the comfort which the suppliant received (e.g. in Pss. VI, XXII, XXVIII, LVI, LXIX).[41] He had heard the "fear not," and then the assurance that Jahweh would not forsake him, but would be with him and be his helper. The cult thus directed these men to hold fast to Jahweh and hope in him. This note they took up, and they then addressed this "hope in God" to themselves.[42] Certainly, the darkness encompassing the suppliant received no explana-

---

[39] Pss. IX. 10 [9], XII. 6, XIV. 6 [5], XVIII. 28 [27], XXXV. 10, CXVI. 6, CXL. 13 [12], CXLVI. 7, CXLIX. 4.

[40] This still does not give a negative answer to the question whether a group which can sociologically be more precisely defined stands behind this self-picture of the man at prayer. On the discussion of this problem see J. J. Stamm, "Ein Vierteljahrhundert Psalmenforschung," in Th. R., 1955, pp. 55ff.

[41] Begrich has given a convincing reconstruction of the priestly oracle of weal on the basis of texts in Deutero-Isaiah, in Z.A.W., 1934, pp. 81ff. Of special importance as showing the existence of this oracle is Lam. III. 55–7: "Then I called on thy name . . . thou didst hear my call . . . thou wert near when I called on thee, and didst say, 'Do not fear'."

[42] Pss. XLII. 6, 12 [5, 11], XXV. 3, 21, XXXVII. 9, 34, LXIX. 4, 7 [3, 6], CXXX. 5ff.

tion, but he knew that he would yet acknowledge Jahweh's help, and was aware that no one who hopes in Jahweh would be put to shame. Thus, the soul is "silent" for God, since from him comes its hope.[43] Nor is it to mind the prosperity of the wicked, for this is brittle and does not last.[44] These and similar thoughts of comfort could afford many a sufferer consolation in grievous trials. Much less often do we find the view which was afterwards to play such a prominent part in the Christian faith, namely that suffering is of service in man's training and refining, and is therefore a positive factor in God's determination for men's salvation. But occasionally we do meet with the confession that Jahweh had "weighed a man down" and "punished" him in order to save him, and that precisely through this suffering he had been brought into a deeper and more personal relationship to God (Pss. LXVI. 10 [11], CXVIII. 18, CXIX. 67, 71). These confessions are a spiritual-isation of the old doxology of judgment, for to those who reflected upon it in retrospect what was at one time regarded as just punishment now appeared as a helpful discipline pointing a man to God. This idea of discipline has its special representative in Elihu, when he was confronted by the complaints of Job (Job XXXIII. 12–33, cf. v. 17ff.). But on the whole we cannot help noticing how difficult it was for Israel to see suffering, which she regarded as something absolutely hostile to life, as relative, and how stumbling her way was to find in divine training a rational view of it, comprehensible to faith.

Another consolation in face of suffering which, although lacking any very broad basis in textual references, still came to have an incalculable influence because of its theological radicality, might be called the consolations of the spiritual. The idea that the oppressed "hid" himself with Jahweh, and that he could "seek refuge" with him, is bound up with the function of the sanctuary as asylum for one who was being pursued. But it became divorced from this sacral institution and, given a spiritualised sense, passed over into the general language of prayer.[45] In some of the psalms this process of spiritualisation led to very radical results. Psalms XVI and LXII begin with the avowal of asylum—and this is also heard at crucial points in Pss. XXVII and XXXVI (Pss. XXVII. 1, 5, XXXVI. 8 [7]). If we listen to these psalms with an ear directed to the question as to what these blessings of being hidden with Jahweh

[43] Ps. LXII. 2, 6 [1, 5], l. דמיה, cf. Ps. XXXVII. 7.
[44] Pss. XXXVII. 1ff., XCII. 8 [7], CXXV. 3; Job XX. 5ff.
[45] Pss. XVII. 8, LVII. 2 [1], LIX. 17 [16], LXI. 5 [4], LXIV. 11 [10].

really consist in, we come upon expressions saying very much more about the bliss of spiritual communion with Jahweh than about outward satisfaction. "Jahweh is my bliss" (טוֹבָתִי), "I have ever set me Jahweh before mine eyes" (Ps. XVI. 2, 8). The last wish which is still open to the man praying in Ps. XXVII is to dwell in the house of Jahweh all the days of his life, in order "to behold the beauty of Jahweh" (לַחֲזוֹת בְּנֹעַם יהוה, Ps. XXVII. 4). The men who pray in these terms are certainly no ascetics—"they feast in the abundance of thy house" (Ps. XXXVI. 9 [8])—but the tenor of these psalms does show clearly how for them everything is lifted into the realm of the spirit. It is an extreme spiritualisation which is attained here—a retreat into the realm of the most sublime communion with God which has made these men practically unassailable from the outside. The succinct statement 'for thy steadfast love is better than life" (Ps. LXIII. 4 [3]) gives a glimpse of how fundamentally the relative importance of all values had changed, for normally life and its enhancement through Jahweh's blessing was at all times the highest of good things for Israel. This discrimination between lovingkindness and life was something wholly new: it signified the discovery of the spiritual as a reality beyond the frailty of the corporeal. This faith no longer had need of anything external, neither the saving history nor objective rites, for Jahweh's salvation appertained to it from within itself. A man can now say to Jahweh in prayer, "Besides thee I desire naught upon earth: my heart and my flesh may fail, but God remains at all times my rock and my portion" (Ps. LXXIII. 25f.). The obscure words "with thee is the fountain of life, and in thy light we see light" (Ps. XXXVI. 10 [9]) probably also belong to this sphere of what is by now an almost mystical spirituality.

The expression "Jahweh is my portion" occurs quite a number of times in connexion with the spiritualised idea of asylum and has a long prehistory.

> Jahweh is my portion (חֶלְקִי) and my cup,
> Thou hast made my lot (גּוֹרָלִי) broad;
> The lines have fallen to me in pleasant places;
> Yes, my heritage (נַחֲלָתִי) pleases me.
> (Ps. XVI. 5f.)

The figure of speech, "portion" and "lot," is allied to an actual usage in sacral law, namely the sacral allocation of land tenure "in the community of Jahweh" (Mic. II. 5). Something of the technical procedure in this apportionment can be gathered from the allocation of the land to the tribes in the Book of Joshua, for tenure was granted by Jahweh not only to the families, but also to the tribes.[46] One tribe alone, Levi, was excepted from this arrangement. But Jahweh did not on that account make less provision for it, for "Jahweh is his portion" (יהוה הוא נחלתו, Deut. x. 9). The Priestly Document too knows of this idea: "I (Jahweh) am thy part (חלק) and portion" (נחלה, Num. xviii. 20). Initially this prescription simply contains a regulation for the maintenance of Levi, and is consequently to be understood in a perfectly material way (Deut. xviii. 1): Levi does not maintain itself by work on the land; it does not in fact hold any land, but lives from the shares in the sacrifices and other cultic payments. But Jahweh's word, "I am thy part," embraced much more than merely a regulation for material maintenance; indeed, its full potential spiritual content was only realised by later generations as they still appealed to the fact that Jahweh was "their portion." It is probable that those who unfolded this ancient phrase in all its amazing content belonged to Levitical circles, if for no other reason than this, that the poets of the Psalms are to be looked for principally among the Levitical temple-singers.[47]

It is in the light of this prehistory that Pss. xvi and lxxiii. 23ff. are to be understood—they are spiritual exegeses of the ancient phrase, "I am thy portion." Jahweh pronounced it, and Levi had accepted it.[48] Here too we are dealing with one of those ancient sacral phrases which were handed on through many generations and all of a sudden released quite unexpected contents. From it was derived the offer of a communion with Jahweh which could not be lost, because it could not be at all touched by disturbances in outward circumstances. But could it really never be lost—even in face of death? It was inevitable that this new idea of a life with Jahweh which survived physical disturbances would have to face up to the reality of death. So it is not at all surprising that precisely Pss. xvi and lxxiii make very radical statements about the relationship to death of the man praying. They are of course very allusive and therefore not in themselves completely unambiguous

[46] G. von Rad, "Verheissenes Land und Jahwes Land im Hexateuch," in Z.D.P.V., 1943, pp. 191ff., reprinted in Ges. Studien, pp. 87ff.

[47] But this spiritualised understanding is in no way due to later attempts to find theological meanings, as can be gathered from the Levitical name Hilkiah ("Jahweh is my portion," II Kings xviii. 37, xxii. 4), which is attested even in the pre-exilic period. How popular must the understanding have been even then when it could determine the name of a child!　　　[48] Cf. also Ps. cxlii. 6 [5]; Lam. iii. 24.

for us from the exegetical point of view. This is especially true of
Ps. XVI:

> Therefore my heart is glad, my soul exults,
>> my flesh also will dwell securely;
> For thou wilt not abandon my life to the realm of the dead,
>> thou wilt not let thy godly one see the pit.
> Thou showest me the way to life,
>> fullness and joy is before thy face,
>> pleasure is in thy right hand for ever.

Unquestionably, the passage can also be taken in the sense of preservation from a death that is hanging over the man who prays—Jahweh will
not let him die at present, but will restore him to life again. On the
other hand, later—at the latest Acts II. 36—the passage became a *locus
classicus* for the doctrine of the resurrection. We do not come very
much further with such texts in cultic or hymnic phraseology by asking
only about their absolute content, as it were about the "poet's understanding of himself": practically everything depends on the meaning
and sense in which they were prayed and repeated on each occasion.
And on that point do we really have such exact knowledge—especially
in what concerns the post-exilic period—that we can make categorical
judgments, as is still done in the exegesis of the Psalms?

With Ps. LXXIII things are, in our opinion, considerably clearer.

> But I am ever with thee: thou hast taken hold of my right hand;
> According to thy counsel wilt thou lead me and hereafter carry me
>> to glory.
> Whom have I in heaven? Besides thee I desire naught on earth.
> My flesh and my heart may fail, but God remains at all times my
>> rock and my part.
> Yea, those who forsake thee perish,
> But my possession is to draw near to God; I have put my refuge in
>> Jahweh.[49]

What is said in vs. 24b no doubt surprises us, but it is neither

---

[49] For the translation and interpretation of vs. 24b cf. J. J. Stamm, *Leiden*, pp. 47f.;
R. Martin-Achard, *From Death to Life*, trans. J. P. Smith, Edinburgh 1960, pp. 161ff.
In this psalm too the idea of dwelling with Jahweh has echoes in the words קרבת
אלהים (H. Birkeland in *Z.A.W.*, 1950, p. 101). It occurs repeatedly in kindred psalms
(Pss. XXIII. 6, XXVII. 4, LXI. 5), and must obviously relate to a group of the Levitical
personnel of the Temple (Ps. LXV. 5 [4]).

untranslatable nor incapable of explanation. The terse form, "God takes a man away" (לקח), belongs in its conciseness to a range of originally mythological concepts current in Israel, and also in Old Babylonia, namely that of "translation." Israel had already given clear expression to the idea that Jahweh had other realms at his disposal, and had the power and liberty to translate men into them, in the story of the ascension of Elijah (II Kings II. 1ff.), or in the note about the translation of Enoch (Gen. v. 24). But in after times the psalmists harked back to this old idea. "God himself will redeem my life, free from Sheol: he will carry me away" (Ps. XLIX. 16 [15]). This statement can hardly be referred to anything other than a life after death, for the thought of the whole psalm revolves, in the sense of the problem of theodicy, around the question of the grace of Jahweh in the life of the individual, and comes to the conclusion that the proud rich must remain in death. This then, death, is the last great separator.[50] And this is obviously the opinion of Ps. LXXIII as well. For neither Ps. XLIX nor Ps. LXXIII can be fitted simply into the series of psalms of lament or thanksgiving—they contain no descriptions of any actual need, with the familiar expressions of deliverance. They are rather pervaded by a strong striving after a principle which does not stop short at a single calamity, but presses forward to the basis of the problem. The poetic form must not make us overlook the fact that these psalms express the theological problem in its most acute form: how is Jahweh's help to and blessing of those who are loyal to him realised in face of the prosperity of the godless? The consolation runs thus: Jahweh holds his pious one fast, and remains his God in every situation in life, and even death cannot remove the communion vouchsafed to him.[51] But it would certainly be wrong to see in this certainty something like a dramatic religious "breakthrough." Our sharp alternative of ante- or post-mortem certainly seems to be a distinction that is alien to these statements in the Psalms: nor are we to imagine that in the atmosphere of Canaan, impregnated as it was with myths, the idea of a life after

[50] P. Volz, "Psalm 49," in Z.A.W., 1937, pp. 235ff. To assume that Ps. XLIX only speaks of a preservation from an evil end (as C. Barth does, Errettung, p. 159), is to break down the whole antithesis of the psalm, for the repeated statement that the rich stay in death would in this case be no answer to this question of the man praying, if the same fate were in store for him.

[51] "The approaches to a belief in an individual resurrection found in the OT are due to a demand for the accomplishment of justice." J. Pedersen, "Wisdom and Immortality," in Vet. Test., Suppl. III (1955), p. 245.

death was some unheard-of novelty, since as early as the time of Ezekiel the cult of a dying and rising god had forced its way into the Temple itself (Ezek. VIII. 14).[52] It is rather the reverse of a break-through: the men praying express a great peace and security; the com-munion with Jahweh is one that cannot be destroyed. The main phrases describing this confidence are "thou art my part" and "I am ever with thee": all else is already really given in the communion that at present exists.[53] What was still needed for its unfolding and its application to the individual was only a special stressing of the unbounded extent of this communion—it reached even over death. For this the old idea of being translated was of help, though now it was obviously looked for less mythologically, as an event taking place after death. It is also easy to imagine that an unconscious influence was exerted by certain ideas which were in the air and which were originally non-Israelite.[54]

A thorough-going change was introduced by Apocalyptic with its expectation of a general resurrection, first apparently only of the righteous (Is. XXVI. 19), and then of a resurrection of all, some "to eternal contempt," others to "eternal life" (Dan. XII. 1–3). The differ-ence is obvious. In the psalms, it was the word of Jahweh addressed to the individual in a wholly personal way which bore him over the threshold of death, because he abandoned himself to it completely. What was characteristic for man's situation over against death was precisely the lack of a generally accepted hope in something beyond, and that inevitability in which nothing remained but to cast oneself on Jahweh's word which alone promised life, and to hide oneself in it before death. On the other hand in Apocalyptic, the resurrection of the dead is merely one act in the great apocalyptic events of the end, the main essentials of which were already fixed in anticipation. These

[52] H. Riesenfeld, *The Resurrection in Ezekiel XXXVII and in the Dura-Europos Paintings*, Uppsala Universitets Årsskrift, Uppsala and Leipzig 1948, pp. 3ff.

[53] "What gives mutual connexion to all these testimonies about the overcoming of death in the life of the individual is the building up of their certainty of the gift of fellowship with God which they enjoy. Because God has spoken to man and speaks to him still, he is freed from the compulsion of having to die and sees ahead of him a path leading to life." Eichrodt, *Theologie*, VOL. III, p. 165.

[54] When Job fancies that he can perhaps expect a turning to him on Jahweh's part even after his death (Job XIV. 13ff.), this too is hardly just the free play of his imagina-tion; he had got hold of an idea which was already somewhere or other in existence in a well-defined shape.

events overtake the whole world and therefore the individual as well, who has to hold himself in readiness for them.

5. Finally, in connexion with Israel's trials and consolations, we must deal with the Book of Job, in which, as in a concave mirror, is gathered together very much of the trials meted out to Israel, and intensified into a superhuman suffering.[55] In the gigantic literary complex which stands under the name of Job, the oldest layer, the narrative prose framework (Job I–II, XLII. 7–17), is of course to be considered separately, for it would be a mistake to try to understand it against the background of a deeply shaken faith. Its place is obviously still prior to the outbreak of the crisis described above. It tells the story of a question raised in heaven and an answer given on the earth. The accuser—by no means an opponent of God from Hell, but an official of the royal household of Jahweh, a kind of heavenly public prosecutor—had on an audience day put the question of whether the piety of Job, who was renowned as completely blameless, was not in principle interested. The question—it is that of the "wholeness" (תֻּמָּה, Job II. 9) of the relationship with God—was definitely put in Jahweh's own interests, and in all that follows the accuser properly appears only as the prolonged arm of Iahweh. Of the heavenly prehistory of his sufferings Job himself knows nothing. It is remarkable too that he does not apply any kind of theological interpretation to his suffering of his own accord: he confines himself to the solemn assertion that he can see nothing in this suffering which must cast doubt on his loyalty to Jahweh. But it would be wrong to understand these two avowals of Job's as evidence of an almost stoical

[55] As we today recognise, the Book of Job belongs to a by no means small group of literary works of the ancient East which are akin to one another in respect of their literary form (they are generally works constructed as dialogues), and which in particular show a clear kinship in content, inasmuch as they raise complaints about suffering, especially innocent suffering, and seek to give an answer to the problem of a theodicy. The prayer of thanksgiving (deriving from Babylon), "I will praise the lord of Wisdom," a dialogue between a sufferer and his friends, and between a master and his slaves, belongs to them. The well-known Egyptian dialogue of a sufferer with his soul ranges itself alongside them. All these texts are translated in *A.N.E.T.* Sumerian fragments of the complaints of a sufferer and the end of his sufferings have recently been discovered (N. S. Kramer, "Man and his God. A Sumerian variation to the 'Job' *motiv*," in *Vet. Test.*, Suppl. III (1955), pp 170ff.). Because of the variety of questions in dispute, the time has not yet come for a thorough comparison of these works. Cf. however J. J. Stamm, *Leiden*. More recent literature on Job—which almost passes all bounds—is given by C. Kuhl, in *Th. R.*, 1953, pp. 163ff., 257ff.; 1954, pp. 261ff.

imperturbability, or of an extreme self-mastery. In his whole behaviour Job shows himself a vulnerable man. What he says is rather to be taken as something quite simple and sober, something self-evident for faith. The two answers are not an extreme achievement of his faith—no, so safe and sheltered is he in his faith that he can only ask with amazement whether one would really grant to God only the power to give, and not the power to take away as well. But in so saying Job justified the "word of honour" which God had given for him before the whole royal household of heaven. This man who was cast into the dust had suffered "for the glory and pride of Jahweh."[56] Job is thus a μάρτυς, a witness in the best sense of the term, for he took up a clearly positive attitude to a concern of God's. After Jahweh's conversation with the accuser, all the heavenly beings—so we have to picture it—must have been eagerly waiting to see whether Job would justify the word of God which was now at stake, or discredit it. Obviously there are connexions between this office and the title "servant" which the narrative so insistently applies to Job (I. 8, II. 3, 7, XLII. 7f.).[57] But it is to quite a different spiritual and religious world that we are transported by the dialogues in chs. III–XLII, which perhaps several hundred years later were incorporated into the pre-exilic prose narrative, for they show a completely different Job—not the man wholly sheltered in his faith and his commitment to God, but one sinking into all the depths of abandonment by God, and accusing him, indeed a blasphemous and scorning Job.

The understanding of this section with the dialogues is made extremely difficult by the lack of a clear progression of thought and a clearly fixed subject of conversation. The problem is presented on wide canvases rather than in clearly defined points. The poet seems to be concerned to elucidate a widespread whole rather than a single truth. Because of this, if, for example, Job expatiates on the general fact that life is suffering (Job VII. 1ff.), or if the friends recite wide-ranging poems about the nemesis which inevitably overtakes the sinner (Job XV. 17ff., XVIII. 5ff.), we must not call this a deviation from the theme. When the theme is interrupted by quite ordinary observations on human suffering or on the phenomenon of evil, the reader often completely loses sight of the main problem of Job. Much of what is said

---

[56] J. G. Herder, *Vom Geist der ebräischen Poesie* (Bibl. theol. Klassiker, VOL. XXX), p. 137.

[57] J. Hempel in *Zeitschrift für systematische Theologie*, 1929, pp. 645f.

refers very slightly or even not at all *ad hominem*: and in addition there is no consistent psychological working out. The building up of the speakers as characters with features of their own is merely begun without being followed out, and in the speeches—those of Job in particular —sections keyed in totally different moods are often placed hard up against one another. Recognition of the highly composite character of the speeches from the point of view of form-criticism further increases the problem of interpretation. Thus, for example, Eliphaz's first speech (Job ivf.) does not in any sense consist of a fairly unified sequence of thought, but is a series of entities of very different kinds, each of which has its own structure of thought and thesis within itself. Eliphaz offers Job at least five different and remarkably slightly connected propositions to ponder. An essay to reconstruct a tolerably unified progression of ideas would fail to recognise that these speeches just do not attempt to solve the problem by this way of a uniform and consistent process of deduction; they do it by striking note after note in differing lines of thought and so move in a much wider stream towards the solution.[58] This opens up a glimpse into the spiritual movement in the dialogues as a whole. These partners in conversation do not take up the thread of conversation from one another—indeed they do not seem even to listen to one another. So the impression is given that each speaks only to the problem round which they all seem to be encamped. Thus, each speech moves from the periphery inwards—and, as we saw, each moves on rather a broad front—without taking any notice worth mentioning of its predecessor. And within the speeches themselves we sometimes come on a completely new beginning. For no one can take Job xvii. iff. as a continuation of ch. xvi. In ch. xvii the culminating point that had been reached is completely removed from sight. In ch. xvi. 18–22 one train of thought reached its end and arrived at a particularly important conclusion, but in ch. xvii a new one starts on its way. It is precisely by means of this discursiveness, which we find hard to bear, that the poet reaches the goal towards which he strives: to some extent he encircles the problem, and by shedding light on it from as many sides as possible and approaching its

[58] Duhm asks in his commentary: "Does Eliphaz intend to teach or warn?" But who is to say that he intends one thing only? This single example itself shows how hazardous it is to keep speaking of the "*schema*," the closed "system" in the theology of the friends. (So e.g. A. Weiser in his commentary, A.T.D., 2nd edn. Göttingen 1956, *passim*.)

solution from as many points of the compass as possible, he succeeds in comprehending the subject under discussion in its totality.[59] If this is a proper way of looking at it, then exegesis will have to be prepared to do greater justice to the contribution made by the speeches of the friends, instead of minimising their arguments to the point of caricature right from the start. Alongside Job's revolutionary argument, and in terms of the effect of breadth mentioned above, this side of the tradition is in actual fact quite indispensable. The expositor must therefore take account of the fact that the individual component parts and sections in this poem are set side by side much more spaciously and in a certain sense much less relatedly and with more independent validity than we in the western world are used to finding in dialogues. The exegete must then show restraint by not drawing things closer together and relating them more to each other than their setting in the poem warrants. Nevertheless in Job's monologue at least, a certain progression of thought can be seen.

In clamorous contrast to the quiet and almost solemn restraint of the prose story, the Job of the dialogue starts by cursing his life and the day appointed as his birthday. To some extent this third chapter contains the spiritual lay-out of the dialogue—it shows the inner realm in which it will unfold itself. In spite of certain points of accord with similar lamentations, in its compactness and sharpness this outburst of despair is something quite new and as yet unheard of in Israel. From the outset we have to take into account more than just a single cause in connexion with the inner prehistory of this religious collapse. Many factors may have been working towards it for a long time. A general loss of authority suffered by the old concepts of faith, an emancipation into a very spiritual religiosity, particularly in circles who thought in

[59] "For the Israelite *thinking* was not the solving of abstract problems. He does not add link to link, nor does he set up major and minor premises from which conclusions are drawn. To him thinking is to grasp a totality. He directs his soul towards the principal matter, that which determines the totality, and receives it into his soul, the soul thus being immediately stirred and led in a certain direction": Pedersen, *Israel I-II*, p. 180; cf. pp. 124ff. But besides this mode of thought, which is alien to us, the poetic element too, i.e. that intractable enthusiasm in portrayal, asserts its claim. Here writes a man who reckons with readers who are able to linger beside the various magnificent pictures and are not merely concerned with the theological content of the various units. How much more briefly it could all have been put! Good observations on this writer's style and method of presentation are to be found in P. Humbert, "Le modernisme de Job," in *Vet. Test.*, Suppl. III (1955), p. 155.

terms of wisdom, a stepping out from the security of traditional sacral orders, a transference of the religious centre of gravity to reflexion and teaching, a radical individualisation of the life of faith—all these may have played a part. What does Job know of the saving orders of the cult or of what Jahweh had rooted in the history? It is in an existence totally without community or saving history that Job in steely isolation carries on his struggle with God. Probably one further thing ought specially to be borne in mind in the search for the reasons for this catastrophe. It has often been remarked that, like all the peoples of antiquity, Israel brought experiences of suffering into causal connexion with evil. It was her deep conviction that every evil act set in progress a bane which sooner or later had to rebound upon the agent. The bane was thus set in motion by the fate-bringing act itself; indeed, it was a part of it. This idea was not so divorced from reality as modern man might imagine. On the one hand, it rested upon rich and ever-fresh experience: and on the other—at least in older times—it was elastic enough to make room even for very mysterious sequences of events. But in Job's extremely individualistic piety, where now only that which happened between God and the as it were absolute individual still had relevance, this idea of bane became very questionable.[60] Let him be shown the evil corresponding to his suffering! (Job vI. 24). Is he to see in his suffering God's verdict of guilty upon him? But he refuses to let himself be declared guilty in this way (הַרְשִׁיעַ, Job x. 2; cf. IX. 29, x. 7). We gather from all this that Job was still far from having absolutely left behind the old idea of the fate-bringing act—it troubles him greatly that his suffering has risen up as a witness against him (Job xvI. 8). Above all, we have to see clearly that of himself Job has nothing to put in the place of the old point of view. The peculiarity of his situation is precisely that, with the breakdown of the old religious ideas, Job saw himself confronted by a theological abyss in which everything that faith was able to say about God was lost, and over which remained only Jahweh in his boundless power and holiness. And now Job passionately contends against the friends on behalf of the incomparable freedom of this absolute Jahweh, whose deeds are uncontrol-

---

[60] This is not of course to say that this was the first crisis in the picturing of the fate-effecting act. As is shown by the psalms mentioned above which treat of theodicy, the crisis goes very much further back. Indeed, the Deuteronomistic idea of the word of Jahweh which brought about judgment was also in itself an important modification.

lable by any human reason. A special part of it is the divine freedom to
root justice where he pleases.[61] It is not as if God were bound to some
norm of right, so that there was, as it were, an umpire who, in case of
a dispute between God and man, could engage both to observe the
rule (Job IX. 32f.). Jahweh is so free and powerful that he himself determines what is right, and is always in the right against man. This is the
root point of Job's supreme trial. Two opposing insights stand before
him. In spite of his suffering he cannot admit that by a grievous sin he
has disturbed his hitherto intact relationship with God. On the other
hand, he knows that this does not at all avail him, for God is completely
free and his right alone is valid. This threatens Job's whole existence
before God, for he believes that he has to look upon himself as guilty—
indeed, he now recognises with increasing dismay in what a hostile
way this absolute power and freedom of God manifest themselves
against man. In this connexion Job cannot comprehend why this
immeasurably powerful God does not magnanimously overlook
frail man, but lies in wait for him and tests him. "Why dost thou
not leave me alone till I but swallow my spittle?" (Job VII. 19). But
what is without parallel is that Job does not hide himself, or flee
from this God, but accepts the battle with him. His complaints are
largely a prayer to Jahweh to preserve the picture of himself in Job's
soul.

Because of the abundance of the themes which Job strikes up, and
the rapid way in which he changes from one to the other, it is far from
easy to see what the real point at issue for Job is in this struggle or why
he accepted it. Much space is taken up by outbursts of terror at the
measurelessness of the power of God and the freedom with which he
makes use of it. In fact, Job's terror and abhorrence can clearly be seen
increasing in his speeches, until in chs. XVI and XVII such a measure of
dread of God is reached as can hardly be surpassed. Here the picture
of God turns completely into that of a demon-God: he gnashes his
teeth upon Job, he "sharpens his eyes" over him—LXX speaks of "eye-
daggers"—he appears to Job now only as a devil's frightening face.
God has seized Job by the neck and dashed him in pieces, pierced him
through his kidneys, and his gall is poured out on the earth. Thus, in
Job's relationship to God there can be discerned a growing estrangement, an ever-widening gulf. He has here sunk down into an abyss of

[61] On this cf. W. Vischer, "Hiob ein Zeuge Jesu Christi," in *Zwischen den Zeiten*,
Munich 1933, pp. 8ff.

terror which far outstrips anything the psalmists had to say.[62] But, in an extremely paradoxical way, with this is interwoven another completely different and opposed movement. Job presses on to God: in all circumstances the important thing is to have speech with him, and in so desiring Job is clearly thinking of a legal contest (Job VI. 29, IX. 15f., 32f., XIII. 3, 13–16, 22). There has to be a verdict between him and God, and he, Job, will force it. What gives him courage for this lawsuit, as well as the certainty that he will be able to stand up to the test, is his "righteousness" alone, to which he holds fast, his "perfection" (תמה) which he does not let go (Job XXVII. 5f.). This insistence of Job's on his own righteousness—which strikes uncomfortably on present-day ears—is the real subject of his whole contention with God, and to it he constantly returns until he unfolds it in its grandest form in the famous declaration of his guiltlessness, the "oath of purification" in ch. XXXI. But are Job's protestations of guiltlessness then to be judged in principle differently from those of the Psalms?

> I clothed myself in righteousness, it was my clothing;
> in justice as a robe and a turban.
>
> (Job XXIX. 14)

These identical words could stand in one of the psalms of the innocent sufferers, the only difference being that Job insists on his צדקה in a very much more impassioned way. When he boasts of his righteousness and the perfection of his relationship to God, he certainly does not thereby regard himself as without sin (Job XIV. 4, IX. 2): he only presupposes a relationship in which God is graciously turned towards man, which he for his part has not broken by any renunciation. On the contrary, it was he who sought it, while God has withdrawn from him into ever deeper concealment. Even the Job remote in his individualistic isolation and struggling for the clarification of his shattered relationship to God still moves wholly within the ideas and concepts by means of which Jahweh had hitherto dealt with his own in the cult. His question is not, as we constantly find said, "the meaning of suffering as such," but precisely that justification of himself which he thinks has been lost. Actually in regard to *genre* too a dependence upon procedures of ancient

---

[62] W. Schadewaldt once spoke of Sophocles as among the Greeks the discoverer of suffering at its most extreme (*Sophocles und das Leid*, Potsdam 1947, p. 19); the same could be said in Israel of the poet who wrote the dialogues in Job.

sacral law can be established. The way in which the material is laid out in the final monologue—oath of purification, appeal for a divine judgment, the divine answer—certainly rests upon a very much older ceremonial in sacral law (Job XXXI).[63] The case in Job XXIII. 3ff. is the same. Here again Job speaks of his wish to be admitted to God's presence, to be submitted to examination (vs. 10).[64] In other cases Job moves in concepts belonging to the sphere of extra-cultic law—he cries out (זעק) for his right in just the same way as someone who is deprived of it raises a complaint before the king (cf. II Kings VI. 26). He conjures the earth not to let his blood trickle away, that his cry may not come to rest.[65] Even in the cry in which he appeals to God as the avenger of blood, he reached back to a very ancient idea—God is the owner of all life: wherever life is threatened by some violence, God's immediate interest is at stake. Job knows this, and therefore makes his solemn appeal to God—against God. In the tremendous tension of his struggle the picture which he has of God threatens to be torn in pieces before his eyes. Something of the sort had already been foreshadowed in ch. XIV. But there Job sought a solution in the sense of a temporal sequence—first the God of wrath acts, and then the God who loves his creature. But now the severance between the protecting God of the tradition and the destructive God of Job's experience has so sharpened that they both exist together. Even if Job suddenly and rapturously experienced the God who was his friend, he is nevertheless not able to delete the reality of the God who is his foe. He makes solemn appeal from the one to the other, and he knows that the God who is his surety, his redeemer, will lead his cause to victory against God the adversary. Everyone who reads the book must see in the two passages, Job XVI. 19ff. and XIX. 23ff., the climax of Job's struggle: nowhere else does such a certainty and consolation enfold him as here. Nevertheless these passages are not to be called the solution, for the dialogue does not

[63] A. Weiser, *Hiob* (A.T.D.), pp. 11, 214. The sequence of the ceremonial is disturbed by the late insertion of the speech of Elihu. Originally, the challenge to God (Job XXXI. 35-7) was certainly immediately followed by God's answer.

[64] For the various testing rituals in connexion with oracles cf. R. Press in *Z.A.W.*, 1933, pp. 121ff., 227ff.

[65] Job XVI. 18ff. The murder cry is the *vox oppressorum*, the most rudimentary appeal for legal protection to the nearest person competent. For the role of the blood, cf. Gen. IV. 10. The fact that Job speaks of his blood makes it again clear that he is using well-defined concepts which are only in the transferred sense applicable to him; cf. Ps. XXX. 10 [9].

of course end here.[66] Besides, God's answer in ch. XL. 1ff.—which is perhaps more original compared with ch. XXXVIIIf.—for its part makes further reference to Job's accusations, a sure sign that for all the comfort to which he has won through, the matter is not yet at its end.

Even with all due reserve in simplifying the inner complexity of the work, these divine answers must be understood as the climax which, as the poet understood it, brings Job's struggles to a conclusion.[67] But it must surprise all who read it that God's answer deals with something completely different from what Job had asked about. Yet this is far from saying that it does not all the same by implication contain a clear answer for Job. To be sure, God does not put it in the way which Job had demanded. Initially his answer consists in a storm of counter-questions, all of which point to the ludicrous limits set to human penetration. In answering Job's question God lifts the veil a little, just so far that Job may see how many more and—in the poet's view at any rate—greater riddles lie behind it. Thus the speech starts by countering all that human *naïveté* which fancies that immediately behind each of a man's problems there equally lies the divine solution ready for him. To this extent God's answer insists upon the absolute marvellousness of his management of the world. Behind each one of its marvels lies another greater marvel, and not one of them does God allow to be taken out of his hand. When Job has doubts about the "wisdom" of God's government of the world (Job XXXVIII. 2), his judgments come much too late. Even at the laying of the foundation stones of the world the heavenly beings struck up songs of praise—they better understood what the situation of this world was (Job XXXVIII. 7). Here it is easy to see that the purpose of the rhetorical counter-questions is not exhausted simply in their making Job aware of the limits of his understanding of the world and ordering him back into his human limitations in relationship to God. What is of greatest importance in the speech is not this negative aspect, for after all in the whole way in which it traverses the

[66] A few verses after the first passage of comfort Job asks that God might lay down a pledge for him with himself—that is, with God himself! (Job XVII. 3f.). Here too then there is a quite similar advance, only it does not move in the concepts of the law of blood, but in those of the law of pledging. But it is not developed beyond this first appeal.

[67] The repeatedly expressed doubts whether the divine discourse and the dialogues belong together are not justified. The course of the dialogues presses forward to some kind of solution (Kuhl, in *Th. R.*, 1954, pp. 303ff.); besides, form-critical considerations rule out the excision of the divine discourse (see above, p. 380, n. 23).

world and its various spheres something very positive is revealed about
the relationship of God to his creation. It is, doubtless, marvellous and
incomprehensible. The fact that rain is poured out on the steppe makes
a mockery of all human ideas of economy, just in the same way as the
life of the wild horse and the wild ox are beyond the possibility of man's
using them; to say nothing of the strange ostrich hen! But nevertheless all this allows man to see that God turns a smiling face to his
creation. That God "rejoices" in his creatures (Ps. CIV. 31) could equally
well be said here too. But in particular he cares for those creatures of
which Job is not even able to think. The whole of creation is dependent
upon him in everything. Psalm CXLV also deals with the praise of all
that lives on earth and extols its creator and preserver:

> The eyes of all wait for thee,
>   and thou givest them their food in due season.
> Thou openest thine hand,
>   and satisfiest all that lives, so that they delight.
> Just is Jahweh in all his ways,
>   and kind in all his doings.
>   (Ps. CXLV. 15–17)

We have already met the formula "just is Jahweh" in the doxologies
of judgment (see above, p. 377, n. 17); the meaning of the avowal is
that Jahweh is innocent of all charges that may be brought against
him. And so for the understanding of the divine answer in Job XXXVIII
it is in our view important that Ps. CXLV, so akin in its spirit to this
answer, sees in the splendour of creation and its maintenance a proof
of the justice of God (cf. also vs. 7). Accordingly, the purpose of the
divine answer in the Book of Job is to glorify God's justice towards
his creatures, and the fact that he is turned towards them to do them
good and bless them. And in the intention of the poem that is also
truly an answer to Job's question. If Job's holding fast to his righteousness was a question put to God, God gives the answer by pointing to
the glory of his providence that sustains all his creation. Of course this
justice of God cannot be comprehended by man; it can only be adored.

The real fascination of this poem lies in its marginal theological
situation—how will Jahweh still be able to express himself in any way
in a situation where the people of God, the cult, and the saving history
no longer have theological relevance? But Jahweh had appeared there
too, outside of these, and had revealed himself in person and with

consolation to one who up till then had only known him by hearsay (Job XLII. 5). If this "solution" in some degree falls short of what the present-day reader looks for, this lies in a peculiarity of the poet's theology which, like the theology of the Wisdom literature in general, can properly only move in utterances about creation, utterances which are of course meant to express to the utmost limits of their capacity God's thoughts of kindness.

5. ISRAEL'S WISDOM DERIVING FROM EXPERIENCE

Like every other nation, Israel understood "wisdom" as a practical knowledge of the laws of life and of the world, based upon experience. The Hebrew word translated as "wise," "wisdom" means, initially, having the experience or the expertise of, let us say, a seaman, a worker in ore, a political adviser, etc.[1] Israel's wisdom is a very complex phenomenon, and it also underwent considerable changes. But the characteristic of practically all that it says about life is this starting point in basic experience. In every stage of culture of course man is set the task of mastering life. To this end he needs to know it, and dare not cease from looking and listening to discover whether in the tangle of events something like conformity to law, an order, cannot be here and there discerned.

This looking and listening is of course particularly intensive in nations' early days. Naturally, the freshness shown when people are open and ready to assimilate and learn unimpeded by teaching or dogmatised experience of any kind is wont soon to give way to a certain dulling and indifference. In Israel too wisdom thus understood had an important function in an early period now hardly datable. But the means of laying hold of and objectifying such orders when once perceived is language. It has been rightly said that the so-called "Twin-formulae," in German *Freund-Feind, Leib-Leben, Liebe-Leid* (friend-foe, body-life, love-suffering), already provide through their linguistic assonance a useful set of concepts.[2] Undoubtedly they are to be understood as primitive attempts to mark off certain orders and tie them down in words. Hebrew too knows an immense number of such formulae, which of course afterwards became more or less literary forms and lost

[1] Even references as late as Jer. x. 9; Is. XL. 20; Ezek. XXVII. 8; Ex. XXXI. 6 (P) use the adjective in that technical sense of experienced, expert, skilled.

[2] A. Heusler, *Die altgermanische Dichtung* (Handbuch der Literaturwissenschaft), Berlin 1924, p. 66. Cf. English "weal-woe."

their old noetic function.[3] Proverbs move on an essentially more ambitious plane. They too formulate recognised and constantly confirmed truths and experiences.[4] Consequently their normal form of expression is the simple statement. But it was also possible to draft them as an admonition, and this was not infrequently done. The words "out of the wicked comes forth wickedness" are designated in 1 Sam. XXIV. 14 [13] as an old proverb. No doubt it called up in people's minds a certain conformity to law beneficial to men. The case is exactly the same with the words "when pride comes, then comes disgrace." The assonant form בא זדון ויבא קלון (Prov. XI. 2) again reminds us what outstanding importance attaches to the word that pins down these garnered truths —only by being formulated is the truth given its sanction.[5]

What these gnomic sayings are really concerned with is made apparent in the great number of paradoxes which they wrested from life and to which they gave form:

"Many a man gives much, and yet becomes richer. Many a man is more niggard than he ought to be and yet becomes poorer" (Prov. XI. 24). Here the mere paradox is expressed, as yet quite without conclusion or teaching. These will certainly follow very soon; but first something much more elementary is taken up—the pinning down of a mere matter of fact.[6] This is the case with the statement that pride goes before a fall (Prov. XVI. 18, XVIII. 12), and many others. These seemingly naïve proverbs have none the less an involved intellectual prehistory. Observation of a large number of identical or similar sequences had to be made before a certain conformity to law could be deduced from them. No one recognised so clearly as Herder the intellectual achievement involved in such a discovery of regularity. "But

[3] Collected in J. Gabor, Der Urrhythmus im Alten Testament, Bei. Z.A.W. No. 52, Berlin 1929; G. Boström, Paronomasi i den äldre hebraiska maschallitteraturen, Lund 1928.

[4] Most certainly a special function was attached to such concise formulae, particularly in the sphere of the early and the earliest administration of justice. Cf. B. Gemser, "The importance of the motive clause in O.T. Law," in Vet. Test., Suppl. 1 (1953), pp. 50ff.

[5] "With a proverb what alone gives the content significance is the form, be that never so primitive or bizarre. . . . This means that with a proverb it is a matter of a truth which is only given its sanction by the form. . . ." W. Preisendanz, Die Spruchform in der Lyrik des alten Goethe und ihre Vorgeschichte seit Opitz, Heidelberger Forschungen 1952, p. 18.

[6] This pure objectivity of the statements acquires a strange depth when the events are referred to Jahweh. "The poor man and the oppressor meet together; he who gave light to both is Jahweh" (Prov. XXIX. 13; cf. Prov. XXII. 2).

let it not be imagined that in every object everyone sees or perceives the same thing."[7] To believe that the teaching as such already lies within the experience is a delusion. The gold coins have still to be shaped out of the crude ore of experience. Thus the concern was, as Herder unsurpassably put it, to establish in each case, in the complex and ambiguous mass of experience, "the clearest and most affecting moment," "the point of greatest light."[8] These maxims will never be understood unless one presupposes as their background a mentality which still had vital questions to put to its environment. The question indeed is whether in the tangle of happenings surrounding man the apprehension of hidden orders is in fact possible. This task is always new—with every changed situation it was essential, for that particular situation, to wrest some form of order from chaos. The task was an unending one, as unending as the manifestations of life. If these maxims show a tendency towards universal validity which seems to us on occasion commonplace, for the men of old it was precisely the break-through to the generally and universally valid that was the most important thing. Such proverbs had the dignity and value of know-ledge painfully garnered. As has already been said in this respect, the pinning down of paradoxical phenomena is especially instructive. That one who is sated tramples honey underfoot, while to the hungry what is bitter tastes sweet (Prov. xxvii. 7); that a gentle tongue breaks bones (Prov. xxv. 15); that he who loves his son chastises him (Prov. xiii. 24, xxiii. 13f.); that the bread of deceit tastes sweet, but the mouth is afterwards filled with gravel (Prov. xx. 17)—these are initially hard and perplexing facts, that is, if they are experienced in the individual case without any other reference. Therefore when behind what seemed to be paradoxical events or facts a hidden order could after all be dis-cerned, the satisfaction was all the deeper. Chaos was once again averted. So wisdom of this kind is undoubtedly a quite elementary form of the mastering of life. We do well not to take it as primarily didactic. No doubt these maxims were soon gathered together, and in the hands of teachers were given their basic function in instruction. But the origin of this discovery of conformity to rule takes place at an earlier time and on a much more elementary plane, and its results served the direct end of safeguarding life and maintaining the self in face of the weari-some consequences and conclusions to which men are forced by

---

[7] *Spruch und Bild bei den Morgenländern* (1792), in *Werke*, ed. B. Suphan, Berlin 1877–1913, VOL. XVI, p. 10.   [8] *Op. cit.*, p. 360.

experience.[9] In every proverb the stable door is only locked after the horse has been stolen.[10] The purpose which these maxims are intended to serve could be called, rather than teaching, an art for living or at least a certain technique for life. The wise men who came later very picturesquely described wisdom as an art of steering (תחבלות, LXX κυβέρνησις, Prov. I. 5), the art of piloting oneself through the confusion of life. Are there rules for this? Is it possible to read off from events, or conduct, or the complex reactions of men, conformities to law, the knowledge of which is of help in life? How do I protect myself from harm? How do I hold my inward and my worldly resources together? How do I meet the claims of others? These maxims, saturated as they are by experience, resemble buoys set out on the sea by which one can find one's position. Herder says very shrewdly that one has not to learn "from" such maxims, but "with their help."[11]

All these maxims, as Herder and Jolles in particular have made clear, have no movement linking them together or drawing conclusions from the events which they record, but are out and out affirmatory.[12] Now, when we bear in mind that every people expended a great deal of trouble and artistry in the formation of this kind of Wisdom literature, and that gnomic apperception is in fact one of the most elegant forms of human thinking and a weapon in the struggle for spiritual content in life,[13] it will be apparent that there are two completely different forms of the apperception of truth for mankind—one systematic (philosophical and theological) and one empirical and gnomic. Each requires the other. Where the one employed by the Wisdom literature is wanting, men are in danger of reducing everything to dogma, and indeed of running off into ideological fantasy. Empirical and gnomic wisdom starts from the unyielding presupposition that there is a hidden order in things and events—only, it has to be discerned in them, with great patience and at the cost of all kinds of painful experience. And this order is kindly and righteous. But, characteristically, it is not understood systematically—and therefore not in such a way as to reduce all the variety experienced and perceived to a general

[9] A. Jolles, *Einfache Formen*, Halle 1930, p. 167.

[10] "In jedem Sprichwort deckt man den Brunnen zu, aber erst, wenn das Kind ertrunken ist," A. Jolles, *op. cit.*, p. 159.

[11] Herder, *Spruch und Bild bei den Morgenländern*, in *Werke*, VOL. XV, p. 11.

[12] A. Jolles, *Einfache Formen*, p. 163.

[13] R. Petsch, *Spruchdichtung des Volkes*, Halle 1938, p. 105.

principle of order, and least of all by the search for a formula which might be spacious enough to comprehend the infinitely varied world of phenomena. This would be the philosophic and systematic way. But, as Jolles says, conceptual thinking cannot possibly apprehend the world to which gnomic thinking applies itself.[14] Wisdom examines the phenomenal world to discern its secrets, but allows whatever it finds to stand in its own particular character absolutely. It is easy to confront certain proverbs with others completely different in content, indeed on occasion absolutely contradictory. Taken strictly, this incongruity is even the rule, for an experience would never have been mentioned or painstakingly formulated if it coincided with those already to hand. Thus wisdom shows not the slightest fear in occasionally formulating antinomies and leaving them unresolved:

He who has insight restrains his words, and he who has a cool spirit is a man of understanding. Even the fool can pass for wise, as long as he keeps silence; for a man of understanding, if he closes his lips (Prov. XVII. 27f.).

Answer not the fool according to his folly, lest you be like him yourself. Answer the fool according to his folly, lest he think himself wise (Prov. XXVI. 4f.).[15]

Thus the experiences always remain open to correction, and are basically capable of enlargement. A philosophical system can in theory be thought of as rounded off, and thus as so comprehensive that the truth contained in it may be described as adequate. But wisdom is always open and never brought to conclusion. Her way of approach to truth is completely different : so too is her openness to correction different from that of philosophy. Her province is not any exclusive understanding of truth, for the proverb which makes a correction does not prove the falsity of the other one; it only leads on to another order which has in the meantime come into the field of vision. What this way of thinking deals with is rather compartments of orders, which it arranges in a row.[16]

[14] A. Jolles, *Einfache Formen*, p. 156.

[15] Cf. Ecclesiastes VII. 3, 9. Zimmerli in *Z.A.W.*, 1933, p. 188.

[16] "When we conceive the world as a multiplicity of individual perceptions and experiences, these perceptions and experiences, when comprehended as a series and put together, admittedly in each case produce *the experience*, but even the sum total of these experiences remains a multiplicity of single entities. Each experience is on each occasion apprehended independently: a conclusion based upon experience is in this way and in this kind of world only binding and valuable in itself and of itself. It is a timeless world . . . because the moments, in their character as isolated, are not

In and accompanying this runs, though not of course everywhere to the same extent, an obvious element of the playful. Who can fail to notice, particularly in the formulation of the paradoxes just touched upon, the delight, and indeed, on occasion, the gaiety lying behind them which often enough over-state the observation to the point of being funny.[17] If the playful is given still freer vein, we meet with the riddle. As is well known, here play is made with the discovery of truth, albeit play with serious realities. For this veiling and unveiling of truths forms part of the most original pleasures of the *homo ludens*.[18] The Wisdom literature of the ancient East seems to have evolved a specially fine cultivation of the riddle. The story of the Queen of Sheba's visit to Solomon, and of the riddles which she asked, is no doubt not contemporary as far as literary form goes with the visit itself. But it fits perfectly into the picture of the mutual exchange which as we know was cultivated by this wisdom's representatives (1 Kings x). In the literature of the Bible the number of express riddles is admittedly very small. But this is unimportant, for stylistically the widespread practice of clothing maxims in metaphor has to be taken in the context of the play with riddles. With the artistic device of metaphor the composer of proverbs puts something well known as a riddle.[19]

> Clouds and winds and yet no rain,
> So is a man who boasts of gifts and never gives.
> > (Prov. xxv. 14)
>
> Like a dog that returns to its vomit,
> So is the fool, who repeats his folly.   (Prov. xxvi. 11)

able together to pass as time. . . . It is impossible to think this world through conceptually, for it is precisely conceptual thinking which this world resists and which on its part destroys this world. Admittedly, here too there is a severing and a binding . . . but the severing preponderates in the bindings, the juxtaposition remains in the relationship, the separation of the members continues in the orders. In a word, this world is not cosmos, but separation, empiricism." A. Jolles, *Einfache Formen*, pp. 155ff.

[17] Cf. Prov. xx. 17, xxvi. 15, xxvii. 15.

[18] Huizinga, *Homo Ludens*, Basel 1944, pp. 171ff. Cf. Samson's very ancient riddle: "What is sweeter than honey? What is stronger than a lion?"—love (Jg. xiv. 18).

[19] In this connexion, B. Gemser, *Sprüche Salomos* (Hb. A.T., Tübingen 1937), p. 3, draws attention to Prov. x. 13, xiii. 19. A good illustration is the story of Darius' pages' nightly competition in riddles (1 Esdras iii). An even richer yield would be brought to light by a careful investigation of the prophetic literature, although here too only Ezek. xvii. 2 is designated as riddle (חידה). But is not Is. viii. 5, about "the waters of Shiloah that flow gently," a discourse in the form of a riddle?

The hearer, who is also thinking along with the speaker, tries to run ahead of the latter and disentangle the meaning from its figurative clothing. Of course, in many cases the pictures have faded into simple metaphors. On the other hand, very much more often we must reckon that the real point of the humour in many of them no longer strikes a chord with us. In this respect the magnificent saying about the crackling of thorns under the pot which sounds like the laughter of fools is almost an exception (Ecclesiastes VII. 6).[20]

But there is a further point connected with this kind of picture which draws comparisons. In the maxim about the clouds and winds without rain and the boastful man, how is the comparison to be taken? (Prov. XXV. 14). Is not more very likely meant than just a comparison chosen more or less casually, for the purpose of illustration; is not the implication rather the existence of a relationship of correspondence between two phenomena lying upon totally different planes? We constantly encounter this sober, recording glance of wisdom out into man's environment—how keenly it was also directed to natural phenomena will be dealt with later on.

> The north wind brings rain,
> gossip in secret, cross looks.   (Prov. XXV. 23)
> When the wood runs short, the fire goes out,
> where there is no slanderer, quarrelling ceases.
> (Prov. XXVI. 20)
> Iron is sharpened upon iron,
> and one man sharpens the behaviour of the other.[21]
> (Prov. XXVII. 17)
> The underworld and Hades are never satisfied,
> and never satisfied are the eyes of man.
> (Prov. XXVII. 20)
> He who touches pitch, it sticks to his hand,
> and he who goes about with the scorner becomes like
> unto him.   (Ecclesiasticus XIII. 1)

[20] "Their [these proverbs'] way of speaking by allusions and pictures lays hold of the plain surface of things, brings them quickly into connexion with something similar from a deeper level, and in this way pushes forward into depths of the world which can no more be expressed in words." Petsch, *Spruchdichtung des Volkes*, Halle 1938, pp. 103f.

[21] Emendation and translation following Gemser, *Sprüche Salomos*, *in loco*. Cf. also Prov. XXIV. 13, XXVI. 11.

These examples, which could easily be multiplied, state analogies between processes in "nature" and in the life of man. Thus the point of these maxims is a comparison of totally different realms of order, which yet reveal analogous phenomena and which can therefore be co-ordinated. We again come up against the proverb about the insatiability of Sheol in the purely scientific context of a numerical proverb (Prov. xxx. 15f.). Such numerical proverbs contained no kind of moral teaching, as was formerly supposed, but are first attempts at the co-ordination of puzzling natural phenomena.[22] So for example Prov. xxx. 15f. deals with a variety of things which can never be satisfied, and Prov. xxx. 24ff. with a number of small but specially "wise" animals. In the proverb in xxx. 18f. four puzzling things are put together under the catchword "way" (דרך) (the way of the eagle in the sky, that of the serpent on the earth, that of a ship on the sea, and the "way" of a man with a maid). It can be seen that all of these are things lying on the margin of what is rationally comprehensible. But these puzzling things must somehow be mastered conceptually, and this is achieved by ranging them in categories. When like can be set alongside like, there is already great gain, for these phenomena now lose the absolutely puzzling quality they had in isolation. Wisdom's constituent is this incisive will for the rational clarification and ordering of the world in which man finds himself, the will to recognise and pin down the orders in both the events of human life and natural phenomena. Unfortunately, only a few texts are available to show the change in the way of looking at nature to which the Enlightenment in the time of Solomon paved the way; they are, however, extensive enough to allow us to recognise the great changeover to a rational way of looking at nature, to the extent of collecting the facts in scientific catalogues. There must have been in Israel as elsewhere "Onomastica," cataloguing compendia, which, starting with the heavens and the weather and going on to the various peoples and animals, enumerated the whole phenomenal world in long series of nouns; for some poems (Job xxxviiiff.; Ps. cxlviii; Ecclesiasticus xliii) quite obviously follow such lists, which are derived from the "Onomastica" known to us from Egypt.[23] But no one need be surprised that, especially in poetry, the

[22] Alt, *K.S.*, vol. ii, pp. 90ff.

[23] G. von Rad, "Hiob 38 und die altägyptische Weisheit," in *Vet. Test.*, Suppl. iii (1955), pp. 293ff., reprinted in *Ges. Studien*, pp. 262ff. In Ecclesiasticus xxxix. 26 the "basic things" which man needs for his physical existence are gathered together—

traditional world view maintained itself alongside of this one—indeed, compared with the new, the former remained predominant. But the new possibilities now opened up for speaking about Creation are apparent in a passage in Job's discourse:

> Didst thou not pour me out like milk,
>   and curdle me as cheese?
> With skin and flesh thou didst clothe me,
>   and knit me together with flesh and bones.
>
> (Job x. 10)

How realistic, observant, rational, and scientific is the description of the formation of man from the liquid sperm, and how patriarchal and sacral the picture in the sources J and E in Genesis sounds in comparison! It all has a very modern ring for us, as indeed it had for its own time as well. Nor would we go wrong if we assumed that this striving after rational insight only prevailed in an educated and learned upper stratum. If we unquestionably have to do here with a scientific way of observation unfolding itself on a rational basis, still it is of the utmost importance to bear firmly in mind that Israel knew neither our concept of "nature" nor the Greek one of a "cosmos." For her the world was not a stable and harmoniously ordered organism, including equally every datum, organic and inorganic alike, and so much to be regarded as a whole that the question of its ultimate determining principle (ἀρχή) was legitimate. Because of this the utmost caution has to be observed in using our concept of "nature," though often of course it can hardly be avoided. (Least of all ought there to be any talk of "nature psalms.") If for the Hebrew the concept of nature was not a given one—and this of course is very difficult for us to picture—the world thus fell

water, fire, iron, salt, wheat-meal, milk, honey, wine, oil, and clothing. For the Egyptian scientific lists, which became standard for Israel, cf. A. H. Gardiner, *Ancient Egyptian Onomastica*, London 1947. For the Sumerio-Babylonian scientific lists, cf. W. von Soden, "Leistung und Grenze sumerischer und babylonischer Wissenschaft," in *Die Welt als Geschichte*, Jahrgang 2, Stuttgart 1936, pp. 411ff. "Numbering, counting, enumerating are means of intellectual orientation. . . . The pedagogical technique of classifying and memorising made the numerical apothegm . . . extremely popular [in the Middle Ages]. Paulinus of Pella . . . set forth 'the ten signs of ignorance'. . . . The author of a codex on deportment knew that the wise Thales himself had written the seven 'curialitates' and seven 'rusticitates' in golden letters on the 'colossus' in Rome": E. R. Curtius, *European Literature and the Latin Middle Ages*, London 1952, p. 510.

much more within the sphere of the imponderable and immeasurable, and he was much less secured over against it through a workable set of concepts than we imagine.[24] The Hebrew's slowness in forming abstract concepts is well known. But just try to imagine an intellectual encounter with and confrontation of the world without our workable abstract concepts! For Israel the world was probably very much more of a process than a thing in being. Since the way of intellectual mastery of this process by means of the consideration of a first principle was not open to her, she was pointed to examination and classification of the individual phenomena, in order to familiarise herself with its external aspect, so far as it could be deciphered at all. But she never found her way to the idea of a cosmos governed throughout by unchangeable laws.[25] The process in which she found herself placed was too mysterious and too much a realm of the action of Jahweh for her to be able to do this. Expressing it somewhat exaggeratedly, to her "world" was a sustaining activity of Jahweh, in which the extraordinary was no more marvellous than the apprehended order. This, however, means that the insights attained into the world surrounding her were in the last analysis orders apprehended by faith. Here it is not, as it were, pure empiricism—if there is any such thing—that finds expression. In the unyielding assumption that in spite of all there must be an order in things was already inherent an implicit faith acquainted with the deep hiddenness of the divine *conservatio* and *gubernatio*. These maxims are the utterances of a humanity which knew itself and its personal life as deeply bound up with what went on in the world around

[24] L. Köhler, *Hebrew Man*, trans. P. R. Ackroyd, London 1956, p. 132.

[25] "It is the characteristic of the Greeks that the world does not confront them confused and cut up into single entities, guided, as the case might be, by whatever may take the fancy of primitive utilitarianism, or the strivings of an existence determined merely by the forces of the instinct. They were endowed with the wonderful gift of seeing everything as a unity and from the point of unity. Even in opposites they did not experience the incompatibility of the contradiction. It was rather that they saw in opposites the complementary poles between which a unity is suspended. It was in disunity that the unity of the world proved itself to them. And their ability to be whole was so great, that the fairest unity seemed to them to come precisely in the joining of opposing forces, in architecture as well as in art and poetry. Harmony is the wonderful name for such a joining wrought out of opposing forces, a word which has unfortunately become so worn out in every-day use, that generally what is understood by it is merely a colourless balance, and people hardly think any longer of the tensions that lie behind it and the effort that it demands." W. Schadewaldt, *Sophokles und das Leid*, Potsdamer Vorträge IV, Potsdam 1947 p 30.

it. While present-day man lives his life very much isolated from the world, and is determined by the feeling of otherness and foreignness to it, Hebrew man felt it to be much more personally related to himself. Its orders had still much to say to him: they were in fact open and flexible towards him. The process in which he found himself was turned to him and his conduct in a relationship of correspondence: it was ready to adapt itself to him in blessing and furtherance, but it was also in a position to affect him penally.

> He who digs a pit (for another) falls into it,
> and he who starts a stone rolling, upon himself will it come back.
> (Prov. XXVI. 27)

Present-day ideas know of no such relationships between what is religious and moral and external consequences, but the ancients firmly believed in them and held it to be the part of wisdom to base the conduct of life on the recognition of such connexions.

Any sound discussion of Israel's wisdom means taking the concept as broadly as it was in fact taken. For her, thinking in terms of wisdom was something common to humanity. Wisdom had to do with the whole of life, and had to be occupied with all of its departments. It was most unfortunate that in the past the Old Testament wisdom was thought of more or less as the product of an exclusive theological school.[26]

Wisdom thus consisted in knowing that at the bottom of things an order is at work, silently and often in a scarcely noticeable way, making for a balance of events. One has, however, to be able to wait for it, and also to be capable of seeing it. In such wisdom is something of the humble—it grows through having an eye for what is given, particularly through having an eye for man's limitations. It always prefers facts to theories. To be wise is therefore just not to think oneself wise. Thinking oneself wise is the hall-mark of the fool, who is no longer open to suggestion, but trusts in himself (Prov. XXVI. 12, XXVIII. 26). Folly is the disregard or transgression or misunderstanding of the orders to which the wise man subordinates himself. The fool knows nothing of the dangers inherent in speaking (Prov. X. 14, XVIII. 2, 6, XXIX. 20f)

---

[26] Thus it is not at all surprising that many echoes of the wise men's thought and of their style have been found in the prophetic writings as well. J. Fichtner, "Jesaja unter den Weisen," in *Th. Lz.*, 1949, pp. 75ff.; J. Lindblom, "Wisdom in the OT Prophets," in *Vet. Test.*, Suppl. III (1955), pp. 192ff.

and in particular the dangers of a rash, uncontrolled behaviour (Prov. XII. 16, XIV. 17, 29, XXIX. 11). Thus the word "folly" does not describe a particular intellectual defect—it is altogether much more related to action than to perception. Folly is a disorder in the centre of a man's life which, however, in the end also results in the loss of his attainment in wisdom. The misconception of the orders about which a man ought to know thus results in particular in rashness and presumption.[27]

So far our concern has been with the basic question of the understanding of the maxims in the Wisdom literature, that is with the general question of the particular form of this intellectual activity, and the object to which it was directed and with which it was occupied. In the process, the distinction between the proverb proper and the artistic maxim and the question as to the latter's *Sitz im Leben* could still remain open, for the artistic maxim too serves the safeguarding of life and the attempt to shape it in the light of particular orders and facts. Only, the environment in which men were set the task of mastering life had to some extent altered. As in Egypt in particular, so in Israel, wisdom had found a place of cultivation at the court. It appears that the newly-arisen court in Jerusalem very soon entered into the general cultural competition and exchange of ideas, for wisdom was reckoned as a high cultural asset, whose cultivation and advance was especially enjoined upon kings. It was really something international and common to all religions. Israel too understood it in this way, for without any scruples she compares the wisdom of Solomon with that of the other peoples (1 Kings v. 10f. [IV. 30f.]). (In what other department would Israel have thus without scruple measured her assets of truth against those of other nations?) Foreign wisdom flowed into her from three sides—the Edomite and Old Arabian south-east, Babylon, and in particular Egypt.[28] It can be seen especially from the relevant Egyptian literature, that wisdom played a great part in the education of the rising generations of the official class. The great Wisdom books all have the form of a master teaching his scholars, and sometimes of the king teaching his son and heir to the throne. Consequently the instruction

---

[27] W. Caspari, "Über den biblischen Begriff der Torheit," in *Neue kirchliche Zeitschrift*, pp. 668ff.

[28] Edomite wisdom is mentioned in Jer. XLIX. 7; Ob. 8; Babylonian in Jer. L. 35, LI. 57; and Egyptian in 1 Kings v. 10 [IV. 30]. The passage in Prov. XXII. 17–XXIII. 11 is taken over directly, with a small number of deviations, from the Egyptian wisdom book of Amenemope. Details in Gemser, *Sprüche Salomos, in loco*.

which follows is almost exclusively admonition, and is chiefly concerned with the behaviour of the official to his superiors and subordinates—it warns against all excess of enjoyment and seeks to train the young man in self-mastery and in particular in the skilful use of speech. It is true, however, that a difference between Egyptian and Israelite wisdom is at once apparent here—Israelite wisdom is not nearly so strongly tied to a class or focused on the world of officials.[29] This difference penetrates right into the inner structure of Israelite wisdom; for while Egyptian wisdom, in keeping with its whole didactic aim, is almost exclusively in admonitory form, what preponderates in Israel's is the maxim which states and affirms, that is, the genuine form of the proverb proper. In fact, even a superficial review shows that a large body of popular proverbs was taken up into the Biblical book of Proverbs, and this means that it expresses in a much more central way what is common to humanity in general with its basic experiences which lie outside of any professional boundaries. Nevertheless the older collections (Prov. x–xxix)—permeated as they are by proverbs about the king, and about behaviour at court, etc.—were no doubt edited at the royal court in Jerusalem.[30] It can be very easily assumed, therefore, that they too—as was completely the case in Egypt—served there in the education and schooling of the rising generation of officials. In Israel as well pains were taken to train young people of high rank. The capacities which the courtier extolled in the youthful David give a clear picture of the capacities which people—or at any rate the storyteller—presupposed in a well-educated young man (I Sam. xvi. 18f.). He had to be extremely good-looking, instructed in the use of weapons, skilful in playing the lyre, and powerful in speech (נבון דבר). It was thus not so very easy to be taken up at court in the direct service of the king. Only those who were particularly skilful were picked out for it (Prov. xxii. 29), for from the time of Solomon onwards the political life even of Israel had become complex, and an official in the diplomatic service had to be competent in a great many things. He had to be a master of foreign languages, and in particular an expert in his own field, that is, as it was then expressed, he had to give counsel to the king (Prov. xv. 22, xx. 8; Tobit iv. 18). Like the "word" for the prophets,

---

[29] Israel did not in any shape or form invent a professional ethos for the courtier or the citizen or for any other class. J. Hempel, *Ethos*, p. 133.

[30] Prov. XIV. 28, 35, XVI. 12, XIX. 12, XX. 2, 8, 26, 28, XXI. 1, XXIII. 3, XXIV. 21, XXV. 3, XXIX. 4, 12, 14, 26, are purely courtly proverbs of the kind.

and "divination" for the priests, for the wise men "counsel" was the proper form of their professional utterance (Jer. XVIII. 18). This giving of counsel always took place in connexion with affairs of state, and it was in this that the test of the official's ability at the court really lay. For in order to be able to give counsel it was not enough to be an expert—a man had also to be able to speak and to state his case convincingly in well-chosen words. Egyptian education made the art of mastering a situation by means of lofty speech the most important subject of study—it was probably the chief goal at which education in the schools aimed.[31] If we look at the extremely large number of maxims in the Biblical book of Proverbs dealing with right speaking and right silence, we see how readily Israel too entered into this high cultivation of rhetoric in the ancient East. Hardly ever was the art of the cultivation of the right word at the right time, the art of the "pleasant word" (אמרי נעם Prov. XVI. 24), more highly esteemed than with her. In its historical writings the Old Testament contains many a finished example of such speeches (Gen. XXIV. 34ff., XLIV. 18ff.; II Sam. XIV. 5ff.). But all are surpassed by the verbal contest in the privy council of Absalom. It shows what giving counsel in matters of high politics meant (II Sam. XVII. 1ff.).

Israel too in her upper classes was thus aware of an ideal of culture, for this wisdom, originally fairly exclusive, was concerned with the totality, the moulding of the whole man. It took as the basis for this a very special picture of man which we already know from the old Egyptian wisdom, namely the man who was silent in the proper way.[32]

[31] Cf., for example, Prov. XXIII. 9, XXV. 9, 11, 15, XXVI. 4f., XXVII. 11, XXIX. 20.

[32] H. Brunner in Ägyptologie (Handbuch d. Orientalistik), Leiden 1952, p. 96. The Hebrew word corresponding to what we understand by "culture" is מוסר. Its root meaning is "chastisement," and we meet it with this meaning in Proverbs too (XIII. 24, XXII. 15, XXIII. 13). But at the same time a usage in the transferred sense is also current, with something like the meaning of "discipline," "instruction." Here the word therefore does not mean chastisement, but already its effect (Jer. V. 3, VII. 28, XVII. 23, XXXII. 33, XXXV. 13). Still further removed is the usage in a few passages in Proverbs where the term has lost the background of penalty, the presupposition of hurting. One "hears" מוסר (Prov. XIX. 27), and one "ignores it" (Prov. XIII. 18, XV. 32). In Prov. XXIII. 23 מוסר is a synonym for בינה and חכמה. In Prov. XIX. 20 it stands synonymously alongside עצה; in Prov. X. 17, XII. 1, XIII. 18, XV. 5, 32 it stands in parallelism with תוכחת, which is better translated by "warning" than "reprimand." Thus the usage is comparable with that of the Greek word παιδεία, which Aeschylus still uses for the chastisement of children, though afterwards with the Sophists it became the epitome of proper fashioning of body and soul. (W. Jaeger, Paideia, trans. G. Highet, Oxford 1939–44, VOL. I, p. 283.)

Its standard is the "man of cool spirit" (קַר רוּחַ, Prov. XVII. 27), who in contrast to the "hot-tempered" man (אִישׁ חֵמָה, Prov. XV. 18, XXII. 24) has his emotions and impulses under control, the "tranquil mind" (לֵב מַרְפֵּא, Prov. XIV. 30, cf. XV. 4), the "slow to anger" (Prov. XIV. 29), who in contrast to the man who is "hasty tempered" (קְצַר רוּחַ, Prov. XIV. 29) will not let the rule of his actions be dictated by any unruly character who comes along. In some of its very important facets, this ideal of culture had affinities with Greek rules of conduct, particularly with the basic one of holding to the mean, with σωφροσύνη and φρόνησις, "the correct recognition of what is proper to the time" (Dornseiff), which were already normative for the early ethic of the nobility (Pindar).[33] But it also has affinities with the "Maze" of the Middle Ages. The story of Joseph, which is a wisdom story throughout, shows us this picture of man in wonderful perfection. In scene after scene it depicts a young man who through discipline, modesty, knowledge, self-mastery, and the fear of God (Gen. XLII. 18) had given a noble form to his whole being, and who in weal or woe always remains the same. Before Pharaoh he proves himself a shrewd counsellor, and before his brothers the man who can be silent, who represses his natural emotions, and finally the one who "covered up all sins with love" (Prov. X. 12).

With this task of education wisdom teaching set itself a new goal. It is clear that a change has come over it compared with the elementary wisdom teaching of the popular proverb spoken of above. But even in this altered aristocratic form it appears as what it always was—an attempt to safeguard life and to master it on the broad basis of experience. However, first of all the sphere of this wisdom teaching is more restricted—it is the sheltered world of a section of higher social standing who have their own particular problems (preservation of property, honour, and position). For another thing, its aim had shifted. It no longer seeks to harken to the most elementary basic orders within which human life in general moves, but applies itself to the cultivation of men and has in consequence become much more directly didactic. This distinction between the wisdom teaching which tries to discover elementary orders and that which educates like a teacher is a necessary one for the understanding of the phenomenon of the Wisdom literature in the Old Testament. Admittedly, it is difficult to decide in detail to which of the two forms a proverb may incline. And such an analysis

[33] E. Schwartz, *Die Ethik der Griechen*, Stuttgart 1951, pp. 52ff., 230.

is made all the more difficult because, as is well known, the editing of the proverbs to make the various collections was from the start undertaken from the point of view of teaching. A large part of the store of popular proverbs must, however, have been of service in this purpose of cultivating men. But in this case we must be clear that we are having to do with a special and secondary application of this store. But it was precisely because of this that the basis of the cultivation of man became so broad—what was proper to a particular social standing had again and again to give way before what is common to all men.

It is impossible to mention all the spheres of man's common life to which these directions for a well-ordered life apply. Becoming a cultured man begins with table manners, and so the teachers of wisdom do not fight shy of giving rules for behaviour at table (Prov. XXIII. 1; Ecclesiasticus XXXI. 12ff.). And it ends at the point where in his action and in the expansion of his ego a man comes up against mysterious limits set for him by God. As will be shown more clearly later on, the determination of these limits was one of the most delicate tasks in this system of the wise men's training for life. All the same, it would be completely wrong to assume that these wisdom teachers started their instruction by beginning with the most outward things and then moving slowly towards God, that is, towards faith and revelation. The opposite is the truth: the starting point of this education is knowledge of God, and of his revelation and commandments. The fear of the Lord, that is, obedience to his will, is the beginning of wisdom (Prov. I. 7, IX. 10, XV. 33; Ps. CXI. 10). The man whom wisdom instructed was a member of the cultic community, his life was subject to manifold cultic ties, in the Temple at the great pilgrimage festivals he heard the peremptory or the comforting voice of Jahweh: to order a man's life in this—that is, the cultic—sphere lay completely outwith the jurisdiction of the teacher of wisdom. But of course a wide sphere still remained unconditioned and unregulated by the cult, where the apodictic commandments in their character as confessional rules forbidding certain things, and much less the conditional law, could give no direction, because no absolute commandment (unless by a most appalling legal casuistry) was of any help at all: and yet in this sphere so many decisions had daily to be made. It is the sphere of the most common and ordinary in daily life, in which the question was not always of murder or adultery or theft, though it was brimful of questions of a different sort. The most ordinary dealings with other people, intelligent and foolish, strangers and the importunate, and particularly with women, raised them. And people had also to learn how to manage money, and their own bodies and—what was hardest of all—their tongue, which had no less than life and death in its power (Prov. XVIII. 21). How many such questions and others like them were raised by one day, and how many decisions were wrested from the person who refused simply to drift. Here the wisdom teacher wanted to help the young man to preserve his strength and fortune and to safeguard his manhood. But he did so not with divine commandments: these he had no authority to give, for his counsels were of course derived essentially from experience. In consequence what he could help the young man with were only "pieces of advice" (עֵצָה). Such counsel does not demand obedience, but it asks to be tested: it appeals to the judgment of the hearer; it is intended to be understood, and to make decisions easier.[34] This attempt at education deriving from faith and cult and knowledge of the commandments, is very much the opposite of certain modern pedagogic projects, in so far as it lacks any presumptuous claim to offer redemption. Instead it is completely non-doctrinaire and non-rigid in character: it has an astonishing ability to adjust itself, without illusion, to what is actual. In its concentration upon the possible it has something decidedly realistic about it, and on occasion it is even opportunist.

Now that the place of wisdom in relationship to the world of the cult and of revelation has been determined, we can finally raise the question of the theological relevance of this wisdom teaching. This question would be much easier to answer if our views were not prejudiced by one or two traditional conclusions of research which have been fairly well established until now. For the question of the theological content of this wisdom teaching has been put far too quickly and far too directly. It was raised by people who came to the teaching from historical books, the commandments, the prophets and the Psalms, and since the range of its utterances is theologically speaking incomparably narrower, and its *motifs* much more monotonous, and since, in contrast with the tenor of the old divine commandments, man with his questions now sets himself in the centre, the obvious conclusion seemed to be that this wisdom teaching expresses a piety that has already become very much secularised and emancipated. To some extent we are dealing with a marginal phenomenon already in grave danger, or theologically speaking with a product of a decaying

[34] Zimmerli, in *Z.A.W.*, 1933, pp. 182ff.

Israel. This optimistically rational piety might have maintained itself for a time, but the inroad of scepticism, and indeed of despair, into it with its diminished vigour was only a matter of time. But so to take the wisdom teaching is completely to misrepresent its nature. It ought not to be at all considered in relation to the central content of Israel's faith and cult, for speaking and commenting on these lay outwith its competence. The function in Israel's life which it claimed as its own was comparatively limited, for its concern was to pin-point and investigate the external and internal orders by which human life is sustained and to which men must give heed. But if in this sphere proper to it wisdom teaching made only very limited theological pronouncements, while at the same time not simply deducing its admonitions and counsels from the existent "law," is this not rather the sign of a piety still retaining its ties with the cult and secure there?[35] Thus, a positive relationship to the world of the cult should rather be the conclusion drawn from the limitations of the subject-matter of the wisdom teaching.[36] For wisdom, questions of faith entered in only on the periphery of its field. It works with reason, in its simplest form as sound common sense: it is reason, and not faith, that must verify and admit that pride goes before a fall, that a dish of herbs where there is love is better than an ox where there is hatred, that bread which is got in an underhand way turns to gravel in the mouth, etc. The wise men made no differentiation between laws ascertained on the basis of different spheres of life (experiences in the "physical" realm, in political and public life, in the sphere of education, etc.)—in fact they did not even differentiate between the utilitarian and the ethical good. This last fact is to be explained by the conviction, deep-rooted in the whole of the ancient world, that the good is always and at the same time the useful. He who sows injustice reaps calamity (Prov. XXII. 8). The honest man walks securely, but he who goes in crooked ways will be found out (Prov. x. 9). To understand this deep conviction, we today have to consider the very different position of the individual in the community. Whoever acted rightly and whoever was a good man was good not only for

[35] The terms *torah*, *mizwah*, and *dabar* are occasionally found, "but it can be proved with absolute certainty that the *termini* mentioned are never used with a legal significance (law, commandments) in the proverbs, but everywhere with a significance which is in the context of wisdom (direction, advice)": J. Fichtner, *Die altorientalische Weisheit in ihrer israelitisch-jüdischen Ausprägung*, Bei. *Z.A.W.* No. 62, Giessen 1933, p. 83.

[36] What a wisdom document looks like when it takes the question of salvation itself as the subject of its investigation can be seen from Ecclesiastes.

himself alone and his isolated existence, but was always good for others and for the community as well. Honesty, self-control, and an even temper were constructive elements for the community and quite automatically brought consideration and esteem. Of course, the conviction that the good is also the useful had considerably deeper roots still for the men of the ancient world, for they were convinced that man was the prisoner of his own actions in a very radical sense. With every good and evil deed he enters upon a nexus of fate. Good and evil alike have to fulfil themselves upon their agent, for the act is in no sense ended with the deed itself. The deed has an element of radiation: it starts a movement for good or for evil, in which the community to which the agent belongs is also interested to a high degree. A man who organises his life properly and who takes his place in a helpful way within the community, who does justice to the claims of others (and of course also to those of God), this man wisdom calls righteous. The collection of proverbs in chs. xff. in particular never tires of praising this righteousness as something constructive and as a surety in life.[37] It is out of place to speak of "retribution," at any rate if we understand by it a forensic act imposed upon the agent from the outside. In fact, a divine norm, on whose violation divine punishment ensues, is never mentioned in these maxims—one seeks all in vain for concepts which are theologically speaking juristic.[38] Even more, the frequent assertion of the nexus between doing good and salvation, and the warnings about the nexus between sin and calamity, in themselves still stand altogether outside of theology. They are part of that teaching and pinpointing of orders and natural laws to which wisdom teaching committed itself, and which we have to understand initially as a wholly secular pursuit. The ever-repeated emphasis of these proverbs is this: remember these laws, of good and evil alike; do not be the fool who disregards these orders, but direct your life according to them; much is in your own power here—for good and evil alike; if you do not want to drift in life, you require a "moral understanding"[39] for all the many

[37] Prov. x. 2, 3, 6, 7, 11, 20, 21, 24, 25, 28, 30, 31, 32, etc. Obviously what we have here is not as yet the later theological concept of "the righteous man" which relates man unilaterally to Jahweh and his commandments. This righteousness of which the older proverbs speak is chiefly a verification in the sphere of the civic and social. Here the righteous man is he who is loyal (cf. Prov. XVII. 15, XVIII. 5, XXV. 5 and some others).

[38] K. Koch, "Gibt es ein Vergeltungsdogma im Alten Testament?" in Z. Th. K., 1955, pp. 2ff.   [39] E. Schwartz, Die Ethik der Griechen, Stuttgart 1951, p. 57.

decisions which will be wrested from you. All this is expressed more comprehensively and yet concisely in the maxim contained in Prov. XVI. 17: "The highway of the upright is avoidance of evil; he who is on guard on his way preserves his life."

What this wisdom teaching has to say only passes over into theology where the subject-matter contains some kind of pointer or reference to Jahweh, his activity, or what pleases or displeases him. In fact, the way in which God is spoken of in these maxims, and what is said about him theoretically and what is not said, is very important. The discussion of this may at the same time be taken as the test of whether the determination stated about the place of wisdom in relationship to the world of the cult and the sacral is justified.[40]

To begin with, we should have to mention a group of proverbs designating God as the one who weighs and tests the hearts of men. The expression is obviously derived from an Egyptian idea: but with how much greater right could it be repeated by Jahwism.[41] This way of speaking of God as the one who tests the heart makes clear at once that the Wisdom literature by no means displays a humanity which believed that it took all its decisions in isolation; on the contrary it saw itself very sharply exposed to a constant divine verdict. A further step in this direction is taken by another group of maxims which speak very directly of the displeasure (or pleasure) which God has in certain practices or ways of human behaviour.[42] To be sure, not all of the decisions which the wisdom teachers wanted to make easier for their pupils were decisions of faith. Whether one should answer a fool or not, or whether one should become surety for debt or not (Prov. XI. 15, XXII. 26)—

[40] In theological colouring these collections show certain differences (even apart from Prov. I–IX). The collection in chs. XXV–XXIX reckons as the oldest: it is also the most "worldly." Compared with it, the collection in chs. X–XXII. 16 says much more about Jahweh, and his will and action. It has been seen as the beginning of that process which became more and more apparent, through which the Wisdom literature became more and more theological, and in consequence the collection has been regarded as later. But the difference can also be connected with a possible special purpose and derivation, of which admittedly we know nothing. We must therefore avoid reconstructing a too straightforward process of development.

[41] Prov. XVI. 2, XVII. 3, XXI. 2, XXIV. 12 (XV. 3, 11). The idea derives from the Egyptian concept of the judgment of the dead, as a result of which the heart of the dead man was weighed in the balance by the god Thot. An illustration is to be found in *Altorientalische Bilder zum Alten Testament*, ed. H. Gressmann, 2nd edn. Berlin and Leipzig 1927, Pl. 203.

[42] Prov. XI. 1, 20, XV. 8, 9, 26, XVI. 5, 7, XVII. 15, XX. 10, 23, XXI. 3, XXII. 11.

these and much else fall within the realm of things indifferent (*Adia-phora*). But it is of course not surprising that in the great majority of the maxims the subject is in some way or another an expression of the will of Jahweh. The point about these maxims, then, is the fact that they recognised this will and applied it to a particular, and generally typical, situation. If in the process some direct assertion is made about Jahweh or his attitude ("it is an abomination to Jahweh if . . ."), it unquestionably gives the maxim greater theological directness; but in principle proverbs which do not name the name of Jahweh are not to be differentiated from the others. The maxims about the witness's utterance in court (Prov. XIV. 25, XIX. 5), about showing favour to one who is guilty (XVIII. 5), about moving boundaries (XXII. 28), etc., make no mention of God, but they nevertheless approximate quite closely to direct commandments of Jahweh (cf. Ex. XX. 16, XXIII. 1ff.; Deut. XIX. 14).[43] If above we recognised the "avoiding of evil"—evil to be understood in the widest sense of the term—as the task of life *par excellence* (Prov. XVI. 17), this has now to be supplemented by the other maxim, "by the fear of Jahweh [that is, by obedience to the command-ments] a man avoids evil" (Prov. XVI. 6).

A third group of maxims is probably the most illuminating theo-logically—it speaks of the limiting of human possibilities by God and God's free action. One maxim says, for example, that a man may deliberate a great deal—the "arrangements of the heart" (מערכי לב) are his own undisputed field, but the (right) answer comes from Jah-weh; that is, much can still happen between the thought and its ex-pression. A man may arrange much for himself, but with speech some-thing incommensurable comes into play; and when one succeeded in finding the right word, this was the inspiration of Jahweh. A similar contrast is found in the maxim given in Prov. XIX. 14: "Home and wealth are inherited from fathers: but a prudent wife is the gift of Jahweh." Inheritance, property, and even a good name are to some extent surveyable quantities which may be entered in the ledgers of life as constants, but in the choice of a life-companion everything is open and uncertain. What these gnomic sayings mean is not of course that the surveyable quantities, like property and the plannings of the human heart, come into being without Jahweh; but reason as it atten-tively examined events continually stumbled on a realm of extreme

---

[43] For a more detailed treatment of these maxims see Fichtner, *Die altorientalische Weisheit*, pp. 24f.

insecurity, something incalculable, and it was here that it met with the action of God in a palpable way.

> A man's heart thinks out a way for itself,
> but Jahweh guides its step.
>
> (Prov. XVI. 9)

> Many are the plans in the heart of a man,
> but it is the purpose of Jahweh that is established.
>
> (Prov. XIX. 21)

> Every way of a man is right in his own eyes,
> but the one who tests the heart is Jahweh.
>
> (Prov. XXI. 2, XVI. 2)

> A man's steps come from Jahweh,
> but man—how could he understand his way?
>
> (Prov. XX. 24)

> There is no wisdom, no understanding, no counsel
> over against Jahweh.
> The horse is harnessed for the day of battle,
> but the victory comes from Jahweh.
>
> (Prov. XXI. 30f.)[44]

These five maxims have it in common that all of them speak in a very radical and comprehensive fashion of the limitations imposed upon human action and discretion. But they do not deal with the well-known subject of the limited powers of humanity and its fallibility— in other words, they are far from seeing human life as somehow tragic. Their concern is rather the limitations set to active life by the fact of being beset behind and before by God. No, a theology cannot be extracted from these maxims. Were one to make the attempt, one would not discover much more than the allusions, frequent enough admit-tedly, to that hidden Nemesis apparent in ever so many events, which has been far too bluntly called "the doctrine of retribution" (as if the wise men were interested in "doctrines"). Indeed, what causes amaze-ment is what is not said about Jahweh. But when these wise men, in giving instruction as to how life was to be mastered, took the view that a man was wise if he always reckoned with God as a limiting factor and as incalculable, this was not at all due to an undermining of

---

[44] Cf. further Prov. XVI. 33, XXI. 1, XXV. 2, XXIX. 26.

theology and a loss of spiritual capital, for in the sphere of the rational and empirical enjoined upon the wisdom teaching, Jahweh could only be comprehended as limitation. What more could they have done theologically than keep setting up these sombre signs on the frontiers of this area? This last-mentioned group of maxims gives an extraordinary glimpse into the intention and insight of these teachers. They are aware that the area which man can grasp with his rational powers (*ratio*) and fill out with his being is really small. Wherever he turns, before he is aware of it he is once more confronted with the perfectly incalculable element in the action of Jahweh. It is affecting to see how such a vital art of mastering life is aware that it must halt at these frontiers—indeed, it even contrives to liquidate itself there, as the last-mentioned maxim so magnificently says (Prov. XXI. 30). It combines two things—man's confidence in his ability to master life and at the same time, with all the wisdom in the world, an awareness of the frontiers and a preparedness to fail in the sight of God. Nothing could be more perverse than to want, under the impression of these maxims, to ascribe to this wisdom teaching a resigned and even tragic attitude to life. The opposite would be more correct, for all the teaching and lessons of experience which the wise men impart to their pupils are designed to serve the end of "strengthening trust in Jahweh" (Prov. XXII. 19).[45] The way in which we are to think of such an ideal of human existence as the wise men envisaged is made clear to us in the story of Joseph. This is the wisdom teaching of the Old Testament at its most distilled, and the sum total of the whole story is expressed when the opinion is given that all human life is completely under the sovereign sway of God (Gen. L. 20).[46] But in so saying the wisdom teaching does not allow itself in any way to be paralysed in its mastering of life. Instead, in a sphere so incomprehensibly beset behind and before by God, it makes bold to give a noble form to an individual's life.

What has been said to some extent outlines the older wisdom teaching. At a later date, not precisely ascertainable, there was a decided movement into the realm of theology. Wisdom teaching became the custodian of centralities of the faith and approached man's environ-

---

[45] The passage Prov. XXII. 17–21 is to be set on a very high plane of theological importance, for here in the programmatic preface we have a correction which Israelite wisdom made on a group of proverbs taken over from Egypt.

[46] G. von Rad, "Josephgeschichte und ältere Chokma," in *Vet. Test.*, Supp. 1 (1953), p. 120, reprinted in *Ges. Studien*, pp. 272ff.

ment with the whole import of the quest for salvation—it asked about the meaning of Creation (Job XXVIII; Prov. VIII. 22ff.). Indeed, in odd inversion of its origin, it increasingly became the form *par excellence* in which all Israel's later theological thought moved.

6. ISRAEL'S THEOLOGICAL WISDOM[1]

What we may call the "human" wisdom of Israel is a phenomenon so complete and convincing in itself that it was first of all necessary to reconstruct it in its peculiar features. But in so doing we by no means exhausted what she understood by wisdom. In later, i.e. post-exilic, Israel a great change in the concept becomes visible. Wisdom is now understood as the divine call to men, and therefore as the mediator of revelation: it is the great teacher of all nations in general and of Israel in particular. Indeed, it is understood as the divine principle bestowed upon the world at Creation. Thus the entire theological thinking of late Judaism came more or less under the sway of wisdom: at any rate it found in the general concept a unity and an all-embracing binding factor such as Israel had not possessed until then. We can therefore say that the realm which the older human and empirical wisdom teaching had excluded with such a clear recognition of its limits was precisely that into which the theological wisdom teaching entered, claimed, and filled. The effective execution of this astonishing change can be ascertained without any difficulty, but as to the way in which the thorough transformation was effected, its causes, the time when it happened, and the men who brought it about, we are completely in the dark. We have no means of bridging the great gap between Prov. X–XXIX on the one hand and Prov. I–IX on the other. But who is to say that we are only to take the change as a more or less unilinear development? Various factors would suggest that we are dealing with ideas which once confronted one another as independent entities and only intermingled at a relatively late date.[2]

The conviction that perfect wisdom is with God alone was certainly

[1] C. Rylaarsdam, *Revelation in Jewish Wisdom Literature*, Chicago 1951; H. Ringgren, *Word and Wisdom, Studies in Hypostatization of Divine Qualities and Functions in the Ancient Near East*, Lund 1947; L. Jansen, *Die spätjüdische Psalmendichtung, ihr Entstehungskreis und ihr Sitz im Leben*, Oslo 1937.

[2] None the less it is easy to see a connexion between the decisive swing over and the strong inner changes which the post-exilic period brought with it. Van Imschoot, "Sagesse et ésprit dans l'Ancien Testament," in *Rev. bib.*, 1938, pp. 28f.

inherent in Jahwism from the beginning.[3] Indeed, it was precisely at the point of the boundlessness of the divine knowledge that man's mad ambition to be like God (Gen. III; Ezek. XXVIII. 1ff.), and his desire to "usurp" (Job XV. 8) something of this wisdom broke out. The same holds true of the idea that Jahweh—*ubi et quando visum est Deo*—could grant to specially chosen men a certain share in this superhuman knowledge. In this sense older Israel understood wisdom as a divine *charisma* with which men were now and then inspired, as for example Solomon with "divine wisdom" (חכמת אלהים, 1 Kings III. 28, v. 9 [IV. 29]). Although the Joseph stories do not in so many words attach the predicate "wisdom" to Joseph, it is nevertheless beyond doubt that they derive his interpretations of the dreams from a special *charisma*, namely one of wisdom, which empowered him to give an interpretation necessarily hidden from the Egyptian wise men (Gen. XLI. 16, 38). In a wholly different sphere, that of art, there was the operation of that "spirit of wisdom" with which Jahweh endowed the builders of the Tabernacle (Ex. XXVIII. 3, XXXI. 3 P). This spirit of wisdom enabled Joshua to lead Israel (Deut. XXXIV. 9). This idea of special endowment with a *charisma* of wisdom which occurs from time to time does not as yet seem to be in principle irreconcilable with the kind of thinking and presuppositions from which the older wisdom teaching started. Thus even in 1 Kings v. 9 [IV. 29], which is perhaps not a very old text but is yet older than Deuteronomy, it is said that God granted great wisdom to King Solomon, and here the narrator is thinking both of the wisdom of Solomon's proverbs and of his insights into the laws of nature. Nevertheless, it must here be stressed, particularly in view of what will follow, that experiential wisdom was in general very far from understanding itself as the fruit of a special divine revelation. It was rather an affair of reason and good common sense, and accordingly it had nothing to do with inspiration.[4] It lacked all direct contact with Jahweh's revelations. But the case is completely different with the wisdom of which Prov. I–IX speaks. There is change too from the point of view of literary style and form-criticism. In Prov. I–IX we are no longer dealing with maxims having a still ascertainable place in the life of the community, and which only subsequently became literature in fairly large collections. In Prov.

---

[3] The references which speak explicitly of Jahweh's wisdom do not start until comparatively late. Is. XXVIII. 29, XXXI. 2; Ps. CXLVII. 5; Prov. III. 19f.; Job IX. 4, XII. 13.

[4] Van Imschoot, in *Rev. bib.*, 1938, p. 26; Rylaarsdam, *Revelation in Jewish Wisdom Literature*, p. 72.

I–IX we find fairly elaborate theological poems showing the ability in each case to handle different literary forms with superb artistry, and they therefore have to be taken from the start as products of a literary theology.[5] Thus their place in the life of the community is also different from that which we may presuppose for Prov. xff.

In the poem on the "Fivefold Blessing of Wisdom" the fear of God and the knowledge of God are celebrated as the first of her gifts (Prov. II. 5–8). This in itself very clearly shows the great change in the claim now made, for hitherto the fear of God was the presupposition, "the beginning" of all empirical wisdom and all discovery of orders. It was out into the world and life that the latter wisdom teaching led a man and taught him his way, while the other makes the claim to lead to God. And this wisdom in no way approaches men in just a neutral guise, as teaching on the lips of a master: much more often it addresses them as a person, an "I" speaking with supreme authority. This address which it utters does not leave man for a moment in doubt that the offer of salvation *par excellence* is issued in it: it has in it throughout something of an impatient ultimatum (Prov. I. 20, VIII. 35). When a man hears this voice, he has entered upon the decision about life and death, for what this wisdom has to bestow is life, life, that is, in the grand sense of the Old Testament, as a saving blessing.[6] We remember that life was offered to older Israel by the commandments, and that Deuteronomy in particular set these ideas on the broadest possible basis. In actual fact, something of the urgency and also the concern of Deuteronomy's preaching, especially that of Deut. xxx. 15ff., is repeated in wisdom's imploring call, though the admonition is not now addressed to Israel as a whole, but personally *ad hominem*, to the individual. And here, in the intensity of this personal call, something really new appeared in Israel. For until now the offer of salvation had not been thus personally proclaimed to the individual, that is, as an offer demanding his whole personal vigilance, and indeed even a real effort on his part.[7] People can "acquire" this wisdom (Prov. IV. 7), "find it" (Prov. III. 13), and "seek after" it (Prov. II. 4), but they can

[5] Prov. VI. 1–19 is a foreign body in this context: the section contains admonitions in the style of the older wisdom teaching.

[6] Prov. III. 18, 22, IV. 13, 22f.

[7] In Deuteronomy, in the effort to give the individual an adequate share in the saving blessings, the blessing of Jahweh reaches individuals through the medium of the people of God which is blessed. Here the saving call is addressed right from the start to the individual.

also "miss" or "forsake" it (Prov. VIII. 36, IV. 6). But wisdom on its side preserves the man who trusts in it, it guides whoever does not rely upon his own understanding and makes him well pleasing in the sight of Jahweh (Prov. VIII. 35). Boström's investigations were the first to show the very personal way in which wisdom desired to enter into the individual's life and the intimacy of its address; Boström demonstrated that wisdom and its invitation have to be understood as the constructive opposite of the *Aphrodite paracyptusa*.[8] In the service of the goddess of voluptuousness women publicly invite men to come to them in order to offer the sacrifice of their chastity: wisdom similarly courts men and allures them to herself, though of course the feast to which she invites has become a marriage feast.[9] Wisdom wants to be a man's sister and intimate friend (Prov. VII. 4). What an odd thing: wisdom personified largely received blood and life from her more sensual opposite, Astarte, the goddess of love!

In spite of its very personal lineaments, theological definition of the wisdom under consideration is impossible. With ben Sirach a few generations later, at the turn of the third and the second centuries, it was identified with the Torah, but in Proverbs, etc., there is clearly no thought of any such direct equation.[10] None the less it is correct to say that wisdom is the form in which Jahweh's will and his accompanying of man (i.e. his salvation) approaches man. Wisdom is the essence of what man needs for a proper life, and of what God grants him. Still, the most important thing is that wisdom does not turn towards man in the shape of an "It," teaching, guidance, salvation or the like, but of a person, a summoning "I." So wisdom is truly the form in which Jahweh makes himself present and in which he wishes to be sought by man.[11] "Whoso finds me, finds life" (Prov. VIII. 35). Only Jahweh can speak in this way. And yet, wisdom is not Jahweh himself: it is something separate from him: indeed, it once designates itself as Jahweh's creature, albeit the first-born of all creatures (Prov. VIII. 22), and identifies itself with the thoughts which God cherished in creating the world (Prov. III. 19).

---

[8] G. Boström, *Proverbiastudien. Die Weisheit und das fremde Weib*, Lund 1935, pp. 15ff.

[9] So particularly Ecclesiasticus LI. 19ff.; Boström, *op. cit.*, pp. 161ff.

[10] Fichtner, *Die altorientalische Weisheit in ihrer israelitisch-jüdischen Ausprägung*, pp. 81ff.

[11] H. J. Kraus, "Die Verkundigung der Weisheit," in *Biblische Studien*, Heft 2, Neukirchen 1951, p. 31.

As was said above, the complete identification of wisdom with the Torah is an accomplished fact with ben Sirach. But this was certainly no absolute innovation, for in the light of this later age's thought this equation has to be regarded as simply a theological conclusion already latent in principle in Prov. I–IX and now come to maturity. But in it the theological concept of wisdom attained such a degree of clarification as to allow the wisdom teaching to draft a tremendous scheme of world history and saving history: wisdom was created by Jahweh before all creation, she came forth from his mouth (Ecclesiasticus I. 4, XXIV. 3). All Creation with all the nations was open before her, and she had searched for a home on earth among men (Ecclesiasticus XXIV. 7). But this first attempt to find a habitation among men failed.[12] God then assigned her a resting-place in Israel, and there, in the form of the Torah, "the Book of the Covenant of God," she took root and grew up into a magnificent tree (Ecclesiasticus XXIV. 12–23). But Jahweh also left a certain portion of wisdom to the nations—"according to his gift," as Sirach says limiting it (Ecclesiasticus I. 10). There is much less reserve in what the great poem about wisdom in Prov. VIII says about the portion of wisdom possessed by the world outside Israel.

> By me kings reign, and rulers decree what is just;
> By me princes and nobles rule, all just judges.
> (Text. emen. Prov. VIII. 15f.)

Here wisdom—the same wisdom as makes the offer of salvation to the men of the people of God—is also designated as a teacher of the Gentiles.[13] It is through her that they enjoy the blessings of law and order: all the wisdom of rulers derives from her. But of course only Israel can boast of the fullness of her gifts. Indeed, it may be said that in such theological reflexions upon history the wise men's aim was nothing less than an aetiology of Israel and Israel's special place among the nations. We can see how life within the Persian Empire, and even more among the Hellenistic hotch-potch of nations, was bound to lead the Jews, because of the very fact that they were faced with the uni-

---

[12] We already hear in Prov. I. 24ff. something of wisdom's disappointment: she has sought and called in vain. R. Bultmann in *Eucharisterion*, pp. 6f.

[13] There is also in Ecclesiasticus XVII. 1ff. a similar theological sketch of the history, which however passes over without any interruption from the Creation to the saving gift of the land (vss. 9ff.). And it too contains a reflexion on Israel's relationship to the nations: "For every nation he appointed a ruler (ἡγούμενος), but Israel is the Lord's portion" (vs. 17).

versal world of nations, to an intensification of their desire to clarify
their own special place in the history of mankind. So Israel once more,
at a very late epoch, found herself again confronted with the task of
understanding herself, in her own sight and in the world's, as Israel.
The force in the view of history thus attained lies in its utterly universal
inclusiveness as well as in the compelling challenge it made to the
responsibility of the individual. But compared with Israel's earlier
attempts to understand herself as the people of God in history, this one
is now slightly tinged with the pallor of theological reflexion. We look
in vain for clear evidence of the direction of this scheme of history
towards a definite historical hour with whose concrete situation Israel
had to identify herself.

That other nations existed in the historical realm was of course for
Israel no specially new insight: what was new was rather the question
of how far they possessed any truth. But an even more urgent factor
at the time was the determination to acquire knowledge of "nature,"
of the world as a totality. We find texts which are only comprehensible
as expressions of an age which asked questions about the meaning of
nature and the totality of the world in a rational sense hitherto unheard
of in Israel. Here the faith of Israel saw itself really confronted with a
new phenomenon, and new insights and experiences, with which it had
to reckon. The poem in Job XXVIII begins with a description of the
astonishing technical abilities of *homo faber*. In his mines he excavates
the mountains and brings treasures to light from their depth. But all
the mastery of the earth of which he is capable cannot hide the bitter
truth that the ultimate secret of the world is hidden from him. We can
see that much more is at stake here than was previously with the
numerical proverbs—it is not the classification of separate strange
phenomena, nor of limited sections of order: it is a totality of knowledge. The question is directed to the world as such and, as Goethe
says, to "what at its core giveth it cohesion." And as it pleads with the
world and interrogates it, it has already the tones of a quest for salvation. For there is no doubt that there is a secret implanted in the world
by God. This secret the poem calls "wisdom." But as it uses this concept the poem thinks of something oddly material, something almost
with a fixed habitation. "God knows the way to her," he "knows her
place" (vs. 23f.), he has "placed her" (vs. 27). But she is simply unattainable by man's technical will and enquiring mind. Verse 22 seems to
indicate that the way to wisdom is only through death and the realm

of death. If the poem originally ended in a deep resignation, further on, in vs. 28, and most certainly at a later date, it was given a positive ending: "But to man he said 'Behold, the fear of the Lord is wisdom, and avoidance of evil is understanding.' "[14] This maxim leads man from those hopeless questions to the questions which had been assigned to him by God. It does this of course quite abruptly in that, without so indicating, it uses the word wisdom in a different sense, namely the usual and popular one. This crude twist at the end of the poem no doubt impairs its ancient grandeur, but it is obviously dictated by a pastoral concern— thou too, O man, hast a portion in the divine wisdom: thy wisdom is the fear of God.[15]

The wisdom poem in Prov. VIII takes us a great step forward. It has three parts. The first (vss. 1–21) and the last (vss. 32–6) are paraenetic, and in the famous middle part (vss. 22–31) wisdom introduces herself in a very strange way, speaking of primeval existence, and of her pre-existence before all the works of Creation. She is created: but she is the first-born of God's works of Creation; she was the dearest child of God and played with Creation and with men. The statements are very illusive, and they could hardly be otherwise at this utmost limit of the possibilities of expression. But it can at any rate be recognised that wisdom was not herself actively engaged in the creation of the world— that would certainly have been expressed much more clearly. It is much more likely that the controversial אמון in vs. 30 should be translated by "darling" or "pet," and that it came to be interpreted as "master workman" only under the pressure of later concepts, as they came to be expressed in the Wisdom of Solomon. Here in Proverbs the author of this poem is obviously only interested in maintaining that wisdom pre-existed before all Creation. In particular the relationship between her and the thing created is described as one of play. Another direction is indicated in Prov. III. 19: "Jahweh by wisdom founded the earth; by understanding he established the heavens." Here we are indeed very close to a concept of co-operation. Wisdom was a means of which Jahweh availed himself; perhaps we could say a constructive principle by which he allowed himself to be guided in the construction of the world.[16] "Sophia" is only expressly designated as the creator of the

---

[14] Thus G. Hölscher and other expositors *in loco*.

[15] The transition in Ps. XIX from 1–7 [6] to 8–15 [7–14] also shows this leading on of wisdom's from the contemplation of the world to the contemplation of the Torah.

[16] See Gemser, *Sprüche Salomos, in loco*. If one considers the way in which Ps.

world in the Wisdom of Solomon (VII. 22). One should therefore not even try to approach Prov. VIII. 22ff. in terms of this specific question, for it speaks about a completely different aspect of the relationship to the world and stands rather beside Prov. III. 19 as complement. What ben Sirach says is again a little different—God "poured out" wisdom (which is created) upon all his works (Ecclesiasticus I. 9). From all this one can see how flexible the concepts still were. At the time of Prov. III. 19 and VIII. 22ff., and even of Jesus ben Sirach, the subject could still be approached in various ways and with the help of different concepts, and each of these expressions was still a bold venture. Even the concept of wisdom as a person, and that of taking her as a "principle," still go side by side. It appears however as if the deepest things which Israel said about God's Creation were given in Prov. VIII. 22ff.—the world and man are joyously encompassed by wisdom. Perhaps we catch something of the meaning if we say that by its wondrousness and the wisdom of its design all Creation transcends itself in the direction of God. It is enclosed by a secret, encompassed by a *doxa*, pointing back to God. Whether any concepts deriving from myth and familiar to contemporaries though no longer known to us rendered the author any assistance in forming this extreme concept of wisdom as a playing child—was it a child of the gods?—is a different question which cannot be discussed here.[17] But we have to give careful heed to the place in theology where these cosmological expressions stand. They are a message of that wisdom which with the force of an ultimatum calls man to a decision about life and death (Prov. VIII. 35). They are therefore merely the first part of the call to man, and serve to strengthen its weight and authority, and to intensify the readiness to listen to it. Thus this poem too contains the twist which we found in Job XXVIII. 28, only it is not so crude nor does it come so abruptly at the very end.

XXXIII. 6 imagines the creation of the world as effected by Jahweh's "word" and "spirit," then the concept חכמה in Prov. III. 19 and basically also that in Prov. VIII. 22 comes remarkably close to the concept of רוח, for here Ecclesiasticus XXIV. 3 on its part seems once more to identify the primordial wisdom with the spirit of God which hovered over chaos. For the use of the concept of wisdom in place of the generally commoner concept of the spirit in the utterances of the Wisdom literature see Van Imschoot, in *Rev. bib.*, 1938, pp. 37ff. The Joseph story says that the "spirit of Elohim" was in Joseph (Gen. XLI. 38). Later on people would surely have spoken of the divine wisdom.

[17] H. Donner has recently very plausibly shown a dependence on the Egyptian concept of *Maat*, in *Zeitschrift für ägyptische Sprache und Altertumskunde*, 1957, pp. 8ff.

But in essence Prov. VIII is very much the same: wisdom is only possible for man by following, by discipleship. Since the text of Prov. VIII is much more positive in what it says about "cosmic" wisdom, the urge towards obedience and following, and so the application to man, is very much stronger than in Job XXVIII. We should therefore not set too much of a gulf between Prov. VIII and Job XXVIII. Only in mood are there great differences; but this derives from the fact that the cosmic wisdom in Job XXVIII appears in the form of a question raised by man which is unanswerable, while in Prov. VIII it speaks to man as the mediator of a revelation. But in both places a portion of this wisdom is promised to man only in virtue of listening and obeying.

Thus a characteristic of these theological reflexions of the Wisdom literature is the determined effort to relate the phenomenon of the world, of "nature" with its secrets of creation, to the saving revelation addressed to man. As we have seen, this theology was much less interested in the phenomenon of history.[18] Faith had apparently—though perhaps only in certain circles—to satisfy considerably increased intellectual pretensions. It is perfectly possible that contact with popular Hellenistic philosophy played a part,[19] but internal conditions and needs in Israel itself were probably more influential. What finds voice here is an Israel which had completely and in all respects emancipated herself from the archaic forms of her faith. This dissociation from the patriarchal concepts of Jahweh's action had already been effected as far as history went in the Succession Document. But now Israel's life also became completely freed from myth in regard to nature, and this certainly did not come about apart from wisdom's strong rational will for knowledge. The concept of miracle had changed. These circles no longer designated as miracle the breaks in the historical nexus and the isolated "signs." Admittedly, even in later ages Jahweh's acts in history counted, as always, as pre-eminently his נפלאות (Pss. LXXVIII. 11, 32, CVI. 7, CXI. 4; Neh. IX. 17). But in the circles of wisdom teaching, interest in the traditions of the saving history had grown weak. It was all the more turned towards the miracle of Creation, its systematic arrangement, its technical riddles and its rules. These are the נפלאות which the Wisdom literature praises.[20] It is here that the Wis-

---

[18] See however J. Fichtner, "Zum Problem Glaube und Geschichte in der israelitisch-jüdischen Weisheit," in *Th. Lz.*, 1951, cols. 145ff.

[19] Eichrodt, *Theologie*, VOL. II, p. 41.

[20] Job v. 9ff., IX. 8ff., XXXVII. 14; Ps. CXXXIX. 14; cf. Jer. x. 12ff.; Ps. CIV. 24.

dom literature becomes enthusiastic, here is the field where it knew itself theologically challenged and where indeed it became productive. What a change there is in the theological situation compared with the teaching about Creation in the Priestly Document in Gen. 1! There, as we saw, Creation opened up the dimension of history and saving history. In order to speak properly about Israel, one had to begin at Creation itself. The task of this priestly theology thus consisted in linking the saving history with Creation, in drawing Creation towards the saving history, because this was the real position where this theology stood.[21] The theological thinking of wisdom ran in exactly the opposite direction. It stood before the world as Creation, and its task was to find a connexion from there with the saving history, that is, with that revelation of Jahweh's will which was pre-eminently turned towards Israel. Its thesis therefore ran: in order to understand Creation properly, one has to speak about Israel and the revelation of God's will granted to her. The rational determination to acquire knowledge which first caused wisdom to direct her attention to the world certainly saw many wonders in it, but it also saw that its real secret evaded her. Least of all did Jahweh's work of creation present itself to wisdom in that ministering function in which it was seen by the priestly teaching in Gen. 1, that is, in the function of opening up and bearing Jahweh's action in history and salvation. We should be justified in saying that only here was the demand to face up to Creation in its whole unmythological worldliness made upon Israel. But what was the connexion between Creation and Jahweh's will for revelation, of whose totality and penetrating power none had better knowledge than these same teachers of wisdom? Their theology masters this tremendous problem not only by relating the cosmic wisdom which is unattainable by natural knowledge to Jahweh's revelation which comes to man, but also even by identifying them! The word which calls man to life and salvation is the same word as that which as wisdom already encompassed all creatures at Creation. It is the same word which God himself made use of as a plan at his creation of the world. Hitherto Israel's contribution to the rational critical knowledge of the world has been counted very small, if not even discounted completely. Over against this, more recent investigation of the Wisdom literature gives a different picture. Israel too put urgent questions to "nature," and penetrated—certainly always from the basis of her faith—to insights of ultimate validity as far as the

[21] See above, pp. 138f.

possibility of knowing the world and its ultimate secrets is concerned. The "No" in Job xxvIII could not have come as a windfall to merely occasional questioning; it sums up the total of a long endeavour after knowledge of the world.

In the light of all this, the later wisdom teachers must have been the representatives of a very comprehensive, indeed a practically encyclopedic, theology, at any rate the most comprehensive one which Israel ever achieved. The encyclopedic endeavour of the older experientially-based wisdom teaching passed over to the later theological teaching. Only with the latter was Israel able to make perfectly universal statements not just about the world and its secrets of creation, but also about the assets of truth which the nations possess. It would not, however, be right to dismiss the cosmological statements simply as "speculations," for in its proper nature this wisdom always understood itself as a process of revelation addressed to man. The place where the cosmological statements stand, as for example those in Prov. vIII. 22ff., is absolutely clear. They are merely the introduction to that wisdom which calls to man; their function is a ministering and motivating one. In the address itself they stand in the background. Their call is therefore far from being wisdom of the kind we find in the mystery religions, which discloses cosmic secrets to the initiate. On the contrary, it addresses itself to the general public (Prov. IX. 3). We cannot however fail to see that the whole call in Prov. vIII also presupposes an intellectual need in man, and reckons with hearers who can only be reached if their will to acquire knowledge is also satisfied. They are therefore told that the wisdom which calls to them has "a cosmic background."[22] Here the statement that the fear of God is the beginning of wisdom has received a far more comprehensive meaning, for it is this cosmic wisdom which gives herself to the man who obeys her. The scope of this wisdom theology was widened for the last time through its fusion with apocalyptic, but this is only heralded in the latest book of the Hebrew canon. The wise man's power extends over the secrets of the future as well.[23] Later wisdom is thus a phenomenon of astonishing complexity.

[22] B. Gemser, *Sprüche Salomos*, on Prov. vIII. 22ff.

[23] Dan. II. 31ff., IV. 16ff., v. 13ff., vII. 1ff., vIII. 1ff., IX. 20ff., x. 1ff.; Wis. vII. 27 and frequently. The way for this connexion of Wisdom literature and apocalyptic had been prepared long in advance, for the Wisdom literature loved to increase the weight of its insights by a prophetic manner of speech. Nevertheless even Ecclesiasticus still claims no knowledge of the future.

In it, Israel's assets of faith were able for the last time, before their ossification in the teaching of the Scribes, to express and present themselves in a completely new form absolutely unknown to older Israel.

The diminished importance of the cult however is surprising. We may not of course deduce from Prov. i–ix a theology that was without a cult or that was even hostile to it. Ben Sirach could even be enthusiastic about the great services of worship,[24] and the wise men of Prov. i–ix too certainly did not deny the cult its place in the post-exilic community. Much becomes clear if we just remember the difference in "offices" and their sphere of responsibility. The ordering of the cult had become an almost esoteric branch of knowledge, and its representatives were the priests. The teachers of wisdom regarded as their task the development of teaching along a completely different line, and in particular in face of questions completely different from those met with by the priests. But even if we guard against radicalisations which oversimplify the issue, the fact remains that, for the wise men in their almost encyclopedic effort, the decisive confrontation of man with Jahweh does not take place in the sphere of the cult with its whole motivation from the saving history. Wisdom's call to men to follow her, her invitation to life, is uttered out in secular life, quite apart from the sacral. The concepts of cult, saving history, and people of God apparently lie outside the field of vision of this call, which is directed to the individual.

Yet the strangest thing of all is that this divine call—where it condescends to such a thing at all—does not legitimate itself from the saving history, but from Creation. This is very similar to the divine utterances in the Book of Job. There too the glory and the power, that is, the divinity of Jahweh, which no doubt is to assail, proves itself from Creation, though admittedly from a Creation which right from the beginning was probably understood as a saving work of Jahweh.

This was thus a very spiritual piety which we can well think of as needing no signs or miracles or cultic symbols as outward sureties. The other side of the renunciation was the conviction of the hiddenness and remoteness of Jahweh's action.

A man's heart thinks out a way, but Jahweh guides his step.
(Prov. XVI. 9)

Of course no faith could have lived by this insight alone—indeed it

---

[24] Ecclesiasticus XLV. 6ff.; especially L. 1ff.

did not have to do so, for in the earlier period Israel's faith rested upon quite other bases than such extreme statements. But what is to happen when wisdom proceeds to understand itself as the representative of the most central concepts of Jahwism, and, bypassing the saving history, goes on to legitimise itself straight from Creation?

7. SCEPTICISM

After all that has been said—the way in which we thought we have to understand Israel's faith in Jahweh—it can be realised that the point where contact with the action of Jahweh in history tended to be lost was always the point when faith was brought into the gravest danger. Accordingly a form of scepticism arose which was specific to Israel, not doubt about the existence of Jahweh—neither Job's despair nor that of the psalms of lamentation led to any dubiety about Jahweh's existence and power—but doubt about his readiness to interfere drastically in history or in the life of the individual.[1] This scepticism is not so very late; even the pre-exilic prophets encountered an astonishingly detached attitude on their contemporaries' part (Is. v. 19; Zeph. i. 12).

It may cause surprise if side by side with these almost cynical voices which cast doubts on Jahweh's might in history we range Ps. xc, which seems to be diametrically opposed to them. But the opening verses of this community lament are themselves characteristic, because they are no longer able to appeal to God's saving acts in history as had been the custom with this class of psalm (cf. Pss. xliv. 2 [1], lxxiv. 2). Like these Ps. xc casts a glance back to the past, but it is a glance which can no longer attach itself to any event in the saving history: the thought of God's eternity was so overwhelming that it swept the imagination away to ever greater distances, back to Creation and beyond it. Thus, the reflexions about man's nothingness in the sight of God occupy a conspicuously large space here, to the extent that there is almost no room left for supplication (and this is after all the most important point in a lament). Supplication only begins towards the end of the psalm. All this is characteristic of the specific note of resignation typical of the whole psalm, which can scarcely bring itself to have

---

[1] To an increasing degree the later period spoke of the impossibility of knowing Jahweh. To know Jahweh was previously the glory and privilege of Israel. But alongside this idea deriving from the distant past—it was not removed—there are more and more references to the incomprehensibility of Jahweh; Jer. xxiii. 23f.; Is. xl. 18, 25; lv. 8f.; Prov. xxx. 1ff.

any confidence. How poor the community has become is shown particularly in vs. 16, which can almost be described as the key to the whole psalm. The "works" of God, the manifestation of which is prayed for, are of course the saving acts of God in history in the past and the present (cf. Ps. XLIV. 2 [1]; Is. V. 12, 19 and frequently). The psalm certainly has knowledge of the glory of God's action in history which he constantly allowed to be revealed to his community, but only as something lost to its own generation. What then is left for the psalmist still to say about God? That he is enthroned in unattainable eternity and that men pass away under his wrath. But this community also knows what it lacks, and it prays God that he may again declare himself anew to it.

The period of the monarchy had already broken in principle with the old drastic idea of Jahweh's action in history. The author of the Succession Document or of the Joseph stories had by now relegated Jahweh's action to a deep concealment. The words interpreting the Joseph stories, which viewed the events as the inextricable intertwining of the evil action of men and the good action of God (Gen. L. 20), were a radical insight and could only be maintained in such a fashion by a strong belief in Jahweh's action in history. For a period which was less sure of itself, this idea of the deep concealment of the action of Jahweh could soon get a very bitter tang. We have already seen, of course, how it was that the later wisdom teaching's belief in Jahweh's action in history grew weak, and how it was his action in Creation that came to the forefront. But were things any more favourably situated for belief there? The resignation in Job XXVIII gives clear enough testimony, and the almost impassioned outbreak of despair at the impossibility of finding God in nature in Prov. XXX. 1–4 automatically ranges these passages alongside Ps. XC. However, only with the Book of Ecclesiastes did this scepticism emerge broadly based and with a hitherto unheard of radicality and weight.[2]

The book appears in the *Gattung* of a royal testament, a class of writing belonging to the court and the wise men, and deriving originally from Egypt. All idea that it contains the personal and individual

---

[2] K. Galling, *Der Prediger* (Hb. A.T. 1, 18), Tübingen 1940; *id.*, "Koheletstudien," in *Z.A.W.*, 1932, pp. 276ff.; W. Zimmerli, *Die Weisheit des Predigers Salomo*, Berlin 1936; J. Pedersen, "Scepticisme israélite," in *Revue d'histoire et de philosophie religieuses*, 1930, pp. 317ff.; A. Lauha, "Die Krise des religiosen Glaubens bei Kohelet," in *Vet. Test.*, Suppl. III (1955), pp. 183ff.

legacy of a solitary thinker has been abandoned. Recent writings have shown that its affinities with the thought of traditional wisdom are in fact very much greater than was once supposed, and that it is only in particular points that Ecclesiastes departs from such traditional wisdom.[3] So the Preacher's book is better understood as a sceptical marginal note on the tradition of the wise men, although of course it is a very bitter one. When it is so taken, we are delivered from the hopeless task of understanding its content as a consistent unity of thought,[4] because it rests wholly upon the traditional themes of the Wisdom literature, though freely glossing them.

The magnificent poem on the basically hopeless cycle of all things which men fail to perceive only because their memory is so short (Ecclesiastes 1. 4ff.), at once opens up the view of the world in which the thought and questioning of Ecclesiastes move. Initially it shows affinities with the later wisdom teaching, for its subject too is nothing less than the whole world. But Ecclesiastes thinks entirely without any reference to history—with him the Wisdom literature lost its last contact with Israel's old way of thinking in terms of saving history and, quite consistently, fell back on the cyclical way of thinking common to the East, the only difference being that in Ecclesiastes this way of thinking is expressed in an utterly secular form. But—and this tragedy is the book's theme—in this world devoid of all action of Jahweh in history, Ecclesiastes seeks for God. It seeks him for men's sake, to find an answer to the question of man's "portion," that is, the place in life assigned to man by God and blessed by him.[5] In this question of the "portion," the "benefit," what is under discussion is the question of the meaning of life: indeed, what it sums up is nothing less than the quest of salvation *per se*, as Ecclesiastes understands it. He investigated life to find a value that could make life worth living, but found that wisdom, riches, toil, and posthumous fame alike were "vanity." Now, in that main question, upon which he passionately insists, Ecclesiastes yet betrays that he is a last descendant of the people of Jahweh, since he knows that everything would be different if Jahweh's action, his work, were revealed to man (Ecclesiastes VIII. 17, XI. 5).

[3] K. Galling, in *Z.A.W.*, 1932, pp. 282ff.
[4] The book is now terminated by two "epilogues" (XII. 9–11 and 12–14). The latter seeks to interpret the contents of the book positively as an admonition to fear God and keep the commandments.
[5] Ecclesiastes II. 10, 21, III. 22, v. 17f., IX. 9.

Ecclesiastes is anything but a nihilistic agnostic. He knows that the world was created by God and that he unceasingly acts upon it. But man's calamity is that he cannot make contact with this divine action, because it is too deeply concealed. Ecclesiastes is in complete agreement with wisdom's traditional outlook that God has appointed its season for all human activity (Ecclesiastes III. 1ff.), and that—putting it in the Greek way—there is a *kairos* for weeping and laughing, and for loving and hating. But—and this is the point where Ecclesiastes' own reflexion begins—what does this mean for men (Ecclesiastes says "for those who work")?

> I saw the toil which God has ordained. . . . He has made everything beautiful in its time. . . .
> Only so that man cannot find out the work which God has done from the beginning.
>
> (Ecclesiastes III. 9ff.)

Ecclesiastes therefore means that the things which God has appointed for men signify only toil. This of course is not God's fault, who makes everything aright. But what help is this to man who cannot "find out" the work of God? There is no coincidence between man's actions and the "time" appointed by God; man always misses the mark. It is a strange discovery! The despair of a wise man at a life which he knows to be completely encompassed by God, but which has nevertheless lost all meaning for him, because this God's activity has sunk down into an unattainable concealment! The reason why this realisation is so devastating for Ecclesiastes is that he knows of no other possibility of coming into contact with God than this empirical way. But the world remains silent in face of his quest for salvation. The result of this absence of answer to his question about God is a "vulnerability on all sides,"[6] and the total insecurity of life is one of the subjects upon which Ecclesiastes expatiates. With him there can be no talk of a message which he had to deliver, since all that is left for him to do is to warn against illusions. Cast your bread upon the waters—after many days you will find it again. Invest your money in different stocks and shares, and you will lose it (Ecclesiastes XI. 1f.).[7] Thus, not even the outcome of insecurity

---

[6] Zimmerli, *Die Weisheit des Predigers Salomo*, p. 20.

[7] H. W. Hertzberg, *Der Prediger*, Komm. A.T., Leipzig 1932, *in loco*. It is taken in a different way by W. Staerk in *Z.A.W.*, 1942–3, pp. 216ff.

can be taken for granted! But what good is it for man to be in a world where the tears of the oppressed flow (Ecclesiastes IV. 1), and slaves ride on horses, and men of superior rank go on foot (Ecclesiastes X. 7)? Very oddly, Ecclesiastes calls a halt just before the point of complete bankruptcy. He does not draw the conclusion come to in the well-known Old Babylonian conversation between the master and his slave.[8] He does not recommend self-destruction: instead, he sees himself suspended over the abyss of despair.

"What I found to be good and fitting is this: to eat and drink and find enjoyment in all the toil which one has under the sun, for that is one's portion" (Ecclesiastes V. 18). In spite of their agreement with similar utterances from ancient Egypt, these maxims of Ecclesiastes are nevertheless to be distinguished fairly radically from that often almost cynical hedonism which of course is so frequently the brother of despair. For his counsels recommending an acceptance and enjoyment of the possible in every case contain a pointer to God: they are in fact the only maxims which bring human action with an almost astonishing directness into connexion with a positive will of God—it "pleases" God (Ecclesiastes IX. 7b).[9] On Ecclesiastes' lips what is said about man's "portion"—the word occurs again in the solemn passage in ch. IX. 7-10—is of great importance, for he now sees one way open to him after all. It may be a very narrow way, but it is nevertheless something apportioned to man by God, and with it he is ready to be content.

There can be no mistake about it: Ecclesiastes is a polemical book. The "wise man" whom it attacks is even mentioned once (Ecclesiastes VIII. 17). But the person intended is not so easy to see. What wise man claimed that he could discern all the work of Jahweh under the sun, "find it out"? This can certainly not be said of the older wisdom teaching, and the later teaching, Prov. I-IX and Ecclesiasticus, was also restrained in its judgment about the possibility of discerning Jahweh on the basis of the world. What is indeed common to them and to Ecclesi-

---

[8] ["Servant,] obey me." "Yes, my Lord, yes." "Now what is good?" "To break my neck, your neck, throw both into the river—that is good" (*A.N.E.T.*, p. 438; *A.O.T.*, p. 287). E. A. Speiser's interpretation—he would see in the conversation merely a parody on obedience to the point of self-immolation—does not square with the weightiness of its philosophy of life (*Journal of Cuneiform Studies*, 1954, pp. 98ff.).

[9] Ecclesiastes II. 25, III. 13, VII. 14, IX. 7ff.

astes is the question directed to the world and life as a whole. This wise man could perhaps rather personify a theology represented by the friends of Job. Admittedly, a deep gulf separates Ecclesiastes from them, as of course from the older wisdom teaching as well, because Ecclesiastes no longer sees a fate-bringing connexion between act and consequence in any shape or form. The idea of the fate-bringing sphere, which in earliest Israel was built into the foundations of the understanding of life, can in Ecclesiastes hardly now be discerned even in outline. He had long ago lost the belief that events in the external world correspond to human behaviour, and are turned towards man in benefit or in punishment.[10] Man and the events in the world outside him had been completely sundered from one another, with the result that he was abandoned like a monad to a process eluding all theological logic. Loneliness surrounds man, for it is not only God who is withdrawn from him. For the man who could compose the reflexions on the cycle of the sun and the waters and the wind, the world too has become an alien entity outside of himself, moving according to rules of its own. This is the explanation of that utter insecurity in regard to life which Ecclesiastes is never weary of revealing from every angle. Insecure are riches, being righteous is insecure (Ecclesiastes VII. 15, VIII. 14ff.), in particular all "that comes," the future, is insecure (Ecclesiastes III. 19, VIII. 7, VI. 12). Death alone is certain, death which awaits all, the clean and the unclean alike, those who offer God sacrifices and those who neglect them (Ecclesiastes IX. 1–3).

Here, at the farthest frontier of Jahwism where Ecclesiastes pitched his camp, arose an idea of life which can with some justification be designated as tragic. Human life is a life which is disposed over. But man is not able to keep in step with the dark divine power to which he is handed over. No matter what trouble he takes, he can never do anything but fail in the attempt to reach accord with the action of this God.[11] Limits that are unsurmountable hinder him from understanding God. No doubt God gives man joy too. But he also brings him into judgment (Ecclesiastes XI. 9). In a word, he is the one stronger than man (Ecclesiastes VI. 10). Thus nothing remained for Ecclesiastes but to submit in deep resignation to this tragic existence. He has no commission to preach. But he speaks in moving and even solemn laments

---

[10] See above, pp. 270f., 384ff.

[11] Complaint about the toil (עִנְיַן עָמָל) pervades the whole book; I. 3, 13, II. 18, 20, 21, 22, III. 10, 13, IV. 4, 8, 9, V. 17, VI. 7, VIII. 15, 17.

of the soul's "toil" which this life prepares for man who cannot in any way master it.[12]

[12] This fundamentally tragic mood is not something absolutely new with Ecclesiastes; it has a certain prehistory. Admittedly we should have to be on our guard against all the gloomy utterances about the frailty and nothingness of human life to which Jahwism, it must be recognised, had an inclination from the beginning. But these are utterances in which the frailty is already understood in the sense of a fated limitation, in the light of which even human failure in the eyes of God is comprehensible and explicable. In respect of this, the form of the argument in Ps. cIII. 14 retains something alien to the class of Psalms—Jahweh knows how "frail a thing" we are (יצר). That is, he knows what can be expected of man and what cannot. This rational grounding of the mercy of Jahweh in his knowledge of the limitations imposed upon men is, on the whole, alien to the prayers of lamentation. Job xIV. 1ff. shows that this argument also admits of an utterly different conclusion. For, if this limitation is true, how is it conceivable that God still makes demands upon this man—indeed, makes great demands upon him?

"The son of earth, born of woman, short are his days and full of unrest.
He comes forth like the flower, and withers, he flees like a shadow and cannot stand.
And over him dost thou hold thine eyes open, dost thou drag him into judgment before thee?
How can one that is clean come from the unclean? There is not one!"

(Translation according to Hölscher, *Das Buch Hiob*, Hb. A.T., 2nd edn. Tübingen 1952.) Here too the incapability is tragically motivated. One further advance is made by the "Babylonian Ecclesiastes," a conversation between a sufferer and his friend, in which human fallibility and falseness are understood as a gift of the gods who created man thus (pp. 279f.).

LIST OF ABBREVIATIONS AND
OF WORKS FREQUENTLY CITED

ALT, A. *K.S.* = *Kleine Schriften zur Geschichte Israels.* 2 vols. Munich 1953–9.

A.N.E.T. = *Ancient Near Eastern Texts relating to the Old Testament*, ed. J. B. Pritchard. 2nd edn. Princeton and London 1955.

A.O.T. = *Altorientalische Texte zum Alten Testament*, ed. H. Gressmann. 2nd edn. Berlin and Leipzig 1926.

A.T.D. = Das Alte Testament Deutsch, edd. V. Herntrich and A. Weiser. Göttingen.

BALSCHEIT, B. *Alter und Aufkommen des Monotheismus in der israelitischen Religion.* Berlin 1938.

BARTH, C. *Errettung* = *Die Errettung vom Tode in den individuellen Klage- und Dankliedern des Alten Testaments.* Basel 1947.

Bei. *Z.A.W.* = Beihefte zur *Zeitschrift für die alttestamentliche Wissenschaft.* Giessen, later Berlin.

Bib. Komm. = Biblische Kommentar, Altes Testament, ed. M. Noth. Neukirchen.

BUBER, M. *Konigtum Gottes.* 2nd edn. Berlin 1936.

B.W.A.N.T. = Beiträge zur Wissenschaft von Alten und Neuen Testament. Stuttgart.

EICHRODT, W. *Theologie* = *Theologie des Alten Testaments.* 3 vols. Leipzig 1933–9. Eng. trans. of VOL. I, *Theology of the Old Testament*, VOL. I, trans. J. A. Baker, London 1961.

Eucharisterion = *Eucharisterion. Festschrift für Hermann Gunkel*, ed. H. Schmidt. Göttingen 1923.

Ev. Th. = *Evangelische Theologie.* Munich.

Festschrift Albrecht Alt = *Geschichte und Altes Testament. Festschrift Albrecht Alt.* Tübingen 1953.

Festschrift für A. Bertholet = *Festschrift für Alfred Bertholet zum 80. Geburtstag gewidmet*, edd. W. Baumgartner, O. Eissfeldt, K. Elliger, and L. Rost. Tübingen 1950.

FICHTNER, J. *Die altorientalische Weisheit in ihrer israelitisch-jüdischen Ausprägung.* Giessen 1933.

GEMSER, B. *Sprüche Salomos.* Tübingen 1937.

GORDON, C. H. *Handbook* = *Ugaritic Handbook.* Rome 1947.

GRESSMANN, H. *Mose und seiner Zeit*. Göttingen 1913.

GUNKEL, H. *Schöpfung und Chaos in Urzeit und Endzeit*. 2nd edn. Göttingen 1921.

—— and J. BEGRICH. *Einleitung in die Psalmen*. Hb. A.T. Tübingen 1933.

HÄNEL, J. *Die Religion der Heiligkeit*. Gütersloh 1931.

Hb. A.T. = Handbuch zum Alten Testament, ed. O. Eissfeldt. Tübingen.

HEMPEL, J. *Ethos* = *Das Ethos des Alten Testaments*. Berlin 1938.

HERRMANN, J. *Die Idee der Sühne im Alten Testament*. Leipzig 1905.

JOHNSON, A. R. *Sacral Kingship* = *Sacral Kingship in Ancient Israel*. Cardiff 1945.

JOLLES, A. *Einfache Formen*. Halle 1930.

KOCH, K. *Sdq im Alten Testament*. Dissertation, Heidelberg 1953.

KÖHLER, L. *Theology* = *Old Testament Theology*, trans. A. S. Todd. London 1957. Trans. of *Theologie des Alten Testaments*. Tübingen 1936.

Komm. A.T. = Kommentar zum Alten Testament, ed. E. Sellin. Leipzig.

KRAUS, H. J. *Gottesdienst in Israel*. Munich 1954.

LEEUW, G. VAN DER. *Phänomenologie der Religion*. Tübingen 1933.

MOWINCKEL, S. *Le Décalogue*. Paris 1927.

—— *Religion und Kultus*. Göttingen 1953.

NOTH, M. *Ges. Studien* = *Gesammelte Studien zum Alten Testament*. Munich 1957.

—— *History* = *History of Israel*. 2nd edn. London 1960. Trans., revised by P. R. Ackroyd, of *Die Geschichte Israels*. Göttingen 1950.

—— *Pentateuch* = *Überlieferungsgeschichte des Pentateuch*. Stuttgart 1948.

—— *Überl. Studien* = *Überlieferungsgeschichtliche Studien I*. Schriften der Königsberger Gelehrten-Gesellschaft. Halle 1943.

Pauly-Wissowa = *Real-Encyclopädie der classischen Altertums Wissenschaft*. Stuttgart.

PEDERSEN, J. *Israel*, 2 vols., here cited as *Israel I–II* and *Israel III–IV*. London 1926, 1940.

RAD, G. VON. *Der Heilige Krieg im alten Israel*. Zürich 1951.

—— *Ges. Studien* = *Gesammelte Studien zum Alten Testament*. Munich 1958.

—— *Studies in Deuteronomy*, trans. D. M. G. Stalker. London 1953. Trans. of *Deuteronomiumstudien*. 2nd edn. Göttingen 1948.

RENDTORFF, R. *Gesetze* = *Die Gesetze in der Priesterschrift*. Göttingen 1954.

Rev. bib. = *Revue biblique*. Paris.

ROST, L. *Thronnachfolge* = *Die Überlieferung von der Thronnachfolge Davids*. B.W.A.N.T. Stuttgart 1926.

ROWLEY, H. H. *The Meaning of Sacrifice in the Old Testament*. Manchester 1950.

SCHAEDER, H. H. *Esra, der Schreiber*. Tübingen 1930.

SCHÖTZ, D. *Schuld- und Sündopfer in Alten Testament*. Breslau 1930.

SELLIN, E. *Geschichte* = *Geschichte des israelitisch-jüdischen Volkes*. Leipzig 1924–32.

—— *Mose* = *Mose und seine Bedeutung für die israelitische und jüdische Religionsgeschichte*. Berlin 1922.

STAMM, J. J. *Leiden* = *Das Leiden des Unschuldigen in Babylon und Israel*. Zürich 1946.

Th. Lz. = *Theologische Literaturzeitung*. Herrnhut.

Th. R. = *Theologische Rundschau*. Tübingen.

Th. W.B.N.T. = *Theologisches Wörterbuch zum Neuen Testament*, ed. G. Kittel. Stuttgart 1930ff.

Th. Z. = *Theologische Zeitschrift*. Basel.

Vet. Test. = *Vetus Testamentum*. Leiden.

WEBER, M. *Ancient Judaism*. Glencoe, Ill., and London 1952.

WELLHAUSEN, J. *Die Composition des Hexateuch*. 2nd edn. Berlin 1889.

—— *Prologomena* = *Prologomena to the History of Israel*, trans. J. S. Black and A. Menzies. Edinburgh 1885. Trans. of *Prologomena zur Geschichte Israels*.

WENDEL, A. *Das Opfer in der altisraelitisch–Religion*. Leipzig 1927.

WESTERMANN, C. *Loben Gottes* = *Das Loben Gottes in den Psalmen*. Berlin 1954.

Z.A.W. = *Zeitschrift für die alttestamentliche Wissenschaft*. Giessen, later Berlin.

Z.D.P.V. = *Zeitschrift des deutschen Palästina Vereins*. Leipzig.

Z. Th. K. = *Zeitschrift für Theologie und Kirche*. Tübingen.

APOCRYPHA

NEW TESTAMENT

NAME AND SUBJECT INDEX